The Plains Sioux and U.S. Colonialism from Lewis and Clark to Wounded Knee

This volume presents an overview of the history of the Plains Sioux as they became increasingly subject to the power of the United States in the 1800s. Many aspects of this story – the Oregon Trail, military clashes, the deaths of Crazy Horse and Sitting Bull, and the Ghost Dance – are well-known. Besides providing fresh insights into familiar events, the book offers an in-depth look at many lesser-known facets of Sioux history and culture. Drawing on theories of colonialism, the book shows how the Sioux creatively responded to the challenges of U.S. expansion and domination, while at the same time revealing how U.S. power increasingly limited the autonomy of Sioux communities as the century came to a close. The concluding chapters of the book offer a compelling reinterpretation of the events that led to the Wounded Knee massacre of December 29, 1890.

Jeffrey Ostler is Professor of History and Department Head at the University of Oregon. He is the author of *Prairie Populism: The Fate of Agrarian Radicalism in Kansas, Nebraska, and Iowa, 1880–1892* (1993).

"Without scrimping on close-up detail or native perspective, Ostler takes the most worked-over of American Indian historical sagas, the Sioux wars, and presents an absolutely riveting, utterly original and consistently persuasive narrative. Framed within the analytical perspective of colonialism, he employs his exhaustive research to demonstrate how little we know until we truly view history 'from the other side.' The story's intense focus on particular actors and Indian decision-making never lets up, and Ostler's concluding argument on the Ghost Dance as spiritual revolution is completely convincing and triumphantly written. With this book the bar has been raised for all historians of Indian–white relations."

 – Peter Nabokov, Professor, Department of World Arts and Cultures
    and American Indian Studies, UCLA

"Offering a compelling rereading of sometimes-familiar histories, Jeffrey Ostler's *The Plains Sioux and U.S. Colonialism from Lewis and Clark to Wounded Knee* takes one inside both the military–political infrastructure of U.S. colonialism and the complex relations of resistance and transformation practiced by Sioux people. Along the way, Ostler brilliantly reveals the fissures, continuities, insufficiencies and power that characterize a century of colonial encounters. His powerfully narrated history offers crucial lessons for anyone considering the dynamics of colonial domination and resistance in Native North America – or elsewhere, for that matter."

 – Philip J. Deloria, Department of History and Program in American
    Culture, University of Michigan

Studies in North American Indian History

Editors

Frederick Hoxie, University of Illinois, Urbana-Champaign
Neal Salisbury, Smith College

This series is designed to exemplify new approaches to the Native American past. In recent years scholars have begun to appreciate the extent to which Indians, whose cultural roots extended back for thousands of years, shaped the North American landscape as encountered by successive waves of immigrants. In addition, because Native Americans continually adapted their cultural traditions to the realities of the Euro-American presence, their history adds a thread of non-Western experience to the tapestry of American culture. Cambridge Studies in North American Indian History brings outstanding examples of this new scholarship to a broad audience. Books in the series link Native Americans to broad themes in American history and place the Indian experience in the context of social and economic change over time.

Also in the series:

RICHARD WHITE   *The Middle Ground: Indians, Empires, and Republics in the Great Lakes Regions, 1650–1815*
SIDNEY L. HARRING   *Crow Dog's Case: American Indian Sovereignty, Tribal Law, and United States Law in the Nineteenth Century*
COLIN G. CALLOWAY   *The American Revolution in Indian Country: Crisis and Diversity in Native American Communities*
FREDERICK E. HOXIE   *Parading through History: The Making of the Crow Nation in America, 1805–1935*
JEAN M. O'BRIEN   *Dispossession by Degrees: Indian Land and Identity in Natick, Massachusetts, 1650–1790*
CLAUDIO SAUNT   *A New Order of Things: Property, Power, and the Transformation of the Creek Indians, 1733–1816*

The Plains Sioux and U.S. Colonialism from Lewis and Clark to Wounded Knee

JEFFREY OSTLER

University of Oregon

CAMBRIDGE
UNIVERSITY PRESS

CAMBRIDGE UNIVERSITY PRESS
Cambridge, New York, Melbourne, Madrid, Cape Town,
Singapore, São Paulo, Delhi, Tokyo, Mexico City

Cambridge University Press
32 Avenue of the Americas, New York, NY 10013-2473, USA
www.cambridge.org
Information on this title: www.cambridge.org/9780521605908

First published 2004
7th printing 2011

A catalog record for this publication is available from the British Library.

Library of Congress Cataloging in Publication Data
Ostler, Jeffrey.
The Plains Sioux and U.S. colonialism from Lewis and Clark
to Wounded Knee / Jeffrey Ostler.
p. cm. – (Cambridge studies in North American Indian history)
Includes bibliographical references and index.
ISBN 0-521-79346-7 – ISBN 0-521-60590-3 (pbk.)
1. Dakota Indians – History – 19th century. 2. Dakota Indians – Government relations.
3. Indians, Treatment of – Great Plains – History. 4. Ghost dance – History.
5. United States – Race relations. 6. United States – Politics and government – 19th
century. 7. United States – Colonization. I. Title. II. Series.
E99.D1O85 2004
978.004′975243 – dc22   2003070009

ISBN 978-0-521-79346-9 Hardback
ISBN 978-0-521-60590-8 Paperback

For my teachers

Contents

Illustrations and Maps

ILLUSTRATIONS

MAPS

Abbreviations

AAG	Assistant Adjutant General
AG	Adjutant General
ARSW	Annual Report of the Secretary of War
ARCIA	Annual Report of the Commissioner of Indian Affairs
CIA	Commissioner of Indian Affairs
CRA	Record Group 75. Letters Received by the Office of Indian Affairs, 1824–81. Cheyenne River Agency. National Archives and Records Administration Microfilm Publications, M234
CR-KC	Record Group 75. Cheyenne River Agency Records. National Archives and Records Administration, Kansas City, Mo.
DMSF	Record Group 393. Records of the United States Army Continental Commands. Division of the Missouri, Special Files Relating to Military Operations and Administration, 1863–85. National Archives and Records Administration Microfilm Publications, M1495
DD	Department of Dakota
DM	Division of the Missouri
DP	Department of the Platte
LT&T	Ivan Stars, Peter Iron Shell, and Eugene Buechel, *Lakota Tales and Texts*, ed. Paul Manhart (Pine Ridge, S. Dak., 1978)
MP	James McLaughlin Papers. Assumption Abbey Archives, Richardton, N. Dak. (microfilm)
OAG	Record Group 94. Letters Received by the Office of the Adjutant General (Main Series), 1871–80. National Archives and Records Administration, Microfilm Publications, M666
OIA	Record Group 75. Letters Received by the Office of Indian Affairs, 1881–1907. National Archives and Records Administration, Washington, D.C.

OSI   Record Group 48. Records of the Office of the Secretary of the Interior, Indian Division. Letters Received, 1881–1907. National Archives and Records Administration, College Park, Md.

PR-KC   Record Group 75. Pine Ridge Agency Records. National Archives and Records Administration, Kansas City, Mo.

RA-KC   Record Group 75. Rosebud Agency Records. National Archives and Records Administration, Kansas City, Mo.

RCA   Record Group 75. Letters Received by the Office of Indian Affairs, 1824–81. Red Cloud Agency. National Archives and Records Administration Microfilm Publications, M234

RCWK   Record Group 94. Reports and Correspondence Relating to the Army Investigations of the Battle at Wounded Knee and to the Sioux Campaign of 1890–91. National Archives and Records Administration Microfilm Publications, M983

RT   Ricker Tablets. Eli Seavy Ricker Papers. Nebraska State Historical Society, Lincoln (microfilm)

SC 188   Record Group 75. Office of Indian Affairs. Special Case 188 (The Ghost Dance, 1890–98). National Archives and Records Administration, Washington, D.C. (microfilm)

STA   Record Group 75. Letters Received by the Office of Indian Affairs, 1824–81. Spotted Tail Agency. National Archives and Records Administration Microfilm Publications, M234

SI   Secretary of the Interior

SRA   Record Group 75. Letters Received by the Office of Indian Affairs, 1824–81. Standing Rock Agency. National Archives and Records Administration Microfilm Publications, M234

SR-KC   Record Group 75. Standing Rock Agency Records. National Archives and Records Administration, Kansas City, Mo.

SW   Secretary of War

Acknowledgments

When I first began working on this book, many scholars and colleagues offered me valuable advice and encouragement. I especially appreciate observations and suggestions given me by Bess Beatty, Tom Biolsi, Cynthia Brokaw, Tom Brossia, Richard Maxwell Brown, Ray DeMallie, Matt Dennis, Joe Fracchia, Shari Huhndorf, Peter Iverson, Jim Mohr, Steve Newcomb, Greg Smoak, Richard White, and the students in my fall 1990 seminar on Wounded Knee. The University of Oregon Office of Research and Faculty Development provided me with critical financial and other support. Fellowships from the Oregon Humanities Center gave me extended time to work on two pieces of the project. Support from the National Endowment for the Humanities came at an especially opportune time, allowing me to do the bulk of the research for the book and begin writing. The Stanley B. Greenfield fund at the University of Oregon enabled me to acquire critical library materials.

I was especially fortunate as the project was in its formative stages to have participated in two seminars sponsored by the Newberry Library. These seminars not only gave me the opportunity to learn from scholars and community leaders like Joe Medicine Crow, Victor Douville, Fred Hoxie, Janine Pease Windy Boy, Pat Albers, Brenda Child, Ray Fogelson, Tsianina Lomawaima, Bea Medicine, Ron McCoy, Jean O'Brien, and Tillie Black Bear, they also allowed me to take part in invaluable discussions about Indians' perspectives on their history. I also learned many important things about the Pequot Powwow.

As the book developed, many Lakota and other Sioux people generously talked with me about their history and culture, answered questions, and shared their hospitality. I am deeply grateful to Ben Black Bear, Tillie Black Bear, Leonard Brughier, Victor Douville, Steve Emery, Mario Gonzalez, Johnson Holy Rock, Craig Howe, Bea Medicine, Tom Short Bull, Albert White Hat, and especially Mike Her Many Horses, who not only invited me to Pine Ridge but came out to salmon country to share his knowledge with me and my students. I'm also grateful to Kelly Morgan and Jerome Kills Small for helping me with translations, Mike Marshall for his assistance with photographs at the Buechel Museum, and Gloria Runs Close to the Lodge for granting me permission to use Calico's account of the 1868 Treaty.

Raymond Bucko, Ray DeMallie, Herbert Hoover, and Harvey Markowitz, each with much greater knowledge of Lakota history and culture than my own, also provided me with many valuable insights. I'm grateful, too, to Father Paul Manhart for providing me with an advance copy of his translation of a portion of *Lakota Tales and Texts* and Todd Kerstetter for his advice about translation.

The research for this book would never have been completed without the dozens of librarians and archivists who assisted me in using materials on-site and responded to written queries and phone calls about sources and reproductions. With apologies to those whose names I may have overlooked, I'd like to thank Joseph James Ahern, John Day, Coi Drummond-Gehrig, Paula Fleming, Ann Jenks, Kenneth Johnson, Susan Humble, Julie Lakota, Deb Lyon, Mary Frances Morrow, Susan Ott, Valerie Porter-Hanson, Richard Sommers, Carey Southwell, Ken Stewart, Mark Thiel, Vyrtis Thomas, Chad Wall, and Keith Winsell. I'm also grateful to Kingsley Bray for sending me copies of his fine, yet difficult to locate, articles; Gary Anderson for his advice about the Campbell Collection at the University of Oklahoma; Eli Paul for his help locating the depredations claims records; Carol Foster for transcribing materials on microfilm; and Mike Brodhead for his very generous hospitality in Kansas City.

As I was writing the book, I was fortunate to find many people who agreed to read drafts and offer advice. Jayna Brown, Phil Deloria, Alex Dracobly, Bryna Goodman, Jerry Green, Shari Huhndorf, Pat Hilden, Robert Johnston, Jim Mohr, Peggy Pascoe, Nic Rosenthal, Gray Whaley, and Richard White all gave me close readings of particular sections of the book (many of these more than once). Arif Dirlik, Joe Fracchia, Randy McGowen, Rosemarie Ostler, and Barbara Welke heroically slogged through the entire manuscript. Comments I received from Fred Hoxie, Neal Salisbury, Frank Smith, and one of the two anonymous readers for the Press were also enormously helpful. I've also appreciated the cheerful advice and hard work of Eric Crahan and Nancy Hulan.

As I complete this book, my thoughts finally turn to family and friends for their support and affection. In addition to those mentioned above, I'd particularly like to acknowledge my parents, Barbara and Don Ostler, and my wife Rosemarie. As well, I can't help but think of the many teachers who have influenced me over the years. I'll always be deeply indebted to Hugh Rush, Lewis Webster, the late Sylvia Scanland, Louis Cononelos, William Mulder, Bing Bingham, Richard Maxwell Brown, and Shel Stromquist for their inspiration and example. I've dedicated this book to them.

Introduction

Colonialism, Agency, and Power

The genesis of this book goes back to 1990 when I was asked to teach a course designed to help history majors understand how historians do their work. I decided to assemble primary and secondary sources about a particular event and give students the opportunity to see firsthand how historians use raw materials to construct their accounts. I don't recall exactly how I chose Wounded Knee. The fact that it was the one-hundredth anniversary of this event, in which the U.S. army slaughtered more than three hundred Lakota Sioux on the Pine Ridge Reservation, influenced me, as did the realization that I knew only the bare outlines of what had happened at Wounded Knee and why. As I examined the sources with my students and read the works of historians and anthropologists, I concluded that existing scholarship fails to provide a satisfactory interpretation of the causes of Wounded Knee. My earlier research on politics and the state suggested to me that important issues had been neglected, in particular, the reasons why the United States sent troops to Pine Ridge and three other Plains (western) Sioux[1] reservations several weeks before the massacre, the army's broader goals in undertaking this campaign, and how the campaign's premises made a massacre likely.

Although I began with Wounded Knee and its immediate context primarily in mind, I moved steadily backward in time. To explain Wounded Knee, I needed to understand the Ghost Dance, a movement that originated in the teachings of a Paiute prophet (Wovoka) in the late 1880s and spread to many tribes in the American West. It became especially important to consider the movement's reception by the Plains Sioux and to analyze critically the army's and many subsequent scholars' contention that military force was necessary to suppress the Sioux Ghost Dance. The claim was that the Sioux

---

[1] In this book, I use the terms *Plains* and *western Sioux* to refer to Sioux people living near or west of the Missouri River. This includes Tetons (Lakota speakers) as well as Yanktons and Yanktonais, who speak the Dakota dialect. For a full discussion of nomenclature, see Chapter 1. The three other reservations were Standing Rock, Cheyenne River, and Rosebud.

ghost dancers had distorted an originally pacific teaching into one of hostility toward whites, yet there were reasons to think this was merely a pretext to justify military action. As I began to think more about the Sioux Ghost Dance, I also realized the need for a better understanding of the conditions in which it emerged. This led me to develop a more complete picture of the economic, social, and political history of the early reservation period beginning in 1877, when the Sioux gave up military resistance to U.S. expansion. As I tried to write that history, however, I could see that many of the conflicts of the late 1870s and 1880s were grounded in an earlier history of relations between the Plains Sioux and the U.S. government. I eventually decided that the logical place for the book to begin was in 1804. That was the year when Lewis and Clark came to western Sioux country, demanding cooperation with the U.S. government and threatening dire consequences if the Sioux refused to comply. Although this book retains its original purpose of explaining Wounded Knee, it does so as part of a more general analysis of Sioux–U.S. interactions in the nineteenth century.

Many of the subjects in the following pages are familiar. It is not as though the Sioux are an obscure tribe that can complain about the lack of scholarly interest in their history. In fact, it could easily be argued that the *last* thing Sioux people need is yet another book about them. Despite the vast literature on the western Sioux, my intention is to offer a new, and I hope useful, perspective on their history by analyzing it through the lens of colonialism.

A colony, in its original meaning from Greek and Roman experience, is a group of people sent to settle a new place while retaining ties to their old country. Colonies are not necessarily in a subordinate relationship to a metropole, although they may come to feel themselves to be and even to sever their formal political relationship with their progenitor, as happened with the American colonies. The expansion of the United States in the nineteenth century also involved the establishment of new colonies that were organized into territories and then states. The process of establishing new colonies has often been described as colonization.

In contrast to colonization, the term *colonialism* makes explicit the fact that expansion almost always involves conquest, displacement, and rule over foreign groups. Colonialism is closely related to imperialism, often confusingly so. Usually, however, imperialism is seen as a process that leads to colonialism, as for example, in the case of Britain's establishment of a trading empire, which eventually led to formal political rule over indigenous people in south Asia and parts of Africa. The problems of definition are complicated by the historical multiplicity of types of imperialism and colonialism.[2]

---

[2] A currently authoritative definition of imperialism and colonialism is provided by Edward W. Said, *Culture and Imperialism* (New York, 1993), 9, who makes a distinction between imperialism as "the practice, the theory, and the attitudes of a dominating metropolitan center ruling a distant territory" and colonialism, "almost always a consequence of imperialism,"

Although Americans have often been reluctant to acknowledge imperialism and colonialism in their history, the expansion of the United States in the nineteenth century clearly involved both, insofar as it entailed the conquest of and eventual rule over Native people.[3] Chapter 1 of this book will offer some observations about the particular characteristics of U.S. imperialism and colonialism.

One of my purposes in using the term colonialism is to name it as a fact of nineteenth-century U.S. history, but I also want to use it as an analytical tool. At one time, histories of colonialism were written mostly from the top down and described a unilateral process by which an imperial power established complete domination over subject peoples. The colonized were acted upon. In recent decades, however, scholars in various parts of the world have paid much greater attention to the process of colonialism from the vantage point of colonized people and have revealed myriad ways in which colonized peoples have resisted, contested, and adapted to colonial regimes.[4] Consistent with this general perspective, this book treats U.S. colonialism as a dynamic and contested process, in other words, a *political* process in the broadest sense of the term.

Thinking of colonialism in these terms allows scholars of Native American history to build on important insights yielded by the past generation of research in their field, while at the same time recalling important themes that

as the "implanting of settlements on distant territory" (also quoted in Bill Ashcroft, Gareth Griffiths, and Helen Tiffin, *Key Concepts in Post-Colonial Studies* [London, 1998], 46). The problem with this definition, however, is that colonialism usually entails the eventual establishment of rule over groups already present in that distant territory. A better set of definitions, including a distinction between colonization and colonialism, is provided in D. K. Fieldhouse, *Colonialism, 1870–1945: An Introduction* (New York, 1981), 1–8. For an important critical discussion that emphasizes the variability of forms of colonialism and the importance of understanding them locally, see Nicholas Thomas, *Colonialism's Culture: Anthropology, Travel, and Government* (Princeton, 1994).

3 Amy Kaplan, "'Left Alone with America': The Absence of Empire in the Study of American Culture," in *Cultures of United States Imperialism*, ed. Amy Kaplan and Donald E. Pease (Durham, 1993), 17, observes that "United States expansionism is often treated as an entirely separate phenomenon from European colonialism of the nineteenth century."

4 One of the most influential sites for work of this sort was in the early phases of the Subaltern Studies project. See Gyan Prakash, "Subaltern Studies as Postcolonial Criticism," *American Historical Review* 99 (December 1994): 1475–90. Examples from other historiographies include Henry Reynolds, *The Other Side of the Frontier: Aboriginal Resistance to the European Invasion of Australia* (Ringwood, Australia, 1982); Ann Laura Stoler, *Capitalism and Confrontation in Sumatra's Plantation Belt, 1870–1979* (New Haven, 1985); J. B. Peires, *The House of Phalo: A History of the Xhosa People in the Days of their Independence* (Berkeley, 1982); Jean Comaroff, *Body of Power, Spirit of Resistance: The Culture and History of a South African People* (Chicago, 1985). For the importance of attention to agency and Native perspectives within a framework of North American colonialism, see Duane Champagne, "A Multidimensional Theory of Colonialism: The Native North American Experience," *Journal of American Studies of Turkey* 3 (1996): 9.

have been forgotten or neglected. In the past twenty years the main keywords of the "new Indian history" and the overlapping field of ethnohistory have been words like *agency, encounter, survival, exchange, negotiation,* and *middle ground.* Work emphasizing these themes has revealed the shortcomings of an earlier historiography that portrayed Indians as no more than victims of European domination and gave little attention to the voices of Native people.[5] The new history has rightly insisted that Indians were historical agents with unique perspectives requiring interpretation through careful attention to specific cultural contexts. In so doing, however, the current generation of scholarship, taken as a whole, has deemphasized questions of power, ideology, and the state.[6] One result of this situation is that much of the recent

---

[5] For a sampling of works that use these keywords or similar concepts see Richard White, *The Middle Ground: Indians, Empires, and Republics in the Great Lakes Region, 1650–1815* (Cambridge, 1991); James Axtell, *Beyond 1492: Encounters in Colonial North America* (New York, 1992); Nancy Shoemaker, ed., *Negotiators of Change: Historical Perspectives on Native American Women* (New York, 1995); Peter Iverson, *"We Are Still Here": American Indians in the Twentieth Century* (Wheeling, Ill., 1998). Influential earlier works that arguably emphasized power at the expense of agency include Dee Brown, *Bury My Heart at Wounded Knee: An Indian History of the American West* (New York, 1971); Francis Jennings, *The Invasion of America: Indians, Colonialism, and the Cant of Conquest* (New York, 1975). Useful discussions of the new Indian history and ethnohistory are Shepard Krech III, "The State of Ethnohistory," *Annual Review of Anthropology* 20 (1991): 345–75; Donald L. Fixico, ed., *Rethinking American Indian History* (Albuquerque, 1997); Richard White, "Using the Past: History and Native American Studies," in *Studying Native America: Problems and Prospects,* ed. Russell Thornton (Madison, 1998), 217–43. Useful discussions of Native American historiography more broadly include R. David Edmunds, "Native Americans, New Voices: American Indian History, 1895–1995," *American Historical Review* 100 (June 1995): 717–40; and Kerwin Lee Klein, *Frontiers of Historical Imagination: Narrating the European Conquest of Native America, 1890–1990* (Berkeley, 1997); and for writing about Native Americans before World War II, see Ellen Fitzpatrick, *History's Memory: Writing America's Past, 1880–1980* (Cambridge, Mass., 2002), 98–140. Though new Indian historians and ethnohistorians have seldom drawn on postcolonial theory and most would resist its critical interrogation of the epistemological bases for writing history and its related move to discourse and representation, postcolonial theory's attention to agency, subaltern voices, cultural difference, and, to a lesser extent, hybridity, suggest broader intellectual affinities. On postcolonial theory, see Arif Dirlik, *The Postcolonial Aura: Third World Criticism in the Age of Global Capitalism* (Boulder, 1997); Peter Childs and R. J. Patrick Williams, *An Introduction to Post-Colonial Theory* (London, 1997).

[6] My argument here is not that the new Indian history and ethnohistory completely ignore such questions, only that they are often eclipsed by more prominent themes. Nor is it difficult to find numerous examples of works that emphasize themes like conquest, colonialism, and genocide, many of which are attentive to questions of indigenous perspectives and persistence. For a few examples, see Patricia Nelson Limerick, *The Legacy of Conquest: The Unbroken Past of the American West* (New York, 1987); Thomas Biolsi, *Organizing the Lakota: The Political Economy of the New Deal on the Pine Ridge and Rosebud Reservations* (Tucson, 1992); Melissa Meyer, *The White Earth Tragedy: Ethnicity and Dispossession at a Minnesota Anishinaabe Reservation, 1889–1920* (Lincoln, 1994); Jean M. O'Brien, *Dispossession by Degrees: Indian Land and Identity in Natick, Massachusetts, 1650–1790* (Cambridge, 1997).

literature tends to minimize the vast imbalance of power between Native peoples and Europeans. Another is that scholars who are sympathetic to Indians' positions and perspectives have largely been uninterested in critically analyzing the ideologies, policies, and on-the-ground actions associated with the United States' conquest of and establishment of colonial rule over Indian people. They have ceded this ground to military and policy historians, who are disciplinarily inclined to privilege the perspectives of government officials and other non-Indian observers.[7]

Of all the insights from the past generation of scholarship, none is more important than the persistence of Native peoples and ways of life. It is no longer possible to think of the "closing of the frontier" in the late nineteenth century as signifying "the last days of the Sioux nation."[8] Like Native people throughout the Americas, the Plains Sioux have survived. At the same time, it is important to keep in mind the general observation that people do not make history "under circumstances chosen by themselves."[9] We also need to be reminded that survival is not the same as freedom. Rather than choosing between a narrative of agency and persistence on the one hand and power, domination, and genocide on the other, my goal has been to write a history that combines these elements and explores their relations. To do this, I have searched for a variety of Sioux voices and tried to interpret them within a changing and diverse cultural context. I have also shown how Sioux individuals made choices – often very different choices – and in so doing actively helped shape the course of events rather than merely being acted upon or responding according to a predetermined cultural script. At the same time, however, there were considerable constraints on indigenous choices. It is important to go beyond merely noting the existence of these constraints to explore how the United States' commitment to an expansionist ideology of manifest destiny, mediated by sometimes contradictory policies and by the decisions of government officials and other European Americans, operated in particular situations.

These observations may convey some idea of what I intend to accomplish by analyzing colonialism as a political process, but to make this more concrete, it may be useful to provide an overview of three interrelated areas of political activity described in this book. The first involves politics among the colonizers. Most middle- and upper-class white Americans shared a similar ideological perspective about the United States' divinely appointed destiny

---

[7] Again, there are exceptions. See Frederick E. Hoxie, *A Final Promise: The Campaign to Assimilate the Indians, 1880–1920* (Lincoln, 1984); Richard White, *"It's Your Misfortune and None of My Own": A History of the American West* (Norman, 1991), 85–118.

[8] Frederick Jackson Turner, "The Significance of the Frontier in American History," in Frederick Jackson Turner, *The Frontier in American History* (New York, 1920), 1–38; Robert M. Utley, *The Last Days of the Sioux Nation* (New Haven, 1963).

[9] Karl Marx, *The Eighteenth Brumaire of Louis Bonaparte* (Moscow, 1934), 13.

as a continental empire and imagined a future in which Indian people would "disappear" (through extermination or assimilation). However, when it came to formulating policies and implementing them in specific situations, U.S. officials and influential citizens had a range of often conflicting ideas and interests. Groups and individuals formed uneasy alliances and frequently clashed. Some of the tensions and conflicts within the U.S. polity can be traced to contradictions within the development of capitalism in North America. Others were related to divisions within the state. Still others stemmed from different responses to the moral dilemmas facing a predominantly Christian nation engaged in an imperial project that required dispossession and threatened extermination. Most European Americans took for granted that the world's peoples could be divided into "races," with the "white race" above all others, although the implications of this belief varied considerably in practice.[10]

A second area of politics emerged when Plains Sioux people interacted with U.S. officials and citizens. Most of these interactions occurred in Sioux country, though some took place when Sioux leaders traveled to Washington and other eastern places. In these encounters, the colonizers and those being subjected to colonization met flesh and blood, face to face. Sometimes the two sides clashed in war, at other times violence erupted from negotiations, but most of the interactions I describe in this book involved nonviolent contests over specific issues. On what terms would trade occur? Under what conditions would militants make peace? Would the Sioux sign a particular treaty, and if so, at what cost? Once the Sioux had been conquered and were living on reservations, a myriad of new issues arose. How would government rations be distributed? Would children be sent to boarding schools? Would U.S. officials try to stop all religious ceremonies or just some? Would the Sioux have to give up more of their land, and if so, could they minimize the loss? Although these discussions were often nonviolent, the Sioux and the government did not enter them on equal terms. Sioux leaders were sometimes able to exercise leverage in negotiations, often by exploiting contradictions among the colonizers. But they were always in a defensive position and subject to U.S. coercion.[11]

---

[10] For useful formulations of the contradictory character of colonialism in general, see John Comaroff and Jean Comaroff, *Ethnography and the Historical Imagination* (Boulder, 1992), 183; Nicholas B. Dirks, ed., *Colonialism and Culture* (Ann Arbor, 1992), 7; Anne McClintock, *Imperial Leather: Race, Gender and Sexuality in the Colonial Contest* (New York, 1995), 15. Recent work on the state, such as Gilbert M. Joseph and Daniel Nugent, eds., *Everyday Forms of State Formation: Revolution and Negotiation of Rule in Modern Mexico* (Durham, 1994), that challenges the coherence and unity of state projects is also relevant here.

[11] Works in Plains history that illuminate politics at this level include Loretta Fowler, *Arapahoe Politics: 1851–1978: Symbols in Crises of Authority* (Lincoln, 1982); Morris W. Foster, *Being Comanche: A Social History of an American Indian Community* (Tucson, 1991); Frederick E.

The third aspect of colonial politics was among the Sioux themselves. The growth of U.S. power during the nineteenth century placed unprecedented stresses on Sioux political structures. Although the Sioux made constructive adaptations to new conditions, they also suffered an increase in destructive factionalism as the vise tightened. In writing about Sioux factionalism, most historians have reproduced the categories, if not the precise language, that U.S. officials used at the time, speaking of "progressives" versus "nonprogressives" (or "hostiles"), with the large majority favoring the former over the latter.[12] Rather than taking sides between two rigidly constructed positions, however, it is more productive to realize that Sioux leaders adopted a *range* of strategies based on reasoned assessments of changing conditions and possibilities. Sioux leaders were not always locked into polar antagonisms. Rather, they adjusted their tactics in light of new circumstances and were responsive to changing opinion among their people. Leaders cooperated among themselves on some initiatives and engaged in the tough political work of mending fences and building unity. Indeed, by focusing too much on factionalism it is possible to fail to appreciate the extent to which Sioux leaders' strategies had a common goal. Obviously, Indians who took up arms against U.S. expansion and who, during the reservation period, used tactics like direct refusal and withdrawal were engaged in resistance to U.S. domination. Yet tactics that involved "accommodation," such as selective cooperation, were also intended to limit or deflect the destructive impact of U.S. policies. Although the consent they entailed may have facilitated certain kinds of hegemony, these tactics, too, involved resistance. As Beatrice Medicine writes of Native responses to colonialism generally, both "confrontation" and "conciliatory acts" were "adaptive strategies to resist total assimilation into a dominant social system and a loss of cultural integrity."[13]

Hoxie, *Parading through History: The Making of the Crow Nation in America, 1805–1935* (Cambridge, 1995).

[12] For works that take the side of "progressives," see George E. Hyde, *Red Cloud's Folk: A History of the Oglala Sioux Indians* (Norman, 1937); George E. Hyde, *Spotted Tail's Folk: A History of the Brulé Sioux* (Norman, 1961); James C. Olson, *Red Cloud and the Sioux Problem* (Lincoln, 1965); Catherine Price, *The Oglala People, 1841–1879: A Political History* (Lincoln, 1996); Robert M. Utley, *The Lance and the Shield: The Life and Times of Sitting Bull* (New York, 1993). A good example of a work that takes the other side is Mari Sandoz, *Crazy Horse: The Strange Man of the Oglalas* (Lincoln, 1942).

[13] Bea Medicine, "Native American Resistance to Integration: Contemporary Confrontations and Religious Revitalization," *Plains Anthropologist* 26 (November 1981): 277. For criticisms of an excessive emphasis on factionalism, see Loretta Fowler, *Shared Symbols, Contested Meanings: Gros Ventre Culture and History, 1778–1984* (Ithaca, 1987), 4–8; Thomas W. Kavanagh, *Comanche Political History: An Ethnohistorical Perspective, 1706–1875* (Lincoln, 1996), xii; Duane Champagne, *American Indian Societies: Strategies and Conditions of Political and Cultural Survival* (Cambridge, Mass., 1989), 4. Rebecca Kugel, *To Be The Main Leaders of Our People: A History of Minnesota Ojibwe Politics, 1825–1898* (East Lansing, 1998), offers a useful corrective to the conventional wisdom that factionalism was largely negative.

Unfortunately, although Sioux leaders shared similar long-term objectives, their disputes became bitter and sometimes turned violent.

Although these three levels of politics can be seen throughout this book, the dynamics of imperialism and colonialism changed over time. Part 1 of this book, "Conquest," begins with the first few decades of the nineteenth century, a period when the Sioux had few interactions with the U.S. government. Their main experience of European Americans was through the fur trade. Although trade promoted limited economic dependency, introduced alcohol into some communities, and placed pressure on bison populations, it also facilitated the acquisition of material goods, including guns and ammunition. These resources helped make it possible for Sioux people to expand their territory at the expense of other tribes. Later, they would support military resistance against the United States. In the long term, the fur trade probably had its greatest impact through its contribution to subsequent phases of American capitalist expansion. The Plains Sioux began to experience these new phases in the 1840s and 1850s, when settlers traveling to Oregon and California invaded their lands, and in the 1860s and 1870s, when their own territory became valuable for mineral wealth. It was at this point that the U.S. government began to exercise power over the Sioux. At first, the Sioux had substantial leverage. In 1868 they were able to force the government to negotiate a treaty that in some ways inscribed Sioux military victories. However, this treaty aggravated already developing divisions between treaty and nontreaty Sioux and contained provisions that eventually led to U.S. control over the Sioux on reservations. In the 1870s, U.S. military power combined with a growing scarcity of game led to the final conquest of Sioux militants and their allies, and the theft of the Black Hills. The first part of the book ends in 1877 with the killing of Crazy Horse, an event that marked the end of Sioux warfare and ushered in a new phase of colonial management.

After 1877, as described in Part 2, "Colonialism," U.S. power manifested itself primarily through reservation agencies administered by the Indian Office (the predecessor to the Bureau of Indian Affairs). Although civilian agents continued to rely on the threat of military force, their primary weapons were economic leverage and new institutions (schools, police, courts). The stated purpose of U.S. policy was assimilation. Although many officials and missionaries were undoubtedly sincere when they professed a desire to rescue savages for civilization, assimilation functioned in the larger scheme of things as a rationale for the dispossession of Indian lands and the destruction of diversity in the name of national homogeneity. In practice, Christian and secular ideas about the common humanity of all peoples were overwhelmed by the corollary belief that existing Indian ways of life were heathen and primitive. The result was a form of management that was at best paternalistic and often simply racist. Remarkably, as the Sioux began living on reservations in the late 1870s, many Sioux leaders genuinely thought they might be able to work out a relationship with the United States that would allow them to preserve some of their land and ways of life, while adjusting to new conditions and demands. By the late 1880s, however, as the United States relentlessly cracked down on Sioux ways of life and demanded further cessions of land, these hopes began to seem elusive.

Part 3, "Anticolonialism and the State," focuses on the emergence of the Ghost Dance and the events that led to Wounded Knee. Under the increasingly oppressive conditions of the late 1880s, a minority of the Plains Sioux embraced Wovoka's prophesies of a cataclysmic event that would either remove European Americans from the western hemisphere or destroy them altogether and usher in a new world. Game would be restored and deceased ancestors returned to life. At most reservations in the western United States where ghost dancing emerged, the Indian Office's civilian agents decided to use "normal" methods to manage the movement, but some agents in charge of the western Sioux reservations were unable to maintain control. Their failures opened the door to a massive military operation, designed in part to demonstrate the continued relevance of the western army. In mid-November 1890, when the army invaded Sioux country, U.S. officials did not deliberately plan a massacre, but their reliance on overwhelming military power to intimidate and coerce eventually had exactly that result.

Wounded Knee was the single most devastating event in Plains Sioux history, but it did not destroy the Sioux nation. In the conclusion to this book I briefly explore some of the actions Sioux people have taken in the twentieth century to deal with Wounded Knee's agonizing legacy. In this way, the book ends where it began, one hundred years after the massacre as Sioux people tried to reckon with its trauma and all that it continues to represent.

PART I

CONQUEST

"Vilest Miscreants of the Savage Race"

The Plains Sioux in an Empire of Liberty

In 1803, when the French sold Louisiana to the United States, the Plains Sioux became subject to the claims of an emerging nation-state with a powerful commitment to territorial expansion. Early American political theorists operated on a grand hemispheric scale, imagining, as Thomas Jefferson did in 1801, that European American settlers eventually would "cover the whole northern, if not southern continent, with a people speaking the same language, governed in similar forms." Such a future had no place for Indians. Jefferson and other imperial planners gave Native people two choices. They could resist and risk being exterminated, or they could assimilate. Either way, North America, if not the entire hemisphere, would eventually be cleansed of ethnically distinct Indian communities.[1]

Why were American political theorists committed to virtually unlimited expansion, and why did the empire they envisioned allow no place for Indians? Founded in opposition to European colonialism (Britain's despotic rule over its North American colonies), the United States understood itself as a fragile experiment in republican liberty. Its future rested on the independence of property-holding citizens, racially defined as "white" and limited to men. Only through holding property could citizens maintain the freedom necessary to exercise vigilance against tyranny. Unlike Europe, where a limited supply of land was monopolized by an aristocratic class, the sheer size

---

[1] Anthony F. C. Wallace, *Jefferson and the Indians: The Tragic Fate of the First Americans* (Cambridge, Mass., 1999), 17 (qtn.), 276; Peter S. Onuf, *Jefferson's Empire: The Language of American Nationhood* (Charlottesville, 2000), 47–50; Reginald Horsman, *Expansion and American Indian Policy, 1783–1812* (East Lansing, 1967), 110–11; Bernard W. Sheehan, *Seeds of Extinction: Jeffersonian Philanthropy and the American Indian* (Chapel Hill, 1973). For a discussion of how attitudes of genocide and ethnocide emerged out of the Revolutionary War experience, see Colin G. Calloway, *The American Revolution in Indian Country: Crisis and Diversity in Native American Communities* (Cambridge, 1995), 292–301.

of the North American continent enabled Americans to imagine escaping a closed system. As the nation's population increased, settlers would occupy new lands in the West and bring new states into the Union (or to form "sister" republics), but this form of colonization would not reproduce the tyranny that British rule had earlier wrought. The United States' control of seemingly limitless space would enable it to overcome the historical tendency of republics to degenerate over time into despotic empires. Territorial expansion was not merely desirable; it was essential to the republican experiment's success. The "founding fathers" envisioned the United States as an imperial power, but in Jefferson's phrase, it would be a kind the world had never known. It would be an "empire for liberty."[2]

Although a republican justification for imperialism rejected forms of capitalist organization that promoted the centralization of political and economic power, and although the language of republicanism could contest special privilege, monopoly, and inequality, Jefferson's theory of empire was consistent with commercial capitalism. Land ownership went beyond simple occupancy; it entailed the right to buy, sell, accumulate, and speculate, and it encouraged claims upon the state to develop internal and overseas markets.[3] A nation committed to the endless expansion of a political economy based on widespread ownership of private property was unable to tolerate the

---

[2] Anders Stephanson, *Manifest Destiny: American Expansionism and the Empire of Right* (New York, 1995), 17–23 (qtn., 22); J. G. A. Pocock, *The Machiavellian Moment: Florentine Political Thought and the Atlantic Republican Tradition* (Princeton, 1975); R. W. Van Alystne, *The Rising American Empire* (Oxford, 1960), 78–99; William Appelman Williams, *Empire As a Way of Life: An Essay on the Causes and Character of America's Present Predicament along with a Few Thoughts about an Alternative* (New York, 1980), 45–62; Drew McCoy, *The Elusive Republic: Political Economy in Jeffersonian America* (Chapel Hill, 1980), 9–10; Robert W. Tucker and David C. Hendrickson, *Empire of Liberty: The Statecraft of Thomas Jefferson* (New York, 1990), 162; John Logan Allen, "Imagining the West: The View from Monticello," in *Thomas Jefferson and the Changing West: From Conquest to Conservation*, ed. James P. Ronda (Albuquerque, 1997), 3–23.

[3] On the centrality of capitalism to modern colonialism, see Arif Dirlik, "Rethinking Colonialism: Globalization, Postcolonialism, and the Nation," *Interventions: International Journal of Postcolonial Studies* 3 (November 2002): 428–48. The debate about the extent to which early American political thought can be characterized as republican or liberal seems to have been resolved in favor of a position that it was a complex blend of both, with liberalism becoming more pronounced over time. See Lance Banning, *The Jeffersonian Persuasian: Evolution of a Party Ideology* (Ithaca, 1978); Joyce Appleby, *Liberalism and Republicanism in the Historical Imagination* (Cambridge, Mass., 1992); Robert E. Shalhope, *The Roots of Democracy: American Thought and Culture, 1760–1800* (Boston, 1990). For the antimonopoly possibilities of radical republicanism, see Sean Wilentz, *Chants Democratic: New York City and the Rise of the American Working Class, 1788–1850* (New York, 1984); Leon Fink, *Workingmen's Democracy: The Knights of Labor and American Politics* (Urbana, 1983); Gerald Berk, *Alternative Tracks: The Constitution of the American Industrial Order, 1865–1917* (Baltimore, 1994); Robert D. Johnston, *The Radical Middle Class: Populist Democracy and the Question of Capitalism in Progressive Era Portland, Oregon* (Princeton, 2003).

permanent coexistence of alternative forms of social organization.[4] Theorists of the American nation did not merely think that they had devised mechanisms for solving particular problems arising under specific historical conditions. They believed that the United States embodied principles that demanded universal adherence. A society organized on the basis of widespread individual ownership of property did not simply suit the temperament of a particular people; it was the highest form of civilization, one that represented humanity's advance beyond primitive forms of social organization. According to this theory, Indians had no right to continue wasteful and inefficient uses of land or to perpetuate barbaric social and religious practices once civilization made its demands. Thus, although U.S. policy recognized Indian tribes as nations with limited sovereignty and made treaties with them, American leaders envisioned nothing less than the eventual extinguishing of all tribal claims to land.

Though many men and women who "settled" western frontiers became virulent Indian haters and advocated extermination, most theorists offered assimilation as an alternative. Assimilation resolved the contradiction between a commitment to dispossession with its implications of genocide on the one hand, and Enlightenment and Christian principles of the common humanity of all people on the other. Seen from one angle, assimilation was antithetical to racial thinking, since it presumed that Native Americans possessed the same innate mental and moral capacities as Europeans. Yet the basic premise of assimilation, that Indian ways of life were inferior, was linked to increasingly systematized theories of racial classification and hierarchy that tended to reinforce ontological thinking about race. Assimilation thus became more a theoretical possibility to be rhetorically proclaimed as civilization's generous gift rather than an actual expectation. American elites eventually tried to resolve the contradiction between imperialism and humanitarianism through the idea that whereas rare individuals might become "civilized," Indians were an inferior race that was inevitably destined to vanish. Although Americans knew at a practical level that Indians

---

[4] Onuf, *Jefferson's Empire*, 76–79, notes that a republic founded in ideological opposition to a strong centralized state placed an especially high premium on patriotism and homogeneity. For accounts of the rise of modern nationalism, see Ernest Gellner, *Nations and Nationalism* (Ithaca, 1983); Etienne Balibar, "The Nation Form: History and Ideology," in *Race, Nation, Class: Ambiguous Identities*, ed. Etienne Balibar and Immanuel Wallerstein, trans. Chris Turner (London, 1991), 86–106; E. J. Hobsbawm, *Nations and Nationalism since 1780: Programme, Myth, Reality*, 2d ed. (Cambridge, 1992); Benedict Anderson, *Imagined Communities: Reflections on the Origin and Spread of Nationalism*, rev. ed. (London, 1991); Anthony D. Smith, *The Nation in History: Historiographical Debates about Ethnicity and Nationalism* (Hanover, N.H., 2000). Although American nationalism was unable to tolerate Native autonomy, recent scholars have explored how Americans appropriated Indianness in constructing national identity. See Philip J. Deloria, *Playing Indian* (New Haven, 1998); Shari M. Huhndorf, *Going Native: Indians in the American Cultural Imagination* (Ithaca, 2001).

ILLUSTRATION 1. Lewis and Clark map. In the early 1800s American leaders often conceived of North America as an empty continent. Library of Congress Geography and Map Division.

controlled a significant proportion of North America, on an ideological level they conceived of the entire continent as empty (see Illustration 1).[5]

Early American imperial thought, then, denied the necessity for colonialism in the sense of rule over others. Settlers would move west, but, in sharp contrast to the colonies under the British empire, they would enjoy the same freedoms as eastern citizens. Nor, according to American theorists, would expansion require permanent rule over subjugated people. During the transition from savagery to civilization, the United States might have to exercise very moderate forms of authority over temporarily enclaved Indian communities, but this was understood to be no more than a fleeting phase within a larger process of dispossession and absorption.

Predictions that settlers would remain free from metropolitan tyranny proved remarkably accurate.[6] But despite prophesies of Indians' rapid disappearance, European Americans consistently overstated their capacity to subdue armed resistance and severely underestimated the pervasiveness of nonviolent Native resistance to dispossession and assimilation. Consequently, building an empire of liberty required the conquest of Indian people as well as the systematic and enduring exercise of power over subjected Indian communities. Native Americans adapted to the new conditions that were being imposed on them, but with very few exceptions, they clung tenaciously to community and tribal affiliations, though these were often reconfigured. In some instances Indians developed new forms of pantribal identity. They refused to accept assimilation, refused to go away. By the end of the nineteenth century, the United States exercised authority over hundreds of indigenous communities on dozens of reservations. U.S. policymakers continued to imagine that through a combination of population decline and assimilation Indians would soon disappear. In practice, however, whether Americans were prepared to acknowledge it or not, the United States was firmly committed to a system of colonial rule.[7]

---

[5] Audrey Smedley, *Race in North America: Origin and Evolution of a Worldview* (Boulder, 1993), 177–81; Richard Drinnon, *Facing West: The Metaphysics of Indian-Hating and Empire-Building* (Minneapolis, 1980), 65–116. However sincere policymakers were about the prospects for assimilation, the discourse of assimilation was always ideological in the sense that it provided a way to evade responsibility for the destructive consequences of expansion. Ultimately, it facilitated fatalistic ideas about the inevitability of Indians' disappearance. Sheehan, *Seeds of Extinction*; Onuf, *Jefferson's Empire*, 51–52; Wallace, *Jefferson and the Indians*, 19–20; Robert F. Berkhofer Jr., *The White Man's Indian: Images of the American Indian from Columbus to the Present* (New York, 1978), 29–30; Brian W. Dippie, *The Vanishing American: White Attitudes and U.S. Indian Policy* (Middletown, Conn., 1982), 3–11.

[6] For a different perspective, however, see William G. Robbins, *Colony and Empire: The Capitalist Transformation of the American West* (Lawrence, 1994).

[7] As this overview makes clear, U.S. imperialism and colonialism in the nineteenth century had distinctive characteristics and contrasted, for example, with various examples of colonialism that involved rule over large populations on other continents. Perhaps the best term for the

In 1803, when the United States claimed sovereignty over Plains Sioux lands, President Jefferson envisioned yeomen farmers eventually extending liberty onto the "open" spaces of the Great Plains. In practical terms, however, Jefferson thought that it would be decades – if not centuries – before this vision was realized. In the meantime, the geopolitical place of the lands acquired under the Louisiana Purchase was defined by more immediate considerations. First, Louisiana was vital for U.S. commercial interests, not only because owning Louisiana assured control over the Mississippi River, but also because it revived the age-old dream of a passage across the continent, one that would place the United States at the center of a worldwide commercial network extending from Europe to Asia. Second, by creating a buffer between the United States and the two remaining European powers, Britain and Spain, the new territory enhanced U.S. strategic interests. Third, as settler-colonists (including slaveowners) and speculators exerted increasing pressure on Indian lands east of the Mississippi River, and as Indians resisted this pressure, Louisiana allowed U.S. officials a way to avoid the contradictions of a policy of "expansion with honor." Instead of abandoning the possibility of assimilation and endorsing extermination, policymakers could move eastern tribes to new locations in the West, where they would ostensibly be protected from overly rapid exposure to civilization and be slowly guided along the proper path.[8]

To begin to exploit Louisiana's benefits, Jefferson sought to establish trading relations with the Indians along the upper Missouri River. This would be commercially beneficial and would draw the tribes away from European

---

U.S. case is *settler-colonialism*, one of several types usefully described in Jürgen Osterhammel, *Colonialism: A Theoretical Overview*, trans. Shelley L. Frisch (Princeton, 1997); and effectively applied to the western United States in Gray H. Whaley, "Creating Oregon from *Ilahee*: Race, Settler-Colonialism, and Native Sovereignty in Western Oregon, 1792–1856," Ph.D. diss., University of Oregon, 2002. As a case of settler-colonialism, the United States bears comparison, among others, to Russia, Canada, Australia, New Zealand, Argentina, Chile, South Africa, Algeria, and Zionism. Depending on several variables, such as specific forms of capitalist production and indigenous population densities and patterns of subsistence, settler-colonialism can lead to various forms of domination and accompanying ideologies, including assimilation, disappearance, and rationales for quasi-permanent governance. For suggestive points of comparison, see George M. Fredrickson, *White Supremacy: A Comparative Study in American and South African History* (New York, 1981), 3–53; Donald Denoon, *Settler Capitalism: The Dynamics of Dependent Development in the Southern Hemisphere* (Oxford, 1983); Patrick Wolfe, "History and Imperialism: A Century of Theory, from Marx to Postcolonialism," *American Historical Review* 102 (April 1997): 388–420; Cole Harris, *The Resettlement of British Columbia: Essays on Colonialism and Geographical Change* (Vancouver, 1997); Gershon Shafir, "Zionism and Colonialism: A Comparative Approach," in *The Israel/Palestine Question*, ed. Ilan Pappé (London, 1999), 81–96; Azzedine Haddour, *Colonial Myths: History and Narrative* (Manchester, 2000).

[8] Tucker and Henderickson, *Empire of Liberty*, 88–89, 95–100; Sheehan, *Seeds of Extinction*, 246; D. W. Meinig, *The Shaping of America: A Geographical Perspective on 500 Years of History: Volume 2: Continental America, 1800–1867* (New Haven, 1993), 4–7, 78–79.

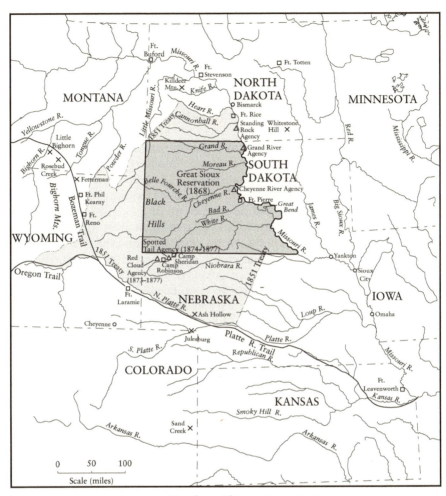

MAP 1. Northern Plains, 1804–1876.

rivals, especially Britain. Accordingly, in sending Meriwether Lewis and William Clark to explore the newly acquired territory, Jefferson placed a great deal of importance on the Sioux. They occupied a powerful position as middlemen in the region's trade.[9]

Relations between the United States and the Sioux did not begin auspiciously. When Lewis and Clark encountered a Sioux village near the mouth of the Bad River (see Map 1) on September 25, 1804, they staged a performance

[9] Anthony F. C. Wallace, "'The Obtaining Lands': Thomas Jefferson and the Native Americans," in *Jefferson and the Changing West*, ed. Ronda, 34; James P. Ronda, *Lewis and Clark among the Indians* (Lincoln, 1984), 30.

designed to impress the Natives with their power. Speaking through an interpreter with only a rudimentary knowledge of the Sioux language (Lakota),
Lewis declared that the Spanish and French fathers had departed and that
a new father, the chief of seventeen nations (the states), had taken their
place. This new father and his people desired intertribal peace and trade.
Following Lewis's speech, the expedition's men marched in military uniform
behind their flag and then Lewis and Clark distributed gifts to the Sioux
leaders.[10]

Problems arose when the Sioux saw that the expedition had given them
only a small portion of its goods and complained that the presents were
inadequate. Faced with these murmurings and the presence of several Sioux
warriors, Lewis tried to intimidate the Indians by firing an airgun "several
times." Although the Sioux had never seen an airgun, they had extensive
experience with European weapons and possessed muskets. Under different
circumstances they might have shown curiosity at a new type of weapon, but
at the moment they gave it little attention. They were confident of their position and continued to press their complaints.[11] Later that day, as the Sioux
tried to prevent an expedition pirogue from leaving shore, Lewis ordered
his men to arms, and Clark issued various threats. By one account, Clark
said he "had more medicine on board his boat than would kill twenty such
nations in one day." By another, he threatened to write to the "great father
the president of the U.S. [and] . . . have them all distroyed [sic] as it were
in a moment."[12] On the twenty-eighth, as Lewis and Clark were about to
resume their journey up the Missouri, the Indians again refused to let them
go. Warriors represented by Black Buffalo took hold of their bowline and
asked for tobacco. Lewis refused, saying he "would not agree to be forced
into any thing." A second group of warriors, led by a man whom Clark
identified as The Partisan, then "[d]emanded a flag & Tobacco."[13] Again,
Clark declared that he "did not mean to be trifled with." Black Buffalo
replied that "he was mad, too" to see the Americans "Stand So much for
1 carrit [sic] of tobacco." Exasperated, Lewis finally threw some tobacco
to Black Buffalo's men. Only then did they release the bowline and allow
the expedition to proceed. Although Lewis and Clark had tried to intimidate the Sioux and gain the upper hand, it was the Sioux who remained

---

[10] Ronda, *Lewis and Clark among the Indians*, 32.

[11] Ibid; Milo M. Quaife, ed., *The Journals of Captain Meriwether Lewis and Seargeant John
Ordway*, Collections of the State Historical Society of Wisconsin, vol. 22 (Madison, 1916),
138 (qtn.). Lewis and Clark fired their airgun on several occasions during their journey and
reported in a manner that reflected a common colonial trope that it "Surprised and astonished
the natives. . . ." Gary E. Moulton, ed., *The Journals of the Lewis & Clark Expedition*, vol. 3
(Lincoln, 1987), 209.

[12] Patrick Gass, *A Journal of the Voyages and Travels of a Corps of Discovery* (Minneapolis,
1958), 51 (1st qtn.); Quaife, ed., *Journals of Lewis and Ordway*, 139 (2d qtn.).

[13] Moulton, ed., *Journals*, 3:124.

undaunted. Frustrated by the expedition's failure to establish dominion over the Sioux, Lewis later pronounced them the "vilest miscreants of the savage race."[14]

What was for Lewis and Clark an unprecedented engagement with an unfamiliar people was for the Sioux another in a familiar series of encounters with non-Indians. For decades Sioux communities had traded with French, British, and Spanish traders. They understood something of the imperial rivalries of European nations, especially as these were played out in competition for trade. The Sioux were interested in learning what Lewis and Clark had to offer, but they were not about to risk destroying their economy for some meager gifts, stories about a chief of seventeen nations, and an airgun. Sioux people did not think much of European nation-states' claims. Ten years earlier, when Jean Baptiste Truteau, an employee of a Spanish trading company, tried to prevail upon the Sioux to "listen to the words of their Spanish father," they pointedly rejected the idea that they had such a relative.[15]

The Sioux Lewis and Clark encountered had lived near the Missouri for a relatively brief period of time, probably no more than two generations. One hundred years before, their ancestors had been living to the east, in present-day Minnesota. In the seventeenth century, when the French first came into Sioux country, they referred to them by an Ottawa term that the French wrote as "Nadouessioux." Eventually, this was shortened to "Sioux." Despite its external imposition, it remains the least confusing umbrella term for all Sioux people. Then, as now, the Sioux formally referred to themselves as *Oceti Sakowin* (Seven Council Fires) and, depending on dialect, as *Dakota* or *Lakota*, a word signifying friendship. It is doubtful that the Seven Council Fires ever existed as a political entity. Rather, this notion expressed an identity based on a shared language, culture, and history. As William Powers observes, the Seven Council Fires (and their subdivisions) were "in a state

---

[14] Quaife, ed., *Journals of Lewis and Ordway*, 142 (1st qtn.); "Lewis and Clarke's Expedition, Communicated to Congress, February 19, 1806," *American State Papers*, vol. 5, class 2, Indian Affairs, vol. 1, # 113, 9th Cong., 1st sess., 714 (2d qtn.). Clark identified the "Partezon's" Lakota name as "Torto-hongar," which Moulton, ed., *Journals*, 3:114, n. 3, translates as war leader (*blotahunka*). French traders and explorers commonly used the term *partisan* as a title for a native war leader. See, for example, M. Perrin du Lac, *Voyages dans les deux Louisanes* (Lyon, 1805), 293: "Chez tous les Sauvages de L'Amérique septentrionale, sans exception, tout homme peut former un parti de guerre et se mettre à la tête; le chef d'une pareille expédition, se nomme *Partisan*." On these events, see also Stephen E. Ambrose, *Undaunted Courage: Meriwether Lewis, Thomas Jefferson, and the Opening of the American West* (New York, 1996), 168–75.

[15] A. P. Nasatir, ed., *Before Lewis and Clark: Documents Illustrating the History of the Missouri, 1785–1804*, vol. 1 (St. Louis, 1952), 270–73 (qtn., 270); George E. Hyde, *Red Cloud's Folk: A History of the Oglala Sioux Indians* (Norman, 1937), 26.

of constant flux, forming temporary alliances, constantly shifting leadership and nuclei of villages and bands."[16]

Opportunities to hunt beaver for trade and bison for subsistence led three groups of the Seven Council Fires, the Lakota-speaking Tetons and the Dakota-speaking Yanktons and Yanktonais,[17] to move westward in the early 1700s. Using guns acquired through trade, they displaced Omahas, Otoes, Iowas, Missouris, and Poncas. By 1770, two Teton subgroups, the Sicangus (Brulés) and Oglalas, were living south of the Great Bend of the Missouri River, where they were under the shadow of the more powerful river tribes, the Arikaras, Mandans, and Hidatsas. Two other Teton subgroups, the Saones and Minneconjous, and some Yanktonai bands were living to the north, east of the Missouri. By this time, the western Sioux had acquired horses and were becoming a buffalo-hunting people.[18]

In the late 1700s a series of smallpox epidemics severely weakened the river tribes. The Oglalas and Brulés took advantage of this situation and moved into the rich buffalo region west of the Missouri, where they became the powerful people that Lewis and Clark encountered. (The village at the mouth of the Bad River was a Brulé band.) During the same period, the Minneconjous and Saones also pushed across the Missouri River to the north, where the latter became differentiated into four subgroups: the Itazipcos (Sans Arcs, or Without Bows), Oohenunpas (Two Kettles), Hunkpapas, and Sihasapas (Blackfeet, not to be confused with the Algonquian tribe of the same name). For the next several decades, the Plains Sioux waged intermittent war against Kiowas, Crows, Shoshones, Assiniboines, and Skidi Pawnees to gain access to new hunting areas. By 1850 the western Sioux, with a population of perhaps fifteen thousand, controlled much of the vast region between the Platte and the Yellowstone.[19]

[16] Raymond J. DeMallie, "Sioux until 1850," in *Plains*, ed., Raymond J. DeMallie, vol. 13, pt. 2, *Handbook of North American Indians*, ed. William C. Sturtevant (Washington, D.C., 2001), 718, 749–50; William K. Powers, *Oglala Religion* (Lincoln, 1975), 21. For a discussion of an emerging Lakota critique of the idea that they are relatively recent migrants, see Mikael Kurkiala, "Objectifying the Past: Lakota Responses to Western Historiography," *Critique of Anthropology* 22 (December 2002): 445–60.

[17] The other four groups of the Seven Council Fires are the Mdewakantons, Wahpetons, Wahpekutes, and Sissetons (collectively known as the Santee or eastern Sioux and speakers of the Dakota dialect). For an authoritative account of Sioux tribal and band names, see DeMallie, "Sioux until 1850," 736–49.

[18] Gary Clayton Anderson, "Early Dakota Migration and Intertribal War: A Revision," *Western Historical Quarterly* 11 (January 1980): 17–36; Richard White, "The Winning of the West: The Expansion of the Western Sioux in the Eighteenth and Nineteenth Centuries," *Journal of American History* 65 (September 1978): 321–23; Frank Raymond Secoy, *Changing Military Patterns of the Great Plains Indians* (1953; Lincoln, 1992), 71–72; James H. Howard, "Yanktonai Ethnohistory and the John K. Bear Winter Count," *Plains Anthropologist* 21 (August 1976): 5–6; Hyde, *Red Cloud's Folk*, 6–18; Kingsley M. Bray, "Teton Sioux Population History, 1655–1881," *Nebraska History* 75 (Summer 1994): 177.

[19] White, "Winning of the West," 324–43; Secoy, *Changing Military Patterns*, 72–75; Hyde, *Red Cloud's Folk*, 18–68. Bray, "Teton Sioux Population," 174, estimates the Teton

Richard White has provocatively described the Sioux movement onto the Plains as "the winning of the West."[20] This phrase has the virtue of reminding us that European Americans did not have a monopoly on expansion. At the same time, however, there were important qualitative differences between the Sioux and U.S. cases. In all likelihood, the stages of Sioux expansion were not planned very far in advance nor centrally coordinated but instead involved a series of pragmatic calculations about exigencies of trade, animal populations, and the relative strengths and weaknesses of rivals and potential allies. The Plains Sioux waged war on other Indian people who stood in the way of their immediate objectives, sometimes developing strong enmities in the process. Unlike European Americans, however, they did not divide the world's people into the civilized and the primitive and imagine an inevitable and total triumph of the former over the latter. Nor did they have anything like the United States' ideologically articulated commitment to an empire that would encompass the entire continent.

Because the Plains Sioux mode of subsistence required bands to move and hunt separately throughout much of the year, Sioux political authority was decentralized. Each of the Seven Council Fires was divided into subgroups known as *oyate*, a term that can be translated as tribe, people, or nation.[21] In turn, each *oyate* consisted of several *tiyospayes*, a term that is commonly glossed as band and literally means a group living together. The *tiyospaye* was the basic social and political unit. A *tiyospaye* typically consisted of no more than a few hundred people, all linked by kinship. More than one *tiyospaye* might camp together for a period of time, and on occasion leaders from several bands might consult and make decisions. But although bands were linked through a common culture, language, and history and there was great deal of interaction, movement, and intermarriage among them, there is little evidence of large multiband councils before the 1850s.[22]

---

population in 1849 at 12,845. To this figure, I have added a portion of the 6,000 combined Yankton and Yanktonai in the early reservation period (Bray, "Teton Sioux Population," 175).

[20] White, "Winning of the West."

[21] To summarize the information presented in the preceding historical narrative, the Tetons had (and still have) seven *oyates* with the Lakota names of Oglalas ("scatter one's own"), Sicangus ("burned thighs," thus the French term, *Brulé*), Minneconjous ("plant by water"), Itazipcos ("without bows," thus the French term, *Sans Arcs*), Oohenunpas ("two boilings," thus Two Kettles), Sihasapas ("blackfeet"), and Hunkpapas ("head of camp circle entrance"). In this book, I have used the Lakota name unless the French or English name is dominant in the historical literature as follows: Oglalas, Brulés, Minneconjous, Sans Arcs, Two Kettles, Sihasapas, Hunkpapas.

[22] Stephen E. Feraca, "The Political Status of the Early Bands and Modern Communities of the Oglala Dakota," *Museum News* 27 (1966): 1; Raymond J. DeMallie, "Pine Ridge Economy: Cultural and Historical Perspectives," in *American Indian Economic Development*, ed. Sam Stanley (The Hague, 1978), 243; Raymond J. DeMallie, "Teton," in *Plains*, ed. DeMallie, 801; Ella C. Deloria, *Speaking of Indians* (1944; Vermillion, S.Dak., 1992), 15.

Generally, each band had one chief (usually called *itancan*, although other terms were used).[23] Some men became chiefs because their fathers had been chiefs; others were recognized for particular accomplishments or abilities. Styles of political leadership varied. Most leaders typically sought consensus through councils of important men and were probably motivated less by a desire for power than a sense of responsibility (sometimes felt as a burden) for the community's well-being. Although band leaders could be authoritarian, in most cases there were checks on undemocratic exercises of power. When a leader transgressed band members' wishes, the people could replace him. Alternatively, a faction that was unsatisfied with a leader could form a new band.

The Plains Sioux did not consist of a fixed number of hermetic communities. Bands were constantly splitting, combining, reforming, cooperating together, and moving away from one another. Intermarriage between bands was common, not only among the western bands but also between the western and eastern Sioux. In the early 1800s the Tetons' relatively higher standard of living drew many Santees, Yanktons, and Yanktonais to their communities. Kingsley Bray's careful reconstruction indicates a Teton (Lakota) population of 8,500 in 1805, 45 percent of the total Sioux population. Lakota numbers increased steadily in the nineteenth century, reaching 16,000 in 1881, 60 percent of the total Sioux population.[24]

Although western Sioux expansion involved warfare, alliances were equally important. Although there was some conflict between Sioux and Cheyenne bands in the 1720s and 1730s and again in the 1790s as Oglalas and Brulés moved into the Black Hills region, by the early nineteenth century, Lakota and Cheyenne communities had established what would become a long-standing alliance.[25] In some instances, Lakota communities established

[23] Powers, *Oglala Religion*, 40–41; Catherine Price, *The Oglala People, 1841–1879: A Political History* (Lincoln, 1996), 6–10, follow Clark Wissler, *Societies and Ceremonial Associations in the Oglala Division of the Teton-Dakota*, Anthropological Papers of the American Museum of Natural History, vol. 11, pt. 1 (New York, 1912), 7–8, and use the term *itancan* for chief and the term *wakiconza* for a separate office with duties to enforce decisions, a distinction similar to the one in DeMallie, "Teton," 802. However, other sources use *wakiconza* or *naca* for chief. See James R. Walker, *Lakota Society*, ed. Raymond J. DeMallie (Lincoln, 1982), 38–39, 178, n. 42; Feraca, "Political Status of Early Bands," 3. Another term that appears in the ethnographic literature is *wicasa yatanpi*, meaning "praiseworthy men," and often referred to as shirtwearer after the scalp shirts worn by holders of the office. According to Powers, *Oglala Religion*, 40; Royal B. Hassrick, *The Sioux: Life and Customs of a Warrior Society* (Norman, 1964), 28–29, this office was distinct from that of chief, but other evidence suggests the term was a synonym for chief. See Stanley Vestal, *Warpath: The True Story of the Fighting Sioux Told in a Biography of Chief White Bull* (1934; Lincoln, 1984), 48; Edmund C. Bray and Martha Coleman Bray, trans. and eds., *Joseph N. Nicollet on the Plains and Prairies: The Expeditions of 1838–39 with Journals, Letters, and Notes on the Dakota Indians* (St. Paul, 1976), 274.

[24] Bray, "Teton Sioux Population," 170–77.

[25] John H. Moore, *The Cheyenne Nation: A Social and Demographic History* (Lincoln, 1987), 75–77, 117–21. Hyde, *Red Cloud's Folk*, 18, 24, provides instances of conflict. However,

alliances with non-Lakotas who were hostile toward other Lakota bands. In 1795 Truteau observed a Saone community living in an Arikara village. The Saones retained a distinct identity, but they had "the same sentiments and character" as the Arikaras. According to Truteau, this internal Saone colony enabled the Arikaras to trade with other Teton bands and to "avoid making too many enemies among the Sioux, who would inevitably overpower them."[26] Much later, in the 1850s, the Minneconjous and Crows reached a peace agreement to allow both groups to hunt in a previously contested buffer zone between the Black Hills and the Powder River. Although some Sioux respected this agreement, the Hunkpapas and Sihasapas did not.[27] Not only do these examples reveal processes of alliance, they underscore that practical decisions were almost always made at the level of individual communities.

As Lakotas interacted with non-Sioux communities, they often absorbed outsiders. Over the years, Cheyenne men and women married into Lakota communities and vice versa. Lakotas also adopted women and children captured in attacks on other tribes.[28] Sometimes, outsiders sought to become Sioux. In the 1830s Poncas joined Lakotas and Yanktons in raids on Pawnee villages evidently for fear that, if they did not, the Sioux would destroy them. Later, the French cartographer Joseph N. Nicollet reported that a band among the Brulés, the "Wazazi" (Wazaza), had been formed by marriages of Sioux and Poncas, who had earlier intermarried with Osages. Apparently, the Ponca-Osages had married Brulés to solidify an alliance undertaken for self-preservation.[29]

Like all Native people of the Americas, the Sioux inhabited a world permeated with living power. From a Judeo-Christian perspective these powers might be described as "supernatural," but Native cosmologies do not conceive of something outside of or above nature. Instead, all that existed – the

---

Cheyenne traditions indicate that any conflict that occurred was minimal. See George Bird Grinnell, *The Fighting Cheyennes* (1915; Norman, 1956), 6; George E. Hyde, *A Life of George Bent Written from his Letters*, ed. Savoie Lottinville (Norman, 1968), 22.

[26] Nasatir, ed., *Before Lewis and Clark*, 310. Bray, "Teton Sioux Population," 177, suggests that this Lakota community was probably a Minneconjou band.

[27] Kingsley M. Bray, "Lone Horn's Peace: A New View of Sioux-Crow Relations, 1851–1858," *Nebraska History* 66 (Spring 1985): 28–47.

[28] John Stands in Timber and Margot Liberty, *Cheyenne Memories* (New Haven, 1967), 121; Stanley Vestal, *Sitting Bull: Champion of the Sioux* (1932; Norman, 1956), 24; R. Eli Paul, ed., *Autobiography of Red Cloud: War Leader of the Oglalas* (Helena, 1997), 140; Walker, *Lakota Society*, 54–55; Hassrick, *The Sioux*, 111–12.

[29] James H. Howard, *The Ponca Tribe*, Smithsonian Institution Bureau of American Ethnology Bulletin 195 (Washington, D.C., 1965), 28; Bray and Bray, eds., *Nicollet*, 261. For an overview of the political economy of intertribal relationships on the Plains, see Patricia C. Albers, "Symbiosis, Merger, and War: Contrasting Forms of Intertribal Relationship Among Historic Plains Indians," in *The Political Economy of North American Indians*, ed. John H. Moore (Norman, 1993), 94–132.

world, the universe – was natural, and nature was saturated with spiritual power.

The Sioux call the spiritual powers of the universe *Wakan Tanka*. This term is usually glossed God, Great Spirit, or Great Mystery. God is a poor translation because it fails to convey any sense of difference between Sioux and Christian religions. Great Spirit, often used to describe a Supreme Being for all Native North Americans, is an inaccurate translation of *Wakan Tanka* (*tanka* means great or large, but the word for spirit is *nagi*, not *wakan*). Great Mystery is a better translation, because *wakan* conveys a sense of incomprehensibility or mysteriousness, but *wakan* can also suggest holiness, sacredness, power, or energy.[30] *Wakan Tanka* is not the Creator of all things nor a being in the same way as the Christian God. Rather, in Scott Howard's useful formulation, *Wakan Tanka* is an "umbrella label for the various *wakan* beings or for *wakan* actions." Although not a person, when calling upon *Wakan Tanka* for assistance, Lakotas often use the kinship term *tunkasila* (grandfather) to show respect and dependence.[31]

Studies of Sioux religion provide useful overviews of cosmology and ritual, but the literature gives little attention to how Sioux religious practices changed with the migration to the new Plains environment in the late 1700s and early 1800s. Some scholars have suggested, however, that one of the most powerful foundations of Plains Sioux religion, the story of the coming of the White Buffalo Calf Woman, reflects these historical transitions. Many versions of this story exist, but they all have the same basic features.[32] The story begins with a time of famine. The Sans Arcs, moving westward, are unable to find buffalo. Two young men, sent out to find game, encounter a beautiful young woman. She explains that she has been sent by the Buffalo tribe with a message for their people. One of the two lusts after the woman and is destroyed. The other returns to the camp, tells the people what he has seen, and they prepare to welcome the visitor. The next day the woman appears at sunrise carrying a pipe. After being welcomed by the chief, she takes the pipe and explains that *Wakan Tanka* has smiled upon everyone

---

[30] For discussions of *wakan*, see William K. Powers, *Sacred Language: The Nature of Supernatural Discourse in Lakota* (Norman, 1986), 120; Raymond J. DeMallie Jr. and Robert H. Lavenda, "*Wakan*: Plains Siouan Concepts of Power," in *The Anthropology of Power: Ethnographic Studies from Asia, Oceania, and the New World*, ed. Raymond D. Fogelson and Richard N. Adams (New York, 1977), 154–56; Albert White Hat Sr., *Reading and Writing the Lakota Language: Lakota Iyapi un Wowapi nahan Yawapi*, ed. Jael Kampfe (Salt Lake City, 1999), 98.

[31] Scott J. Howard, "Incommensurability and Nicholas Black Elk: An Exploration," *American Indian Culture and Research Journal* 23, no. 1 (1999): 115. See also Powers, *Oglala Religion*, 45–46.

[32] Powers, *Oglala Women*, 50. Versions of the story of the coming of the White Buffalo Calf Woman can be found in Frances Densmore, *Teton Sioux Music and Culture* (1918; Lincoln, 1992), 63–66; Joseph Epes Brown, ed., *The Sacred Pipe: Black Elk's Account of the Seven Rites of the Oglala Sioux* (Norman, 1953), 3–9.

present, as all belong to one family. She, in fact, is their sister. The woman then explains that she represents the Buffalo tribe and that the sacred pipe she carries is a gift from them to the people. After instructing the women, children, and men of their duties and obligations, she lights the pipe and offers it to the earth and the four directions. She puffs the pipe, passes it to the chief and then leaves. As the people watch her depart, the woman becomes a white buffalo calf. According to some traditions, the White Buffalo Calf Woman not only gave the Sacred Pipe to the San Arcs on this occasion, she also brought the seven rituals central to the practice of Plains Sioux religion. Other traditions, however, suggest that the western Sioux received the seven rituals at different times. Using these rituals, the Plains Sioux had become a Buffalo Nation, strong, generous, and enduring.[33]

By becoming a Buffalo Nation, the Plains Sioux had in some ways enacted a universal process by which people moving into a new country come to see themselves as a chosen people, as Elliott West suggests in writing about the migration of the Cheyennes onto the Plains.[34] As with the notion of the Sioux winning of the West, however, it is important to bear in mind critical distinctions between Sioux and U.S. approaches to the Plains. Americans' belief in themselves as a chosen people, a people with a "manifest" destiny to build an empire with world-historical significance, entailed comprehensive ideas about their superiority and ultimate place in the world that went far beyond the Sioux sense of themselves. The western Sioux made the Plains their world, but they knew there would always be other people on the Plains and that there were other worlds beyond. In contrast, Americans saw their mission as nothing less than to make the whole continent – indeed, the whole world – conform to their belief that they had achieved the highest form of human existence in history. For Americans, extending the domain of civilization involved not just using the resources of the continent, but re-creating its entire face. The Plains would be thoroughly transformed. Abstract grids would be placed on it, sod overturned, fields fenced, and the land made to conform to a single standard.[35] Rather than sanctioning this kind of

---

33 The seven ceremonies the White Buffalo Calf Woman gave the Lakotas are *Inipi* (the sweat-lodge, or ritual of purification), *Hanbleceya* (seeking a vision), *Wanagi Yuhapi* (ghost-keeping), *Wiwanyang Wacipi* (the sun dance), *Hunkapi* (the making of relatives), *Isnati Awicalowan* (preparing a girl for womanhood), and *Tapa Wankayeyapi* (the throwing of the ball). Powers, *Oglala Religion*, 89–103; and DeMallie, "Teton," 806–08, offer succinct descriptions of these ceremonies. Brown, ed., *The Sacred Pipe*, 44, states that two of the rituals (*Inipi* and *Hanbleceya*) were in use before the Sacred Pipe; Powers, *Oglala Women*, 48, indicates that the White Buffalo Calf Woman instructed the Sans Arcs in all seven rituals. For the idea of the Plains Sioux as a Buffalo Nation, see Julian Rice, *Ella Deloria's "The Buffalo People"* (Albuquerque, 1994).

34 Elliott West, *The Contested Plains: Indians, Goldseekers, and the Rush to Colorado* (Lawrence, 1998), 76.

35 This process bears comparison to the "high modernist" state projects analyzed in James C. Scott, *Seeing Like a State: How Certain Schemes to Improve the Human Condition Have*

domination over the land, the White Buffalo Calf Woman instructed her people how to receive the gifts offered from the world's spiritual powers so they could "walk the red road," to use a common Sioux metaphor.[36] Although this vision entailed progress in the sense of moving from hardship (famine) to prosperity, walking the red road had more to do with maintaining a carefully balanced way of life through ritual and daily practices. These continually reminded people of their dependence on the life-giving powers that suffused the world. American visions of empire had religious sanction, but the destiny of God's chosen people had far different ramifications.

Eventually, the Plains Sioux would be forced to contend with the full expression of the United States' vision of empire. In the early nineteenth century, however, the Sioux gained most of their knowledge of European Americans through a group whose practical interests were not conspicuously imperial: fur traders.

A U.S.-sponsored fur trade was slow to develop. In 1809 the Missouri Fur Company established a post near the mouth of the Bad River, not far from Lewis and Clark's initial encounter with the Sioux. The outbreak of war with Britain in 1812 blocked shipping through New Orleans and forced the Missouri Company to abandon its posts upriver of Council Bluffs. Trade did not revive until after the Panic of 1819, when several companies established posts along the Missouri. By 1827, one of these outfits, the American Fur Company – known simply as "The Company" – had established a monopoly over the upper Missouri trade. Over the next three decades competitors attempted to break this company's hold on the upper Missouri trade, but they were never successful.[37]

In retrospect it is easy to see the fur trade as the thin end of the wedge that would ultimately force the western Sioux into economic and political dependency. At the time, however, most Sioux did not regard the trade as a step in this direction. If anything, by Plains Indians' ways of thinking, it was the outside traders who were dependent. One trader reported that Crees thought of his ilk as "poor people who could not exist without them, because we must have buffalo robes or we should perish from the cold." Most Plains Indians willingly hunted more bison than necessary for subsistence and processed the robes (later, hides) to sell for weapons, ammunition, metal tools, clothing, decorative ornaments, sugar, coffee, clay pipes, blankets, and

Failed (New Haven, 1998), and to the general model of North American frontier processes in William Cronon, George Miles, and Jay Gitlin, "Becoming West: Toward a New Meaning for Western History," in *Under an Open Sky: Rethinking America's Western Past*, ed. William Cronon, George Miles, and Jay Gitlin (New York, 1992), 3–27.

36 This metaphor appears, among other places, in Raymond J. DeMallie, ed., *The Sixth Grandfather: Black Elk's Teachings Given to John G. Neihardt* (Lincoln, 1984).

37 David J. Wishart, *The Fur Trade of the American West, 1807–1840: A Geographical Synthesis* (Lincoln, 1979), 42–74.

tobacco. In most cases, these items had self-evident uses. In other instances, Indians invented new uses for European goods, such as cutting arrowheads from frying pans.[38]

Nonetheless, there were serious disadvantages to the trade. Hunting bison for the market was one of many causes that contributed to the decline of bison populations in the 1840s and 1850s.[39] Another arguably negative consequence was the labor required of women to process hides. Although men spent more time hunting to kill animals for trade than they would have otherwise, the additional labor paid off handsomely. In other words, killing ten animals – five for subsistence and five for hides – required less than twice as much time and effort than killing five for subsistence. On the other side of equation, because it took twice the amount of labor to process ten hides as five, female labor increased in direct proportion to any increase in hunting for the market. Measuring this division of labor's exploitation, however, is complicated by the fact that we know little about how trade goods reduced female labor in other areas.[40]

There is little ambiguity when it comes to assessing the impact of alcohol. Whiskey was easily the least expensive way to procure furs and skins, especially when it was mixed with river water and adulterated with condiments like chewing tobacco, molasses, and peppers. It was also a necessary weapon in the trade wars that erupted among rival firms.[41] Alcohol abuse had many

---

[38] J. N. B. Hewitt, ed., *Journal of Rudolph Friederich Kurz: An Account of His Experiences among Fur Traders and American Indians on the Mississippi and the Upper Missouri Rivers*, Smithsonian Institution Bulletin 115, trans. Myrtis Jarrell (Washington, D.C., 1957), 154 (qtn.); John E. Sunder, *The Fur Trade on the Upper Missouri, 1840–1865* (Norman, 1965), 134–35; *Message from the President of the United States in Compliance with a Resolution of the Senate Concerning the Fur Trade, and Inland Trade to Mexico*, 22d Cong., 1st sess., 1831–32, S. Doc. 90, serial 213, 65–68; Densmore, *Teton Sioux Music and Culture*, 438.

[39] For explanations of the bison's decline, see Dan Flores, "Bison Ecology and Bison Diplomacy: The Southern Plains from 1800 to 1850," *Journal of American History* 78 (September 1991): 465–85; Dan Flores, "The Great Contraction: Bison and Indians in Northern Plains Environmental History," in *Legacy: New Perspectives on the Battle of the Little Bighorn*, ed. Charles E. Rankin (Helena, 1996), 3–22; Elliott West, *The Way to the West: Essays on the Central Plains* (Albuquerque, 1995), 51–83; West, *Contested Plains*, 90–92; William A. Dobak, "Killing the Canadian Buffalo, 1821–1881," *Western Historical Quarterly* 27 (Spring 1996): 33–52; Andrew C. Isenberg, *The Destruction of the Bison: An Environmental History, 1750–1920* (Cambridge, 2000). In my view, some of this literature sensationalizes examples of Indians wasting buffalo to obtain hides, robes, or tongues, and goes too far in the direction of blaming Indians for the problems they faced as bison populations collapsed.

[40] Alan Klein, "The Political-Economy of Gender: A 19th Century Plains Indian Case Study," in *The Hidden Half: Studies of Plains Indian Women*, ed. Patricia Albers and Beatrice Medicine (Lanham, Md., 1983), 143–73.

[41] *Message Concerning the Fur Trade*, 23–24; Hiram Martin Chittenden, *The American Fur Trade of the Far West: A History of the Pioneer Trading Posts and Early Fur Companies of the Upper Missouri Valley and the Rocky Mountains and the Overland Commerce with Santa Fe*, 2 vols. (1902; Stanford, 1954), 1:26–31; Sunder, *Fur Trade*, 9, 56, 113–17; Elliott Coues, ed., *Forty Years a Fur Trader on the Upper Missouri: The Personal Narrative of*

negative consequences. Since northern Plains Indians had no experience with alcohol, they frequently followed the example of their suppliers and drank to excess.[42] Routine conflicts that might have been resolved without violence often escalated to the point of bloodshed. In 1842 David D. Mitchell, superintendent of Indian affairs at St. Louis, stated that "upwards of *five hundred men*, belonging to these prairie tribes, have been killed during the last two years, in drunken broils [*sic*]."[43] Although this was probably an exaggeration, it accurately captured the undoubtable fact of an increase in alcohol-related violence.

One notable instance of alcohol's role in conflict involved an ongoing struggle between two rival Oglala leaders, Bull Bear and Smoke. In the late 1830s whiskey flowed freely into the North Platte region when new traders tried to undercut the American Fur Company's monopoly. At the same time, Oglalas loyal to Smoke chafed under the authoritarian chieftainship of Bull Bear. A series of quarrels, fueled by alcohol, eventually led to Bull Bear's death at the hands of young men affiliated with Smoke in November 1841. This incident marked a serious rupture in Oglala social relations. A few years later Francis Parkman wrote that the Oglalas told him that since the death of Bull Bear "the people had been like children that did not know their own minds." Although a feud such as this was not unprecedented, alcohol undoubtedly exacerbated the situation and hindered a peaceful resolution.[44] The available evidence mainly documents conflict between men, but drinking probably contributed to male violence against women as well.

Although drinking was a problem, communities had resources to combat it. Many leaders resisted the introduction of alcohol into their communities, and most Plains Sioux did not consume alcohol at all during this period. In the early 1830s Clear Blue Earth curbed drinking among the Brulés by establishing tighter organizational control over his people. Young men, seeing how easily whiskey led to violence, pledged never to touch a drop. As Beatrice Medicine points out, such pledges were similar to other vows that

---

Charles Larpenteur, 1833–1872, 2 vols. (New York, 1898), 1:57–58, 1:74–76, 1:229–32, 2:416–17.

[42] For a discussion of how European Americans provided Indians a model of "drunken mayhem," see Craig MacAndrew and Robert B. Edgerton, *Drunken Comportment: A Social Explanation* (Chicago, 1969), 139–49.

[43] *ARCIA*, 1842, 27th Cong., 2d sess., 1842–43, H. Ex. Doc. 2, serial 418, 426. Accounts of violence connected with drinking can be found in Rufus B. Sage, *Rocky Mountain Life, or, Startling Scenes and Perilous Adventures in the Far West, During an Expedition of Three Years* (1858; Lincoln, 1982), 116–21; Hewitt, ed., *Journal of Kurz*, 176–77; Paul, ed., *Autobiography of Red Cloud*, 156–64.

[44] Francis Parkman, *The Oregon Trail* (1849; New York, 1950), 156; Kingsley M. Bray, *The Political History of the Oglala Sioux: Part 2: Breaking the Oglala Hoop, 1825–1850: Section 1: 1825–1841*, English Westerners' Special Publications, American Indian Studies Series No. 4 (London, 1985), 10–21; Hyde, *Red Cloud's Folk*, 52–55; Price, *Oglala People*, 22–24.

were central to masculine identity like going on a war party or dancing in the Sun Dance.[45]

Most Plains Sioux bands avoided the brunt of the most disastrous consequences of the fur trade. In 1837 smallpox on board an American Fur Company steamship spread throughout the upper Missouri region. Although the Mandans were hit hardest (90 percent of their population died), some Sioux bands living on the river north of Fort Pierre also suffered significant losses. Fortunately, many Sioux bands below Fort Pierre had been inoculated against smallpox in an 1832 government program. Others living away from the Missouri avoided the trading posts once they learned of the epidemic.[46]

Although the majority of Plains Sioux communities maintained a friendly, if sometimes strained, relationship with traders, there was always a persistent undercurrent of discontent. In the mid-1850s Edwin Denig, a long-time employee of the American Fur Company, wrote that Hunkpapas, Sihasapas, and Sans Arcs had been consistently hostile toward traders. He singled out the Hunkpapa chief Little Bear, whose "hatred for the white man" led him to seek the "destruction of all traders in the country." In 1853 when the American Fur Company tried to build a winter camp near Little Bear's village, his "soldiers (*akicita*) cut up the carts, killed the horses, flogged the traders and sent them home." Little Bear and others "threaten to burn up the forts, make no buffalo robes except what they want for their own use and wish to return to their primitive mode of life."[47]

Denig's characterization of the Hunkpapas, Sihasapas, and Sans Arcs as completely hostile to traders was clearly overdrawn. At one time or another, they all sought western goods.[48] Nonetheless, his account makes clear that some Sioux had serious reservations about the fur trade. Denig did not inquire into the sources of the hostility he recorded, but it is easy to identify

---

[45] Stanley Vestal, *Warpath: The True Story of the Fighting Sioux Told in a Biography of Chief White Bull* (1934; Lincoln, 1984), 249; George E. Hyde, *Spotted Tail's Folk: A History of the Brulé Sioux* (Norman, 1961), 26–29, 41; Beatrice Medicine, "An Ethnography of Drinking and Sobriety Among the Lakota Sioux," Ph.D. diss., University of Wisconsin, 1983, 50–51.

[46] Annie Heloise Abel, ed., *Chardon's Journal at Fort Clark, 1834–1839* (1932; Lincoln, 1997), 123–37; Barton H. Barbour, *Fort Union and the Upper Missouri Fur Trade* (Norman, 2001), 136–38; Russell Thornton, *American Indian Holocaust and Survival: A Population History since 1492* (Norman, 1987), 94–99; Edwin Thompson Denig, *Five Indian Tribes of the Upper Missouri*, edited and with an introduction by John C. Ewers (Norman, 1961), 27–28; Howard, "Yanktonai Ethnohistory," 47–48; Bray, "Teton Sioux Population History," 178; Clyde D. Dollar, "The High Plains Smallpox Epidemic of 1837–38," *Western Historical Quarterly* 8 (January 1977): 23–24; Michael K. Trimble, "The 1832 Inoculation Program on the Missouri River," in *Disease and Demography in the Americas*, ed. John W. Verano and Douglas H. Ubelaker (Washington, D.C., 1992), 261–63; John E. Sunder, *Joshua Pilcher: Fur Trader and Indian Agent* (Norman, 1968), 123.

[47] Denig, *Five Indian Tribes*, 26–27.

[48] Patterns of Hunkpapa trade are described in Robert M. Utley, *The Lance and the Shield: The Life and Times of Sitting Bull* (New York, 1993), 38–40.

them. Traders brought whiskey and disease. They cut down trees for fire-wood and to fuel steamboats. Through their own hunting and their en-couragement of Indian hunting, they depleted game. The trade encouraged intertribal conflict by promoting the availability of arms and ammunition. The Plains Sioux knew about European American settler-colonists to the east from Santees and Yanktons. Perhaps some saw the fur trade as the first stage of a larger process with worse consequences to come.

For the most part, however, Plains Sioux in the 1820s and 1830s had little reason to think Americans would pose a serious threat. In 1823 an army expedition under the command of Colonel Henry Leavenworth came up the Missouri River to punish the Arikaras for attacking a party of trappers. Yankton and Lakota warriors joined the expedition. When the Sioux arrived at the Arikara village ahead of Leavenworth, they easily forced the Arikaras to take refuge in their fortified village. The Americans had promised to storm the village, but Leavenworth failed to attack. The Sioux looked on with contempt.[49] Two years later St. Louis trading interests persuaded Congress to authorize a commission to visit the tribes of the upper Missouri. This commission, escorted by troops under General Henry Atkinson, convinced several western Sioux leaders to sign a treaty. Although the treaty stated that the Indians recognized "that they reside within the territorial limits of the United States, acknowledge their supremacy, and claim their protection," the signers probably understood it not as an admission of U.S. sovereignty but as a friendly trade agreement between equals.[50]

Although settlers did not yet desire the lands of the Great Plains, the western Sioux began to experience indirect effects of agrarian expansion in the 1840s. An ever-growing number of migrants on their way to an imagined paradise in Oregon began to pass through southern Lakota country as they traveled up the Platte and North Platte rivers. These Jeffersonian trespassers would soon be joined by Mormons, following their own visions of Zion in the Great Salt Lake Valley, and then by people pursuing a novel dream that America's founders had not foreseen: California gold.

In 1841 fewer than 100 emigrants crossed the Plains; four years later the number rose to over 2,500. In September 1845 Thomas H. Harvey, superin-tendent of Indian affairs at St. Louis, reported that Indians protested "that the

---

[49] Col. H. Leavenworth to Brig. Gen. H. Atkinson, 20 Oct. 1823, *South Dakota Historical Collections* 1 (1902): 210–23; Roy W. Meyer, *The Village Indians of the Upper Missouri: The Mandans, Hidatsas, and Arikaras* (Lincoln, 1977), 54; Hyde, *Red Cloud's Folk*, 38; Chittenden, *Fur Trade of the Far West*, 588–96.

[50] Charles J. Kappler, ed., *Indian Affairs: Laws and Treaties*, 5 vols. (Washington, D.C., 1904–1941), 2:227–32, 2:235–36 (qtn., 2:227–28); Roger L. Nichols, ed., "General Henry Atkinson's Report of the Yellowstone Expedition of 1825," *Nebraska History* 44 (June 1963): 65–82; Kingsley M. Bray, *The Political History of the Oglala Sioux: Part 1: Making the Oglala Hoop, 1804–1825*, English Westerners' Special Publications, American Indian Studies Series No. 2 (London, 1982), 29–38.

whites have no right to be in their country without their consent; and the upper tribes, who subsist on game, complain that the buffalo are wantonly killed and scared off."[51] Although recent scholarship has questioned the claim that emigrants killed or "scared off" many bison, overland travelers contributed to game scarcity when their own livestock consumed early spring grasses. Emigrants also damaged Indians lands by cutting already scarce timber for fuel.[52]

As George Hyde observes, Lakotas were "puzzled" by these "new white people," whose purposes were far more opaque than the traders'. Nonetheless, Lakotas' history of commercial relationships with Americans suggested ways of interacting with emigrants. If they were going to consume the resources of Sioux lands, they should pay. Along the trail, Oglalas and Brulés demanded provisions and specie as compensation for the overlanders' destructive impact on game, grass, and timber. Emigrants usually complied, but because they regarded the land as a wilderness unencumbered by legitimate ownership claims, they viewed Indian demands as extortion. Good Americans that they were, they called on the government to stop these affronts.[53]

Lakota anger at the overlanders increased when cholera, measles, and smallpox struck in 1849. Brulés were hit particularly hard, losing around 500 of their 3,500 people. Traders along the Platte reported that the Sioux thought cholera had been "introduced by the whites, for the purpose of causing their more speedy annihilation." Probably on the basis of evidence like this, Hyde writes that "most Indians believed that these diseases were forms of magic which the whites were employing against them." Sioux medical practice did recognize that many illnesses were caused by "evil spirits," although there were other explanations, such as exposure to contaminating influences, eating the wrong foods, inhaling contaminants, the transgression of taboos, and the improper performance of rituals. Perhaps, then, the Sioux (or, at least some of them) understood the late 1840s epidemics as inflicted not by magic but through seemingly prosaic means, although still perhaps involving intentional malice. Then, too, not all Sioux necessarily attributed these outbreaks to the intentional actions of non-Indians. In July 1849 Captain Howard Stansbury, head of an expedition of the Army Corps of Topographical Engineers, encountered a Sioux band along the North Platte. From James Bordeaux, a French trader who was married into this band, Stansbury learned that they had contracted cholera on the South Platte and

---

[51] John D. Unruh Jr., *The Plains Across: The Overland Emigrants and the Trans-Mississippi West, 1840–60* (Urbana, 1979), 119; *ARCIA*, 1845, 29th Cong., 1st sess., 1845–46, S. Doc. 1, serial 470, 536.

[52] West, *Way to the West*, 53–56, 77; *ARCIA*, 1851, 32d Cong., 1st sess., 1851–52, S. Ex. Doc. 1, serial 613, 289; *ARCIA*, 1852, 32d Cong., 2d sess., 1852–53, H. Ex. Doc. 1, serial 673, 357.

[53] Hyde, *Red Cloud's Folk*, 56; Unruh, *Plains Across*, 169–70.

had "fled to the emigrant-road, in the hope of obtaining medical aid from the whites." Stansbury directed the expedition's physician to prepare some medicine for this and another nearby camp, where another trader, Joseph Bissonnette, lived. According to Stansbury, the Sioux "swallowed the medicine with great avidity, and an absolute faith in its efficacy." The most likely interpretation of this episode is that Lakotas, acting on a common distinction between native and non-native diseases, sought western medicine for what they understood to be a non-native disease.[54] Perhaps the Sioux Stansbury encountered understood cholera as the result of Americans' magic, but, if so, it is surprising that they turned to their destroyers for relief.

Whether overlanders intentionally inflicted disease or not, Sioux people living along the Platte could see that cholera, measles, and smallpox were associated with an escalating invasion. In 1849, the first year of the rush to California gold, 25,000 emigrants crossed the Plains, five times more than the highest previous year.[55] This meant even more wagons crushing the grass and pulverizing dirt into dust, more trees cut down, more grass eaten by cattle and sheep, more bison killed and driven away. For the first time, Lakotas sensed the serious possibility of being overwhelmed and having to fight for their land.

These impressions were enhanced by the fact that the overlanders were backed by the military. In late spring 1845, 250 dragoons under the command of Stephen W. Kearny marched from Fort Leavenworth up the Platte, taking the north fork to Fort Laramie and beyond. Kearny informed Pawnees, Lakotas, Cheyennes, and Arapahoes that "the road opened by the dragoons must not be closed by the Indians, and that the white people traveling upon it must not be disturbed, either in their persons or property." With the certitude required of a colonel, Kearny reported to his superiors that "the Indians will remember and observe what has been told them on this subject."[56]

Historians have offered different interpretations of Indian responses to Kearny's show of force. Francis Parkman wrote that when the tribes near Fort Laramie "saw the white warriors... they were lost in astonishment at their regular order, their gay attire, the completeness of their martial equipment,

[54] Hyde, *Spotted Tail's Folk*, 50–52; Bray, "Teton Sioux Population History," 180; *ARCIA*, 1850, 31st Cong., 2d sess., 1850–51, H. Ex. Doc. 1, serial 595, 49 (1st qtn.); Hyde, *Red Cloud's Folk*, 64 (2d qtn.); Howard K. Stansbury, *Exploration and Survey of the Valley of the Great Salt Lake of Utah*, 32d Cong., Spec. sess., 1851, S. Ex. Doc. 3, serial 608, 44–45 (3d, 4th qtns.). For Sioux ideas about the causes of disease, see Hassrick, *The Sioux*, 288–91; Stephen R. Riggs, *Tah-Koo Wah-kan; or, the Gospel Among the Dakotas* (Boston, 1869), 376–77; Powers, *Oglala Women*, 96; James Owen Dorsey, "A Study of Siouan Cults," in *Eleventh Annual Report of the Bureau of Ethnology* (Washington, D.C., 1894), 496. For the distinction between native and non-native disease, see Powers, *Oglala Religion*, 129–30.
[55] Unruh, *Plains Across*, 84–85.
[56] *ARSW*, 1845, 29th Cong., 1st sess., 1845–46, S. Doc. 1, serial 470, 211.

and the size and strength of their horses." When Kearny ordered his men to fire one of the expedition's two howitzers, "[m]any of the Arapahoes fell flat on the ground, while others ran away screaming with amazement and terror."[57] Ethnohistorian Catherine Price rightly rejects Parkman's account, filled as it is with typical colonial tropes of natives overwhelmed by the mere sight of Europeans. Attempting to read the situation from a Native perspective and knowing that Lakota culture valued giving gifts to show honor, Price argues that the gifts Kearny gave Lakota leaders "seemed to indicate the high esteem in which Kearny and his troops held them."[58] But this interpretation, too, is highly doubtful. Their culture was not so hermetically alterior as to prevent Lakotas from grasping the obvious fact of Kearny's intent to intimidate. The Lakotas were undoubtedly impressed by the howitzers (they had never seen weapons of such size before), but they likely evaluated the potential threat of these weapons according to pragmatic considerations about their capacity to inflict damage under specific conditions, conditions over which mounted Indian warriors would have had some control. Although we do not know exactly what the Lakotas thought of Kearny's show of force, events would show that many were willing to fight Americans, howitzers or no.

The Kearny expedition was a sign that U.S. imperialism was entering a new phase on the Plains. Before the mid-1840s, American thinkers had envisioned the region's place abstractly in a hypothetical empire, but as settlers put pressure on Indian lands to the east and then as settlers migrated across the Plains, U.S. officials were developing specific policies with on-the-ground implications for Plains people. The main policy of the 1840s was known as the "reservation system." Although formally a new policy, it was rooted in the contradictory history of earlier policies. As we saw at the beginning of this chapter, early theorists of empire like Thomas Jefferson tried to evade the contradiction between their desire for Indian lands and their belief in Enlightenment and Christian moral principles. They relied on the hope that Indians would voluntarily relinquish their lands and embrace American cultural and religious norms. In this way, the United States could have "expansion with honor." By the 1820s, as it became increasingly clear that eastern tribes were unwilling to give up their lands or ways of life, government officials began to enact Jefferson's contingency plan: removal. Under removal, Indian tribes

---

[57] Parkman, *Oregon Trail*, 183–84. Parkman was not an eyewitness to the events he described and most likely got his information while drinking Madeira with Kearny at Fort Leavenworth a year later. See Mason Wade, ed., *The Journals of Francis Parkman*, 2 vols. (New York, 1947), 2:422. Edward Lazarus, *Black Hills/White Justice: The Sioux Nation Versus the United States, 1775 to the Present* (New York, 1991), 14, strikes a Parkmanesque note in writing of how the Indians "watched in bewilderment as the American sabres sparkled in the sun."

[58] Price, *Oglala People*, 28.

would be encouraged and forced, if necessary, to relocate to the semiarid region west of the Mississippi. This region would be set aside as "Indian Territory." A "Permanent Indian Frontier" would separate tribes from the corrupting elements of civilization (traders, alcohol, and squatters). Under the tutelage of missionaries they would gradually become civilized.[59]

Some Native leaders signed removal treaties and moved "voluntarily" for fear of refusal's consequences. The army forced others west at bayonet point. In all, the government removed directly or indirectly at least 100,000 eastern Indians. Thousands died along the many trails of tears that mocked any pretense to honor.[60] By the time removal was accomplished the assumptions behind the Permanent Indian Frontier were already obsolete. Even as relocated tribes tried to get their bearings in new lands, they witnessed settlers building cabins and clearing fields. The idea that had once comforted the consciences of humanitarians, that the isolation of the Plains would protect Indians so that they could be slowly nurtured toward civilization, was further undermined by the overland trail along the Platte. In the late 1840s U.S. officials decided on a modified form of colonial management. Instead of the Permanent Indian Frontier, the United States would now force Plains tribes onto reservations. As with earlier policies, Indians would "exchange" some of their lands for the time and material resources necessary to begin assimilating into the dominant society.[61]

To implement this scheme on the northern and central Plains, the government convened a gathering of the region's tribes at Horse Creek, a tributary of the North Platte several miles down river from Fort Laramie, in September 1851. The written text of the resulting treaty (the Fort Laramie or Horse Creek Treaty) specified the territory of each tribe and called for intertribal peace. It also stated that the tribes recognized the right of the United States to establish roads and military posts within these reservations and pledged to respect the passage of emigrants. In exchange, the government would provide annuities of $50,000 to all the tribes over the next fifty years. These

---

[59] On the continuity between Jefferson's thinking and removal, see Sheehan, *Seeds of Extinction*, 245–50; Wallace, *Jefferson and the Indians*, 273–75. For the emergence of the removal policy in the 1820s, see Francis Paul Prucha, *The Great Father: The United States Government and the American Indians*, 2 vols. (Lincoln, 1984), 1:179–213; Anthony F. C. Wallace, *The Long, Bitter Trail: Andrew Jackson and the Indians* (New York, 1993), 30–56; Michael D. Green, "The Expansion of European Colonization to the Mississippi Valley, 1780–1880," in *The Cambridge History of the Native Peoples of the Americas: Volume 1, North America*, pt. 1, ed. Bruce G. Trigger and Wilcomb E. Washburn (Cambridge, 1996), 481–88, 510–19; Ronald N. Satz, *American Indian Policy in the Jacksonian Era* (Lincoln, 1975); Michael Paul Rogin, *Fathers and Children: Andrew Jackson and the Subjugation of the American Indian* (New York, 1975).

[60] Russell Thornton, "Cherokee Population Losses during the Trail of Tears: A New Perspective and a New Estimate," *Ethnohistory* 31 (November 1984): 289–300.

[61] For the origins of the reservation system, see Robert A. Trennert Jr., *Alternative to Extinction: Federal Indian Policy and the Beginnings of the Reservation System, 1846–51* (Philadelphia, 1975), 16–60.

annuities would be distributed by government officers at agencies on or near each tribe's reservation.[62]

It is difficult to know for sure what the Sioux understood they were doing when they signed this treaty. As they gained more experience with treaties, they came to understand much more about American protocols and customs, but in 1851 Sioux leaders knew little about this aspect of U.S. colonialism. Although the traders present would have been able to interpret the proceedings and explain the treaty text, Sioux leaders probably did not understand many of the treaty's provisions and implications. Furthermore, those who "touched the pen" considered themselves to be validating all that had been said on both sides during the entire proceedings rather than just the text. At the very least, Sioux leaders understood the treaty as providing compensation for damage caused by overland migration. Shortly after the treaty, Indian superintendent Mitchell reported that the Indians regarded the distribution of presents at Horse Creek as "full payment" for former complaints for the "destruction of their buffalo, timber, grass, etc."[63]

The Fort Laramie Treaty was deeply flawed. One problem that the government failed to take into account was the decentralized and voluntary character of Plains Sioux political organization. For that reason, the treaty lacked widespread legitimacy. Of the six Sioux leaders who signed the treaty, four were Brulé, one Two Kettle, and the other Yankton. Although these men were probably authorized to speak for their own bands, they did not necessarily represent all the bands within these *oyate*, and they certainly did not represent other *oyate*. Numerous Oglalas were at the council and many presumably approved of what they understood the treaty to mean, but none of them signed. There were few, if any, representatives of Sans Arcs, Hunkpapa, Minneconjou, Sihasapa, or Yanktonai communities and no signers.[64] Government officials attempted to overcome this problem by ordering the Sioux to choose a "head chief." Band leaders chose Brave Bear, a Brulé, for this

---

[62] Cheyennes, Arapahoes, Crows, Assiniboines, Gros Ventres, Mandans, and Arikaras also signed the treaty. Kappler, ed., *Indian Affairs: Laws and Treaties*, 2:594–95. For accounts of the treaty council, see *ARCIA*, 1851, serial 613, 288–90; Hiram Martin Chittenden and Alfred Talbot Richardson, eds., *Life, Letters and Travels of Father Pierre-Jean De Smet, S.J., 1801–1873*, 4 vols. (New York, 1905), 2:675–84; LeRoy R. Hafen, *Broken Hand: The Life of Thomas Fitzpatrick: Mountain Man, Guide and Indian Agent*, rev. ed. (Denver, 1973), 284–301. The boundaries of the 1851 reservation, shown in Map 1, encompassed most of the lands in the 1868 Great Sioux Reservation.

[63] Raymond J. DeMallie, "Touching the Pen: Plains Indian Treaty Councils in Ethnohistorical Perspective," in *Ethnicity on the Great Plains*, ed. Frederick C. Luebke (Lincoln, 1980), 40; *ARCIA*, 1851, serial 613, 289.

[64] Kappler, ed., *Indian Affairs: Laws and Treaties*, 2:596, lists Mah-toe-wha-you-whey (Mato Oyuhi [Brave Bear], Brulé), Mah-kah-toe-zah-zah (Makatozaza [Clear Blue Earth], Brulé), Bel-o-ton-kah-tan-ga (Blotahunka Tanka [Grand Partisan, or Great Leader], Brulé), Nah-ka-pah-gi-gi (Nakpazizi [Yellow Ears], Brulé), Mak-toe-sha-bi-chis (Mato Sabic'iye [Smutty Bear, or more accurately, Bear Who Blackens Himself], Yankton), Meh-wah-tah-ni-hans-kah (Mawatani Hanska [Long Mandan], Two Kettle).

novel office despite his protests that he was a young man without experience who did not desire to be "chief of the Dahcotahs." Still, decreeing a "head chief" did not change political realities.[65]

An even more fundamental problem was that the United States did not view the treaty as an agreement between equal sovereigns. The treaty was merely a temporary convenience of a relentlessly expansionist nation-state. In the years before the 1851 Treaty the United States had become committed to a particularly aggressive phase of empire building. Following the war of 1812, which secured U.S. economic independence, the United States embarked on two decades of vigorous continental expansion and economic growth. By the mid-1840s America was poised to gain sovereignty over Oregon and to embark on a war of conquest with Mexico. Between 1845 and 1848, U.S. territory increased by 67 percent.[66]

Manifest destiny, a term coined in 1845, did not entail fundamentally new ideas. Americans had always seen their nation fulfilling a providential design for the spread of special qualities. The 1840s version of manifest destiny, however, crystallized and intensified these themes. In addition, influenced by new pseudoscientific theories about race, manifest destiny linked American national identity more than ever before to an elaborate racial hierarchy in which whites were supreme.[67] A speech by Missouri Senator Thomas Hart Benton in 1846 articulated a racialized ideology of manifest destiny and spelled out its implications for the continent's Native peoples. Benton focused on the historical destiny of what he called the "Caucasian" or "White race." Of all the world's "races," only the "White race" had obeyed God's command "to subdue and replenish the earth." Beginning in western Asia, "Whites" had followed the setting sun "in obedience to the great command." They moved into Europe and then to the "New World," where they found "new lands to subdue and replenish." Defying even the most optimistic predictions, "the van of the Caucasian race" moved rapidly over the Allegheny Mountains, into the Mississippi Valley, and by 1846 had reached the shores of the Pacific. Soon, Benton predicted, the United States would establish a

[65] DeMallie, "Touching the Pen," 44. Matters were further complicated when the Senate amended the treaty to reduce the annuities from fifty years to ten years with a possible five-year renewal. Although one Sans Arcs and another Minneconjou joined five Brulés and five Oglalas in signing this amendment, many bands were not represented. See Harry Anderson, "The Controversial Sioux Amendment to the Fort Laramie Treaty of 1851," *Nebraska History* 37 (September 1956): 201–20.

[66] U.S. Bureau of the Census, *Historical Statistics of the United States: Colonial Times to 1970*, pt. 1 (Washington, D.C., 1975), 428.

[67] Recent works on manifest destiny include Thomas R. Hietala, *Manifest Design: Anxious Aggrandizement in Late Jacksonian America* (Ithaca, 1985); Stephanson, *Manifest Destiny*. Reginald Horsman, *Race and Manifest Destiny: The Origins of American Racial Anglo-Saxonism* (Cambridge, Mass., 1981), emphasizes the increasingly racialized character of manifest destiny in the 1840s and 1850s. For racial thought covering these decades see also Berkhofer, *White Man's Indian*, 55–59; Smedley, *Race in North America*, 231–44.

ILLUSTRATION 2. John Gast, *American Progress*. This 1873 lithograph of John Gast's 1872 painting represents classic themes of manifest destiny: the progress of civilization and the inevitable disappearance of Indians and the wilderness to which they belonged. Library of Congress Prints and Photographs Division, LC-USZ62-737.

commercial empire in the Pacific, thus allowing the "Caucasians" to reinvigorate the "Mongolian, or Yellow race." As for the continent's native inhabitants: although the "White race" possessed a destiny, the "Red race" had only a fate. History showed that Indians had "disappeared from the Atlantic coast: the tribes that resisted civilization, met extinction."[68] (For a visual representation of these themes, see Illustration 2.)

Assimilation or extinction – these were the alternatives Benton offered Indian people. Typical of Americans when discussing the "fate" of Indians, Benton used the passive voice, as though extinction would happen without human agency. But behind Benton's phrasing were both a history and future of intentional acts of genocide and ethnocide. The actual implications of a national commitment to the ideology of manifest destiny varied from situation to situation and changed over time. In the early 1850s on the Platte River trail it would serve to justify extermination.

[68] Quoted in William M. Meigs, *The Life of Thomas Hart Benton* (Philadelphia, 1904), 309–10.

2

"Futile Efforts to Subjugate Them"

Failures of Conquest

The United States' conquest of the Plains Sioux was not an easy process. It was one thing for Lewis and Clark to fire their airgun, or for General Atkinson to get some leaders to sign a document stating (in English) that they acknowledged the "supremacy" of the United States, or for Colonel Kearny to fire his howitzers and imagine his audience cowering in fear. It was quite another for the United States to establish real control over the Sioux and their allies on the northern Plains. The Plains Sioux eventually gave up military resistance, though only after more than twenty years of war.

Conflict began in summer 1854 when a Mormon emigrant allowed an ox to stray. On August 17, a Minneconjou named High Forehead, who was staying with Brave Bear's people, shot the animal. Brave Bear offered to make restitution, but army officers at Fort Laramie decided to teach the Sioux a lesson. Two days later, a hot-headed young lieutenant named John L. Grattan, who reportedly had said that he wanted to "crack it to the Sioux," took twenty-nine men, two howitzers, and a drunk interpreter to Brave Bear's camp to demand the Mormon ox thief's arrest. When High Forehead refused to give himself up, Grattan ordered his men to fire. Their volley was met by a charge of a few hundred Sioux fighters. Grattan's troops turned and ran but the Sioux killed them to a man. Brave Bear, injured in the fight, later died. To avenge his death, some of Brave Bear's relatives attacked a mail train in November, killing three. Over the next several months the Sioux occasionally harassed overland travelers and raided horses, but there were no further attacks.[1]

Although some army officers who investigated the affair were sharply critical of Grattan, higher officials quickly assumed the classic western pose

[1] *Report of the Secretary of War in Compliance with a Resolution of the Senate . . . Respecting the Massacre of Lieutenant Grattan and his Command by Indians*, 34th Cong., 1st sess., 1855–56, S. Ex. Doc. 91, serial 823; George E. Hyde, *Red Cloud's Folk: A History of the Oglala Sioux Indians* (Norman, 1937), 72–75 (qtn., 72).

of the "injured innocent"[2] and dubbed the incident the "Grattan massacre." As a massacre, it had to be avenged. The following year, the War Department dispatched brevet General William S. Harney to Fort Leavenworth, where he assumed command of 600 men and marched up the Platte, by one account declaring, "By God, I'm for battle – no peace." To prevent Lakotas who desired to avoid conflict from becoming Harney's targets, Thomas Twiss, the Indian Office's agent at the Upper Platte Agency, informed leaders that they would be considered friendly if they camped on the south side of the Platte. Those remaining on the north side would be declared "hostile." Despite Twiss's instructions, Brave Bear's band, now led by Little Thunder, remained north of the Platte at Ash Hollow on Blue Water Creek. According to Lakota sources, Little Thunder, Iron Shell, and other leaders thought they could convince Harney of their peaceful intentions.[3] On September 3, 1855, Harney approached Little Thunder's camp of 250. The Indians tried to engage him in discussion, but within minutes Harney's men attacked. They killed at least 86, over half of whom were women and children, and took 70 women and children captive. In contrast to Harney's sanitized version of the slaughter, Lieutenant G. K. Warren wrote in his journal of "wounded women and children crying and moaning, horribly mangled by the bullets." Frank Salaway, a trader who arrived at Ash Hollow shortly after the massacre, heard from Harney's interpreter that soldiers took an infant from a woman who had been shot through the leg. The child was "put up as a target and shot at by some of the soldiers who killed it."[4]

After Ash Hollow Harney went to Fort Laramie, where he demanded the surrender of the warriors who had attacked the mail train the previous November. He then marched to Fort Pierre and ordered representatives of the seven Lakota tribes and the Yanktonais to convene the following spring so that he could dictate a treaty for them to sign. In May all except the Oglalas gathered. Harney directed each tribe to select a head chief who would appoint subchiefs and a police force. The head chief would be responsible for the good behavior of his people. President James Buchanan failed to submit

[2] Patricia Nelson Limerick, *The Legacy of Conquest: The Unbroken Past of the American West* (New York, 1987), 35–54.

[3] Robert M. Utley, *Frontiersmen in Blue: The United States Army and the Indian, 1848–1865* (New York, 1967), 115–16 (qtn., 115); *ARCIA*, 1855, 34th Cong., 1st sess., 1855–56, S. Ex. Doc. 1, serial 810, 400–01; George E. Hyde, *Spotted Tail's Folk: A History of the Brulé Sioux* (Norman, 1961), 68–72; Richmond L. Clow, "Mad Bear: William S. Harney and the Sioux Expedition of 1855–1856," *Nebraska History* 61 (Summer 1980): 133–38; Susan Bordeaux Bettelyoun and Josephine Waggoner, *With My Own Eyes: A Lakota Woman Tells Her People's History*, edited and introduced by Emily Levine (Lincoln, 1998), 55.

[4] *ARSW*, 1855, 34th Cong., 1st sess., 1855–56, H. Ex. Doc. 1, serial 841, 49–51; Bettelyoun and Waggoner, *With My Own Eyes*, 55–58; James A. Hanson, *Little Chief's Gatherings: The Smithsonian Institution's G. K. Warren 1855–1856 Plains Indian Collection and The New York States Library's 1855–1857 Warren Expeditions Journals* (Crawford, Nebr., 1996), 106; Frank Salaway interview, 1906, RT, tablet 27, roll 5.

Harney's treaty to the Senate; the House, treating it as an administrative matter, refused to provide appropriations for Indian police uniforms.[5]

Although intended to inspire terror and create submission, Harney's actions had the opposite effect among many Sioux. Those who were disposed to fight the Americans hardened their resolve. Others developed a new hatred of the U.S. military and a new commitment to armed resistance. One Lakota for whom Ash Hollow was a formative experience was Crazy Horse, then in his early teens and living with Little Thunder's people. On the day of Harney's attack, Crazy Horse was hunting, but returned that evening to find the bodies of his relatives hacked by swords and destroyed by guns. Soon after, Crazy Horse vowed to become a leader of his people and to fight the Americans, if necessary for the rest of his life.[6]

A year after Harney's attack, militants circulated a pipe summoning all Lakotas to a council to be held the following year at Bear Butte on the northeastern edge of the Black Hills. At minimum five thousand attended and the number may have been closer to ten. One Lakota told Lieutenant Warren that when the people had gathered "their hearts felt strong at seeing how numerous they were.... [I]f they went to war again they would not yield so easy as they did before." To defend western Sioux territory, the council adopted specific measures. No non-Indians, except traders, could travel north of the North Platte or west of the Missouri, and no roads could be constructed in this area. All bands would refuse to sign treaties and war would be resumed against the Crows to gain access to buffalo herds west of the Powder River.[7]

For the next several years, militants aggressively carried out this policy, stopping government expeditions from entering the Black Hills, raiding trading posts, refusing to accept annuities, and threatening bands that did. In June 1862 two militants killed Bear's Rib, a Hunkpapa, when he received

[5] Hyde, *Spotted Tail's Folk*, 74; Clow, "Mad Bear," 142–46; Alban W. Hoopes, "Thomas S. Twiss, Indian Agent on the Upper Platte, 1855–1861," *Mississippi Valley Historical Review* 20 (December 1933): 358; *Council with the Sioux Indians at Fort Pierre*, 34th Cong., 1st sess., 1855–56, H. Ex. Doc. 130, serial 859, 1–2, 6–7; *Estimate for Payment to Certain Indians*, 35th Cong., 1st sess., 1857–58, H. Ex. Doc. 136, serial 959.

[6] Mari Sandoz, *Crazy Horse: Strange Man of the Oglalas* (Lincoln, 1942), 73–81, 98–100. For Crazy Horse's biography, see also Joseph M. Marshall III, "Crazy Horse (Tasunke Witko)" in *Encyclopedia of North American Indians*, ed. Frederick E. Hoxie (Boston, 1996), 137–39; Keith A. Winsell, "Crazy Horse" in *Notable Native Americans*, ed., Sharon Malinowski (New York, 1995), 95–98; Virginia Driving Hawk Sneve, *They Led a Nation* (Sioux Falls, S.Dak., 1975), 26–27; Richard G. Hardorff, *The Oglala Lakota Crazy Horse: A Preliminary Genealogical Study and an Annotated Listing of Primary Sources* (Mattituck, N.Y., 1985).

[7] *Explorer on the Northern Plains: Lieutenant Gouverneur K. Warren's Preliminary Report of Explorations in Nebraska and Dakota, in the Years 1855–'56–'57* (Washington, D.C., 1981), 52. The council's decisions are reconstructed in Kingsley M. Bray, "Lone Horn's Peace: A New View of Sioux-Crow Relations, 1851–1858," *Nebraska History* 66 (Spring 1985): 39, 42–43.

annuities at Fort Pierre. A letter signed by ten Hunkpapas and addressed to the Upper Missouri Indian agent explained that they had "notified the Bear's Rib yearly not to receive your goods; he had no ears, and we gave him ears by killing him. We now say to you, bring us no more goods; if any of our people receive any more from you we will give them ears as we did the Bear's Rib."[8]

During these years, some Sioux turned away from armed resistance. Consider, for example, another member of Little Thunder's band, Spotted Tail. When Harney attacked, Spotted Tail was thirty years old and a leading advocate of using force to halt U.S. expansion. Spotted Tail defended his people at Ash Hollow and was among those Harney later ordered arrested. At first, Spotted Tail resisted the idea of surrendering, but he eventually did so out of respect for the elders of his band. He also feared what might happen to his wife and child, who had been taken captive. Certain he was going to the gallows, Spotted Tail came to Fort Laramie singing his death song. Instead of hanging Spotted Tail, government officials sent him to Fort Leavenworth prison. By the time he was released a year later, Spotted Tail had decided on a different approach. Undoubtedly, the sheer size of Fort Leavenworth and the knowledge that it was only one of many similar installations convinced Spotted Tail that war would be futile. In addition, as he learned more about Americans, Spotted Tail decided he could protect his people best through diplomacy.[9]

In the late 1850s and early 1860s nonmilitant bands did their best to avoid trouble and keep from starving. Although the government encouraged these bands to take up farming, most continued to rely on hunting and gathering. Not only did the Plains Sioux prefer this way of life, they were deeply suspicious of the motives behind American exhortations to take up the plow. In 1856 Oglalas and Brulés declared that "the real object" of the government's encouragement of farming was to "confine the Indians to a small tract of country to live on corn for food, and take away from them all the rest of the Indian country, and give it and the buffalo to whites." By the late 1860s, however, game was becoming so scarce along the Missouri River that many Sioux there were forced into dependence on government annuities

[8] *Explorer on the Northern Plains*, 18–20; *ARCIA*, 1858, 35th Cong., 2d sess., 1858–59, H. Ex. Doc. 2, serial 997, 437, 443; *ARCIA*, 1862, 37th Cong., 3d sess., 1862–63, H. Ex. Doc. 1, serial 1157, 336–40; Robert M. Utley, *The Lance and the Shield: The Life and Times of Sitting Bull* (New York, 1993), 47–51 (qtn., 49). For a discussion of the cultural meaning of having no ears, see Raymond J. DeMallie, "'These Have No Ears': Narrative and the Ethnohistorical Method," *Ethnohistory* 40 (Fall 1993): 515–38.

[9] Hyde, *Spotted Tail's Folk*, 75–82; Keith A. Winsell, "Spotted Tail" in *Notable Native Americans*, ed., Malinowski, 410–14; Sneve, *They Led a Nation*, 36–37. Not all Lakotas who were imprisoned at Fort Leavenworth drew the same conclusions as Spotted Tail. Red Leaf, for example, continued to advocate armed resistance until 1868. Hyde, *Spotted Tail's Folk*, 78; Bettelyoun and Waggoner, *With My Own Eyes*, 155, n. 9.

supplemented by limited farming. One group moved to Fort Laramie, where they become known as the Wagluhe band, meaning that they were like men who lived with their wives' relatives, that is, hangers-on, loafers. Others moved south along the Republican River, where buffalo were plentiful. Still others, more inclined to fight, went north to the Powder River country and became closely tied to militant Minneconjous, San Arcs, and Hunkpapas.[10]

Full-scale war broke out on the northern Plains in the 1860s. The immediate trigger was an uprising of the eastern Sioux against Minnesota settlers in 1862. As troops moved to suppress this revolt, many Sioux fled west and found refuge with Yanktons, Yanktonais, and Lakotas.[11] The next summer General Henry H. Sibley and General Alfred Sully led expeditions into the recently organized Dakota Territory to subjugate the Sioux once and for all. In September, near Whitestone Hill, Sully attacked a village of about 4,000 Sioux and claimed to have killed 300 warriors with only 22 soldiers lost. The following July he attacked another large village near Killdeer Mountain and reported killing another 100 to 150 Sioux.[12]

In this campaign, as in others, the army presumed that an overwhelming victory would cause Indians to realize the futility of resistance and that they would then submit to their fate. Thus, after Killdeer Mountain Sully claimed that "in spite of their boasts and threats" the Sioux would never again "attempt to unite and make a stand."[13] But events soon proved this to be wishful thinking. Sioux losses were significant (though Sully may have overstated them)[14] and persuaded some militants to consider making peace, but most looked toward tactical revisions – greater vigilance and revised methods of

---

[10] *ARCIA*, 1856, 34th Cong., 3d Sess., 1856–57, H. Ex. Doc. 1, serial 893, 648 (qtn.); *ARCIA*, 1868, 191; Ernest L. Schusky, *The Forgotten Sioux: An Ethnohistory of the Lower Brule Reservation* (Chicago, 1975), 56–57; Hyde, *Spotted Tail's Folk*, 91–95; Hyde, *Red Cloud's Folk*, 97–98; Catherine Price, *The Oglala People, 1841–1879: A Political History* (Lincoln, 1996), 44.

[11] For scholarly accounts of this uprising see Roy W. Meyer, *History of the Santee Sioux: United States Indian Policy on Trial* (Lincoln, 1967), 72–132; Gary Clayton Anderson, *Kinsmen of Another Kind: Dakota-White Relations in the Upper Mississippi Valley, 1650–1862* (Lincoln, 1984), 177–280. For Dakota accounts, see Gary Clayton Anderson and Alan R. Woolworth eds., *Through Dakota Eyes: Narrative Accounts of the Minnesota Indian War of 1862* (St. Paul, 1988).

[12] Utley, *Frontiersmen in Blue*, 270–78; Louis Pfaller, "Sully's Expedition of 1864: Featuring the Killdeer Mountain and Badlands Battles," *North Dakota History* 31 (January 1964): 25–77.

[13] Brig. Gen. Alfred Sully to Maj. Gen. John Pope, 18 Aug. 1864 in "Official Correspondence Pertaining to the War of the Outbreak, 1862–1865," *South Dakota Historical Collections* 8 (1916): 331 (1st qtn.); Brig. Gen. Alfred Sully to AAG Dept. of the Northwest, 11 Sept. 1864, "Official Correspondence," 320 (2d qtn.).

[14] The possibility that Sully inflated the number of Indians he killed is suggested by information in Pfaller, "Sully's Expedition," 50, that Indians claimed that they had suffered only thirty-one dead at Killdeer Mountain.

defense – rather than a major strategic shift. Proponents of armed resistance were passionately committed to defending their land and way of life. They were willing to endure great hardship and suffering to turn back the American invasion. Although they were not able to prevent conquest, as we will see, they were able to limit U.S. power and win significant concessions.

Four months after Killdeer Mountain, in late November, violence erupted to the west when Colonel John M. Chivington and the Colorado Third Cavalry slaughtered more than two hundred peaceful Cheyennes at Sand Creek. Soldiers mutilated the bodies of many of the dead, taking scalps and severed genitals as trophies.[15] Word of Sand Creek and its atrocities spread throughout the Plains, inflaming Cheyennes, Arapahoes, and Lakotas against Americans. Cheyenne and Sioux war parties had already been attacking emigrant parties, stages, and ranches from the North Platte southwest to Denver. Within weeks after the massacre at Sand Creek, Spotted Tail, formerly an advocate of peace, joined in an attack on a stage station, telegraph office, and army post at Julesberg, Colorado.[16]

The war expanded in 1865 when miners began to use a new route to Montana called the Bozeman Trail. This road left the Oregon Trail at Fort Laramie and cut through the heart of northern Lakota territory. When militants harassed travelers along the trail, the government built a series of forts. Lakotas, Arapahoes, and Cheyennes resolved to fight this new invasion. Although technically legal,[17] the Indians had legitimate cause to regard the Bozeman Trail forts as a violation of the spirit of the 1851 agreement, which they believed permitted travel on the North Platte road alone. Following the government's bungled attempt to get the militants to make peace in mid-1866, war resumed. The Indians achieved a major victory in December 1866 when they used a decoy party to lure a force of eighty men under the command of Colonel William J. Fetterman into an ambush that resulted in the death of Fetterman and all of his men.[18]

The Sioux called this victory *Wasicu Opawinge Wicaktepi* (They Killed One Hundred Whites), but the army named it the Fetterman Massacre. As such, it needed to be avenged. The commander of the Division of the Missouri, General William Tecumseh Sherman, called for acting "with

[15] *Report of the Secretary of War Communicating . . . the Evidence Taken . . . by a Military Commission, Ordered to Inquire into the Sand Creek Massacre*, 39th Cong., 2d sess., 1866–67, S. Ex. Doc. 26, serial 1277; George Bird Grinnell, *The Fighting Cheyennes* (1915; Norman, 1956), 165–80; Stan Hoig, *The Sand Creek Massacre* (Norman, 1961).

[16] James C. Olson, *Red Cloud and the Sioux Problem* (Lincoln, 1965), 9–11; Hyde, *Spotted Tail's Folk*, 105–06.

[17] The United States wrote into the 1851 Treaty the right to establish roads in Indian country. See Charles J. Kappler, ed., *Indian Affairs: Laws and Treaties*, 5 vols. (Washington, D.C., 1904–1941), 2:594.

[18] Olson, *Red Cloud and the Sioux Problem*, 27–51; Robert M. Utley, *Frontier Regulars: The United States Army and the Indian, 1866–1891* (Lincoln, 1973), 98–107.

vindictive earnestness against the Sioux, even to their extermination, men, women and children."[19] In this climate any clash could become an occasion for the army to make inflated claims. In August 1867, when troops repelled an attack on a corral near Fort Phil Kearny, the officer in charge reported no fewer than 60 Indians killed and 120 severely wounded. These figures were wildly exaggerated; probably no more than 5 or 6 Sioux died in what became known as the Wagon Box fight. To the south, Indians attacked several points along the North and South Platte, imperiling the construction of the Union Pacific Railroad.[20]

In theory the United States could have deployed enough military power over a long enough period of time to have forced the Sioux and their allies to abandon their effort to shut down the Bozeman Trail. In practical terms, however, the government faced significant constraints on the exercise of its power in this particular situation. After the Civil War, public officials were eager to reduce the army's size, yet the army retained important commitments. Radical Republican reconstruction policies required a large military presence in the South. In the West the surge in overland travel combined with the construction of the Pacific railroad increased demands for military protection. Finite resources were spread thinly over a rapidly expanding empire. When it came to the Bozeman Trail, U.S. officials saw a trade-off between protecting travelers and protecting crews that were surveying and building the Union Pacific. Local economic interests wanted to keep the road open, but the transcontinental railroad was a national priority and its backers were politically influential. Moreover, another new railroad, the Northern Pacific, would soon make the Bozeman Trail obsolete.[21]

In addition to these geopolitical considerations, a new surge of self-styled "humanitarian" concerns about Indians added pressure to end warfare on the Plains. At the close of the Civil War many northerners hoped to extend the moral reformation of American society that had resulted in slavery's abolition. One obvious target was the nation's relations with Indians. It was not difficult to find shocking cases of fraud and corruption in the management of Indian affairs. The reformers' main criticism, however, was that national expansion was proceeding at the expense of honor. "Friends of the Indians" rejected the view that Indians were responsible for conflict and argued instead that "in a large majority of cases Indian wars are to be traced to the aggressions of lawless white men." Rather than relying on military methods,

---

[19] James R. Walker, *Lakota Society*, ed. Raymond J. DeMallie (Lincoln, 1982), 145; *Letter of the Secretary of the Interior, Communicating... Information Touching on the Origins and Progress of Indian Hostilities on the Frontier*, 40th Cong., 1st sess., 1867, S. Ex. Doc. 13, serial 1308, 27 (qtn.).

[20] Olson, *Red Cloud and the Sioux Problem*, 64–65, 60.

[21] Russell F. Weigley, *History of the United States Army* (New York, 1967), 262, 266–67; Robert Wooster, *The Military and United States Indian Policy, 1865–1903* (New Haven, 1988), 13–40; Olson, *Red Cloud and the Sioux Problem*, 62, 71–72.

Indian policy should apply the principles of Christian humanitarianism – kindness, honesty, and justice. This would bring peace to the West, save Indians from extermination, and guide them toward citizenship in a Christian civilization.[22]

Most army officers regarded "Indian lovers" (Sherman's private term) as sentimental dreamers who knew little about Indians and lacked essential masculine qualities of toughness and sound judgment. Just as military leaders expressed contempt toward Indian men for their supposed lacked of self-discipline, honesty, and respect for property and women, they feminized the "Friends of the Indians" as soft-headed and emotional.[23] In the face of criticism, army officials strongly defended their methods and argued that their role in Indian affairs should be expanded, not contracted. In 1849, when Indian affairs were transferred from the War Department to the newly created Department of the Interior, the army had gladly given up what it regarded as an onerous burden. Now, however, army officials argued that they should assume full control over Indian affairs.[24]

From one angle, it might appear as though the positions of the humanitarians and the army were diametrically opposed. However, America's recent history had shown that the impulses to uplift and punish were not inherently at odds. In the 1830s and 1840s most abolitionists regarded the use of force to end slavery as a moral contradiction, but in the 1850s a growing number came closer to John Brown's belief that "the crimes of this *guilty land: will* never be purged *away*, but with Blood."[25] War's crucible fused the two goals of destroying slavery and subjugating the South. By 1865 most

---

[22] *Condition of the Indian Tribes: Report of the Special Joint Committee*, 39th Cong., 2d sess., S. Rept. 156, 1866–67, serial 1279, 5 (qtn.); Robert Winston Mardock, *The Reformers and the American Indian* (Columbia, Mo., 1971), 8–46; Francis Paul Prucha, *American Indian Policy in Crisis: Christian Reformers and the Indian, 1865–1900* (Norman, 1976), 3–29; Richard White, *"It's Your Misfortune and None of My Own": A History of the American West* (Norman, 1991), 102–04.

[23] Michael Fellman, *Citizen Sherman: A Life of General William Tecumseh Sherman* (New York, 1995), 266 (qtn.); Robert G. Athearn, *William Tecumseh Sherman and the Settlement of the West* (Norman, 1956), 246–50; Paul Andrew Hutton, *Phil Sheridan and His Army* (Lincoln, 1985), 98–99, 181–82. Although these views were dominant among western army officers, a minority shaded toward the humanitarian position at times. See Richard N. Ellis, "The Humanitarian Generals," *Western Historical Quarterly* 3 (April 1972): 169–78; and for an overview of the range of military opinion, Sherry L. Smith, *The View from Officers' Row: Army Perceptions of Western Indians* (Tucson, 1990).

[24] Agitation for transfer of Indian affairs to the War Department began in 1866 and continued, ultimately without success, through 1880. See Francis Paul Prucha, *The Great Father: The United States Government and the American Indians*, 2 vols. (Lincoln, 1984), 1:549–60; Donald J. D'Elia, "The Argument over Civilian or Military Indian Control, 1865–1880," *Historian* 24 (February 1962): 207–25; Loring Benson Priest, *Uncle Sam's Stepchildren: The Reformation of United States Indian Policy, 1865–1887* (New Brunswick, 1942), 15–27.

[25] Quoted in Stephen B. Oates, *To Purge This Land with Blood: A Biography of John Brown*, 2d ed. (Amherst, Mass., 1984), 351. For violence in the abolitionist movement, see James

northerners regarded four years of death as the terrible but necessary price of moral progress. If the South's defiance had caused the North to become the instrument of God's wrath, what would happen if Indians rebuked the earnest appeals of good Christian men? What if tribes refused to sign treaties and embrace civilization? In such cases, said the Indians' friends, the president should call out "mounted troops for the purpose of conquering the desired peace."[26]

Although reformers' ideas did not become formalized until the declaration of President Ulysses S. Grant's "peace policy" in 1869, they affected events on the Plains two years earlier by encouraging the creation of the Indian Peace Commission. The four civilians on this commissions hoped that "peaceful negotiation would succeed," but the three army officers "had no hope of peace until the Indians were thoroughly subdued by force of arms."[27] The commission negotiated treaties with southern Plains tribes but was unable to do the same in the north. The commissioners believed that any effective agreement would require the support of Red Cloud, whom Americans had seized upon as the chief architect of the Fetterman ambush and preeminent leader of the "hostiles." Red Cloud refused to meet with the commission, although he sent word that "whenever the military garrisons at Fort Phil Kearney and Fort C. F. Smith were withdrawn, the war on his part would cease."[28] As they were not authorized to make this concession, the commissioners retreated to Washington.

When the commissioners returned to the Plains in 1868, they had authority to accept Red Cloud's demands. That summer the army reluctantly abandoned the Bozeman Trail posts. After burning the forts, Red Cloud and his band spent the next several weeks hunting, leaving the commissioners to cool their heels. It was not until November that Red Cloud appeared at Fort Laramie. Months before, several nonmilitant Oglala and Brulé leaders had signed the treaty. Red Cloud and several others from the north now added their marks.[29]

Brewer Stewart, *Holy Warriors: The Abolitionists and American Slavery* (New York, 1976), 151–74; Benjamin Quarles, *Black Abolitionists* (New York, 1969), 224–43.

[26] *Report of Indian Peace Commissioners*, 40th Cong., 2d Sess., 1867–68, H. Ex. Doc. 97, serial 1337, 2. An especially searching analysis of Indian reformers' ideology during this period is Richard Slotkin, *The Fatal Environment: The Myth of the Frontier in the Age of Industrialization, 1800–1890* (Middletown, Conn., 1985), 316–31.

[27] *Report of Indian Peace Commissioners*, 2. The members were Commissioner of Indian Affairs Nathaniel G. Taylor, Missouri Senator John B. Henderson, Samuel F. Tappan, John B. Sanborn, General Sherman, Major General Alfred H. Terry, and retired General William Harney.

[28] Ibid., 5. As Price, *Oglala People*, 67–68, 81–82, points out, U.S. observers consistently overstated Red Cloud's actual political position. Robert W. Larson, *Red Cloud: Warrior-Statesman of the Lakota Sioux* (Norman, 1997), 99–100, discusses controversies about his involvement in the Fetterman ambush.

[29] Olson, *Red Cloud and the Sioux Problem*, 76–81; Price, *Oglala People*, 81–83.

A Lakota account of the treaty negotiations, narrated many years later by Calico, an Oglala leader, offers insight into how the Sioux understood the agreement they made with the United States. Calico called the negotiations *Putinhinsapa Wolakota*. *Putinhinsapa* means Blackbeard and was a reference to one of the commissioners, John B. Sanborn.[30] *Wolakota* is an abstract noun meaning peace or friendship and is formed from the root word upon which Lakota identity is based (the verb *lakolya* means to make friends). For the Sioux, then, the 1868 Treaty entailed the making of a permanent peace between two equal parties. Calico's memory of Sanborn's words reveals his understanding of the nature of the peace. Sanborn told the Sioux that he had come to "put the fire out," or in other words, to end the war. To do this, he promised to give them draft animals "gentle enough for our old women to work with" as well as cows, sheep, pigs, chickens, horses, wagons, and plows. Each family would be given a house and "$500.00 from Tunkasila [the President] for his own use." To make his promises clear, Sanborn showed the Sioux a picture of a "wood frame building...with a corral beside it and all the animals...standing in their stalls." Significantly, the picture also included "an old tipi with a Lakota with a feather in his hair and pipe bag." Sanborn explained, "You can live in these houses and still live in your old way."[31]

Transcripts of councils held prior to the 1868 negotiations offer additional insight into Lakota views. Leaders had repeatedly complained, in Spotted Tail's words, that "[t]he country in which we live is cut up by white men, who drive away all the game." Some pointed to forts, others roads, and still others steamboats as the reason why the buffalo had been scared or driven away. The Sioux called on U.S. officials to remove these causes of the bison's decline and wash the blood from the land.[32] With these complaints as background, it is clear that Sioux leaders understood the treaty's provisions for annuities, rations, livestock, farm equipment, and houses as payment for the destruction of game and as signs of peace.

Portions of the text of the treaty reflected Sioux understandings of the agreement. Article 1 stated that the "Government of the United States desires peace, and its honor is hereby pledged to keep it. The Indians desire peace,

---

[30] William Garnett interview, 1907, RT, tablet 2, roll 1.

[31] Calico, "Blackbeard Treaty," narrated to Henry Marrowbone in 1922, copy in the author's possession. I am grateful to Gloria Runs Close to the Lodge for giving me permission to use this account.

[32] *Papers Relating to Talks and Councils Held with the Indians in Dakota and Montana Territories in the Years 1866–1869* (Washington, D.C., 1910), 49–50, 85, 88–89, 97–98 (qtn., 49). References to washing the blood from the land appear in *Proceedings of a Board of Commissioners to Negotiate a Treaty or Treaties with the Hostile Indians of the Upper Missouri* (Washington, D.C., 1865), 57, 64, 81, 83, 105. See also Jeffrey Ostler, "'They Regard Their Passing as *Wakan*': Interpreting Western Sioux Explanations for the Bison's Decline," *Western Historical Quarterly* 30 (Winter 1999): 475–97.

and they now pledge their honor to maintain it." Furthermore, the treaty inscribed Sioux military victories along the Bozeman Trail by formalizing the abandonment of the military posts along the Bozeman Trail and stipulating that the Powder River country would be considered "unceded Indian territory." Americans could not settle or travel through this area without Sioux permission. At the same time, however, the treaty set the stage for dispossession. Article 11 qualified the meaning of "unceded Indian territory" by stipulating that the Sioux had the right to occupy areas outside the permanent reservation only "so long as the buffalo may range thereon in such numbers as to justify the chase." Sioux territory would then be limited to the reservation, as defined in Article 2, shown in Map 1.

Other provisions of the treaty further threatened Sioux territorial integrity. Article 11 required the Indians not to interfere with the Union Pacific and Northern Pacific railroads. Although these roads were outside the new reservation boundaries, their construction would create new pressures for further land cessions. Furthermore, Article 11 allowed "railroads, wagon-roads, mail-stations, or other works of utility or necessity ... [to] be constructed on the lands of their reservation." The Sioux could not veto these intrusions. They would be compensated, but the government would set the amount. Overall, it is doubtful that the Sioux realized the implications of these provisions or that they understood the treaty as involving a land cession at all.

Other parts of the treaty opened the door to assertions of U.S. sovereignty over the Sioux. Article 1 required the Indians to deliver anyone accused of wrongdoing for trial and punishment under U.S. law, a significant blow to tribal law. Under Article 10 the United States agreed to provide annuities of clothing and other articles for thirty years and rations for four years. The Sioux regarded these annuities and rations as payment for destroyed game, but U.S. officials saw them as temporary expedients in the service of assimilation. Other provisions that linked the distribution of annuities and rations to new forms of government supervision also threatened Sioux autonomy. Article 10 required an "exact" annual census, Article 4 specified that annuities would be distributed at a new agency on the Missouri River, and Article 7 required parents to "compel their children" between ages six and sixteen to attend school. Several articles (3, 6, 8, 10, and 14) contained provisions to encourage agriculture and the privatization of communal lands. Some of these provisions fulfilled the promises of farm animals, wagons, and equipment that Calico recalled, but the United States did not intend the treaty to protect Sioux ways of life. Despite the tipi, feather, and pipe bag in Sanborn's picture, the words of the treaty were designed to erase Sioux ways of life.[33]

---

[33] The text of the treaty and a list of signers is in Kappler, ed., *Indian Affairs: Laws and Treaties*, 2:998–1007. On Sioux understandings of the treaty, see Roxanne Dunbar Ortiz, *The Great*

When the civilian members of the peace commission finally obtained Red Cloud's coveted mark on their document, they believed that conflict between the United States and the Sioux would soon come to an end. This optimism was naïve for three reasons.[34] First, peace would only occur if the government were to guarantee the integrity of Sioux territory, but there was little in American history to suggest confidence on this score. The second was that Sioux leaders who signed did not realize that the treaty contained many of the provisions it did. When the Oglalas and Brulés learned that the government, citing Article 4, planned to remove them to a new agency on the Missouri, they were dismayed and sent a delegation to Washington. On June 10, 1870, when Interior Secretary Jacob Cox went over the text in detail, Red Cloud declared that this was "the first time I have heard of such a treaty. I never heard of it and do not mean to follow it." He had agreed to "make peace" after the "forts were removed," but that was all.[35] Third, many militants refused to sign the treaty. Some of those who had fought with Red Cloud to close the Bozeman Trail, such as Crazy Horse, Black Twin, Big Road, and Hump (also known as High Backbone), opposed the treaty and remained willing to fight. Furthermore, many Lakotas and Yanktonais on the upper Missouri, who were more concerned about the forts and steamboat travel along the Missouri than the Bozeman Trail, were skeptical that the treaty would halt the American invasion. Sitting Bull, Black Moon, and Spotted Eagle were among the prominent war leaders among these groups.

After the dismantling of the Bozeman Trail forts, the main area of conflict shifted to the upper Missouri. In late August 1868 Sitting Bull and other nonsigners attacked Fort Buford. Built opposite the mouth of the Yellowstone in 1866, this fort, as Robert Utley observes, was an especially "detested emblem of the white invasion." Lakotas and Cheyennes killed three soldiers, seriously wounded three others, and made off with over two hundred head of cattle. They continued to raid the upper Missouri forts (Buford, Rice, and Stevenson) as well as Fort Totten in the Devil's Lake area. Within two

---

Sioux Nation: Sitting in Judgement on America (New York, 1977), 106, 115, 122, 123, 135, 142–43.

34 Catherine Price, "Lakotas and Euroamericans: Contrasted Concepts of 'Chieftainship' and Decision-Making Authority," *Ethnohistory* 41 (Summer 1994): 447–63; Price, *Oglala People*, 16, 33–34, 59–60, 143, argue that the central problem in U.S.–Lakota relations was the ethnocentric failure of U.S. officials to grasp the decentralized character of Lakota political organization and their assumption that there was a single leader with supreme authority. But officials were not so blind as to fail to perceive the absence of central authority; indeed, they tried to overcome this by designating head chiefs. The problem lay more in their unbounded faith in the righteousness of their cause and their ability to effect transformations.

35 *New York Times*, 11 June 1870, p. 1; see also the accounts of this delegation in Hyde, *Spotted Tail's Folk*, 175–81; Olson, *Red Cloud and the Sioux Problem*, 96–113. The result of this delegation's visit was that the government dropped its efforts to relocate the Oglalas and Brulés, but it would soon revive this idea.

years, however, the upper Missouri militants had decided on a new, defensive policy. Northern Lakotas and Cheyennes began to winter north of the Yellowstone in northeastern Montana and to spend summers south of the Yellowstone. Should the United States encroach on this area, they would defend themselves, but would not attack otherwise.[36] This new policy brought them into closer contact with the Lakotas, Cheyennes, and Arapahoes who had defeated the army along the Bozeman Trail in 1865–1868. By the early 1870s a center of armed resistance had formed between the Yellowstone and the Black Hills. The geographical concentration of the militants meant that if the U.S. army tried to invade the region, it would face a formidable alliance of all northern Plains Indians still willing to fight.

During these years, Sioux militants attempted to create new forms of centralized authority to resist a sustained invasion. Associates of Sitting Bull undertook one initiative. According to One Bull, Sitting Bull's nephew and adopted son, Sitting Bull was chosen to be "War Chief – Leader of the entire Sioux nation" in an impressive ceremony attended by four thousand Indians. By this ceremony, One Bull explained, Sitting Bull had become chief over the Yanktonais, Sihasapas, Hunkpapas, and Minneconjous. Sitting Bull's new authority was linked to the need for unified action in the war against the United States. His supporters told him, "When you tell us to fight, we shall fight, when you tell us to make peace, we shall make peace." At the same ceremony, Gall was made "2nd in command as War Chief" and Crazy Horse was made "head war chief over the Oglalla's [sic]; Cheyennes & Arapahoes."[37] In practice, however, it would be difficult for Sitting Bull or Crazy Horse to exercise absolute authority. As we will see in the next two chapters, Sioux decision-making processes would remain decentralized. Unity was difficult to sustain.

The first test of the new defensive policy came in fall 1871 when surveyors entered the Yellowstone Valley to locate a route for the Northern Pacific Railroad. The next spring Spotted Eagle informed Colonel David S. Stanley that he would "fight the rail road people as long as he lived, would tear

---

[36] Utley, *Lance and the Shield*, 71–72, 78, 84, 90–94 (qtn., 71).

[37] "Information in Sioux and English with Regard to Sitting Bull," Walter S. Campbell Collection, box 104, folder 11, Western History Collections, University of Oklahoma Library, Norman. Campbell used this information in his biography of Sitting Bull, written under a pen name. See Stanley Vestal, *Sitting Bull: Champion of the Sioux* (1932; Norman, 1957), 91–95. Utley, *Lance and the Shield*, 87, provides a similar account. Gary Clayton Anderson, *Sitting Bull and the Paradox of Lakota Nationhood* (New York, 1996), 63, suggests that One Bull's account was exaggerated and argues that Sitting Bull was not chosen as "Supreme Chief of the Sioux Nation" but was rather made a *wakiconza*. Yet One Bull's account indicates only that Sitting Bull was made war leader, not "head chief," and that his authority applied only to a portion of the militants. It is likely that the term used was not *wakiconza*, which refers either to an enforcer of decisions or a band leader, but *ikicize itancan* (war leader). In a song from around 1876 Sitting Bull referred to himself as "Ikicize imatancan qon [k'on]" ("a war chief I have been"). See Campbell Collection, box 104, folder 18.

up the road and kill its builders." That summer the government authorized two military expeditions of more than one thousand troops to ensure the safety of Northern Pacific engineers. Sioux forces were unable to engage U.S. troops under favorable conditions and could only harass them occasionally. In one skirmish in early August, known by the excessively dignified title of the Battle of Arrow Creek, Lakotas killed one civilian and a soldier and wounded two other soldiers. U.S. forces wounded six Lakotas and killed two. After this incident, the engineers abandoned their work and sought refuge at a nearby fort, thus confirming the soundness of the Indians' strategy. American actions suggested that the Sioux and their allies could stop the railroad from being built just as they had earlier forced the United States to abandon the Bozeman Trail forts. The Indians had other reasons to reaffirm opposition to the Americans. At the end of the Arrow Creek incident, Lakotas watched from a nearby bluff as four U.S. soldiers lifted the body of Plenty Lice, a Hunkpapa killed in the fighting, and heaved it onto a campfire. This was an outrage they did not easily forget.[38]

In summer 1873 another army expedition escorted Northern Pacific employees into the Yellowstone Valley. In early August Hunkpapas and Minneconjous tried to ambush two companies of Seventh Cavalry scouts commanded by Lieutenant Colonel George Armstrong Custer. Custer almost met his demise three years prematurely, but avoided the trap and pursued the militants to the Yellowstone River. The militants used buffalo hide boats to cross, but the Americans lacked this technology and could only lob cannon shells across the river. So ended the "Battle of the Yellowstone."[39] This clash coincided with the Panic of 1873, which halted the Northern Pacific's construction at Bismarck for six years. In all likelihood, the militants deduced that their own resistance had stopped the railroad's construction.

In retrospect it may seem that the nontreaty bands' pursuit of war was unrealistic, but they had ample cause to think they could prevail. By the early 1870s, bison populations had declined severely for some distance west of the Missouri and south of the Black Hills, but large herds remained in what is now northeastern Wyoming, northwestern South Dakota, western North Dakota, and eastern Montana. The militants were well armed. Although they had suffered some defeats, they had an impressive record of avoiding destructive engagements and checking the American advance. Furthermore, they had reason to think that the spiritual powers of the universe, accessible through ceremony and proper moral behavior, would continue to assist them.

At first glance, it might appear that the treaty bands' rejection of armed resistance meant they had fundamentally different ideas about the future from the nontreaty bands. Yet although leaders of the treaty, or agency,

[38] Utley, *Lance and the Shield*, 106–11 (qtn., 107).
[39] Ibid., 112–14.

bands were willing to make certain accommodations to the United States, they did so reluctantly and often only in a limited area. They made only the necessary trade-offs to gain something or prevent losses in another area. In the early 1870s, the goal of most agency leaders was to preserve basic patterns of life with little modification.

Although in some sense colonized by the 1868 Treaty, the agency bands retained significant practical sovereignty in the early 1870s. By this time, the government had established four main agencies for the western Sioux; the Red Cloud Agency for the Oglalas; the Spotted Tail Agency for the Brulés; the Cheyenne River Agency for the Minneconjous, Sans Arcs, and Two Kettles; and the Standing Rock Agency for the Hunkpapas, Sihasapas, and Yanktonais.[40] Government agents saw themselves as preparing the ground for the eventual assimilation of the Sioux, but at this stage, they could do little except try to persuade and cajole Indians to take up farming or wear "civilized" clothing. In practice, the agencies conformed to the Sioux notion that they were nothing more than a place to receive payment for ceded land (the Lakota term for agency is *owakpamni oyanke*, distribution place). Although some treaty bands established semipermanent camps at or near their respective agencies in the 1870s, others, especially early in the decade, traveled extensively, continuing to pursue variations on earlier subsistence patterns, occasionally coming to their agency to collect annuities and interact with other bands. Treaty bands felt free to cross and recross formal reservation boundaries as they wished, showing no recognition of these lines as having any practical significance. When at the agencies, Sioux people addressed the government agents as *ate* (father), but this did not signify an acceptance of U.S. paternalism. Instead, they used this kinship term to call on agents to fulfill their obligations. Just as a father should provide for his children, so agents should ensure the timely delivery of annuities and rations, provide useful advice, and look out for Indians' well-being.

During these years, as a prelude to initiating specific programs for assimilation, the agents began trying to assert their authority over the Sioux. When they did, they often met strenuous opposition. On October 22, 1874, at Red Cloud Agency, for example, Agent J. J. Saville, a physician selected by the Episcopal Church under Grant's peace policy, ordered agency employees to cut down a pine tree, strip its branches, and bring it to the agency. When some Oglalas asked about the tree, they learned that the agent intended it as a pole to fly the flag of the United States.[41] Oglalas would have seen the

---

[40] In addition to these agencies, the Lower Brulé and Crow Creek agencies were located near the Big Bend of the Missouri and the Yankton Agency was located farther down the Missouri near the Nebraska border.

[41] Accounts of this incident can be found in Hyde, *Red Cloud's Folk*, 220–22; Olson, *Red Cloud and the Sioux Problem* 169–70; Price, *Oglala People*, 135–37; Larson, *Red Cloud*, 158–59. I have relied on these and on Garnett interview, tablet 1, roll 1. A less reliable

American flag as a type of *wapaha*, a term for the feathered staffs their own military societies carried in public performances.[42] They had seen the American flag many times before at the head of columns of U.S. troops and at military posts, such as nearby Camp Robinson. They recognized it as a symbol of U.S. authority. Within hours, Oglalas demanded that Saville halt work on the flagpole. When the agent ordered his employees to continue, several Oglalas used tomahawks to destroy the pole. Saville then sent for soldiers from nearby Camp Robinson. When troops arrived, fighting almost broke out, but key leaders, notably Young Man Afraid of His Horses, intervened.[43]

With the Stars and Stripes now flying, Saville tried to extend U.S. sovereignty by taking a census. Like other Indians, Oglalas were wary of being counted. Not only might a census reduce their "official" population, thus giving the government a pretext for reducing annuities and rations, a census was another sign of U.S. authority. Some Oglala leaders, Red Cloud among them, adamantly refused to be counted. By threatening to withhold rations and annuities and to call in troops, Saville eventually secured the co-operation of other Oglala leaders. These leaders feared the consequences of military intervention and judged that cooperation on the census might allow them to influence the agent on other matters. They persuaded their people to submit to enumeration. Nonetheless, Saville was unable to control the process. When the count was complete, it showed an *increase* in the number of Indians at Red Cloud Agency from 6,500 to 9,339 with several hundred more out hunting.[44]

Agency employees, who oversaw the census, lacked sufficient knowledge of the Indians to prevent them from being counted multiple times and including deceased relatives and unborn children in their reports. Mixed-blood interpreters and "squawmen" (non-Indian men with Indian wives), who assisted with the count, were better informed, but the very source of their knowledge – their relationships to Lakota people – led them to tolerate, if not encourage, resistance.

As the flagpole and census incidents show, the assertion of U.S. power at the agencies met with only limited success. This was true not only because of

---

account is Charles W. Allen, *From Fort Laramie to Wounded Knee: In the West That Was*, edited and with an introduction by Richard E. Jensen (Lincoln, 1997), 14–25.

[42] Walker, *Lakota Society*, 78; James R. Walker, *Lakota Belief and Ritual*, ed. Raymond J. DeMallie and Elaine A. Jahner (Lincoln, 1980), 265.

[43] Young Man Afraid of His Horses is a good example of a mistranslation of a Lakota name. As Stephen Return Riggs, *Dakota Grammar, Texts, and Ethnography*, Contributions to North American Ethnology, vol. 9, ed. James Owen Dorsey (Washington, D.C., 1893), 230, points out, his father's name, Tasunke Kokikapi, literally means "They (the foe) fear even his horse."

[44] *ARCIA*, 1875, 250; Hyde, *Red Cloud's Folk*, 222–23. Matthew G. Hannah, "Space and Social Control in the Administration of the Oglala Lakota ('Sioux'), 1871–1879," *Journal of Historical Geography* 19, no. 4 (1993): 425, notes the importance of Saville's use of influential Oglala leaders as a step toward more effective methods of colonial management.

resistance from below but also because of uncertainties and contradictions from above. At the Red Cloud and Spotted Tail agencies, these factors combined to work against establishing permanent locations, obviously a crucial precondition for promoting assimilation. Officials in Washington, eager to reduce transportation costs, wanted the agencies situated on the Missouri, but most Oglalas and Brulés preferred their agencies to be located far to the west. Their agents generally supported this view. The result was that the government moved the two agencies several times between 1870 and 1878 – sometimes on or near the Missouri, sometimes far away. This constant relocation meant that the agents spent the bulk of their energies setting up the basic infrastructure of an agency only to have to dismantle it and start over someplace else. Although the Oglalas and Brulés might have welcomed the fact that constant relocation diminished agents' capacities, the experience of constantly being forced to move contributed to a sense of powerlessness. In 1876 one Lakota chief noted that the government had promised his people a permanent home, but "we have been moved five times." Perhaps, he observed with bitter humor, the government should "put the Indians on wheels and you can run them about wherever you wish."[45]

Even at agencies that remained in a single place, the Sioux made little movement toward assimilation in the first half of the 1870s. Although agents frequently professed great optimism that Sioux men would soon be spending their days behind a plow, this seldom happened. Many members of treaty bands planted a few acres of corn and vegetables. A handful tried to establish larger farms only to be defeated by grasshoppers and drought. Some agents adopted a realistic position about farming. After a couple of years in charge of the Grand River Agency (established in 1869 and shortly thereafter renamed Standing Rock Agency), it dawned on agent J. C. O'Connor that the "character of the country" was far more suited for stockraising than extensive farming. Furthermore, since Indian men were used to "the chase" and were "little inclined for farming operations," stockraising was a good match to "their habits."[46]

Nor did missionaries, civilization's unofficial vanguard, make much progress. In the early 1870s far more prospectors, railroad surveyors, and soldiers populated western Sioux country than evangelists. In 1870, Father Pierre-Jean De Smet, a Jesuit priest known to Indians throughout the West

---

[45] Hyde, *Spotted Tail's Folk*, 186–90; Hyde, *Red Cloud's Folk*, 182–202; Olson, *Red Cloud and the Sioux Problem*, 114–43; Price, *Oglala People*, 92–114; Edward E. Hill, *The Office of Indian Affairs, 1824–1880: Historical Sketches* (New York, 1974), 147–48, 176–77, 202–03; *Report and Journal of Proceedings of the Commission Appointed to Obtain Certain Concessions from the Sioux Indians, December 26, 1876*, 44th Cong., 2d sess., 1876–77, S. Ex. Doc. 9, 1876, serial 1718, 8 (qtn.).

[46] *ARCIA*, 1872, 261. On the failures of farming at this agency, later known as Standing Rock Agency, see *ARCIA*, 1873, 23–31; *ARCIA*, 1874, 246; *ARCIA*, 1875, 245.

as "Black Robe," preached along the Missouri and baptized more than four hundred Sioux (though, like his earlier baptisms at the 1851 Horse Creek council, with indeterminate long-term effect). The following year the Jesuits sent two missionaries to Grand River Agency. They built a church and schoolhouse, but within weeks departed, "disillusioned and defeated." It was not until six years later that the Benedictine Order established a mission at Standing Rock Agency.[47] The constant movement of the Red Cloud and Spotted Tail agencies hindered the establishment of permanent missions there until the late 1870s. Only at Cheyenne River Agency, where Thomas L. Riggs established a Congregational mission in 1872, was there a permanent Christian presence.[48]

Before the United States could begin systematically to implement an agenda of assimilation, the Sioux would need to become economically dependent on the government. In the early 1870s, most Sioux bands left their agencies to hunt bison at some point during a given year. In addition to keeping them culturally tied to their usual ways of life, this practice allowed them an independent source of food and hides, both for their own use and for trade, as well as freedom from agents' oversight. Once bison herds ceased to exist, Indians would be more closely bound to the agencies, and agents would be able to use food as a weapon to compel compliance. The demise of the bison would also force nontreaty bands to give up armed resistance and live at the agencies. This time was fast approaching. Already there had been a substantial decline in bison populations as a result of hunting, mostly by Indians, for external markets. In the early 1870s, however, the political economy of bison destruction underwent a significant transformation when capitalists who controlled new tanning technologies opened up new markets for hides. To satisfy these markets, non-Indian hunters invaded the Plains, armed with large-bore rifles equipped with telescopic sights and a range of several hundred yards. Great Plains bison became gun belts for British soldiers in India, drive belts for industrial machinery in Liverpool, and luxury

---

47 Hiram Martin Chittenden and Alfred Talbot Richardson, eds., *Life, Letters and Travels of Father Pierre-Jean De Smet, S.J., 1801–1873*, 4 vols. (New York, 1905), 2:678–79, 3:932; Mary Claudia Duratschek, *Crusading along Sioux Trails: A History of the Catholic Indian Missions of South Dakota* (St. Meinrad, Ind., 1947), 60–72; Ross Alexander Enochs, *The Jesuit Mission to the Lakota Sioux: Pastoral Theology and Ministry, 1886–1945* (Kansas City, 1996), 10–25; ARCIA, 1871, 525; John J. Killoren, *"Come, Blackrobe": De Smet and the Indian Tragedy* (Norman, 1994), 342 (qtn.); ARCIA, 1876, 38–40; ARCIA, 1877, 73.

48 Thomas Lawrence Riggs, "Sunset to Sunset: A Lifetime with My Brothers, the Dakotas," *South Dakota Historical Collections* 29 (1958): 134–39; ARCIA, 1873, 232. The Protestant Episcopal Church briefly established a mission at Spotted Tail Agency in 1875, but it was not until 1879, after the agency's location was finally determined, that this denomination established a permanent mission at the renamed Rosebud Agency. ARCIA, 1875, 254; ARCIA, 1878, 40; ARCIA, 1879, 42. At Red Cloud Agency (renamed Pine Ridge), the Episcopal Church began establishing a mission in 1878. ARCIA, 1878, 38; ARCIA, 1879, 40.

furniture in Manhattan townhouses. Within a decade the animals were on the brink of extinction.[49]

By the early 1870s Americans had accumulated substantial knowledge of western Sioux territory. Scientific and military expeditions had traveled through the region, recording information about its topography, resources, and people. Painters and writers like George Catlin and Francis Parkman had given the American public an extensive set of representations of the Sioux and their land. Still, Americans thought of Sioux country largely as a region on the way to someplace else, an empty desert through which the transcontinental railroad was forced to pass. But Sioux country was about to become important in its own right. As Americans consumed the country's dwindling numbers of bison, cattlemen occupied the newly vacant range. Farmers, too, were moving into the zone between the humid prairies and the drier plains. As they did, regional boosters began to talk of how the plow could release the soil's moisture and thereby transform the continent's interior desert into a lush garden peopled by millions.[50] U.S. citizens also began to imagine vast riches beneath the earth. The series of mining rushes that began in 1849 engendered a mania for new strikes everywhere. Thus far, miners had experienced the Sioux mainly as an obstacle on the way to wealth in California, Colorado, or Montana. But many Americans were certain that deep within the heart of Sioux territory, in the Black Hills, lay hidden magnificent deposits of gold.

Some scholars have argued that the Sioux attributed only economic significance to the Black Hills in the 1870s and that the idea of the Black Hills as "sacred" emerged only in the twentieth century when the Sioux needed new arguments in their fight to regain them. Recent Lakota representations of the Black Hills are undoubtedly conditioned by present-day needs and involve, to some extent, the "invention of tradition." Nonetheless, as Linea Sundstrom has persuasively argued, the Black Hills played an important role in Lakota mythology and were a crucial site for religious ceremonies, especially the Sun Dance and vision quests. That Sioux leaders stressed the economic value of the Black Hills in the 1870s does not prove the absence of religious value. It only means that in the context of U.S. efforts to force the Sioux to sell the Black Hills in the mid-1870s, economic discourse assumed

---

[49] Hyde, *Spotted Tail's Folk*, 227, 240; Hyde, *Red Cloud's Folk*, 193; Tom McHugh, *The Time of the Buffalo* (New York, 1972), 253; Andrew C. Isenberg, *The Destruction of the Bison: An Environmental History, 1750–1920* (Cambridge, 2000), 130–43. David D. Smits, "The Frontier Army and the Destruction of the Buffalo: 1865–1883," *Western Historical Quarterly* 25 (Autumn 1994): 313–38, argues that the army itself conducted a policy of destroying the bison, but Isenberg, *Destruction of the Bison*, 129, effectively responds that "Sherman commended the hunters but he did not command them."

[50] Henry Nash Smith, *Virgin Land: The American West as Symbol and Myth* (New York, 1950), 210–13.

priority. For several interconnected reasons – economic, religious, and political – the Plains Sioux looked upon the Black Hills as the center of their land, indeed, as the very heart of the earth.[51]

Until 1874 the army tried to deter prospectors from pursuing persistent rumors of Black Hills gold. Their main concern was that an invasion of miners would strain scarce resources by creating demands for protection from Indian attacks. Military planners hoped eventually to locate a fort in the Black Hills to subdue Sioux, Cheyenne, and Arapahoe militants, but this initiative would be politically tricky and require careful timing.[52] Military officials' thinking about the Black Hills was also affected by their responsibility to enforce the 1868 Treaty. Army officers did not especially like this document. They thought it reflected the hopeless naïvete of reformers. It was also a reminder of the humiliation of abandoning the Bozeman Trail forts. On the other hand, the army had to be sensitive to critics. As we have seen, the army was trying to wrest control over Indian affairs from the Indian Office. To assure skeptics, it could not openly support treaty violations. Significant economic pressures existed to open up the Black Hills, especially from boosters in places like Yankton, Cheyenne, and Sioux City. However, the railroads themselves were not eager to move in this direction. At the moment, they preferred that soldiers guard their employees and passengers on already existing lines.[53]

These calculations changed radically after the Panic of 1873. Suddenly, opening the Black Hills became a national priority. Should gold be discovered in the Black Hills (many Americans were certain the god of manifest destiny had placed it there), a host of benefits would follow. An influx of new gold would alleviate the scarcity of money and stimulate business. A gold rush would provide a safety valve for mounting social unrest by opening opportunities for unemployed workers.[54] As the value of the Black Hills

---

[51] Donald Worster, *Under Western Skies: Nature and History in the American West* (New York, 1992), 136–47; Eric Hobsbawm and Terence Ranger, eds., *The Invention of Tradition* (Cambridge, 1983); Linea Sundstrom, "The Sacred Black Hills: An Ethnohistorical Review," *Great Plains Quarterly* 17 (Summer/Fall 1997): 185–212. The Black Hills are referred to as the "heart of the earth" and Harney Peak as the "center of the earth" in Raymond J. DeMallie, ed., *The Sixth Grandfather: Black Elk's Teachings Given to John G. Neihardt* (Lincoln, 1984), 310, 295. In 1876, Running Antelope (Hunkpapa) told U.S. officials that the Sioux looked toward the Black Hills as the "center of their land." *Report and Journal of Proceedings*, 48.

[52] Olson, *Red Cloud and the Sioux Problem*, 171–72; Watson Parker, *Gold in the Black Hills* (Norman, 1966), 10–23; Donald Jackson, *Custer's Gold: The United States Cavalry Expedition of 1874* (New Haven, 1966), 6–11; Howard Roberts Lamar, *Dakota Territory, 1861–1889: A Study of Frontier Politics* (New Haven, 1956), 149–50; Hutton, *Sheridan and His Army*, 290; Robert Lee, *Fort Meade and the Black Hills* (Lincoln, 1991), 2–3.

[53] On the Northern Pacific's demands for military resources, see Hutton, *Sheridan and His Army*, 171–72.

[54] Slotkin, *Fatal Environment*, 355–56.

soared, the Grant administration's peace policy began to wane. In part this was because the peace policy had not led to peace. From 1869 through 1873, the United States waged war against Apaches, Arapahoes, Cheyennes, Comanches, Kiowas, and Modocs.[55] On the northern Plains the 1868 Treaty was supposed to guarantee that the Sioux would live quietly under the tutelage of good Christian agents. Instead, the Sioux were defying American imperatives either through armed resistance or opposition to government authority at the agencies. Americans who had once favored a policy of kindness were losing patience. Perhaps it was time for harsher measures.

A retreat from liberalism toward Indians was linked to broader national trends. By the early 1870s many supporters of Radical Reconstruction, who had once advocated the use of state power to ensure political and civil rights for freed slaves, thought the time had come to withdraw troops from southern states. Freedmen would have to fend for themselves. The Panic of 1873 reinforced the growing conservatism of the northern bourgeoisie, which responded to sharpening class conflict by vigorously asserting the rights of property, the priority of national economic development, and the necessity for social order. By contesting these principles, labor agitators, angry farmers, nonsubmissive blacks, and militant Indians threatened to destroy the nation.[56]

In this climate, Lieutenant General Phil Sheridan, commander of the Division of the Missouri, had little difficulty persuading the Grant administration to authorize a military expedition into the Black Hills. Sheridan's stated objective was to establish a fort close to the militants' stronghold. Although he downplayed the possibility that the Black Hills would yield gold, it is inconceivable that a man with Sheridan's acumen for long-range strategic planning would have failed to grasp the implications of a Black Hills bonanza.[57] If rumors of gold were verified, a mining rush would be unstoppable. Almost certainly, Indians would defend themselves against this invasion and attack the gold diggers. The army's mission in the Black Hills would quickly change from arresting miners to fighting Indians.

In late July 1874 members of the army expedition found a few flecks of Black Hills gold. The expedition's commander, Lieutenant Colonel Custer, immediately reported the discovery of "gold among the roots of the grass." In the fall and spring private expeditions set out for the "New El Dorado." Humanitarians, always a minority but one close to President Grant's ear,

---

[55] An overview of conflicts in these years can be found in Robert M. Utley, *The Indian Frontier of the American West, 1846–1890* (Albuquerque, 1984), 157–64, 170–78.

[56] Eric Foner, *Reconstruction: America's Unfinished Journey, 1863–1877* (New York, 1988), 448–54, 485–511, 524–34. Slotkin, *Fatal Environment*, 358–70, shows how the national media linked representations of Indian savagery, Negro lawlessness, and labor agitation to construct an ideological justification for seizure of the Black Hills.

[57] *ARSW*, 1874, 43d Cong., 2d sess., 1874–75, H. Ex. Doc. 1, serial 1635, 24–25; Hutton, *Sheridan and His Army*, 290–91.

called on the government to enforce the 1868 Treaty. In contrast, the army, western politicians, local and national business interests, and most of the general public wanted to open the Black Hills. Although the army officially discouraged miners from trespassing on the Great Sioux Reservation, its pursuit of violators was halfhearted.[58] Grant hoped he could resolve the issue by convincing the Sioux to sell or lease the Black Hills. In June 1875 the president authorized a commission headed by Iowa Senator William B. Allison to accomplish this purpose. When Lakotas rebuffed the commission's offer of $100,000 per year to lease the Hills or $6,000,000 for their outright sale, Allison returned to Washington.[59]

Grant now faced a serious dilemma. Politically, it would be next to impossible to stop hundreds of citizens from pursuing their God-given right to search for wealth. Yet failure to remove the intruders would be a serious breach of the peace policy. Forced to choose between expansion and honor, Grant, not unlike many of his predecessors, sacrificed the latter. On November 3, 1875, before the sympathetic audience of Secretary of War William W. Belknap, Interior Secretary Zachariah Chandler, General George Crook, and General Sheridan, Grant outlined plans designed to lead to war. The president would not rescind orders banning citizens from the Great Sioux Reservation, but troops would be withdrawn from the Black Hills. This would open the floodgates to a full-scale invasion of the Hills. The inevitable Indian attacks on miners would provide a pretext for a final conquest of the northern militants. The government would demand that the agency Sioux sell the Black Hills at whatever price it decreed and threaten to starve them if they refused. To avoid antagonizing his humanitarian advisors, Grant did not announce these plans.[60] In the West, however, the withdrawal of troops quickly became known. Where they had once come by the dozen, argonauts by the hundreds now arrived daily. In January 1876 there were approximately four thousand illegal occupants of the Black Hills.[61]

In preparation for war the government launched a verbal assault on the "untamable and hostile" bands under Sitting Bull and other chiefs of "less note." Like Lewis and Clark, who demonized the Sioux as the "vilest miscreants of the savage race," government officials expressed outrage at the militants' defiance: "They set at defiance all law and authority, and boast that the United States authorities are not strong enough to conquer them.

---

58 Jackson, *Custer's Gold*, 81–91; Edgar I. Stewart, *Custer's Luck* (Norman, 1955), 64–68; Evan S. Connell, *Son of the Morning Star* (San Francisco, 1984), 246–47; Slotkin, *Fatal Environment*, 355–57 (qtn., 357); Parker, *Gold in the Black Hills*, 29–36; ARSW, 1875, 44th Cong., 1st sess., 1875–76, H. Ex. Doc. 1, serial 1674, 69–70.

59 Olson, *Red Cloud and the Sioux Problem*, 199–213; Hyde, *Red Cloud's Folk*, 239–46.

60 ARSW, 1876, 44th Cong., 2d sess., 1876–77, H. Ex. Doc. 1, pt. 2, serial 1742, 28, 440–41. An especially useful account of these decisions is John S. Gray, *Centennial Campaign: The Sioux War of 1876* (Ft. Collins, Colo., 1976), 23–26.

61 Parker, *Gold in the Black Hills*, 71.

The United States troops are held in contempt, and . . . they laugh at the futile efforts that have thus far been made to subjugate them, and scorn the idea of white civilization." The militants' crimes did not consist simply of a list of alleged treaty violations. It was their refusal to bow to the dictates of the manifest destiny of a superior people that demanded the use of military force to "*whip* them into subjection."[62]

On December 3, Interior Secretary Chandler ordered all "hostile Sioux Indians residing outside of their reservations" to report to the agencies by the end of January. If they refused, the Interior Department would request the military to force them to comply.[63] Most of the militant bands had never signed the 1868 Treaty, but even so, the treaty gave them the right to occupy lands outside the reservation boundary. To no one's surprise, the militants did not leave their hunting grounds. The army began mobilizing troops.

Grant's plan to provoke a war went off without a hitch, but the war itself did not follow the intended script. Although Sheridan hoped to strike the militants in their winter camps, cold weather and heavy snow slowed troop deployment. Soldiers attacked an Indian village on the Powder River on March 17, 1876, but quickly withdrew in the face of a counterattack. It was not until June that the army was prepared to move against the militants' stronghold. When they did, disaster struck. Inspired by a prophesy of victory that Sitting Bull received at a Sun Dance, the Sioux mounted a ferocious attack against Crook at Rosebud Creek on June 17, forcing him to retreat. Eight days later Custer and his Seventh Calvary rode into a large village of Sioux and Cheyennes on a stream the Indians called the Greasy Grass. On July 4, as the United States celebrated the one hundredth anniversary of the signing of the Declaration of Independence, shocking news of Custer's defeat at the Little Bighorn began to arrive.[64]

---

[62] E. C. Watkins to CIA, 9 Nov. 1875, in *Military Expedition against the Sioux Indians*, 44th Cong., 1st sess., 1876–76, H. Ex. Doc. 184, serial 1691, 8–9.

[63] SI to SW, 3 Dec. 1875, in ibid., 10.

[64] For military developments leading to the Little Bighorn, see Utley, *Frontier Regulars*, 248–58; Gray, *Centennial Campaign*, 35–171; for Sitting Bull's vision, see Vestal, *Sitting Bull*, 148–51; Utley, *Lance and the Shield*, 137–38. Recent works on the Little Bighorn include John S. Gray, *Custer's Last Campaign: Mitch Boyer and the Little Bighorn Reconstructed* (Lincoln, 1991); James Welch with Paul Stekler, *Killing Custer: The Battle of the Little Bighorn and the Fate of the Plains Indians* (New York, 1994); Gregory F. Michno, *Lakota Noon: The Indian Narrative of Custer's Defeat* (Missoula, 1997); Larry Skelnar, *To Hell with Honor: Custer and the Little Bighorn* (Norman, 2000).

3

"Doubtless an Unauthorized Promise"

The Politics of the Great Sioux War

Military historians have usually characterized the Little Bighorn as a temporary, if spectacular, setback for the United States. After Custer's demise, the usual story goes, the army regrouped and scored a series of crippling blows against the Sioux and their allies. Within a year, the militants had submitted to their fate as a conquered people.[1] In fact, the dynamics were more complicated than this suggests. Concerns about military harassment and dwindling food supplies played a part in decisions to surrender, but so did concessions the militants forced U.S. officials to make. What historians have called the Great Sioux War consisted of politics more than battles, and it did not result in a completely vanquished foe.

From the outset, the victors at the Little Bighorn realized that they would continue to face danger from U.S. troops. On the day after the killing of Custer, Indians scouts reported the approach of soldiers from the north. Before leaving, however, the Indians buried their own dead and stripped the bodies of the Seventh Cavalry, taking guns, ammunition, saddles, boots (useful for leather), coins, shirts, pants, belts, chewing tobacco, and coffee. Boys counted coup on the dead by stabbing them or shooting arrows, while grieving women slashed some of the bodies. A few Cheyennes, whose relatives were cut down at Sand Creek almost thirteen years before, severed some of the soldiers' hands and feet. That evening and the next day, they started moving. For a few weeks the five to six thousand people in the militants' camp

---

[1] Robert M. Utley, *Frontier Regulars: The United States Army and the Indian* (Lincoln, 1973), 267–81; Stephen E. Ambrose, *Crazy Horse and Custer: The Parallel Lives of Two American Warriors* (New York, 1975), 451–74; Paul Hedren, "The Great Sioux War: An Introduction," in *The Great Sioux War, 1876–77: The Best from "Montana: The Magazine of Western History,"* ed. Paul Hedren (Helena, 1991), 1–21; Jerome A. Greene, *Yellowstone Command: Colonel Nelson A. Miles and the Great Sioux War, 1876–1877* (Lincoln, 1991); Charles M. Robinson III, *A Good Year to Die: The Story of the Great Sioux War* (New York, 1995).

stayed together, singing "kills" songs to celebrate *Pehin Hanska kasota kin*, the destruction of Long Hair. In late July or early August they decided to break into smaller groups to facilitate hunting.[2]

During these weeks the militants saw few signs of the army. Two days after the battle General Alfred H. Terry's troops found the bodies of Custer and his men beginning to rot in the early summer heat. Too demoralized to pursue the Indians, Terry ordered his men to bury the dead and then retreated to a camp on the Yellowstone River. General Crook had earlier returned to a post in northern Wyoming after the Battle of the Rosebud. Throughout July, Terry and Crook remained in camp nervously awaiting reinforcements.[3]

With the arrival of fresh troops – "Custer avengers" – Crook and Terry returned to the field in early August. After several days, with supplies running short and the only Indian trails weeks old, Crook and Terry decided to go to the Yellowstone River for new supplies. As they made their way down the Powder River, a cold rain fell. Many soldiers had scurvy, dysentery, and rheumatism. Upon reaching the Yellowstone, Terry and Crook bickered over a possible plan of action before deciding to go their separate ways. Terry swung north, but his scouts were unable to find the slightest sign of Indians, and he called off his campaign on September 5.[4] In the meantime, Crook, having run low on rations, was marching south from the Heart River toward the Black Hills. On the eighth, scouts belonging to an advance guard under Captain Anson Mills approached Slim Buttes, as shown in Map 2, just north of the Black Hills. There they sighted a camp of Minneconjous, Oglalas, Brulés, and Cheyennes.[5]

Near dawn the next morning, Mills attacked. Because he did not achieve complete surprise, the Indians were able to flee to the surrounding bluffs and

---

[2] Wooden Leg, *Wooden Leg: A Warrior Who Fought Custer*, interpreted by Thomas B. Marquis (1931; Lincoln, 1962), 258–71, 276–80; Kate Bighead in Thomas B. Marquis, *She Watched Custer's Last Battle* (Hardin, Mont., 1933), 5–6; John Stands in Timber and Margot Liberty, *Cheyenne Memories* (New Haven, 1967), 205–07; Stanley Vestal, *Warpath: The True Story of the Fighting Sioux Told in a Biography of Chief White Bull* (1934; Lincoln, 1984), 200–05; Raymond J. DeMallie, ed., *The Sixth Grandfather: Black Elk's Teachings Given to John G. Neihardt* (Lincoln, 1984), 192–98; Jerome A. Greene, ed., *Lakota and Cheyenne: Indian Views of the Great Sioux War, 1876–1877* (Norman, 1994), 37, 40, 64; James Welch with Paul Stekler, *Killing Custer: The Battle of the Little Bighorn and the Fate of the Plains Indians* (New York, 1994), 179–86; John S. Gray, *Centennial Campaign: The Sioux War of 1876* (Ft. Collins, Colo., 1976), 338–45, 357; Peter John Powell, *People of the Sacred Mountain: A History of the Northern Cheyenne Chiefs and Warrior Societies, 1830–1879: With an Epilogue, 1969–1974*, 2 vols. (San Francisco, 1981), 2:1042–46.

[3] Gray, *Centennial Campaign*, 192–211.

[4] Ibid., 212–38, 241; John G. Bourke, *On the Border with Crook* (New York, 1891), 344–61; John F. Finerty, *War-Path and Bivouac: The Conquest of the Sioux* (Chicago, 1890), 226–33.

[5] ARSW, 1876, 44th Cong., 2d sess., 1876–77, H. Ex. Doc. 1, serial 1742, 506–507; Bourke, *On the Border*, 365–69; Finerty, *War-Path and Bivouac*, 241–48; Gray, *Centennial Campaign*, 243–46; Jerome A. Greene, *Slim Buttes, 1876: An Episode of the Great Sioux War* (Norman, 1982), 35–50.

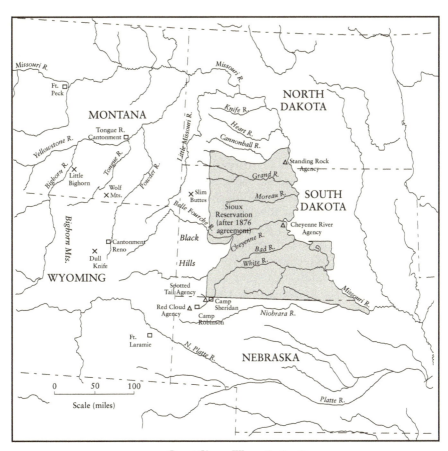

MAP 2. Great Sioux War, 1876–1877.

ravines and send word to nearby camps. By the time Crook reached Mills's position, Lakota reinforcements had arrived. The result was a standoff. Two U.S. soldiers and one scout were killed and between six and twelve Indians died. After the skirmish, the troops raided the Indian village. They found beadwork, quillwork, parfleches, buffalo robes, paint, and five thousand pounds of dried meat. They also discovered several items from the Seventh Cavalry. What they did not take, they burned. The following morning, their stomachs full for the first time in days, the troops resumed their march toward Custer City. In October Crook announced the termination of this campaign.[6]

[6] *ARSW*, 1876, serial 1742, 509–12; Finerty, *War-Path and Bivouac*, 249–57; Gray, *Centennial Campaign*, 246–54.

Although the United States had so far failed miserably to achieve its goal of subjugating the militants, it was making much better progress with its other war aim: gaining fictive legal title to the Black Hills. On September 7, a U.S. commission headed by George W. Manypenny, a leading humanitarian, arrived at Red Cloud Agency to secure Oglala leaders' consent to an "agreement." (Congress had abolished treatymaking in 1871.) Manypenny and his colleagues informed the Oglalas that Congress had decreed that the Sioux Nation must give up the part of their reservation west of the 103d meridian, an area that included the Black Hills. They must also surrender unceded lands under Article 16 of the 1868 Treaty in northeastern Wyoming and southeastern Montana. The commissioners made clear that if the Oglalas refused, Congress would cut off their rations, the army would punish them, and the government would take the Black Hills anyway.[7] After days of tense discussions, some of the leaders at Red Cloud Agency signed. The commissioners then traveled to Spotted Tail, Standing Rock, Cheyenne River, Crow Creek, Lower Brulé, and Santee agencies. Although the 1868 Treaty required that three-fourths of all adult men agree to any changes, the Manypenny Commission obtained the marks of only 10 percent. Nonetheless, they were confident that their work was legal and left Indian country with "our hearts full of gratitude to God, who had...directed our labors to a successful issue."[8]

Many Sioux were critical of those who signed the 1876 agreement. In 1879, for example, Sitting Bull informed a newspaper reporter that Red Cloud and Spotted Tail were "rascals" for selling "our country without the full consent of our people." Sitting Bull's anger is understandable, but, short of returning to war, Red Cloud and Spotted Tail had few alternatives. The army had assumed control over the western Sioux agencies in July and was in a strong position to exact retribution.[9] Sioux who signed the Black Hills agreement made strong claims on the U.S. government while protesting what they were being forced to do. On September 22, Young Man Afraid of His Horses explained that his mark was "to signify the Great Father has fed and clothed me a hundred years and given me wagons and cattle." Fire

---

[7] *Report and Journal of Proceedings of the Commission Appointed to Obtain Certain Concessions from the Sioux Indians, December 26, 1876*, 44th Cong., 2d sess., 1876–77, S. Ex. Doc. 9, serial 1718, 4–5, 29; Charles J. Kappler, ed., *Indian Affairs: Laws and Treaties*, 5 vols. (Washington, D.C., 1904–1941), 1:168–71. The commission's members included H. C. Bulis, Newton Edmunds, Rev. H. B. Whipple, A. G. Boone, A. S. Gaylord, Gen. H. H. Sibley, and J. W. Daniels.

[8] James C. Olson, *Red Cloud and the Sioux Problem* (Lincoln, 1965), 225–29; Edward Lazarus, *Black Hills/White Justice: The Sioux Nation Versus the United States, 1775 to the Present* (New York, 1991), 90–92; *Report and Journal of Proceedings*, 7 (qtn.); Kappler, ed., *Indian Affairs: Laws and Treaties*, 2:1002.

[9] Robert M. Utley, *The Lance and the Shield: The Life and Times of Sitting Bull* (New York, 1993), 207 (qtn.); ARSW, 1876, serial 1742, 445.

Thunder took a different, though complementary, approach. When it was his turn to sign, he "came up holding his blanket before his eyes and signed blindfolded."[10]

Fire Thunder's gesture offered a pointed commentary on earlier remarks by one of the commissioners, Episcopal Bishop Henry B. Whipple. When the commissioners had first come to Red Cloud Agency, Whipple told the Oglalas that the "Great Father does not wish to throw a blanket over your eyes, and to ask you to do anything without first looking at it." Days later, Whipple was pleased to observe that the Indians now "understand everything perfectly plain" and that there was therefore "no blanket over any one's eyes."[11] Fire Thunder's action rebuked Whipple's happy interpretation of the proceedings.

As the Manypenny Commission pursued its work, army officers began to prepare for a winter campaign. Lieutenant General Phil Sheridan established two bases near the heart of the militants' strength. One, the Tongue River Cantonment, commanded by Colonel Nelson A. Miles, was at the confluence of the Tongue and the Yellowstone. The other, commanded by Crook, was Cantonment Reno, on the Powder River near the Big Horn Mountains.[12] The rivalry between these two officers would shape the course of events in important ways.

Though a hero in the Civil War, Nelson Miles's advancement in the army had not kept pace with his insatiable ambition. Despite family connections to General in Chief of the Army, William Tecumseh Sherman (Miles had married Sherman's niece, Mary Hoyt Sherman), Miles was still a colonel in 1876. He was especially bitter that Crook had been promoted over him to brigadier general three years before. As Crook went into action against the Sioux, Miles was far away, impatiently commanding Fort Leavenworth. After the Little Bighorn, however, Sheridan ordered Miles to reinforce the army on the northern Plains. Finally, Miles hoped, he would gain the generalship he had so long been denied.[13]

Crook was not as self-promotional as Miles, but he, too, sought credit for ending the Great Sioux War. After winning distinction in the Civil War, Crook had developed a reputation as one of the western army's premier Indian fighters. He was known especially for his innovative use of Indian scouts

---

[10] *New York Herald*, 23 Sept. 1876, p. 7.

[11] *Report and Journal of Proceedings*, 32, 35.

[12] Paul Andrew Hutton, *Phil Sheridan and His Army* (Lincoln, 1985), 322.

[13] Robert Wooster, *Nelson A. Miles and the Twilight of the Frontier Army* (Lincoln, 1993), 1–83; Peter R. DeMontravel, *A Hero to His Fighting Men: Nelson A. Miles, 1839–1925* (Kent, Ohio, 1998), 46–80; Robert M. Utley, "Nelson A. Miles," in *Soldiers West: Biographies from the Military Frontier*, ed. Paul Andrew Hutton (Lincoln, 1987), 213–18; Martin F. Schmitt, ed., *General George Crook: His Autobiography* (Norman, 1946), 183, n. 14.

and for relentless pursuit of his enemies. After the Battle of the Rosebud, the first failure of his career, Crook eagerly sought redemption.[14]

The first action took place in Miles's area of operation. On October 10, as Miles's supply trains moved up the Yellowstone, they encountered fire from Sioux snipers. Six days later, amid continued firing, Lieutenant Colonel Elwell S. Otis discovered a message to Miles from Sitting Bull, posted on a stake, which demanded that the army leave, warning, "If you don't, I will fight you again." On the twentieth, Miles responded to the militants' overtures for a meeting and found himself face to face with Sitting Bull. Miles demanded that Sitting Bull surrender, Sitting Bull told Miles to take his soldiers out of his country, and then shooting began. Five Lakotas were killed; U.S. casualties were two wounded.[15]

Five days later three Minneconjou leaders who had been with Sitting Bull, Red Skirt, Bull Eagle, and Small Bear approached Miles and indicated their willingness to go to the Cheyenne River Agency. The next day they and other Sans Arcs leaders representing about two thousand people agreed to surrender. They left five hostages to guarantee their arrival at the agency. Elated, Miles proclaimed "the beginning of the end."[16]

To secure this agreement, Miles had to make concessions. One Minneconjou, Spotted Elk (also known as Big Foot), later stated that Miles agreed to allow his people to conduct a buffalo hunt before going to the agency and promised them rations, guns, and ammunition. According to Spotted Elk, Miles also said he would move the Cheyenne River Agency "to the fork of the Cheyenne" (the mouth of the Belle Fourche). Miles himself reported only that the surrendering Sioux would have to turn in their weapons at the agency and "such horses as the Government should require," with the proceeds from their sale going to purchase livestock. Miles probably did say things to the Indians about moving the agency but without informing his superiors.[17]

Miles's agreement with the Minneconjous and Sans Arcs quickly broke down. Those contemplating surrendering, Miles related, were "very

[14] Jerome A. Greene, "George Crook," in *Soldiers West*, ed. Hutton, 115–22; Charles M. Robinson III, *General Crook and the Western Frontier* (Norman, 2001).

[15] *ARSW*, 1877, 45th Cong., 2d sess., 1877–78, H. Ex. Doc. 1, serial 1794, 489–492 (qtn. 491); Utley, *Lance and the Shield*, 168–69; Greene, *Yellowstone Command*, 81–104; Col. W. H. Wood to AAG DD, 1 Mar. 1877, DMSF, roll 4; Nelson A. Miles, *Personal Recollections and Observations of Nelson A. Miles*, 2 vols. (1896; Lincoln, 1992), 1:225–26.

[16] Col. Nelson A. Miles to AAG DD, 27 Oct. 1876, DMSF, roll 4 (qtn.); Miles to Gen. A. H. Terry, 28 Oct. 1876, DMSF, roll 4; Greene, *Yellowstone Command*, 108. The hostages were Red Skirt, White Bull, Black Eagle, Sun Rise, and Foolish Thunder.

[17] Wood to AAG DD, 1 Mar. 1877 (1st qtn.); Miles to Terry, 28 Oct. 1876 (2d qtn.). See also Harry Anderson, "Nelson A. Miles and the Sioux War of 1876–77," *The Westerners Brand Book* (Chicago) 16 (June 1959): 26. For additional evidence that Miles promised a "reservation on the Belle Fourche," see Brig. Gen. George Crook to AAG DM, 8 Jan. 1877, DMSF, roll 4.

suspicious" and "afraid that some terrible punishment will be inflicted upon them" once they reached Cheyenne River. Given the army's desire to avenge Custer, these were reasonable fears, to say the least. Although Miles assured them that they would be safe at the agency, could they trust him, and even if they could, was he in a position to guarantee their safety? Because of these concerns, only two hundred actually went to the agency. Most who contemplated surrender had second thoughts and either returned to Sitting Bull's camp or joined Crazy Horse.[18]

In the meantime, to the south, Crook was preparing for a winter campaign. To defeat the militants, Crook and Sheridan believed, it would be necessary to deter the Sioux at Red Cloud and Spotted Tail agencies from providing material support and manpower to the militants, as they had done the previous summer. To accomplish this, Sheridan wanted Crook to disarm all Indians at both agencies, but Crook feared that this would damage his efforts to recruit Sioux scouts to accompany the expedition. Thus, he decided to disarm only Red Cloud's and Red Leaf's bands. He sent troops to their camps on October 23. The soldiers found few weapons, but they allowed Pawnee scouts to seize 750 ponies. Soon after, Crook informed Red Cloud that the government was "deposing" him as "chief" of the Oglalas and that henceforth Spotted Tail would be "head chief" over the Sioux at Red Cloud and Spotted Tail agencies.[19] After this, Crook enlisted 155 Sioux, Cheyenne, and Arapahoe scouts to join a force of more than 200 already enlisted, mostly Shoshones and Pawnees, to accompany him in his upcoming expedition against the Sioux and Cheyenne militants. In addition to paying the scouts, Crook provided each man with a horse (many from the raid on Red Cloud and Red Leaf), ammunition, a gun, and the opportunity to keep captured horses.[20] Crook also offered to help the Sioux scouts in their effort

---

[18] Miles to Terry, 28 Oct. 1876 (qtn.); Lieut. Col. George Buell to AG DD, 2 Dec. 1876, DMSF, roll 4; Greene, *Yellowstone Command*, 109; Anderson, "Miles and the Sioux War," 27.

[19] Hutton, *Sheridan and His Army*, 325–26; AAG DP to AAG DM, 24 Oct. 1876, DMSF, roll 4; Brig. Gen. George Crook to AAG DM, 30 Oct. 1876, DMSF, roll 4; Bourke, *On the Border*, 387–88; Jerome A. Greene, "The Surrounding of Red Cloud and Red Leaf, 1876: A Preemptive Maneuver of the Great Sioux War," *Nebraska History* 82 (Summer 2001): 69–75. A simultaneous operation was carried out to disarm the Indians at Cheyenne River and Standing Rock. See *ARSW*, 1876, serial 1742, 469–70; Brig. Gen. Alfred A. Terry to Lieut. Gen. P. H. Sheridan, 26 Oct. 1876, DMSF, roll 4.

[20] John G. Bourke diary, 9, 2 Nov. 1876, vol. 14, roll 2, 1378–79, 1352–53, United States Military Academy Library, West Point, N.Y. (microfilm). On the role of scouts in this campaign see Thomas W. Dunlay, *Wolves for the Blue Soldiers: Indian Scouts and Auxiliaries with the United States Army, 1860–90* (Lincoln, 1982), 82–84; Loretta Fowler, *Arapahoe Politics, 1851–1978: Symbols in Crises of Authority* (Lincoln, 1982), 58–63; George Bird Grinnell, *Two Great Scouts and Their Pawnee Battalion: The Experiences of Frank J. North and Luther H. North* (Cleveland, 1928), 253–81; Robert Bruce, *The Fighting Norths and Pawnee Scouts: Narratives and Reminiscences of Military Service on the Old Frontier* (Lincoln, 1932), 48–54. On scouts in general, see also David D. Smits, "'Fighting Fire with Fire':

to prevent the government from moving them to Indian Territory, a subject that had come up during the Manypenny Commission's recent visit. On November 8, Three Bears and Fast Thunder, Oglala headmen and spokesmen for the scouts, informed Crook that in exchange for their help they wanted to go to Washington to speak against removal. Three days later, they placed another issue on the table. As Fast Thunder put it, "the reason I am going out to fight the northern hostiles is that the country up there was given by the Great Father and I want to get it back."[21] In the months to come, Lakotas would continue to explore this possibility, and it would play a central role in negotiations.

When Crook set out for the north in November, he hoped to surprise and destroy Crazy Horse's camp. After arriving at Cantonment Reno on November 18, Crook sent six Arapahoe and eight Sioux scouts, who learned that Crazy Horse was camped near the site of the Little Bighorn battlefield. Soon after, however, another scout reported that Crazy Horse's people were aware of his approach. Crook then turned his attention to a camp of about 1,500 Cheyennes under the leadership of Dull Knife (also known as Morning Star) in the Big Horn Mountains. On the twenty-third Crook ordered Colonel Ranald S. Mackenzie to start out with eight hundred cavalry and most of the scouts. The next day, scouts determined the location of the camp, and Mackenize prepared to attack.[22]

The Cheyennes were aware of Crook's arrival at Cantonment Reno from their own scouts. On the morning of the twenty-fourth, an eighty-year-old holy man, Box Elder, had a vision of soldiers coming. When they heard his prophesy, many Cheyennes urged the women and children to hide in the surrounding rimrocks, leaving a small force of men to guard the camp. However, the Kit Fox warrior society, with quirts in hand, threatened to punish anyone who left. That evening, the Kit Foxes held a dance to celebrate their recent killing of thirty Shoshones. The dancing ended just before light

---

The Frontier Army's Use of Indian Scouts and Allies in the Trans-Mississippi Campaigns, 1860–1890," *American Indian Culture and Research Journal* 22, no. 1 (1998): 73–116.

[21] Bourke diary, 8, 11 Nov. 1876, vol. 14, roll 2, 1367–70, 1385–86 (qtn., 1386). Although the Sioux at Cheyenne River, Standing Rock, Crow Creek, and Lower Brulé convinced the Manypenny Commission to drop its demand that they be moved to Indian Territory, at Spotted Tail and Red Cloud agencies leaders proposed sending a delegation to investigate Indian Territory's suitability. This delegation, headed by Spotted Tail, arrived in Indian Territory on November 11 and returned around December 12 having decided against moving. *Report and Journal of Proceedings*, 19–21, 25–28; George E. Hyde, *Spotted Tail's Folk: A History of the Brulé Sioux* (Norman, 1961), 258–59; Lieut. Horace Neide to CIA, 15 Dec. 1876, STA, roll 841; Maj. J. W. Mason to AAG DP, 21 Dec. 1876, STA, roll 841.

[22] Bourke diary, 18 Nov., 21 Nov., 30 Nov. 1876, vol. 14, roll 2, 1391, 1403–1406, 1409; Brig. Gen. George Crook to Lieut. Gen. P. H. Sheridan, 23 (two telegrams), 28 Nov. 1876, DMSF, roll 4; Col. R. S. Mackenzie to Brig. Gen. George Crook, 26 Nov. 1876, enclosed in Crook to Lieut. Gen. P. H. Sheridan, 30 Nov. 1876, DMSF, roll 4.

was about to break in the east. Just then, Mackenzie's troops stormed up a dry creek bed and into the camp.[23]

The Cheyennes had time to gather children and old people, some horses and weapons, and items vital to the tribe's religious life, but little else. Most of the women and children fled up a nearby ravine. At the top, the women established breastworks and stood, some in nothing more than cotton dresses, singing to the men below to have courage. Unable to regain the village, the Cheyennes fought to recover some of the horses they had left behind and to prevent the soldiers from getting within range of the women and children. Soon after taking the camp, the army began to burn it. In advance of the flames, soldiers and scouts seized buffalo robes, skins, guns, war drums, and items taken at the Little Bighorn. Dense smoke billowed as fire consumed the Cheyennes' tipis, their stores of dried meat and pemmican, their clothing, war bonnets, and shields. That night in the subzero cold, Dull Knife's people stood atop a ridge and built small fires for warmth. In the distance they could see the army's inferno.[24]

Mackenzie reported that his forces found twenty-five dead Cheyennes. Other Cheyennes probably died, their bodies recovered by their own people or undiscovered. Over the next few days, as they fled toward Crazy Horse's camp, a few more died of wounds suffered in the fighting and some starved or froze to death. At least fourteen Cheyenne babies died of exposure. Dull Knife's people lost most of their possessions – their tipis, food supplies, tools, most of their clothing, and several hundred ponies. The United States suffered six soldiers killed and twenty-six wounded.[25]

Several days later, the Cheyennes reached Crazy Horse's camp, more than one hundred miles to the north in the Tongue River valley. For the Lakotas, the pitiable condition of the refugees and their stories of death and suffering drove home the risks of war. The addition of more than a thousand people to the three thousand already present strained scarce resources. The Lakotas provided the Cheyennes with food, shelter, clothing, tobacco, and horses. Some Cheyennes later praised Crazy Horse's people for their generosity, but others believed their allies had been stingy.[26]

The arrival of the Cheyennes found Lakota leaders in the midst of intense discussions, triggered by Drum on His Back, an Oglala who had recently arrived to persuade the militants to surrender. Several weeks before at Red

[23] George Bird Grinnell, *The Fighting Cheyennes* (1915; Norman, 1956), 369–75; Powell, *People of the Sacred Mountain*, 2:1052–58; Stands in Timber and Liberty, *Cheyenne Memories*, 214–16.

[24] Bourke diary, 30 Nov. 1876, vol. 14, roll 2, 1417–25, 1430–32; Powell, *People of the Sacred Mountain*, 2:1058–70; William Garnett interview, 1907, RT, tablet 2, roll 1.

[25] Mackenzie to Crook, 26 Nov. 1876; Bourke diary, 30 Nov. 1876, vol. 14, roll 2, 1425; Powell, *People of the Sacred Mountain*, 2:1069–70; Wooden Leg, *Wooden Leg*, 287.

[26] Wooden Leg, *Wooden Leg*, 286–87; Powell, *People of the Sacred Mountain*, 2:1071.

Cloud Agency, Drum on his Back had grown furious with the Manypenny Commission's demands and the agency leaders' failure to reject them. On September 19 he took up a Winchester rifle in one hand and a war club in the other and forced the commission's proceedings to a temporary halt. A few days later he rode north, reaching Crazy Horse's camp in early December. Although the sources do not reveal the substance of Drum on His Back's arguments, he probably hoped to convince the militants to bring their spirit of defiance to the agencies. To remain at war would be futile, but strong, unified political action might prevent further dispossession and even lead to the return of confiscated lands.[27]

The presence of the Cheyenne refugees undoubtedly had an impact on the discussions in Crazy Horse's camp, although the significance of their plight was subject to varying interpretations. On one hand, they afforded evidence of the high cost of war, yet proponents of continued militancy could argue that sufficient vigilance and unity could have saved them. According to reports from Sioux who later surrendered at Cheyenne River Agency, Crazy Horse and most of the Oglala leaders favored continuing to fight, while most Minneconjou and Sans Arcs leaders were disposed to consider terms for peace. These cleavages, however, were not firm. Lame Deer and Black Shield, Minneconjou chiefs, and Spotted Eagle, a Sans Arcs leader, were inclined toward militancy, as were many of the young warriors within less militant bands.[28]

Although the sources reveal little about the opinions of women, they were likely more inclined to peace than war. This does not imply that gender divided Sioux people into haters and lovers of war; the situation was more complicated than that. Sioux girls were taught to honor the war deeds of brothers and other male relatives; wives and mothers celebrated the coups of husbands and sons. Historically, women had occasionally gone on war parties and a few gained fame as warriors. For most Sioux women, however, status and identity were closely linked to domestic responsibilities. Obligations to their families, the constant dread of being attacked, and too many days without enough food led many to seek an end to the fighting.[29] Sioux

[27] Col. W. H. Wood to AAG DD, 24 Jan., 16 Feb. 1877, DMSF, roll 4; *New York Times*, 22 Sept. 1876, p. 5; Garnett interview, tablet 2, roll 1; George W. Manypenny, *Our Indian Wards* (Cincinnati, 1880), 355–56; Harry H. Anderson, "The War Club of Sitting Bull the Oglala," *Nebraska History* 42 (March 1961): 55–61. Drum on His Back, also known as Sitting Bull and Packs the Drum, was a nephew of Little Wound, the son of Bull Bear, who had been killed by warriors of Smoke's band in November 1841 (see Chapter 1). Thus, his mission involved an effort to reunite the Oglala people.

[28] Wood to AAG DD, 24 Jan., 16 Feb. 1877; Col. W. H. Wood to AAG DD, 28 Dec. 1876, DMSF, roll 4; Lieut. R. H. Day to Post Adjt., Fort Buford, 14 Apr. 1877, DMSF, roll 4.

[29] For nineteenth-century Lakota women, see Raymond DeMallie, "Male and Female in Traditional Lakota Culture," and Beatrice Medicine, "'Warrior Women': Sex Role Alternatives for Plains Indian Women," both in *The Hidden Half: Studies of Plains Indian Women*,

and Cheyenne women rarely spoke in councils, but they could influence their husbands as well as younger brothers, nephews, sons, grandsons, and brothers-in-law. In all these relationships they commanded respect. Since men who advocated war often spoke of the need to defend women and children, women who favored surrender could turn this argument to their advantage when they appealed to male relatives. In this way, women indirectly influenced public discourse.

Unable to reach a consensus on the major issue, the leaders in Crazy Horse's camp agreed on a provisional course of action. They decided to allow Drum on His Back and a delegation of fifteen to go to Miles's post on the Tongue River and talk with him about possible terms of peace. As they came within sight of their destination on December 16, a group of Crow scouts from the post ambushed them, killing five, including Drum on His Back. The Crows had acted without Miles's permission, but the ambush severely damaged the argument that Miles could be trusted and tilted the balance against advocates of surrender.[30]

Six days later, two Minneconjou headmen, Fool Bear and Important Man, came to Crazy Horse's camp with another overture. Acting as emissaries from the five hostages who had remained with Miles in late October (see earlier) and had since gone to Cheyenne River Agency, they carried terms from Colonel W. H. Wood, the chief military officer there, that those who surrendered would have to give up their weapons and horses but would not be imprisoned or punished. Fool Bear and Important Man reported that the Minneconjous and Sans Arcs were "disposed to listen." The Oglalas and Cheyennes said they would "never submit" to such terms "as long as they lived" and "abused" the two men.[31]

According to Fool Bear and Important Man, the militants were preparing for a long fight. The two men focused particularly on "a great medicine man," who had recently assumed Custer's Indian name of "Long Hair" and was in "constant communication with the spirit of General Custer." Long Hair said that he had once been a "friend of the whites," but now that they were trying to "deprive me of my home and country," his people should never submit to them. Long Hair's communication with Custer's spirit had given him formidable powers. Not only was he invulnerable to being penetrated by bullets, he had recently "made" eight cases of ammunition. These powers, he claimed, would be effective for seven more months.[32]

ed. Patricia Albers and Beatrice Medicine (Lanham, Md., 1983), 237–65, 267–80; Marla N. Powers, *Oglala Women: Myth, Ritual, and Reality* (Chicago, 1986).

[30] Wood to AAG DD, 24 Jan., 1 Mar. 1877; Col. W. H. Wood to AAG DD, 21 Feb. 1877, DMSF, roll 4; Col. Nelson A. Miles to AAG DD, 17 Dec. 1876, DMSF, roll 4; Thomas H. Leforge, *Memoirs of a White Crow Indian*, told by Thomas B. Marquis (1928; Lincoln, 1974), 269–71; DeMallie, ed., *Sixth Grandfather*, 199–200.

[31] Wood to AAG DD, 24 Jan. 1877.

[32] Ibid. This medicine man was identified as Yellow Grass in Wood to AAG DD, 16 Feb. 1877.

Mari Sandoz suggests that Long Hair's production of ammunition was a trick designed to strengthen the courage of his people.[33] Perhaps, but chicanery was not necessarily involved. It was culturally possible for a Lakota *wicasa wakan*[34] to be in communication with Custer's ghost. Lakotas believed that the *nagi* (spirits or ghosts) of people who had died, including enemies, remained near their place of death afterward and that those with spiritual power could communicate with them. The living could offer spirits gifts and, in turn, spirits could intervene in human affairs.[35] How might Custer's spirit have enabled Long Hair to produce ammunition? The English translation of Fool Bear and Important Man's account states that Crazy Horse "made" the ammunition, implying an ex nihilo creation. It is more likely, however, that Long Hair used his ability to communicate with Custer's spirit to have ammunition brought to him. Some weeks earlier a small party of Cheyennes had visited the Greasy Grass and recovered large quantities of ammunition. A few days later this party came across Dull Knife's band and helped guide them to Crazy Horse's camp, bringing their cargo with them.[36] This was probably the channel through which Long Hair induced Custer's spirit to act.

Whatever the cultural logic behind Long Hair's abilities, he wanted the army to know about his powers. Accordingly, he instructed Fool Bear and Important Man to explain the situation when they returned to the Cheyenne River Agency. Though army officers would have scoffed at the idea of a Sioux medicine man communicating with a slain lieutenant colonel, Long Hair's pronouncements revealed that the army faced a determined foe, one

---

[33] Mari Sandoz, *Crazy Horse: The Strange Man of the Oglalas* (Lincoln, 1942), 350.

[34] This term, usually translated as medicine man, is better glossed as holy man or spiritually powerful man.

[35] James R. Walker, *Lakota Belief and Ritual*, ed. Raymond J. DeMallie and Elaine A. Jahner (Lincoln, 1980), 119–24, 137, 142; Arthur Amiotte, "The Lakota Sun Dance: Historical and Contemporary Perspectives," in *Sioux Indian Religion: Tradition and Innovation*, ed. Raymond J. DeMallie and Douglas R. Parks (Norman, 1987), 87. See also Aaron McGaffey Beede, *Sitting Bull–Custer* (Bismarck, N.Dak., 1913), 49, which relates a story that after Custer's death, Sitting Bull "talked with his ghost" and it predicted Sitting Bull's death. See also a painting by No Two Horn in James R. Grossman, ed., *The Frontier in American Culture: An Exhibition at the Newberry Library, August 26, 1994–January 7, 1995: Essays by Richard White and Patricia Nelson Limerick* (Berkeley, 1994), 42, showing Custer's ghost emerging from his body. It is significant that Long Hair's ability to communicate with Custer's spirit would continue for seven months from the time of Fool Bear and Important Man's visit (late December), thus marking one year after his death. This corresponded to the amount of time that Sioux people generally thought a spirit would remain before departing for the next world. See Alice C. Fletcher, "The Shadow or Ghost Lodge: A Ceremony of the Ogallala Sioux," in *Reports of the Peabody Museum of American Archaeology and Ethnology, Vol. 3, 1880–1886* (Cambridge, Mass., 1887), 296; Royal B. Hassrick, *The Sioux: Life and Customs of a Warrior Society* (Norman, 1964), 38; William K. Powers, *Oglala Religion* (Lincoln, 1974), 93.

[36] Wooden Leg, *Wooden Leg*, 282–86.

that would not be easily defeated. Long Hair may have had a subtle effect on the U.S. military's calculations of the costs of war and, in this way, an impact on the course of events.

For the militants to succeed, however, they could not afford defections. To prevent them, Crazy Horse was willing to use his force of *akicitas* (police). After a few days in Crazy Horse's camp, Fool Bear and Important Man persuaded the families of the hostages to leave for the agency. As they prepared to depart, however, Crazy Horse told them that they "would be followed and killed." A few nights later these families departed in secret, but Crazy Horse and "a good many of his warriors" overtook them, shot their horses, took their guns and knives, and forced them to return. The next morning, evidently thinking that Crazy Horse would be afraid to act in "broad daylight," they decided to leave "in the presence of all the people." Again, Crazy Horse used force to block their departure, although he did allow Fool Bear and Important Man to leave. On December 27 the two men traveled fifty miles but then decided to return to Crazy Horse's camp and try one more time. Finally, they succeeded in "stealing away" four lodges of the hostages' relatives.[37]

By this time, Miles was eager for a fight. Things had not gone well for him over the past few weeks. First had come news of Mackenzie's attack on Dull Knife's village, a great victory for General Crook but not for Colonel Miles. Then came what Miles described as the "most unfortunate affair" of the Crow scouts' ambush of Drum on His Back. On December 18 Miles finally had some good news when one of his lieutenants, Frank D. Baldwin, found Sitting Bull's camp on Ash Creek, south of Fort Peck. The army killed only one Indian but destroyed some of the camp's possessions and food. With the thermometer reading forty below, Miles was eager to build on this victory and informed General Terry on the twentieth that "I shall now endeavor to strike the large camp, under Crazy Horse."[38]

Historians have usually portrayed the militants as afraid to engage the army. Yet, even as Miles was planning to move against Crazy Horse, Crazy Horse had already begun an offensive of his own, hoping that successful military action would strengthen his people's resolve to hold out. On December 18 Indians attacked a U.S. mail train and eight days later raided the cattle

---

[37] Wood to AAG DD, 24 Jan. 1877. Although many in the camp probably regarded Crazy Horse's use of force as consistent with his authority as war leader, the Minneconjous' and Sans Arcs' primary loyalty was to their own leaders and relatives. It is likely that there were strong divisions of opinion in Crazy Horse's camp about the legitimacy of his use of force. Ethnographic material on *akicitas* can be found in James R. Walker, *Lakota Society*, ed. Raymond J. DeMallie (Lincoln, 1982), 28–34, 74–94.

[38] *ARSW*, 1877, serial 1794, 493–94; Miles to AAG DD, 17 Dec. 1876 (1st qtn.); Col. Nelson A. Miles to Gen. A. H. Terry, 20 Dec. 1876, DMSF, roll 4 (2d qtn.); Greene, *Yellowstone Command*, 140–45.

herd at Tongue River Cantonment. On the twenty-ninth, just as Crazy Horse predicted, Miles began pursuing the raiders up the Tongue River. There was some minor skirmishing on New Year's Day and again on January 3. As U.S. forces approached Crazy Horse's village on the eighth, the Indians sent decoys to lure the soldiers into an ambush. When the decoys advanced too quickly, the warriors behind them were forced to come into the open. What followed was an inconclusive clash known in the annals of U.S. military history as the Battle of Wolf Mountains. Historians have asserted that Crazy Horse was a "defeated man now, and he knew it," but the only evidence for this is Miles's own report, which described the Indians' losses as "severe" and claimed that Crazy Horse's "strength and prestige" had been "broken." Although Crazy Horse was disappointed that the ambush scheme had failed, only two or three of his men had been killed. He was neither broken nor defeated. After the Wolf Mountains fight, the Sioux and Cheyennes quickly moved camp. Miles ordered his forces to retreat.[39]

A week later, Sitting Bull arrived in Crazy Horse's camp. Despite Baldwin's attack a month earlier, Sitting Bull carried impressive quantities of beads, blankets, and tobacco, as well as fifty cases of ammunition he had obtained from trading buffalo robes to Métis traders near the Canadian border. Sitting Bull also brought a long history of remarkable deeds, one that could inspire people with hope and a sense of possibility. The last time Sitting Bull and Crazy Horse were together, they had killed Custer. Not surprisingly, Sitting Bull's appearance heartened the war advocates. According to a Minneconjou named Eagle Shield, heralds went through the camp, "directing all the Indians to get themselves in good condition for fighting." The young men, he reported, were all "eager for a fight." The situation, then, was exactly the opposite of what Miles claimed. The militants were not demoralized nor afraid. Indeed, they hoped that the army would pursue them so they could destroy them and were disappointed to learn that Miles's troops had returned to their post.[40]

---

[39] *ARSW*, 1877, serial 1794, 494–96; Don Rickey Jr., "The Battle of Wolf Mountain," *Montana: The Magazine of Western History* 13 (Spring 1963): 44–54. For historians' assessments, see Ambrose, *Crazy Horse*, 458 (qtn.); Robinson, *Good Year to Die*, 314–24; Greene, *Yellowstone Command*, 182; Welch with Stekler, *Killing Custer*, 240; Jeffrey V. Pearson, "Nelson A. Miles, Crazy Horse, and the Battle of Wolf Mountains," *Montana: The Magazine of Western History* 51 (Winter 2001): 67. For Miles's assessment see *ARSW*, 1877, serial 1794, 495. Miles's only evidence for casualties was the amount of blood in the snow; Wooden Leg, *Wooden Leg*, 293, states that one Cheyenne and two Lakotas were killed. DeMontravel, *Hero to His Fighting Men*, 97–99, provides a more restrained interpretation of the significance of Wolf Mountains.

[40] Lieut. R. H. Day to Col. W. B. Hazen, 25 Nov. 1876, DMSF, roll 4; Wood to AAG DD, 16 (qtn.), 21 Feb. 1877. The Métis Sitting Bull traded with were probably one of many groups that hunted and traded in southern Saskatchewan. See Marcel Giraud, *The Métis in the Canadian West*, 2 vols., trans. George Woodcock (Lincoln, 1986), 2:402–05.

Despite the war advocates' resolve, however, they were unable to prevent a growing wave of defections. In late January various parties left for the agencies: several Cheyennes under Little Wolf; about seventy-five Oglalas, Brulés, and Minneconjous led by Eagle Pipe; and more than two hundred Minneconjous, Sans Arcs, and Two Kettles led by Red Horse, White Eagle, and Spotted Elk. Crazy Horse's *akicitas* tried to stop them, taking some arms and horses, but it proved impossible to police the village's borders. Nonmilitants who remained hoped that emissaries for peace would come from the agencies. On February 10, two Brulés, Charging Horse and Make Them Stand Up, reached Spotted Tail Agency with a message from the "hostile camp." Many people "are anxious for Spotted Tail to go there to them with tobacco.... They want to come in and live in peace."[41]

With the militants unable to engage the army anytime soon and with supplies running low, Sitting Bull decided to depart for Canada. Before leaving, Sitting Bull tried to persuade Crazy Horse to join him. Mari Sandoz suggests that Crazy Horse decided against going to "Grandmother's Country" because it was even colder in the north, but there were other possible reasons. More a warrior than a diplomat, Crazy Horse may have preferred to make a stand in his own country rather than having to establish new relations with the Indian and Métis people of southern Canada and the Canadian government.[42] Then, too, he may have feared that an attempt to move his people north would cause a mass exodus to the agencies. In any event, Sitting Bull left for Canada in early February. The main body of the Cheyennes went to the Big Horn Mountains, while Crazy Horse moved toward the Powder and Little Powder rivers.[43]

Over the next few months, most of the militants decided to surrender. In some ways, the process resembled a breach in a dike. At first only a few people left for the agencies, but soon more people followed. When this happened, it became increasingly difficult to persuade the rest to stay. With their unity broken, even the most hard-core advocates of war decided they had

---

[41] Lieut. W. P. Clark to Lieut. John G. Bourke, 24 Feb. 1877, DMSF, roll 4; Lieut. J. M. Lee to Lieut. J. G. Bourke, 6 Mar. 1877, DMSF, roll 4; Col. W. H. Wood to AAG DD, 27 Feb. 1877, DMSF, roll 4; Lieut. Horace Neide to Lieut. John G. Bourke, 10 Feb. 1877, DMSF, roll 4 (qtn.).

[42] Sandoz, *Crazy Horse*, 355–56. Already the Hunkpapa band leader, Black Moon, had crossed into Canada with about 350 people; according to Swelled Face in Wood, AAG DD, 21 Feb. 1877, Sitting Bull had sent them "to get ammunition and to induce the Red River Indians to join the hostiles" and was planning to follow them soon. Although an alliance between Sitting Bull and the Métis was unlikely, it was reasonable for Sitting Bull to consider it in view of the 1869–1870 Métis uprising and continued Métis unrest. See Thomas Flanagan, *Louis "David" Riel: "Prophet of the New World"* (Toronto, 1979); George F. G. Stanley, "The Half-Breed 'Rising' of 1875," *Canadian Historical Review* 17 (December 1936): 399–412.

[43] DeMallie, ed., *Sixth Grandfather*, 202; Lieut. W. P. Clark to Lieut. J. G. Bourke, 3 Mar. 1877, DMSF, roll 4.

no choice but to lay down their arms. The army's potential to inflict catastrophic damage combined with unreliable food supplies defined the context in which this process occurred. But except for Mackenzie's attack on Dull Knife's band, the army was never able to score a major victory. In fact, the Indians' ability to avoid military defeat forced Miles and Crook to rely on diplomacy. Although the militants were unable to avoid surrendering, they did win important concessions.

As in the fall, Miles was ahead of Crook on the diplomatic front, although this was due more to Indians' initiative than his own. When Miles's troops returned to their post after the skirmish at Wolf Mountains, they brought with them between six and nine Cheyenne captives, all women and children. The day before the skirmish, this party had been returning to Crazy Horse's camp from a visit to relatives. They had mistaken the smoke from Miles's camp for their own. Among the captives was Sweet Taste Woman, whose sister was married to a leading warrior and religious leader, White Bull (also known as Ice). As an elder (she was about fifty years old), Sweet Taste Woman commanded respect among her people and had powerful social connections. Among the Cheyennes, the relationship between a woman and her sister's husband was close and relatively relaxed.[44]

Tired of seeing her people suffer and die, Sweet Taste Woman saw her capture as an opportunity to broker peace talks between Miles and her people. Though his motives differed, Miles decided to send Sweet Taste Woman and interpreter John Brughier to the Cheyenne village. Before they left, Sweet Taste Woman explained to Miles that he should send tobacco, a sign of peace, as well as other presents: sugar, coffee, bacon, and beans. Sweet Taste Woman and Brughier left the Tongue River Cantonment on February 1 and reached the Cheyenne camp on the Little Bighorn a few days later.[45] Although Miles stated in his official correspondence that the terms were unconditional surrender, as Harry H. Anderson points out, Cheyenne sources show that Sweet Taste Woman brought assurances from Miles that "if the Indians surrendered they would be given a place to live in their own country." It was one thing for the Cheyennes to contemplate surrendering if it meant having their leaders imprisoned and being forced to live in Indian Territory. It was much easier if it meant they could live permanently in their own land.[46]

---

[44] Bighead in Marquis, *She Watched Custer's Last Battle*, 8; Wooden Leg, *Wooden Leg*, 290–96; Grinnell, *Fighting Cheyennes*, 384; Stands in Timber and Liberty, *Cheyenne Memories*, 219–22; ARSW, 1877, serial 1794, 495; Powell, *People of the Sacred Mountain*, 2:1074–75; E. Adamson Hoebel, *The Cheyennes: Indians of the Great Plains*, 2d ed. (Ft. Worth, 1978), 35.

[45] Col. Nelson A. Miles to AAG DD, 23 Feb. 1877, DMSF, roll 4; Miles, *Personal Recollections*, 1:239; Wooden Leg, *Wooden Leg*, 295–96; Stands in Timber and Liberty, *Cheyenne Memories*, 222–23. On Brughier, see John S. Gray, "What Made Johnnie Brughier Run," *Montana* 14 (Spring 1964): 34–49.

[46] Harry H. Anderson, "Indian Peace-Talkers and the Conclusion of the Sioux War of 1876," *Nebraska History* 44 (December 1963): 246–47. Anderson relies on information provided by

Under Cheyenne decision-making processes, a body known as the council chiefs (also known as peace chiefs) first considered the matter. Unable to reach consensus, they turned it over to the warrior societies, but they, too, were divided and returned the issue to the council chiefs. After two days of inconclusive discussions, they settled on a provisional course of action. They would move closer to Miles's post, send a delegation to see him, and then try to decide. A small group of Minneconjous in the Cheyenne camp, led by Hump, accompanied them. Some days later, when the Cheyennes came to the Tongue River, Sweet Taste Woman, Brughier, and several peace advocates, including White Bull, Two Moons, and Hump, went ahead, reaching Miles's post on February 19. Miles quickly recognized White Bull and Two Moons (Sweet Taste Woman probably described them to him), rode up to them, shook their hands, and called them by name. The next day Miles offered to make White Bull a scout, and he agreed. Other Cheyennes and Lakotas said they would remain behind as hostages. Four days later, the rest started back to the main camp, now on the Powder River, returning on March 4.[47]

As the Cheyennes began discussing Miles's response, another option opened up. A party of Lakotas representing Spotted Tail came to urge them to surrender at the Spotted Tail and Red Cloud agencies on the White River. According to Wooden Leg, they offered assurances that the Indians at those agencies were being well fed and that no one was being punished for killing Custer. Likely, they also spoke of the possibility of the Cheyennes having an agency of their own.[48] Once more, it was impossible to achieve consensus. Finally, in late February the council chiefs decided to allow individual families to act on their own. The largest group of Cheyennes – between eight and nine hundred – decided to go to the White River agencies, where they surrendered in March and April. A smaller group of about three hundred,

---

John Stands in Timber, a Cheyenne historian and grandson of Sweet Taste Woman, in Verne Dusenberry, *The Northern Cheyenne*, Montana Heritage Series Number 6 (Helena, 1955), 4–5. Although there is no independent corroboration of this evidence, it is very likely reliable in view of evidence discussed throughout this chapter that Miles and Crook made these kinds of promises. For background on the Northern Cheyennes' land situation in 1877, see Orlan J. Svingen, *The Northern Cheyenne Indian Reservation, 1877–1900* (Niwot, Colo., 1993), 3–7; Hoebel, *Cheyennes*, 106–16.

47 Wooden Leg, *Wooden Leg*, 296–97; Miles to AAG DD, 23 Feb. 1877; Grinnell, *Fighting Cheyennes*, 385–86; Powell, *People of the Sacred Mountain*, 2:1089–90. On the council (peace) chiefs, see George Bird Grinnell, *The Cheyenne Indians: Their History and Ways of Life*, 2 vols. (New Haven, 1923) 1:336–44; Stan Hoig, *The Peace Chiefs of the Cheyennes* (Norman, 1980), 3–14; Hoebel, *Cheyennes*, 43–53.

48 Wooden Leg, *Wooden Leg*, 298; ARSW, 1877, serial 1794, 496–97; Lieut. W. P. Clark to Lieut. John G. Bourke, 24 Feb. 1877, DMSF, roll 4. Already some Cheyennes had decided to go to these agencies. Little Wolf and a party of about twenty people had left the Cheyennes when they were still with Crazy Horse in late January; they reached Camp Robinson on February 28. Clark to Bourke, 24 Feb. 1877; Thomas R. Buecker and R. Eli Paul, eds., *The Crazy Horse Surrender Ledger* (Lincoln, 1994), 101.

mostly relatives of White Bull and Two Moons, surrendered to Miles on April 22.[49]

Miles was furious when he learned that most of the Cheyennes were going to surrender at agencies controlled by Crook. The Cheyennes – all of them – had been within his grasp, and now Crook had snatched them away. Miles immediately wrote to Washington claiming that Spotted Tail's messengers had given ammunition to the Cheyennes and had "promised them the opportunity of obtaining abundant ammunition at the agencies, which is doubtless an unauthorized promise." Miles did not name Crook, but he clearly implied that his rival was not playing fair.[50] In truth, however, both commanders played the game of making promises that went beyond their authority.

The Lakota delegation that convinced the Cheyennes to surrender to Crook was as much the result of Spotted Tail's initiative as it was of Crook's. Naturally, Crook desired to win the militants' surrender with minimum generosity. In early January Crook's subordinate at Red Cloud Agency, Major Julius W. Mason, approached Spotted Tail about the possibility of going to Crazy Horse's village. Despite the fact that many of the militants were angry with him over his position on the Black Hills, Spotted Tail was a skilled diplomat with significant resources. Not only was he Crazy Horse's uncle, he had many followers with strong ties to people in the militants' camps. As the government's recognized chief at the White River agencies, he was in a strong position to determine the material conditions for those who surrendered. Spotted Tail was willing to negotiate with the militants, but only if he could offer favorable terms. When Crook insisted on unconditional surrender, Spotted Tail told Mason no.[51]

Mason then recruited a delegation of thirty Oglalas led by Hunts the Enemy (later known as George Sword). Departing Red Cloud Agency in late January, the delegation found Crazy Horse around February 11 camped with a small group of relatives on the Powder River, separate from the main Oglala village. After distributing tobacco, the delegates explained the purpose of their visit. At first, according to a military report, "their speeches were not

49 Wooden Leg, *Wooden Leg*, 298–300; *ARSW*, 1877, serial 1794, 497; Powell, *People of the Sacred Mountain*, 2:1124–28; Gray, *Centennial Campaign*, 350–51; Greene, *Yellowstone Command*, 196–98. Thirty to forty under White Hawk decided against surrendering and instead joined Lame Deer's Minneconjous. Another group of a similar size, consisting mostly of Kit Fox warriors and their families, decided to hold out, although they eventually went into Red Cloud Agency. Hump and a small group of Lakotas surrendered to Miles on April 20.
50 *ARSW*, 1877, serial 1794, 496–97; Oliver Knight, "War or Peace: The Anxious Wait for Crazy Horse," *Nebraska History* 54 (Winter 1973): 530.
51 Hyde, *Spotted Tail's Folk*, 15; Kingsley M. Bray, "Crazy Horse and the End of the Great Sioux War," *Nebraska History* 79 (Fall 1998): 103; Anderson, "Indian Peace-Talkers," 239–41.

responded to," but at a subsequent council, Crazy Horse said "the smoke was good." He further stated that he would "send for all the Indians and let them decide what they would do; that if he told them to stay they would do so, even if they were to die; but he would let them say." From this, it was clear that Crazy Horse had decided to give up forcing people to remain with him against their will.[52] After this council the Hunts the Enemy delegation proceeded to the main Oglala village. Their spokesman, Iron Hawk, said that they wanted to seek peace and would move slowly toward Red Cloud Agency over the next several weeks. Hunts the Enemy, however, had not been able to guarantee acceptable terms for surrender. Thus, as he neared Red Cloud Agency, Iron Hawk asked Hunts the Enemy or some of his men to "come to me again, or else send your men to me."[53]

Even before Hunts the Enemy reached Crazy Horse's camp, Crook was revising his position on the terms of surrender. In early February, when Crook learned that Miles had supposedly scored a major victory at Wolf Mountains, he decided he was in trouble. It was not clear to Crook if the Hunts the Enemy initiative would succeed, and if so, how fast. Unless he acted quickly, the war might be over and Miles would have won it. Crook had intelligence that Crazy Horse's people would respond positively to an overture from Spotted Tail. He decided to do what it would take to get Spotted Tail to convince Crazy Horse to come in.[54]

On February 12 Spotted Tail departed with two hundred Brulés. Crook's aide, Lieutenant John G. Bourke, recorded in his diary that Crook told Spotted Tail "that no stipulations would be approved that did not involve the surrender of arms, ponies, and ammunition." Bourke further noted, however, that the ponies taken from the militants would be distributed to Spotted Tail and his men, thus allowing Spotted Tail to give the ponies back as gifts. Moreover, although no one involved made a record of Crook's agreement with Spotted Tail, Crook's later actions indicate that he authorized Spotted Tail to tell the militants that he would try to secure a new agency for them in the north. The possibility of an agency in the north was especially attractive. Not only did the northern militants regard the lands north and west of the Black Hills as their home, but also an agency of their own would

---

[52] Clark to Bourke, 3 Mar. 1877 (qtn.); Lieut. W. P. Clark to Lieut. John G. Bourke, 8 Mar. 1877, DMSF, roll 4; Garnett interview, tablet 2, roll 1; Red Feather interview, 8 July 1930, in Eleanor H. Hinman, ed., "Oglala Sources on the Life of Crazy Horse," *Nebraska History* 57 (Spring 1976): 25–26; Bray, "Crazy Horse and the End of the Great Sioux War," 103–04.

[53] George Sword, "Miwakan Yuha Tohan Oyakapi [Sword's Deeds Related]," Franz Boas Collection, American Philosophical Society, Philadelphia, 22–24, 95–96 (qtn., 96). For discussions of this text, see Elaine A. Jahner, "Transitional Narratives and Cultural Continuity," in *American Indian Persistence and Resurgence*, ed. Karl Kroeber (Durham, 1994), 149–80; Raymond J. DeMallie, "'These Have No Ears': Narrative and the Ethnohistorical Method," *Ethnohistory* 40 (Fall 1993): 527–32.

[54] Anderson, "Indian Peace-Talkers," 242–43; Neide to Bourke, 10 Feb. 1877.

allow them retain their autonomy and ensure that they not be subordinate to the leaders of the treaty bands at Red Cloud and Spotted Tail agencies.[55] It is also likely that Spotted Tail obtained Crook's agreement to help prevent the government from forcing his people to Indian Territory or the Missouri River.[56]

As Spotted Tail headed toward Crazy Horse's village, members of his party fanned out. North of the Black Hills, they began to encounter Lakotas and Cheyennes who were on their way to the agencies or were considering coming in. Spotted Tail's party assured these people that they would be well-treated and offered to escort them to the White River. It was at this point that members of Spotted Tail's party encountered the main camp of the Cheyennes and persuaded most of them to surrender to Crook. Sometime between the fifteenth and twentieth of March, Spotted Tail reached Crazy Horse's camp. Upon learning that Crazy Horse was out hunting, Spotted Tail sent two of the men in the camp to take tobacco to him. They returned empty-handed. Unfortunately, there is little documentation for the discussions that undoubtedly ensued, but a few days later, Crazy Horse's father told Spotted Tail that his son "makes peace the same as if he were here, and shakes hands through his father, the same as if he himself did it." Crazy Horse had decided to give up his lifelong fight against the United States. It was a painful decision, so painful that he could not bear to be present.[57]

By the time Spotted Tail returned to his agency on April 5, small groups were beginning to surrender there and at Red Cloud Agency. Over the next several weeks, these numbers increased dramatically. Although intelligence indicated that Crazy Horse's people were making their way south, Crook and his subordinates were concerned that they would change their minds. U.S. officials knew that agency leaders were worried that the government

---

[55] Bourke diary, 13 Feb. 1877, vol. 19, roll 2, 1835; Schmitt, ed., *General George Crook*, 217; Anderson, "Indian Peace-Talkers," 244; Bray, "Crazy Horse and the End of the Great Sioux War," 106. On Crook's advocacy of a northern agency, see Chapters 4 and 5.

[56] Although the threat of removal to Indian Territory had subsided, Lakotas continued to be wary of the possibility of removal, and rightly so, as Sheridan and Sherman advocated moving the Sioux to Indian Territory when the war ended. See Gen. W. T. Sherman to Gen. P. H. Sheridan, 11, 21 Apr. 1877, DMSF, roll 4; Olson, *Red Cloud and the Sioux Problem*, 231; Manypenny, *Our Indian Wards*, 345–50; Richmond L. Clow, "The Sioux Nation and Indian Territory: The Attempted Removal of 1876," *South Dakota History* 6 (Fall 1976): 466–73. Brulés had bitter memories of the Missouri, having lived there from 1868 to 1871. They were subject to disease and whiskey and there was little game or timber. See Hyde, *Spotted Tail's Folk*, 146–69.

[57] Lieut. J. M. Lee to Lieut. J. G. Bourke, 10 Mar. 1877, DMSF, roll 4; Col. R. S. Mackenzie to Lieut. John G. Bourke, 17 Mar., 1 Apr. 1877, DMSF, roll 4; Brig. Gen. George Crook to Lieut. Gen. P. H. Sheridan, 25 Mar. 1877, DMSF, roll 4; Lieut. W. P. Clark to Lieut. J. G. Bourke, 2 Apr. 1877, DMSF, roll 4; Lieut. J. M. Lee to AAG Dist. of the Black Hills, 2, 5 (qtn.) Apr. 1877, DMSF, roll 4.

was going to remove them to the Missouri River. If these rumors reached the militants, there was every reason to think that they might return to war or join Sitting Bull in Canada.[58] Determined that Crazy Horse not escape his grasp, Crook asked Red Cloud to go to Crazy Horse's camp. To gain his cooperation, Crook promised to restore Red Cloud to the government's favor, which he had lost when Crook "deposed" him as "head chief" of the Oglalas the previous October. In early April Red Cloud agreed to go. Besides the promise of a northern agency, he carried gifts of horses, blankets, sugar, and tobacco. Crazy Horse and the other leaders affirmed their decision to make peace and decided to do so at Red Cloud rather than Spotted Tail Agency.[59]

Crazy Horse and his people surrendered to the United States on May 7, 1877. Five miles from Red Cloud Agency, Crazy Horse, followed by leading Oglala warriors, met Crook's subordinate, Lieutenant William P. Clark. After dismounting, Crazy Horse shook hands with Clark and invited him to smoke a pipe. He Dog, one of Crazy Horse's closest friends, presented Clark with his war headdress, his war shirt, a buffalo robe, and his war horse. Crazy Horse gave his war bonnet and war shirt to Red Cloud. A few hours later, Crazy Horse, Little Hawk, Little Big Man, Big Road, and He Dog approached the agency at the head of an impressive procession. First came two hundred mounted warriors, bearing rifles, lances, and shields. They were followed by seven hundred women and children. The line of people and animals (there were more than two thousand horses, an uncountable number of dogs, and a few mules) went on for two miles.[60] As they approached the agency, Crazy Horse's people began to sing. Non-Indian observers later wrote that they sang a "hymn of peace," but the songs they sang more likely recounted deeds of war.[61]

---

[58] Capt. Anson Mills to AAG Dist. Black Hills, 6 Apr. 1877, DMSF, roll 4; Brig. Gen. George Crook to Lieut. Gen. P. H. Sheridan, 13, 19 Apr. 1877, DMSF, roll 4.

[59] Brig. Gen. George Crook to Lieut. Gen. P. H. Sheridan, 18 Apr. 1877, DMSF, roll 4; Garnett interview, tablet 2, roll 1; He Dog, "History of Chief Crazy Horse," in *The Killing of Chief Crazy Horse: Three Eyewitness Views by the Indian, Chief He Dog; the Indian-White, William Garnett; the White Doctor, Valentine McGillycuddy,* ed. Robert A. Clark (1976; Lincoln, 1988), 51–53.

[60] *Chicago Tribune,* 8 May 1877, 5; *New York Herald,* 7 May 1877, 10; Bourke diary, 6 May 1877, vol. 20, roll 2, 1984–86; Bourke, *On the Border,* 412–13; He Dog, "History of Chief Crazy Horse," 57; Short Buffalo interview, 13 July 1930, in Hinman, ed., "Oglala Sources," 40; "Eagle Hawk Narrative," in *The Surrender and Death of Crazy Horse: A Source Book about a Tragic Episode in Lakota History,* ed. Richard G. Hardorff (Spokane, 1998), 135–41. The government recorded 899 in Crazy Horse's band. See Buecker and Paul, eds., *Crazy Horse Surrender Ledger,* 14.

[61] Bourke diary, vol. 24, roll 2, 27. Although Sandoz, *Crazy Horse,* 361, states that they were "chanting the peace song of the Lakotas," as far as I can tell, there is no tradition of such a

If the outcome of the Great Sioux War is to be measured in a comparison of lives lost, the Sioux and Cheyennes clearly won – by a margin of almost two to one.[62] Mackenzie's destruction of Dull Knife's village and some of the subsequent skirmishes took their toll, but the militants' victory at the Little Bighorn and their subsequent ability to avoid a more devastating defeat forced the United States to make significant concessions. Nonmilitant Indians made an important contribution to this outcome by brokering the agreements. Had Miles and Crook not made the promises they did, the war would have ended differently. Many more people might have gone to Canada. The militants might have continued to fight. They had sufficient ammunition, and although they had faced sporadic game shortages, they could have supported themselves for several months or more.

The militants would have preferred that the United States had never invaded their territory, destroyed most of their game, and forced them to fight. Having taken up arms, many did not want to put them down. But the militants had done much to affect conquest's terms. Although it is hard to avoid reading this moment in light of what would happen later, Crazy Horse and his people had real reason for hope as they rode toward Red Cloud Agency. Much had been lost. No longer would they have the freedom they had once enjoyed. But peace offered significant advantages: an end to the ravages of intertribal warfare, an end to costly resistance to the United States, and freedom from fear and hunger. Many writers have expressed skepticism about the seriousness of Crazy Horse's commitment to create a new way of life, but as Kingsley Bray points out, the gift of his war shirt to Red Cloud was a "startling gesture of conciliation."[63]

Vital questions remained. Would the government act on Crook's promise to create a northern agency? Americans had lied and broken agreements before. What if the United States forced the Oglalas to live in a cramped space on the Missouri River or in Indian Territory? Who could be sure that the army would not imprison or hang the killers of Custer? Or maybe the army would simply slaughter them all. Into an uncertain future, Crazy Horse and his people rode with songs of victory filling the air.

---

song. Nor can I find evidence for Sandoz's observation that an officer remarked, "By God, this is a triumphal march, not a surrender," also reported in Ambrose, *Crazy Horse and Custer*, 462.

[62] According to the careful tally in Greene, *Yellowstone Command*, 233, from February 1876 through December 1877, U.S. forces suffered 283 killed. Greene estimates that 150 Indians were killed, a figure that includes noncombatants killed in direct conflict with U.S. forces but not those who died of starvation or exposure.

[63] Bray, "Crazy Horse and the End of the Great Sioux War," 112. Larry McMurtry, *Crazy Horse* (New York, 1999), 112, for example, concludes that Crazy Horse was "not tamable, not a man of politics."

4

"Force Is the Only Thing"

The Killing of Crazy Horse

Four months after Crazy Horse shook hands with Lieutenant Clark, he was killed under circumstances that remain cloudy and controversial. As Crazy Horse was being confined to a guardhouse, someone (exactly who is unclear) pierced his abdomen with a knife or bayonet. He died a few hours later. For Lakotas, the killing of Crazy Horse was (and remains) a defining moment in their history. Several keepers of the pictographic records of annual events painted on hides, known as *waniyetu iyawapi* (winter counts), depicted 1877–1878 as the year in which *Tasunka Witko Ktepi* (they killed Crazy Horse). The keeper of one Oglala winter count, Calico, was so distressed by the killing of Crazy Horse that he ended his record that year. It was as though history itself had come to an end.[1]

In explaining the killing of Crazy Horse, most historians have focused on rumors, innuendoes, intrigues, betrayals, and secret plots that occurred at the agency in the days and weeks prior to Crazy Horse's death. In their view his death resulted from a conspiracy led by Red Cloud, who supposedly saw Crazy Horse as a rival and was consumed by jealousy over his popularity. Other historians have rejected the idea that Crazy Horse was a victim of a conspiracy. They have faulted him for his unwillingness to cooperate with Red Cloud and other Oglala leaders, as well as his intransigence toward government officials. Presumably, his stubbornness led to his death. Other

---

[1] Winter counts that designate 1877–1878 as the killing of Crazy Horse include No Ears (Oglala), Short Man (Oglala), both in James R. Walker, *Lakota Society*, ed. Raymond J. DeMallie (Lincoln, 1982), 148; High Hawk (Brulé) in Edward S. Curtis, *The North American Indian*, vol. 3 (Cambridge, Mass., 1908), 180; Battiste Good (Brulé) in Garrick Mallery, *Picture-Writing of the American Indians*, Tenth Annual Report of the Bureau of American Ethnology, 1888–89 (Washington, D.C., 1893), 327; White Bull (Minneconjou) in Stanley Vestal, *Warpath: The True Story of the Fighting Sioux Told in a Biography of Chief White Bull* (1934; Lincoln, 1984), 270. For an overview of the Calico winter count, I am grateful to Mike Her Many Horses for a presentation he gave at the University of Oregon on March 11, 1997.

writers, even those sympathetic toward Crazy Horse, have suggested a similar explanation. Because Crazy Horse was inherently incapable of adapting to reservation life, his life was destined to come to a tragic end. The problem with these interpretations is that they focus too much on individual Lakotas' flaws and intratribal politics. In so doing, they neglect to analyze the broader context. To understand the events that led up to Crazy Horse's death, we need to consider how U.S. policies set parameters for government officials' decisions and constrained the ability of Lakotas to act. As we saw in the previous chapter, a critical consideration in Crazy Horse's decision to surrender was General Crook's promise of an agency of his own in the north. Crazy Horse and his people were deeply attached to the country north and west of the Black Hills and did not wish to live under the authority of the treaty band leaders. More than any other factor, it was the government's failure to deliver on the promise of a northern agency that led to the deterioration in relations between Crazy Horse and U.S. officials in the weeks before his death.[2]

From the outset, Crazy Horse made it clear that good relations with the United States would depend upon securing a northern agency. On May 25, when General Crook came to Red Cloud Agency to meet Crazy Horse for the first time, Crazy Horse knelt before Crook and took his hand. Later that day at a council Crazy Horse reminded Crook about his desire for an agency of his own:

You sent tobacco to my camp and invited me to come in. When the tobacco reached me I started and kept moving till I reached here. I have been waiting ever since arriving, for Gen. Crook, and now my heart has been made happy. In coming this

---

[2] The strongest statement of a Red Cloud conspiracy is Stephen E. Ambrose, *Crazy Horse and Custer: The Parallel Lives of Two American Warriors* (New York, 1975), 463–73; see also Mari Sandoz, *Crazy Horse: Strange Man of the Oglalas* (Lincoln, 1942), 360–413; Mike Sajna, *Crazy Horse: The Life Behind the Legend* (New York, 2000), 308–21. Larry McMurtry, *Crazy Horse* (New York, 1999), 116–17, notes that Crazy Horse was alienated by the government's broken promises, though his narrative gives greater emphasis to Red Cloud's and Spotted Tail's jealousy of Crazy Horse; George E. Hyde, *Red Cloud's Folk: A History of the Oglala Sioux Indians* (Norman, 1937), 295–98, emphasizes Crazy Horse's intransigence toward U.S. officials; Catherine Price, *The Oglala People, 1841–1879: A Political History* (Lincoln, 1996), 160–63, faults Crazy Horse for his refusal to cooperate with Oglala leaders; James C. Olson, *Red Cloud and the Sioux Problem* (Lincoln, 1965), 242–43, notes that the government's failure to deliver on the northern agency contributed to Crazy Horse's rebelliousness but suggests that Crazy Horse would have been unable to adjust to reservation conditions anyway; Robert W. Larson, *Red Cloud: Warrior-Statesman of the Lakota Sioux* (Norman, 1997), 211–16, offers a neutral synthesis of competing viewpoints while still focusing mainly on local politics. For an overview of the literature on Crazy Horse, see Richard S. Grimes, "The Making of a Sioux Legend: The Historiography of Crazy Horse," *South Dakota History* 30 (Fall 2000): 277–302.

way I picked out a place where I wish to live hereafter. I put a stake in the ground to mark the spot.[3]

Driving a stake into the ground had strong resonances within Lakota culture. During battle warriors sometimes fastened themselves to the ground with a lance, picket pin, or small stake until they were released by other warriors or the enemy was driven off. These acts displayed individual courage and faith in the abilities of comrades.[4] By a similar logic, Crazy Horse's stake revealed a determination not to be moved from his chosen spot. The stake also had meaning as part of a Lakota dialogue with U.S. expansion. Lakotas were well aware of Americans' use of stakes to mark mining claims and railroad routes, and Crazy Horse expected General Crook to give the same recognition to his stake as to any other. With this in mind, we can see that Crazy Horse's gesture of kneeling before Crook did not convey a sense of subjugation. Instead, it was at once an acknowledgment of Crazy Horse's dependence on Crook to carry out his promise and a demand that he do so.

Crook probably realized that the government was not going to meet this demand, although he kept this knowledge to himself. Indeed, Crook never proposed a separate agency for Crazy Horse. The most he did was to recommend to Generals Sheridan and Sherman (in April) that the Red Cloud and Spotted Tail agencies be moved to the north, one to the mouth of the Tongue River and the other to the mouth of the Powder. This would not have satisfied Crazy Horse. He wanted his own agency. Crook's plan would also have provoked substantial opposition among the western Sioux, because it did not simply call for an expansion of the existing reservation. The new reservation, located in Montana, would have been created at the price of the liquidation of almost all the existing Great Sioux Reservation; the net reduction of western Sioux lands would have been close to 25 percent. In any case, Crook was unable to persuade Sheridan and Sherman to support this plan. In the short term, they wanted to move the Oglalas and Brulés to the Missouri River. Their long-term goal was to concentrate all northern Plains Indians in Indian Territory.[5]

---

[3] *Cheyenne Daily Leader*, 26 May 1877, p. 4 (qtn.); John G. Bourke diary, n.d., vol. 24, roll 2, 33, United States Military Academy Library, West Point, N.Y. (microfilm); William Garnett interview, 1907, RT, tablet 2, roll 1. It is unclear where Crazy Horse placed this stake. Lieut. C. A. Johnson to CIA, 4 June 1877, RCA, roll 721, reported that Crazy Horse's people wanted their agency "near to Bear Buttes." However, according to He Dog's interview, 7, 13 July 1930, in Eleanor H. Hinman, ed., "Oglala Sources on the Life of Crazy Horse," *Nebraska History* 57 (Spring 1976): 20, 25, Crazy Horse wanted his agency on Beaver Creek west of the Black Hills.

[4] Clark Wissler, *Societies and Ceremonial Associations in the Oglala Division of the Teton-Dakota*, Anthropological Papers of the American Museum of Natural History, vol. 11, pt. 1 (New York, 1912), 24–25.

[5] For the outlines of this proposal, see Brig. Gen. George Crook to Lieut. Gen. P. H. Sheridan, 20 Apr. 1877, DMSF, roll 4. I estimate that the total area of Crook's proposed reservation would

It appears that Crook hoped to finesse his inability to deliver on the northern agency by encouraging Crazy Horse and other former militants to visit Washington. Following Crazy Horse's remarks at the council, Man Afraid of His Horses reminded Crook of Oglala opposition to living on the Missouri River or in Indian Territory. Crook promised that he would soon ask several Lakota leaders to accompany him to Washington to talk to the new President (Rutherford B. Hayes) about these issues.[6] Once the delegates were in Washington, Crook could say a few mild things in favor of the idea of a northern agency, while avoiding any mention of his unauthorized promise. It would be left to the president or interior secretary to say no. At the same time, Crook could remain on good terms with Crazy Horse and other Lakota leaders by opposing plans to move them to the Missouri or Indian Territory. In this way, Crook could achieve his overriding priority, which was to maintain order at the agencies.

Three days after Crook's visit to Red Cloud Agency, the Oglalas witnessed an event that must have raised doubts about Crook's willingness to fulfill his promises. As we saw in the previous chapter, the Cheyennes had surrendered with the understanding that they would be given a reservation in the north. In late April, however, Crook and Mackenzie informed them that the government intended to send them to Indian Territory to live with their southern relatives. Although the Cheyennes objected, Crook and Mackenzie remained firm. Having surrendered, the Cheyennes had lost their leverage and now had no choice but to move south. On May 28 the Oglalas watched as one thousand Cheyennes left for Indian Territory under military escort.[7]

Despite this evidence of Crook's fallibility, Crazy Horse seems to have continued believing in the possibility of a northern agency. During the next several weeks there were tensions at Red Cloud Agency, but none of these was serious enough to disrupt relations between Crazy Horse and U.S. officials. In early July, for example, when agency officials asked former militants to sign receipts for rations, Crazy Horse and others refused, saying they would not sign any papers at all, possibly because they feared that officials were trying to trick them into signing documents that ceded land or sanctioned removal. In late August, Agent James Irwin would contend that these actions

have been about 28,000 square miles compared to 38,000 in the Great Sioux Reservation after the Act of February 28, 1877, according to *ARCIA*, 1877, 247. For Sherman's and Sheridan's desire to have the agencies located on the Missouri River, see Gen. W. T. Sherman to Lieut. Gen. P. H. Sheridan, 9, 11, 21 Apr. 1877, DMSF, roll 4. Crook's plan also would have encountered opposition from Montana citizens and the Northern Pacific railroad.

[6] Garnett interview, tablet 2, roll 1.

[7] *Testimony Taken by a Select Committee of the Senate Concerning the Removal of the Northern Cheyenne Indians*, 46th Cong., 2d sess., 1879–80, S. Rept. 708, serial 1899, 3–5, 14–15; Peter John Powell, *People of the Sacred Mountain: A History of the Northern Cheyenne Chiefs and Warrior Societies, 1830–1879: With an Epilogue, 1969–1974*, 2 vols. (San Francisco, 1981), 2:1149–51; Johnson to CIA, 4 June 1877.

demonstrated Crazy Horse's stubborn opposition to the government. But by that time government officials were seeking evidence against Crazy Horse.[8] At the time of the event, officials did not see it as a sign of irrevocable intransigence. Indeed, in late July, when Crook gave permission to Oglalas and Brulés to have a buffalo hunt and informed them that the Indian Office had approved a delegation to Washington, Crazy Horse joined other Oglalas in expressing approval. According to William Garnett, an agency interpreter, Crazy Horse frequently asked Garnett questions about traveling east and was learning to "use the fork at the table" in preparation for this trip.[9]

Crazy Horse's presence did create some strains among the Oglalas, though they did not indicate irreconcilable differences. Evidence of tensions appeared in dramatic fashion at a reenactment of the Battle of the Little Bighorn that was held in conjunction with a Sun Dance that Crazy Horse sponsored sometime in July.[10] Crazy Horse's warriors played themselves and members of the agency bands took the part of the army. Although both sides had agreed beforehand to strike their opponents lightly, during the performance Crazy Horse's warriors took up their war clubs, struck the "Custer Indians" forcefully, and fired their revolvers into the air, driving "the army" off the grounds.[11]

[8] James Irwin to CIA, 13 July, 31 Aug. 1877, RCA, roll 721.

[9] Benjamin Shopp to CIA, 15 Aug. 1877, RCA, roll 721; Garnett interview, tablet 2, roll 1. Crook likely promised the Oglalas and Brulés that they could have a buffalo hunt at the May 25 council, as it was referred to in Lieut. W. P. Clark to Lieut. W. A. Schuyler, 13 June 1877, DMSF, roll 4. Garnett was the son of Looks at Him, an Oglala, and Richard Brooke Garnett, who commanded Ft. Laramie from 1852 to 1854. Charles W. Allen, *From Fort Laramie to Wounded Knee: In the West That Was*, edited and with an introduction by Richard E. Jensen (Lincoln, 1997), 229–30, n. 7.

[10] Garnett interview, tablet 2, roll 1, states that this Sun Dance was held three miles northwest of Red Cloud Agency. In the 1960s, however, Oglalas identified a site on Beaver Creek, much nearer the Spotted Tail Agency, as the location for the Sun Dance. See Edward Kadlecek and Mabell Kadlecek, *To Kill an Eagle: Indian Views on the Last Days of Crazy Horse* (Boulder, 1981), 91–92, 143.

[11] Garnett interview, tablet 2, roll 1, states that this "battle" occurred during the part of the Sun Dance where there is usually a "sham battle." Ethnographic accounts of the Lakota Sun Dance indicate that the only time during the Sun Dance in which there was mock fighting was during the cutting of the center pole for the Sun Dance, when four men or women would strike the tree as though it was an "enemy" while recounting their own war deeds or those of relatives. See J. R. Walker, *The Sun Dance and Other Ceremonies of the Oglala Division of the Teton Dakota*, Anthropological Papers of the American Museum of Natural History, vol. 16 (New York, 1917), 106; Frances Densmore, *Teton Sioux Music and Culture* (1918; Lincoln, 1992), 112; Royal B. Hassrick, *The Sioux: Life and Customs of a Warrior Society* (Norman, 1964), 282; William K. Powers, *Oglala Religion* (Lincoln, 1975), 96. From Garnett's account, it seems unlikely that the sham battle occurred in conjunction with the cutting of the pole. Accounts of particular Sun Dances, however, indicate that there was more flexibility within the Sun Dance for improvisations of the sort Garnett described than might be apparent from ethnographic accounts, which are biased in favor of identifying common patterns rather than historical variations. See, for example, the account of a Sun Dance in the

Although this episode probably aggravated simmering disputes about the recent past, the fact that it occurred during a Sun Dance indicated that factionalism was not so entrenched as to preclude all grounds for common identity and action. Through this and other Sun Dances held that summer, Plains Sioux communities sought spiritual power that would help them in the months to come. In doing so, they renewed their relationships to human and nonhuman relatives and strengthened their commitment to the well-being of their people as a whole. Sioux who danced or participated as leaders, healers, helpers, relatives, and friends did not think of themselves as going through the motions of a dying people's last traditional ceremony. Even though the United States had forced them onto reservations, the Sun Dance established a powerful space for them to renew the world and themselves as a people within it.[12]

Relations between U.S. officials and Crazy Horse did not deteriorate until mid-August when Crook decided to cancel the buffalo hunt he had earlier promised.[13] At one level, Crook's reason for canceling the hunt was related to Lakota factionalism. After a council on July 27, Young Man Afraid of His Horses proposed that a feast be held at Crazy Horse's camp the next day. At this point, Red Cloud abruptly left the room. That evening two unnamed people from Red Cloud's band informed Agent Irwin that there was "considerable dissatisfaction among them as to the proposition to hold the feast with Crazy Horse." Since Crazy Horse was a very recent arrival, they explained, it was only right that any feasts be hosted by Red Cloud. The two men also alleged that Crazy Horse was "waiting for a favorable opportunity to leave the agency and never return." Should he be allowed to go on the buffalo hunt, his band "would go on the war path and cause the Government infinite trouble and disaster."[14]

Crook was certainly aware of this intelligence. Officials at Spotted Tail Agency also informed him sometime around August 5 that Spotted Tail and other Brulé leaders were concerned that if the former militants at Spotted

summer of 1875, during which Sitting Bull staged a surround of enemies in Powell, *People of the Scared Mountain* 2:928–29, and the discussion of a Sun Dance in Chapter 8 of this book.

[12] Arthur Amiotte, "The Lakota Sun Dance," in *Sioux Indian Religion*, ed. Raymond J. DeMallie and Douglas R. Parks (Norman, 1987), 76, explains that the "tasks of sacrifice" in the Sun Dance are done "in order that the world may be recreated and that man be reactivated with the *wakan* forces of the universe." Joseph Epes Brown, ed., *The Sacred Pipe: Black Elk's Account of the Seven Rites of the Oglala Sioux* (Norman, 1953), 72, points out that participants in the Sun Dance are instructed "to offer your body as a sacrifice in behalf of all the people, and through you the people will gain understanding and strength." For the theme of renewal, see Howard L. Harrod, *Renewing the World: Plains Indian Religion and Morality* (Tucson, 1987).

[13] Lieut. Col. L. P. Bradley to AAG DP, 16 Aug. 1877, in Bourke diary, n.d., vol. 24, roll 2, 54.

[14] Shopp to CIA, 15 Aug. 1877.

Tail Agency joined Crazy Horse's band in a buffalo hunt, many would "slip away" and join Sitting Bull in Canada. If this were to happen, Brulé leaders evidently feared that it would empower those in the U.S. government who wanted to force the Brulés to move to the Missouri River or Indian Territory. With these dangers in mind, Brulé leaders decided not to take part in the hunt.[15] Yet divisions among Lakotas alone were not responsible for Crook's decision to cancel the hunt. For one thing, the main axis of factionalism – nontreaty (militant) versus treaty (agency) leaders – had emerged from a long history of divergent responses to U.S. expansionism. Furthermore, the fact that U.S. officials exercised substantial discretionary authority created a situation in which Lakota leaders had a strong incentive to try to influence them. In this particular situation, agency leaders who were suspicious of Crazy Horse knew that rumors of his impending departure would be of particular interest. Because these rumors were plausible, the concerns of leaders like Spotted Tail were genuine, but again, the reality of their fears was in the end a measure of U.S. power.

Crook's cancellation of the buffalo hunt marked a turning point in U.S. relations with Crazy Horse. Shortly after this decision was announced, on August 17, Agent Irwin and Lieutenant Clark both urged Crazy Horse to join the delegation to Washington planned for mid-September. The next day, however, Crazy Horse informed Clark that he had decided not to go. He proposed instead that several of his own men take his place and that Spotted Tail, Little Wound, Red Cloud, and other agency leaders not be a part of the delegation.[16]

George Hyde argues that Crazy Horse refused to go to Washington because he "suspected a trap" and suggests that this was typical of "his type of mentality." For Hyde, Crazy Horse was a "primitive man of action who hated the whites and all their ways." In sharp contrast to Spotted Tail, Crazy Horse lacked the capacity to understand the value of cooperating with U.S. officials and instead cared only about a silly matter like a buffalo hunt. The buffalo hunt, however, was not trivial. Not only did it mean food, clothing, and obtaining items for trade, from Crazy Horse's perspective the hunt was an emblem of Crook's good faith. Furthermore, Crazy Horse's position did not indicate an atavistic hatred of whites. Instead, Crazy Horse's demand that the delegation include members of his band clearly shows that he realized the importance of diplomacy. Foremost in Crazy Horse's mind was the northern agency. In 1930, He Dog recalled that Crazy Horse would have been willing to go to Washington "if they would have the agency moved

---

[15] Jesse M. Lee, "Gen. Jesse M. Lee's Account of the Killing of Chief Crazy Horse at Fort Robinson, Nebr.," in *Crazy Horse: The Invincible Chief*, ed. E. A. Brininstool (Los Angeles, 1949), 17–18 (qtn., 18).

[16] Lieut. W. P. Clark to Gen. George Crook, 18 Aug. 1877, in Bourke diary, n.d., vol. 24, roll 2, 72–76.

over to Beaver Creek" (on the western edge of the Black Hills in eastern Wyoming).[17] Crazy Horse probably hoped to gain a firm commitment on the northern agency before agreeing to join the delegation.

Some Oglalas later linked Crazy Horse's reluctance to travel to Washington to Oglala plots against him. According to Garnett, Crook's cancellation of the buffalo hunt led Crazy Horse to believe vicious rumors that had been whispered to him for weeks. Garnett focused particularly on a "half-blood" woman with a "captivating gaze" who set out to "imbue [Crazy Horse's] mind with poisons," telling him that the trip to Washington was a "trick to get him out of the country and keep him, that if he went away he would not be allowed to return." Although Garnett did not name this "evil woman," he was undoubtedly referring to Helen Laravie (or Larrabee), the daughter of a Lakota woman and a non-Indian trader, who married Crazy Horse shortly after his surrender. In 1930, He Dog and Little Killer offered a variation on Garnett's account by contending that Spotted Crow and other unnamed "jealous" Indians told Crazy Horse "a lot of stories" to make him fear for his life if he went to Washington. According to Eagle Hawk, one story they told was that "[i]f you go to Washington, . . . they are going to stuff you in the mouth of a cannon and kill you."[18]

Some historians have relied uncritically on these accounts. Stephen Ambrose argues that the stories being whispered into Crazy Horse's ear were all part of a plot by Red Cloud to prevent him from going to Washington where he would be "feasted and petted by the United States Government, made into a big man, [and] perhaps elevated to the chieftainship of all the Sioux." According to Ambrose, it was Red Cloud himself who arranged to have the "young and pretty" Laravie sent to Crazy Horse's lodge in order to fill his head with rumors. When Crazy Horse decided not to go to Washington, he unwittingly fell into the "trap" Red Cloud had set for him. All of this makes for a great story, but it is unlikely that Red Cloud could have managed events so thoroughly, even had he wanted to.[19]

The problem with relying on accounts by Garnett, He Dog, Little Killer, and Eagle Hawk is not that they fabricated information or had poor memories. People near Crazy Horse truly feared that the United States was planning to kill Crazy Horse or put him away in prison. No doubt Crazy Horse

---

[17] George E. Hyde, *Spotted Tail's Folk: A History of the Brulé Sioux* (Norman, 1961), 280–81; He Dog interview, 7 July 1930, in Hinman, ed., "Oglala Sources," 20; Irwin to CIA, 31 Aug. 1877.

[18] Garnett interview, tablet 2, roll 1; He Dog interview, 13 July 1930, and Little Killer interview, 12 July 1930, in Hinman, ed., "Oglala Sources," 25, 44. On Crazy Horse's marriage to Laravie, see Richard G. Hardorff, *The Oglala Lakota Crazy Horse: A Preliminary Genealogical Study and an Annotated Listing of Primary Sources* (Mattituck, N.Y., 1985), 34–35; "Eagle Hawk Narrative," in *The Surrender and Death of Crazy Horse: A Source Book about a Tragic Episode in Lakota History*, ed. Richard G. Hardorff (Spokane, 1998), 141.

[19] Ambrose, *Crazy Horse and Custer*, 467.

himself worried about these possibilities. Nonetheless, the theory of a conspiracy overstates the capacity of some Oglalas to manipulate others and makes Crazy Horse the passive victim of a massive plot. Furthermore, it leaves little room for analyzing the role of the decisions and actions of U.S. officials.

Until mid-August officials at Red Cloud Agency maintained reasonably good relations with Crazy Horse. The crucial question is why relations soured to the point that officials decided to have Crazy Horse arrested. This decision cannot be taken for granted. To simply say that Crazy Horse became increasingly obstinate and that officials therefore ordered his arrest implies that these officials had no alternatives and were merely captive to events. Officials were free to interpret Crazy Horse's actions and respond to them in any number of ways.

The most important official at Red Cloud Agency was Lieutenant William Philo Clark, Crook's man on the ground. Clark was born in 1845 and graduated from West Point in 1868. He joined the Second Cavalry and came under Crook's command in 1876. Crook assigned Clark command of Camp Robinson during the critical period during and after the militants' surrender. Clark was deeply interested in American Indian folklore and religion. In 1881 the army commissioned Clark to prepare a study of sign language and Plains Indian ethnography. This study, *The Indian Sign Language*, was published in 1885, a year after Clark's death.[20]

In pursuing his interests, Clark occasionally crossed cultural boundaries. In 1881 Clark asked and received permission from a Cheyenne holy man at Fort Keogh, Montana, to join a sweat lodge ceremony. As the heat increased inside the lodge, Clark's hair became so hot he could hardly stand to touch it. He became "dazed and dizzy" and the "perspiration ran off my body in huge drops." Unable to speak Cheyenne or use signs in the darkness, Clark could not make known his discomfort at being "physically and mentally cooked." He could have "raised some of the skins which formed the covering to the lodge," but "my pride would not let me do this." Fortunately for Clark, someone raised the lodge covering and "the cool air swept gratefully over me."[21]

In 1877 Clark was just beginning to become an "expert" on Indians. His inexperience was revealed during a feast held after the May 25 council between Crook and Oglala leaders noted above. To honor Clark and Crook, Lakotas offered them some dog meat. Clark was disgusted by the idea of

---

[20] Robert A. Clark, ed., *The Killing of Chief Crazy Horse: Three Eyewitness Views by the Indian, Chief He Dog; the Indian-White, William Garnett; the White Doctor, Valentine McGillycuddy* (1976; Lincoln, 1988), 137–39; Paul Andrew Hutton, *Phil Sheridan and His Army* (Lincoln, 1985), 341–42; *Army and Navy Register*, 27 Sept. 1884, p. 1; W. P. Clark, *The Indian Sign Language* (Philadelphia, 1885).

[21] Clark, *Indian Sign Language*, 367.

eating dog, but he knew that if he refused it, his hosts would be insulted. So, he offered a dollar to a Lakota to eat the meat for him. Taking the role of the all-knowing initiate, Clark explained to Crook that it would be all right if he did the same. Imagine, then, Clark's chagrin when Crook replied that he had eaten dog meat many times before, that he "could eat anything the Indians could eat," and then tasted some and pronounced it "nice."[22] Over the next few months, a no doubt humbled Clark tried to rise to the example of his superior officer. Clark visited Crazy Horse frequently, smoked with him, and talked with him at length. For his part, Crazy Horse continued to invite Clark to social occasions and offer him dog. Clark learned to swallow his disgust and proudly informed Crook that he was on "excellent dog-eating terms" with Crazy Horse.[23]

On one level, stories of army officers eating the flesh of dogs and burning up in sweat lodges reveal a desire American men often felt for the wild and primitive. They also reenact myths of frontier heroes like Daniel Boone and Natty Bumppo, who live among Indians and become like them but always as advance agents of an aggressively expanding empire.[24] These stories also show that army officers sought knowledge about Indians for specific purposes. Before entering the Cheyenne sweat lodge, Clark took off his military uniform, but upon exiting, he put it back on and then returned to his office to report on his experiences to army officials. At a deeper level, though, it wasn't enough to observe and talk with Indians. It was necessary to know them through actually becoming like them, if only momentarily. Anyone could know that Indians ate dog, but for civilization to demonstrate its superiority over savagery, it was necessary for men like Crook and Clark to master savagery on its own terrain.

Clark may have felt some genuine affection for Crazy Horse during his dog-eating days, but his "friendship" with Crazy Horse was paternalistic and highly contingent. In the same way that Andrew Jackson spurned his Cherokee "red children" when they rejected his advice that they move to

[22] Garnett interview, tablet 2, roll 1. Lakotas prepared and ate dog as part of formal ceremonies such as the installation of new officers in a warrior society or the Hunka ceremony, in which people were made relatives, and in conjunction with feasts following councils. See Hassrick, *The Sioux*, 24, 89, 157–59; James R. Walker, *Lakota Society*, ed. Raymond J. DeMallie (Lincoln, 1982), 64–65; James R. Walker, *Lakota Belief and Ritual*, ed. Raymond J. DeMallie and Elaine A. Jahner (Lincoln, 1980), 238–39.

[23] Lieut. W. P. Clark to Brig. Gen. George Crook, 18 Aug. 1877, in Bourke diary, n.d., vol. 24, roll 2, 72–76.

[24] E. Anthony Rotundo, *American Manhood: Transformations in Masculinity from the Revolution to the Modern Era* (New York, 1993), 227–32; Richard Slotkin, *The Fatal Environment: The Myth of the Frontier in the Age of Industrialization, 1800–1890* (Middletown, Conn., 1985), 65–68, 104–06. Gail Bederman, *Manliness and Civilization: A Cultural History of Gender and Race in the United States, 1880–1917* (Chicago, 1995), links masculinity and primitivism to discourses about race, civilization, and imperialism.

Indian Territory in the early 1830s, Clark was angry when Crazy Horse resisted his fatherly authority. On August 18, the day Crazy Horse told Clark he would not go to Washington, Clark reported that he had "kindly but firmly" explained to Crazy Horse why he should go to Washington and why it was unreasonable for him to dictate the composition of the delegation. When Crazy Horse stood firm, Clark decided to change tactics: "Force is the only thing that will work out a good condition in this man's mind; kindness he only attributes to weakness." His power would have to be "broken."[25] The exact consequences of an initiative to "break" Crazy Horse were unclear, but Clark's response greatly increased the likelihood that Crazy Horse would be arrested and killed.

Given Clark's position as a trained military officer charged with managing Indians, it is hardly surprising that he responded to Crazy Horse's resistance as he did. On the other hand, Clark had other options. He could have told Crazy Horse that he would try to convince Crook to change his mind about the buffalo hunt. He could have assured him that he would argue for a northern agency if he changed his mind about Washington. He could have asked Crook to come at once to the agency, invite all the leaders to a council, and see what he could do to build a new reservoir of trust.

Although Clark appeared determined to "break" Crazy Horse, Crook remained interested in exploring other options. Events far from Sioux country provided him with an opportunity to devise a new initiative. On May 7, the same day Crazy Horse surrendered, a few hundred Nez Percé Indians had staged an impressive demonstration at Fort Lapwai, Idaho. Dressed in their finest clothes and proudly singing, they protested U.S. demands that they move to a reservation. When General Oliver O. Howard threatened war and arrested one of their leaders, Toohoolhoolzote, other leaders decided they had no choice but to comply.[26]

A month later, as the Nez Percés were completing preparations to move, a group of Nez Percé youths killed four settlers, including one who had killed the father of one of the youths two years before. Other young Nez Percés, enraged at Indian-hating settlers, killed several others. Fearing the wrath of the U.S. government, the Nez Percés abandoned their plans to move to the reservation and prepared to defend themselves. On June 17 U.S. troops attacked the Nez Percé camp at White Bird Canyon on the Salmon River. The Nez Percé killed thirty-four U.S. soldiers and suffered only three wounded.

[25] Clark to Crook, 18 Aug. 1877. For Jackson's paternalism, see Michael Paul Rogin, *Fathers and Children: Andrew Jackson and the Subjugation of the American Indian* (New York, 1975).

[26] Alvin M. Josephy Jr., *The Nez Perce Indians and the Opening of the Northwest* (New Haven, 1965), 496–97, 502–08.

Over the next two months, the Nez Percés eluded and outfought the army, all the while moving eastward to the Bitterroot Mountains along the Idaho–Montana border and then southeast along the Continental Divide.[27]

On August 23 the Nez Percés crossed into Yellowstone National Park and entered General Crook's Department of the Platte. At one level, Crook found this development alarming. As Alvin Josephy explains, "[t]he emergence of the hostile Nez Perces on the plains, flaunting their successes over the soldiers, might be the signal for new uprisings by all the tribes."[28] On the other hand, this danger presented an opportunity to change Crazy Horse's mind about the trip to Washington. In late August Crook began assembling a force to attack the Nez Percés should they move west or south out of Yellowstone Park. Crook envisioned a force of two hundred or more scouts, led by Lakota leaders, including Red Cloud, Spotted Tail, Crazy Horse, and Touch the Clouds, a Minneconjou who represented the former militants at Spotted Tail Agency.[29] Although Crook did not outline his intentions in so many words, he obviously hoped that giving Crazy Horse the opportunity to pursue and possibly fight the Nez Percés would make up for the canceled buffalo hunt and convince him to join the Washington delegation. Perhaps, too, he hoped that the shared experience of a scouting expedition would diminish tensions among Lakota leaders. Crook had effectively used scouts this way before and had reason to think that Crazy Horse would be attracted to the idea of leading warriors into battle against an enemy, even if it was in the service of the United States.

Clark informed Crazy Horse and Touch the Clouds of Crook's proposal at a meeting on August 31.[30] Some historians have suggested that Crazy Horse was suspicious that the army did not really intend to send him against the Nez Percés. Once he enlisted, the army would force him to attack Sitting Bull, who was rumored to have crossed from Canada into northern Montana. Thus, he rejected Crook's plan.[31] Several other writers have argued that Crazy Horse was willing to go but that he became the victim of an intentional mistranslation. Mari Sandoz, for example, quotes Crazy Horse saying, "We came in for peace. . . . We are tired of war and talking of war . . . but still we want to do what is asked of us and if the Great Father wants us to fight we will go north and fight until not a Nez Perce is left." Sandoz contends

[27] Ibid., 512–26; Merrill D. Beal, *"I Will Fight No More Forever": Chief Joseph and the Nez Perce War* (Seattle, 1963), 45–170.

[28] Josephy, *Nez Perce Indians*, 597–600 (qtn., 600).

[29] AAG DP to Lieut. Gen. P. H. Sheridan, 28, 29 Aug. 1877, DMSF, roll 5; AAG DP to AAG DM, 30 Aug. 1877, DMSF, roll 5; AAG DP to Brig. Gen. George Crook, 30 Aug. 1877, DMSF, roll 5; Lieut. Gen. P. H. Sheridan to Maj. Hart, 30 Aug. 1877, DMSF, roll 5; *Cheyenne Daily Leader*, 2 Sept. 1877, p. 6.

[30] Lieut. Col. L. P. Bradley to Lieut. Gen. P. H. Sheridan, 31 Aug. 1877, DMSF, roll 5. See also AAG DP to Brig. Gen. Crook, 31 Aug. 1877, in Bourke diary, n.d., vol. 24, roll 2, 55.

[31] Olson, *Red Cloud and the Sioux Problem*, 243; Larson, *Red Cloud*, 213.

that interpreter Frank Grouard ("the Grabber") mistranslated Crazy Horse's words, saying that he would "fight until not a white man is left." This renewed Clark's and Crook's suspicions and set Crazy Horse up to be arrested and killed.[32]

The story of a mistranslation is unlikely if for no other reason than that Clark probably would have detected such a blatant error. Clark undoubtedly knew a few Lakota words. One of the first he would have learned would have been *wasicun*, the word usually translated "white man." This word sounds quite a bit different than *Poge Hloka*, the Lakota word for Nez Percé. Furthermore, Clark was already becoming proficient in sign language and used it as "a check upon unreliable interpreters." Clark easily could have cleared up such a simple mistranslation.[33] Indeed, there are good reasons to think that Clark had a reasonably good idea of Crazy Horse's true intentions by the end of this meeting. Historians who have recounted the story of a mistranslation have often implied that the meeting between Touch the Clouds, Crazy Horse, and Clark ended after Grouard's mistranslation. According to Garnett, however, after Grouard finished translating, Clark summoned Garnett and requested him to ask Crazy Horse "if he would not go out with the scouts, and some of his men; that the Nez Percés were out and up in the country where he used to roam." By Garnett's account, Crazy Horse said that he would not. Crazy Horse then told Clark that he was going out to hunt and ridiculed Clark for being "too soft" to fight the Nez Percés himself.[34] Garnett's recollections make it clear that Clark realized that the discussion was about fighting the Nez Percés. If there had been a mistranslation, Clark was not deceived by it. But although Clark had an accurate grasp of Crazy

---

[32] Sandoz, *Crazy Horse*, 392. Other works that tell the story of a mistranslation include Ambrose, *Crazy Horse and Custer*, 467–68; Ralph K. Andrist, *The Long Death: The Last Days of the Plains Indian* (New York, 1964), 299; Ian Frazier, *Great Plains* (New York, 1989), 104–05; Charles M. Robinson III, *A Good Year to Die: The Story of the Great Sioux War* (New York, 1995), 338; Sajna, *Crazy Horse*, 312–13. The story of a mistranslation also surfaces in the 1996 television movie *Crazy Horse*, produced by Turner Network Television, when Crazy Horse, who throughout the film has been fluent in English, now speaks in Lakota. Subtitles reveal that Crazy Horse intends to fight the Nez Percés. Acting on behalf of Red Cloud, however, Grouard willfully changes these words as he puts them into English.

Grouard was the son of a Mormon missionary and a Polynesian woman. In 1865 at the age of fifteen he ran away from his home in Utah, and a few years later was either captured or voluntarily joined Sitting Bull's people. He later lived with the Oglalas. See Robert M. Utley, *The Lance and the Shield: The Life and Times of Sitting Bull* (New York, 1993), 94, 352, n. 6; Joe DeBarthe, *Life and Adventures of Frank Grouard*, edited and with an introduction by Edgar I. Stewart (Norman, 1958).

[33] Clark, *Indian Sign Language*, 5. The signs for "Nez Percé" and "whites" are somewhat similar but different enough to avoid confusion: the sign for Nez Percé involves passing the index finger of the right hand under the nose, while the sign for "whites" involves passing the same finger in front of the eyes in order to convey the notion of a hat. See Clark, *Indian Sign Language*, 269, 402–03.

[34] Garnett interview, tablet 2, roll 1.

Horse's intentions, he was not happy about the situation. Crazy Horse was openly mocking Clark and defying him. After his meeting with Crazy Horse, Clark reported that Crazy Horse and Touch the Clouds told him that "they were going north on the warpath."[35] This report might appear to confirm the story that Clark was deceived by Grouard's mistranslation. It is more likely, however, that Clark, angry at Crazy Horse, misrepresented his intentions.

Crook was alarmed when he learned of Clark's report that Crazy Horse intended to go to war. Crook decided to shelve his plan of using a force of Lakota scouts against the Nez Percés and hurried to Red Cloud Agency. Shortly after arriving on September 2, Crook ordered Lieutenant Colonel Luther P. Bradley, the commander at Camp Robinson, to "surround and disarm" Crazy Horse's band the next morning. Later that day, however, Crook canceled these orders. Crook had two reasons for his reversal. First, he feared that an operation against Crazy Horse would alarm a group of seventy-five Lakotas, who had been with Lame Deer's band when it had been attacked by Nelson Miles on May 8 and were now approaching Spotted Tail Agency.[36] Second, a visit from the agent at Spotted Tail Agency, Lieutenant Jesse M. Lee, raised doubts in Crook's mind about Clark's report of Crazy Horse's intentions. The day after Crazy Horse's conversation with Clark, Touch the Clouds and Crazy Horse had come to Spotted Tail Agency and given Lee an account of their meeting with Clark. According to Lee, Touch the Clouds told Clark:

that when he came here [to the agency] he had promised absolute peace; but that the Great Father, Gen. Crook and others, had deceived him, and now wanted him and his people to go on the warpath – a thing which he violently condemned as a breach of promise; that at first it was to give up his gun, and he did it; then it was to enlist as a scout to keep peace and order at the Agency, and he did that; then he was asked to throw away the buffalo hunt, and he did that, too! Then, like a horse with a bit in his mouth, his head was turned toward Washington, and he looked that way. Now, the Great Father, the "Gray Fox" (Crook) and "White Hat" (Clark) put blood on their faces and turned them to war; that he and Crazy Horse had been deceived and

---

[35] Lieut. W. P. Clark to Major Daniel W. Burke, 31 Aug. 1877, quoted in Lee, "Lee's Account," 19–20. In a later report, Lieut. W. P. Clark to CIA, 10 Sept. 1877, STA, roll 841, Clark said nothing to indicate he thought Crazy Horse was going to go to war, but that Crazy Horse had "told me that he did not like the country about here, that he never promised to stay here, and that he was going North with his band."

[36] Brig. Gen. George Crook to Lieut. Gen. P. H. Sheridan, 31 Aug., 3 Sept. 1877, DMSF, roll 5; Lieut. Gen. P. H. Sheridan to Gen. E. D. Townsend, 1 Sept. 1877, RCA, roll 721; Lieut. Col. L. P. Bradley to AG DP, 7 Sept. 1877, DMSF, roll 4. For movements of people with Lame Deer, see Jerome A. Greene, "The Lame Deer Fight: Last Drama of the Sioux War of 1876–1877," *By Valor and Arms: Journal of American Military History* 3, no. 3 (1978): 11–21; ARSW, 1877, 45th Cong., 2d sess., 1877–78, H. Ex. Doc. 1, serial 1794, 526; Capt. Daniel W. Burke to AAG DP, 23 July 1877, DMSF, roll 4; AAG DP to AAG DM, 5 Sept. 1877, DMSF, roll 4.

lied to; but now they would do as "White Hat" said, and war it should be! They would all go north to fight, and when they met the Nez Percés (meaning they would conquer them) all would soon be peace.[37]

When Lee reported this information, Crook replied that he was glad Lee had come and that he did not want "to make a mistake, for it would, to the Indians, be the basest treachery to make a mistake in this matter." Crook decided to meet with Crazy Horse the next morning to determine his intentions for himself.[38]

On the morning of the third, as Crook was preparing to leave for Crazy Horse's camp, an Oglala named Woman's Dress told Crook that Crazy Horse planned to kill him. According to Garnett, Crook received this news "with some incredulity," but Clark nonetheless urged him to cancel the meeting. When Baptiste Pourier, a cousin of Woman's Dress, assured Crook that Woman's Dress was reliable, Crook decided to take Clark's advice.[39] This moment was crucial, as it closed off an opportunity for Crazy Horse and Crook to reach some understanding. Though Crook would not have been able to deliver on the northern agency, he might at least have found a way to reduce tensions. But instead of meeting with Crazy Horse, Crook made plans to have him arrested.

It is unclear what motivated Woman's Dress to tell his story. Perhaps he genuinely believed it, or perhaps he was acting on behalf of Crazy Horse's rivals. Whatever the case, the more important question is why U.S. officials reacted the way they did to Woman's Dress's story. Although most historians have passed over it, Clark's advocacy of Crazy Horse's arrest was particularly important. As we have seen, Clark had been "kind" to Crazy Horse in June and July. When Crazy Horse did not respond properly to Clark's friendship, Clark turned against him, concluding that he only understood "force" and that he had to be "broken." By this time, Clark was determined to believe the worst about Crazy Horse. Indeed, it is remotely possible that Clark himself put Woman's Dress up to the story. (If there *must* be a conspiracy, why exclude Clark as a suspect?)

---

37 Lee, "Lee's Account," 20–23 (qtn. 21). This account, which is consistent with Lieut. J. M. Lee to CIA, 30 Sept. 1877, RA-KC, book 2, is corroborated by Louis Bordeaux interview, 1907, RT, tablet 11, roll 3; Baptiste Pourier interview, 1907, RT, tablet 13, roll 3; Red Feather interview, 8 July 1930, in Hinman, ed., "Oglala Sources," 30.

38 Lee, "Lee's Account," 23.

39 Garnett interview, tablet 2, roll 1; Lieut. W. P. Clark to CIA, 10 Sept. 1877, STA, roll 841; Bourke diary, n.d., vol. 24, roll 2, 43–44; Red Feather interview in Hinman, ed., "Oglala Sources," 27. Ambrose, *Crazy Horse and Custer*, 469, assumes that Woman's Dress was a *winkte* (a term that literally means "wishes to be a woman" and has often been described as an example of the general phenomenon of male *berdaches* in American Indian societies). No source I know indicates that Woman's Dress was a *winkte*. I have heard, although have been unable to confirm it, that Woman's Dress's name came from an episode in which he took a Shoshone woman's dress during a raid.

Crook's position was more neutral. On one hand, Crook had strong reasons to believe Woman's Dress. Clark, his trusted subordinate, urged him to do so, and Pourier also vouched for Woman's Dress. Furthermore, like all army officers, Crook was culturally trained to think of Indians as potentially devious. But that could work both ways. Perhaps it was Woman's Dress who was deceitful. Crook probably had some doubts that Crazy Horse intended to kill him. His careful questioning of Clark and Pourier gives this impression, as does his statement several years later that he regretted having canceled the meeting.[40] Crook may have recalled how Crazy Horse had knelt before him and shaken his hand the first time they met. Was he really the sort of man who would kill another in cold blood? Perhaps it seemed to Crook that Clark was pursuing his case against Crazy Horse a little too vigorously. Or, Pourier may have hesitated an instant before saying that Woman's Dress was a reliable man.

Even if Crook thought that Crazy Horse intended to kill him, we cannot assume that Crook's only option was to order his arrest. Crook could have gone ahead with the meeting and taken precautions to protect himself. He could also have delayed the meeting pending further inquiries. Although these were real alternatives, it is not surprising that Crook did what he did. Crook's highest priority was to maintain order. From this perspective, whether he thought Crazy Horse intended to kill him or not, Crook had other reasons for deciding to arrest Crazy Horse. Sooner or later, it would become clear that Crook could not deliver on the northern agency. Crook had once hoped that if Crazy Horse went to Washington he might be convinced to drop this demand, but given his response to the canceled buffalo hunt, it was unlikely that Crazy Horse would ever accept a permanent home at Red Cloud Agency. At the very least, Crazy Horse would continue to cause trouble at the agency. It was possible that he would leave the agency and head north, if not to fight, perhaps to join Sitting Bull in Canada.

Crook realized, however, that arresting Crazy Horse would be risky, as it would likely lead to unrest among former militants at Red Cloud and Spotted Tail agencies. To guard against this, Crook and other army officers met with key Oglala leaders, including Red Cloud, Red Dog, Young Man Afraid of His Horses, Little Wound, Slow Bull, American Horse, Yellow Bear, Blue Horse, and Three Bears. These leaders agreed to provide a force of Lakota scouts to assist U.S. troops in arresting Crazy Horse the next morning.[41]

When Crazy Horse had surrendered four months before, most of these leaders would have hoped to avoid the kind of situation they now faced.

---

[40] According to Garnett interview, tablet 2, roll 1, in 1889 Crook "remarked thoughtfully that he always thought he should have gone to that council."

[41] Ibid. On the mobilization of the scouts and soldiers, see Bourke diary, n.d., vol. 24, roll 2, 46; AAG DP to AAG DM, 5 Sept. 1877, DMSF, roll 4; Clark to CIA, 10 Sept. 1877.

Although some of them were suspicious of Crazy Horse from the outset and others had come to see him as a threat to order, it would be a mistake to think that the majority were eager to have Crazy Horse arrested. Why, then, did they cooperate? American Horse provided an answer at a meeting he and other leaders held with Agent Irwin on August 31. For the past several days, American Horse related, he and the other band leaders had been meeting daily to discuss how to "quiet" Crazy Horse and "bring him into a better state of feeling." These leaders had tried to get Crazy Horse to meet with them, but, said American Horse, "we can do nothing with him – he has not attended our councils." Earlier that day, American Horse continued, a council of over eight hundred Oglalas had resolved that "we want no more fighting" and to "live in peace." His people wanted to have their agency remain on the White River. There they could "learn to take care of ourselves and not hav[e] the Great Father always feeding us." To do this, American Horse asked the "Great Father" to provide seeds, livestock, wagons, and tools "for the land he has taken from us." He also expressed his hope that a delegation of Oglalas would soon go to Washington to "talk friendly and earnestly with the Great Father about our present condition and our future prospects."[42]

American Horse's statement suggests that Oglalas who were willing to cooperate in arresting Crazy Horse had motives other than long-standing jealousy. American Horse and the leaders he spoke for on August 31 would have preferred that the United States and its people go away and return the land they had stolen. Under present circumstances, however, they felt their best hope was to use diplomacy to avoid further disaster. As we have seen, the great fear for Lakotas at Red Cloud and Spotted Tail agencies was that the U.S. government would move them to the Missouri River or Indian Territory. In early September, many leaders worried that if they refused to cooperate with Crook, he would cancel the Washington trip, and even worse, send in troops, events that would increase the likelihood of removal. Such considerations led them to profess loyalty to the government and agree to help arrest Crazy Horse.

The government report of American Horse's speech did not fabricate his words or misrepresent his basic position, but it contained silences. We can only imagine what American Horse and the other Oglala leaders felt when they agreed to help arrest Crazy Horse. Some, no doubt, were glad to see a rival eliminated. Some believed that Crazy Horse deserved what he was getting; many leaders had found his refusal to join in their previous councils frustrating.[43] Others, however, probably concluded that Crazy Horse was not entirely to blame. Young Man Afraid of His Horses, who had earlier suggested that a feast be held at Crazy Horse's camp, likely regretted that Red

---

[42] James Irwin to CIA, 1 Sept. 1877, RCA, roll 721.
[43] Price, *Oglala People*, 162.

Cloud had rejected this suggestion. Not all the leaders would have regarded Crazy Horse's confrontational style as wholly illegitimate, though circumstances forced them to act against him. Whatever their thinking, Oglala leaders must have found this moment terribly agonizing. Yes, they would cooperate with the United States, but it would be with sorrow and with anger.

On the morning of September 4 a force consisting of eight companies of the Third Cavalry and about four hundred Indians (mostly Lakotas with some Arapahoes and Cheyennes) marched to Crazy Horse's camp. When they arrived, they found the camp deserted. Crazy Horse had gone toward Spotted Tail Agency with his first wife, Black Shawl, and his friends Kicking Bear and Shell Boy.[44] That afternoon, Crazy Horse reached Touch the Clouds's camp, about three miles from Spotted Tail Agency. Fearing that Crazy Horse and Touch the Clouds were planning to lead the former militants there on a "merciless slaughter of unsuspecting and innocent whites," Lee and Captain Daniel W. Burke, the commander of Camp Sheridan, sent White Thunder and about three hundred Brulés to Touch the Clouds's camp to escort Crazy Horse to the agency headquarters. As they came in, Spotted Tail arrived with another three hundred Brulés.[45]

It soon became apparent that Crazy Horse did not intend to start a war. Instead, he wanted to move to Spotted Tail Agency in order to escape the turmoil at Red Cloud. "They have misunderstood me and misinterpreted me there," Crazy Horse explained. "I was talked to night and day and my brain is in a whirl. I want to do what is right." Spotted Tail agreed that Crazy Horse could live at his agency provided that he consented to "listen to me" since he was "chief." Lee told Crazy Horse that he was willing to have him transferred. However, he would need to take Crazy Horse back to Red Cloud Agency to make arrangements with authorities there.[46]

Although historians have often portrayed Crazy Horse as the passive victim of a massive conspiracy, an obstinate opponent of progress, or scornful of appropriate Lakota political customs, his decision to go to Spotted Tail Agency reveals that he was capable of creative and constructive action. True, Crazy Horse was worried and confused. ("My brain is in a whirl," he said.)

[44] Bradley to AG DP, 7 Sept. 1877; Garnett interview, tablet 2, roll 1.

[45] Lee, "Lee's Account," 25–26 (qtn., 25); Lee to CIA, 30 Sept. 1877.

[46] Lee to CIA, 30 Sept. 1877. Crazy Horse's plan to move to Spotted Tail Agency was probably born in the desperate moment when he learned that troops and scouts were moving against his camp. Quite possibly, Black Shawl suggested the idea. Sick with either tuberculosis or blood poisoning (see Hardorff, *Oglala Lakota Crazy Horse*, 34–35; V. T. McGillycuddy, "Dr. V. T. McGillycuddy's Recollections of the Death of Crazy Horse," in *Crazy Horse*, ed. Brininstool, 43–44), Black Shawl may have requested to be taken to see her mother, who lived at Spotted Tail Agency, or to see a particular healer there; part of her motivation may have been to get Crazy Horse away from Red Cloud Agency.

Very likely, the government's reluctance to act on the northern agency had caused Crazy Horse to give serious thought to leaving Red Cloud Agency for the north. But instead of finding Crazy Horse frozen by fear, plotting a new war, or stubbornly refusing to cooperate with other Lakota leaders, we see him requesting to live at his uncle's agency. As late as twenty-four hours before his death, Crazy Horse and Spotted Tail, with Lee's support, had reached an agreement that would have kept him alive. Unfortunately, however, key government officials remained adamant that Crazy Horse be arrested.

On the morning of September 5 Lee, Crazy Horse, and about a dozen Lakota leaders set off in the direction of Red Cloud Agency. Lee sent a dispatch to Clark informing him that Lee had promised Crazy Horse that he could state his case and asking whether he should take Crazy Horse to Red Cloud Agency or Camp Robinson. Four miles from the agency, Lee received Clark's answer: Lee was to take Crazy Horse to Lieutenant Colonel Bradley, the commander at Camp Robinson.[47] When Lee and Crazy Horse arrived there late that afternoon, the post adjutant informed Lee that Crazy Horse was to be turned over to Captain James Kennington, the officer of the day. Before doing this, Lee went to Bradley's office to explain "the circumstances under which he was secured and brought there" and to request that Crazy Horse be "permitted an interview." Bradley replied that orders had already been issued and that he was powerless to change them. Not even General Crook could rescind them. (The orders called for Crazy Horse to be transported to Omaha. From there, he probably would have been sent to prison at Fort Marion, Florida.) Still hoping that Bradley might change his mind and hear Crazy Horse the next morning, Lee turned Crazy Horse over to Kennington. Lee assured Crazy Horse he would not be harmed.[48]

By this time hundreds of Lakotas had gathered. They watched as Kennington and one or two Sioux scouts led Crazy Horse to a nearby building. Judging from his lack of resistance, most writers have assumed, quite reasonably, that Crazy Horse did not realize what was happening until he walked into the building and saw several Indians, their legs in irons.[49] No more than half a minute, probably less, passed from the moment Crazy Horse entered the guardhouse to the moment he was mortally wounded. Not surprisingly, the eyewitness accounts differ about what happened during these seconds. This much is clear: when Crazy Horse saw he was about to be confined, he tried to escape, using his knife to strike against those escorting him and nearby U.S. soldiers and Indians. A hand-to-hand struggle ensued between

[47] Lee, "Lee's Account," 30.

[48] Lee to CIA, 30 Sept. 1877 (qtns.); Lee, "Lee's Account," 31–32; Bradley to AG DP, 7 Sept. 1877.

[49] Sandoz, *Crazy Horse*, 407–08; Ambrose, *Crazy Horse and Custer*, 472; McMurtry, *Crazy Horse*, 130.

Crazy Horse and his old friend, Little Big Man, now a scout. Some accounts suggest that Little Big Man stabbed Crazy Horse, probably not intentionally, but in an effort to subdue him. Others indicate that William Gentles, the sentinel posted at the guardhouse, drove his bayonet into Crazy Horse's side or back.[50] Realizing that his friend was probably going to die, Touch the Clouds wanted to move Crazy Horse to a Lakota lodge, but U.S. officials ordered him to be taken to the office of the post adjutant, where he died six hours later around 11:30 P.M.[51]

As Crazy Horse took his last breath, according to some writers, his friend Touch the Clouds said, "It is well. . . . He has looked for death and it has come." These are sad and moving words, but it is doubtful that Touch the Clouds said them. The original source for this quotation is a report written by Lieutenant Colonel Bradley two days later. The problem is that Bradley wasn't there when Crazy Horse died, and no one who was present recorded these words.[52] It is unlikely that Bradley intentionally fabricated this story. He probably heard it second- or thirdhand. In any case, Bradley embraced this account, as it supported the impression he and other officers were trying to create that the large majority of Lakotas accepted Crazy Horse's death. Bradley did acknowledge that "there was a great deal of excitement" after Crazy Horse's death, but "it is quieting down. The leading men of his band, 'Big Road,' 'Jumping Shield', and 'Little Big Man,' are satisfied that his death is the result of his own folly, and they are on friendly terms with us." Clark echoed these views: "The excitement caused by [Crazy Horse's] death is subsiding. . . . Some few are still making threats, but the majority consider his death to be a blessing to his people."[53]

Bradley and Clark seriously distorted Lakota sentiments. Consider, for example, Fast Thunder, one of the leaders of the Lakota scouts. By the government's system of classification, Fast Thunder was a "friendly" Indian. Yet according to his grandson, Mathew King, Fast Thunder was angry enough after Crazy Horse's death to seriously consider leading the scouts to war against the United States. Realizing this would be futile, however, "he left the fort and camped someplace in the hills . . . to cool down." There, he

[50] For a thorough analysis of seventeen eyewitness accounts of these events, see James N. Gilbert, "The Death of Crazy Horse: A Contemporary Examination of the Homicidal Events of 5 September 1877," *Journal of the West* 32 (January 1993): 5–21.

[51] Lee, "Lee's Account," 33–34; McGillycuddy, "McGillycuddy's Recollections," 45–46; Lieut. W. P. Clark to Brig. Gen. George Crook, 6 Sept. 1877, in Bourke diary, n.d., vol. 24, roll 2, 66–67; Clark to CIA, 10 Sept. 1877.

[52] Ambrose, *Crazy Horse and Custer*, 474 (qtn.). See also Bradley to AG DD, 7 Sept. 1877; Price, *Oglala People*, 162. According to McGillycuddy, "McGillcuddy's Recollections," 46, those present when Crazy Horse died were Kennington, Lieut. H. R. Lemly, John Provost, Touch the Clouds, Crazy Horse's father, and a relative of Crazy Horse's mother.

[53] Bradley to AG DP, 7 Sept. 1877; Lieut. W. P. Clark to Lieut J. G. Bourke, 9 Sept. 1877, in Bourke diary, n.d., vol. 24, roll 2, 71.

and his followers "smoked the peace pipe."[54] Far from indicating that the Lakotas considered Crazy Horse's death a "blessing," the absence of further violence testified to Lakotas' pragmatism and self-control.

It is certainly possible to find fault with Oglalas for the killing of Crazy Horse. Although Red Cloud probably did not orchestrate a conspiracy, he did little to establish good relations with Crazy Horse. For his part, Crazy Horse might have been less defiant of government officials and more willing to cooperate with agency leaders, especially in late August and early September when tensions were high. In the end, however, U.S. policies and the decisions of government officials established the broader context in which Crazy Horse was killed.

The key factor that led to the deterioration of relations between Crazy Horse and U.S. officials was Crook's inability to deliver a northern agency. This alienated Crazy Horse and contributed to intratribal factionalism. Had Crazy Horse been given his own agency, he and other Oglala leaders would have had little reason for conflict. At one level, the way the northern agency issue played out resulted from the discretionary decisions of one individual. But, although Crook, like other officials, had some latitude in making decisions, his choices were consistent with broader policy objectives. Unable to militarily defeat the Sioux (or, at least, to do it quickly enough to satisfy public opinion and a penurious Congress), Crook, like his rival Miles, turned to diplomacy to secure the militants' surrender. Typical of U.S. officials in negotiating with Indians, however, Crook was less than forthcoming. Despite the virtually insurmountable obstacles to a northern agency, obstacles that Crook surely appreciated, he nonetheless gave Crazy Horse the impression that a northern agency was a realistic possibility.

In the final analysis, Crook's objective, like other military and civilian officials charged with executing a national Indian policy premised on manifest destiny, was to establish control over the Sioux as a necessary step toward their eventual assimilation. When Crazy Horse refused to comply with this priority and insisted that U.S. officials deliver on earlier agreements, he became a threat to order and therefore became subject to arrest. Crazy Horse's death was not inevitable. At several moments along the way, key players, including Crazy Horse himself, could have made decisions that would have resulted in a different outcome. Nonetheless, the killing of Crazy Horse was more than a historical accident or simply a tragedy. It was a logical consequence of U.S. policies for governing a newly conquered people.

[54] Kadlecek and Kadlecek, *To Kill an Eagle*, 125–26.

PART 2

COLONIALISM

5

"We Were Raised in This Country"
Claiming Place

Plains Sioux communities and individuals experienced their own history in different ways. In one way or another, the mid-1870s were years of deeply painful transition for all of them. The taking of the Black Hills, the end of armed resistance, the decimation of the buffalo, confinement to a reservation, and the death of Crazy Horse all marked the loss of autonomy and self-determination. By the late 1870s, the Sioux had become a captive people.[1]

In describing Plains Sioux history in the late 1870s and 1880s, historians have often turned to the metaphor of dying, writing books with titles like *The Long Death* and *The Last Days of the Sioux Nation*.[2] Plains Sioux people were undoubtedly demoralized and even despairing during these years. Nonetheless, even after being forced onto a reservation, the western Sioux tried to shape their own future as best they could. In Frederick Hoxie's terms, they sought to transform the "prison" of the reservation into a "homeland."[3] A critical aspect of this for Sioux leaders was to ensure that their people could have their agencies located where they wanted on the reservation. Neither the Sioux nor the government objected to the location of Cheyenne and Standing Rock agencies, but in 1877 the government continued to try to move the Red Cloud and Spotted Tail agencies to the Missouri River on the eastern part of the reservation. Oglalas and Brulés strenuously opposed these efforts. Furthermore, as we have seen, some army officials wanted to liquidate the Great Sioux Reservation altogether and relocate all the western Sioux to Indian Territory. Sioux leaders at all the agencies fought this scheme.

[1] Mary E. Young, "Captives within a Free Society," in *American Indian Policy Review Commission Final Report*, 2 vols. (Washington, D.C., 1977), 1:47–82.
[2] Ralph K. Andrist, *The Long Death: The Last Days of the Plains Indian* (New York, 1964); Robert M. Utley, *The Last Days of the Sioux Nation* (New Haven, 1963).
[3] Frederick E. Hoxie, "From Prison to Homeland: The Cheyenne River Indian Reservation before WW I," *South Dakota History* 10 (Winter 1979): 1–24.

For several months, as we saw in the last chapter, many Oglala and Brulé leaders had protested being moved to Indian Territory or the Missouri River and had been trying to organize a delegation to go to Washington. Although the Indian Office authorized a delegation in late July, tensions at Red Cloud Agency consistently threatened these plans. Finally, on September 17, 1877, a delegation of ten Oglalas and three Arapahoes from Red Cloud Agency and ten Brulés from Spotted Tail Agency left for the east. They were accompanied by Agent Irwin, Lieutenant Clark, and several interpreters.[4] This delegation was a carefully chosen mix of leaders from treaty and nontreaty bands. At least eight of the twenty Sioux delegates had been to Washington before, some more than once. Others, however, including seven who had surrendered the previous spring, had never traveled beyond the Great Plains.[5] One of the former militants was He Dog. As his wagon was about to leave Camp Robinson for the railhead, his wife, Rock, had to be pulled from his wagon. She and others no doubt feared that their relatives would be claimed by deadly illness or imprisonment.[6]

After boarding the train at Sidney, Nebraska, the delegates traveled to Chicago, where they spent the night of September 21. Although we have no direct evidence of the delegates' intentions, it seems that they were alert to opportunities to gain favorable newspaper coverage. A *Chicago Tribune* reporter observed that the delegates were "sharp looking chaps,... dressed in the costumes of the plains, their faces well ochred, and wearing huge earrings and immense silver crosses, with an abundance of eagle feathers." Significantly, this reporter noted, each had "his calumet in his hand as an evidence of their mission of peace." Conceivably, the writer himself (an amateur ethnographer?) was responsible for this interpretation of the calumet, but it was quite possibly based on information from the Indians themselves. As the reporter rode with some of the delegates in an omnibus to the hotel, Spotted Tail explained to him that "he had great hopes for the future of

---

[4] The delegates from Spotted Tail Agency were Spotted Tail, Spotted Tail's son (Young Spotted Tail or Little Spotted Tail), Swift Bear, Good Voice, Ring Thunder, Hollow Horn Bear, White Tail, Red Bear, Touch the Clouds, and Little Hawk. The Red Cloud Agency delegates were Red Cloud, Young Man Afraid of His Horses, Little Wound, American Horse, Yellow Bear, Three Bears, Little Big Man, He Dog, Big Road, Iron Crow, and three Arapahoes, Black Coal, Sharp Nose, and Friday. The interpreters were James Merivale, William Garnett, Leon Palliday, Antoine Janis, and F. C. Boucher. See *Chicago Tribune*, 22 Sept. 1877, p. 2; *New York Herald*, 25 Sept. 1877, p. 7. For a discussion of the meaning of this trip for the Arapahoes, see Loretta Fowler, *Arapahoe Politics, 1851–1978: Symbols in Crises of Authority* (Lincoln, 1982), 63–66.

[5] Former militants were Red Bear, Touch the Clouds, Little Hawk, Little Big Man, He Dog, Big Road, and Iron Crow. Red Cloud, Spotted Tail, Swift Bear, Good Voice, Ring Thunder, Little Wound, American Horse, and Yellow Bear had previously been to Washington.

[6] *Chicago Tribune*, 22 Sept. 1877, p. 2. The 1886 census of Pine Ridge lists He Dog's wife as Rocks; the 1887 census gives her name as Rock. See Indian Census Rolls, 1885–1940, Pine Ridge, National Archives and Records Service, M595, rolls 362, 363.

his people, if they were only given a chance and treated with some degree of fairness by the whites." In this context, Spotted Tail may well have explained the calumet's meaning, knowing that Chicagoans might read of it the next day.

Although the delegates were serious about their purpose, this did not prevent them from enjoying their stay in Chicago. Once they arrived at the Sherman House, the *Tribune* reported, they "tested the springing qualities" of the sofas and chairs "to an alarming extent," no doubt sharing private jokes about Americans and their furniture. Following supper they "repaired to their room, where casino and poker for small stakes and 'jack-pots' entertained them for some hours."[7]

The delegates left Chicago the next day and arrived in Washington (*Otonwahe*)[8] on September 24, where they were ushered to the Continental Hotel. When General Crook arrived the next morning, Spotted Tail reminded him that he had promised to house the delegates at Washington House, where they had stayed in the past. Spotted Tail refused to say another word to his old friend until this oversight was corrected. Crook immediately paid a visit to Interior Secretary Carl Schurz. Within the hour the delegates were on their way to their preferred accommodations.[9]

Later that day Spotted Tail and Red Cloud gave interviews to a reporter from the *New York Herald.* As in Chicago, the two chiefs saw this as an opportunity to shape American opinion. Spotted Tail explained that the delegates had come to Washington to stop the government from putting them on "some place or reservation that did not suit them." Red Cloud seconded Spotted Tail's views and told of how his people had "lost quite a number of their children through fever" when they had lived on the Missouri a few years before. Red Cloud also related the story of Mackenzie's raid on his camp the previous October, contending that the army's confiscation of his people's horses was entirely without justification. "He intends when he sees the President to ask him to be paid for the horses that were taken from him," the *Herald* sympathetically explained. "He felt very indignant at this humiliation, as did all his young men."[10]

The next day the delegates met with Irwin, Crook, and William Welsh, a Christian humanitarian, to prepare for their meeting with President Hayes the following afternoon.[11] Although these men had very different long-term

---

7 *Chicago Tribune,* 22 Sept. 1877, p. 2. On the importance of humor in Indian life, see Vine Deloria Jr., *Custer Died for Your Sins: An Indian Manifesto* (New York, 1969), 148; Keith H. Basso, *Portraits of "The Whiteman": Linguistic Play and Cultural Symbols among the Western Apache* (Cambridge, 1979).

8 The word *otonwahe* refers to any town or city but was applied to Washington in particular.

9 *New York Herald,* 25 Sept. 1877, p. 7; Herman J. Viola, *Diplomats in Buckskins: A History of Indian Delegations in Washington City* (Washington, D.C., 1981), 125–26.

10 *New York Herald,* 25 Sept. 1877, p. 7.

11 Ibid., 27 Sept. 1877, p. 7.

goals, in the short term they all wanted to keep the Spotted Tail and Red Cloud agencies in the same general area. Irwin, Crook, and Welsh opposed relocation because they feared it would hinder the progress of civilization. From their perspective, the only way Indians would ever trust the United States would be for the government to treat them fairly. Crook was in a particularly tight spot. The former militants were still hoping for a northern agency. The situation would be bad enough when they were told this was impossible, but it would be far worse if they were then forced to live on the Missouri.

That same day, President Hayes met with Interior Secretary Schurz, also to plan for the upcoming meeting. Elected in the aftermath of the Little Bighorn, Hayes wanted to settle the "Sioux problem" once and for all. Although he had never given a great deal of attention to Indian affairs, Hayes was favorably inclined to the views of humanitarian reformers.[12] Some of the men Hayes would meet the next day were the killers of Custer, but he had no wish to see the iron hand of retribution fall upon the entire Sioux nation. He was willing to listen to the delegates' grievances and to assure them that their "Great Father" held their well-being close to heart. If they were treated fairly, Hayes believed, the Sioux and Arapahoes might put away their suspicions of the government and begin to embrace civilization.

On the twenty-seventh the delegates, along with Crook, Clark, Irwin, and Welsh, went to what Lakotas called *Tunkasila Oti* (Grandfather's House). Historians of U.S.–Indian diplomacy have often written of Indians calling on the "Great Father" or "the Great White Father." It is doubtful that any tribe ever used a term signifying "whiteness" for the president, although many tribes addressed presidents as "father," or, in the case of the Sioux, "grandfather." Herman Viola explains that Indians' use of these kinship terms was "a diplomatic device rather than an expression of subordination."[13] In addressing the president as grandfather, the Sioux delegates hoped to turn American paternalism to their advantage by reminding presidents of their power (were not grandfathers able to take effective action?) and calling on them to fulfill their obligations and promises (did not grandfathers keep their word?).

When the delegates arrived at the White House, they were ushered directly into the East Room. Assembled there were most of the members of Hayes's cabinet as well as John Q. Smith and Ezra A. Hayt, the outgoing

[12] Ibid. For Hayes's views on Indian policy, see Ari Hoogenboom, *The Presidency of Rutherford B. Hayes* (Lawrence, 1988), 153–71; Robert Winston Mardock, *The Reformers and the American Indian* (Columbia, Mo., 1971), 151–59.

[13] Viola, *Diplomats in Buckskins*, 94; see also Raymond J. DeMallie, "Touching the Pen: Plains Indian Treaty Councils in Ethnohistorical Perspective," in *Ethnicity on the Great Plains*, ed. Frederick C. Luebke (Lincoln, 1980), 50. In some situations, however, Lakotas distanced themselves from relationship with the president by referring to him as "your [the commissioners'] president." Calico, "Black Shields Account," copy in the author's possession.

and incoming commissioners of Indian affairs, Episcopal Bishop Henry B. Whipple, a prominent reformer, and several important women, including the president's wife, Lucy. After Lieutenant Clark introduced the delegates to the president, Welsh began the presentation of the Indians' case. "These red men," he observed, "claimed to be [the president's] children, and therefore had a claim upon his generosity and justice." The "special subject of their visit," Welsh continued, "is to present their objections to removing to the Missouri." If they were forced to lived there, Welsh explained, they could not become "civilized, as their women would become corrupt, and other evils follow to the men by the influence of bad white men." The Sioux wanted to remain where they were and have the government "assist them in agricultural pursuits. They were all anxious for civilization and want to become citizens."

Red Cloud followed by explaining that his people desired to "walk in the broad road, so that they may grow and prosper like the white people." This would not be possible if he was forced to live on the Missouri, as "there is too much whiskey there. If I go there I will come to nothing at all." These arguments skillfully played to Red Cloud's audience. As Robert W. Larson points out, the reference to whiskey especially appealed to "Lemonade Lucy" Hayes, a temperance advocate. Several other speakers spoke in a similar vein, saying that they "wanted to be civilized" and, in Little Big Man's translated words, "did not want to remove."[14]

The next morning, Spotted Tail advanced another line of argument. Instead of talking about his desire for civilization, Spotted Tail focused on past wrongs, pointing out, for example, that he had signed the Black Hills agreement only because the government had "frighten[ed] us into this business." With this as an example, Spotted Tail then bluntly informed the president: "You take our lands from us," adding that "your people make roads and drive away the game, and thus make us poor and starve us." Evidently hoping that Hayes had a sense of justice, Spotted Tail appealed to the universal proposition that all nations "ought to hold on to [their land] as their own." "The country I live in is mine," he said, "I love it. This is why I talk as I do."

After several more speeches, Hayes responded that the Lakotas would have to move to the Missouri for the upcoming winter because their supplies had already been sent there and they would starve if they did not. When spring came, however, "you shall select for your permanent abode such land on your reservation as you like best," even holding out the possibility that the northern Lakotas could have an agency on the Tongue River. Hayes's only stricture was that they choose these lands according to their potential for "cultivation." "Game is fast disappearing," he admonished, "and you cannot always live as hunters." To this, the president added a great deal of fatherly

[14] *New York Times*, 28 Sept. 1877, p. 5; Robert W. Larson, *Red Cloud: Warrior-Statesman of the Lakota Sioux* (Norman, 1997), 220.

advice about how his children ought to set their hearts on churches, schools, and houses.[15] By this time, late Friday afternoon, the meeting adjourned for the weekend.

Although the Sioux delegates had secured a critical concession, they still hoped to convince Hayes to change his mind about forcing them to spend even one winter on the Missouri. To increase their chances of this, they spent the weekend doing political work. On Sunday, having learned that Hayes regularly attended the Foundry Methodist Church, some of the delegates went there for services. No doubt, the Indians had their own ethnographic interest in investigating other religious practices. More to the point, however, their attendance also made a useful statement about their willingness to follow the road to "civilization." Later that day, some of the delegates met with a *New York Herald* reporter, helping him write a sympathetic story for the Monday edition. Through the *Herald*, the delegates informed the American public of their past hardships on the Missouri and rebutted the argument that it would be impossible to ship supplies from the Missouri to their present agencies. Because the additional cost of moving supplies appeared to be the main obstacle, the delegates volunteered to transport these supplies from the Missouri. True, they acknowledged, the government would have to provide wagons and pay wages, but this would be a valuable investment in its long-term policy of promoting Indian progress. "Wagons are great civilizers," the delegates pointed out.[16]

The next day, October 1, the delegation returned to the White House. Unlike their previous meetings, when the delegates had worn "full savage costume" (see Illustration 3), this time they were attired in "citizens' dress." It is unclear whether their change of clothes was the idea of someone like Crook or Welsh or if it originated with the delegates themselves. Whatever the case, their appearance in western clothing dramatized their willingness to change. As Spotted Tail told Hayes, "you said you wished us to live like white-men, and so we are to-day dressed in white men's clothes." Hayes conceded that the delegates' appearance was evidence of their "wish to live like white people," but he insisted that "it is too late in the season... to move the supplies." Hence, the Oglalas and Brulés would have to go to the Missouri.[17]

The day after their final meeting with Hayes, the delegates made one last appeal to Interior Secretary Schurz. Although Lakotas formally addressed Schurz as *ate* (father), among themselves they jokingly called him *Hinhan kin* (the Owl), a name that captured his bearded face with two eyes peering

[15] *New York Times*, 29 Sept. 1877, pp. 1–2.

[16] *New York Herald*, 1 Oct. 1877, p. 7.

[17] *New York Times*, 2 Oct. 1877, p. 1. The delegates could have worn western clothing during all of their visits, as the Indian Office gave them suits upon their arrival in Washington. See *New York Times*, 26 Sept. 1877, p. 1.

ILLUSTRATION 3. Sioux delegation to Washington, 1877. Although the delegates dressed in "native costume" for this photograph, a few days later they donned "western clothing" to illustrate their willingness to become "civilized." Rutherford B. Hayes Presidential Center, Fremont, Ohio.

through spectacles. Red Cloud and Spotted Tail told Schurz that their people were not going to like the idea of going to the Missouri and that they might "scatter all over the country" when they heard the news. Like a good school teacher, however, Schurz instructed them that there "are many things that are not as you desire and many that are not as we desire." As "wise men," he said, "we have to accommodate ourselves to things as they are."[18]

Despite Schurz's and Hayes's contention that the Sioux had no alternative other than moving to the Missouri, the only obstacle to transporting supplies to the Indians rather than moving the Indians to the supplies was that it would cost more. Against this, however, the delegates made a persuasive case for the advantages of allowing their people to haul the supplies. Moreover, moving several thousand people to the Missouri and back again the next spring also involved costs. The government would have to pay for wagons to transport people, and Indians' cattle and horses might die along the way. There were

[18] George E. Hyde, *Spotted Tail's Folk: A History of the Brulé Sioux* (Norman, 1961), 292; *New York Times*, 3 Oct. 1877, p. 5.

also potential human costs. A move in the late fall or early winter risked exposing old people and children to bad weather and more might die over the winter. Then, too, forcing the former militants to move increased the chances that some of them would try to join Sitting Bull in Canada.

In all likelihood, Hayes's refusal to budge had less to do with economics than politics. Hayes and other officials saw value in making some concessions to the Sioux, but they could only go so far without meeting strong opposition. Fifteen months after the Little Big Horn a good part of the American public, along with many of the nation's political and intellectual leaders, favored a policy of dealing firmly with the Sioux. For years, such people said, the government had coddled the Indians. Huge sums from the public treasury had been spent maintaining them in idleness. Under the influence of misguided and ill-informed humanitarians, weak men had been running Indian agencies. Indians had developed little respect for the U.S. government and were constantly making outrageous demands. Instead of the government dealing with Indian leaders as though they were heads of state, it should teach its wards some lessons. Hayes and Schurz were under pressure to draw a line. They already risked criticism for not forcing the Sioux to Indian Territory or the Missouri. If they yielded to the delegates on everything, it would be a sure sign of the administration's weakness.[19]

Although the Sioux delegates were not able to persuade the president to let them stay where they were for the winter, they did secure a critical concession. Hayes had committed the government to allow the Oglalas and Brulés to select permanent sites for their agencies in places of their own choosing on the Great Sioux Reservation. Removal to Indian Territory or relocation to the Missouri had been defeated, at least for now.

To gain this concession, the delegates had to work together effectively. Scholars have often emphasized that Indian communities under colonialism were crippled by factionalism. Nonetheless, Native leaders were sometimes able to overcome tendencies toward divisiveness.[20] In this instance, Sioux leaders, who only a year before had been committed to very different

[19] The Hayes administration's policy toward the Sioux would probably not have much effect on whether or not New York went Republican in 1880. Nonetheless, a perception of weakness might damage Interior Secretary Schurz's efforts to reform the Indian Office and thwart the army's efforts to take control of Indian affairs. On these issues, see Francis Paul Prucha, *The Great Father: The United States Government and the American Indians*, 2 vols. (Lincoln, 1984), 1:549–53, 586–89; Loring Benson Priest, *Uncle Sam's Stepchildren: The Reformation of United States Indian Policy, 1865–1887* (New Brunswick, 1942), 15–20, 68–69; Hans L. Trefousse, *Carl Schurz: A Biography* (Knoxville, 1982), 242–43; Mardock, *Reformers and the American Indian*, 159–61; Hoogenboom, *Presidency of Hayes*, 154; Donald J. D'Elia, "The Argument over Civilian or Military Indian Control, 1865–1880," *Historian* 24 (February 1962): 207–25.

[20] For a valuable discussion of the shortcomings of scholars' treatment of factionalism, see Rebecca Kugel, *To Be the Main Leaders of Our People: A History of Minnesota Ojibwe Politics, 1825–1898* (East Lansing, 1998), 7–9.

strategies, worked together toward a common aim. Surely there were tensions among these leaders and potential for strong disagreement later. For the moment, however, they had cooperated effectively. The delegates' success also depended on their ability to turn the government's rhetoric to their advantage. Recognizing the value of appearing to be receptive to U.S. policies, the delegates repeatedly expressed their wish to "become like the white man" and be "civilized."[21] To some extent, the delegates' use of this language was tactical. On the other hand, many Sioux leaders were genuinely willing to "become like the white man," though only in the limited sense that they wanted to prosper and were willing to incorporate certain elements of American ways of life to do so. As we will see in Chapter 7, for example, the Plains Sioux sometimes expressed willingness to send their children to school, but they did not think this was the first step toward assimilation. Instead, they realized the practical advantages of having their children learn to read and write in English and in this limited sense becoming "like whites."

By the time the delegates returned home on October 11, a Dakota winter was fast approaching. Most of the Lakotas were resigned to going to the Missouri and began to prepare for this untimely move as best they could. Many of the Sans Arcs, Minneconjous, and northern Oglalas, however, talked of staying where they were or going to Canada. A report by Lieutenant Clark indicates that the northerners remained angry at the leaders who had signed the Black Hills agreement, contending that "Red Cloud or any other old buffalo bulls" had no right to "give away what did not belong to them." Because the sale of the Black Hills lacked legitimacy, the former militants further argued, "the lands round" the Black Hills (the unceded territory of the 1868 Treaty) "are still theirs," a position that allowed them to stake a claim to an agency of their own in the north. When the Lakotas finally started for the Missouri in late October, the northerners went with them, but Lieutenant Jesse Lee, the agent at Spotted Tail, feared that "this move will prove disastrous and that many Indians will scatter and bad consequences may follow."[22]

---

[21] It seems likely that both of these terms were translations of *wasicuniciyapi*, which literally means "they make themselves *wasicun*." *Wasicun* is commonly translated as "white man," though the term does not refer to skin color. According to William K. Powers, *Sacred Language: The Nature of Supernatural Discourse in Lakota* (Norman, 1986), 39, *wasicun* derives from a term referring to anything that is *wakan* (sacred or powerful) and seems to have been applied to European Americans because they were perceived as being *wakan*, as having certain powers. Eugene Buechel, comp., *A Dictionary – Oie Wowapi Wan of Teton Sioux*, ed. Paul Manhart (Pine Ridge, S.Dak., 1983), 551, however, speculates that it may mean a person wearing bad clothes. Powers, *Sacred Language*, 38–40, points out that many Lakotas say that the term is derived from *wasin* (fat) and *icu* (to take), and thus means "person who steals bacon." I have also heard the term glossed as "fat takers."

[22] *Chicago Tribune*, 12 Oct. 1877, p. 1; Lieut. W. P. Clark to CIA, 7 Nov. 1877, STA, roll 841; Lieut. J. M. Lee to CIA, 31 Oct. 1877, STA, roll 841; James C. Olson, *Red Cloud and the Sioux Problem* (Lincoln, 1965), 254.

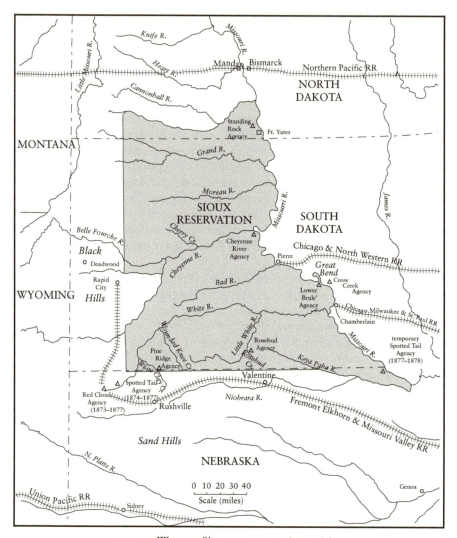

MAP 3. Western Sioux country, 1877–1889.

Under military escort, Lakotas traveled in two separate groups of between four and five thousand each. Those from Red Cloud Agency set out toward the Great Bend of the Missouri, while the Spotted Tail Indians headed toward the old Ponca Agency, seventy-five miles downstream from the Great Bend in northern Nebraska (see Map 3). Within a few days, about two thousand northerners in the Spotted Tail column decided to travel with Red Cloud, promising Agent Lee to rejoin Spotted Tail later. Upon their arrival in Red Cloud's camp on November 6, Lieutenant Clark reported that they were "wild, stubborn, and restless and still smarting under the bitter feelings engendered by the killing of Crazy Horse." Clark was dismayed to learn that the northerners were carrying Crazy Horse's body with them, for this showed that even in death Crazy Horse "exercises an influence for evil." Historians Edward Kadlecek and Mabell Kadlecek have pointed out that descendants of Crazy Horse's followers maintain that Crazy Horse had already been buried. The Kadleceks note, however, that Crazy Horse's relatives were carrying a spirit bundle that had been prepared earlier in a Spirit Keeping ceremony. This, they plausibly suggest, "may be the origin of the story."[23]

The two columns of people toiled slowly east under miserable conditions, enduring days of rain, sleet, and snow without sufficient clothing or provisions. Around November 22 Red Cloud's column reached the forks of the White River, sixty miles from the Missouri. Irwin and most of the troops went ahead to obtain supplies. By this time, some northerners had already broken for Canada. Now, with the soldiers away, most of the remainder seized the opportunity to leave. By late November only 300 of the 2,000 militants remained with Red Cloud's people. Soon, newspapers were reporting rumors of "Indian outrages" such as attacks on stage lines and ranches. The town of Deadwood was supposedly "surrounded by Indians."[24] To make matters worse for U.S. officials, around November 30, with high temperatures only in the teens, Red Cloud announced that his people refused to go another mile. Rather than continue to the Missouri, they would remain camped for the winter at the confluence of the White and Little White Rivers. Soon thereafter, Spotted Tail's people stopped fifty-five miles short of the Missouri, near the mouth of the Keya Paha River, in northern Nebraska.[25]

Upon learning of these events, the general of the army, William Tecumseh Sherman, exploded. For months Sherman had watched in frustration as other officials failed to deal with the Sioux as he thought they should. As far as Sherman was concerned, the Sioux should have been moved to the Missouri

---

[23] Lee to CIA, 31 Oct. 1877; Capt. Joseph Lawson to AG DD, 4 Dec. 1877, OAG, roll 283; Clark to CIA, 7 Nov. 1877; James Irwin to CIA, 7 Nov. 1877, RCA, roll 721; Edward Kadlecek and Mabell Kadlecek, *To Kill an Eagle: Indian Views on the Last Days of Crazy Horse* (Boulder, Colo., 1981), 67.

[24] Olson, *Red Cloud and the Sioux Problem*, 255; James Irwin to CIA, 26 Nov. 1877, RCA, roll 721; Lieut. R. W. Hoyt to Post Adjt., Cheyenne Agency, 27 Nov. 1877, RCA, roll 721; Lawson to AG DD, 4 Dec. 1877; *New York Herald*, 5 Dec. 1877, p. 7 (qtns.); *Chicago Tribune*, 2 Dec. 1877, p. 5, 5 Dec. 1877, p. 2; *Cheyenne Leader*, 20 Dec. 1877, p. 4; R. Blakeley to S. J. R. McMillen, 26 Nov. 1877, OAG, roll 283.

[25] Lieut. Gen. P. H. Sheridan to Gen. W. T. Sherman, 1 Dec. 1877, OAG, roll 283; *Annual Report of the Chief Signal-Officer of the Army, 1878*, 45th Cong., 3d sess., 1878–79, H. Ex. Doc. 1, pt. 2, serial 1848, 234; Lieut. J. M. Lee to CIA, 11 Dec. 1877, STA, roll 842. Some of Spotted Tail's people remained near this stopping point, while others camped along the Niobrara, and others on Ponca Creek, west of Fort Randall. Lieut. J. M. Lee to CIA, 26 Jan. 1878, STA, roll 842; E. K.(?) Valentine to Frank Welch, 26 Feb. 1878, STA, roll 842. Hyde, *Spotted Tail's Folk*, 288, says that Spotted Tail's main camp was on Rosebud Creek; evidence I have seen, however, indicates that it was probably on the Keya Paha.

River, if not Indian Territory, months ago – at gunpoint, if necessary. Instead, humanitarians and other sentimentalists had treated Sioux chiefs as though they were heads of state. Sherman could do little, however. The Great Sioux War was over, the agencies had been returned to the control of the Indian Office, and the president was listening to people like William Welsh and George Crook, one of Sherman's least favorite generals.

The flight of the northerners to Canada and the refusal of the remaining Sioux to continue to the Missouri provided Sherman with an opportunity to press for military involvement. On December 1 he instructed General Sheridan not to allow Red Cloud's people "to have a pound of food anywhere except at their proper Agency, and consider them as hostile unless they submit to authority." Sheridan replied that he "fully concur[red]" with Sherman, but wondered if he had the authority to withhold rations. He advised Sherman to consult with Interior Secretary Schurz before taking any action. Sherman agreed to do this, while in the next breath repeating his orders to withhold rations from Red Cloud's people.[26] In the end, though, Sherman was unable to starve Red Cloud's people into submission. Agent Irwin protested that Sherman's orders would be a serious violation of the trust Red Cloud had placed in the government and threatened to resign unless they were revoked. Crook also appealed to military authorities to allow Red Cloud's people to remain where they were for the winter. In the face of these objections, the War Department overruled Sherman.[27]

One reason for Irwin's and Crook's support of the Lakotas' decision to stop short of the Missouri was that they feared further unrest. Already, they had lost control of the majority of the northerners. It was possible that others – even Lakotas who had lived at the agencies for years – might defect. Indeed, throughout the winter government officials were forced to contend with efforts by Sitting Bull to exploit widespread feelings of discontent at the Red Cloud and Spotted Tail camps.

Sitting Bull learned about the situation in late November when the first people to break away from Red Cloud's column arrived in Sitting Bull's camp at East End Post. This group, which included relatives of Crazy Horse, informed Major James W. Walsh of the North-West Mounted Police that Crazy Horse himself had led them to Canada. On his deathbed, they explained, Crazy Horse said, "I have always wanted to go to the land of the white mother, but my father persuaded me to stay here. I shall be dead in

---

[26] Gen. W. T. Sherman to Lieut. Gen. P. H. Sheridan, 1, 3 Dec. 1877, OAG, roll 283; Lieut. Gen. P. H. Sheridan to Gen. W. T. Sherman, 2 Dec. 1877, OAG, roll 283; Lieut. Gen. P. H. Sheridan to Gen. A. H. Terry, 3 Dec. 1877, OAG, roll 283.

[27] James Irwin to CIA, 13 Dec. 1877, RCA, roll 721; James Irwin to CIA, 17 Dec. 1877, RCA, roll 722; Brig. Gen. George Crook to AAG, 6 Dec. 1877, OAG, roll 283; Acting CIA to James Irwin, 4 Dec. 1877, OAG, roll 283; George W. McCrary to SI, 11 Dec. 1877, OAG, roll 283; Gen. W. T. Sheridan to Lieut. Gen. P. H. Sherman, 14 Dec. 1877, OAG, roll 283.

a few minutes and will then go to the white mother's country. I want you all to follow me; you see the Americans want to kill us." Whether Crazy Horse spoke these words or not, he continued to be a symbol of resistance, inspiring his people to take action.[28]

Sitting Bull welcomed the arrival of Crazy Horse's relatives and the news they brought. Since crossing into Canada in May, Sitting Bull had had some success in creating a new base for Sioux autonomy. Building upon the good relations that Black Moon, Four Horns, and other Lakota leaders had established with Canadian officials before his arrival, Sitting Bull obtained assurances from Canadian officials that they would not allow U.S. troops to pursue him as long as his people obeyed Canada's laws. The Canadians appeared sympathetic to Sitting Bull's stories about his mistreatment in the United States. Buffalo were abundant north of the border, and it was easy to trade for ammunition.[29] It would be a mistake, then, to conclude with Robert Utley that because Sitting Bull's "defensive policy . . . against white encroachment had failed utterly" his "self-esteem had probably never plunged lower." Sitting Bull's policies had not entirely succeeded, but the story wasn't over. The arrival of Crazy Horse's people presented the possibility, as Gary Anderson points out, that the "Sioux nation would reconstruct itself north of the border."[30]

When Sitting Bull learned of the unrest to the south, he sent messengers to the United States to persuade more Lakotas to join him. One emissary who reached Red Cloud's camp in early January 1878 reportedly urged "the Indians at all the Agencies" to join Sitting Bull, "and when they all arrived there they would unite and make war upon the American Government." More than one hundred of the northerners responded to this invitation and left on January 10.[31] Three days later, according to Bull Eagle, a scout from Cheyenne River Agency, the situation remained volatile at Red Cloud's camp. Many people "advocated war, the breaking up of all the Agencies, and all going back to their hunting grounds." Soon after, Big Road, one of the delegates to Washington the previous fall, led a small group to Canada. At

[28] *Bismarck Tri-Weekly Tribune,* 20 Dec. 1877, p. 2.

[29] Robert M. Utley, *The Lance and the Shield: The Life and Times of Sitting Bull* (New York, 1993), 183–89; Gary Clayton Anderson, *Sitting Bull and the Paradox of Lakota Nationhood* (New York, 1996), 108–11; Stanley Vestal, *Sitting Bull: Champion of the Sioux: A Biography* (1932; Norman, 1957), 207–13; Joseph Manzione, *"I Am Looking to the North for my Life": Sitting Bull, 1876–1881* (Salt Lake City, 1991), 43–51; Gary Pennanen, "Sitting Bull: Indian without a Country," *Canadian Historical Review* 51 (June 1970): 125–26.

[30] Utley, *Lance and the Shield,* 189; Anderson, *Sitting Bull,* 116. As evidence of his assessment, Utley (p. 190) cites a statement Sitting Bull made to a *New York Herald* reporter that he was "nothing" and that he was "neither a chief nor a soldier." Rather than indicating low self-esteem, this statement was probably a ritualistic profession of humility.

[31] Major Charles G. Bartlett to AAG DD, 29 Jan. 1878, RCA, roll 722 (qtns.); James Irwin to CIA, 12 Jan. 1878, RCA, roll 722.

the same time, Touch the Clouds left for the Cheyenne River Agency to live with his Minneconjou relatives.[32]

As the winter wore on, Agent Irwin became increasingly frustrated with the "whole Sioux outfit" and wrote that they will "never be cured of their <u>importance</u> and <u>arrogance</u> and <u>willfull</u> [sic] <u>stubbornness</u> until they are made to feel the power of the government." In most of his communications with the Indian Office over the previous months, Irwin had drawn a distinction between "his" Indians (who were loyal) and the northerners (who were the sole source of rebellion). But when unrest continued after these troublemakers left for Canada, Irwin was certain that "my Indians are in communication with Sitting Bull" and "concoct[ing]" some kind of "deviltry."[33] Although Irwin's report raised the possibility that the Lakotas' lack of submissiveness might provoke military action, their attitude of defiance probably worked to their advantage, because it ultimately pressured Irwin and other officials in the field to support the Lakotas' goals for fear that if they did not, they would lose control of the situation altogether.

The possibility of open revolt increased significantly in mid-February when the Indian Office decided that the permanent location for the Red Cloud Agency would have to be near the Missouri to reduce the costs of shipping supplies. By this time, acting on their agreement with President Hayes the previous fall, Red Cloud's people had reached a consensus for a site on White Clay Creek, far to the west. To mark this decision, Red Cloud and others had traveled to White Clay and driven a stake in the ground. Despite Irwin's earlier outburst against the "arrogant" and "willful" Sioux, he opposed the government's rejection of White Clay, knowing that if the president's promise was broken, the Oglalas would "get ugly."[34]

Red Cloud's people were undoubtedly outraged when they learned of the Indian Office's decision. Nonetheless, their response was remarkably restrained. Perhaps because they feared that an attitude of open defiance risked military action, they decided upon a course of using diplomacy to

---

[32] Bartlett to AAG DD, 29 Jan. 1878 (qtn.); James Irwin to CIA, 27 Jan. 1878, RCA, roll 721. Although Bull Eagle described Big Road as wanting to go to Canada, other evidence indicates that he went reluctantly. See Turning Bear and Little Big Man to the President of the U.S., 1 Aug. 1878, RCA, roll 723; interview with Skunk Horse, enclosed in V. T. McGillycuddy to CIA, 7 Oct. 1879, RCA, roll 724.

[33] James Irwin to CIA, 20 Feb. 1878, RCA, roll 722 (underlining in original).

[34] CIA to W. M. Leeds, 18 Feb. 1878, RCA, roll 722; Ben Tibbetts to Major P. D. Vroom, 26 Apr. 1878, RCA, roll 723; James Irwin to CIA, 17 Feb. 1878, RCA, roll 722. Commissioner of Indian Affairs Hayt anticipated that Irwin would object that this decision contravened the president's promise and argued that the president had only "contemplated sending out proper persons to examine and decide on [a] new location with consent of the Indians." Still, Hayt was presenting the Oglalas with a fait accompli. CIA to Leeds, 18 Feb. 1878.

secure their interests. After several councils Oglala leaders in mid-March authorized Red Cloud to write to the president, reminding him that his people "had done what you asked us to do when were in Washington" and asking him "as friends" to allow them to live at White Clay. "We were raised in this country," Red Cloud patiently argued, "and know where we would like to live." Over the next weeks, Oglalas repeatedly insisted on their desire to move to White Clay. By this time, numerous printed copies of the proceedings at Washington the previous fall were circulating at Red Cloud's camp. Though most Oglalas could not read this document, they knew it contained the president's promise, and so they constantly waved copies before the eyes of their agent and other officials who visited their camp. In this way, they turned the written text, so often an enemy, to their advantage.[35]

By this time, Spotted Tail's people had also chosen a permanent place for their agency, near the confluence of Rosebud Creek and Little White River, about one hundred miles west of the Missouri. Aware that the government was threatening to overrule the Oglalas' choice, Spotted Tail's people feared that they, too, would be forced to live on or near the Missouri. Agent Lee argued passionately against such a decision, emphasizing that Spotted Tail's people regarded the president's promise as "bound up with such solemnity that it could not be broken." "We took the Great Father's word in our heart and in our hands," they told Lee, "and with our old and young – the sick and the dying, we came through storms and sufferings to this place, and we never cast our Great Father's words aside – we keep these and hold them fast." Should this promise be broken, Lee predicted, "many of the young men, and perhaps some of the old ones, will quit the agency."[36]

Throughout the spring and into the summer, Red Cloud's and Spotted Tail's people were anxious and uncertain about what would happen. Rumors came that they would be allowed to go to the places they had chosen. With relief, even joy, people began preparations to move camp. But, then, like the sudden shift of a prairie wind, new delays and new rumors arose. Perhaps another commission was coming, and what would be the result of that? New demands to live on the Missouri? New threats of starvation and exile if they refused? During this time, some Lakotas undoubtedly argued that they should defy the government and go to the places they had chosen without official permission. Others probably argued for seeking refuge with Sitting

---

[35] Red Cloud to Major P. D. Vroom, 14 Mar. 1878, RCA, roll 723; J. H. Hammond to CIA, 3 Apr. 1878, RCA, roll 722. According to the *New York Times*, 15 July 1878, p. 1, these pamphlets were published by the Union Pacific Railroad. The Union Pacific opposed locating the Sioux agencies on or near the Missouri because this would discourage settlement in north central Nebraska.

[36] Lieut. J. M. Lee to CIA, 20 Apr. 1878, STA, roll 842 (underlining in original).

Bull. For the moment, however, they decided to remain where they were and await more definite news.[37]

On June 20 Congress authorized funds for a commission to resolve the location of the two agencies once and for all. This commission, headed by Colonel D. S. Stanley and accompanied by Commissioner of Indian Affairs Hayt, arrived at the temporary Spotted Tail Agency on July 5. When Hayt explained to Spotted Tail's people that it was imperative for them to live near the Missouri to "avoid the expense of overland transportation," Spotted Tail found it difficult to contain his anger. He "complained bitterly of being delayed so long this summer upon the Missouri" pointing out that this had caused "many deaths in his camp" and reminding the commissioners of the president's promise.[38] Spotted Tail bluntly informed the commissioner of Indian affairs that he was a "bald-headed liar" and stated that his people would break camp with or without the government's permission.[39]

The Brulés' determination to resist convinced officials that it would be futile to try to keep their agency on the Missouri. On July 13 Interior Secretary Schurz authorized funds to move them to a place near the one they had earlier chosen, two and one-half miles up the Rosebud. Two weeks later, the Brulés started west to their new agency. The journey was slow and, for many, painful. The government had promised to arrange sufficient wagons to transport those who could not walk, but by August 8 none had appeared. According to Special Agent William J. Pollock, old and lame people had to walk under a "broiling sun." All the while, others "murmur[ed] imprecations against the govt and the agent because transportation has not been furnished." Eleven days later, with seventy miles remaining, wagons were still unavailable. It was not until September 1 that the last of the Brulés reached the place they desired for their home, henceforth known as Rosebud Agency. Most had walked the entire way.[40]

After their conference with Spotted Tail, the Stanley commission traveled to Red Cloud's camp, arriving there on July 10. The next day Red Cloud offered them a brief overview of the history of relations between his people and the United States. "The land of the Dakotas was once large and covered with buffalo and grass," Red Cloud began. When the "white men came . . . we fed and clothed them. When sick we watched over them." But then, "white people poured into our country" and began to "divide up our land and tell

---

[37] On the general mood of anxiety and uncertainty among the Oglalas, see James Irwin to CIA, 14 May 1878, RCA, roll 722.

[38] *ARCIA*, 1878, 156. The other members of the commission were J. M. Haworth, formerly an agent for the Kiowas, and Rev. Alfred L. Riggs, a missionary at Santee Agency.

[39] *Omaha Weekly Herald*, 19 July 1878, p. 5. Lakotas frequently associated Americans' baldness with their mendacity. See Kay Graber, ed., *Sister to the Sioux: The Memoirs of Elaine Goodale Eastman, 1885–91* (Lincoln, 1978), 88.

[40] C. Terry to CIA, 13 July 1878, STA, roll 842; William J. Pollock to CIA, 15, 22 July, 8 (qtns.), 19 Aug. 1878, STA, roll 843; *ARCIA*, 1878, 38.

us what part they would give us." When this happened, and when "[w]e saw white men . . . bringing starvation upon us and our children," the Sioux were forced to "fight and kill white men." After the 1868 Treaty, Red Cloud continued, the "white men . . . found our gold," and "more commissioners" came to "cheat us out of more than half of the little land [the government] pretended to give us forever." The only reason the Sioux had not been destroyed altogether was because "the white man's God will not let you starve us to death." With this history in mind, Red Cloud concluded by pleading with the commissioners: "Give us back our self-reliance. Give us our manhood, and a hope in the future. Something to live for. We do not want to be paupers, we want to be men."[41] After he had finished speaking, Red Cloud produced a copy of the proceedings the previous fall and showed the commissioners the president's promise that the Oglalas "would be allowed to select any location within their reserve for their permanent home." Red Cloud and the other leaders had fought hard to get Hayes to utter these words nine months before. Although Red Cloud himself could not read, he was able to bring these words once again to life. It was a persuasive performance. One of the commissioners, J. M. Haworth, immediately declared that "Red Cloud had made a good speech, and that he was right."[42]

Two days later, on the thirteenth, twenty Oglala leaders led the commissioners (minus Hayt, who returned to Washington) on a tour of Lakota country. After almost three weeks spent examining possible locations for the Red Cloud Agency, the commissioners concluded that the new agency should be located in the southwest corner of the reservation on Wounded Knee Creek and named "Ogalalla" or "Pine Ridge." This was not the exact spot where Red Cloud had placed his stake, but it was close. The commissioners strongly recommended against a Missouri River location. If the Oglalas were forced to live on the Missouri, "they must be paupers dependent on the government forever," whereas if they were located on the lands recommended, "within ten years they have a fair and good prospect of becoming self-supporting." Even from the standpoint of economy, always Washington's paramount concern, the Missouri was not necessarily cheaper. Because the Indians would need timber for houses, and because there was little timber on the Missouri, it would have to be imported at considerable expense. Wounded Knee, however, had ample timber.[43]

By convincing this commission to recommend against the Missouri, the Oglalas had won a significant battle. But it remained to be seen what higher officials would decide. Hayt, for one, insisted that the Oglalas live on the Missouri. On the other hand, Schurz was more sympathetic to the idea of allowing the Red Cloud Agency to be located elsewhere. If the Oglalas wanted

[41] *The Council Fire and Arbitrator* 7 (October 1884): 140.
[42] *ARCIA*, 1878, 156 (1st qtn.); *New York Times*, 15 July 1878, p. 1 (2d qtn.).
[43] *ARCIA*, 1878, 157–59 (qtns., 158).

to live far from the Missouri, Schurz argued that the costs of transportation should be subtracted from their rations. This position reconciled the often antagonistic priorities of economy and order. Economy would not be sacrificed if Red Cloud's people chose the place for their agency. At the same time government officials would avoid having to contend with the unrest that would inevitably follow a broken promise.[44]

Further complications arose when the Oglalas considered the commission's recommendation. On August 30 they insisted that their agency be located on White Clay Creek, since Wounded Knee was dry in the summer and froze over in the winter. By early September officials in Washington had informally decided against an agency on the Missouri, but they had yet to approve an alternative. Nor had they authorized local officials to begin making preparations to secure transportation for a possible move. With cold weather fast approaching, Irwin appealed directly to Schurz to avoid "repeat[ing] the frightful experiment of last winter in moving six thousand destitute people at such a season."[45]

On September 19 Red Cloud's people decided to force the issue by announcing that they would set out for White Clay on the twenty-first. They instructed Irwin to inform President Hayes that they "do not do this to defy or hurt the feelings of the Great Father, but because it is their duty to do the best they can to protect their women & children." By the twenty-fifth the Oglalas were on their way to White Clay Creek. The "unaccountable delay has made them angry & they are not now to be trifled with," Irwin warned. This move might easily have been a disaster. Fortunately, however, the full fury of winter did not descend that year until well into December. Although the government failed to supply transportation, the Oglalas managed to make the 170-mile journey without serious problems. In late November they arrived at White Clay Creek, the exact spot that Red Cloud had earlier staked.[46]

A few months later, on February 8, 1879, government officials and Oglala leaders met at White Clay Creek to lay the cornerstone for a schoolhouse at the new agency, henceforth known as Pine Ridge Agency. Into a cedar box government officials placed several documents: a report of an earlier commission to the Sioux, some agency records, copies of laws relating to Indian policy, and an almanac. Before placing this box beneath the cornerstone, one

---

[44] *New York Times,* 15 July 1878, p. 1, 18 July 1878, p. 1; James Irwin to SI, 5 Sept. 1878, RCA, roll 722.

[45] James Irwin to CIA, 30 Aug. 1878, RCA, roll 722; Irwin to SI, 5 Sept. 1878.

[46] James Irwin to CIA, 19 (1st qtn.), 25 (2d qtn.) Sept. 1878, RCA, roll 722; *ARCIA,* 1878, 36–37; James Irwin to CIA, 25 Nov. 1878, RCA, roll 723. For temperatures, see *Annual Report of the Chief Signal-Officer of the Army, 1879,* 46th Cong., 2d sess., 1879–80, H. Ex. Doc. 1, pt. 2, serial 1908, 432.

of the officials asked Oglala leaders if they would like to contribute something. James O'Beirne, a special agent from the Indian Office, reported that Red Cloud placed in the box a gold ring and called upon "Almighty God [to] put it into the hearts of the white man, not to disturb us in our present home, but allow us to remain here in peace." Adding a bracelet to the box, Little Wound expressed the hope that "the white man would not attempt to remove his people from where they now are." After the cedar box had been placed in the earth, Red Cloud laid the cornerstone and then drove a "wooden spike home, which fastened the first jointing of the sills." O'Beirne remarked that the "Indian Chiefs . . . quietly went their way, evidently much impressed with the importance of what had been . . . auspiciously commenced."[47]

Though an auspicious occasion for all, Oglalas and government officials had different ideas about what had taken place. For the Americans, a cornerstone for a schoolhouse signified a crucial first step on a path leading to assimilation. For the Indians, however, the cornerstone was a sign of permanence and self-determination. When O'Beirne reported that Red Cloud drove a wooden spike *home*, he (probably inadvertently) captured the meaning of Red Cloud's act. This was the second time Red Cloud had driven a stake into the earth at White Clay Creek. His people had won the right to live in this place. Like other western Sioux communities at the beginning of the reservation period, they would continue to fight to make their agency a place of their own.

[47] James O'Beirne to CIA, 12 Feb. 1879, RCA, roll 725.

6

"I Work So Much it Makes Me Poor"

The Reservation Economy

Sometime in late May 1882, several thousand bison appeared on the Great Sioux Reservation about one hundred miles west of the Standing Rock Agency. According to James McLaughlin, the Standing Rock agent, the Indians knew "instinctively" that the buffalo had arrived, even though "it had been many years since the buffalo had sought the hunting-grounds of that part of the reservation." With this "rich store of succulent meat in sight," McLaughlin continued, "it was not possible that the Indians could be held in check." On June 10, more than six hundred Standing Rock Lakotas and Yanktonais left the agency. Days later, they located the herd and killed five thousand bison.[1]

McLaughlin's contention that the Indians knew "instinctively" that the bison had arrived revealed the common tendency of Americans to represent Indians as primitives, so close to nature as to be almost animal-like. (The Standing Rock hunters themselves probably attributed their knowledge of the bison's presence to a combination of spiritual and empirical sources.) With its tone of light-hearted nostalgia, McLaughlin's and other similar accounts of the "last buffalo hunt" also reflected the standard trope of the "vanishing Indian." Like most Americans of the time, McLaughlin saw history as the outworking of inevitable laws of "progress." These laws decreed that the buffalo must disappear and that, when they did, Plains Indians would either die off or be assimilated by a supposedly superior "civilization." In this narrative, the last buffalo hunt decisively marked the end of a way of life. There was little room for continuity between the past and the future.[2]

---

[1] James McLaughlin, *My Friend the Indian* (1910; Lincoln, 1989), 97 (qtn.), 101, 109, 114. McLaughlin, p. 110, estimated there were 50,000 animals in the herd, probably an overestimate. A version of this chapter appeared as "'The Last Buffalo Hunt' and Beyond: Plains Sioux Economic Strategies in the Early Reservation Period," *Great Plains Quarterly* 21 (Spring 2001): 115–30.

[2] On the theme of the vanishing Indian, see Brian W. Dippie, *The Vanishing American: White Attitudes and U.S. Indian Policy* (Middletown, Conn., 1982). For another account of a "last

The near extinction of the bison certainly marked a transition in Plains Sioux history, one marked by deep pain. Nonetheless, because they had no choice but to live through this transition, Sioux people created continuities from the past to the present. Even as the buffalo disappeared, many Sioux thought that they might someday return, though others were less hopeful that this would occur, at least anytime soon. Whatever their views on the return of the buffalo, all western Sioux communities worked to construct economies that would allow them to survive, and if possible, live well under new conditions.[3] The actions and words of Sitting Bull offer some insight into Plains Sioux perspectives during the early reservation period. In these years, Sitting Bull often wore a "bunch of shed buffalo hair painted red, fastened on the side of his head" as a reminder of the coming of the White Buffalo Calf Woman. This indicated more than a simple nostalgia for an irretrievable past. For Sitting Bull, the story of the coming of the White Buffalo Calf Woman continued to have meaning. During a period of great difficulty, *Wakan Tanka* had taken pity on the Lakota people through her. As Sitting Bull explained to a *Chicago Tribune* reporter in 1879, "[y]ou must not think that the Great Spirit does not watch me as closely as he watches you. He put me on these prairies, and he has permitted me to thrive with them. I know that he is watching me, and he will never leave me to starve. When the buffalo are gone he will give me something else."[4]

During the early reservation period the western Sioux received a significant portion of their food, clothing, and material goods directly from the United States. Under the terms of the 1868 Treaty, the government was obligated to provide clothing to every person on the reservation annually for thirty years. The treaty also required the government to provide other "necessities," a requirement that it fulfilled by providing stock cattle, wagons, agricultural implements, material for housing, and household furnishings. The terms of the 1876 agreement, by which the Sioux were forced to cede the Black Hills, required the government to provide daily to every person one-and-a-half pounds of beef, one-half pound of flour, one-half pound of corn, and small

buffalo hunt," see Thomas Lawrence Riggs, "Sunset to Sunset: A Lifetime with My Brothers, the Dakotas," *South Dakota Historical Collections* 29 (1956): 228–43.

[3] Richard White, *The Roots of Dependency: Subsistence, Environment, and Social Change among the Choctaws, Pawnees, and Navajos* (Lincoln, 1983), 199–211; and Thomas Biolsi, *Organizing the Lakota: The Political Economy of the New Deal on the Pine Ridge and Rosebud Reservations* (Tucson, 1992), 23–31, describe Plains Indians during this period as becoming economically dependent, though for an argument that the Oglala Sioux were relatively self-sufficient from 1890 to 1914, see Paul Robertson, *The Power of the Land: Identity, Ethnicity, and Class among the Oglala Lakota* (New York, 2002), 45–75.

[4] Frances Densmore, *Teton Sioux Music and Culture* (1918; Lincoln, 1992), 458 (1st qtn.); *Chicago Tribune*, 5 July 1879, p. 1 (2d qtn.).

quantities of coffee, sugar, and beans. These rations were to continue "until the Indians are able to support themselves."[5]

There were several problems with annuities. Although the 1868 Treaty stipulated that issues of clothing should be made by the first of August, the government often missed this deadline by months.[6] Leaders at Cheyenne River explained the hardships from a late issue:

Last winter our people all left their Camps and came to the agency expecting every day to get our goods but we did not get them for several weeks.... The weather was very cold and many of our people almost perished because they had no clothing and many of them that had poultry and small stock at home found much of it frozen when they got back.[7]

When annuities eventually arrived, they were often of inferior quality. Elaine Goodale, who taught at Lower Brulé and Pine Ridge in the 1880s, observed that annuity goods like clothing, shoes, or flannel "were nearly worthless and a burden to recipients." Goodale did note, however, that the Sioux gained some benefit from these goods by selling them to nearby settlers. In other instances, Indians found unintended uses for otherwise useless items. One schoolteacher, for example, recalled that Lakotas at Cheyenne River cut the leather from government-issue boots to make "extra-fine hunting lariats." Although the Sioux judged annuities by their practical value, government agents valued them much more for their capacity to promote "civilization." In 1884, when the Cheyenne River agent learned that only 500 of the requested 825 men's suits had arrived, he complained to Washington not that the shortage would cause 325 men to freeze but that it would adversely affect his campaign to promote the wearing of western clothing. Because annuities were a tool of assimilation, it was important for the agents to control them. Thus, even though the sale or barter of annuity goods displayed an entrepreneurialism that arguably coincided with the values of American capitalism, the agents regarded these acts as crimes and frequently arrested offenders. This response to unauthorized enterprise underscores that assimilation was not simply a matter of encouraging certain kinds of behavior but was instead a project of control.[8]

---

[5] Charles J. Kappler, ed., *Indian Affairs: Laws and Treaties*, 5 vols. (Washington, D.C., 1904–1941), 2:1001, 1:170.

[6] See, for example, L. F. Spencer to CIA, 10 Jan. 1889, RA-KC, book 15, which complained that annuities typically did not arrive at Rosebud Agency until midwinter.

[7] Little No Heart, The Charger, and Spotted Eagle to CIA, 10 Sept. 1883, OIA, file 19056–1883.

[8] Kay Graber, ed., *Sister to the Sioux: The Memoirs of Elaine Goodale Eastman, 1885–91* (Lincoln, 1978), 63 (1st qtn.); Kunigunde Duncan, *Blue Star: Told from the Life of Corabelle Fellows* (Caldwell, Idaho, 1938), 99 (2d qtn.); William A. Swan to CIA, 7 Jan. 1884, CR-KC, box 263; For examples of bartering or selling annuity goods, see J. A. Stephan to Acting CIA, 25 Feb. 1880, SRA, roll 851; V. T. McGillycuddy to CIA, 16 Nov. 1880, RCA, roll 726; for arrests for the sale of annuity goods, see Cheyenne River Agency Diary, 13 Dec. 1887, 18 Feb. 1889, CR-KC, box 273; L. F. Spencer to CIA, 21 Dec. 1888, RA-KC, book 15.

There were also problems with treaty rations. On paper, rations afforded a minimally adequate diet, though one substantially below that enjoyed before reservation confinement.[9] Sometimes, however, the United States failed to provide sufficient and timely rations. Mary Collins, a missionary at Cheyenne River, observed in 1887 that the Indians "are hungry this week. They have received no beef issue for a long time."[10] A related problem was that the cattle delivered by contractors in the fall tended to "shrink" during the winter. One agent stated that it was common for an animal weighing one thousand pounds in October to weigh only seven hundred pounds by the spring. During a severe winter – hardly uncommon – shrinkage could be worse. As this agent noted, "all loss, by death, or otherwise, during a severe winter is borne by the Indians, and not by the Government."[11]

Because rations were barely sufficient, the Sioux had to be constantly on guard against any initiative that would reduce them further. The government's usual practice at the western Sioux agencies was to issue beef "on the hoof." Every two weeks at the agency or at scattered locations on the reservation, U.S. officials released cattle to band leaders. After the men shot the cattle, women joined them in skinning and butchering the animals.[12] Many U.S. officials objected to this practice. Not only did it reinforce "barbaric" behavior like eating offal, it gave Indians a rationale to own weapons and acquire ammunition.[13] For these reasons, the Indian Office preferred cattle to be killed and butchered by agency employees. It would then be issued "on the block" or frozen for later issue.

Sioux leaders strenuously objected to issuing beef on the block. As indicated by the fact that the Sioux called issue day *wanasapi*, the word for a communal buffalo hunt, "hunting" cattle allowed them to exercise valued skills and to perform "traditional" roles.[14] Beef on the block also

[9] Richard H. Steckel and Joseph M. Prince, "Tallest in the World: Native Americans of the Great Plains in the Nineteenth Century," *American Economic Review* 91 (March 2001): 287–94.

[10] Louis P. Olson, "Mary Clementine Collins: Dacotah Missionary," *North Dakota History* 19 (January 1952): 73. See also H.C. Bulis to CIA, 28 Feb. 1879, RA-KC, book 5. According to Luther Standing Bear, *Land of the Spotted Eagle* (1933; Lincoln, 1978), 57, when Lakotas first encountered beef they disliked it because it smelled bad.

[11] J. George Wright to CIA, 28 Jan. 1890, RA-KC, book 16. The agent at Cheyenne River noted that a shrinkage of 20 to 30 percent was common. *ARCIA*, 1889, 130.

[12] For descriptions of the issue of cattle, see Graber, ed., *Sister to the Sioux*, 59–60; Charles A. Eastman (Ohiyesa), *From the Deep Woods to Civilization: Chapters in the Autobiography of an Indian* (1916; Lincoln, 1977), 79–80.

[13] "Report of William H. Waldby" in *Report of the Board of Indian Commissioners, 1887* in *Annual Report of the Secretary of the Interior, 1887*, 50th Cong., 1st sess., 1887–88, H. Ex. Doc. 1, pt. 5, serial 2542, 925–26; Benjamin H. Miller to SI, 4 Nov. 1889, Reports of Inspections of the Field Jurisdictions of the Office of Indian Affairs, Record Group 75, National Archives and Records Administration, Microfilm Publications, M1070, roll 36.

[14] Florentine Digmann, "History of the St. Francis Mission, 1886–1922," unpublished manuscript, n.d., series 7, box 14, folder 7, p. 5, Holy Rosary Mission Records, Marquette University Special Collections, Milwaukee.

ILLUSTRATION 4. Rations line. Lakota women regularly stood in line waiting to receive rations of flour, beef, coffee, and sugar. Denver Public Library, Western History
Collection, X-31445.

threatened to diminish Indians' control over their lives. It was one thing
to have government officials release cattle and have Indians take over from
there. It was quite another for Indians to contemplate the prospect of government officials throwing them pieces of beef. Sioux women, who stood in
line to obtain rations of coffee, sugar, and flour (see Illustration 4), already
resented the fact that "the clerks and assistants when making issues, throw
the rations to the Indian women in a very disrespectful manner, 'as if they
were dogs.'" Furthermore, issuing beef directly to individuals threatened the
authority of band leaders.[15]

The Sioux also objected to issuing beef on the block because this method
cost them important parts of the animal. In 1882 the agent at Pine Ridge
reported that the Oglalas were "peculiarly sensitive on this beef question,"
since by killing cattle themselves, "they are enabled to make use of at least
a fifth quarter in nutriment in the way of intestines, liver, etc." Beef on the
block also deprived Lakotas of the animals' hides.[16] Indians used a small
number of these hides for making moccasins and other leather goods. They

---

[15] CIA to L. F. Spencer, 7 Dec. 1888, RA-KC, box A-357.
[16] V. T. McGillycuddy to CIA, 16 Dec. 1882, PR-KC, box 35. Documentation of the Indian
Office's objections to the system of issuing on the hoof and of Lakota opposition can also
be found in V. T. McGillycuddy to CIA, 21 Oct. 1879, RCA, roll 724; J. A. Stephan, 31
Aug. 1880, SRA, roll 852; James G. Wright to CIA, 3 June 1885, RA-KC, book 11. Plans
for issuing on the block threatened Lakotas with the loss of hides because they called for the
agents to sell the hides to pay for extra employees to kill and butcher cattle.

sold the large majority to traders at prices between $2.50 and $4.00 each. A hide was worth a hundred pounds of flour and some kerosene oil or a pair of women's shoes and a ham.[17] With people struggling just to survive, any innovation that threatened to deprive them of a valuable source of food and income was certain to meet resistance. In 1889 the agent at Rosebud predicted that any change in the present system of issuing beef would result in "open revolt." Although the agents were able to make some progress in implementing issuing on the block, the Rosebud agent's remarks suggest that issuing live cattle remained the most common method.[18]

Lakotas at Rosebud and Pine Ridge faced another threat to their supply of rations. Unlike the situation at Cheyenne River and Standing Rock, where the government conducted accurate censuses in the 1870s, the count at Rosebud and Pine Ridge remained inflated into the 1880s. Brulés and Oglalas resisted an accurate census; one reason was that they realized it would probably result in a reduction of rations. Accurate counts did not take place until 1886 at Pine Ridge and 1890 at Rosebud.[19]

Overall, although the western Sioux usually had enough to eat in the 1880s, this was true only because they defeated government efforts to cut back on minimally adequate rations and, as will be discussed later, were able to supplement rations through other means. Because the Sioux were dependent on the government for food, agents often used rations as a weapon to compel compliance. As we will see in later chapters, they commonly threatened to withhold rations for refusing to send children to schools and for holding social dances and religious ceremonies.

The western Sioux also became dependent on the United States for shelter during the 1880s. Lacking new supplies of buffalo hides for tipis, Indians were forced to use government-issued canvas. As the decade wore on and the government gave them building materials for log houses and provided them with stoves, the western Sioux increasingly lived within four walls, at least during the winter months.[20] To some extent Sioux people saw advantages in

---

[17] On the hide trade and prices paid for hides, see James. G. Wright to CIA, 28 May 1885, RA-KC, book 11; James McLaughlin to CIA, 7 Sept. 1889, MP, roll 33. A list of prices at the store of E. J. deBell, a licensed trader at Rosebud agency, shows prices of $3.00 for 100 pounds of flour, 35¢ for a gallon of kerosene oil, women's shoes from $1.50 to $3.00 a pair, and hams at 15¢ per pound. J. George Wright to CIA, 1 Mar. 1890, RA-KC, book 16.

[18] J. George Wright to CIA, 19 Nov. 1889, RA-KC, book 16.

[19] My statement about Standing Rock and Cheyenne River is based on my analysis of population reports in *ARCIA*, 1876–1890. On the census at Pine Ridge and Rosebud, see V. T. McGillycuddy to CIA, 16 Oct. 1885, PR-KC, box 36; *ARCIA*, 1886, 78; James C. Olson, *Red Cloud and the Sioux Problem* (Lincoln, 1965), 306–07; Thomas Biolsi, "The Birth of the Reservation: Making the Modern Individual among the Lakota," *American Ethnologist* 22, no. 1 (1995): 28–53; Lieut. Col. J. S. Fletcher Jr. to AAG DP, 31 July 1886, OIA, file 21655–1886; *ARCIA*, 1889, 161; *ARCIA*, 1891, 410–11.

[20] In 1890 "but few Indians" at Rosebud were not living in "houses of their own construction." *ARCIA*, 1890, 62.

building houses. Having endured several moves in the 1870s, Oglalas and Brulés, for example, realized that the construction of houses was a safeguard against being relocated yet again. Then, too, a well-constructed cabin with a warm stove had its attractions in certain months.[21] Nonetheless, many Sioux fiercely resisted being forced to accept the new ways. To convince them to build houses, the Indian Office resorted to cutting back on issues of canvas.[22]

As with annuities, the government's effort to encourage the Sioux to live in log houses was linked to its larger goal of promoting "civilization." Once again, however, the Sioux used material resources for their own purposes. For example, agents hoped that when Indians built cabins they would scatter across the prairie in Jeffersonian fashion, thus eroding community and tribal institutions and affiliations. At Pine Ridge, however, the Oglalas built their new houses along streams, thus creating elongated villages.[23] This modification of the old camp circle meant that people continued to live in relative proximity and allowed the *tiyospaye* to continue to function as the basic unit of Lakota life. Indeed, the relative permanence of houses would make it more difficult for the government to atomize Oglalas in the future. Furthermore, policies of assimilation presumed that once the Sioux had adopted the accouterments of civilization (western clothing and shelter) they would undergo a corresponding internal change, as if pouring wine from one bottle to another would change the wine. In many subtle ways, however, Sioux people proved adept at re-creating familiar cultural patterns under new conditions. Thus, Indians who lived in log houses in the winter frequently moved into tipis during warmer weather. Photographs taken during the 1880s and 1890s often show a tipi to the side of a cabin (see Illustration 5). Others show temporary summer encampments consisting entirely of tipis.

In addition, the Sioux modified their new houses to suit their tastes. Instead of papering the walls of their houses with floral prints, they used muslin to make large wall coverings, called *ozan*, the name for a tipi's dew covering. According to Ella Deloria, they painted these with "lively black and white drawings of historical scenes of hunting or battles or peacemaking between tribes, and courtship scenes, games, and [other] activities of the past." People visited one another just to see these pictographs and hear stories about them.[24]

[21] Speech of Three Bears in V. T. McGillycuddy to the President of the United States, 26 May 1879, RCA, roll 724. Though cabins were warm, the lack of ventilation may also have contributed to disease. See Ella C. Deloria, *Speaking of Indians* (1944; Vermillion, S.Dak., 1992), 55; Graber, ed., *Sister to the Sioux*, 45.

[22] Raymond J. DeMallie, "Pine Ridge Economy: Cultural and Historical Perspectives," in *American Indian Economic Development*, ed. Sam Stanley (The Hague, 1978), 254.

[23] *ARCIA*, 1884, map between pp. 38–39.

[24] John A. Anderson, Henry W. Hamilton, and Jean Tyree Hamilton, *The Sioux of the Rosebud: A History in Pictures* (Norman, 1971), 71, 112, 213; Deloria, *Speaking of Indians*, 56–57.

ILLUSTRATION 5. Cabin with tipi. Although Plains Sioux people built log cabins in the 1880s, they continued to live in tipis, especially during the warmer months. Denver Public Library, Western History Collection, X-31387.

Although the near extinction of the bison meant that Plains Sioux communities were unable to live as they had in the past, to a surprising extent the Sioux were able to hunt deer, pronghorn antelope, and other game in the 1880s. After the buffalo disappeared, White Bull recalled, people at Standing Rock, few of whom had guns or ammunition, "made arrows and kept them hid and would...hunt small animals."[25] Although small game was important primarily as a source of food, Indians used elk, deer, and pronghorn hides for moccasins and other clothing. They also sold hides or traded them for other goods. The trader at Cheyenne River reported that in 1883 he purchased $11,000 worth of skins and furs from Indians.[26]

Indians frequently left the reservation to pursue small game. In 1887 Wyoming ranchers complained that Sioux hunting parties were "killing off all the game." In response, the agent at Pine Ridge wrote that because "deer and antelope are very plentiful in southeastern Wyoming," it was difficult

---

[25] Walter S. Campbell Collection, box 106, notebook 47, p. 10, Western History Collections, University of Oklahoma Library, Norman. Other sources that indicate that hunting was an important source of subsistence in the 1880s and 1890s are Vine V. Deloria Sr., "The Standing Rock Reservation: A Personal Reminiscence," *South Dakota Review* 9 (Summer 1971): 175; Thomas E. Mails, *Fools Crow*, assisted by Dallas Chief Eagle (1979; Lincoln, 1990), 73.

[26] J. F. Cravens to CIA, 19 Nov. 1877, CRA, roll 129; *Testimony Taken by a Select Committee of the Senate Concerning the Condition of the Indian Tribes in the Territories of Montana and Dakota*, 48th Cong., 1st sess., 1883–84, S. Rept. 283, serial 2174, 89.

to prevent Oglalas from leaving the reservation to hunt there. The following year settlers along the Cannonball River protested to the Standing Rock agent that "two roving bands of Sioux Indians...are carrying on an indiscriminate slaughter of Antelope." Despite these complaints, however, non-Indian hunters probably posed the greatest threat to game. As one hunter boasted to White Bull in 1883: "After we have cleaned up the buffalo, we are going to clean up the deer."[27]

Elaine Goodale provided an account of the activities of one Sioux hunting party. In summer 1889, Goodale accompanied Whirling Hawk, his family, and a few other families on a hunting expedition to the Sand Hills of Nebraska. In addition to killing several pronghorn, this hunting party was on the lookout for anything edible. One hot July day as the party was traveling, Goodale was "startled to see men and boys leap suddenly from their seats and race ahead of the wagons, yelling and throwing off their clothes as they ran." Soon, they were "dashing into a shallow pond, madly chasing a flock of half-grown wild ducks, not yet able to fly. Screaming with joy, they plunged after the terrified birds as they dove and rose and dove again, finally seizing and wringing their necks and casting them triumphantly on shore." Not long after, the party enjoyed an "impromptu feast." On other days, Goodale shared in meals of badger, skunk, and mud turtle.[28]

Goodale's narrative brings to light another important aspect of early reservation-era economic strategies. Although the Sioux are well-known as a hunting people, their diet included a variety of plant foods. Lakota names for the summer months show the importance of some of these foods: *Wipazutkan Waste Wi* (June, the months when service berries are good); *Canpasapa Wi* (July, the month when the choke cherries are black); and *Kantasa Wi* (August, the month when the plums are red). In summer 1889, Goodale observed women and children gathering wild cherries, *tinpsila* (wild turnips), rose-hips, mint, and balm. These were important sources of nutrition.[29]

---

[27] H. D. Gallagher to CIA, 21 Oct. 1887, PR-KC, box 36 (1st qtn.); Lewis A. Dodge to James McLaughlin, 7 July 1888, SR-KC, box 302 (2d qtn.); Stanley Vestal, *Warpath: The True Story of the Fighting Sioux as Told in a Biography by Chief White Bull* (1934; Lincoln, 1984), 240 (3d qtn.). On non-Indian hunters' impact on pronghorn, see Connie Marie Greenquist, "The American Pronghorn Antelope in Wyoming: A History of Human Influences and Management," Ph.D. diss., University of Oregon, 1983, 86–87.

[28] Graber, ed., *Sister to the Sioux*, 95–113 (qtn., 102).

[29] Ibid., 101, 104. Gathering continued to be an important economic activity. Madonna Swan, a Lakota woman who grew up on the Cheyenne River Reservation, observed that one of her grandmothers spent time gathering turnips and berries in the 1930s. She also recalled picking cherries and plums and collecting acorns with her mother and another grandmother. Mark St. Pierre, *Madonna Swan: A Lakota Woman's Story as Told through Mark St. Pierre* (Norman, 1991), 12, 23. For an overview of the Sioux diet before and during the reservation period, see

Although hunting and gathering revealed the persistence of older ways of life, other economic strategies in the 1880s involved innovation and the creative use of government resources. The U.S. project of assimilation envisioned Indian families eventually becoming commercial farmers. To implement this policy, government agents provided Indians with agricultural tools and seeds. These resources (supplemented by equipment and supplies Indians obtained on their own) enabled many Sioux to work small plots of land, usually less than five acres, seldom more than ten or twenty. These gardens were usually located along creek bottoms where there was water at least part of the year. Families grew *wayahota* (oats), *wagmeza* (corn), *wagmu* (squash and pumpkins), *blo* (potatoes), and *spansniyutapi* or *wagmuspansni* (watermelons; literally, "they eat it raw" or "uncooked squash").[30] Indians also raised chickens and turkeys. As early as 1883, "a large number of poultry of all kinds" could be found in Pine Ridge communities. With a bureaucrat's pseudo-precision, the agent at Cheyenne River reported 1,957 "domestic fowl" in 1887.[31]

Although Plains Sioux people (especially men) often spoke scornfully of farming as something inimical to their identity altogether (and, at best, women's work), most could have easily found ancestors only a generation or two before with extensive horticultural experience. Many bands had planted crops in the late 1700s and early 1800s while living near the Missouri. The very name of the Minneconjous, "Planters beside the Stream," revealed an older history of woodland subsistence patterns. More recently, the Corn band of the Brulés had grown corn (although not without enduring a fair amount of ridicule from other bands). Furthermore, the Plains Sioux had historical ties to corn-growing people – eastern Dakotas and Arikaras, for example.[32] Sioux women probably did most of the farm work in the 1880s. In part, this was because of men's antipathy toward farming, but also because Sioux men engaged in work that took them away from the household (see later). Nonetheless, many men – especially older men – took up farming.

Ethel Nurge, "Dakota Diet: Traditional and Contemporary," in *The Modern Sioux: Social Systems and Reservation Culture*, ed. Ethel Nurge (Lincoln, 1970), 35–91.

[30] L. W. Bauer, "Little White River Farming District, An Approximate Report," c. 1887, RA-KC, box A-357, folder labeled "1887." This report noted that there were twenty-two families farming in this particular district. Of these, seventeen had five or fewer acres under cultivation. McLaughlin at Standing Rock reported in 1887 that "every family" was "engaged in cultivating farms ranging in size from garden patches to 40-acre fields, quite a number having between 10 and 15 acres under cultivation, and few have from 20 to 40 acres each." *ARCIA*, 1887, 48.

[31] V. T. McGillycuddy to CIA, 8 Oct. 1883, PR-KC, box 36 (1st qtn.); *ARCIA*, 1887, 18 (2d qtn.).

[32] William K. Powers, *Oglala Religion* (Lincoln, 1975), 26; George E. Hyde, *Spotted Tail's Folk: A History of the Brulé Sioux* (Norman, 1961), 43–44; Julian Rice, *Ella Deloria's "The Buffalo People"* (Albuquerque, 1994), 181–82.

Robert Higheagle, who grew up at Standing Rock, recalled that he often saw grandfathers "out in the fields early in the morning with the hoe."[33]

For decades U.S. officials had talked about a future in which Indian people would support themselves through agriculture. This fantasy was especially absurd when it came to people living on the northern Great Plains where the growing season was short, the soil often poor, and rainfall usually scarce. Most government agents who actually lived in the region eventually grasped these facts. Although some agents feared that cattle raising would retard Indians' progress toward civilization by reinforcing their "nomadic love of roaming," they eventually concluded that this was the only plausible way for them to achieve economic self-sufficiency.[34]

Peter Iverson has pointed out that it was fairly easy for Indian people in North America who were familiar with horses and hunting to adapt to cattle ranching. For men who were raised in a society that measured status by the number of horses owned and valued skill in riding and knowledge of animals, the idea of herding cattle was far more attractive than tending to a patch of corn and melons. Owning several head of cattle provided men with the opportunity to build a reputation for generosity, crucial to achieving prominence.[35]

At Standing Rock and Cheyenne River, the army provided stock cattle as compensation for the confiscation of Sioux ponies in 1876 (see Chapter 4). People did not forget this outrage, but they did start building a livestock population. The government issued 647 cows and 9 bulls at Cheyenne River in 1877 and 1878, resulting in 2,600 head of cattle in 1880 and 5,400 in 1887. In 1890 Cheyenne River Indians provided one-fourth of the beef required for the agency's rations. To White Swan and Charger, leaders at Cheyenne River, stock raising looked like the best road to follow. They requested in 1890 that half of the money the government planned to spend to acquire plows be used to buy stock cattle instead.[36] The increase in these herds was the result of hard work, planning, and knowledge of animals. The Sioux used mowing machines to cut hay, and they constructed stables to shelter

[33] Patricia C. Albers, "Autonomy and Dependency in the Lives of Dakota Women: A Study in Historical Change," *Review of Radical Political Economics* 17, no. 3 (1985): 118–19; Robert Higheagle Manuscript, Campbell Collection, box 113, folder 10, p. 88.

[34] James McLaughlin to My Dear Captain, 25 Apr. 1883, MP, roll 20. By 1889 McLaughlin was "prepared to advocate the abandonment of agriculture, except in the cultivation of vegetable gardens, and have the Indians turn their attention to stock-growing exclusively." *ARCIA*, 1889, 166.

[35] Peter Iverson, *When Indians Became Cowboys: Native Peoples and Cattle Ranching in the American West* (Norman, 1994), 53–54.

[36] Lieut. George Brown to Post Adjt., 14 Aug. 1879, CRA, roll 131; *ARCIA*, 1880, 20; *ARCIA*, 1887, 18; *ARCIA*, 1890, 42; Statement of White Swan and Charger, 2 Jan. 1890, OIA, file 108–1890. At Standing Rock, there were 6,550 cattle in 1891. *ARCIA*, 1891, 325. At Pine Ridge, 500 cows, heifers, and bulls were issued as an "experiment" in 1879. By 1890, the people of Pine Ridge had 10,900 cattle. *ARCIA*, 1880, 40; *ARCIA*, 1890, 51–52.

their animals from cold Dakota winds.[37] After the winter of 1886–1887, the agent at Standing Rock noted that losses of Indian cattle had been about 30 percent. Far more would have died had the Indians not fed their cattle with the bark of cottonwood trees, just as they had fed their horses in seasons past. Losses to non-Indian ranchers in the region were far higher.[38]

Cattle ownership was concentrated in a few hands. The agent at Cheyenne River reported in 1887 that half of the 5,400 cattle there were owned by eight "half breeds," a pattern that probably prevailed at other agencies. Evidence from Pine Ridge indicates that some "full bloods" also had large holdings of livestock. Yet, such concentrations did not exclude widespread ownership of at least some cattle. Most families had a few head by the late 1880s.[39]

In providing Indians with stock cattle, agents wanted them to behave like expectant capitalists. Each family was supposed to calculate the advantages that would come from increasing the size of its own herd so that it could eventually sell surplus animals. Most Sioux, however, thought about their cattle in a broader social context. The Sioux had always recognized certain individual property rights, but proper uses of property – what could be done with a deer that had been killed or with a cow? – were regulated by notions of reciprocal obligations among kin within the *tiyospaye*. Sioux people often gave cattle to needy relatives or killed them for a feast. Such responsibilities could require substantial resources. In June 1887, for example, one thousand people attended a dance at Hump's camp near the mouth of Cherry Creek. All needed to be fed.[40]

Government agents punished Indians who managed their stock cattle in a way inconsistent with the spirit of capitalism. In September 1885 at Pine Ridge, for example, White Horse, He Crow, and Good Boy were found guilty

---

[37] *ARCIA*, 1883, 37; *ARCIA*, 1884, 20; *ARCIA*, 1889, 130; *ARCIA*, 1890, 51–52, 59.

[38] *ARCIA*, 1887, 48–49. In 1890 the Standing Rock agent reported that 5,500 tons of hay had been cut. *ARCIA*, 1890, 37.

[39] *ARCIA*, 1887, 18. Although it is impossible to document the distribution of cattle at any of the other agencies, complaints by the Pine Ridge agent against "squaw men" and "half-breeds" of "cheating full blood Indians out of their stock or stealing it outright" suggest a concentration of cattle along these lines. H. D. Gallagher to CIA, 21 Jan. 1890, PR-KC, box 37. Claims filed at Pine Ridge in 1891 and 1892 by people whose property was destroyed by ghost dancers in late 1890 and early 1891 indicate that most Oglalas had a few head of livestock. This observation is based on my sampling of every tenth (beginning with claim 3) of the 609 claims filed at Pine Ridge, most of which show a claim for at least a few head. It is also noteworthy that Oglala leaders (whose claims did not fall into my sampling sequence, but that I also checked) made claims for fairly large numbers of livestock. For example, Fast Thunder made a claim for fifty-six head of cattle, Young Man Afraid of His Horses filed one for forty-seven head, and American Horse filed a claim for sixty-two head. These claims are enclosed in the report of James A. Cooper, 25 Feb. 1892, OIA, file 7805–1892. These records are described in R. Eli Paul, "Dakota Resources: The Investigation of Special Agent Cooper and Property Damage Claims in the Winter of 1890–91," *South Dakota History* 24 (Fall/Winter 1994): 212–35.

[40] Charles E. McChesney to CIA, 15 June 1887, OIA, file 15967–1887.

of shooting stock cattle and sentenced to a fine of $30 or fifty days hard la-bor.[41] These men were not incapable of planning for the future, but they found other needs more compelling. In this way, too, Sioux economic strate-gies showed continuity with earlier ways of life. Nonetheless, Sioux people did not simply enact a cultural script that conformed to a static set of values. The opportunities and pressures of colonialism encouraged some Sioux to contest "customary" notions of proper behavior and to begin to move in the direction of individual acquisitiveness. Those who moved this way, however, were subject to community discipline. "[O]ut of spite or revenge," the Pine Ridge agent reported, "evil-disposed Indians have . . . maimed or killed their neighbor's cattle."[42]

The western Sioux also increased their horse herds in the 1880s. Even though the army took away most of the horses of the Cheyenne River Indians in 1876, they did not confiscate those belonging to mixed-bloods and squaw men. Through trade with these people and perhaps with Indians from other reservations, other Cheyenne River Indians reacquired horses. In 1878 there were only 606 horses reported at Cheyenne River, but this number increased to 2,785 in 1887.[43] At Pine Ridge Red Cloud remained angry about the army's confiscation of his people's horses in 1876, but the government had not taken horses from all Oglala bands. By 1889 over 9,000 horses were reported at Pine Ridge.[44]

Because Indians depended upon reservation rangeland to graze their horses and cattle, they tried to prevent encroachments by outside stock. In 1887 the agent at Rosebud determined that there were 2,500 head of non-Indian-owned cattle grazing illegally north of the Nebraska state line, on the southeastern part of the reservation. According to the agent, when the Brulés contested the ranchers' practices, the ranchers said they would pay 25¢ per head to graze on the reserve. But Brulés vetoed this plan, first because they wanted $1.00 per head, second, because they feared that any funds collected would disappear in Washington. When non-Indians contin-ued to graze on their land, Brulés burned the grass to stop them. The agent tried to prevent illegal grazing, but it was difficult to do so. His entire force of Indian police would have had to patrol the range, impossible in view of their other responsibilities. Not surprisingly, then, illegal grazing continued. In 1889 Swift Bear and other Brulés protested to the Commissioner of Indian

---

[41] V. T. McGillycuddy to CIA, 19 Sept. 1885, PR-KC, box 36. See also Cheyenne River Agency Diary, 14 May 1888. On the frequency of killing stock cattle and regulations against it, see also Acting CIA to V. T. McGillycuddy, 16 May 1885, PR-KC, box 7; *ARCIA*, 1889, 156.

[42] *ARCIA*, 1884, 37. The Standing Rock agent also reported three arrests for "maiming cattle" in *ARCIA*, 1890, 41.

[43] Theodore Schwan, "Number Head Domestic Animals on Cheyenne River Indian Reserva-tion," 10 Nov. 1878, CRA, roll 130; *ARCIA*, 1887, 18. Of the twenty-eight people listed as having horses in Schwan's 1878 report, seven, listed as "Indian" and of mixed ancestry, accounted for 440 of the 606 head.

[44] *ARCIA*, 1889, 156.

Affairs that "the whole country in the vicinity of Turtle Creek has been covered with cattle belonging to parties residing in Nebraska, many of whom are professional cattle and horse thieves."[45]

Thus far, we have seen the Plains Sioux working in a variety of ways to feed themselves and to prevent government initiatives that would diminish treaty rations. They also creatively exploited the limited opportunities of the reservation economy.

One important source of income in the 1880s was hauling freight. This practice originated in fall 1878 when the government employed two hundred men to carry supplies from the Missouri to the new Rosebud and Pine Ridge agencies. Those hauling to Rosebud were paid 25¢ per hundred pounds; those to Pine Ridge received $30 per month.[46] What began as an improvisation to meet the exigencies of a particular situation quickly became institutionalized. As soon as the first wagons arrived at the agencies, they were sent back to the Missouri and to the rail station at Sidney, Nebraska. Soon, the agents were calling for the government to issue additional wagons so that more Lakotas could haul freight. By October 1879, Oglalas had carried 2 million pounds of freight and earned $41,000; the Rosebud agent reported in August 1880 that all the freighting for the agency was being done by Indians. Government officials usually imagined that Indians would learn the arts of civilization behind a plow, not a freight wagon. But the discourse of civilization required them to admit that any kind of labor was a step in the right direction. Indeed, government observers were ecstatic about the success of the "experiment" of Indian freighting. Not only had "the most sanguine expectations as to cheap transportation been fully realized," wrote one official, but the "Indians' hereditary prejudice against labor has been broken down."[47]

The Sioux would have been surprised by the idea that they had never worked before. They embraced this particular form of labor not because they had undergone some moral transformation, but because it provided a practical way to obtain wagons, it was a source of income, and it offered some freedom of movement. Indeed, they found freighting attractive precisely because it required rather little alteration in the patterns of their lives, unlike some other government schemes for their improvement.

[45] L. F. Spencer to CIA, 23 June 1887, RA-KC, book 13; Swift Bear et al. to CIA, 13 Apr. 1889, RA-KC, book 15. Trespassing was also a problem at Pine Ridge and Cheyenne River. See A. J. Willard to SI, 23 Apr. 1888, OIA, file 10868–1888; H. D. Gallagher to Acting CIA, 15 June 1888, PR-KC, box 54; Charles E. McChesney to CIA, 5 July 1886, OIA, file 17906–1886.

[46] William J. Pollock to CIA, 6 Oct. 1878, STA, roll 843; James Irwin to CIA, 11 Nov. 1878, RCA, roll 723.

[47] J. H. Hammond to CIA, 5 Dec. 1878, RCA, roll 722; V. T. McGillycuddy to CIA, 16 May 1879, RCA, roll 724; *ARCIA*, 1879, 39; *ARCIA*, 1880, 45; William J. Pollock to CIA, 31 Jan. 1879, STA, roll 844 (qtn.).

Hauling freight continued to be a significant source of income in the 1880s. From 1884 to 1890, Rosebud freighters moved more than 2 million pounds year from the railhead at Valentine, Nebraska, earning an annual average of about $14,000.[48] In the early 1880s between 700 and 800 Pine Ridge freighters netted between $35,000 and $41,000 annually, but after 1885, when the railroad was extended west to Rushville, only twenty-five miles south of the agency, their earnings dropped substantially. Reports for 1888 and 1890 show that total income from freighting at Pine Ridge was around $10,000 per year.[49] At Standing Rock and Cheyenne River agencies on the Missouri, there was no freighting until the late 1880s, when the government started to ship some supplies via rail (to Mandan for Standing Rock and Pierre for Cheyenne River), resulting in total annual earnings of around $3,000.[50] Some evidence indicates that the agents tried to control the allocation of freighting work so that they could use it to encourage (or compel) certain kinds of behavior. In 1890, for example, the Pine Ridge agent reported that he tried to give the work to Indians who had previously invested their income in farm implements and household goods.[51]

Sioux people earned small amounts of income from several other activities. For example, Corabelle Fellows, a day school teacher at Swift Bird's camp at Cheyenne River, informed the agent in 1884 that Hairy Dog Bear had "finished chopping his five cords of wood for the school. It is all measured correct, and good wood as far as I am a judge. I measured it myself and believe it five good cords. He did it as I directed and at your terms $4.00 a cord, making $20.00 coming to him." In 1889 the Standing Rock agent reported that during the previous year Indians had sold 1,800 cords to the agency and to a military contractor. At Cheyenne River, Charger's band regularly sold wood to Missouri River steamboats.[52] Other Indians sold hay to feed to agency livestock.[53]

Some men and women worked directly for the government. At Standing Rock, for example, Indian laborers hauled water from the Missouri River

[48] *ARCIA*, 1885, 41; *ARCIA*, 1886, 297; *ARCIA*, 1888, 54; *ARCIA*, 1889, 161; *ARCIA*, 1890, 59.

[49] *ARCIA*, 1881, 47–48; *ARCIA*, 1883, 35; *ARCIA*, 1884, 38; *ARCIA*, 1885, 35; *ARCIA*, 1888, 50; *ARCIA*, 1890, 51.

[50] *ARCIA*, 1888, 59; *ARCIA*, 1889, 170.

[51] *ARCIA*, 1890, 51.

[52] Corabelle Fellows to C. E. McChesney, 27 Oct. 1884, CR-KC, box 232; *ARCIA*, 1889, 169; Samuel Charger, "Biography of Martin Charger," *South Dakota Historical Collections* 22 (1946): 20. For other examples, see Charles E. McChesney to CIA, 27 Aug. 1888, OIA, file 21979–1888; Capt. J. W. Bell to CIA, 12 July 1886, PR-KC, box 36.

[53] For example, CIA to Charles E. McChesney, 17 Feb. 1886, CR-KC, box 265, authorized $56 to purchase hay "for subsistence of ponies belonging to the Indian police." CIA to L. F. Spencer, 29 July 1889, RA-KC, box A-358, authorized purchase of one hundred tons of baled hay at $10 per ton and thirty tons of stacked hay at $4.50 per ton for "Agency and police stock." Both these documents specified that purchases were to be made from Indians.

for use at the agency. When a new water system was constructed in 1889, they dug trenches for it. Indians plowed and harvested the agency farm, herded agency livestock, and put up fences.[54] They built houses, schools, and other agency buildings, made harnesses, repaired wagons, and worked on the agency police force. By the late 1880s a few taught in the government and mission day schools.[55]

Much of this work was casual labor at a rate as low as 50¢ per day, though some work paid more. In 1888 the five assistant carpenters at Standing Rock earned between $120 and $360 per year (an apprentice carpenter made $60); other semiskilled workers received similar rates. The captain of the police and his two lieutenants made $15 per month; the twenty-four privates, $10. The annual salary for teachers was $600; for assistant teachers it was $480.[56] The best jobs went to mixed bloods and relatives of prominent leaders, especially those whom agents regarded as "progressive" or were trying to co-opt. Some positions went to students who returned from off-reservation boarding schools such as Carlisle and Hampton or who had graduated from the on-reservation industrial and agricultural schools. Men held by far the majority of agency jobs. There were, however, some female teachers in the 1880s.[57] Women also did some domestic work at the agencies' headquarters.[58]

Protestant and Catholic missions also provided a few opportunities for paid labor. In 1882, for example, female missionaries at Oahe, a Congregational mission at Cheyenne River, were paying a young Sioux woman 50¢ for washing and 25¢ for ironing. Lakotas also helped build a Catholic church for the St. Francis mission at Rosebud in 1890. Although the priests hoped that Indians would "haul stones for a house for the Great Spirit" without requesting earthly benefits, the fathers eventually had to pay them to accomplish God's work.[59]

[54] James McLaughlin to CIA, 8 May 1888, 5 Dec. 1889, MP, roll 33.

[55] CIA to James McLaughlin, 3 July 1890, SR-KC, box 303; McLaughlin to CIA, 8 May 1888; CIA to James McLaughlin, 21 Oct. 1890, SR-KC, box 303; *ARCIA*, 1888, 60–62.

[56] "Report of Irregular Employees at Standing Rock Agency Dakota for the Month Ending June 30, 1879," SRA, roll 851; McLaughlin to CIA, 8 May 1888; CIA to McLaughlin, 21 Oct. 1890; *ARCIA*, 1888, 61–62.

[57] Of the six Indian teachers at Standing Rock in 1888, three (Jennie Primeau, Maria L. Van Solen, and Rosa Bearface) were female. *ARCIA*, 1888, 61–62.

[58] Cheyenne River Agency Diary, 1 Aug. 1886, for example, noted that "Mrs. Eagle Man commenced cooking for prisoners at noon." H. D. Gallagher to CIA, 24 Mar. 1890, PR-KC, box 37, wrote that he intended to fill the positions of assistant cook, assistant laundress, and assistant seamstress with "Indian girls of the proper age who had made a meritorious record" at Carlisle.

[59] Louisa Irvine to Mary C. Collins, 26 Jan. 1882, South Dakota Conference United Church of Christ Archives, Oahe Mission Collection, box 16, Center for Western Studies, Augustana College, Sioux Falls, S.Dak.; Digmann, "History of the St. Francis Mission," 17.

There were few opportunities for employment off the reservation. In fall 1887 fourteen men from Standing Rock labored for about two weeks on a Missouri River steamship at the rate of $1 per day, but such work was unusual.[60] Although some Sioux may have worked occasionally for non-Indian ranchers, there is little evidence of much off-reservation labor in the 1880s.[61] Most settlers were too poor to hire extra labor. On her trip to the Sand Hills in 1889, Elaine Goodale and her Sioux companions encountered several pioneer families living in "soddies," their children in rags and without shoes. One morning several settlers called upon the Indians "to try to 'make a trade,'" offering "broken-down hacks and worthless old shotguns." No wonder Lakotas "showed some contempt for the white man's poverty."[62]

The only significant source of off-reservation income in the 1880s was through Wild West shows. At a time when Americans were demanding that the Sioux cease being Indian, it is ironic that many of them found employment in an American industry that paid them for being the most "Indian" of all Indians.[63] William "Buffalo Bill" Cody opened his first show in 1883. At first, Cody hired Pawnees to entertain audiences by attacking the Deadwood mail coach. For the 1885 season, Cody added to his list of employees the most famous Indian name in all of North America, Sitting Bull, giving the "renowned Sioux chief" second billing just below himself.[64]

Sitting Bull did not so much perform in these shows as occupy iconic space. Instead of having him participate in attacks on the ever-imperiled Deadwood stage or kill Custer, Cody used him to introduce the show, displaying him prominently in the opening parade and introducing him to (often jeering) crowds. Sitting Bull's role was simply to stand expressionlessly in buckskin, paint, and a headdress, thus to be viewed as an ethnographic display, a sign of authenticity, and captive to civilization. For his services from June to October 1885, Cody paid Sitting Bull $50 a week and a bonus of $125 (the other five Hunkpapas who accompanied Sitting Bull were paid $25 a month).[65]

When Cody wanted to employ Sitting Bull again for the 1886 season James McLaughlin, the Standing Rock agent, refused to give permission.

---

[60] Issac P. Baker to James McLaugh[li]n, 14 Apr. 1888, SR-KC, box 302.

[61] Not until the 1920s and 1930s did non-Indian ranchers and farmers in Nebraska began to employ Lakotas from Pine Ridge and Rosebud. See Gregory Gagnon and Karen White Eyes, *Pine Ridge Reservation: Yesterday and Today* (Interior, S.Dak., 1992), 21; DeMallie, "Pine Ridge Economy," 259, 263.

[62] Graber, ed., *Sister to the Sioux*, 98–99.

[63] Phyllis Rogers, "'Buffalo Bill' and the Siouan Image," *American Indian Culture and Research Journal* 7, no. 3 (1983): 43–53, argues that the Wild West shows created the image of the Sioux as standing for all Indians.

[64] L. G. Moses, *Wild West Shows and the Images of American Indians, 1883–1933* (Albuquerque, 1996), 21–27, 30.

[65] Ibid., 27; Don Russell, *The Lives and Legends of Buffalo Bill* (Norman, 1960), 316.

Cody then went to Pine Ridge, where he hired twenty-nine men at $25 per month to accompany his show.[66] Although Cody obtained authority from the Indian Office to hire these people, over the next few years agents from Cody's and other shows descended on Nebraska towns like Rushville and Gordon to recruit Oglalas, often without the government's authorization. In 1889, the Pine Ridge agent complained that there were more than two hundred Oglalas away "for the circus, Wild West exhibitions, [and] quackmedicine business." Half of these "are absent... without permission from the Department."[67]

It is difficult to determine the actual economic benefits Indians gained from working in Wild West shows. At the rate of $25 per month, the two hundred Oglalas employed by the shows in 1889 would have made a total of $5,000 per month. Assuming an average stint of four months, they would have netted an aggregate of $20,000, an amount twice that earned by freighting the same year. (Some were away much longer, especially those who went to Europe.)[68] If a good portion of this money returned to the reservation, it would have been a significant economic benefit to many families. The Pine Ridge agent argued that Oglala communities gained little from the shows. In "the great majority of cases," he contended, Indians traveling with shows "do not send a dollar home to their families during their absence," and almost always they "return to their homes perfect wrecks physically, morally, and financially." Although people employed by the shows undoubtedly spent a good portion of their pay, the Pine Ridge agent's assessment of the situation, so obviously colored by his opposition to Indians leaving the reservation, seems extreme. There is every reason to think that show Indians sent some of the money they earned back to the reservation. Furthermore, Cody's contracts generally included a "hold back" provision, by which Indians received one-third of their wages upon returning home.[69]

Cody's and other Wild West shows provided some economic advantages to Indians and offered an opportunity to gain knowledge of other parts of the world. Cody and others treated their employees reasonably well. However, any assessment of these enterprises must take into account the fact that they exploited colonial conditions to create economic and cultural capital. Furthermore, by legitimizing America's history of conquest, the shows

---

[66] Moses, *Wild West Shows*, 31–32.

[67] *ARCIA*, 1889, 153. According to H. D. Gallagher to CIA, 17 Apr. 1889, PR-KC, box 36, sixty-two Indians left the agency without permission with the Kickapoo Medicine Co. Other outfits that recruited near Pine Ridge were Adam Forepaugh's circus and Carver's Wild America. H. D. Gallagher to CIA, 8 May 1888, PR-KC, box 36; "List of Indians Absent," c. July 1889, PR-KC, box 36; H. D. Gallagher to CIA, 17 Apr. 1890, PR-KC, box 37.

[68] For a discussion of Indians' experiences and perceptions of Europe while traveling with the shows, see Rita G. Napier, "Across the Big Water: American Indians' Perceptions of Europe and Europeans, 1887–1906," in *Indians and Europe: An Interdisciplinary Collection of Essays*, ed. Christian F. Feast (Aaachen, 1987), 383–401.

[69] *ARCIA*, 1889, 153; Moses, *Wild West Shows*, 199.

sanctioned the ongoing subordination of Indian people as well as laying the cultural groundwork for overseas imperialism.[70]

In addition to working for wages, Indians also gained income through trading their own products. One important source of income was beadwork. Western Sioux women began using beads to decorate robes, shirts, pipe bags, cradles, and moccasins as early as the late 1700s. Beadwork expanded steadily from the 1860s through the 1890s. A portion of this growth can be attributed to the conditions of enforced idleness for women in the early reservation period. At Pine Ridge, for example, it was a common joke during this time that "if anything didn't move, an Oglala woman would bead it." Although most beadwork circulated within the nonmarket economy of the *tiyospaye*, women produced some beadwork for sale or trade to settlers. One authority notes that settlers "often furnished the garment to be decorated and dictated the style."[71]

Sioux people also sold objects such as pipes, drums, war shirts, war clubs, and shields to collectors of Indian artifacts. At the 1881 Pine Ridge Sun Dance, for example, Lieutenant John G. Bourke purchased several pipes and was offered, but apparently declined to buy, a wooden "medicine saucer." In addition, some Native artists sold ledger drawings.[72] Although these transactions were to some extent "voluntary," they occurred in the context of government policies that both limited the value of some of the items Indians traded (a war shield had little practical use in 1881) and shaped the economic conditions that pressured Indians into trading. Overall, collections of Indian artifacts were not built primarily with items acquired through trade. Bourke obtained several items in his collection as a result of the army's raid on Dull Knife's village in November 1876.[73]

[70] Richard White, "Frederick Jackson Turner and Buffalo Bill," in *The Frontier in American Culture: An Exhibition at the Newberry Library, August 26, 1994–January 7, 1995: Essays by Richard White and Patricia Nelson Limerick*, ed. James R. Grossman (Berkeley, 1994), 27, 39; Jonathan D. Martin, "'The Grandest and Most Cosmopolitan Object Teacher': *Buffalo Bill's Wild West* and the Politics of American Identity, 1883–1899," *Radical History Review* 66 (Fall 1996): 115–19.

[71] Richard Conn, *A Persistent Vision: Art of the Reservation Days* (Denver, 1986), 56–58. Marla N. Powers, *Oglala Women: Myth, Ritual, and Reality* (Chicago, 1986), 137 (1st qtn.); Graber, ed., *Sister to the Sioux*, 98, 105; Carrie A. Lyford, *Quill and Beadwork of the Western Sioux* (Lawrence, 1940), 58 (2d qtn.). For a discussion of the production of beadwork during this period by Kiowa women, see Jacki Thompson Rand, "Primary Sources: Indian Goods and the History of American Colonialism and the 19th-Century Reservation," in *Clearing a Path: Theorizing the Past in Native American Studies*, ed. Nancy Shoemaker (New York, 2002), 151–53.

[72] John G. Bourke diary, 22 June 1881, vol. 41, roll 3, 1528, United States Military Academy Library, West Point, N.Y. (microfilm); Janet Catherine Berlo, "A Brief History of Lakota Drawings, 1870–1935," in *Plains Indian Drawings, 1865–1935: Pages from a Visual History*, ed. Janet Catherine Berlo (New York, 1996), 34–39.

[73] Joseph C. Porter, *Paper Medicine Man: John Gregory Bourke and His American West* (Norman, 1986), 64. According to Luther Standing Bear, *My People the Sioux*, ed. E. A.

In their reports to Washington, agents praised some Indians for their willing-ness to work, but they castigated others for sitting around eating government beef, drinking government coffee, and telling stories about the good old days. (Especially clever agents coined phrases such as the "ancient order of aborig-inal coffee coolers" to ridicule people who resisted their efforts to improve them.)[74] The problem with the agents' division of their colonial subjects into two groups – those who worked and those who did not – was not so much that it flunked the test of cultural relativism (as if refusing to work was culturally prized) as that it was empirically false. All Sioux people engaged in various forms of productive labor during the 1880s.

In addition to social labor, such as bearing and raising children, tending to the sick, making clothing, and preparing foods, Sioux people hunted, gath-ered, planted, and harvested. To gain extra income, they sold hides, hauled freight, cut wood, made beadwork, built schools and houses, and worked for the government. This income was vital to their economic strategies because it allowed them to obtain additional food, clothing, and guns and ammunition for hunting beyond what the government provided through treaty rations and annuities. Sioux people also used their income to purchase things like tobacco, colored cloth, beads, dye (for face painting), coffee, shawls, and saddles. These items were not strictly necessary in terms of life or death, but they marked the difference between simple survival and the hope of liv-ing well.[75] Extra income was also crucial for collective projects. When six Brulés were arrested for stealing horses and killing a non-Indian in 1880, Rosebud Indians raised $332.80 to hire lawyers for their defense. Eight years later, when Cheyenne River Indians heard of yet another government scheme to take more of their land, they collected $400 to send their leaders to Washington.[76]

Depending on their means and inclinations, individuals and groups pursued different economic strategies. Because of access to weapons and

---

Brininstool (1928; Lincoln, 1975), 210, an agent at Rosebud acquired "a great many Indian relics" by illegally trading government-issue horses.

[74] V. T. McGillycuddy to whom it may concern, 23 Apr. 1883, PR-KC, box 53.

[75] These are some of the items from a list provided by O. M. Carter, 1 May 1880, STA, roll 845. On the use of dye for face and body painting, see J. B. Tripp Jr., "Rosebud before 1905," in *Early Dakota Days: Stories and Pictures of Pioneers, Cowboys, Indians,* comp. Winifred Reutter (White River, S.Dak., 1962), 214. Government-licensed and off-reservation traders undoubtedly gouged their customers when they could. However, because there was some competition among traders, Lakotas were able to exercise leverage. Traders noted that to retain Indians' business, they had to offer a *"sinte"* (tail), a small present at the end of each transaction, which added significantly to their costs each year. See E. D. Pratt to CIA, 21 June 1878, STA, roll 843; Oscar M. Carter to John Cook, 31 May 1880, STA, roll 845. H. D. Gallagher to CIA, 15 Sept. 1887, PR-KC, box 36, argued that between the three licensed traders at Pine Ridge and traders at nearby towns, there was too much competition.

[76] John Cook to CIA, 7 Aug. 1880, RA-KC, book 8; Spotted Tail to SI, 1 Oct. 1880, RA-KC, book 8; Charles E. McChesney to CIA, 25 Jan. 1888, OIA, file 2800–1888.

proximity to game, some Sioux were able to hunt more than others. Some were able to earn money by freighting or cutting wood. Others did not have these opportunities or chose not to pursue them. Clearly, some families within particular communities had greater wealth than others and some communities were economically better off than others. But all western Sioux communities pursued strategies that involved some combination of the activities discussed earlier. It was not so much the divergence in these strategies themselves that caused government agents to divide Indians into "progressives" who worked and "nonprogressives" who did not. These categories were political labels, which agents applied according to positions leaders took on issues such as allotment, education, and cultural transformation.

The Plains Sioux probably found some kinds of work enjoyable. Gardening, caring for horses, or freighting offered many people a certain measure of autonomy and satisfaction. Even under the best conditions, however, the Sioux struggled to survive. In 1883 a member of a government commission asked Charger, a Sans Arcs leader at Cheyenne River, if the Indians at his agency "want to learn to work and be like white men." Charger replied, "I am trying to be like a white man," but "I work so much it makes me poor."[77] Many forms of labor revealed the brutal facts of colonial domination. Not only was hauling water for the Standing Rock Agency back breaking and mind numbing, it must have been deeply alienating for people to place their bodies in the service of those who had taken their land and thought of themselves as a superior race. It also must have been painful to go onto the prairie and gather the bleached bones of buffalo and other animals as many Brulés did in 1886. The 330 tons of bones the Brulés collected and hauled to Valentine to be shipped to fertilizer factories provided an important source of income. At the same time, however, each bone gathered was a bitter reminder of all that had been lost.[78]

---

[77] *Testimony Taken by a Select Committee*, 100.
[78] James Wright to CIA, 4 Sept. 1886, RA-KC, book 12. For a discussion of the bison bone trade on the upper Missouri, see LeRoy Barnett, "Ghastly Harvest: Montana's Trade in Buffalo Bones," *Montana: The Magazine of Western History* 25 (Summer 1975): 2–13.

7

"Just as Well with My Hair on"
Colonial Education

In September 1879 Richard Henry Pratt, a balding former soldier, traveled
to Rosebud Agency to announce his intention to take several Sioux children
to his new boarding school at Carlisle, Pennsylvania. After Pratt explained
his purpose, Spotted Tail replied in words something like these: *Wasicun
kin oyasin wamawicanons'a na iwicatonpisni.* When this statement was
translated – "The white people are all thieves and liars" – and when Spotted Tail went on to say that Brulés did not want their children to learn to
steal and lie, Pratt must have worried that his mission would fail. Eventually, though, he persuaded Spotted Tail, Two Strike, Milk, White Thunder,
and others to send some of their children to Carlisle. Pratt then went to Pine
Ridge where he secured additional students. He left Sioux country with sixty
boys and twenty-four girls.[1]

The Carlisle Indian Industrial School was a particularly visible manifestation of a shift in European Americans' thinking about the process of assimilation. In earlier decades, it was assumed that the transition from "savagery"
to "civilization" would be slow and would depend on prolonged separation
of Indians from contaminating influences of civilization. By the 1870s, however, with the completion of the transcontinental railroad, the continent's
resources were available for incorporation into a rapidly developing industrial empire. It no longer seemed possible for western Indians to remain
separate from American life. As ethnographer Alice Fletcher wrote, "the Indian is caught in the rush of our modern life, and there is no time for him to
dally with the serious questions that are upon him." As never before, Indians
would have to change or be overwhelmed.[2]

---

[1] Richard Henry Pratt, *Battlefield and Classroom: Four Decades with the American Indian,
1867–1904*, edited and with an introduction by Robert M. Utley (New Haven, 1964), 221–
26 (qtn., 222); David Wallace Adams, *Education for Extinction: American Indians and the
Boarding School Experience, 1875–1928* (Lawrence, 1995), 48.

[2] Frederick E. Hoxie, *A Final Promise: The Campaign to Assimilate the Indians, 1880–1920*
(Lincoln, 1984), 43–44 (qtn., 27–28).

Shifts in theories of social evolution facilitated the notion that assimilation could be accomplished with relative ease. Although John Wesley Powell, the most influential anthropological thinker of the late nineteenth century, persisted in seeing a wide gap between primitive and civilized peoples and was pessimistic about Indian capacities to make progress, others imagined that the transformation process could be accelerated. The key was to establish the proper environment. Thus, reformers called for the government to abolish reservations, force Indians to take up individual allotments, and establish an educational program that would remove Native American children from tribal influences and quickly transform them into American citizens. Armed with certain knowledge of their own superiority, boundless optimism in humanity's plasticity, and unflappable confidence in their ability to direct social evolution, the "friends of the Indians" launched the most comprehensive and sustained assault on Native ways of life in U.S. history.[3]

No one was more sanguine about the uses of social engineering than Richard Henry Pratt. All that was required, in his opinion, was the destruction of reservations and the exposure of detribalized Indians to American institutions. Pratt went so far as to propose that the government take all the Indians in the United States and distribute an equal number to each county. In the meantime, Pratt was able to gain government authorization for a more modest proposal. Citing his success teaching Indian prisoners at Fort Marion, Florida, Pratt persuaded the army to let him take some of the prisoners to Hampton Institute, established in 1868 to educate free blacks. He also secured permission to recruit additional students from western reservations. Fearing that the American public would not accept Indians if they were associated with African Americans, however, Pratt began searching for an alternative to Hampton. Eventually, the army allowed him to use the abandoned military barracks at Carlisle.[4]

---

[3] Ibid., 17–39; Curtis M. Hinsley Jr., *Savages and Scientists: The Smithsonian Institution and the Development of American Anthropology, 1846–1910* (Washington, D.C., 1981), 125–43; George W. Stocking Jr., *Race, Culture, and Evolution: Essays in the History of Anthropology* (1968; Chicago, 1982), 116, 128–29. For the ideas and activities of Indian reformers in the late 1870s and 1880s, see also Loring Benson Priest, *Uncle Sam's Stepchildren: The Reformation of United States Indian Policy, 1865–1887* (New Brunswick, 1942), 66–252; Henry Eugene Fritz, *The Movement for Indian Assimilation, 1860–1890* (Philadelphia, 1963), 198–221; Robert Winston Mardock, *The Reformers and the American Indian* (Columbia, Mo., 1971), 192–210; Wilbert H. Ahern, "Assimilationist Racism: The Case of the 'Friends of the Indian,'" *Journal of Ethnic Studies* 4 (Summer 1976): 23–32; Francis Paul Prucha, *The Great Father: The United States Government and the American Indians*, 2 vols. (Lincoln, 1984), 2:609–715; Alexandra Harmon, "When Is an Indian Not an Indian?: The 'Friends of the Indian' and the Problems of Indian Identity," *Journal of Ethnic Studies* 18 (Summer 1990): 95–123.

[4] Prucha, *Great Father*, 2:695–97; Donal F. Lindsey, *Indians at Hampton Institute, 1877–1923* (Urbana, 1995), 6–9, 27–30. Matthew G. Hannah, "Space and Social Control in the Administration of the Oglala Lakota ('Sioux'), 1871–1879," *Journal of Historical Geography* 19, no. 4 (1993): 427, further points out that keeping children at Carlisle would allow the

The Sioux parents who allowed their children to go to Carlisle probably did not fully grasp Pratt's larger agenda, as he infamously phrased it before an audience of reformers, to "kill the Indian...and save the man." In September 1879 Pratt said nothing to Sioux leaders about his theories of social evolution and their implications for cultural destruction. Instead, he spoke to them of the practical advantages of education. Not only could educated young men earn high wages stringing telegraph wires, they could "write letters for you, interpret for you, and help look after your business affairs in Washington." Indeed, had the Sioux been educated, Pratt suggested, the Black Hills might not have "passed from you." Ironically, this argument conceded Spotted Tail's point that whites were liars and thieves. Indians would need to educate themselves so that they could effectively counter European-American mendacity.[5]

It was not as though Sioux leaders had never thought about these issues. Far more than Pratt, they wanted their people to prosper and to develop effective means of countering future government initiatives to take more of their land. Unlike Pratt, in fact, they thought education might eventually help them *recover* stolen land. When Sioux leaders thought about schools, however, they assumed these would be built on their reservation. One of their main concerns about Carlisle was its location. Not only was it painful for parents to contemplate not seeing their children for years, but also they must have wondered what would it be like for them to travel so far from home. Would they arrive safely? And, once at Carlisle, what would it be like for them to be separated from their families and ways of life? Would they get sick and die? Would Pratt really teach them useful things? Parents surely knew he would make their children wear "white man's clothing," but did they realize he was planning to cut their hair?

As parents surely anticipated, their children's journey to Carlisle was distressing, even traumatic. One boy who traveled east in fall 1879 was Standing Bear's son, Kills Plenty. He later recalled that when he and his companions got off the train in (of all places) Sioux City, Iowa, they were greeted by a large crowd of onlookers, who "tried to give the war-whoop and mimic the Indian." Two years earlier, when the Sioux delegates to Washington had arrived in Chicago, they too had been greeted by "war whoops." Whereas adult men had been able to laugh, however, the children naturally became

government to exercise leverage over parents and thus "encourage good behavior." According to Elaine Goodale Eastman, *Pratt: The Red Man's Moses* (Norman, 1935), 221, Pratt stated in 1884: "There are about 260,000 Indians in the United States, and there are 2,700 counties. I would like to divide them up in the proportion of about nine Indians to a county." I am grateful to the mathematician Joseph Fracchia for pointing out the error in Pratt's division.

5 Isabel C. Barrows, ed., *Proceedings of the National Conference of Charities and Correction at the Nineteenth Annual Session Held in Denver, Col., June 23–29, 1892* (Boston, 1892), 46 (1st qtn.); Pratt, *Battlefield and Classroom*, 223 (other qtns.).

"wrought up and excited, and...did not like this sort of treatment." Later, as the train continued east, the "big boys were singing brave songs, expecting to be killed any minute."[6]

As an institution of assimilation, Carlisle was designed not merely to teach Indians the three R's but to remake them at their very core. One aspect of this project involved renaming. Soon after his arrival at Carlisle, Kills Plenty's teacher wrote several words on a blackboard. An interpreter explained that each of the words was "a white man's name." The students were to come, one by one, and point to one of the names, which would then be his own. The first boy who was summoned was unsure what to do and looked at the others as if to say "Is it right for me to take a white man's name?" After a long time, he uneasily pointed to one of the names. The teacher then wrote the name on a piece of tape and sewed it on the back of the boy's shirt. When Kills Plenty's turn came, he pointed to the name "Luther." At the end of the day, there was a roomful of Sioux boys with the "names of white men sewed on our backs."[7]

Some days later, an interpreter told Kills Plenty (now Luther Standing Bear) and the other boys that a barber would soon arrive. That evening Robert American Horse protested to a group of boys, "If I am to learn the ways of the white people, I can do it just as well with my hair on." The students resolved to resist, but there was little they could do. On the appointed day, the boys were summoned one by one from their classroom to an adjacent room. Luther Standing Bear never forgot how the barber "motioned me to sit down" nor the moment when he "commenced to work." When it was over, "it hurt my feelings to such an extent that the tears came into my eyes." He could not recall whether the barber "noticed my agitation or not, nor did I care. All I was thinking about was that hair he had taken away from me."[8]

Hair cutting was painful for many reasons. Zitkala-Ša (Red Bird), an eight-year-old Yankton Sioux girl sent to a Quaker missionary school, objected to having her hair cut because "among our people, short hair was worn by mourners, and shingled hair by cowards." More immediate, though, was the way the ordeal affected the body. Years later, Zitkala-Ša could still recall "the cold blades of the scissors against my neck" and the sound of the blades "gnaw off one of my thick braids." After this, she "lost my spirit" and felt like "one of many little animals driven by a herder." When Luther Standing

---

[6] Luther Standing Bear, *My People the Sioux*, ed. E. A. Brininstool (1928; Lincoln, 1975), 130–31; *Chicago Tribune*, 22 Sept. 1877, p. 2.

[7] Standing Bear, *My People*, 137. For an overview of students' initial responses to Indian boarding schools, see Michael C. Coleman, *American Indian Children at School, 1850–1930* (Jackson, Miss., 1993), 79–100.

[8] Standing Bear, *My People*, 140–41.

Bear became "bald-headed," he felt he was "no more [an] Indian, but would be an imitation of a white man." Overall, hair cutting was probably the most traumatic of boarding schools' operations in identity transformation. By contrast, when students began to wear "civilized" clothing, they often complained that it was uncomfortable, but they did not find it nearly as invasive as losing their hair.[9]

Besides having to assume the external trappings of civilization, students were subjected to a daily routine of what David Wallace Adams refers to as "relentless regimentation." Every activity was governed by an exacting schedule, signaled by bells and bugles, each with rules, regulations, commands, and penalties for infractions. Constant military drilling reinforced this regime. In these ways, boarding schools were similar to the modern prison. Both tried to produce, in Michel Foucault's terms, "subjected and practised bodies."[10] In the end, however, boarding schools were not able to achieve their ultimate goal of complete transformation. Standing Bear's phrase – an *imitation* of a white man – is revealing of both the boarding schools' power and its limits. In the long run, hair cutting and other alterative procedures did not ultimately destroy the identity of Indian children. In large measure this was because of the resilience of students themselves. Zitkala-Ša eventually recovered her spirit and, like Luther Standing Bear, became an advocate for Indian people in the outside world. Indeed, by bringing together Indian people from many different communities, boarding schools often encouraged the emergence of a pantribal Indian identity.[11] Contradictions within American culture could also limit the power of boarding schools. Cutting the hair of young boys and girls met assimilation's requirements of transformation *and* imitation, but teenage girls with short hair were poor copies of prevailing norms. Thus, boarding schools usually allowed girls in their teens to keep their hair long, although they had to adopt styles that conformed to standards of middle-class Anglo-American femininity.[12] Overall, however, although boarding schools did not destroy Indian identity, many

[9] Agnes M. Picotte, foreword to Zitkala-Ša, *Old Indian Legends* (1901; Lincoln, 1985), xii; Zitkala-Ša, "The School Days of an Indian Girl," *The Atlantic Monthly* 85 (February 1900): 187; Standing Bear, *My People*, 141; Adams, *Education for Extinction*, 103–08.

[10] Adams, *Education for Extinction*, 117–21 (qtn., 117); Michel Foucault, *Discipline and Punish: The Birth of the Prison*, trans. Alan Sheridan (New York, 1979), 138.

[11] Picotte, foreword to Zitkala-Ša, *Old Indian Legends*, xiii–xvi; Frederick E. Hoxie, "Exploring a Cultural Broderland: Native American Journeys of Discovery in the Early Twentieth Century," *Journal of American History* 79 (December 1992): 980–81; K. Tsianina Lomawaima, *They Called it Prairie Light: The Story of Chilocco Indian School* (Lincoln, 1994).

[12] Brenda J. Child, *Boarding School Seasons: American Indian Families, 1900–1940* (Lincoln, 1998), 30. On the absence of cutting girls' hair at Carlisle, see Luther Standing Bear, *Land of the Spotted Eagle* (1933; Lincoln, 1978), 189.

ILLUSTRATION 6. Spotted Tail and children at Carlisle. South Dakota State Historical Society.

students were deeply scarred by their experiences. Only the most resilient children later wrote about their experiences, whereas those who suffered deeper damage did not.

Despite Pratt's assurances to the parents of children he took with him in fall 1879, some of the parents petitioned the government in January 1880 for permission to visit Carlisle to "see for ourselves how they live, and are taken care of." Perhaps because officials realized that to deny this request would make it harder to gain parents' cooperation in the future, they reluctantly agreed. In June a delegation from Rosebud (Spotted Tail, Two Strike, Black Crow, White Thunder, and Iron Wing) and Pine Ridge (Red Cloud, Little Wound, Red Dog, Red Shirt, and American Horse) spent a week at Carlisle before traveling on to Washington. On their return trip, the delegates stopped again at Carlisle. A few, most notably Spotted Tail, defied Pratt and took their children back with them, though not without posing before a camera (see Illustration 6). Upon their return, others called on their agent to have their children sent home.[13]

Clearly, the delegates were not happy with what they saw at Carlisle. Unfortunately, however, the only source that gives an account of their views was a report written by Pratt, and his objective was to defend himself rather than neutrally describe parents' concerns. According to Pratt, Spotted Tail began by objecting to the school's "soldier methods," by which Pratt initially thought he meant the school's use of military uniforms and military drills. However, when Episcopal Bishop William H. Hare showed Spotted Tail a photograph of his own son at "one of the best schools in the country dressed in a uniform with a gun in his hand," Spotted Tail said he was not against uniforms and drilling but confining children to the guardhouse. Pratt then explained that the guardhouse was only used for just cause and pointed out that Spotted Tail's own son (nine-year-old Little Scout) had been sentenced for "fighting with one of the other boys." When he explained these facts, Pratt wrote, Spotted Tail "walked out." Having obviously implied that Spotted Tail had acted impetuously, Pratt turned to his central contention that the chief's sole purpose in conducting his "fault finding crusade" was to pressure Pratt to hire his son-in-law, Charles Tackett, who had earlier accompanied the students as an interpreter.[14] The obvious flaw in Pratt's interpretation, however, was that by his own admission *all* of the delegates objected to Carlisle's methods. As George Hyde points out, it is absurd to think that Red Cloud, for one, would have lodged spurious complaints against Carlisle simply to help Spotted Tail get a job for Tackett.[15]

[13] Spotted Tail et al. to Friend, 14 Jan. 1880, enclosed in Cicero Newell to CIA, 14 Jan. 1880, STA, roll 845 (qtn.); American Horse to H. McK. Heath, 9 Jan. 1880, enclosed in V. T. McGillycuddy to CIA, 10 Jan. 1880, RCA, roll 726; John Cook to CIA, 21 Apr. 1880, STA, roll 845; George E. Hyde, *A Sioux Chronicle* (Norman, 1956), 53–54; Lieut. R. H. Pratt to Acting CIA, 24 June 1880, STA, roll 845; *ARCIA* 1880, 45.

[14] Pratt to Acting CIA, 24 June 1880 (qtns.). On Little Scout, see Pratt, *Battlefield and Classroom*, 237; George E. Hyde, *Spotted Tail's Folk: A History of the Brulé Sioux* (Norman, 1961), 311.

[15] Hyde, *Spotted Tail's Folk*, 324. Hyde, *Sioux Chronicle*, 54, states that a group of "Quaker ladies" was also present on this occasion. Although Quaker women were involved in the founding of Carlisle, the women present were part of a party of Episcopalian visitors

What bothered Pratt's visitors was the discrepancy between the description he had given the previous fall and what they now saw before their very eyes. In his recruitment speech, Pratt had said much about education's practical benefits, but not a word about haircuts, guardhouses, or military drills. The Sioux were not opposed to military training per se. In earlier times, boys had learned to become warriors by playing games, observing the action while accompanying war expeditions, and, as they grew older, through participation in warrior societies. But Pratt's methods were not designed to produce men who could fight. Instead, as he wrote in his first annual report, wearing uniforms and drilling had taught boys "obedience and cleanliness, and given them a better carriage." Although Pratt's report indicated that Spotted Tail had no objection to military drilling, it is likely that he and other leaders recognized these exercises for what they were, attempts to make students submit to a new kind of authority. The guardhouse made Pratt's objective painfully clear. Sioux parents did not believe that children had the right to do anything they pleased. Locking children away, however, violated their sense of appropriate methods for correcting misbehavior. Sioux parents rarely used corporal punishment, relying instead on verbal admonition and social pressure to encourage proper conduct.[16]

Although most of the parents who traveled to Carlisle in June 1880 wound up allowing their children to remain at the school, they fully expected them to return home after three years, the period of time Pratt had originally told parents he would keep their children. In May 1882, however, Pratt informed the Rosebud agent that most of the students should remain at Carlisle. Cyrus, the son of Windy, for example, was an "active, promising, student," who could benefit from "several years longer at the school." Parents unanimously opposed this amendment to Pratt's plans. In June the Rosebud agent informed Pratt that he was unable to offer any "inducement" to persuade parents to allow their children a "longer stay away from their families." Luther Standing Bear, who returned to Rosebud to assist in the cause of recruitment, explained that "so many had died there that the parents of the Indian boys and girls did not want them to go." Indeed, in Carlisle's first two years,

sponsored by Hare. Pratt, *Battlefield and Classroom*, 235–37; Philip S. Benjamin, *The Philadelphia Quakers in the Industrial Age, 1865–1920* (Philadelphia, 1976), 113. For a defense of Pratt, see Everett Arthur Gilcreast, "Richard Henry Pratt and American Indian Policy, 1877–1906: A Study of the Assimilation Movement," Ph.D. diss., Yale University, 1967, 63–66.

[16] *ARCIA*, 1880, 180 (qtn.); Royal B. Hassrick, *The Sioux: Life and Customs of a Warrior Society* (Norman, 1964), 315–21; Ella C. Deloria, *Speaking of Indians* (1944; Vermillion, S.Dak., 1992), 23–29, 37–41. The fact that the delegates, at least according to Pratt, did not object to having their children's hair cut probably means only that they judged it would be best to criticize Carlisle in ways that could create alliances with "friends of the Indian." As Adams, *Education for Extinction*, 121–22, points out, many reformers objected to harsh forms of punishment; some, especially Quakers, had reservations about military training.

at least sixteen children from all tribes died at the school, and eight others died after being sent home. High mortality continued to be a problem at Carlisle and the other boarding schools Plains Sioux children attended in the 1880s.[17]

Naturally, it was painful enough for parents to lose children under any circumstances, but it was worse when they died so far away. Often parents did not even know a child was sick, only to receive the shocking news of a death. It only added to parents' distress when the bodies of children were not returned home. Like all people, the Plains Sioux had meaningful rituals to deal with the loss of a loved one. Sioux women painted red the face of the deceased, dressed the body in beautiful clothing (including moccasins that had been beaded or quilled on the soles), and placed eagle feathers in the hair. When the body was placed onto a scaffold or into a coffin, mourning relatives gave away many of the deceased's possessions. Mothers often remained near the body for four days while fathers went to a hill to pray.[18]

Many families performed a ceremony known as *Wanagi Yuhapi* (Spirit Keeping or Ghost Keeping). In this ritual, a lock from the deceased's hair is cut and put into a "spirit bundle" containing a pipe and other objects. The spirit bundle is kept in a special lodge and ritually fed. At the end of the prescribed period of time (one or two years), the spirit is released, and the relatives of the deceased give away virtually all of their belongings. This ritual not only reinforced values of reciprocity and enabled relatives to go through a structured process of grieving, it also ensured that the spirit of the deceased would successfully travel along the *Wanagi Tacanku* (the Spirit Road, i.e., the Milky Way) to *Wanagi Yata* or *Makoce* (Place or Land of the Spirits).[19] To perform this ceremony, it was necessary for parents to have their deceased child's body.

When Ernest White Thunder and Maud Swift Bear died in December 1880, their fathers, both prominent leaders at Rosebud, petitioned the Indian

[17] Lieut. R. H. Pratt to John Cook, 22 May 1882, RA-KC, box A-356; John Cook to Lieut. R. H. Pratt, 6 June 1882, RA-KC, book 9; Standing Bear, *My People*, 162; *ARCIA*, 1880, 179; *ARCIA*, 1881, 184. For discussions of the health problems and high mortality rates at Indian boarding schools during this period, see Adams, *Education for Extinction*, 130–35; Lindsey, *Indians at Hampton*, 222–24.

[18] Standing Bear, *My People*, 159; Marla N. Powers, *Oglala Women: Myth, Ritual, and Reality* (Chicago, 1986), 93–95.

[19] For accounts of the Spirit Keeping ceremony, see Powers, *Oglala Women*, 98–100; William K. Powers, *Oglala Religion* (Lincoln, 1975), 93–95; Hassrick, *The Sioux*, 38, 302–05; Frances Densmore, *Teton Sioux Music and Culture* (1918; Lincoln, 1992), 77–84; Aaron McGaffey Beede, "Letting Go of the Ghost," Aaron McGaffey Beede Papers, Elwyn B. Robinson Dept. of Special Collections, University of North Dakota, Grand Forks, 50–65. For Lakota views on the afterlife, see James R. Walker, *Lakota Belief and Ritual*, ed. Raymond J. DeMallie and Elaine A. Jahner (Lincoln, 1980), 71; Powers, *Oglala Religion*, 53; Ronald Goodman, *Lakota Star Knowledge: Studies in Lakota Stellar Theology*, 2d ed. (Rosebud, S.Dak., 1992), 21–23.

Office to have their bodies sent home. The Acting Commissioner of Indian Affairs denied this request because it would encourage demands that "the bodies of all pupils who may die" at any off-reservation Indian school be returned, a policy that was not "practicable."[20] Although U.S. officials were willing to devote considerable expense toward twisting the arms of Indian parents into parting with their children, the cost of shipping the bodies of children to grieving parents was too much to bear.

Parents, then, had many reasons to keep their children at home, and they frequently resisted efforts to take their children to off-reservation schools. In 1886 Carlisle recruiters "visited every camp" at Rosebud and held "numerous councils with the Indians, using every possible argument and persuasion," but they were unable to secure a single additional pupil. The same year, when officials of Haskell Institute in Lawrence, Kansas, tried to find students at Cheyenne River, the agent reported that the "Indians of this agency are very much opposed to sending their children to schools off the Reservation." It would be impossible to obtain students "without using force." In this instance, because parents had made their attitude so plain, their agent refused to allow school officials to even try to recruit. Horace R. Chase, the superintendent of the Indian Industrial School at Genoa, Nebraska, also found it difficult to obtain students. "It is a most humiliating task," Chase complained in 1888, "to go out among the camps and settlements and try to overcome the ignorant prejudices of the Indians and induce them to accept the blessings of a free education."[21] Although Chase presumably returned with a few children, his self-pity was a measure of defeat.

Often, however, recruiters were eventually able to obtain parents' consent. In part this happened because some Sioux leaders concluded that boarding schools offered benefits. Leaders' protests that children weren't learning to read and write revealed a desire that they do so, and over time, children gained competence in these areas. Furthermore, students were acquiring trades such as carpentry, tinning, and harness making. They were also gaining knowledge of the ways of European Americans and establishing useful relationships with non-Indians and Indians of other tribes. These experiences and resources might be keys to survival in the next generation and beyond. Concrete advantages also derived from cooperating with the government (or, to put it another way, not cooperating had disadvantages). As noted earlier, the Brulé leaders who met in June 1882 unanimously rejected Pratt's request to keep most of their children. When fall came, however, thirty-five students from Rosebud were enrolled at Carlisle, a decrease of only one over the previous year. Twelve of these were students who had previously

[20] Acting CIA to John Cook, 27 Jan. 1881, RA-KC, box A-355.
[21] J. George Wright to CIA, 24 Mar. 1890, RA-KC, book 16; Charles E. McChensey to CIA, 5 Oct. 1886, OIA, file 27035–1886; *ARCIA*, 1888, 266.

enrolled, twenty-one others were new students, and the status of two is unclear.[22]

Why had parents agreed to something they apparently did not want? No one (literally) put a gun to their head, but there were more subtle forms of coercion. Because the Sioux were directly or indirectly dependent on the government for their material well-being, colonial officials had substantial leverage. A family's refusal to send a child to Carlisle might cost a wagon, livestock, access to wage work, or it might result in a reduction of rations. Furthermore, Sioux leaders recognized the value of choosing their fights carefully. In this particular instance, Brulés at Rosebud were concerned about new threats to their land. In February 1882 the congressional delegate from Dakota Territory, Richard F. Pettigrew, introduced a bill to create a commission for negotiating with the western Sioux to reduce their reservation by half; in May the *Black Hills Daily Times* urged the government "to extinguish the Indian title . . . to Indian reservations." To resist further land loss, many Brulés concluded that it would be best to gain (or avoid losing) political capital by cooperating on Carlisle.[23]

All told, a significant number of Sioux children spent some time in off-reservation boarding schools during the 1880s. A rough estimate would be that around two hundred children from Rosebud and one hundred from Pine Ridge attended Carlisle between 1879 and 1890, while one hundred children from Standing Rock and a similar number from Cheyenne River attended Hampton during these years.[24] The Indian Industrial School at Genoa, Nebraska, which opened in 1884, enrolled more than one hundred additional children at any given time (most of these were from Rosebud). A few western Sioux children were also sent to the Lincoln Institute in Philadelphia and other off-reservation schools.[25]

[22] *ARCIA*, 1882, 177; *ARCIA*, 1883, 39, 161.

[23] *Congressional Record*, 47th Cong., 1st sess., 1882, 13, pt. 2:1304; *Black Hills Daily Times*, 6 May 1882, p. 2. Brulé leaders who hoped to succeed Spotted Tail after his death in August 1881 (see Chapter 9) had an additional reason to try to gain political capital by cooperating on Carlisle.

[24] For Carlisle, I am relying on *ARCIA*, 1880, 178; *ARCIA*, 1882, 177; *ARCIA*, 1883, 161; *ARCIA* 1884, 186; *ARCIA* 1885, 214; *ARCIA*, 1886, 18; *ARCIA*, 1887, 257; Lieut. R. H. Pratt to L. F. Spencer, 18 Feb. 1889, RA-KC, box A-358. For Hampton, I am relying on *ARCIA*, 1878, 173; Pratt, *Battlefield and Classroom*, 198–202; Lindsey, *Indians at Hampton*, 34–36; *ARCIA*, 1885, 238; *ARCIA*, 1891, 510. On Sioux children from Standing Rock at Hampton, see Paulette F. Molin, "'To Be Examples to . . . Their People': Standing Rock Sioux Students at Hampton Institute, 1878–1923 (Part One)," *North Dakota History* 68, no. 2 (2001): 2–23.

[25] For numbers at Genoa, see *ARCIA*, 1884, 207; *ARCIA*, 1886, 8; *ARCIA*, 1887, 243. In 1884, the Rosebud agent reported that seven children had been sent to the Lincoln Institute, thirteen to Episcopal mission schools, and twenty-five to Catholic schools. *ARCIA*, 1884, 45–46. For a while Standing Rock children were sent to St. Mary's Training School in Fehanville, Illinois. *ARCIA*, 1884, 55; *ARCIA*, 1885, 55. Probably because four of these

As significant numbers of boarding school graduates returned home in the mid- and late 1880s, it was clear that the institutions had altered them, though seldom in ways that corresponded to the hopes of either Indian parents or non-Indian reformers. According to Luther Standing Bear, "some of the returned Carlisle students were ashamed of their old people and refused to shake hands with them; some even tried to make them believe they had forgotten the Sioux language." Other returnees wanted to fit in but felt out of place. In early January 1891, just days after the Wounded Knee massacre, Plenty Horses, a young man who had spent five years at Carlisle, shot and killed Lieutenant Edward Casey. At his trial in May, Plenty Horses said that when he had returned to his people "I was an outcast among them. I was no longer an Indian. I was not a white man. I was lonely. I shot the lieutenant so I might make a place for myself among my people."[26]

Eventually, most graduates eased their way back into the lifeways of their people, in part because they had few alternatives. A handful of returnees, like Luther Standing Bear, who taught school, kept a small store, and became an assistant minister, managed to find work commensurate with their education. Most did not.[27] By the late 1880s, assimilationists were wringing their hands over the "relapse problem." According to the agent at Rosebud, the majority of the seventy pupils who had returned from off-reservation schools had "retrograded to a greater or less extent, to blanket or camp life, and resumed the Dakota language in ordinary conversation."[28] Of course, for many Sioux parents, the "relapse problem" was not a problem at all. It was heartening when children put aside western clothing, embraced their native tongue, and grew their hair long again.

Given complete freedom of choice, most Sioux parents would have preferred their children never to see the inside of boarding school walls. If there had to be schools, however, parents preferred them to be located close to home. In 1885 Cheyenne River leaders informed the Indian Office that they did not want their children sent to Hampton. Instead, they wanted a "school like a Hampton" on the reservation.[29] Not only did parents believe that children

died, however, this connection was short lived. See James McLaughlin to Rev. A. Asher, 22 Apr. 1885, MP, roll 20.

[26] Standing Bear, *My People*, 191 (1st qtn.); Julia B. McGillycuddy, *Blood on the Moon: Valentine McGillycuddy and the Sioux* (1941; Lincoln, 1990), 272 (2d qtn.); Robert M. Utley, "The Ordeal of Plenty Horses," *American Heritage* 26 (December 1974): 15–19, 82–86.

[27] For the problem of inadequate employment, see *ARCIA*, 1891, 516. For Indians' complaints about this problem, see James L. McLaughlin to CIA, 19 July 1887, MP, roll 33. For Standing Bear, see Richard N. Ellis, "Introduction," in Standing Bear, *My People*, xii–xiv.

[28] *ARCIA*, 1887, 260; L. F. Spencer to CIA, 18 Apr. 1887, RA-KC, book 13 (qtn.). For a fuller discussion of the problems facing former students, see Adams, *Education for Extinction*, 273–306; Coleman, *American Indian Children*, 178–89.

[29] Little No Heart et al. to CIA, 12 Aug. 1885, OIA, file 19094–1885.

were less likely to become sick if they remained in their own country, they could visit their children frequently and keep a close eye on what the schools were doing.

The number of seats in on-reservation boarding schools steadily increased during the 1880s. At Standing Rock in the early years of the decade the government assumed control over an industrial farm school, originally begun by Benedictine monks, then constructed a second school. By the late 1880s the two schools enrolled more than two hundred students. The Episcopalians added another school in 1889.[30] At Cheyenne River, where the Episcopal Church was already operating a girls' boarding school (St. John's), a government boarding school for boys capable of enrolling sixty students opened in 1881. Three years later, the Congregationalists established another school on the eastern side of the Missouri River at Oahe.[31] Pine Ridge had no boarding schools until December 1883, when the government built one with an eventual capacity of two hundred. Five years later, the Jesuits added a second school at the Holy Rosary Mission.[32] Boarding school capacity was lowest at Rosebud. Although the Indian Office promised to build a boarding school there, it never followed through, probably because of fears that it would compete with Genoa, which was heavily dependent on Rosebud students. The only boarding schools at Rosebud were St. Mary's (Episcopal) and St. Francis (Catholic), which opened in the middle of the decade.[33]

Reservation boarding schools carried out many practices that parents found objectionable. Julia McGillycuddy, the wife of Pine Ridge agent Valentine McGillycuddy, told a story that supposedly took place the day the new boarding school opened. The agent had the blinds drawn so that parents could not see what was happening within the school's walls. Just as a teacher raised the shears to cut the hair of one of the boys, however, "a breeze blew back the shade from the window" and everyone yelled, "*Pahin kaksa, Pahin kaksa!* . . . They are cutting the hair." Then, "through doors and windows the children flew; down the steps, through gates and over fences in a mad flight toward the Indian villages." This story, almost certainly invented or

---

[30] *ARCIA*, 1879, 49; *ARCIA*, 1883 49; *ARCIA*, 1884, 55; *ARCIA*, 1888, 60; *ARCIA*, 1890, 38.

[31] William H. Hare to CIA, 15 Nov. 1880, CRA, roll 131; *ARCIA*, 1880, 20; *ARCIA*, 1881, 26; *ARCIA*, 1885, 19; *ARCIA*, 1890, 43, 330; Thomas Lawrence Riggs, "Sunset to Sunset: A Lifetime with My Brothers, the Dakotas," *South Dakota Historical Collections* 29 (1958): 194.

[32] *ARCIA*, 1884, 39; *ARCIA*, 1885, 36; *ARCIA*, 1886, 77; *ARCIA*, 1889, 155; *ARCIA*, 1890, 55; *Red Cloud's Dream Come True: Holy Rosary Mission, 1888–1963, Pine Ridge, S.D.* (n.p., 1963), 10; Ross Alexander Enochs, *The Jesuit Mission to the Lakota Sioux: Pastoral Theology and Ministry, 1886–1945* (Kansas City, 1996), 29; Robert W. Galler Jr., "A Triad of Alliances: The Roots of Holy Rosary Indian Mission," *South Dakota History* 28 (Fall 1998): 144–60.

[33] *ARCIA*, 1883, 44; *ARCIA*, 1886, 81; *ARCIA*, 1891, 417.

embellished by the agent, his wife, or both, undoubtedly reflects the attitudes of Oglala parents and echoes actual episodes of protest. But its tone of lighthearted nostalgia at once trivializes Indian resistance and understates the repressiveness of McGillycuddy's regime. Over the years, boys routinely had to submit to what one Pine Ridge teacher realized was "the humiliation of having their long hair cropped."[34]

Overall, however, the experience of students in reservation boarding schools was less traumatic than in off-reservation schools.[35] For one thing, visits from relatives mitigated homesickness. At Pine Ridge, when parents came to the agency to pick up rations (usually every two weeks), children were allowed to spend the day with them. Parents and other relatives frequently asked school officials for permission to take children home for a few days, pleading that the child was sick or was needed to care for a relative. In his duties as agency physician at Pine Ridge, Charles Eastman, a Santee Sioux, heard many appeals for written excuses from school. "I would argue the matter with parents as tactfully as I could," he recalled, "but if nothing else could win the coveted paper, the grandmother was apt to be pressed into the service, and her verbal ammunition seemed inexhaustible."[36]

Children did not always obtain permission before leaving school. When the boys and girls at St. Francis boarding school heard the sound of drums from Two Strike's camp, recalled Father Florentine Digmann, "there was no holding them." Students' capacity to run away allowed them and their parents to win modest concessions. To stem the tide of unauthorized absences, St. Francis gave permission for students to spend Sunday after Mass with their families. Even this was not enough; eventually the Rosebud agent had to station a policeman at St. Francis in order to "compel [*sic*] a full attendance."[37] Children usually ran away simply because they detested school, but as Ella Deloria, a Yankton Sioux scholar, explains, "kinship and its duties," particularly the need to be with sick or dying relatives, frequently compelled children to go home. Even well-intentioned school officials, Deloria notes, failed to comprehend children's commitment to the "old ideal,

[34] McGillycuddy, *Blood on the Moon*, 206; Thisba Hutson Morgan, "Reminiscences of My Days in the Land of the Ogallala Sioux," *South Dakota Historical Collections* 29 (1958): 24. A priest at Rosebud's St. Francis boarding school recalled that "it was quite a ceremony, when boys of ten or twelve years were taken to school and had to get their hair cut. It cost often tears to both boys and parents, the latter would wrap them up and take them home for a keepsake." Florentine Digmann, "History of the St. Francis Mission, 1886–1922," unpublished manuscript, n.d., series 7, box 14, folder 7, p. 5, Holy Rosary Mission Records, Marquette University Special Collections, Milwaukee.

[35] For a general discussion of reservation schools, see Adams, *Education for Extinction*, 30–36.

[36] Charles A. Eastman (Ohiyesa), *From the Deep Woods to Civilization: Chapters in the Autobiography of an Indian* (1916; Lincoln, 1977), 82.

[37] Digmann, "History of St. Francis Mission," 4 (1st qtn.); "Chronicle St. Francis Mission, St. Francis, South Dakota, 1886–1928," series 2/1, box 1, folder 6, p. 4, Holy Rosary Mission Records; J. George Wright to CIA, 8 (?) Nov. 1889, RA-KC, book 16 (2d qtn.).

that relatives and their needs and happiness comes first." Running away sometimes resulted in tragedy. In January 1889 two young boys "skipped out" from the boarding school at Oahe and started for home. According to the missionaries, because it was warm weather and their families were sure to bring them back, no one pursued them. Suddenly, though, the air turned cold. One of the boys reached home but the other was found frozen.[38]

Summer vacations tempered the oppressiveness of reservation boarding schools. When the school year ended at Carlisle or Hampton, Indian students either remained there or were sent to local non-Indian farm families under the "outing" program. By contrast, although students at Pine Ridge boarding school had to wear heavy brogans nine months of the year, when June arrived, they could return to the comfort of their moccasins.[39] Children could listen to grandmothers and grandfathers tell stories, go hunting with an uncle, or learn beadwork from an aunt.

Children were able to create some space for cultural expression within the schools. Thisba Hutson Morgan, a teacher at the Pine Ridge boarding school, recalled that "nothing made the little girls happier than to be given needles, thread and scraps of cloth from the sewing room to entertain themselves during their play periods." They used these materials to make camps, complete with tipis two-feet tall, and "Indian dolls made from sticks, covered with brown cloth, with beads for eyes and real hair clipped from their own braids." Using empty thread spools and salvaged boxes, girls made wagons to take the dolls from one camp to another, where they would prepare a feast "from scraps brought from the kitchen."[40]

Teen-age girls also devised ways to express themselves within the confines of externally imposed requirements. Although the head matron at Pine Ridge insisted that girls wear their hair in a single braid instead of the current fashion of two braids, Morgan observed that girls made the best of the situation by braiding each other's hair in highly intricate braids "using four, five and sometimes seven strands." In this way, they were able to "soften the discipline of the one braid." At times, girls chose not merely to create new possibilities within prescribed constraints but openly to transgress the school's policies. According to Morgan, "when something at the school had really gone wrong" and the "girls felt a spirit of rebellion within them," they

---

[38] Deloria, *Speaking of Indians*, 71 (1st qtn.); Thomas L. Riggs to Alfred Riggs, 28 Jan. 1889, South Dakota Conference United Church of Christ Archives, Oahe Mission Collection, box 4, Center for Western Studies, Augustana College, Sioux Falls, S.Dak. (2d qtn.).

[39] On the "outing" program at Carlisle, see Adams, *Education for Extinction*, 156–63. Morgan, "Reminiscences," 26, recalled that students wore "awful brogans furnished by the United States Government. They limped and shuffled about trying to learn to walk in the heavy things that were blistering their feet, some leaving bleeding sores which often became badly infected."

[40] Morgan, "Reminiscences," 28–29. See also Riggs, "Sunset to Sunset," 194, for an account of young girls "playing camp" at the Oahe school.

would "suddenly appear with their hair in two braids and their eyebrows plucked." This was a double offense against the school's rules.[41]

Unfortunately, Morgan was silent about what qualified as something "really gone wrong" and what happened when girls defied the rules. Nonetheless, her recollections reveal that Indian children frequently contested the authority of boarding schools. The administrators were never able to establish complete control. In part this was because schools lacked the resources and the will to establish total regimentation, but it was also because of children's individual and collective creativity.

Many parents "voluntarily" sent their children to reservation boarding schools, but consent meant an agonizing calculation of weighing schools' limited advantages against their more obvious disadvantages and then factoring in the costs of refusal. Many parents said no. Authorities frequently used harsh methods to fill reservation boarding schools. In 1883 the Standing Rock agent decreed that each band would be required to furnish a quota of children for the agency's boarding schools and that failure to comply would result in a reduction of rations proportional to the shortfall. The Pine Ridge agent simply arrested boys and girls who refused to enroll.[42]

The emerging system of Indian education also included day schools. The Indian Office built a handful of day schools in the early 1880s, but it was not until mid-decade that the government initiated a comprehensive program of day school education at the western Sioux agencies. By 1890 Cheyenne River had eight government day schools, Rosebud thirteen, Standing Rock seven, and Pine Ridge eight. In addition, there were as many as nine denominational day schools at Cheyenne River and at least one at Standing Rock in 1890. By this time, there was sufficient capacity for a majority of children of school age to attend a day school. Although few Sioux children attended every day, most did at least some of the time. (A photograph of a day school and its students is shown in Illustration 7.)[43]

Some assimilationists promoted day schools as a way to ensure that the boarding schools received a steady supply of well-prepared students. Others, however, worried that day schools were weak tools. As U.S. Indian school

[41] Morgan, "Reminiscences," 26, 28.

[42] James McLaughlin to CIA, 13 Nov. 1883, OIA, file 21325–1883; Morgan, "Reminiscences," 24.

[43] *ARCIA*, 1881, 49; *ARCIA*, 1883, 50; *ARCIA*, 1885, 17, 36, 42, 54–55; *ARCIA*, 1886, 52; *ARCIA*, 1887, 19, 43; *ARCIA*, 1888, 54; *ARCIA*, 1890, 37–38, 42, 53, 60; Riggs, "From Sunset to Sunset," 254–56, 275; Richmond L. Clow, ed., "Autobiography of Mary C. Collins, Missionary to the Western Sioux," *South Dakota Historical Collections* 41 (1982): 11. Figures in *ARCIA*, 1891, 506–07, indicate that there was sufficient capacity for about two-thirds of all children of school age to attend day schools at Cheyenne River, Standing Rock, and Pine Ridge, though for less than half at Rosebud, and that the number of students who attended at one time or another was at capacity.

ILLUSTRATION 7. Reservation day school and pupils. Nebraska State Historical Society, RG2969:2–99.

superintendent John N. Oberly saw it, the "barbarian child of barbarian parents" was temporarily exposed to "the superior race to which his teacher belongs," but at the end of the day, the child "returns...to eat and play and sleep after the savage fashion of his race." Oberly favored a compulsory education law that would require all Indian children to attend boarding schools. Only this would "cure the Indian race of savagery."[44]

Someone sitting in a Washington office might have easily concluded from reports coming in from the agents in Sioux country that the eyes of more and more Indian parents were opening to the blessings of the schoolhouse. In 1885 from the Cheyenne River Agency came news of "an increased desire upon the part of the Indians to send their children to school." The next year, the "majority" of the Cheyenne River Sioux were "willing and anxious" to have their children attend day schools. In 1888 the interest of parents was "greater than ever before." Evidently, Cheyenne River schools were bursting at their seams as eager parents rushed to enroll daughters and sons. Either that or the agents were plagiarizing previous reports.[45]

An agent at Rosebud was far more candid when he wrote that "it is easy to say that the Indians pine for educational advantages, but I do not find it so." Hoping, perhaps, to deflect attention from his own incapacities by denigrating Indians, this agent elaborated:

[44] Prucha, *Great Father*, 2:705; *ARCIA*, 1885, cxi, cxiv (qtns.).
[45] *ARCIA*, 1885, 17; *ARCIA*, 1886, 52; *ARCIA*, 1888, 26.

[P]arents are continually inventing some frivolous excuse upon which to formulate a reason for detaining their children at home, and, as a rule, would infinitely prefer to have them spend their time killing small game with a bent stick and a feathered dart. As a result, the labor of keeping up school attendance is a constant struggle for the agent.... Only in isolated cases can credit be attached to Mr. and Mrs. Lo. There are camps on this agency where the mere mention of a prospective school operates like a red rag on an enraged bull.[46]

Agents had to use every weapon in their arsenal to fill the day schools. Their first line of offense was to try to convince parents of education's benefits, an effort that drew upon the time-honored tactic of mixing platitudes with veiled threats and hinted promises. Failing this, agents threatened to deny rations to families who refused to give up their children to civilization and on occasion carried out these threats. Agents used their police force to hunt down truants; one went so far as to detail a policeman to each school.[47]

Parents belonging to bands that opposed farming and strongly resisted the government's efforts to suppress dancing, giveaways, and other cultural practices were the most likely to refuse to send their children to school. Parents from bands that pursued a strategy of selective cooperation were less likely to resist, though they had several concerns. At Pine Ridge, for example, none of the school rooms were sealed or plastered and consequently they were cold and leaky. Teachers tacked pieces of canvas to the ceiling joists, but the air currents tore these loose and made a "continual flapping which interferes with the children's studies." On several occasions during the winter of 1888–1889, the Pine Ridge day schools had to be closed "because it was impossible to keep from suffering."[48] Parents also complained that their children went hungry. As Elaine Goodale, a teacher who was appointed Supervisor of Education Among the Sioux, observed, this was because the noontime meal at a day school consisted of "nothing but one hardtack and part of a cup of coffee."[49] There were also worries about

---

[46] *ARCIA*, 1887, 43.

[47] James McLaughlin to CIA, 14 Apr. 1886, MP, roll 32; *ARCIA*, 1891, 525–26; V. T. McGilly-cuddy to CIA, 19 Sept. 1885, OIA, file 22331–1885; V. T. McGillycuddy to CIA, 2 Mar. 1886, PR-KC, box 36; H. D. Gallagher to CIA, 27 Jan. 1890, PR-KC, box 37; James G. Wright to CIA, 12 Apr. 1886, RA-KC, book 12; Wright to CIA, 8 (?) Nov. 1889.

[48] CIA to H. D. Gallagher, 15 Oct. 1889, PR-KC, box 9; H. D. Gallagher to CIA, 21 Nov. 1889, PR-KC, box 37 (1st qtn.); Benjamin H. Miller to SI, 4 Nov. 1889, Reports of Inspections of the Field Jurisdictions of the Office of Indian Affairs, 1873–1900, Record Group 75, National Archives and Records Administration, Microfilm Publications, M1070, roll 36 (2d qtn.).

[49] Kay Graber, ed., *Sister to the Sioux: The Memoirs of Elaine Goodale Eastman, 1885–91* (Lincoln, 1978), 123 (qtn.). On the lack of food at day schools, see also Ethel C. Jacobsen, "Life in an Indian Village," *North Dakota History* 26 (Spring 1959): 73. On Elaine Goodale's work as an educator, see Ruth Ann Alexander, "Finding Oneself through a Cause: Elaine Goodale Eastman and Indian Reform in the 1880s," *South Dakota History* 22 (Spring 1992): 1–37.

disease. In winter 1888–1889, measles spread through both day and boarding schools. The following year many children died from whooping cough
and influenza.[50]

Parents were often disappointed in the quality of instruction. Not surprisingly, given the low rate of pay and undesirable living conditions, work in
reservation day schools did not always attract the most competent teachers.
Elaine Goodale's inspection of the schools revealed that "[e]verything was
copied off the board on slates with no explanation." When confronted with
their lack of success, teachers' "stock excuse was the bald assumption that
'Indians just won't talk American,' or 'You can't learn them sums; they've
not got the head for it.'" Goodale, who was able to converse in Lakota,
pointed out that Indians resented this kind of "indifferent or patronizing
attitude." Ella Deloria, who attended the St. Elizabeth's mission school at
Standing Rock in the 1890s, criticized school teachers for their ignorance of
their students' native language. If a teacher corrected a student by saying,
"You won't do that again, will you?," the likely answer would be "yes."
A teacher might think this response perverse and punish the child without
realizing that Dakota/Lakota speakers respond to such questions by saying,
"Yes (you are right that I will not)."[51]

Despite these problems, however, most parents probably regarded day
schools as a preferable alternative to boarding schools. In 1889 Little Wound
told government commissioners that when the "younger ones" ran away
from the Pine Ridge boarding school, "they may freeze to death going home."
For this reason, he explained, "we want these little schools so that when it is
cold they will not have to go so far to school." Day schools were also more
susceptible to parental influence. According to the Pine Ridge agent, parents
frequently threatened to take their children from day schools rather than
permit their hair to be cut. Consequently, many students had long hair, and
teachers were forced to adopt a policy of "gradually gaining the consent of
parents to have it done without disturbing their schools." In general, Sioux
people favored day schools for the same reason that led some assimilationists
to reject them: At the end of the day, children returned home.[52]

---

[50] *ARCIA*, 1889, 133, 159, 168; *ARCIA*, 1890, 39, 44–45; J. George Wright to CIA, 12 Feb.
1890, RA-KC, book 16.

[51] Graber, ed., *Sister to the Sioux*, 124, 123 (see also Goodale's report in *ARCIA*, 1890, 276);
Deloria, *Speaking of Indians*, 71. Teachers at mission schools were more likely to know some
D/Lakota than those at government schools. In 1887, however, the Indian Office adopted an
English-only policy at mission schools (modified the next year to allow use of native-language
Bibles). *ARCIA*, 1887, xxii; *ARCIA*, 1888, xvii.

[52] *Report and Proceedings of the Sioux Commission*, 51st Cong., 1st sess., 1889–90, S. Ex.
Doc. 51, serial 2682, 109; Gallagher to CIA, 21 Nov. 1889. For a discussion of how Lakotas
shaped day schools to their own ends in subsequent decades, see Thomas G. Andrews,
"Turning the Tables on Assimilation: Oglala Lakotas and the Pine Ridge Day Schools, 1889–
1920s," *Western Historical Quarterly* 33 (Winter 2002): 407–30.

Before the 1880 schools were something that U.S. officials occasionally talked about, but very few Sioux children had been exposed to European-American education. Ten years later, however, the large majority had spent some time in a government or mission day school, and a sizeable number had attended reservation or off-reservation boarding schools. By 1890 schools were a solid presence in the lives of the western Sioux.

Beyond teaching students to read and write, schools offered the Sioux new lessons about the long-term intentions of the United States. Before the late 1870s the western Sioux perceived the main threat from U.S. expansion to be loss of land and game as well as physical destruction. Whether they tried to resist this expansion militarily or diplomatically, Sioux leaders generally hoped to prevent European Americans from overrunning their lands, and then, to find a way to live with them in greater or lesser proximity. In the 1850s, 1860s, and 1870s, the Sioux undoubtedly grasped the fact that some European Americans ultimately desired to force them to live in radically new ways, but it was not until the 1880s that they fully realized what this might mean. When their children were taken to distant institutions, when their names were changed, their hair cut, and speaking their language banned, Sioux people apprehended that European Americans were not content to confine them to reservations and make them farm. They wanted to eradicate the entire Sioux way of life. Schools were not the only indication of a European American commitment to cultural genocide. Along with the government's educational program came an assault on the cultural and religious practices that had sustained Sioux communities for generations.

8

"All Men Are Different"

The Politics of Religion and Culture

Sometime in spring 1881 an Oglala named Rocky Bear vowed to *Wakan Tanka* that if his deathly ill wife was healed, he would dance in *Wiwanyang Wacipi*, the Sun Dance. Because Rocky Bear was the first Oglala to announce an intention to dance, he was chosen to be the leader of the Sun Dance that summer.[1]

Preparations for the Sun Dance began almost as soon as Rocky Bear announced his intention. *Wicasa wakans* (holy men) burned sweetgrass and offered pipes to the heavens, the earth, and the four directions, praying for good weather. Drummers made sure their equipment was in good order; singers composed and practiced songs. Those who would play important roles in the ceremonies of the Sun Dance meditated on their duties. Mentors carefully instructed the dancers about proper procedures. The dancers purified themselves in sweat lodges, prepared offerings of tobacco, and thought of their purpose in undertaking this extremely arduous ordeal. Relatives of the dancers and parents of babies who would have their ears pierced during the dance prepared material goods and food to give away.[2]

On June 20, 1881, approximately 3,500 people (mostly Oglalas, but also some Brulés) gathered at the designated place, three miles south of Pine Ridge

---

[1] John G. Bourke diary, 20 June 1881, vol. 40, roll 3, 1459–60, United States Military Academy Library, West Point, N.Y. (microfilm). *Wiwanyang Wacipi* literally means "looking at the sun they dance." For an overview of the Sun Dance throughout the Plains region, see JoAllyn Archambault, "Sun Dance," in *Plains*, ed. Raymond J. DeMallie, vol. 13, pt. 2, *Handbook of North American Indians*, ed. William C. Sturtevant (Washington, D.C., 2001), 983–95.

[2] On preparations for the Sun Dance, see Frances Densmore, *Teton Sioux Music and Culture* (1918; Lincoln, 1992), 98–104; James Owen Dorsey, *A Study of Siouan Cults*, Eleventh Annual Report of the Bureau of American Ethnology, 1894 (Washington, D.C., 1894), 451–53; J. R. Walker, *The Sun Dance and Other Ceremonies of the Oglala Division of the Teton Dakota*, Anthropological Papers of the American Museum of Natural History, vol. 16, pt. 2 (New York, 1917), 62–96.

Agency, just over the border in Nebraska.[3] After receiving instructions from a crier, they formed a procession, led by a man bearing a ribbon-decorated pipe, a drummer, and a dozen singers. Fifteen minutes later they arrived at the site of a cottonwood tree, which had earlier been chosen to stand in the center of the dance enclosure. After warriors charged the tree, a group of ten men and five young women came forward, offering ponies, cloth, and other valuable items. Four of the men, each in turn, recited a war deed and with an axe struck the tree, each on a different quarter. When they were finished, Red Whirlwind, the daughter of Little Wound, took an axe and cut down the tree to shouts of victory. Carriers then placed the tree on skids and took it to the dance grounds, where they laid it on the earth.[4] While praying, singing, and making offerings to the poor, people prepared the tree to stand in the center. They cut off the lower limbs, painted the trunk, and attached a crossbar to the tree. They also placed pieces of scarlet cloth in the upper branches and attached to the tree a medicine bundle and two rawhide figures – one an Indian, the other a buffalo.[5]

The morning and early afternoon of the next day were devoted to constructing the Sun Dance enclosure. Participants built a structure of about sixty feet in diameter made of cottonwood saplings and branches. It would shelter spectators, singers, and drummers. All this time, people on horseback, in wagons, and on foot, continued to arrive. By midafternoon there were as many as eight thousand people. This included almost everyone from Pine Ridge, Sioux from other agencies, and several non-Indian spectators.[6] Around three o'clock a series of processions began in which men of different

---

[3] Bourke diary, 20 June 1881, vol. 40, roll 3, 1473; Bourke diary, 22 June 1881, vol. 41, roll 3, 1529.

[4] Ibid., 20 June 1881, vol. 40, roll 3, 1454–77. Ella Deloria, "The Sun Dance of the Oglala Sioux," *Journal of American Folk-Lore* 42 (October–December 1929): 397, n. 4, reports that four young women cut into the tree ceremonially and then men cut down the tree. Densmore, *Teton Sioux Music and Culture*, 113, indicates that four women cut into the tree and that the first of them cut it to the ground.

[5] Bourke diary, 21 June 1881, vol. 41, roll 3, 1489–92. Although Bourke did not note that the tree was painted nor that there was a medicine bundle attached to the tree, both were almost certainly the case. A medicine bundle containing what Arthur Amiotte, "The Lakota Sun Dance: Historical and Contemporary Perspectives," in *Sioux Indian Religion*, ed. Raymond J. DeMallie and Douglas R. Parks (Norman, 1987), 83, describes as "the sacred implements for making life – the *wahintke* (hide-tanning tool), the knife, a piece of *papa* (dried meat) with an arrow struck through it, a woman's sewing awl, a tent stake for staking out a horse" was a common feature of the ceremony. A similar bundle is described by Densmore in *Teton Sioux Music and Culture*, 118. On the painting of the pole, see Densmore, *Teton Sioux Music and Culture*, 116; Joseph Epes Brown, ed., *The Sacred Pipe: Black Elk's Account of the Seven Rites of the Oglala Sioux* (Norman, 1953), 78; Deloria, "Sun Dance of the Oglala Sioux," 398.

[6] Bourke diary, 20 June 1881, vol. 40, 1474; 21 June 1881, vol. 40, 1485; 22 June 1881, vol. 41, 1507. Western Sioux people routinely traveled to other agencies to attend sun dances. See James McLaughlin to CIA, 15 Aug. 1883, OIA, file 15399–1883; James G. Wright to CIA,

bands danced to and from the center. They fired guns at the two rawhide figures, eventually severing the strings that held them to the crossbar.[7] At intervals, women entered the circle with gifts of blankets and cloth. All the while, holy men pierced babies' ears and distributed gifts. Later, the twenty-seven dancers – those who had made vows and would dance the next day – and their helpers joined a ceremony in which Rocky Bear set a buffalo head on a bed of sage in a sacred place near the pole. Near the buffalo head the dancers placed ceremonial pipes on a small frame. That evening the dancers, already weary from lack of food and water, danced to and from the sacred tree, blowing on whistles made from the wing bones of eagles.[8]

The following day, the dancers arose with the sun, purified themselves in sweat lodges, and had their bodies painted. After these preparations, the crier summoned all the people to the enclosure, where holy men, the dancers, and some of the dancers' relatives formed a procession into the circle. A holy man burned sweetgrass and then lit the ceremonial pipe, held it to the sky, the earth, and the four directions, and offered it to the dancers.[9] Then, the opening song of the Sun Dance was sung. Unfortunately, the sources do not reveal which song was used. One possibility is a song used around the same time at Standing Rock Agency:

Tunkasila	Grandfather
ho uwayin kte	a voice I will send
namah'on ye	hear me
maka sitomniyan	all over the earth

21 July 1883, RA-KC, book 9; V. T. McGillycuddy to CIA, 27 June 1883, PR-KC, box 35, vol. 4.

[7] Densmore, *Teton Sioux Music and Culture*, 118, indicates that the figure of the man and the buffalo symbolized "that the enemy and also the buffalo had been conquered by supernatural help." However, Walker, *Sun Dance*, 108, suggests that the images, both of which had exaggerated erect penises, symbolized, in the case of the man, "*Iya*, the patron God of libertinism," and in the case of the buffalo, "*Gnaski*, the Crazy Buffalo, the patron God of licentiousness." On Bourke's observations of the phallic nature of these symbols, see his diary, 21 June 1881, vol. 40, roll 3, 1489, and the drawing at the end of vol. 40, roll 3.

[8] Bourke diary, 21 June 1881, vol. 40, roll 3, 1492–96; Bourke diary, 21 June 1881, vol. 41, roll 3, 1497–1505. Bourke's account says that a "buffalo head" was used, which is consistent with Walker, *Sun Dance*, 94. Buffalo skulls were also used. See Alice Fletcher, "The Sun Dance of the Ogalalla Sioux" in *Proceedings of the American Association for the Advancement of Science, 1882* (Salem, Mass., 1883), 583; Densmore, *Teton Sioux Music and Culture*, 99, 127; Brown, ed., *Sacred Pipe*, 91. Bourke's account of all the dancers placing pipes on a frame near the buffalo head is at variance with Densmore's account, based on conversations with informants at Standing Rock, which indicates that the leader of the dancers placed a single pipe with the bowl resting on the skull and the stem supported by "a slight frame of sticks." Densmore, *Teton Sioux Music and Culture*, 127. These variations, undoubtedly, reflect different local traditions as well as some degree of permissible improvisation.

[9] Bourke diary, 22 June 1881, vol. 41, roll 3, 1507; Densmore, *Teton Sioux Music and Culture*, 123–25.

ho uwayin kte	a voice I will send
namah'on ye	hear me
tunkasila	grandfather
wanikte lo	I will live
epe lo	I have spoken[10]

Shortly before noon, the dancers made their sacrifices. Pretty Enemy, the only woman to dance, kept a promise she had made several months before when she and her husband left Sitting Bull's Canadian camp in the dead of winter. Starving, cold, and on the verge of despair, they prayed that if they lived they would dance in the Sun Dance. A holy man cut four pieces of flesh from each of Pretty Enemy's shoulders in fulfillment of her vow.[11] Some of the male dancers also gave pieces of flesh, while others had holy men make two incisions in their upper chest and insert a skewer beneath the skin. By this means, they were attached to a rawhide rope, which was attached to the sacred tree, from which they tried to break themselves free.

One dancer, Bull Man, danced for over an hour. Four times he fainted and was revived by his helper but the skewers refused to rip through his flesh. At one point, six women (probably relatives), offered pieces of their own flesh so that Bull Man's agony could end. Finally, the holy men concluded that Bull Man had suffered enough and removed the skewers. As the dancers suffered, more gifts were given. Bolts of calico, shawls, parasols, gowns, shirts, silver belts, beads, pieces of colored glass, jewelry, willow mats, and Navajo blankets lay on the ground, waiting to be claimed by those in need. After the dancers had completed their sacrifices, at about three o'clock in the afternoon, the Sun Dance was over.[12]

Those who participated in the 1881 Pine Ridge Sun Dance did not think of themselves as belonging to a dying people. The United States had taken much of their land, sanctioned the destruction of the buffalo, and forced them to live on a reservation, but as they came together in late June, with the sun at its highest point in the sky and the earth so obviously alive, they felt encouraged and renewed. Participating in "the great corporate prayer, the highlight of Dakota life," they remembered that *Wakan Tanka* had taken pity on them in the past and could do so again. By sharing their material resources, strengthening bonds with relatives, feasting, singing, drumming, and dancing, Sioux people felt that they could do more than merely survive. They could live well, enjoying cultural autonomy and self-determination. Through having their children's ears pierced, they could ensure that the next

---

[10] Densmore, *Teton Sioux Music and Culture*, 130. I have slightly altered Densmore's translation.

[11] Bourke diary, 22 June 1881, vol. 41, roll 3, 1508, 1514.

[12] Ibid., 1514–28.

generation heard the "voices of the spirits and of the grandfathers," thus ensuring the perpetuation of their way of life.[13]

Although the 1881 Pine Ridge Sun Dance reproduced familiar rituals and meanings, it differed from sun dances held just a few years before. One new development was the presence of dozens of non-Indian observers. At least seven military officers, several agency officials, as well as a contingent of cowboys from neighboring ranches attended. The following year's dance came under scientific scrutiny when ethnologist Alice Fletcher came to observe.[14] It is difficult to know what the Plains Sioux thought about having non-Indians observe the Sun Dance. Lieutenant John G. Bourke's account of the 1881 dance at Pine Ridge indicates that he was welcome. Because he was General Crook's *mnisapa wicasa* (secretary; literally, "ink man"), dance leaders provided Bourke with "every facility in acquiring a knowledge of this great Dance." They allowed him and agent Valentine McGillycuddy to walk within the Sun Dance enclosure, though they were not permitted to go between the buffalo head and the sacred tree.[15]

Although Bourke's account indicates that the Sun Dance leaders were delighted to have their agent and an army lieutenant within their holy spaces, other evidence suggests that Sioux people did not welcome Americans' prying eyes. After attending the 1882 Sun Dance, Alice Fletcher wanted to observe other private ceremonies such as vision seeking. Oglalas objected, telling her, "The white people do not understand us, they laugh at our sacred things, and they will laugh at these things which they did not know before."[16] Although Fletcher did not report the circumstances in which Oglalas had observed non-Indians laughing at their religious practices, they must have had the Sun Dance in mind. Why, then, did they allow outsiders to observe? Although the Indian Office had not yet tried to stop sun dances at the western Sioux agencies, Oglalas must have heard talk of this possibility and recognized it as a serious threat. Given these circumstances, it seems that they hoped to educate Americans about the Sun Dance so it could continue.

[13] Ella C. Deloria, *Speaking of Indians* (1944; Vermillion, S.Dak., 1992), 33 (1st qtn.); Amiotte, "Lakota Sun Dance," 84 (2d qtn.). On the significance of ear piercing as a metaphor for being willing "to listen to and accept a significant message," see Raymond J. DeMallie, "'These Have No Ears': Narrative and the Ethnohistorical Method," *Ethnohistory* 40 (Fall 1993): 521.

[14] "Conference Held at Sun Dance of Ogalalla Sioux Indians at Pine Ridge Agency Dakota," 22 June 1881, OIA, file 11106–1881; Bourke diary, 21 June 1881, vol. 40, roll 3, 1485; Fletcher, "Sun Dance," 580; Joan Mark, *A Stranger in Her Native Land: Alice Fletcher and the American Indians* (Lincoln, 1988), 79–82.

[15] Bourke diary, 22 June 1881, vol. 41, roll 3, 1520.

[16] Alice C. Fletcher, "The Elk Mystery or Festival: Oglala Sioux," *Reports of the Peabody Museum of American Archaeology and Ethnology, Vol. 3, 1880–86* (Cambridge, Mass., 1887), 280.

As Lieutenant Bourke observed the dance in 1881, Oglalas made every effort to explain it to him. One Oglala, for example, told Bourke that "the object of the Sun Dance was 'to make the grass grow.'"[17] Later, as Bourke watched the dancers struggling to break free of the sacred tree, Red Dog said, "My friend, this is the way we have been raised. Do not think this strange. All men are different. Our grandfathers taught us to do this. Write it down straight on the paper." Red Dog, it seems, hoped that Bourke's new knowledge of the Sun Dance and his ability to convey this to other European Americans might lead them to adopt Red Dog's own position of cultural pluralism. In a pre-Boasian era, however, few Americans were ready to accept Red Dog's position. Bourke was no exception, and he responded to Red Dog with a brief lecture on social evolution. It was true, he admitted, that "all men are different" and that this is "your religion, the religion of your grandfathers." Indeed, Bourke said, "our grandfathers used to be like yours hundreds and thousands of years ago." But "now we are different," he continued, "[y]our religion brought you the buffalo, ours brought us locomotives and the talking wires." In his diary, Bourke described the "bloody drama" of the Sun Dance as affording a glimpse into "Red-hot Hell."[18]

U.S. officials' first attempts to stop sun dances usually failed. In 1880 the agent at Standing Rock, Joseph A. Stephan, reported that he warned Running Antelope, Iron Horse, and Eagle Man not to hold a Sun Dance they were planning. When they went ahead, Stephan "deemed it wise not to use the full extent of my authority to prevent the movement." Stephan's most immediate problem was the weakness of the agency's Indian police force. Only fourteen of the thirty policemen had weapons, and nine of those had been assigned to the Cheyenne River Agency. Stephan could have requested troops from the commander at nearby Fort Yates, Lieutenant Colonel W. P. Carlin, but Stephan and Carlin were fighting over the control of reservation timber and exchanging heated allegations about responsibility for Indian prostitution and alcohol abuse.[19]

Stephan's inability to act reveals that what Thomas Biolsi terms "administrative technologies of power" remained undeveloped. Although officials in charge of western Sioux agencies began to build police forces shortly after 1878, the year the Indian Office first authorized them, lack of resources made their task difficult.[20] Agents were often unable to provide recruits with

---

[17] Bourke diary, 21 June 1881, vol. 41, roll 3, 1498–99. On the theme of the Sun Dance's renewal of the world, see Amiotte, "Lakota Sun Dance," 76; Howard L. Harrod, *Renewing the World: Plains Indian Religion and Morality* (Tucson, 1987), 115–56.

[18] Bourke diary, 22 June 1881, vol. 41, 1523–24, 1528.

[19] J. A. Stephan to CIA, 6 July 1880, SRA, roll 852. Conflicts between the Standing Rock agents and the military at Fort Yates can be traced in SRA, 1877–1880, rolls 848–852.

[20] Thomas Biolsi, *Organizing the Lakota: The Political Economy of the New Deal on the Pine Ridge and Rosebud Reservations* (Tucson, 1992), 3; William T. Hagan, *Indian Police and*

decent weapons. In the words of one agent, this had a "thoroughly demoralising effect" on police morale.[21] Even something as simple as uniforms presented a problem. Plains Sioux men were highly attuned to the symbolism of attire. The way they painted themselves, the feathers they wore, and the staffs they carried all conveyed important messages about past accomplishments and present status. Not surprisingly, then, the Indian police at Rosebud expressed displeasure at having to wear gray uniforms. Not only were these uniforms shabby hand-me-downs worn by guards at the 1876 Centennial Exhibition, their color was the same as the uniforms of the Confederate States of America. According to Rosebud agent John Cook, Indians asked why the "Great Father" did not provide them with the same uniform as his own soldiers rather than the "dress and uniform of the Great Father's late enemies." (Eventually, gray gave way to blue.)[22]

Low pay also hindered recruitment and retention. Congress was as devoted to the ideals of civilization as any American institution, but it was interested in achieving these ideals with the minimum possible impact on the public purse. Consequently, the Indian Office was chronically underfunded and had to purchase its technologies for domination on the cheap. In the early 1880s the pay of Indian police was $8 per month for officers and $5 for privates. By contrast, in the late 1870s the army paid Indian scouts $13 per month and an additional $9 for the use of their horses. Because they were poorly paid, the police at the Cheyenne River Agency were exposed to "the ridicule of other Indians."[23]

To strengthen its capacity to suppress "heathenish dances, such as the sun-dance, scalp-dance, etc.," the Interior Department directed the Indian Office in December 1882 to establish courts of Indian offenses. These courts, composed of "progressive" Indian leaders, would convict and sentence Indians for offenses like dancing, polygamy, opposition to schools, giving away annuity goods, and intoxication.[24] Rosebud agent James Wright attempted to wield his new weapon in spring 1883 when he informed Brulé leaders of the new edict banning the Sun Dance and asked them to organize a Court

Judges: Experiments in Acculturation and Control (New Haven, 1966), 42; Mark R. Ellis, "Reservation *Akicitas*: The Pine Ridge Indian Police, 1879–1885," *South Dakota History* 29 (Fall 1999): 189.

[21] John Cook to CIA, 25 Aug. 1881, RA-KC, book 8.

[22] *ARCIA*, 1880, 46 (qtn.); Hagan, *Indian Police and Judges*, 45; Ellis, "Reservation *Akicitas*," 196, 198. On the importance of attire and regalia, see James R. Walker, *Lakota Belief and Ritual*, ed. Raymond J. DeMallie and Elaine A. Jahner (Lincoln, 1980), 270–81.

[23] Hagan, *Indian Police and Judges*, 43; V. T. McGillycuddy to CIA, 4 Aug. 1879, RCA, roll 724; Theodore Schwan to CIA, 26 July 1880, CRA, roll 131 (qtn.).

[24] *Report of the Secretary of the Interior*, 1883, 48th Cong., 1st sess., 1883–84, H. Ex. Doc. 1, pt. 5, serial 2190, xi; Hagan, *Indian Police and Judges*, 104–125; Francis Paul Prucha, *The Great Father: The United States Government and the American Indians*, 2 vols. (Lincoln, 1984), 2:646–48.

of Indian Offenses. But not a single leader was willing to serve on the court. From the "Indian stand point," Wright was forced to explain to Washington, "the offenses as set forth, and for which punishment is provided, are no offenses at all." As for the Sun Dance, though Wright expressed "in the strongest terms the wishes of the 'Great Father' and my own," he "might as well expect to be obeyed in an order for the Sun to stand still, as in one to suspend or do away with the dance."[25] Wright might have used the police to discourage the dance before it began or to break it up once it was underway, but Wright did not try this tactic. It probably would have failed and might easily have resulted in bloodshed. Agents were usually unwilling to risk open conflict for fear that an episode of violence would reflect badly on their competence.

Although leaders at Rosebud continued to refuse to organize a Court of Indian Offenses, they did agree not to hold a Sun Dance in 1884. Convinced that Brulés had taken an irreversible step toward progress, Wright was dismayed when he learned the following spring that efforts were underway to organize a Sun Dance. Taking "prompt and decisive action," Wright was able to secure "a very reluctant abandonment." Still, in the weeks after the Sun Dance ordinarily would have been held, Indians attributed sickness, death, and severe storms to the dance's suppression and consequently demanded Wright's removal. Some Brulés probably continued to hold small sun dances in remote areas, but the 1883 Sun Dance turned out to be the last one permitted by the government at Rosebud until the 1920s.[26]

Wright's success in suppressing the Sun Dance at Rosebud was probably primarily because of his use of economic weapons. In May 1886 Wright requested permission to withhold issues of oxen, wagons, harnesses, and other agricultural implements until August when the time for holding a Sun Dance had passed. This allowed him to threaten those considering organizing a dance with the loss of valuable material goods.[27] Wright had other resources at his disposal. He controlled the allocation of freighting and other agency work, he was capable of withholding rations, and he was able to issue passes for travel to other agencies.

The sources for the suppression of the Sun Dance at Pine Ridge reveal deeper complexities. In spring 1883, when Agent McGillycuddy informed Oglalas of the government's order banning the Sun Dance, the Oglalas responded in much the same way as the Brulés. A forceful minority of leaders,

---

[25] *ARCIA*, 1883, 42 (1st qtn.); James G. Wright to CIA, 21 July 1883, RA-KC, book 9 (2d qtn.).

[26] *ARCIA*, 1884, 48; *ARCIA*, 1885, 44 (qtn.); John A. Anderson, Henry W. Hamilton, and Jean Tyree Hamilton, *The Sioux of the Rosebud: A History in Pictures* (Norman, 1971), 156.

[27] *ARCIA*, 1886, 82; James G. Wright to CIA, 27 May 1886, RA-KC, book 12. For a discussion that identifies the police as central to suppressing the Sun Dance, see Clyde Holler, *Black Elk's Religion: The Sun Dance and Lakota Catholicism* (Syracuse, 1995), 116–17.

---

led by Red Cloud, protested that "neither by treaty [n]or otherwise have they relinquished their inherent right of participation in this practice." Oglalas went ahead and held a Sun Dance that summer.[28] Instead of following the Indian Office's directive to create a Court of Indian Offenses, McGillycuddy organized an Agency Council, a body that consisted of one hundred men by 1885. McGillycuddy evidently preferred a large council to a three-man court because he thought he could use it more effectively to undermine the Oglalas' system of *tiyospaye*-based political leadership. In May 1884 McGillycuddy persuaded this council to assist him in stopping the Sun Dance.[29]

McGillycuddy's summary of his discussion with the Agency Council reveals a careful blend of blackmail and bribery. The council, McGillycuddy reported, "fear that a resort to <u>forcible</u> interference on the part of the police would lead to more or less bloodshed." Rather than risk violence and its consequences, the council endorsed McGillycuddy's plan to withhold rations for four weeks from "all Indian families found participating in the dance." If this did not work, the council agreed to support the use of force.[30] McGillycuddy also offered rewards. "As an offset" to the Sun Dance, he allowed Young Man Afraid of His Horses, the president of the council, to lead a party to the Crow Reservation. He also authorized parties led by Little Wound and Blue Horse to travel to the Wind River Reservation to trade for freighting ponies.[31]

Members of the Agency Council must have found it agonizing to cooperate with McGillycuddy's suppression of the Sun Dance. Consider the situation of Little Wound. Only three years before he had watched as his daughter Red Whirlwind cut the sacred tree. He himself had danced in the Sun Dance, and his body bore the scars as a permanent reminder of his ordeal and its meaning.[32] Many other members of the council had danced in the Sun Dance, and even if they had never danced themselves, it was important to them all. Why, then, did they accept their agent's will? Probably the most compelling reason was their fear that the government would use force to suppress the dance and that this would provoke bloodshed. In addition, cooperation brought important material advantages (and prevented such losses). McGillycuddy's authorization of journeys to the Crow and Wind River reservations suggests that the agent would give priority to Young Man Afraid of His Horses, Little Wound, and Blue Horse in allocating freighting work. In addition, leaving the reservation provided opportunities to hunt, thus enabling Oglalas to add to their supplies of food and clothing, always

---

[28] V. T. McGillycuddy to CIA, 27 June 1883, PR-KC, box 35.
[29] V. T. McGillycuddy to CIA, 4 May 1884, 12 Mar. 1885, PR-KC, box 36. By 1885 McGillycuddy was calling the Agency Council the Board of Councilmen.
[30] McGillycuddy to CIA, 4 May 1884 (underlining in original).
[31] V. T. McGillycuddy to CIA, 1 June 1884, OIA, file 10836–1884.
[32] Walker, *Lakota Belief and Ritual*, 67.

a critical consideration. Visiting other tribes also afforded the opportunity to share stories of past raids and battles and, in the case of the Crows, to make friends with former enemies. As Young Man Afraid of His Horses later pointed out, the Oglalas and the Crows both shared similar problems. "[T]he white man is crowding us, and will want to crowd us still more," he explained. Therefore, "I want to visit the Crows and plan with them for the protection of our people." Finally, Oglalas were interested in renewing ties with relatives whom the Crows had captured in the days of conflict between the two tribes.[33]

An account of the Pine Ridge Sun Dance's suppression by the mixed-blood interpreter William Garnett suggests another important factor in the thinking of members of the Agency Council. In a 1907 interview Garnett related that when the time had come to announce the 1884 Sun Dance, the leader of dance, No Flesh, sought McGillycuddy's permission. When McGillycuddy informed No Flesh that he would not allow the Sun Dance, No Flesh asked the agent how he could fulfill his vow to dance. (Failure to fulfill such vows could have serious consequences.)[34] According to Garnett, McGillycuddy replied that "the Indians could go out on the hills and fast and suffer and go into their sweat houses and have their 'carvers' do the usual cutting of flesh as a sacrifice to their God in the sweat houses – do this as they were used to doing in times of stress or urgency when they could hold no regular dance." No Flesh assented to this plan, but, because no "white man had told the agent how to suspend the dance," he wanted to know who had told him. Garnett related that he himself told McGillycuddy what to tell No Flesh but that the agent did not "give Garnett away."[35]

---

[33] Lieut. M. W. Day to Brig. Gen. George Crook, 26 Jan. 1889, OIA, file 5119–1889. Young Man Afraid of His Horses visited the Crow Reservation for the first time in November 1883. See Frederick E. Hoxie, *Parading through History: The Making of the Crow Nation in America, 1805–1935* (Cambridge, 1995), 141–42. I am grateful to Mike Her Many Horses for alerting me to the desire of Oglalas to find out about captive relatives among the Crows.

[34] For example, Densmore, *Teton Sioux Music and Culture*, 101, points out that "[m]ore than one man who disregarded his vow to the sun had perished in a lightning flash; or if he escaped punishment himself, it was known that disaster had befallen his family or his horses."

[35] William Garnett interview, 1907, RT, tablet 1, roll 1. In an e-mail communication, Raymond A. Bucko, the author of *The Lakota Ritual of the Sweat Lodge: History and Contemporary Practice* (Lincoln, 1998), informed me that he had never heard of giving flesh in the sweat lodge ceremony (*inipi*) but did not rule out the possibility. Conversations I have had with Lakota people about Garnett's story reveal a divergence of opinion about whether or not one could fulfill a Sun Dance vow in the sweat lodge or some similar way. On the basis of these conversations and the general theoretical assumption that ritual practice is situational and contingent, I am inclined to think that No Flesh and others had no obvious solution to their problem. It was probably the case, although I cannot find ethnographic evidence to verify it, that precedents existed for using alternative means to fulfill a Sun Dance vow in times of emergency, as Garnett's account indicates. On the other hand, since Lakotas, then as now, had strong opinions about proper procedures, some may have thought the only way to fulfill a vow was in the Sun Dance itself.

It is certainly possible that Garnett's account of his own role in these ne-gotiations is accurate. Yet one cannot help but wonder if members of the Agency Council or even No Flesh himself suggested this plan to McGilly-cuddy with the knowledge that the agent was open to finding a way to let No Flesh fulfill his vows without having a Sun Dance. Whatever the channels of communication and suggested procedure, the general outlines of Garnett's account are confirmed in a biography of McGillycuddy written by his wife, Julia McGillycuddy. She wrote that the "proclamation" her husband issued banning the Sun Dance specified that individuals who had made vows "must go to some secluded spot in order to execute their promise."[36]

McGillycuddy probably thought of this concession as a temporary evil to facilitate the long-term goal of promoting complete assimilation. From his perspective, it would have been better to let No Flesh fulfill his vow than to use military force, because having to rely on the army would reflect poorly on his managerial competence. Oglala leaders would have drawn different implications from their agent's concession. Although they probably grasped something of McGillycuddy's ultimate agenda, they could use his conces-sion to claim a permanent space for having small sun dances as long as they were held discretely and did not interfere with activities like farming. Oglala leaders could also interpret McGillycuddy's concession as indicating his will-ingness to tolerate any religious ceremony that could be conducted in private: vision seeking, keeping the spirits of loved ones who had died, honoring girls when they became women, praying with the pipe, and purification in sweat lodges.

For Agency Council leaders to cooperate in stopping the 1884 Sun Dance, then, did not mean the complete eradication of Lakota religious expression. Even rituals associated with the Sun Dance could continue. For example, although parents had generally had children's ears pierced during the Sun Dance, this practice continued in other contexts.[37] None of this is to deny the great loss Plains Sioux people suffered when the United States suppressed the Sun Dance. The point is that the richness of Sioux religious practice offered abundant means for gaining access to the spiritual powers of the universe. Finally, although Plains Sioux communities were forced to abandon large public sun dances in the 1880s, they continued to hold dances in secret. Many leaders, undoubtedly, saw the possibility that if they kept this ceremony alive, a time would come when conditions would change and they would be able once again to hold large public dances. (This, in fact, has happened.)[38]

---

[36] Julia B. McGillycuddy, *Blood on the Moon: Valentine McGillycuddy and the Sioux* (1941; Lincoln, 1990), 168. McGillycuddy's actual orders in V. T. McGillycuddy to CIA, 1 June 1884, do not say anything about this concession.

[37] Walker, *Lakota Belief and Ritual*, 192.

[38] Amiotte, "Lakota Sun Dance," 75; William K. Powers, *Oglala Religion* (Lincoln, 1975), 120; Holler, *Black Elk's Religion*, 133; Archambault, "Sun Dance," 989–92.

Already in this book, we have seen several instances in which Sioux leaders hoped they had reached a permanent settlement with U.S. officials on a particular matter only to discover that officials wanted more. Land, of course, is a prime example of this phenomenon of "never enough." In the areas of religion and culture, too, the Indian Office was not content with suppressing the Sun Dance. In the 1880s government officials were determined to suppress all of heathenism's manifestations.

Another of the Plains Sioux' most cherished rites was *Wanagi Yuhapi* ("Spirit Keeping" or "Ghost Keeping"). As described in Chapter 7, many families kept the spirit of a deceased relative for a year or more in a "spirit lodge" before releasing the spirit. After this, the family gave away the household's material possessions. Spirit Keeping reinforced a communal ethos, helped relatives deal with emotions of loss and grief, and ensured that the deceased would arrive safely in the next life. Compared to the Sun Dance, Spirit Keeping was a relatively private affair. All members of the community might attend the final giveaway, but even this, the most public aspect of the ritual, was not a tribal event.

At Pine Ridge, McGillycuddy's successor, Hugh D. Gallagher, began targeting Spirit Keeping in 1887. Gallagher regarded certain practices that accompanied Spirit Keeping, such as mourners lacerating their bodies, as "barbaric." But his main objection was to the "giving away and destruction of property at the death of a member of the family." Spirit Keeping reinforced communal values and stood as an obstacle to Indians' development of bourgeois notions of property.[39] All Oglalas, regardless of their attitudes toward the United States on other matters, were deeply distressed by what Gallagher himself called his "war" against Spirit Keeping. At first, Gallagher hoped that some of the supposedly "progressive" Indians would willingly give up this ritual. In "combating this evil," however, Gallagher was surprised when he found himself "opposed by every Indian upon the reservation." Little Wound, Young Man Afraid of His Horses, and Red Cloud, leaders who had not always agreed, unanimously opposed the ban on Spirit Keeping. In December 1888 they informed the "Great Father" that in "stopping our Ghost Lodges" he had "made us ashamed," or to translate the Lakota word they probably used (*istelya*) another way, he had dishonored them and lowered them to the level of the nonhuman. Hoping that the president might be able to grasp the concept of cultural pluralism, they asked him to "consider that we are Indians."[40]

[39] *ARCIA*, 1888, 49. Rosebud Agent J. George Wright's objections to Spirit Keeping were much the same. See *ARCIA*, 1890, 62.

[40] *ARCIA*, 1888, 49; Little Wound, Young Man Afraid of His Horses, and Red Cloud to the Great Father, 10 Dec. 1888, PR-KC, box 54. I am grateful to Jerome Kills Small for explaining the meaning of *istelya*.

Oglalas made every effort to resist the government's assault on Spirit Keeping. According to the Wounded Bear winter count, a bereaved family defied the ban and performed the ceremony in 1888–1889. Oglalas also exploited a loophole in the language of the ban prohibiting "the giving away and destruction of property at death." Instead of performing this ceremony after the death of the individual, they held it a few hours before the person actually died. It is difficult to gauge Gallagher's success in suppressing Spirit Keeping. Father Florentine Digmann, who came to Pine Ridge in August 1888, recalled that "ghostlodges" were "in vogue" at the time, but that Gallagher, a practicing Catholic, "soon abolished them." Almost certainly, however, the government's ban against Spirit Keeping did not result in its complete elimination.[41]

Besides moving against sites of obvious religious activity, the Indian Office also tried to suppress cultural practices of any sort, even when their purpose was mainly social. Western Sioux people loved to dance. The painter George Catlin wrote in 1841 that "I saw so many of their different varieties of dances amongst the Sioux, that I should almost be disposed to denominate them the '*dancing Indians*.'" Although other tribes might have quarreled with the idea of Sioux superiority in this or any other regard, Catlin's observation captured a cultural commitment that remained very much alive half a century later. In the 1880s the most common dance on the Great Sioux Reservation was the Omaha Dance (also known as the Grass Dance). People danced to a variety of songs expressing themes of bravery and generosity. There was always a feast and a giveaway. Other popular social dances included the Night Dance, in which young men and women danced together under adult supervision, the Rabbit Dance, and the Owl Dance. Dancing changed a great deal during the early reservation period. Some dances, such as those previously sponsored by warrior societies, probably declined, while new dances emerged.[42]

During the 1880s agents boasted that they had put an end to dancing of any sort everywhere under their jurisdiction. From Cheyenne River William

---

[41] Stephen E. Feraca, ed., *The Wounded Bear Winter Count* (Kendall Park, N.J., 1994), 23; *ARCIA*, 1888, 49; Florentine Digmann, "History of the St. Francis Mission, 1886–1922," unpublished manuscript, n.d., series 7, box 14, folder 7, p. 15, Holy Rosary Mission Records, Marquette University Special Collections, Milwaukee.

[42] George Catlin, *Letters and Notes on the Manners, Customs, and Condition of the North American Indians*, 2 vols. (London, 1841), 1:244 (italics in original); Clark Wissler, *Societies and Ceremonial Associations in the Oglala Division of the Teton-Dakota*, Anthropological Papers of the American Museum of Natural History, 11, pt. 1 (1912): 48–52, 78–79; Densmore, *Teton Sioux Music and Culture*, 468–77; Ben Black Bear Sr. and R. D. Theisz, *Songs and Dances of the Lakota* (Aberdeen, S.Dak., 1976), 19–20; Royal B. Hassrick, *The Sioux: Life and Customs of a Warrior Society* (Norman, 1964), 156–59; Thomas E. Mails, *Fools Crow*, assisted by Dallas Chief Eagle (1979, Lincoln, 1990), 82; Samuel Charger, "Biography of Martin Charger," *South Dakota Historical Collections* 22 (1946): 19.

Swan reported in August 1883 that he had "broken up entirely the dancing on this agency." How had he done this? "I tore down the Indian dance house," he crowed, "and took away from them their drum." In a penetrating ethnographic observation, Swan informed Washington bureaucrats that this drum was a "dancing musical instrument." But tearing down one dance house and confiscating a single drum hardly eliminated the Cheyenne River Indians' capacity to sing and dance. Undoubtedly, even as Swan was penning his report, Indians throughout his jurisdiction were moving their feet to the heartbeat of grandmother earth. Swan's own reports indicate his failure to suppress dancing. In 1885 Swan noted that he sent police to "Sans Arc[s] Camp to stop Grass Dance and arrest Ring leaders" and went to "stop Dancing on Bad River and at Pierre." Dancing had been cut off in one place, but like a hydra, it had sprung up in three. Swan's successor, Charles McChesney, had to admit that in at least two villages, one at Cherry Creek and the other on the upper Cheyenne River, Indians were spending "most of their time in dancing."[43]

Over the course of the 1880s Sioux people were able to preserve some space for social dancing. At Pine Ridge, for example, in 1885 Agent McGilly-cuddy promulgated rules against dancing and drumming on the Sabbath and arrested violators. Although oppressive, these rules at the same time bore witness to the limits of McGillycuddy's power, as they had the effect of establishing the legality of dancing and drumming on the other six days. One of the reasons Sioux people were able to protect dancing was their ability to articulate effective arguments. In 1883, for example, White Ghost, a Lower Yanktonai chief at Crow Creek Agency, told a government commission that when he went to visit "the Great Father in Washington" he had seen "amusements of all kinds. . . . I saw the white people, both men and women, dancing together. . . . Well, we dance here too, and use a drum, and I think we gain a great deal by these dances." But what about the argument that dancing was bad because it took Indians away from their farms? White Ghost was ready with a reply: "If we dance a part of the time we feel brighter, and then we turn out again and open up our farms and work hard."[44]

---

[43] William A. Swan to CIA, 11 Aug. 1883, CR-KC, box 263; Cheyenne River Agency Diary, 24 July 1885, CR-KC, box 273; *ARCIA*, 1887, 20. On the drum as the "heartbeat of *unci* (grandmother) earth," see Severt Young Bear and R. D. Theisz, *Standing in the Light: A Lakota Way of Seeing* (Lincoln, 1994), 47.

[44] V. T. McGillycuddy to CIA, 2 July 1885, PR-KC, box 36; *Testimony Taken by a Select Committee of the Senate Concerning the Condition of the Indian Tribes in the Territories of Montana and Dakota*, 48th Cong., 1st sess., 1883–84, S. Rept. 283, serial 2174, 113. For a discussion of the politics of suppressing dancing on the southern Plains, see Clyde Ellis, "'There is No Doubt . . . the Dances Should be Curtailed': Indian Dances and Federal Policy on the Southern Plains, 1880–1930," *Pacific Historical Review* 70 (November 2001): 543–69.

In the same way that U.S. officials intended to transform grass dancers into Bible readers, they sought to replace the practices of native healers with those of western physicians. From the seventeenth century on, American doctors, especially in frontier regions, had borrowed freely from Indian doctors. "Indian cures" enjoyed widespread currency in popular culture. Although the authority of scientific professional medicine was gaining strength in the late nineteenth century, many western doctors nonetheless remained sympathetic to Indian medicine. From the standpoint of the Indian Office's policy of assimilation, however, native medicine was yet another symptom of savagery. Commissioner of Indian Affairs Hiram Price offered a typical formulation of the issue when he wrote in his 1883 annual report that the "evil influence of the native 'medicine men' is one of the greatest obstacles to be overcome in the civilization of the Indian."[45]

Unlike the case of the Sun Dance, the Indian Office did not ban native medical practices. Officials realized that an outright prohibition against native medicine would provoke enormous opposition and leave the Indian Office open to charges of callous disregard for Indians' welfare. Thus, they encouraged agents and missionaries to promote the voluntary acceptance of western medicine.

Proponents of western medical practices often claimed they were gaining ground. Mary Collins, a missionary at Running Antelope's village at Standing Rock, asserted that she was "fast supplanting the old medicine man who was only a conjurer or a witch at the best." As proof, she related what happened when she was called one day to see a sick child. Before entering the house, Collins noticed several green watermelon rinds. Within the house, several men and women were rattling a wash boiler full of chains and tin cups to scare away an evil spirit. Ever officious, Collins ordered everyone to leave except the child's grandmother and parents. Over the grandmother's denial that the child had eaten any watermelons, Collins administered an emetic and "[i]t was soon proven that his stomache [*sic*] was over loaded with the melons." According to Collins, the grandmother and parents "cried out, 'She is Wakan[.]' 'She saw inside the child and knew what was there.'"[46]

Dr. Z. T. Daniel, the physician at Cheyenne River Agency, also declared a victory for civilization. In 1889 when a government commission visited the agency (see Chapter 10), Daniel's office "was packed each day with patients, and evenings they had me going through their camps." The medicine men "are the most insuperable obstacles in the path of [the Indians'] general

---

[45] Paul Starr, *The Social Transformation of American Medicine* (New York, 1982), 48–49, 79–144; Virgil J. Vogel, *American Indian Medicine* (Norman 1970), 124–47; *ARCIA*, 1883, xliii (qtn.). See also *ARCIA*, 1884, xxxvi; *ARCIA*, 1886, xl–xli; *ARCIA*, 1889, 13; *ARCIA*, 1890, xix–xx.

[46] Richmond L. Clow, ed., "Autobiography of Mary C. Collins, Missionary to the Western Sioux," *South Dakota Historical Collections* 41 (1982): 44.

advancement toward civilization," but, Daniel observed, their pernicious influence persisted only because they were unable to travel to the distant camps.[47]

Collins and Daniel both held a flawed theory of culture change to say nothing of an inflated sense of their own role in effecting it. The extension of the kingdom of God (for Collins) or civilization (for Daniel) involved a step-by-step substitution of native with non-native practices. Although many Sioux were willing to use western medicine in some situations, few saw its occasional use as a replacement for native healing methods. Consistent with their pragmatic evaluation of the efficacy of medical practice, the Plains Sioux incorporated European American medical practices into an already existing range of specialized approaches to treating specific ailments.

In the absence of a detailed study of Sioux medicine during this period, it is impossible to provide more than a brief overview. The ethnographic literature makes a distinction between two types of practitioners. *Wicasa wakan* ("sacred" or "powerful" men) and *winyan wakan* ("sacred" or "powerful" women) were capable of calling on *wakan* beings for spiritual power to assist humans in a variety of ways, including healing. *Pejuta wicasa* and *pejuta winyan* (literally, "grassroots" men and women) knew how to use herbs to treat a variety of ailments. These methods were not mutually exclusive. As the ethnomusicologist Francis Densmore pointed out, it was "not unusual for the same man [or woman] to use more than one of these methods, but he was best known by the one which he employed the most."[48]

In the early 1900s at Standing Rock, Densmore collected substantial information from several medicine men, who were widely known for their ability to treat specific ailments. Using visionary power, prayers, songs, and plants, individual healers were known for their ability to treat consumption, scrofula, wounds, headaches, heart trouble, tonsillitis, rheumatism, stomach pains, and broken bones.[49] Physicians employed by the U.S. government often dismissed the claims of Sioux healers. For example, J. M. Woodburn, the Rosebud Agency physician, regarded most of Lakota medicine as involving little more than the use of the "tom-tom" and other "noisy doings." Nonetheless, Woodburn was forced to admit that "[s]ome of their remedies are extremely efficacious." He was especially impressed by Sioux doctors'

---

[47] *ARCIA*, 1889, 133.

[48] Powers, *Oglala Religion*, 56; Densmore, *Teton Sioux Music and Culture*, 245. Marla N. Powers, *Oglala Women: Myth, Ritual, and Reality* (Chicago, 1986), 96, uses the term *wapiye winyan* ("curing woman") as a synonym for *pejuta winyela* (a variant of *pejuta winyan*). However, Densmore, *Teton Sioux Music and Culture*, 245, uses the term *wapiya* for one who "'conjured' the sick," and thus presumably as a kind of *wicasa wakan* or *winyan wakan*. Densmore also provides another term, *wakanhan*, for a "conjurer" who relied on sacred stones to heal the sick.

[49] Densmore, *Teton Sioux Music and Culture*, 244–76.

abilities to set fractures and repair dislocations. In a similar way, James R. Walker, who became agency physician at Pine Ridge in 1896 and established close relations with several *wicasa wakans*, contended that "most of their medicines are inert, and...their practices consist mostly of mysticism and trickery." Still, Walker conceded, their ceremonies "beget an expectation of relief so that when the medicine man suggests that there is relief the patient declares he feels it."[50]

In the 1880s serious weaknesses in the Indian Office's medical program precluded a head-to-head test of western versus native medicine.[51] For one thing, a position that required riding around an Indian reservation in the dead of a Dakota winter with little monetary compensation did not attract the most qualified personnel. Although some of the doctors the Indian Office employed were devoted and a portion of those were competent, others failed to inspire confidence. The reputation of American-style medicine was hardly advanced when a government physician misdiagnosed a skin ailment as smallpox, as happened at Rosebud in 1880. Six years later, Captain J. W. Bell, temporarily in charge at Pine Ridge, complained that the agency physician was "totally unfit and incompetent" and observed that none of the Indians were "willing to take his prescriptions." Bell could hardly blame them, because he did not trust this physician with his own health.[52]

Another problem was that the Indian Office failed to provide adequate resources. Supplies of medicine often ran low, and it was impossible for physicians, even when willing and able, to attend to more than a small portion of the Indians under their jurisdiction. The Indian Office failed to provide many doctors with a team of horses and a wagon to visit outlying areas. Distances made it impossible for physicians to respond rapidly to particular cases of illness. The policy of encouraging Indians to live apart from one another only exacerbated the difficulties facing a doctor who sincerely desired to see as many patients as possible.[53] Any serious effort to improve the health of Indians would have required the employment of additional assistants, nurses, and the construction of a hospital at each agency. The

---

[50] *ARCIA*, 1889, 162; Walker, *Lakota Belief and Ritual*, 10. For a brief overview of Lakota medical practices, see Hassrick, *The Sioux*, 288–91.

[51] For an overview of the problems in the government's Indian health program in the late 1800s and early 1900s, see Prucha, *Great Father*, 2:841–47; for a discussion of a similar situation, see Robert A. Trennert, *White Man's Medicine: Government Doctors and the Navajo, 1863–1955* (Albuquerque, 1998), 59–76.

[52] Cicero Newell to CIA, 1 Mar. 1880, RA-KC, book 7; Capt. J. W. Bell to CIA, 1 June 1886, PR-KC, box 36. See also the complaints against the Standing Rock Agency physician in James McLaughlin to CIA, 2 Sept. 1889, MP, roll 33.

[53] Ambler Caskie to James McLaughlin, 12 Aug. 1889, MP, roll 33; *ARCIA*, 1889, 133, 162; Kay Graber, ed., *Sister to the Sioux: The Memoirs of Elaine Goodale Eastman, 1885–91* (Lincoln, 1978), 45; *ARCIA*, 1890, 62–63.

government built a hospital at Standing Rock in 1889, but not at the other agencies. There remained a chronic shortage of personnel.[54]

Even when the Indian Office and missionaries succeeded in delivering medical treatment, a corresponding decline in the influence of native healers did not result. A Lakota who swallowed a dose of cod liver oil did not suddenly adopt the worldview of the prescribing physician. Western medicine was worth trying, and it sometimes worked, but its efficacy did not mean that native medicine was any less valuable. Nor did western medical techniques necessarily remain under the control of Americans. Evidence suggests that Sioux healers sometimes incorporated specific practices. For example, Dr. Woodburn complained that many of his "patients" were actually "medicine men." Only through using the "utmost tact and rigid questioning" was Woodburn able to determine whether these men wanted the medicine for their own families or "whether they were describing the symptoms of a patient of their own." Charles A. Eastman, a mixed-blood Santee Sioux with a degree in medicine from Boston University who worked as the government physician at Pine Ridge in the late 1880s, observed that Oglala doctors "call[ed] at my office to consult me, or 'borrow' my medicine."[55]

Native doctors who used western medicine were especially interested in acquiring treatments for patients afflicted with European-introduced diseases. Over the years, Sioux healers had developed some methods for treating such ailments, but with only mixed success. Shooter, one of Densmore's informants, told her that "in the old days the Indians had few diseases," and so it was possible for a "medicine-man" to treat "one special disease." A "medicine man would not try to dream of *all* herbs and treat *all* diseases, for then he could not expect to succeed in all." This, Shooter remarked, was "one reason why our medicine-men lost their power when so many diseases came among us with the advent of the white man."[56] Rather than try to use their own methods to devise treatments for new diseases, Sioux doctors often tried to borrow already-developed western practices.

By 1890 Plains Sioux people had been exposed to western medicine more than ever before, but the practice of native medicine had hardly declined. Although this represented a victory for cultural persistence, Indian practitioners had a difficult time combating the serious health problems that resulted from the conditions of reservation life.

---

[54] *ARCIA*, 1889, 168; *ARCIA*, 1890, 45, 63.

[55] *ARCIA*, 1889, 162; Charles A. Eastman (Ohiyesa), *From the Deep Woods to Civilization: Chapters in the Autobiography of an Indian* (1916; Lincoln, 1977), 123. A useful discussion of the interactions between western and native medicine is Mary-Ellen Kelm, *Colonizing Bodies: Aboriginal Health and Healing in British Columbia, 1900–50* (Vancouver, 1998), 153–72.

[56] Densmore, *Teton Sioux Music and Culture*, 244–45 (italics in original).

Reports from the Standing Rock Agency show a high death rate during the 1880s. The lowest death rate reported during the decade was 31.6 per 1,000 in 1884–1885. In three years (1881–1882, 1888–1889, and 1889–1890), the death rate exceeded 50 per 1,000. Measles, influenza, and whooping cough claimed many victims, but the most consistent killer was tuberculosis in its two forms, consumption (pulmonary tuberculosis) and scrofula (glandular tuberculosis).[57] Plains Sioux people had probably suffered from tuberculosis in earlier times, but it did not become a serious problem until the reservation period.[58] Several factors would have contributed to the rise of tuberculosis. Houses were poorly ventilated and dried expectorant from infected persons accumulated in the dirt floors. Tipis had far better air circulation, and the frequent movement of camps in earlier times discouraged the development of unsanitary conditions. Poor diet, including infected beef, as well as social stress, emotional anguish, and the decline of physical activity were also likely relevant.[59]

Thus far in this chapter, we have been mostly concerned with the government's suppression of Plains Sioux religious and cultural practices. Ultimately, however, the project of assimilation entailed not just the eradication of the barbarism of the Sun Dance but Indians' willing embrace of Christianity. During the 1880s, as the government ratcheted up its assault on Lakota culture and religion, missionary activities increased correspondingly. Missionaries were optimistic that through God's grace Plains Sioux people would accept Christianity, and they baptized many Sioux Indians. But baptism usually did not entail conversion in the sense that missionaries understood this process. Nor did it mean a rejection of Sioux identity.

[57] These figures are based on reports in *ARCIA*, 1880–1891. By comparison, the mortality rate in New York City in the same decade was between 25 and 30 per 1,000; the national rate in 1900 was 17.2. See Gretchen A. Condran, "Changing Patterns of Epidemic Disease in New York City," in *Hives of Sickness: Public Health and Epidemics in New York City*, ed. David Rosner (New Brunswick, 1995), 29; U.S. Department of Commerce, Bureau of the Census, *Historical Statistics of the United States: Colonial Times to 1970*, 2 vols. (Washington, D.C., 1975), 1:59.

[58] Washington Matthews, "Consumption among the Indians," *Transactions of the Third Annual Meeting of the American Climatological Association*, 1886 (New York, 1887), 239–40; Aleš Hrdlička, *Tuberculosis among Certain Indian Tribes of the United States*, Bureau of American Ethnology Bulletin 42 (Washington, D.C., 1909), 1–2; John B. McDougall, *Tuberculosis: A Global Study in Social Pathology* (Baltimore, 1949), 243; Jane E. Buikstra, "Introduction," in *Prehistoric Tuberculosis in the Americas*, Northwestern University Archeological Program Scientific Papers 5, ed. Jane E. Buikstra (Evanston, Ill., 1981), 1–14.

[59] Hrdlička, *Tuberculosis*, 12–14, 30–32; James D. Walker, "Tuberculosis among the Oglala Sioux Indians," *Southern Workman* 35 (1906): 379–84; Michael E. Teller, *The Tuberculosis Movement: A Public Health Campaign in the Progressive Era* (Westport, Conn., 1988), 18–20; René Dubos and Jean Dubos, *The White Plague: Tuberculosis, Man and Society* (Boston, 1952), 193–207.

Under President Ulysses S. Grant's peace policy, Catholics gained exclusive rights to preach the gospel at Grand River (Standing Rock) Agency and established a mission there in 1876. Episcopalians were given Red Cloud (Pine Ridge), Spotted Tail (Rosebud), and Cheyenne River, where they began missionary work in the late 1870s. Congregationalists also established a mission outpost at Cheyenne River in 1872.[60] In 1881 the government ended the policy of giving a single church monopoly rights at a particular agency; under the new policy of free competition for souls, several new missions were founded. By 1890 three different churches were engaged in mission work at Pine Ridge, Standing Rock, and Rosebud. Cheyenne River still had two.[61]

Missionaries commonly offered remarkable figures to support claims about the progress of their work. In 1889, for example, an Episcopalian catechist at Pine Ridge reported that 165 Indians had been baptized during the previous year and that 2,200 – about half of all Oglalas – now belonged to his church.[62] Perhaps this many Oglalas had at one time or another received baptism, but it is doubtful that more than a handful had become Christian in any meaningful sense. Standing Rock Agent James McLaughlin, himself a Catholic, offered a more realistic assessment when he complained in 1886 that "there is very little sincerity in the religious professions of any of the Indians of this agency." Indians seldom attended "divine services," and when they did it was "almost invariably for a selfish object" such as to be "flattered and feasted."[63] We need not endorse McLaughlin's denigration of Indians' motives for attending church to accept his point that church attendance seldom signified an inner transformation.

Some writers have made much of the fact that Red Cloud and Spotted Tail requested Catholic priests to come to their agencies in the late 1870s.[64] Yet these chiefs had their own reasons for wanting the Black Robes to come. One was that the more churches at their agencies, the more difficult it would be for the Indian Office to move them yet again. Another was that they hoped

---

[60] Prucha, *Great Father*, 1:517–18; Ray H. Mattison, "Indian Missions and Missionaries on the Upper Missouri to 1900," *Nebraska History* 38 (June 1957): 144–45. As noted in Chapter 2, missions were established at Cheyenne River in 1872 (Congregationalist), Standing Rock in 1876 (Catholic), Red Cloud in 1878 (Episcopalian), and Spotted Tail in 1879 (Episcopalian).

[61] Prucha, *Great Father*, 1:522–24. At Standing Rock, Congregationalists established a mission in 1883; Episcopalians followed in 1884. *ARCIA*, 1883, 50–51; *ARCIA* 1885, 55. Presbyterians established a mission at Pine Ridge in 1886 or 1887; Catholics opened one in 1887. *ARCIA*, 1887, 42; Ross Alexander Enochs, *The Jesuit Mission to the Lakota Sioux: Pastoral Theology and Ministry, 1886–1945* (Kansas City, 1996), 29; Robert W. Galler Jr., "A Triad of Alliances: The Roots of the Holy Rosary Indian Mission," *South Dakota History* 28 (Fall 1998): 144–60. At Rosebud, a Catholic mission began in 1886; there was a Presbyterian mission by 1890. *ARCIA*, 1886, 82; *ARCIA*, 1890, 62.

[62] *ARCIA*, 1889, 158.

[63] James McLaughlin to Rev. M. Marty, 11 Feb. 1886, MP, roll 20.

[64] Enochs, *Jesuit Mission*, 24–26.

the Catholic priests would establish effective mission schools. Already there was an Episcopal-run school at Rosebud, but Spotted Tail protested in 1879 that at the rate things were going, no one attending the school would learn English for a "hundred winters." As George Hyde observes, Spotted Tail "did not care a jot about white men's religion," but he "learned to value the ability to speak, read, and write English."[65]

Red Cloud and Spotted Tail also saw the advantages of having two groups of competing missionaries. This would allow them to play the churches off each other and use one or both groups as allies vis-à-vis government officials. At the very least, Christian missionaries brought tangible benefits, not the least of which was food. As Sitting Bull once joked upon being told that there were no fewer than four hundred Christian denominations in the United States, it would be good to have a minister from every one of them at Standing Rock. That way his people would have more to eat.[66]

If the benefits of interchurch competition encouraged the Sioux to seem more interested in Christian truths than they actually were, at a deeper level rivalries between the churches, especially Protestant versus Catholic, could undermine Christianity's credibility. Father Digmann revealed something of the intensities of these divisions when he complained that Episcopal missionaries tried to "alienate the Indians from us" by saying that "we were Jesuits expelled already from Germany as disturbers of the peace" and accusing them of "praying to statues." According to McLaughlin, such disputes did little to help the gospel advance. "[S]eeing the whites disagreeing among themselves" he reported, the Indians at Standing Rock "are either confounded ... or become distrustful and indifferent."[67]

Though the missionaries overstated the numbers of Christian converts and the depth of their transformation, some Sioux did experience some kind of conversion. It is worth considering what such experiences may have involved. Some conversion stories seem to reveal a sudden, thoroughgoing transformation of the sort that conformed to missionaries' expectations. For example, an account of the conversion of Francis (Saswe) Deloria, a Yankton Sioux, told by his grandson, Vine Deloria Sr., seems to suggest an awareness of baptism's capacity for redemption from sin. As a boy, Francis Deloria had a vision in which he killed four Sioux men. When he became a young man, Francis killed the four men, just as foretold in his vision. In each instance, his reasons were legitimate (two of the cases involved in-laws who were wife

[65] Spotted Tail et al. to Our Agent, enclosed in H. C. Bulis to CIA, 17 Mar. 1879, STA, roll 843; George E. Hyde, *Spotted Tail's Folk: A History of the Brulé Sioux* (Norman, 1961), 295.

[66] Gary Clayton Anderson, *Sitting Bull and the Paradox of Lakota Nationhood* (New York, 1996), 148.

[67] Digmann, "History of St. Francis Mission," 7; James McLaughlin to CIA, 18 July 1887, MP, roll 33. See also, Graber, ed., *Sister to the Sioux*, 48.

beaters), but he was deeply troubled nonetheless. As Vine Deloria Sr. related, "[a]fter he killed the fourth man, Grandfather could never drink a cup of water or coffee in peace. The minute he looked into that cup, he would see the face of one of the men he had killed, with a sort of a snarling smile. So he used to shut his eyes to drink." When missionaries first came to the Yankton reservation, Francis Deloria welcomed them and sent his children to their school. Eventually, in 1871, he was baptized and afterward told the presiding Episcopal missionary, "I have been such an awful sinner that it seems to me you would need to take five or six barrels of water to wash away my sins." Later at a feast, Deloria picked up his cup of coffee wondering which of the four faces would look back at him. "But there was no face, no face at all. For Francis Deloria, his sins were gone."[68]

When Vine Deloria Sr. told this story about his grandfather, he was a retired Episcopal priest and related it in terms of salvation from sin. Yet Francis Deloria's "conversion" probably involved pragmatic, political considerations as well. In another interpretation of the story, Vine Deloria Sr.'s son, Vine Jr., notes that when the missionaries first arrived, Francis "saw that they represented the kind of life that the Yanktons would have to live in the future." The "old ways were gone," Francis realized, "and now that the Yanktons were now restricted to a small tract of land, they would have to support themselves in the white man's way." With this in mind, Francis and other Yankton leaders requested the missionaries to help them. As for baptism, Vine Deloria Jr.'s telling of the story suggests that Francis understood it more as a ritual for healing than salvation from sin. After killing the four men, Francis began to see their faces "whenever he would try to drink any liquids." The faces appeared as "reflections, taunting him and uttering threats only he could hear." It was not, then, that Francis felt guilty; rather, he was tormented by spirits who sought revenge. Naturally, Francis – himself a medicine man – "consulted the other Yankton medicine men about a cure for this condition." None was able to help him. In the meantime, by Vine Jr.'s account, Francis sought the missionaries for other reasons. After a few years, Francis was baptized, though with some reluctance. At a feast to celebrate his conversion, Francis "looked in his coffee cup and for the first time in years did not see any of the dead man's faces." Baptism had provided the cure that eluded the Yankton medicine men.[69]

Other evidence indicates that Sioux people often understood Christian ritual primarily in terms of its power to heal. According to Christopher Vecsey, Martin M. Marty, a Benedictine monk, who arrived at Standing Rock in 1876, was "reputed . . . to have the power to cure smallpox with his prayers." While at Rosebud in 1887, Father Digmann and other missionaries had a

---

[68] Vine V. Deloria Sr., "The Establishment of Christianity among the Sioux," in *Sioux Indian Religion*, ed. DeMallie and Parks, 91–111 (qtns., 104–05).

[69] Vine Deloria Jr., *Singing for a Spirit: A Portrait of the Dakota Sioux* (Santa Fe, 2000), 35–36.

"special eye on the sick, that they should not go without being baptized."
Pursuit of the dying, however, led to cultural misunderstandings. Since so
many of those who were baptized died shortly after, Brulés attributed their
deaths to "the pouring on of the water" (a literal rendering of the Lakota
term for baptism, *mniakastan*). By Digmann's account, the missionaries gradually convinced Brulés that sickness, not baptism, was responsible for these
deaths. In so doing, however, they became trapped by the discourse of healing. Digmann noted that after being baptized at the age of eighty, chief Two
Strike never again suffered from the fainting spells that had earlier afflicted
him. Throughout the remaining years of his life, he ascribed his continued
health to baptism and often said "Baptism was good medicine."[70] Missionaries were undoubtedly frustrated when Indians reached conclusions like this.
For them, healing was ultimately instrumental, a means of furthering Indian
acceptance of the gospel. For Indians, however, healing was often an end in
itself, one that fell short of recognizing the necessity for salvation from the
condition of original sin.

Another instance, related by Ella Deloria (Vine Deloria Sr.'s sister), suggests further ways that conversion could be a healing process. A woman
had dreamed of the Thunder Beings but because the *heyoka* ceremony had
been suppressed, she was unable to "appease the thunders." Consequently,
she "wept in terror each time there was a cloud in the sky" for fear that a
storm would build and she would be struck by lightning. Finally, she sought
relief from a Christian minister and was "cured of her fears" and became a
"Christian, a real one." Undoubtedly, this woman's commitment to Christianity was genuine, but her understanding of Christianity, it would seem,
remained distinctively indigenous. The story carries no sense of a recognition
of sin. Rather, it illustrates the ability of a Christian holy man to remedy a
specific spiritual ailment.[71] In other ways, too, Sioux people became Christians to find relief from particular problems. Elizabeth Winyan, an eastern
Sioux who served for years as a "native helper" at the Congregationalist
mission at Cheyenne River, became a Christian, at least in part, to escape an
abusive husband.[72]

Sioux people often referred to Christian priests and ministers as *wicasa
wakan*, the same word they used for their own specialists who were capable
of mediating between humans and the *wakan* beings of the universe.[73] To the
extent that a Sioux *wicasa wakan* used ritual to tap into distinctive aspects

[70] Christopher Vecsey, *Where the Two Roads Meet* (Notre Dame, 1999), 8; Digmann, "History
of the St. Francis Mission," 12.

[71] Deloria, *Speaking of Indians*, 63. For explanations of *heyoka* ceremonies, see Walker, *Lakota
Belief and Ritual*, 155–57; Hassrick, *The Sioux*, 272–77.

[72] Thomas Lawrence Riggs, "Sunset to Sunset: A Lifetime with My Brothers, the Dakotas,"
South Dakota Historical Collections 29 (1958): 191.

[73] See the entries under "minister" and "priest" in John P. Williamson, *An English-Dakota
Dictionary* (1902; Minneapolis, 1992), 108, 152.

of *Wakan Tanka,* so too a Christian *wicasa wakan* would have used unique means to gain access to powerful beings previously unknown to the Sioux. A Sioux "convert" to Christianity might well change some of his or her beliefs and behaviors and might regard certain rituals as more efficacious than others (at least, that is, for the present time). Such moves, however, were consistent with Sioux religious practice, which had always been open to new ways to obtain sacred power. Scott Howard offers a useful distinction between Christianity, which is "exclusive, regarding other religions and systems of thought as incorrect or 'pagan,'" and historic Sioux religion, which "did not rest on actual propositions or on doctrinal statements of belief" and was therefore "inclusive – capable of including many rituals and practices."[74] Conversion, therefore, usually did not involve replacing one belief system with another, but instead involved a process of incorporating Christian elements into a context that, although undergoing change, remained distinctively Lakota.[75]

When they first encountered missionaries, Sioux people probably did not realize the universality of Christianity's claims. As time went on, however, it became clearer that although Indians might appropriate certain Christian practices on their own terms, this approach was actually not what Christians had in mind. Though some Sioux adopted a pragmatic attitude toward the missionaries, if for no other reason than political and material considerations, others came to oppose Christianity. Among these was Sitting Bull. Aaron McGaffey Beede, an Episcopal missionary at Standing Rock in the early 1900s, concluded that Sitting Bull had no objection to Christianity as such, regarding it as one of many manifestations of a "fundamentally

---

74 Scott J. Howard, "Incommensurability and Nicholas Black Elk: An Exploration," *American Indian Culture and Research Journal* 23, no. 1 (1999): 119. Howard's comments are made in the context of the recent debate about the nature of Black Elk's "conversion" to Christianity in the early 1900s and offer a satisfactory alternative to Michael F. Steltenkamp, *Black Elk: Holy Man of the Oglala* (Norman, 1993), who argues that Black Elk became a Christian in the full sense that he regarded Christianity as ultimately superior to "traditional" Lakota religion; and Julian Rice, *Black Elk's Story: Distinguishing Its Lakota Purpose* (Albuquerque, 1991), who contends that Black Elk's Christianity was merely expedient. For other work that recognizes Black Elk's Christianity as genuine but not a repudiation of Lakota religion, see Raymond J. DeMallie, "Nicholas Black Elk and John G. Neihardt: An Introduction," in Raymond J. DeMallie, ed., *The Sixth Grandfather: Black Elk's Teachings as Given to John G. Neihardt* (Lincoln, 1984), 1–74; Holler, *Black Elk's Religion.*

75 William K. Powers, *Voices from the Spirit World: Lakota Ghost Dance Songs* (Kendall Park, N.J., 1990), 10, describes this process as "Lakotafication," a concept similar to the more generic "indigenization," as used, for example, in J. Jorge Klor de Alva, "Aztec Spirituality and Nahuatized Christianity," in *South and Meso-American Native Spirituality: From the Cult of the Feathered Serpent to the Theology of Liberation,* ed. Gary H. Gossen, in collaboration with Miguel León-Portilla (New York, 1993), 173–97. For a nuanced discussion of the relationship between Catholicism and Lakota religion, see Harvey Markowitz, "Converting the Rosebud: A Culture History of Catholic Mission and the Sicangu Lakotas, 1886–1916," Ph.D. diss., University of Chicago, 2002.

Catholic" religion. On occasion, Beede claimed, Sitting Bull prayed to Jesus, and he regarded Mary "as a human incarnation of that mystical 'Mother' whom all the old-time Dakotas were taught to adore." Nonetheless, Sitting Bull opposed Christianity because he "felt that the Church was in some way leagued with the U.S. government in crushing the Dakota nationality" and because of objections to the "requirement of the Church that he should utterly abandon the religion of his fathers in order to share in the rites of the church." Mary Collins, who carried on a long-running debate with Sitting Bull about religion, confirmed that "he hated Christianity and found great satisfaction in taking my converts back into heathendom while of course I felt equal satisfaction in converting his heathen friends."[76]

By the late 1880s, missionaries had become an institutionalized presence in Plains Sioux country, one now firmly linked to an increasingly active and coercive state. Sioux responses to Christianity had always involved political considerations, but the stakes now were higher. More clearly than ever before, the message of the gospel was being articulated in conjunction with a state-directed project of assimilation involving boarding schools, prohibitions against religious and cultural practices, and, as we will see in the next two chapters, attacks on indigenous political leadership and further confiscation of land. As always, Sioux leaders and their people faced agonizing decisions. Many bands would continue to pursue a strategy of trying to make pragmatic compromises with the new order in the hope of preventing damaging losses and possibly making limited gains that could later be built upon. Members of bands with this orientation tended to make accommodations with Christianity, trying to get what they could from the missionaries while preserving space for their own spiritual practices. Bands that were committed to more direct forms of resistance, however, adopted a more confrontational approach to the missionaries' message and actions. Yet even for those most hostile to Christianity, it could not be ignored. Christianity had to be taken into account, argued against, and even partially incorporated, before it could be rejected. This helps explain why, as we will see in later chapters, the Ghost Dance used central themes of Christianity in its effort to renew a world that western civilization had destroyed.

[76] Aaron McGaffey Beede, *Sitting Bull-Custer* (Bismarck, N.Dak., 1913), 44–45; untitled and undated manuscript in Mary Collins Family Papers, box 2, folder 35, South Dakota Historical Society, Pierre.

9

"Great Trouble and Bad Feeling"

Government Agents and Sioux Leaders

From the outset, as the United States tried to establish control over the Plains Sioux, the government's relationship with Sioux leaders was structured by a basic contradiction. On one hand, U.S. officials were dependent on native leaders, at times going so far as to declaring a particular leader "head chief" of the Sioux nation or one of its subdivisions.[1] On the other hand, the government's goal of assimilation called for the eventual destruction of native political organization.

Commissioner of Indian Affairs Thomas Jefferson Morgan forcefully articulated this imperative and its relationship to broader goals when he wrote: "It has become the settled policy of the Government to break up reservations, destroy tribal relations, settle Indians upon their own homesteads, incorporate them into the national life, and deal with them not as nations or tribes or bands, but as individual citizens. The American Indian is to become the Indian American."[2] In the 1880s, as government agents tried systematically to advance this agenda, the contradictions became especially sharp. To advance assimilation, agents tried to destroy the power of some leaders, but in doing so, they had to enlist help from others. Agents' efforts to eliminate chiefs largely failed. Their major effect, it seems, was to aggravate internal divisions among the Sioux.

One of the best-known instances of factionalism among the Sioux in the early reservation involved Spotted Tail and Crow Dog, a headman in the Brulés' Orphan band. Crow Dog had lived with Sitting Bull in Canada before coming to Rosebud sometime in the late 1870s. In writing about this conflict and its violent conclusion, most historians have followed the contours of

---

[1] Examples include the government's selection of Brave Bear as "head chief" of the Sioux in 1851 (Chapter 1) and Spotted Tail of the Brulés and Oglalas (Chapter 3).
[2] *ARCIA*, 1890, vi.

the arguments at the time, taking one side or the other.[3] A more useful approach, however, is neutrally to analyze this dispute in relationship to the contradictions of U.S. policies.

By the early reservation period, Spotted Tail was the preeminent leader of the Brulé people. Some of the militant Brulés who surrendered in 1877 only grudgingly accepted his authority and sharply criticized him for signing away the Black Hills. Nonetheless, in the late 1870s, most of his people accepted and valued Spotted Tail's leadership.[4] Spotted Tail had been instrumental in blocking the United States from removing the Brulés to Indian Territory or the Missouri River, and he effectively negotiated with government officials on matters ranging from the method of issuing beef to non-Indian trespass on reservation lands.[5] Spotted Tail's authority was linked to his control over two important institutions. He oversaw the distribution of annuities, a practice that symbolized his position as primary intermediary between the Brulés and the United States and one that was probably generally accepted as necessary to ensure equity. In addition, his powerful *akicita* (soldiers), consisting of as many as three hundred men, policed the reservation and maintained order.[6]

---

[3] George E. Hyde, *Spotted Tail's Folk: A History of the Brulé Sioux* (Norman, 1961), 308–36, takes Spotted Tail's side; Richmond L. Clow, "The Anatomy of a Lakota Shooting: Crow Dog and Spotted Tail, 1879–1881," *South Dakota History* 28 (Winter 1998): 209–27, takes Crow Dog's. Sidney L. Harring, *Crow Dog's Case: American Indian Sovereignty, Tribal Law, and United States Law in the Nineteenth Century* (Cambridge, 1994), 100–41, offers a more balanced analysis, though on key points adopts a pro–Crow Dog perspective. For biographical information on Crow Dog, see Hyde, *Spotted Tail's Folk*, 312–13; Leonard Crow Dog and Richard Erdoes, *Crow Dog: Four Generations of Sioux Medicine Men* (New York, 1995), 23.

[4] When General George Crook appointed Spotted Tail "head chief" of the Brulés and the Oglalas in October 1876 (see Chapter 3), this merely ratified the relationship he had with his own people, while giving him no standing at all with the Oglalas. My interpretation differs from Clow, "Anatomy of a Lakota Shooting," 212, n. 8, who argues that Spotted Tail's position as "head chief" was "unrecognized by most tribesmen," and Harring, *Crow Dog's Case*, 120, who contends that Spotted Tail lacked "complete legitimacy" because his power was not "derived from the traditional consensus model of the selection of Brule chiefs," and instead was based, "at least in part,...on the army and the Indian agent." It is true that Spotted Tail's authority depended on his success in dealing with U.S. officials, but most Brulés accepted this situation. It is also true that Spotted Tail's authority lacked "complete legitimacy" in that some Brulés questioned or objected to his decisions, but this was common in "traditional" Lakota politics.

[5] Spotted Tail to CIA, 10 Oct. 1879, enclosed in Cicero Newell to CIA, 10 Oct. 1879, STA, roll 844; Spotted Tail et al. to Our Agent, enclosed in H. C. Bulis to CIA, 17 March 1879, STA, roll 843.

[6] Cicero Newell to CIA, 15 Mar. 1880, STA, roll 845; John Cook to CIA, 21 Apr., 12 July 1880, STA, roll 845. On the size of the *akicita* in September 1877, see Jesse M. Lee, "Gen. Jesse M. Lee's Account of the Killing of Chief Crazy Horse at Fort Robinson, Nebr.," in *Crazy Horse: The Invincible Chief*, ed. E. A. Brininstool (Los Angeles, 1949), 26. On the customary duties of Lakota *akicita*, see James R. Walker, *Lakota Society*, ed. Raymond J. DeMallie (Lincoln, 1982), 28–34, 74–94.

As government officials tried to implement assimilation at Rosebud Agency, they acted in contradictory ways. Hoping to show Brulés the value of farming and western lifestyles in general, the Indian Office built a large, two-story house for Spotted Tail in 1879.[7] At the same time, Rosebud agents tried to gain control over Spotted Tail's police. First, they tried to organize a rival force. When this failed, they allowed Spotted Tail's force to operate as the agency's official force but reduced its size.[8] These actions aggravated existing tensions at Rosebud and created new ones. Spotted Tail's house contributed to the perception in some quarters that he was growing rich at the expense of the tribe, with some Brulés probably seeing it as evidence that he had been bribed into selling the Black Hills.[9] In the past, Spotted Tail had been able to maintain the loyalty of the several Brulé bands by using the *akicita* as a form of patronage, but the reduction in its size made this more difficult. Presumably to keep the peace with potential rivals, he appointed Crow Dog as police captain, but this move could not completely overcome the new structural constraints.[10]

Rosebud agents continued to fight with Spotted Tail over the police. Shortly after the arrival of a new agent, John Cook, in April 1880, Spotted Tail ordered the *akicita* to enforce a boycott of two licensed traders. Cook saw this action as a challenge to his authority and ordered one policeman, Thunder Hawk, to go to the site of the boycott and "dismiss the police he found performing unlawful duty." When Thunder Hawk declined, Cook himself went to "the scene of the disturbance" and demanded the police to "at once withdraw." The police replied that they were there "in obedience to the orders of the chief, Spotted Tail." Cook informed them that they were not allowed to take orders from anyone without his approval. With Thunder Hawk's help, Cook finally succeeded in dispersing the police. In a long "interview," described by Cook as "quite warm at intervals," Spotted Tail insisted that the police belonged to him but agreed to refer the matter to a tribal council and act upon their advice. According to Cook, "[t]he council was held, and the result proved satisfactory to me." Within a few days, the police had resumed their duties, and, according to Cook, Spotted Tail

[7] C. Terry to CIA (two letters), 3 June 1879, STA, roll 844; Hyde, *Spotted Tail's Folk*, 317–18.

[8] Henry Lelar to William J. Pollock, 30 Sept. 1878, STA, roll 843; C. Terry to CIA, 31 Aug. 1879, STA, roll 844; Cicero Newell to CIA, 4 Sept. 1879, STA, roll 844; Cicero Newell to My Dear Col., 22 Oct. 1879, STA, roll 844; Hyde, *Spotted Tail's Folk*, 311–12.

[9] Hyde, *Spotted Tail's Folk*, 317. Hyde, *Spotted Tail's Folk*, 313–14; and Clow, "Anatomy of a Lakota Shooting," 217, discuss criticisms of Spotted Tail for collecting grazing fees from Nebraska ranchers and keeping them for his personal use, but I have been unable to find original documentation for this.

[10] It is unclear when Crow Dog became captain of the police, but he was dismissed in late February 1880. See Cicero Newell to My Dear Col., 24 Feb. 1880, STA, roll 845.

apologized to the traders, saying "he had been agent so long that he forgot his Great Father had sent him one!"[11]

Thinking he had won a major victory, Agent Cook began cultivating a group of rival leaders to further undermine Spotted Tail's power. At a council on May 13, Cook met with several headmen, including Thunder Hawk, Quick Bear, and Crow Dog. They signed a letter to the Commissioner of Indian Affairs in which they stated their support for the agent and raised questions about Spotted Tail's leadership. They expressed particular concern about Spotted Tail's role as part of a delegation, scheduled to depart soon, to inspect the boarding school at Carlisle, Pennsylvania. The signers of the letter objected that Spotted Tail was "not telling us what he will do when he gets there; all the young head men are dissatisfied; although he is our chief, I hope you will not listen to what he says."[12] As we saw in Chapter 7, Spotted Tail was dismayed by what he saw at Carlisle and took some of his children home with him. For Washington officials, Spotted Tail was now an enemy of civilization. Even before Spotted Tail returned to Rosebud, Interior Secretary Carl Schurz sent a letter to Cook denouncing him.[13] When Spotted Tail returned, Cook and an emerging block of rival leaders seized the opportunity to discredit him.

According to Cook, at a council of the "best" Indians held on July 9, Spotted Tail was "openly charged with deceit, corruption, and treachery." Not only on his recent trip to Carlisle, but in "times and ways without number," he had "deprived them of their just rights and had exerted his influence towards their retrogression rather than their advancement." The council called for the division of the Brulés into two bands so that Spotted Tail would no longer control the distribution of annuities and "retain his baleful influence." Cook, it appeared, had delivered a serious blow to Spotted Tail's power. Two days later, however, a larger council of Brulé leaders, one that included Spotted Tail, overturned the previous council's decisions and decreed that Spotted Tail would continue to have "management & controll [*sic*] of the distribution of the Brule Annuities." Cook's report of this meeting gave two reasons, both plausible, for the outcome. The first was that Brulé leaders feared that the "breaking of Spotted Tail" was "an entering wedge to the displacement of all of the rest." The second was that Spotted Tail used his "magnetic influence" to sway wavering Brulés to his side.[14]

---

[11] *ARCIA*, 1880, 46–47. Spotted Tail's boycott of the traders was evidently because they had combined to raise prices. See CIA to John Cook, 30 Apr. 1880, STA, roll 845.

[12] Quick Bear et al. to CIA, 14 May 1880, STA, roll 845. Other signers of this letter included Standing Bear, Afraid of Hawk, Crazy in Lodge, Big Star, White Thunder, Good Voice, White Crane Walking, Burning Breast, Black Horn, Red Fish, and Brave Bull.

[13] This letter is referred to in John Cook to CIA, 9 July 1880, STA, roll 845.

[14] Ibid.; John Cook to CIA, 12 July 1880, STA, roll 845.

Cook's ploy of using a poorly organized faction to bring down Spotted Tail had clearly failed. The agent tried to remove the sting of defeat by blustering that the chief was an "inveterate termigant [*sic*] and tyrant." But the decision of the council suggested that Spotted Tail still commanded significant support among his people. Indeed, the July crisis convinced Cook that he had no choice but to tolerate Spotted Tail's power. Never again did he challenge the chief.[15]

Some evidence suggests that Crow Dog and Spotted Tail attempted to overcome their disagreements after the July 11 council. Although Crow Dog had been dismissed from the police force five months earlier, either by Spotted Tail or Agent Cicero Newell, sometime in mid-July Spotted Tail reappointed Crow Dog to the force and made him captain. For a time, the two men were apparently on reasonably good terms. Later in July, six members of the tribal police, sent to recover some horses that ranchers had stolen from the Brulés, killed a non-Indian. Crow Dog and Spotted Tail worked together to arrest the six policemen and hand them over to military authorities for trial.[16]

Nonetheless, tensions continued to surface over the next several months. In February 1881 Swift Bear, Two Strike, White Thunder, and Crow Dog complained to an unnamed "friend in Congress" that Spotted Tail had grown rich from the sale of their land and that when "the railroad is built through this country," he will "again receive pay for it in secret." They also contended that Spotted Tail had made "all our people angry" by bringing his children home from Carlisle the previous summer. Interestingly, these complaints were forwarded to the Indian Office by William J. Cleveland, an Episcopal missionary at Rosebud. Ever since 1879 when Spotted Tail demanded that the Episcopalians be replaced with Catholics, Cleveland had reason to oppose Spotted Tail. For their part, Crow Dog and his allies must have realized that Cleveland was likely to second their criticisms of Spotted Tail and give them leverage with his influential friends in the East.[17]

We know few details about what happened between the two men until July 4, when Crow Dog confronted Spotted Tail following holiday festivities

---

[15] Cook to CIA, 12 July 1880.

[16] Newell to My Dear Col., 24 Feb. 1880; Hyde, *Spotted Tail's Folk*, 315–16; John Cook to CIA, 9 Aug. 1880, STA, roll 845; *ARCIA*, 1880, 47.

[17] Swift Bear, Two Strike, and White Thunder to My Friend in Congress, 26 Feb. 1881, enclosed in William J. Cleveland to CIA, 26 Feb. 1881, OIA, file 4761–1881 (1st qtn.); Swift Bear, Two Strike, White Thunder, and Crow Dog to My Friend in Congress, 26 Feb. 1881, enclosed in Cleveland to CIA, 26 Feb. 1881 (2d qtn.). Hyde, *Spotted Tail's Folk*, 330, argues that after sending this letter and realizing it had no effect, Crow Dog and his friends gave up on nonviolent means for removing Spotted Tail and began to plot his murder, though there is no concrete evidence for this view. Clow, "Anatomy of a Killing," 219, uses the 26 Feb. 1881 letters as examples to support his argument that Spotted Tail's actions clearly violated Lakota cultural norms and that he was rapidly losing support among his people. Yet there is no evidence for this view beyond the statements of Spotted Tail's opponents.

at the agency. Crow Dog may have pointed a gun at Spotted Tail, although Crow Dog later denied this. Later that day, Spotted Tail complained to Cook of "the hostile demonstrations that were being made against him by [Crow Dog] and his faction." Soon after, Cook dismissed Crow Dog from the police force.[18] Before this date, there is no hint in the record that either man threatened violence against the other. After July 4, however, both Crow Dog and Spotted Tail had reason to fear for their lives.

Crow Dog killed Spotted Tail one month later, on August 5. The shooting took place following a meeting of tribal leaders. During this council (or as it was adjourning), several Brulés criticized Spotted Tail for having taken the wife of a man named Medicine Bear some days before.[19] George Hyde rejects the story of a dispute about a woman as a pure fabrication. Richmond Clow, however, offers a letter from Reverend Cleveland written one day after the killing as evidence to the contrary. According to Cleveland, when Spotted Tail "ran off" with another man's wife, "the affection & respect of the people was so thoroughly estranged from him especially by this last dirty deed that no one seemed to be surprised that he was shot." Although Cleveland's letter offers strong support for the existence of a dispute about a woman, it does not necessarily mean that, in Cleveland's words, "the people" were united in a "growing hatred and jealousy" of Spotted Tail.[20] Given Spotted Tail's advocacy of Catholic instead of Episcopalian missionaries, to say nothing of Cleveland's beliefs about proper sexual conduct, Cleveland was scarcely a neutral observer.

Assessing the morality of Spotted Tail's actions from a Sioux perspective is complicated. It was not uncommon for a Sioux man to take up with the wife of another man. The word for this, *wiinahme*, conveys a sense of a man hiding or concealing another man's wife. A husband, of course, would see theft and betrayal in such an act, but a wife might see freedom. In Plains Sioux society, as in most societies, significant tensions surrounded obligations of marriage. Wives often left husbands and could find support among the new husband's relatives. On the other hand, relatives of a jealous husband sometimes killed the new lover, and a jealous husband might cut off a nose or ear of a former wife (hence, the need for hiding). To mediate conflicts, a new husband or his relatives might give something of value to the jilted husband in restitution.[21]

---

[18] Hyde, *Spotted Tail's Folk*, 330; *Black Hills Daily Times*, 17 Mar. 1882, p. 4 (qtn.), 21 Mar. 1882, p. 4.

[19] Medicine Bear is the name given in Julia B. McGillycuddy, *Blood on the Moon: Valentine McGillycuddy and the Sioux* (1941; Lincoln, 1990), 177; Crow Dog and Erdoes, *Crow Dog*, 34.

[20] Hyde, *Spotted Tail's Folk*, 333–34; Clow, "Anatomy of a Lakota Shooting," 222; William Cleveland to William H. Hare, 6 Aug. 1881, William H. Hare Papers, box 1, folder 38, Center for Western Studies, Augustana College, Sioux Falls, S.Dak.

[21] Marla N. Powers, *Oglala Women: Myth, Ritual, and Reality* (Chicago, 1986), 87–89.

With this in mind, it is hardly surprising that Spotted Tail's action provoked anger among many Brulés, especially the woman's former husband
and his relatives (Crow Dog was possibly among them).[22] Yet it is not clear
that Spotted Tail violated obvious tribal norms. At his trial, Crow Dog himself did not argue that it was wrong for Spotted Tail to take another man's
wife nor did he charge Spotted Tail with failing to provide compensation.
The allegation was more specific: "he ought to have bought [a wife] from
some man having more than one."[23] Many Brulés probably agreed. Spotted
Tail already had four wives to say nothing of a reputation as a woman-
izer. (According to one source, Spotted Tail was nicknamed "Speaking with
Women.")[24] Still, it was hardly unprecedented for a tribal leader to do something like this. There is every indication that the woman went willingly, and
besides, Spotted Tail offered restitution. Although his action was controversial, it is highly doubtful that it discredited him to the extent Cleveland
claimed.

Crow Dog left the council before Spotted Tail. He was in a wagon with his
wife, Pretty Camp, and their child. Soon after, Spotted Tail left on horseback.
Both men were headed toward the agency, a few miles from the council site.
According to Crow Dog's trial testimony, he stopped to fix a loose board
from his wagon that had fallen to the ground. A few moments later Spotted
Tail approached at a full gallop. Spotted Tail slowed to a walk, searched
for a weapon, and then pulled a pistol on Crow Dog. Before Spotted Tail
could fire, Crow Dog drew his gun and fired the fatal shot. The prosecution,
however, argued that the loose board was a ruse and that the killing was an
act of cold-blooded murder. Several Brulés testified that they had witnessed
the shooting and that Spotted Tail did not have a gun.[25]

Historians have followed the structure of the arguments in Crow Dog's
trial and have contended either that Crow Dog intended to kill Spotted Tail
or vice versa.[26] No one, however, has considered the possibility that neither
man intended to kill the other and that both acted in self-defense.

---

[22] Although Cleveland to Hare, 6 Aug. 1881, says that Crow Dog was "no relation" to the
woman, Crow Dog and Erdoes, *Crow Dog*, 34, suggests Medicine Bear was a "relative and
friend" of Crow Dog.

[23] *Black Hills Daily Times*, 21 Mar. 1882, p. 4.

[24] Crow Dog and Erdoes, *Crow Dog*, 34.

[25] *Black Hills Daily Times*, 17 Mar. 1882, p. 4; 18 Mar. 1882, p. 1; 20 Mar. 1882, p. 4; 21
Mar. 1882, p. 4.

[26] Clow, "Anatomy of a Lakota Shooting," 223; Mary Crow Dog and Richard Erdoes, *Lakota
Woman* (New York, 1990), 182; Crow Dog and Erdoes, *Crow Dog*, 35, argue that Crow
Dog fired in self-defense. Hyde, *Spotted Tail's Folk*, 332, argues that Crow Dog planned to
kill Spotted Tail. More than other historians, Harring, *Crow Dog's Case*, 121–25, shows
awareness of the limitations of the evidence, but in endorsing the legitimacy of Crow Dog's
claim to self-defense, his narrative implies that Spotted Tail intended to kill him.

Despite much of the trial testimony, it is doubtful that Spotted Tail was unarmed. Spotted Tail usually carried a revolver, and common sense suggests he probably had one on August 5.[27] Furthermore, affidavits gathered after the trial offer substantial evidence that Spotted Tail was armed, that Calls on the People, the wife of Spotted Tail's friend High Bear, took his pistol after he was shot and gave it to Spotted Tail's son, and that Spotted Tail's family gave horses to witnesses willing to testify that Spotted Tail was unarmed.[28] If Spotted Tail was armed, however, it does not mean that he intended to kill Crow Dog. Seeing Crow Dog crouched behind a wagon, Spotted Tail may well have drawn his gun as a defensive measure.

On the other hand, it is doubtful that Crow Dog planned to kill Spotted Tail. If, as Spotted Tail partisans like Hyde have argued, Crow Dog began plotting Spotted Tail's death several months before, why did it take him so long to do it and why didn't he choose more favorable circumstances? As Crow Dog's defense attorney pointed out, if he was planning a murder, Crow Dog would not have risked the lives of his wife and child.[29] Crow Dog probably was fixing his wagon when he saw Spotted Tail. When Spotted Tail drew his weapon, Crow Dog might well have feared that Spotted Tail intended to kill him. Crow Dog, too, would have drawn his gun, also in self-defense. Perhaps, then, the killing of Spotted Tail involved neither cold-blooded murder nor self-defense in the face of murderous intent, but rather mistaken judgments on the part of both men.

No matter how the killing happened, however, analyses that take one side or the other overlook the broader context in which Spotted Tail was killed. As we have seen, conflict between the two men became serious only when government agents tried to use Crow Dog to destroy Spotted Tail's power. Once the conflict began, basic conditions of reservation life made it difficult to resolve. In earlier times, rivals could go their separate ways, but now they were forced to coexist within an ever-contracting space with diminishing resources. Under these conditions, it became increasingly difficult to resolve conflicts.

Government officials seized upon the killing of Spotted Tail to advance their stalled agenda for assimilation. The day after the killing, Rosebud Agent Cook reported that "the murder" was the result of a "well-matured plan" by a few "conspirators" to make one of their own number head chief. Having

---

[27] In an affidavit dated 15 Feb. 1883, Brave Bull stated that Spotted Tail "always carried" a revolver. See Crow Dog Trial and Related Papers, folder 3, South Dakota Historical Society, Pierre.

[28] Affidavits of No Flesh, 5 Jan. 1883, V. T. McGillycuddy, 6 Jan. 1883, Pretty Camp, 31 Jan. 1883, William Garnett, 20 Feb. 1883, William Henry Wright, 25 Sept. 1883, in Crow Dog Trial and Related Papers, folder 3.

[29] *Black Hills Daily Times*, 23 Mar. 1882, p. 1.

exposed this plot and therefore the illegitimacy of any claim the conspirators might make to succeed Spotted Tail, Cook then indicted the institution of head chief as a "hindrance to civilization" and called for its abolition.[30] Cook also tried to use the killing to subject the Brulés to the authority of U.S. legal institutions. In the aftermath of Spotted Tail's death, a Brulé council convened to ensure that relatives of the deceased did not seek revenge. Following customary practices, the council arranged for Crow Dog's family to give Spotted Tail's relatives horses, blankets, and a sum of money. These gifts were not intended to offer compensation, as if a human life could be valued in these terms. Rather, as Sidney Harring points out, the "goal was the termination of the conflict and the reintegration of all persons involved into the tribal body."[31]

Instead of letting this settlement stand, Cook, with the Indian Office's support, ordered Crow Dog's arrest and began making arrangements to prosecute him on murder charges in U.S. territorial court. In March 1882 this court convicted Crow Dog of murder and sentenced him to death. In December 1883, the U.S. Supreme Court overturned his conviction on the grounds that the U.S. courts had no jurisdiction in a dispute involving Indians on a reservation. Crow Dog returned to Rosebud, and as we will see, became an important leader in the Ghost Dance movement.[32]

Historians have seen Spotted Tail's death as a critical turning point in Brulé history. Hyde argues that the government "took advantage of the murder" to break the tribal organization and put the Brulés "under the control of their white agent." The killing of Spotted Tail, Hyde concludes, "ended the history of the Brulé Sioux as a tribe." It is true that Spotted Tail was an unusually skilled leader, but Brulé political autonomy had never depended upon a single chief. During the 1880s Brulé band leaders continued to operate with some effectiveness, albeit under increasingly onerous constraints. Evidence of the durability of Brulé leadership can be found in government agents' denunciations of recalcitrant band leaders long after Spotted Tail's death. It can also be found in leaders' efforts to halt illegal grazing on the reservation and to stop further land thefts. Brulé leaders were unable to stop

---

[30] John Cook (per Henry Lelar) to CIA, 6 Aug. 1881, RA-KC, book 8. See also John Cook to CIA, 13 Aug. 1881, RA-KC, book 8.

[31] Harring, *Crow Dog's Case*, 104. Details of the settlement vary slightly; see Harring, *Crow Dog's Case*, 110; Hyde, *Spotted Tail's Folk*, 333; Crow Dog and Erdoes, *Crow Dog*, 36; Clow, "Anatomy of a Lakota Shooting," 224.

[32] Harring, *Crow Dog's Case*, 110–14, 129–32. Harring observes that although the Supreme Court decision in *ex parte Crow Dog* affirmed tribal sovereignty, it contained "a strong tone of racism, combined with a clear message that tribal law was somehow transitory, a mechanism to assist in the inevitable transition from savagery to civilization" (p. 132). The decision invited the Major Crimes Act of 1885, which asserted U.S. jurisdiction over Indians charged with major crimes and was intended to undermine tribal autonomy and hasten assimilation.

all U.S. initiatives, but they were no less successful than leaders at other Sioux agencies.[33]

Efforts to undermine the power of chiefs had different results at other agencies. At Pine Ridge, Valentine McGillycuddy's assault on Red Cloud did little damage to the targeted chief. Instead, it resulted in the demise of a powerful agent.

No one personified the spirit of coercive assimilation at the heart of U.S. policy better than McGillycuddy. From the moment he assumed charge of Pine Ridge in 1879, it was clear that he possessed unusual zeal. In June the Indian Office authorized an expenditure of $2,500 for the construction of a house for Red Cloud in his capacity of "head chief" of the Oglalas. Unlike the Rosebud agent, who simply went along with a similar proposal for Spotted Tail, McGillycuddy argued successfully that the government allocate only $500 to a house for Red Cloud and spend the rest on houses for other chiefs and on agency buildings.[34]

Although McGillycuddy praised Red Cloud in March 1880 for "behaving in an exemplary manner," a few months later he decided to "depose" him as head chief. The immediate cause of this decision was Red Cloud's support for larceny charges brought against T. G. Cowgill, a licensed trader at Pine Ridge. In McGillycuddy's mind, these charges were "intended to reflect on myself as agent." In acting against Red Cloud, McGillycuddy made the same move as Cook at Rosebud. He turned to other leaders for support. On July 27 McGillycuddy confidently reported that the "Indians are holding councils day and night looking towards the final deposing of Red Cloud as chief." Yet five weeks later, American Horse wrote "the Great Father" that at a council "called to determine who should be the head chief of the nation" Red Cloud had been chosen "almost without opposition, as only five votes were cast against him." American Horse further reported that "[o]ur agent is trying through some of our young men and a few of his police to throw Red Cloud away.... This the nation does not want, and it is only bringing great trouble and bad feeling among our people."[35] Although American Horse's

[33] Hyde, *Spotted Tail's Folk*, 335; L. F. Spencer to CIA, 21 Feb. 1887, RA-KC, book 13; L. F. Spencer to Col. August V. Kautz, 23 (?) Feb. 1888, RA-KC, book 14; L. F. Spencer to CIA, 19 Feb. 1889, RA-KC, book 15; J. George Wright to CIA, 12 Feb. 1890, RA-KC, book 16. On Brulé resistance to illegal grazing, see Chapter 6; on opposition to ceding additional land, Chapter 10.

[34] C. Terry to CIA, 3 June 1879, RCA, roll 724; V. T. McGillycuddy to CIA, 9 Sept. 1879, RCA, roll 724; V. T. McGillycuddy to CIA, 2 Dec. 1879, RCA, roll 725.

[35] V. T. McGillycuddy to CIA, 16 Mar., 27 July 1880, RCA, roll 726; American Horse to the Great Father, 4 Sept. 1880, RCA, roll 726. According to Red Cloud to the Great Father, 4 Sept. 1880, RCA, roll 726, more than one hundred leaders attended this council. McGillycuddy's decision to depose Red Cloud may also have been influenced by his resistance to the agent's efforts to establish a police force, as suggested, for example, in V. T. McGillycuddy

report may have overstated Oglala harmony, it showed that McGillycuddy was unable as of yet to exploit factionalism.

Most agents would have retreated at this point, but McGillycuddy was different. Years later, interpreter William Garnett recalled that McGillycuddy had a "revengeful and unrelenting nature" and described him as "overbearing," "tyrannous," "haughty," and "domineering." He was not the sort of man to take no for an answer. Two weeks after the Oglalas affirmed their support for Red Cloud, McGillycuddy declared that Red Cloud had been "deposed by majority of Indians on account [of] false charges brought against me in Washington." This was nothing less than a bald-faced (or, as Lakotas might have said, bald-headed) lie.[36]

To weaken Oglala support for Red Cloud, McGillycuddy used his control over material resources to drive a wedge between him and other chiefs. McGillycuddy began giving permission to Young Man Afraid of His Horses to leave the reservation to hunt and visit the Crow Reservation. He also made special issues of wagons and other goods to leaders who "cooperated" with him.[37] At one time McGillycuddy may have toyed with the idea of declaring Young Man Afraid of His Horses "head chief."[38] Eventually, however, he decided to use the "friendly" chiefs for the moment, while taking steps to diminish their power in the future. To accomplish the latter, McGillycuddy decentralized the issue of annuities. In 1879 he issued annuities in bulk to seven chiefs; three years later, he issued them to sixty-three heads of families. "This method," the agent claimed, is "rapidly breaking up the tribal system and the power of the chiefs."[39]

In April 1882 Red Cloud struck back at McGillycuddy, charging him with theft of annuities and calling for his removal. One month later, a council of many of the chiefs McGillycuddy was trying to coopt (Young Man Afraid of His Horses, Little Wound, American Horse, No Flesh, and Blue Horse) requested the government to provide them with stock cattle and wagons and affirmed their support for the agent. According to McGillycuddy's summary of this council, the chiefs "very much regret the feeling that has prompted

to CIA, 4 Aug. 1879, RCA, roll 724. See also the discussion in Mark R. Ellis, "Reservation *Akicitas*: The Pine Ridge Indian Police, 1879–1885," *South Dakota History* 29 (Fall 1999): 190–95.

36 William Garnett interview, 1907, RT, tablet 2, roll 1; V. T. McGillycuddy to CIA, 18 Sept. 1880, PR-KC, box 35.

37 V. T. McGillycuddy to To Whom It May Concern, 24 Feb. 1881, PR-KC, box 53; V. T. McGillycuddy to CIA, 7 Nov. 1881, 24 Mar. 1882, PR-KC, box 35; V. T. McGillycuddy to CIA, 22 Apr. 1882, PR-KC, box 53; V. T. McGillycuddy to To Whom It May Concern, 23 Dec. 1882, PR-KC, box 53; V. T. McGillycuddy to CIA, 6 Nov. 1883, 20 Dec. 1884, PR-KC, box 36.

38 A hint of this is in McGillycuddy's statement, after deposing Red Cloud, that Young Man Afraid of His Horses was "tacitly recognized" as head chief. See V. T. McGillycuddy to [illegible], 27 Dec. 1881, PR-KC, box 53.

39 *ARCIA*, 1882, 37–38 (qtn., 38).

Ex-Chief Red Cloud to adopt his present course, and that the same does not meet with their approval."[40] This summary undoubtedly simplified a complex set of views in a self-serving way. As events would show, however, most of these leaders were now willing to support the agent.

Although McGillycuddy represented cooperating chiefs as "progressives," these leaders were less concerned to follow American scripts of social evolution than to ensure the survival of their people under dangerous conditions. Their deepest fear, as conflict between Red Cloud and McGillycuddy escalated in the summer, was that the government would send troops onto the reservation. The crisis came to a head in August. On the thirteenth Red Cloud and dozens of supporters signed a petition demanding that the government remove McGillycuddy within sixty days or they would "take upon ourselves the responsibility of politely escorting him out of our country." McGillycuddy immediately requested permission to arrest this petition's leading signers – Red Cloud, He Dog, No Water, Cloud Shield, and American Horse.[41] The agent also threatened military intervention. On the eighteenth several chiefs met in council and discussed "the question of 'troops or no troops.'" Faced with an ultimatum to support the agent or have the army called in, they informed "the Great Father" that "we do not require the presence of troops here" and that "we agree to settle the trouble with the aid of the Police."[42]

The next day, McGillycuddy summoned Red Cloud to his office. After rebuffing the agent several times, Red Cloud finally appeared, mainly because McGillycuddy threatened to call in troops if he continued to resist. Once Red Cloud arrived, the agent read him a warrant for his arrest, but instead of following through on this warrant, McGillycuddy simply "informed the Police, Chiefs, and Indians that I should hold them responsible for his future conduct" and sent the chief back home.[43] Although the available evidence offers little insight into why McGillycuddy did not actually arrest Red Cloud, the most likely explanation is that the agent feared that he would suffer from adverse publicity. Had Red Cloud beeen manacled and thrown on a train to a military prison, dozens of reporters would have clamored for interviews and broadcast Red Cloud's version of events. McGillycuddy would have realized that from New York to San Francisco he would stand accused of being a thief and a tyrant.

In his reports to Washington, McGillycuddy tried to make it seem as though he was in control at the agency, but this was far from true. One

---

[40] V. T. McGillycuddy to CIA, 5 Apr., 4 May 1882, PR-KC, box 35.

[41] Red Cloud et al. to SI, 13 Aug. 1882, OIA, file 15826–1882; V. T. McGillycuddy to CIA, 17 Aug. 1882, PR-KC, box 35.

[42] V. T. McGillycuddy to CIA, 20 Aug. 1882, PR-KC, box 35 (1st qtn.); statement of Little Wound et al., 18 Aug. 1882, OIA, file 15850–1882 (2d qtn.).

[43] McGillycuddy to CIA, 20 Aug. 1882. CIA to V. T. McGillycuddy, 19 Aug. 1882, PR-KC, box 6, authorized Red Cloud's arrest.

drawback to McGillycuddy's tactic of threatening to call in the troops was that it undermined the confidence of some agency employees and missionaries and gave his opponents an opportunity to exploit their fears. In a letter of August 23 several agency employees and residents complained that McGillycuddy was "to blame for the present disturbance as it results entirely from a personal quarrel between him and Red Cloud." They refuted the idea that Red Cloud has a "hundred warriers [sic] who desire to go upon the war path." Instead, they pointed out, Red Cloud had merely requested the Indian Office to send an inspector to Pine Ridge. Turning the tables on McGillycuddy, they worried that the agent was going to provoke "an Indian war" and backed Red Cloud's request for an inspector.[44] Some of the signers may have had long-standing grievances against the agent. Yet one of them, T. G. Cowgill, had been on the other side of the McGillycuddy–Red Cloud feud two years before (see earlier). Obviously, McGillycuddy's heavy-handed tactics had created genuine alarm and had provided his enemies an opening.

Instead of having its desired effect, McGillycuddy's campaign against Red Cloud resulted in a government investigation. In September the Indian Office sent Inspector William J. Pollock to investigate affairs at Pine Ridge. Lakotas referred to these inspectors as *igmu tanka* (mountain lion; literally "big cat"), apparently because they were always ready to pounce on someone.[45] In this case, McGillycuddy was the prey. Pollock concluded that Red Cloud could not be expected to cooperate with an agent who "lost no opportunity to humiliate and to heap indignity upon him, who called him liar, fool, [and] squaw."[46] Two other inspectors also visited Pine Ridge. One concurred with Pollock, but the other stated that McGillycuddy was guilty of nothing more than "technical irregularities" and lauded him as one of the finest agents in the service. In the end, the Indian Office did not dismiss McGillycuddy. If McGillycuddy was stealing government property, he covered his tracks well enough to remove hard evidence. That left the issue of the agent's imperiousness toward Red Cloud. Although Red Cloud agitated for McGillycuddy's removal during a visit to Washington in January 1883, officials were reluctant to act.[47]

By spring 1883 the crisis appeared to be over. McGillycuddy reported that conditions at Pine Ridge were "in a more harmonious condition at this agency than have been known for years" and praised Red Cloud for agreeing

---

[44] T. G. Cowgill et al. to CIA, 23 Aug. 1882, OIA, file 15595–1882. This letter was also signed by J. G. Edgar, the agency clerk, James F. Oldham, the chief of police, Fordyce Grinnell, the agency physician, Julia Draper, a missionary, and several other agency employees and residents.

[45] McGillycuddy, *Blood on the Moon*, 228.

[46] Quoted in James C. Olson, *Red Cloud and the Sioux Problem* (Lincoln, 1965), 283–84.

[47] Ibid., 284 (qtn.); *Council Fire and Arbitrator* 6 (February 1883): 22.

to "work with the agent." In June Red Cloud told his people that the "agent is a good man and is not stealing."[48] One could attribute the new mood at Pine Ridge to McGillycuddy having "put down" his antagonist, as James Olson suggests.[49] It is more likely, however, that the agent felt pressure to reduce tensions at Pine Ridge lest Washington officials conclude he was an incompetent manager.

Despite the new harmony, however, McGillycuddy continued to try to isolate Red Cloud. In spring 1884, as we saw in Chapter 8, McGillycuddy organized an Agency Council. The agent's immediate goal was to stop the Sun Dance, but he also saw the new council as a way to diminish Red Cloud's power. The Agency Council, McGillycuddy reported, was composed only of "delegates from the different villages," who represented the "working and progressive element" of the Oglalas and stood for the "proper management of the agency irrespective of the Indian Chiefs." Although McGillycuddy's language suggested the creation of a completely novel, "American" form of government, in fact the new body was simply a tribal council limited to leaders from bands of the agent's choice. Red Cloud and other "nonprogressives" were excluded.[50]

Red Cloud opposed the creation of the Agency Council and its decision to support McGillycuddy's efforts to suppress the Sun Dance. He was also worried about the possible loss of tribal lands. In 1884 Congress passed the Dawes Sioux Bill (not to be confused with the better-known Dawes Severalty Act of 1887), which called for the reduction of the Great Sioux Reservation and the allotment of tribal lands. To defeat this new bill and to help him resist McGillycuddy's continuing effort to undermine his authority, Red Cloud sought help from an influential non-Indian ally, Thomas Augustus Bland.[51] Bland's arrival at Pine Ridge in late June reignited the Red Cloud–McGillycuddy feud.

Bland was an agrarian radical (he would support the Populist Party in the early 1890s) with a searching critique of mainstream "humanitarian" reformers' emphasis on individual land ownership as the salvation of Indians. Bland opposed allotment of land not only because he regarded it as a scheme of monopolistic railroad corporations and other interests, but also because he harbored serious doubts about the ultimate superiority of a system of private property. In 1884 Bland was the editor of the influential *Council Fire* and a member of the Indian Rights Association (IRA), organized two years before. Bland's unorthodox position on allotment, however, would soon lead him to break with the IRA and organize the National Indian Defence

---

[48] V. T. McGillycuddy to CIA, 27 Mar., 26 June 1883, PR-KC, box 35.
[49] Olson, *Red Cloud and the Sioux Problem*, 285.
[50] V. T. McGillycuddy to CIA, 4 May 1884, PR-KC, box 36.
[51] *Council Fire and Arbitrator* 7 (June 1884): 103. For further discussion of the Dawes bill, see Chapter 10.

Association (NIDA).[52] Bland probably became acquainted with Red Cloud in the late 1870s, during one of the chief's visits to Washington. On Christmas Day 1882 Bland and his wife, Cora, invited the famous Oglala chief to a "literary reception" at their home in Washington, where he received praise for his "advocacy of the ways and pursuits of civilization."[53]

In 1884, when Bland set off for Dakota Territory, his primary purpose was to encourage Sioux opposition to the Dawes bill. Bland probably did not intend to start a fight with McGillycuddy, but he must have realized that a red carpet would not await him. Upon Bland's arrival at Pine Ridge on June 28, McGillycuddy promptly ordered him off the reservation. Bland produced a letter from Interior Secretary Henry M. Teller authorizing his visit, but the agent was unimpressed and ordered the Indian police to escort Bland to Nebraska, where he stayed with a local rancher. The next day Red Cloud and other Oglala leaders visited Bland and informed him of their grievances against the agent: his suppression of the Sun Dance, his favoritism toward leaders of the Agency Council, and his threat to withhold rations from anyone attending the current meeting. One leader, No Water, suggested that the agent might "get so swelled up that he will blow up or blow away.... This country is ours, it don't belong to McGillycuddy." Bland encouraged the Oglalas not to act precipitously and to wait for him to persuade Washington officials to dismiss the agent. Bland expressed confidence that they would do this, since McGillycuddy had openly defied Secretary Teller's order to allow him on the reservation.[54]

Removing McGillycuddy was not as easy as Bland predicted. Teller shared some of Bland's skepticism about allotment and may have been inclined to believe the charges Bland leveled against McGillycuddy in the *Council Fire* after his return to Washington.[55] But powerful figures, such as Senator Henry L. Dawes, dismissed Bland as "a very strange man" and defended

[52] Benjamin Heber Johnson, "Red Populism? T. A. Bland, Agrarian Radicalism, and the Debate over the Dawes Act," in *The Countryside in the Age of the Modern State: Political Histories of Rural America*, ed. Catherine McNicol Stock and Robert D. Johnston (Ithaca, 2001), 15–37; Thomas W. Cowger, "Dr. Thomas A. Bland, Critic of Forced Assimilation," *American Indian Culture and Research Journal* 16, no. 4 (1992): 79–83; Jo Lea Wetherilt Behrens, "In Defense of 'Poor Lo': National Indian Defense Association and *Council Fire*'s Advocacy for Sioux Land Rights," *South Dakota History* 24 (Fall/Winter 1994): 159–60. On the split between the IRA and NIDA, see also Chapter 10.

[53] *Council Fire and Arbitrator* 6 (Jan. 1883): 6.

[54] T. A. Bland to SI, 21 July 1884, Special Files of the Office of Indian Affairs, 1807–1904, file 264, "Ejection of T. A. Bland from the Pine Ridge Reservation by Agent V. T. McGillycuddy, 1882–1885," Record Group 75, National Archives and Records Administration, Microfilm Publications, M574, roll 73, (hereafter special file 264); W. J. Godfrey to To Whom It May Concern, 3 July 1884, special file 264; *Council Fire and Arbitrator* 7 (July–August 1884): 101–03 (qtn., 101).

[55] Bland's attacks on McGillycuddy began in the July–August 1884 issue of the *Council Fire* and continued for several issues. On Teller's opposition to allotment, see Francis Paul Prucha,

McGillycuddy for his "integrity and wisdom."[56] With most of the "friends of the Indian" on Dawes's side, it would have been difficult for Teller to discharge McGillycuddy on Bland's word alone. Furthermore, McGillycuddy himself had written repeatedly to Washington about Sioux resistance. Oglalas opposed to allotment were tearing up survey stakes, Red Cloud and his allies were "dancing, feasting, and counciling day and night," and some extremists were openly threatening "the early assassination of the agent, members of the police, and friendly chiefs." Although Secretary Teller could read these reports as signs of McGillycuddy's mismanagement, perhaps the agent was valiantly upholding law and order.[57]

Caught between conflicting voices, Teller decided to take the well-trodden path of least resistance and order yet another investigator, Henry Ward, to visit Pine Ridge. On November 19 Ward reported that McGillycuddy had been justified in expelling Bland from the reservation because he "deliberately and apparently intentionally placed himself in antagonism to the agent." Another factor that favored McGillycuddy, at least in the short term, was the election of Grover Cleveland, the first Democratic president in twenty-four years. Fearing that the Democrats' lengthy absence from the public trough would trump their campaign promises for civil service reform, Teller wanted to make it as difficult as possible for them to replace Republicans under his jurisdiction. Thus, he reappointed McGillycuddy to a four-year term two months before Cleveland was to assume office.[58]

With the new administration in power, Red Cloud, with Bland's assistance, continued his efforts to have a new agent. On March 18, 1885, Red Cloud met with President Cleveland and informed him that "[o]ur agent is a bad man. He steals from us, and abuses us, and he has sent all of the good white men out of our country, and put bad men in their places." The Cleveland administration was sympathetic toward replacing McGillycuddy but, having campaigned for civil service, was hesitant to replace him without sufficient cause. Accordingly, the Interior Department summoned McGillycuddy to Washington in April to give his side of the story. Rather than make a decision at this point, administration officials next decided to wait for the results of a congressional investigation headed by Democratic Congressman William S. Holman of Indiana.[59]

As part of an itinerary that included visits to several western reservations, the Holman committee arrived at Pine Ridge on July 22. Holman was

American Indian Policy in Crisis: Christian Reformers and the Indian, 1865–1900 (Norman, 1976), 246–47.

[56] *Springfield (Mass.) Republican*, 7 Aug. 1884, p. 8.

[57] V. T. McGillycuddy to CIA, 13 July 1884 (two letters), PR-KC, box 36.

[58] Henry Ward to SI, 19 Nov. 1884, special file 264; Olson, *Red Cloud and the Sioux Problem*, 298; McGillycuddy, *Blood on the Moon*, 233.

[59] *Council Fire and Arbitrator* 8 (April 1885): 53 (qtn.); *Council Fire and Arbitrator* 8 (May 1885): 65–69; Olson, *Red Cloud and the Sioux Problem*, 300–01.

well-disposed to Red Cloud. During Red Cloud's trip to Washington in March, the congressman had invited the chief to his house and listened sympathetically to his complaints. Unlike many of McGillycuddy's previous investigators, Holman did not focus on narrow allegations of malfeasance. Instead, he questioned the agent's management style. Holman pointedly asked McGillycuddy if it was not true that his actions had "alienate[d]" Red Cloud from "all civilization movements?" McGillycuddy responded that he had never seen any "solid work on the part of Red Cloud or his people toward progress" and that Red Cloud thought he was "independent of the Government." When Holman pointed out that the United States had often found it desirable to "recognize the chiefship of Indians for the express purpose of increasing their importance in directing the action of their tribes," the agent retorted that this was desirable only if "the strong control of the chief is exercised toward progress." Red Cloud had been useful in 1868, but now he was a "stumbling block."[60]

This exchange highlighted the basic contradiction toward Indian leaders in U.S. policy. Holman and McGillycuddy agreed that in the long run chiefs would become obsolete. For now, however, the United States needed chiefs to encourage their people to progress to that point. Their disagreement was about which chiefs would promote progress and under what circumstances.

Red Cloud attempted to maneuver within these contradictions. Knowing that Americans were impressed by outward signs of "civilization," Red Cloud began wearing western-style dress. This helped him persuade sympathetic non-Indians that he wanted to "live like the white people." While in Washington in March, for example, Red Cloud had impressed a *New York Sun* reporter with his "respectable suit of black, with a white 'boned' shirt, turn down collar and black tie." Holman, too, found these signs convincing. Was it not true, he asked McGillycuddy, that Red Cloud "wears the costume of the white man" and that he "keeps the American flag floating over his band?" The agent conceded that it was, but the real test was his willingness to take up the plow. On this, Red Cloud failed miserably.[61]

Managers of Democratic Party patronage undoubtedly hoped that the Holman report would provide ample ammunition to sink McGillycuddy. However, the committee's Republicans prevented a recommendation for the agent's dismissal. Instead, the report offered two sets of criteria for a "good" Indian agent (one of these was Republican and applicable to McGillycuddy, the other Democratic and an implicit rebuke). By this time, the Cleveland administration had concluded that the only way to discharge McGillycuddy

[60] *Report of the Special Committee of the House of Representatives...to Inquire into the Expenditure of Public Money in the Indian Service*, 49th Cong., 1st sess., 1885–86, H. Rept. 1076, serial 2438, 49, 32 (qtns., 32).

[61] *New York Sun*, quoted in *Council Fire and Arbitrator* 8 (May 1885): 84; *Report of the Special Committee to Inquire into the Expenditure of Public Money*, 33.

was to provoke him into committing a suitable transgression. In May 1886 the Indian Office ordered the agent to fire his clerk. When he refused, Interior Secretary L.Q.C. Lamar relieved him. The new agent, Hugh D. Gallagher, was a Democrat from Holman's state of Indiana.[62]

The immediate cause of McGillcuddy's removal was the Democrats' appetite for patronage, but McGillycuddy likely would have kept his post had he not been so vulnerable. The agent's downfall can be traced to his attempt to destroy Red Cloud in 1880. Red Cloud had substantial resources to resist McGillycuddy. He had the support of his own band and became a rallying point for discontented Oglalas in other bands. He was able to recruit influential non-Indian allies to his cause and raise serious doubts about the Pine Ridge agent in Washington. Red Cloud's actions sometimes risked provoking violent retribution, but the possibility of violence could work in Red Cloud's favor. McGillycuddy's threats to use force cost him the allegiance of some of his employees and raised additional questions about his draconian methods.

Although it failed, McGillycuddy's attack on Red Cloud was not without destructive consequences. Among these was the wedge he drove between Red Cloud and other leaders. Following the agent's dismissal, Oglala leaders took steps to overcome these divisions. At a council held on July 26, 1887, Red Cloud and Young Man Afraid of His Horses smoked the pipe, shook hands, and agreed to "do all in their power and in harmony to help their tribe in every possible way." Red Cloud said that "he now considers himself and Young-Man-Afraid-of-His-Horses as one man, and they will pull together and hereafter sit side by side in council as brothers."[63] This reconciliation was an Oglala achievement, not the least because they had been able to replace an agent whose approach was confrontational and divisive with one who tried to reduce factional tensions. One of Gallagher's main reforms was to abolish the Agency Council, which, as we have seen, excluded Red Cloud. Although he did not say so in his official report, this move meant that Gallagher recognized an inclusive tribal council as the main body for articulating Oglala views. Gallagher realized that this action threatened to damage relations with Young Man Afraid of His Horses, who had been the Agency Council president. Young Man Afraid was willing to accept the abolition of the council, but he worried that the agent "was going to withdraw all favors from him." To counter this, Gallagher allowed Young Man Afraid to continue his practice of visiting the Crows.[64]

---

[62] *Report of the Special Committee to Inquire into the Expenditure of Public Money*, x, lxiii; Olson, *Red Cloud and the Sioux Problem*, 304–05, 307; McGillycuddy, *Blood on the Moon*, 248–50. A temporary agent, Captain James Bell, assumed charge in May; Gallagher began his term in October. *ARCIA*, 1887, 40.

[63] "Report of William H. Waldby" in *Report of the Board of Indian Commissioners, 1887* in *Annual Report of the Secretary of the Interior*, 1887, 50th Cong., 1st sess., 1887–88, H. Ex. Doc. 1, pt. 5, serial 2542, 932.

[64] *ARCIA*, 1887, 42; H. D. Gallagher to CIA, 25 July 1887, PR-KC, box 36 (qtn.).

Historians have interpreted the reconciliation of Red Cloud and Young Man Afraid of His Horses as the ending of a political rivalry. By this way of thinking, Young Man Afraid had sided with McGillycuddy against Red Cloud because he was angry that Red Cloud had usurped his father's position as head chief. Supposedly, he wanted to restore the prominence of his family and perhaps even become head chief himself. Though this interpretation gives Young Man Afraid the dignity of acting in his own interests, rather than as a pawn of a government agent, it assumes the universality of a particular type of political motivation. Sioux leaders were certainly capable of acting self-interestedly. However, Young Man Afraid's differences with Red Cloud stemmed less from political ambition than from a commitment to a particular strategy for helping his people in difficult times. Both in his relations with U.S. authorities and other Oglala leaders, Young Man Afraid generally acted as a peacemaker, a role which he assumed because of his position as a *Wicasa Yatanpi* (praiseworthy men, commonly known as shirtwearers).[65]

When Red Cloud and Young Man Afraid of His Horses smoked the pipe in July 1887, they showed the durability of Sioux political institutions. They also revealed inadequacies of classifying leaders as "progressives" or "non-progressives." Red Cloud's confrontational style makes it easy to see him as opposed to "progress," yet Young Man Afraid also rejected assimilation. During the McGillycuddy years, Young Man Afraid cooperated with the government in limited ways but only because he concluded it was a tactical necessity. Although Red Cloud and Young Man Afraid often appeared to have irreconcilable differences during those years, their differences had more to do with means than ends. New conditions after McGillycuddy's departure made it possible for them to find common ground. As we will see in the next chapter, the unity they established would help them resist a new U.S. effort to take additional Sioux land in the late 1880s.

Although most U.S. Indian agents tried to "break" the power of chiefs who stood in their way, some tried subtler approaches. Of all the agents in western Sioux country, James McLaughlin was the most experienced. After four years at the Devil's Lake Agency, McLaughlin assumed charge of Standing Rock in 1881, where he remained until 1894. McLaughlin took great pride in his knowledge of Indians and his ability to befriend them. In his autobiography *My Friend the Indian*, McLaughlin contrasted himself to other agents.

---

[65] Olson, *Red Cloud and the Sioux Problem*, 271; Robert W. Larson, *Red Cloud: Warrior-Statesman of the Lakota Sioux* (Norman, 1997), 227; Joseph Agonito, "Young Man Afraid of His Horses: The Reservation Years," *Nebraska History* 79 (Fall 1998): 120. For Young Man Afraid's position as a shirtwearer, see He Dog interview, 7 July 1930, in Eleanor H. Hinman, ed., "Oglala Sources on the Life of Crazy Horse," *Nebraska History* 57 (Spring 1976): 10. For a discussion of shirtwearers, see Chapter 1. Not all shirtwearers interpreted their duties the same way; Young Man Afraid had his own political style.

"[I]nstead of sitting in my office and waiting for the Indian to come to me," he wrote, "I went to the Indian." This duty, the agent pointed out, was "not always congenial." Sometimes it "led to things and places that I would not have elected to seek out." McLaughlin did not specify what barbaric scenes he had witnessed in which savage corners of the world, but through it all he had become "very close to the red man." He had learned that "under the blanket in which the Indian shrouded himself, there was a heart and mind altogether human, but undeveloped." McLaughlin "made friends" with former Hunkpapa "hostiles" such as Gall and Crow King. He tried, with less success, to win over Sitting Bull.[66]

McLaughlin first met Sitting Bull on September 8, 1881, at Fort Yates, where, after four years in Canada, the chief was on his way to prison at Fort Randall. Many years later, McLaughlin recalled that his first impression was of "a stocky man, with an evil face and shifty eyes." Two years later, when Sitting Bull was transferred to Standing Rock, he demanded that McLaughlin list him first on the agency rolls and appoint twenty-four of his men as headmen. McLaughlin reported that he "heard this inflated nonsense through to the end," but then "explained to [Sitting Bull] his status, together with the rules and regulations governing the Indian service." McLaughlin described his new ward as "an Indian of very mediocre ability," who was at the same time "pompous, vain, and boastful."[67]

The situation was ripe for McLaughlin to launch the kind of all-out attack on Sitting Bull that Cook and McGillycuddy initiated against Spotted Tail and Red Cloud. Instead, McLaughlin decided to use the arts of friendship and persuasion. To do this, he offered to demonstrate the superiority of American ways of life by taking Sitting Bull on a tour of one of civilization's great showcases, St. Paul, Minnesota.[68]

McLaughlin and Sitting Bull arrived in St. Paul on March 14, 1884. Their party included Sitting Bull's nephew, One Bull, and McLaughlin's wife, Mary, a mixed-blood Sioux who served as interpreter. McLaughlin's week-long itinerary featured a series of displays illustrating European American ingenuity and material comfort. Sitting Bull toured the offices of the *Pioneer Press*, "witnessing typesetting, job printing, telegraphing, [and] telephone exchange." He visited a mercantile establishment, where he viewed an "immense supply of provisions" and took his first ride on an elevator. At another stop, firemen demonstrated the operation of their engines and extension ladders and "slid down bars from . . . their sleeping room."

McLaughlin took Sitting Bull to the Catholic cathedral, the state capitol, and on a drive around St. Paul's residential neighborhoods. Sitting Bull was

[66] Louis L. Pfaller, *James McLaughlin: The Man with an Indian Heart* (New York, 1978); James McLaughlin, *My Friend the Indian* (1910; Lincoln, 1989), ix–xi, 3 (qtns.), 34.

[67] McLaughlin, *My Friend the Indian*, 182 (1st qtn.); *ARCIA*, 1883, 49 (other qtns.).

[68] James McLaughlin to CIA, 7 Mar. 1884, OIA, file 5115–1884.

ushered to a boot and shoe factory, where he was measured for a "high cut pair of shoes." These shoes – polished – appeared within twenty minutes. Another firm produced a pair of pants even faster, "in two minutes time." Sitting Bull witnessed the making of cigars, the sale of hats, and the milling of grain. At the Second National Bank, he was shown through "all the vaults" and saw "kegs and boxes of silver & gold." A bank official held $400,000 in U.S. bonds and informed Sitting Bull that they were equal in value to all the silver and gold in the room. This official then allowed Sitting Bull to hold this remarkable stack of paper in his own hand for a brief moment.

By McLaughlin's account, Sitting Bull was pleased with what he saw. He "expressed much satisfaction" at the *Pioneer Press*. He was so taken with the firemen sliding down their poles that he requested an encore. And, he "appreciated" the opportunity not only to see but to touch the paper representation of fabulous wealth. After returning to the agency, McLaughlin was cautiously optimistic. Sitting Bull was a "very stubborn and self-willed man," he wrote, but "[h]is eyes have been opened."[69]

Over the next few years, McLaughlin continued to tutor Sitting Bull in the ways of civilization. Shortly after returning to Standing Rock, the agent arranged for Sitting Bull to join a Wild West show run by Alvaren Allen, the proprietor of the hotel that hosted Sitting Bull in St. Paul. In September Sitting Bull traveled to New York and Philadelphia with the Allen show. The following year, Sitting Bull signed on with Buffalo Bill Cody and visited Montreal, Washington, and St. Louis, and in 1888, Sitting Bull again visited Washington as part of a tribal delegation to discuss a possible land cession.[70]

Contrary to McLaughlin's hopes, the more Sitting Bull saw of the ways of European Americans, the more negative he became. Upon returning from the East, Sitting Bull frequently ridiculed McLaughlin's claims about "the greatness of the white men's civilization." The "whitemen loved their whores more than their wives," he told his people. They "dressed them better and were [m]ore tenderly affectio[n]ate to them." Furthermore, despite what McLaughlin always said, Americans didn't consider their president "sacred." "[H]alf of the people in the hotels were always making fun of him." Sitting Bull was an excellent mimic, and he frequently amused his friends and relatives by showing them how a white man danced with a white woman or by imitating "the manners of McLaughlin." Once at a banquet in Bismarck, he took a napkin from the table and sat down on it, saying to his companions in sign language, "What is good for a white man's face is fit for an Indian's ass."[71]

[69] James McLaughlin to Maj. J. M. Stevenson, 13 May 1884, MP, roll 20.
[70] Robert M. Utley, *The Lance and the Shield: The Life and Times of Sitting Bull* (New York, 1993), 262–65, 274–76.
[71] Notes enclosed in A. McG. Beede to W. S. Campbell, 23 Dec. 1929, Walter S. Campbell Collection, box 107, folder 3, Western History Collections, University of Oklahoma Library, Norman.

But what about elevators, factories, and fire engines? If Sitting Bull "expressed much satisfaction" at these demonstrations, it was probably for different reasons than McLaughlin hoped. (Imagine the jokes Sitting Bull told his friends back home about the firemen sliding down poles!) Sitting Bull never became convinced that the ways of middle-class Minnesotans or Pennsylvanians were right for his people. Near the end of his tour with Cody, he told a reporter that he was "sick of the houses and the noises and the multitudes of men" and to missionary Mary Collins, he said he would rather "die an Indian than live a white man." Sitting Bull was amazed to learn that U.S. citizens would part with a silver dollar for his autograph and gladly received their *mazaska* (money; literally, white metal) to distribute among his people.[72] Nonetheless, he was highly critical of a society governed by money. For Sitting Bull, there was something troubling in the fact that Americans stamped their coins with the image of an eagle. "And so, now," he once said, "the eagle sits upon money, and money rules over the people."[73] Sitting Bull also worried about alcohol abuse. Having observed frequent drunkenness in American cities, he remarked that the "'soul' of a whiteman is so odored with whiskey that it will have to hang-around here on earth for hundreds of years before the winds and storms will purify it [so] that the [people] in the other life can endure the smell of it there." The consequences of civilization might well prove disastrous. "With whiskey replacing the buffaloes," Sitting Bull lamented, "there is no hope for Indians."[74]

McLaughlin soon realized that Sitting Bull was not drawing the proper lessons from his exposure to civilization. After Sitting Bull returned from touring with Cody in 1885, McLaughlin complained that his pupil "has not profited by what he has seen, but tells the most astounding falsehoods to the Indians." Among these was that the president had told him that "he was the only great Indian living & that he made him head chief of all the Sioux, that all the Indians must do his bidding, that he was above his Agent and could remove the agent... when he chose." McLaughlin came close to having Sitting Bull arrested, but settled instead on forbidding him from going with Cody the following year.[75]

Despite these tensions, there was surprisingly little conflict between McLaughlin and Sitting Bull until the time of the Ghost Dance. When he wasn't traveling, Sitting Bull spent much of his time quietly at his camp on Grand River forty miles southwest of the agency. In the late 1880s he

---

[72] *St. Louis Sunday Sayings*, 4 Oct. 1885, in Campbell Collection, box 113, folder 7 (1st qtn.); Utley, *Lance and the Shield*, 269 (2d qtn.).

[73] "*Yukan lehantu kin wanbli kin he mazaska kin el yanke. Na mazaska [kin] he oyate kin kaska awicaye.*" Reply to question about Sitting Bull's prophesies, Campbell Collection, box 104, folder 11.

[74] Notes enclosed in Beede to Campbell, 23 Dec. 1929.

[75] James McLaughlin to Gen. S. C. Armstrong, 9 Nov. 1885, MP, roll 20 (qtns.; underlining in original); Utley, *Lance and the Shield*, 266.

became less opposed to education and encouraged his people to farm as a means of self-preservation. In April 1888 McLaughlin was forced to concede that Sitting Bull's "behavior... has been all that could be desired."[76]

Some historians have suggested that by the late 1880s Sitting Bull "was losing what little influence that he possessed." True, leaders like Gall, John Grass (Sihasapa), Mad Bear (Yanktonai), Two Bears (Yanktonai), and Big Head (Yanktonai) took a much more active role in everyday agency affairs. They emerged as spokesmen in councils with government commissions in 1888 and 1889. Yet, Sitting Bull remained a powerful figure. He took an active role in organizing Sioux opposition to land cessions and was a member of a Standing Rock delegation to Washington in October 1888. Not everyone agreed with him, but his voice could not be ignored.[77] McLaughlin realized that Sitting Bull continued to be an influential force for the old ways, and he came to hate the chief for spurning his offers of friendship. As we will see, McLaughlin's simmering hatred of Sitting Bull contributed to his decision to arrest the chief in fall 1890, a decision that played a crucial role in the events leading to Wounded Knee.

[76] James McLaughlin to Paul C. Blum, 9 Apr. 1888, MP, roll 20.
[77] Gary Clayton Anderson, *Sitting Bull and the Paradox of Lakota Nationhood* (New York, 1996), 149. Although Anderson states that McLaughlin recognized Grass as head chief of the agency, I can only find evidence that he recognized him as "head chief of the Blackfeet Sioux." See *ARCIA*, 1887, 52.

10

"Enough to Crush Us Down"

Struggles for Land

Ever since the early nineteenth century, Americans had envisioned the possibility that western Sioux territory might eventually become part of a vast kingdom of yeoman farmers. Prior to the 1880s, however, there were few signs of this vision becoming a reality. The Plains Sioux knew European Americans mainly as hide traders, whiskey dealers, miners, freighters, surveyors, soldiers, and ranchers. The plow was seldom seen. All this changed with the Great Dakota Boom in 1878. As the national economy recovered from a five-year depression, railroads shot from Iowa and Minnesota across the western prairies. The result was an outbreak of "Dakota fever." The fertile soils of eastern Dakota Territory and a series of unusually wet years sustained this epidemic for almost a decade. Between 1878 and 1887, Americans filed for more than 24 million acres of Dakota land.[1]

Given Dakota fever's intensity and duration, it is easy to assume that settlers were behind U.S. efforts to force the Sioux to cede portions of their reservation in the early 1880s. In fact, settlers wished to go no farther west than they had to. Even in the late stages of the boom plenty of land was available east of the Missouri.[2] Demands for opening the Great Sioux Reservation came instead from local and regional capitalists. When the Chicago and North Western Railroad reached Pierre in 1880, and then, a year later, when the Chicago, Milwaukee and Saint Paul completed a line to Chamberlain, it seemed only a matter of months before the rails would extend to Deadwood or Rapid City in the Black Hills. Local boosters were certain their towns were destined to become the new Chicago, but railroad officials would build west only if sufficient local traffic existed to fill their cars. A

---

[1] Herbert S. Schell, *History of South Dakota*, 2d ed. (Lincoln, 1968), 158–61.
[2] Homesteaders did not begin taking up land west of the Missouri until the early 1900s. Ibid., 223–24; Paula M. Nelson, *After the West Was Won: Homesteaders and Town-Builders in Western South Dakota, 1900–1917* (Iowa City, 1986), 12–23.

simple right-of-way across the reservation would not suffice; Sioux land would have to be occupied by settlers.[3]

Unlike the taking of the Black Hills, a project planned at the highest levels of the federal government, the first attempt of the 1880s to obtain additional Sioux land came from territorial leaders. In August 1882 Dakota Territory's delegate to Congress, Richard F. Pettigrew, introduced a rider to an appropriations bill authorizing a commission to negotiate a land agreement with the Sioux. A month later Interior Secretary Henry M. Teller appointed a three-man commission, headed by Newton Edmunds, a Yankton banker who had been governor of Dakota Territory from 1863 to 1866. The other members of the commission were Peter C. Shannon, former Chief Justice of the Dakota territorial Supreme Court, and James C. Teller, the secretary's younger brother.[4]

Edmunds and his colleagues were eager to minimize any obstacles to the rapid completion of their work. One inconvenience was Article 12 of the 1868 Treaty, which required that three-fourths of adult Sioux men agree to any land cession. In his initial instructions Commissioner of Indian Affairs Hiram Price assumed that Edmunds would adhere to Article 12. However, Edmunds contended that the rejection of this provision in 1876, when the government took the Black Hills, furnished "ample precedent" for ignoring it now. This argument – that a treaty once broken could be broken again – persuaded Price to accept Edmunds's proposal. He would secure signatures from an unspecified number of chiefs and headmen so long as these amounted to "as full a representation of each tribe or band as may be possible."[5]

Between October 18 and December 21, 1882, the Edmunds Commission secured the marks of dozens of leaders at Pine Ridge, Rosebud, Standing Rock, and Cheyenne River agencies.[6] Although there is no record of the

---

[3] H. Roger Grant, *The North Western: A History of the Chicago & North Western Railway System* (DeKalb, Ill., 1996), 59–60; John W. Cary, *The Organization and History of the Chicago, Milwaukee & St. Paul Railway Company* (New York, 1981), 267; Herbert Welsh, *Report of a Visit to the Great Sioux Reserve Made in Behalf of the Indian Rights Association* (n.p., 1883), 1–2; Howard Roberts Lamar, *Dakota Territory, 1861–1889: A Study of Frontier Politics* (New Haven, 1956), 178. Some local interests feared the consequences of opening the reservation, however. Cattlemen feared an influx of competing homesteaders, while some regional speculators feared that opening new lands would depress the value of their current holdings.

[4] *Letter from the Secretary of Interior, Transmitting…Report of Commissioner of Indian Affairs Submitting Copies of Sioux Agreements to Cession of Land to the United States*, 48th Cong., 1st sess., 1883–84, S. Ex. Doc. 70, serial 2165 (hereafter Edmunds report), 3–4. On Edmunds, see George E. Hyde, *A Sioux Chronicle* (Norman, 1956), 111; Schell, *History of South Dakota*, 86–88, 105–08; Lamar, *Dakota Territory*, 95–97, 102–06; Doane Robinson, *History of South Dakota Together with Personal Mention of Citizens of South Dakota*, 2 vols. (n.p., 1904), 1:789.

[5] Edmunds report, 4–5, 7–9 (qtn., 9).

[6] Ibid., 31–41. The commission also visited Crow Creek and Lower Brulé agencies but was unable to secure any signatures there. Hyde, *Sioux Chronicle*, 128–36; Ernest L. Schusky,

commission's councils, evidence gathered a year later through an investigation headed by Massachusetts Senator Henry L. Dawes indicates that the
Edmunds Commission tried to conceal the fact that the document the leaders signed called for the cession of land. According to testimony by Little
Wound, for example, the commissioners told the Indians at Pine Ridge that
the agreement simply authorized dividing the Great Sioux Reservation into
separate reservations. The commission said nothing about the "Great Father having what was left." Even Pine Ridge agent Valentine McGillycuddy
testified that although the Edmunds Commission told the Oglalas that the
reservation would be divided, "[t]here was no particular mention made of
any portion of the reservation remaining after this division was made."[7]

Although Edmunds and the other members of the commission left Sioux
country confident they had done the work necessary to open large portions
of the reservation to settlement, the agreement never became law. According
to George Hyde, problems began when the commissioners sent word of
their triumph to Yankton, where newspapers "blossomed out with glowing
descriptions of the immense tracts of Sioux land that would soon be open
to white settlement." These newspapers, in turn, found their way into the
hands of Pine Ridge "squawmen," who "communicated to the chiefs and
the headmen, and then the camps began to buzz like a hive of angry bees."
For the first time, the Oglalas recognized that the commission had tricked
them into signing away their land. Red Cloud began "preaching a holy war
against Edmunds and his land agreement." Although Hyde's account offers
a stirring example of Indian resistance, unfortunately there is no evidence to
support it. Neither Red Cloud nor other Sioux leaders mounted a significant
protest against the Edmunds agreement until the Dawes Committee began
its investigation some months later.[8]

Opposition to the Edmunds agreement emerged mainly through the actions of a new wave of "humanitarian" reformers. As we saw in Chapter 2,
reformers had played a crucial role in shaping the Grant administration's

---

The Forgotten Sioux: An Ethnohistory of the Lower Brule Reservation (Chicago, 1975),
116–19.

[7] *Testimony Taken by a Select Committee of the Senate Concerning the Condition of the Indian
Tribes in the Territories of Montana and Dakota*, 48th Cong., 1st sess., S. Rept. 283, 1883–
84, serial 2174 (hereafter Dawes report), 143 (1st qtn.), 148 (2d qtn.). See also Welsh, *Report
of a Visit*, 26–27, 38–39. Despite the efforts by Edmunds and his colleagues to conceal their
purpose, many Sioux were evidently suspicious. At Cheyenne River, for example, Bull Eagle
and Spotted Eagle told a newspaper reporter: "we have no land to spare; we want it all for
ourselves and children, and we will make no treaty." *Black Hills Weekly Times*, 19 Aug. 1882,
p. 4. See also McGillycuddy's account of how Yellow Hair handed him a round ball of earth,
saying that he was handing him the balance of his people's land (Dawes report, 148–49).

[8] Hyde, *Sioux Chronicle*, 119, 121. In meeting with U.S. officials in Washington in January
1883, Red Cloud did not raise the issue of the Edmunds agreement, and instead demanded
a new agent and compensation for the ponies confiscated in 1876. *New York Times*, 30 Jan.
1883, p. 1.

"peace policy" of the late 1860s. During the 1870s, however, U.S. Indian policy became more militarized and national elites grew wary of social reform. By the late 1870s the "friends of the Indian" had lost momentum. In 1879, however, three events – the Cheyenne outbreak, the Ponca controversy, and the Ute uprising – galvanized public interest in "the Indian problem." In addition, Americans recognized that western tribes would soon face unprecedented pressures from settlers and developers. As always, humanitarians wished for an honorable expansion. Civilization must liquidate tribal lands, of that there was no doubt. In fulfilling the divine command, however, the United States should adhere to principles of honesty and justice.[9]

The most influential of several new reform organizations was the Indian Rights Association (IRA). It was founded in Philadelphia in December 1882 by Herbert Welsh, the nephew of William Welsh, a leading figure under Grant's peace policy. To develop an agenda and stake its claim to authority, the IRA had to locate and publicize specific abuses. The Edmunds Commission presented a fine opportunity. Using information from local missionaries, the IRA began making formal inquiries and protests. In late February Welsh went to Washington to lobby against the Edmunds agreement. Another IRA member, Charles Painter, enlisted Eliphalet Whittlesey, chair of the Board of Indian Commissioners, and ethnologist Alice C. Fletcher to contact key senators.[10] Reformers' lobbying produced two concrete results. On March 2, the Senate passed a resolution creating a committee to investigate the "feasibility and propriety of proposed reduction" of the Sioux Reservation. This committee, with Senator Dawes at its head, gathered the evidence of the Edmunds Commission's improprieties discussed earlier. The next day, Congress addressed the Edmunds Commission's failure to secure the signatures of three-fourths of the adult men. Responding to these concerns, the Interior Department instructed the Edmunds Commission to return to Sioux country and satisfy the three-fourths requirement.[11]

If government officials wanted signatures, Edmunds decided, that's what he would give them. At Pine Ridge, the commission's interpreter, Reverend

[9] Robert Winston Mardock, *The Reformers and the American Indian* (Columbia, Mo., 1971), 168–201; Frederick E. Hoxie, *A Final Promise: The Campaign to Assimilate the Indians, 1880–1920* (Lincoln, 1984), 1–14.

[10] William T. Hagan, *The Indian Rights Association: The Herbert Welsh Years, 1882–1904* (Tucson, 1985), 1–19, 40; W. H. Hare to Herbert Welsh, 23 Oct. 1882, Indian Rights Association Papers, Historical Society of Pennsylvania, Philadelphia, microfilm, roll 1; H. Swift to Herbert Welsh, 2 Nov. 1882, Indian Rights Association Papers, roll 1; H. Burt to Herbert Welsh, 15 Nov. 1882, Indian Rights Association Papers, roll 1; T. L. Riggs to CIA, 12 Feb. 1883, in Edmunds report, 43–44. Hyde, *Sioux Chronicle*, 131, writes that when Congress convened in December 1882, "the air was filled with ugly rumors concerning... the Sioux land commission," but the *New York Times*, 10 Feb. 1883, p. 1, noted that the Edmunds agreement "has not attracted much attention."

[11] *Congressional Record*, 47th Cong., 2d sess., 1884–85, 14, pt. 4:3556, 3574, 3699; *U.S. Statutes at Large* 22 (1883): 624; Hyde, *Sioux Chronicle*, 137.

Samuel Hinman, secured as many as he could, but he neglected the pesky fact that signers be at least eighteen years old. Hinman's list included one hundred and forty boys, one as young as three and several others under ten years of age. The reverend defended himself to the Dawes Committee by stating that he objected when the first boy came forward to sign, but that a chief protested that because the boy was "a member of the warriors' lodge and draws rations for his family, he has all the rights of an adult." This may have explained one or two signatures, but it could hardly have explained more than a hundred.[12]

In the end, the Edmunds Commission was unable to escape reformers' surveillance. Beginning in May 1883, a steady stream of investigators – first the IRA's Welsh, then members of the Board of Indian Commissioners, and finally Senator Dawes's committee – collected abundant testimony of the Edmunds Commission's misdeeds. This evidence did not damn the commission in the eyes of Dakota Territory's citizens, but it allowed critics to issue a searing denunciation when they met in October at the first annual Lake Mohonk Conference. Supporters were unable to resuscitate the Edmunds agreement.[13]

The humanitarians' quarrel with the Edmunds Commission was less about ends than means. Those who saw themselves as the Indians' friends were devoted to privatizing tribal lands, but they wanted to do it without violating previous treaties. In March 1884 reformers introduced the Dawes Sioux Bill, which provided the Sioux "ample justice" by requiring adherence to the three-fourths requirement and offering what its drafters regarded as generous compensation. Strenuous opposition from Thomas Augustus Bland's National Indian Defence Association (NIDA) slowed down passage of the Dawes Bill, but it eventually became law on April 30, 1888. Coming on the heels of the 1887 Dawes Severalty Act, a more general piece of legislation that announced Congress' intent to implement the policy of allotment, the Dawes Bill signaled a renewed assault on Sioux lands.[14]

Plains Sioux leaders following these developments realized the necessity of finding new forms of collective action. Accordingly, in 1886 Sitting Bull paid a visit to the home of his old enemies, the Crows, where he met close to one hundred Indians from Cheyenne River and several more from Pine Ridge. Although the main purpose of these journeys was commercial and

---

[12] Dawes report, 140, 299, 202 (qtn.); Welsh, *Report of a Visit*, 29–30.

[13] Welsh, *Report of a Visit*; Dawes report, passim; *Fifteenth Annual Report of the Board of Indian Commissioners for the Year 1883* (Washington, D.C., 1884), 33–43.

[14] Hagan, *Indian Rights Association*, 41–43, 56–58 (qtn., 43); Francis Paul Prucha, *The Great Father: The United States Government and the American Indians*, 2 vols. (Lincoln, 1984), 2:635–37; *Sixth Annual Report of the Executive Committee of the Indian Rights Association, 1888* (Philadelphia, 1889), 5–6.

social, Sitting Bull seized the opportunity to agitate against recent efforts to begin allotting the Crow Reservation. In a speech at the nearby Little Bighorn battlefield and in several councils at Crow Agency, Sitting Bull exhorted the Crows to resist allotment. According to U.S. officials, the Crows had favored allotment, but Sitting Bull's "machinations and insidious counsels" provoked substantial opposition.[15] Although we lack direct evidence of Sitting Bull's intentions, it is likely that he hoped that promoting intertribal opposition to allotment would prevent further dispossession of his own people. Other leaders tried different approaches. In late 1887, following the passage of the Dawes Severalty Act and with the Dawes Sioux Bill pending, efforts were underway at several agencies to collect money to fund a delegation to Washington. By January 1888 Cheyenne River Lakotas had raised $400 and were sending emissaries to Standing Rock and Rosebud to encourage fund-raising there. Pine Ridge Indians were also raising money; their agent blamed the NIDA for this agitation.[16]

Although the Indian Office did not approve a delegation to Washington, it could not prevent mounting opposition to land cession. In June 1888 Cheyenne River Agent Charles McChesney reported that two-thirds of the Indians there were "strongly opposed" to the Dawes Bill. James McLaughlin thought it would not be difficult to get the bill approved at Standing Rock except "for the pressure that will be brought by Indians of the other Sioux Agencies." Although McLaughlin's observations were self-serving ("his" Indians would surely do what was right in the absence of outside agitation), his report made clear that the western Sioux bands were pressuring each other to stand firm against new assaults on their land. Indeed, in mid-July, delegates from Standing Rock and other western Sioux agencies met at Rosebud. Elaine Goodale, who attended the council, reported that a delegate from

[15] Henry E. Williamson to James McLaughlin, 7 Sept. 1886, Records of the Crow Agency, box 13, Record Group 75, National Archives and Records Administration, Denver; J. G. Walker and James R. Howard to CIA, 27 Sept. 1886, OIA, file 26352–1886 (qtn.); Henry E. Williamson to CIA, 27 Sept. 1886, OIA, file 26353–1886. On resistance to allotment at Crow Agency before Sitting Bull's visit, see Frederick E. Hoxie, *Parading through History: The Making of the Crow Nation in America, 1805–1935* (Cambridge, 1995), 146–48. The evidence for Sitting Bull's visit from the Standing Rock side is slender. Louis L. Pfaller, *James McLaughlin: The Man with an Indian Heart* (New York, 1978), 396, n. 52, cites two letters from McLaughlin about this visit, McLaughlin to CIA, 3 Sept. 1886, 14 Oct. 1886, OIA, files [2]4394–1886, 28062–1886, though neither actually mentions it. Relying on oral history, however, Mrs. J. F. Waggoner, "Sitting Bull at the Agency," Walter S. Campbell Collection, box 104, folder 14, Western History Collections, University of Oklahoma Library, Norman, notes that Sitting Bull visited the Crow Reservation sometime after 1885. According to Thomas M. Heski, *The Little Shadow Catcher, Icastinyanka Cikala Hanzi: D. F. Barry, Celebrated Photographer of Famous Indians* (Seattle, 1978), 67, Sitting Bull was tried at Standing Rock for his activities at Crow Agency.
[16] Charles E. McChesney to CIA, 25 Jan. 1888, OIA, file 2800–1888; James McLaughlin to CIA, 23 Feb. 1888, MP, roll 33; L. F. Spencer to CIA, 15 Nov. 1887, RA-KC, book 14; H. D. Gallagher to CIA, 12 Dec. 1887, PR-KC, box 36.

Standing Rock "delivered a message from Sitting Bull, forbidding them to sign." Another speaker captured the prevailing mood of the meeting: "Be the ink black or red, we will not touch the pen, we will not even look at the paper."[17]

A commission to secure Sioux agreement to the Dawes Bill arrived at the Standing Rock Agency on July 21. The commission's chair was Richard Henry Pratt, well-known to the Sioux as the head of Carlisle Indian School. The other commissioners were William J. Cleveland, an Episcopal missionary at Rosebud, and John V. Wright, a former Confederate colonel from Tennessee. Three days after their arrival the commissioners began their work by informing the six hundred Indians present that they had hundreds of copies of the bill in the Dakota language, each with a map of the proposed cession. Each man, they explained, was to take his personal copy of these documents. Those who could read could study the text on their own, while others (the majority) would have to depend on "the boys and girls who have been to school." If the commissioners expected a massive rush for these documents, they were disappointed. The Sioux took only fifty copies of the bill. The commissioners explained that the Indians thought they "would commit themselves . . . to the acceptance of the provisions of the bill if they took the printed copies." Although this was probably not literally true, it was accurate in a more general sense. Most Standing Rock Sioux felt that they already knew enough about the bill to reject it. There was no reason to study the text. To do so would only give the commissioners legitimacy.[18]

The next day, Wright informed the Standing Rock Sioux that they had two choices. They could either continue to "get your living from the Government," or they could learn to make their living themselves "like men." The first option, besides being unmanly, was untenable. The problem was that the president "does not own the money that is in his strong box." Should the Indians refuse the president's plan for them to support themselves, "then the white people may say: 'If these people will not work and help themselves we will not give them any money; we will elect no man to office who will give them more money.'" At this not very subtle threat, the government stenographer recorded, there was "commotion among the Indians."[19]

---

[17] Charles E. McChesney to CIA, 26 June 1888, OIA, file 16455–1888; James McLaughlin to Gen. [Samuel C.] Armstrong, 5 May 1888, MP, roll 20; Elaine Goodale, "Will the Indians Sign?" *The Independent*, 16 Aug. 1888, p. 6. On arrangements for the mid-July council, see also Herbert Welsh to SI, 5 July 1888, OSI, file 3126–1888.

[18] *Letter from the Secretary of the Interior Transmitting . . . Report Relative to Opening a Part of the Sioux Reservation*, 50th Cong., 2d sess., 1888–89, S. Ex. Doc. 17, serial 2610 (hereafter Pratt report), 30–33, 56–62 (qtn., 61); Jon L. Wakelyn, *Biographical Dictionary of the Confederacy* (Westport, Conn., 1977), 449. A copy of the Dakota version of the bill is enclosed in Herbert Welsh to SI, 10 July 1888, OSI, file 3145–1888.

[19] Pratt report, 64. For an optimistic assessment of the first two days' events, see Capt. R. H. Pratt to SI, 25 July 1888, OSI, file 3561–1888.

The only option for the Sioux, Wright and the other commissioners argued, was to become self-sufficient, and the only way to do this was to sign the bill. The western Sioux had 22 million acres of land, far more than they needed. If they sold half of it, the government would make it available to homesteaders at 50¢ an acre and place the proceeds from these sales in a permanent fund of at least $1,000,000 (and as high as $5,500,000 if all of the land was sold). Half of the interest on this fund (5 percent per annum) would go to education and agriculture; the other half would be paid in cash. Indians who took up individual allotments would receive agricultural assistance and an additional $20 in cash. These provisions, the commissioners emphasized, were "kind, generous, ample, [and] plenty." The Indians could sign a black paper and tell "the Great Father that they think he is wise and they will go in the road which he points out to them." Or, they could sign a red paper and tell him that "they do not want to hear any more of his words; that, although they have not got any more buffalo, or any more deer, and the white people are crowding around here like a great flood, yet they think they can take care of themselves without his help."[20]

That night the Standing Rock Indians held their own council. Speaker after speaker stated his opposition to the bill, and the council did not adjourn until dawn. A few hours later, the Indians gathered before the Pratt Commission to announce their decision. Their spokesman, John Grass, a Sihasapa leader, began by arguing that the bill offered insufficient compensation. Five percent per year on $1,000,000, Grass observed, would yield $50,000. After half of this went to "educational and industrial purposes," what would be left? "[W]e calculated on it, together with the number of Indians that it would be given to," Grass reported, and "it made us feel very bad." (At this point, the stenographer recorded "laughter.") Half of $50,000 divided among over 20,000 Sioux would yield "about $1 apiece."[21]

Grass then turned to one of the least favorite topics of U.S. commissioners, the history of previous treaties. Many of the Indians who signed the 1868 treaty, Grass contended, "claim they only gave them a right of way for a railroad." "Perhaps," Grass suggested, the commissioners "changed the paper so that they would take the whole country." Even so, had the government "made the payments that they promised at that time, it would have been all right." But this had not happened. "You owe us for land that you have already bought," Grass declared, "and you ought to pay us that first." Grass further disputed the reservation's northern boundary at the Cannonball River. When he had signed the 1876 Black Hills agreement, Grass

[20] Pratt report, 66–69, 72–76 (1st qtn., 69, other qtns., 76). For the provisions of the legislation, see the Pratt report, 35–43, and the summary in *ARCIA*, 1888, lxxiii–lxxiv.
[21] Pratt report, 77–78. The *Bismarck Daily Tribune*, 29 July 1888, p. 1, describes the late night/early morning council. Its coverage of the Pratt Commission noted several other all-Indian councils, mostly held in the evening or at night.

explained, he had done so with the understanding that the northern border would be the Heart River, farther north. Given these past injustices, his people did not want to sign the black paper, the one that signified approval of the Dawes Bill. Nor would they sign the red. "Now you have heard. There is nothing else for us to say. We are through."[22]

As some of the Indians began to disperse, Pratt quickly launched into a rebuttal of Grass. His first move was to brush aside the uncomfortable subject of treaty history. "Whether these treaties are true or false," Pratt announced, "they represent a state of affairs that is established beyond all dispute; and all talk against them is idle, useless, and a waste of time." It was pointless to talk about "old things." Pratt then tried to counter Grass's argument that the bill didn't provide fair compensation. Having just declared a moratorium on discussion of "old things," Pratt now summoned history for his own purposes. "What makes your land ... worth anything at all?" he asked the Indians. In 1868, "you could not have sold the whole of [your land] for 10 cents an acre." But now that the "white man" had arrived with his towns and railroads, "your land [is now] worth something." Rather than spurning the government's offer, the Sioux should be grateful that their land had any value at all![23]

Pratt then called on Wright to respond to Grass's critique of the bill's terms. It was unfair of Grass to say that the Sioux would only get $1 each for the land, Wright argued. Five percent on $1 million was only a minimum. If all the land was sold, it would bring over $5 million into the fund. Furthermore, in addition to a cash payment the bill provided for the purchase of cattle. Indians who took up allotments would get additional benefits. In the meantime, they would continue to receive treaty rations and annuities. Rather than scorning these terms, the Sioux should appreciate what the "white people" were doing for them. For the support of the Sioux and other Indian tribes, they paid $7 million annually into "the Great Father's Treasury." Many were "getting tired of it," and who could blame them? Would not the Sioux "get tired if you had to feed the Arickarees every year besides feeding yourselves?" As for Grass's refusal to sign either paper, this was impossible. "We have come here to obey the orders of the Great Father" and so must the Sioux. They did not have to agree to the bill, Wright explained, but if "you refuse it, you must refuse it in the way he says." They must sign either the black paper or the red.[24]

Following this, Pratt gave Grass a chance to reply. Instead of offering a point-by-point rebuttal, however, the Sioux' spokesman protested that the commissioners had talked so much. If all their words were "put together and put on top of us," Grass observed, it would be "enough to crush us down."

---

[22] Pratt report, 78–79.
[23] Ibid., 80.
[24] Ibid., 81–84 (qtns., 82, 84).

By contrast, "I did not say very much," and he would say little now. (In fact, by this time, the commissioners had spoken about seven hours, while Grass's speech – the only Indian speech – had lasted no more than an hour.) Grass intended to avoid a war of words. The commission could stay for months, but "we can't say anything different. We will not sign those papers."[25]

It is easy to see why the Standing Rock Sioux refused to sign the black document, but why were they so adamant about not signing the red one? Some writers have suggested that the Sioux feared a "cunning trick – the red paper might turn black before it reached Washington."[26] Perhaps some Sioux thought the commissioners would literally turn the red document black, but such statements more likely expressed metaphorically the fear that the commissioners would alter the document's wording or distort its meaning. Furthermore, there was something qualitatively different about actually marking a paper in opposition rather than not signing anything at all. For one thing, Indians must have feared that U.S. officials would use their marks on the red paper to identify them and their descendants forevermore as enemies. For another, the commissioners' process was likely to undermine solidarity. Under rules in which individuals were asked to come forward serially and make a choice to sign one of two documents, it was far more likely that they would fear to be on the losing side and thus sign the black paper. It would be much easier to preserve unity against the bill by rejecting the process of signing altogether.

When Grass announced the Indians' decision, it was a Friday. Pratt decided to adjourn until the following Monday (July 30). All that week and into the next the commissioners tried everything they could think of. They brought in Dakota Territorial Governor Louis K. Church, who urged the Sioux to accept the will of the "Great Father," who "holds out his hand in friendship." Agent McLaughlin, who later claimed to have reservations about the bill, swallowed them long enough to recount its many advantages. McLaughlin also implored the Standing Rock Sioux to drop their claim that "commissioners in the past have deceived you." He did not deny deceit's existence, but instead urged that "the past be entirely wiped out."[27] The commissioners themselves made more speeches, hoping that the force of repetition would wear down a captive audience.

---

[25] Ibid., 85. My estimate of total speaking time is an extrapolation based on the knowledge that Wright's opening speech took three hours (p. 70).

[26] Elaine Goodale Eastman, *Pratt: The Red Man's Moses* (Norman, 1935), 175; Robert M. Utley, *The Lance and the Shield: The Life and Times of Sitting Bull* (New York, 1993), 274 (qtn.). See also Mary Collins's statement in *Proceedings of the Sixth Annual Meeting of the Lake Mohonk Conference, 1888* (n.p., 1888), 20. Hyde, *Sioux Chronicle,* 191, notes that the commission's choice of colors was not especially inspired, because for the Sioux red symbolized "life and happiness," while black was a "bad color."

[27] Pratt report, 87–88; James McLaughlin, *My Friend the Indian* (1910; Lincoln, 1989), 274–75.

Forced into continuing a conversation they did not want, Grass and the other Standing Rock speakers could only repeat their objections to the bill and their allegations of past injustice and deception. When Standing Rock leaders kept bringing up history, the commissioners tried to put a stop to it by grilling Grass on his claim that the 1876 Manypenny Commission had deceived the Sioux about the reservation boundaries. This led to a series charges and countercharges.[28] By August 1, the commissioners showed signs of losing control. At one point, Judge Wright began shaking his fists and gesticulating wildly. This prompted Gall, the leading spokesman of the Hunkpapas, to object that Wright made "so many signs with your hands that I am afraid of you" and that he spoke to them "just the same as to children." Wright offered a partial apology for his behavior the next day. When "I shake my fists and make gestures," he said, people think "I am getting mad," but "I was not mad – only in earnest." This explanation did little, however, to counter Gall's charge of paternalism. Indeed, Wright continued to talk in exactly the same way. Later, in taking up the Indians' allegation that the commissioners were threatening them, Wright offered an analogy of a "little boy" who wanders off in the direction of a dangerous river. It would be a threat for a father to say to him, "'If you do not come back, I will whip you,'" but it is not a threat if a father says, "'Come back, my son, do not go to the river; it is dangerous, you might be drowned.'"[29] While the Standing Rock Sioux would have questioned Wright's distinction between legitimate and illegitimate paternalism, their immediate objection to this analogy might well have been its denial of the whip Wright and his colleagues so obviously held. The commissioners repeatedly told the Indians that if they refused to sign, it would be "like slapping your Great Father in the face." If they "throw him away he will throw you away."[30]

Despite the threat of incurring the U.S. government's wrath and all that implied (loss of rations, annuities, and total dispossession), the people of Standing Rock held firm. Over and over their leaders implored the commissioners to stop talking and go home. As the days dragged on, Sitting Bull urged his people to pack up their wagons and demanded of the commissioners, "how many months you expect us to stay here, and by what time you will call it a decision." Gall informed the commissioners that "our crops are being ruined" and wanted to know "who is going to pay us for them."[31] Later, Grass pointedly remarked that, because the commissioners were "getting

---

[28] Although Sioux leaders accused the Manypenny Commission of lying about the reservation boundaries in 1876 (see, e.g., Gall's statement in Pratt report, 107), Grass argued only that his signature had been contingent on the boundaries being changed (p. 79). Thus, although two interpreters who had been present in 1876, Louis Agard and William Halsey, testified in support of Pratt (p. 103), their testimony contradicted only Gall's, not Grass's, position.

[29] Pratt report, 103–24 (qtns., 116, 119, 124).

[30] Ibid., 95, 102.

[31] Ibid., 116 (1st qtn.); *Bismarck Daily Tribune*, 3 Aug. 1888, p. 1 (2d qtn.).

good salaries every day," it made no difference "how many days you stay in a place." By contrast, the Indians needed to return to their fields. Miffed at what he took to be Grass's implication that he was benefitting financially from his work as a commissioner, Pratt shot back that "it does not make any difference whether I am at home or here, my salary is just the same." This response, however, missed the point. The commissioners could afford to draw out the proceedings indefinitely, but the Indians could not.[32]

On August 7 the commissioners finally let the Standing Rock Sioux return to their homes, although they stayed at the agency for two more weeks. Pratt said he would throw open his arms to anyone who wanted to sign either of the two papers, but only twenty-two were willing. (All signed the black.) The commissioners went on to the Crow Creek and Lower Brulé agencies and secured some signatures, but they realized it would be futile to go to Pine Ridge, Rosebud, or Cheyenne River. By this time, Pratt was desperate. After dashing off to Madison, Wisconsin, to consult with Interior Secretary William Vilas, Pratt hastily called a general council of chiefs from the six agencies. This council convened at Lower Brulé on September 24. Pratt and Wright made one last effort to convince these leaders that the government would never give them better terms and that they should sign now. Almost all said no.[33]

Many proponents of taking Sioux land believed that Congress should simply pass a law enacting their will without going to the trouble of gaining Sioux consent. Only two years earlier, the Supreme Court had dealt a major blow to tribal sovereignty by ruling in *United States v. Kagama* that Congress had plenary power over Indian affairs.[34] Nonetheless, key government officials remained committed to an "honorable" cession. In October Interior Secretary Vilas invited Sioux leaders to Washington and offered to amend the terms of the original bill. The major change was the price of the land. For the first three years, land would be sold to settlers at $1 per acre, for two years after at 75¢ an acre, and thereafter at 50¢. Fourteen of the delegates agreed to these terms, but the other forty-seven stated that they would not sell their land unless the price was $1.25 per acre, "just what the Government sells its land for." Nothing had been resolved, but the stage was set for a new commission to bring a revised proposal to Sioux country.[35]

---

[32] Pratt report, 131–32.

[33] Ibid., 8–12, 196–226.

[34] Arguments for seizure appeared in the *Bismarck Daily Tribune*, 8 Aug. 1888, p. 2; *Minneapolis Evening Journal*, 8 Aug. 1888, p. 4; *Congressional Record*, 50th Cong., 2d sess., 1888–89, 20, pt. 2:1493. For the *Kagama* case, see Sidney L. Harring, *Crow Dog's Case: American Indian Sovereignty, Tribal Law, and United States Law in the Nineteenth Century* (Cambridge, 1994), 142–49.

[35] Pratt report, 13, 227–49; *New York Times*, 16 Oct. 1888, p. 1 (qtn.).

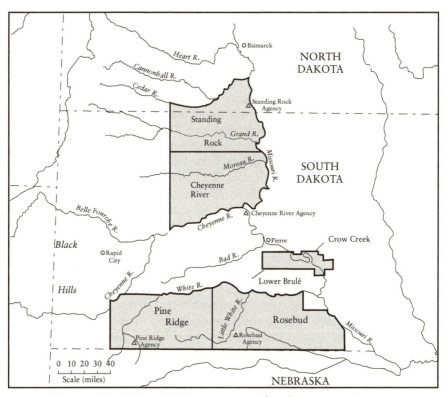

MAP 4. Western Sioux reservations after the 1889 cession.

The new measure, approved by Congress on March 2, 1889, offered some concessions. The price of lands sold in the first three years would be $1.25. The subsequent prices remained the same as those Vilas had offered in October, but after ten years the government promised to buy all unsold lands for 50¢ an acre. The new bill also guaranteed a minimum of $3 million in a permanent fund and specified that the government would bear all expenses (surveying and administration) rather than having them deducted from the land sales. The bill increased the size of allotments from 160 to 320 acres and granted $50 instead of $20 to those who took up allotments. It also addressed a long-standing grievance by offering compensation for ponies confiscated from Red Cloud and Red Leaf in 1876.[36] The boundaries of the new reservations are shown in Map 4.

For the third time in eight years, a U.S. commission would to try to force the western Sioux to give up a substantial portion of their land. The

---

[36] Charles J. Kappler, ed., *Indian Affairs: Laws and Treaties*, 5 vols. (Washington, D.C., 1904–1941), 1:328–39.

commission consisted of two politicians, William Warner, governor of Missouri, and former Ohio governor Charles Foster. Foster, a political crony of newly elected President Benjamin Harrison, saw his appointment as a rare opportunity. The "Indian is a queer character and pretty soon he will become extinct," Foster told a newspaper reporter. If a man wanted the experience of serving on an Indian commission, "he has no time to lose." Although Foster was appointed chair, the most important commissioner was General George Crook. Having secured the rank of Major General and closing in on retirement, Crook enjoyed his life of dinner parties, banquets, hunting trips, and an occasional post inspection. He had turned down the job a year before (Pratt was not the first choice). With Pratt's failure, however, government officials prevailed on Crook as the one man with the knowledge and diplomatic tact to carry out this important errand for civilization.[37]

The Crook Commission, as it became known, arrived in Sioux country on May 31 and did not leave until August 7. A minority favored signing from the beginning. Most mixed bloods saw advantages in taking up allotments and genuinely believed that their people would be better off if they cooperated with the United States (though some with large cattle herds feared that ceding land would restrict their access to the range).[38] Only a few full bloods favored the bill outright. Most of these were unusual men. Standing Bear, probably the first Lakota to own a store, found the bill attractive not only for its promise of 640 acres but also because taking an allotment would allow him to travel without a pass.[39] George Sword, the police captain at Pine Ridge, was another strong advocate of the bill. As a young man, Sword had compiled an impressive war record, including fighting against U.S troops. After a time, though, he concluded that "the white people always won the victory" and took a new name, *Miwakan Yuha* (literally, "A Sword He Has"), "because the leaders of the white soldiers wore swords." Sword was "determined to adopt the customs of the white people, and to persuade my people to do so." Though many Lakota leaders advocated selective adoption of American ways of life, Sword went farther in the direction of acculturation than most.

---

[37] *Report and Proceedings of the Sioux Commission*, 51st Cong., 1st sess., 1889–90, S. Ex. Doc. 51, serial 2682 (hereafter Crook report), 15; Jerome A. Greene, "The Sioux Land Commission of 1889: Prelude to Wounded Knee," *South Dakota History* 1 (Winter 1970): 47–48 (qtn., 47); Maj. Gen. George Crook to SW, 8 June 1888, OSI, file 2809–1888; Martin F. Schmitt, ed., *General George Crook: His Autobiography* (Norman, 1946), 267–84.

[38] On the support of mixed bloods for the bill, see Hyde, *Sioux Chronicle*, 210–11; Paul Robertson, *The Power of the Land: Identity, Ethnicity, and Class among the Oglala Lakota* (New York, 2002), 21. Greene, "Sioux Land Commission," 57, notes that most mixed bloods at Cheyenne River opposed the bill.

[39] Hyde, *Sioux Chronicle*, 209; Luther Standing Bear, *My People the Sioux*, ed. E. A. Brininstool (1928; Lincoln, 1975), 211; Crook report, 51; Maj. Gen. George Crook to Chief Standing Bear, 26 Aug. 1889, General George Crook Correspondence, 1864–1908, Hayes Memorial Library, Fremont, Ohio (microfilm, University of Oregon Library, Eugene).

From his position as semipermanent head of the Indian police (he was not a band leader), he assisted in the suppression of Lakota religious practices and was a strong advocate of farming and allotment.[40]

By far the majority of Lakotas, Yanktons, and Yanktonais opposed the bill. Everywhere Crook and his colleagues went they faced this fact. At Rosebud, their first stop, "[v]ery few, if any, of the prominent men" favored the bill, and aversion was even stronger at Pine Ridge. Although most Sioux at Lower Brulé were favorably disposed, at Crow Creek opponents and proponents were evenly divided. When Crook got to Cheyenne River, he found "almost unanimous opposition to the ratification of the bill." Sentiment against the bill was equally strong at Standing Rock.[41]

Indians reiterated many of arguments from the year before. At Cheyenne River, for example, White Swan spoke of past commissions whose "words were rich with the promises we were to get," but the promises had gone to the "white people," leaving the Indians with only the words. Many speakers objected that the price was still not high enough. Swift Bird demanded "$1.25 per acre for all, good and bad." At Standing Rock, John Grass pointed out that few settlers would take up land at the maximum price. Instead, they would wait until the land was only 50¢ an acre. (Grass's remarks were prescient; the Sioux received only 57¢ per acre for the 1889 land cession, as drought and low farm prices discouraged settlement.)[42]

Although some Sioux suggested that price remained the major stumbling block, others expressed serious misgivings no matter what the terms. To counter the argument that the Sioux had more land than they needed, White Swan reminded the commissioners of the Christian story when "there was only one man created on the world, and they went to work and took a bone out of that man and made a woman and they had connection, and that way the white people have grown on this world." In the same way, White Swan continued, his own people "are going to spread and there is going to be more

---

[40] James R. Walker, *Lakota Belief and Ritual*, ed. Raymond J. DeMallie and Elaine A. Jahner (Lincoln, 1980), 74 (qtns.). Sword became captain of the Pine Ridge Indian policy shortly after its organization in 1879. See Julia B. McGillycuddy, *Blood on the Moon: Valentine McGillycuddy and the Sioux* (1941; Lincoln, 1990), 113, 121. He retained that position throughout the 1880s. Sword's activities are documented in George Sword to CIA, 16 Aug. 1882, OIA, file 15651–1882; Pratt report, 249; statement of Fast Thunder, enclosed in H. D. Gallagher to CIA, 9 April 1889, OIA, file 9707–1889. Although Sword cooperated in the government's suppression of Lakota religion, he later played a crucial role in communicating Lakota traditions to James Walker. See Walker, *Lakota Belief and Ritual*, 21–23; Elaine A. Jahner, "Transitional Narratives and Cultural Continuity," in *American Indian Persistence and Resurgence*, ed. Karl Kroeber (Durham, 1994), 162–63.

[41] Crook report, 16–21 (qtns., 16, 20).

[42] Ibid., 161 (1st qtn.), 164 (2d qtn.), 196; Herbert T. Hoover, "The Sioux Agreement of 1889 and Its Aftermath," *South Dakota History* 19 (Spring 1989): 70. Although a few settlers rushed to take up land in early 1890, Nelson, *After the West Was Won*, 12, notes that settlement of the West River country did not begin in earnest until the turn of the century.

people here." The Sioux had just as much right to multiply and replenish as European Americans. At Rosebud, High Hawk made the same point in an earthier way. "I expect my children to have children and grandchildren, and get all over the country," High Hawk said. The commissioners, however, "want me to cut off my 'tool' and not make any more children."[43]

To break down Sioux opposition, Crook used some of the same tactics as Pratt. Crook and the other commissioners adomonished the Sioux to quit "growling about the past," scolded them for for "slap[ping] the Great Father in the face," and warned of the dire consequences that would follow should they "turn your backs" on him.[44] On the other hand, the 1889 commissioners were careful not to shake their fists or browbeat leaders into admissions of wrong. Instead of "talking the Indians to death," they afforded them ample opportunity to ask questions and make speeches.[45] Crook, Foster, and Warner often talked down to their audience, but they were much less condescending than their predecessors the year before and often flattered key leaders.[46] When daily councils adjourned, the commission provided feasts and watched Indians perform Omaha dances (to the missionaries' dismay, Crook even permitted such spectacles on Sunday). Crook himself spent hours "tuning up the Indians," as he put it in his diary.[47]

Crook, Foster, and Warner portrayed themselves as honest and trustworthy men. Before an audience of Cheyenne River Indians Foster congratulated himself that "[w]e have been told at other places that we are the only Commission that ever came out that was not bald headed."[48] Foster had apparently learned of the Sioux association of Americans' bald headedness and their proclivity to lie.[49] Yet whereas it was true that the commissioners' heads still had hair (although Foster's and Crook's hairlines were receding noticeably – see Illustration 8), it did not necessarily follow that U.S. officials with hair were honest. Many Sioux did not trust General Crook. Take Little No Heart, for example. Several years before, he had referred to the general as *Skopa*. This word means crooked or warped and is therefore a

---

[43] Crook report, 162, 52.

[44] Ibid., 84, 114.

[45] Warner concluded a fairly short speech, especially by the standards of the Pratt Commission, by observing that "there is no death so terrible as that of the man who is talked to death," a remark that was met by "great cheering." Ibid., 84.

[46] An example of condescension was Crook's observation at Rosebud that if the Sioux didn't start working "the Government will have to send out dolls and rattles to amuse you." Ibid., 50. For an instance of flattery, see Foster's comment that he was "greatly pleased with the speech of American Horse" and that "if he had the education of a white man he would sit in the Great Council of the nation." Ibid., 91.

[47] George Crook, diary, 1, 2, 8, 17, 19 (qtn.), 24–28 June, 20, 21, 26, 30 July 1889, Crook-Kennon Papers, U.S. Army Military History Institute, Carlisle Barracks, Pa.; *Word Carrier* 18 (September 1889): 2.

[48] Crook report, 157.

[49] On the association between baldness and lying, see Chapter 5, note 39.

ILLUSTRATION 8. Crook Commission. Left to right: General George Crook, Charles Foster, William Warner. State Historical Society of North Dakota, 0022H29.

literal translation of Crook's name; as in English, *skopa* can also be used figuratively to mean dishonest. In 1889, when Little No Heart spoke before the commission, he did not call Crook "crooked," but he did note that previous commissioners had "been fooling us." He objected to having commissioners ask for his trust when "white people" in the Black Hills had "cigar[s] in their mouths" while his own people were "getting poorer all the time." Little No Heart's refusal to sign the bill rejected Crook's argument that he could be trusted.[50]

In the end, however, Crook secured the necessary three-fourths assent to the March 2, 1889, legislation. Why did Crook succeed where Pratt failed? One factor was that Crook had more money. Congress appropriated $18,000 for the Pratt Commission, but authorized Crook to spend $25,000. The general's "war chest" funded his policy of liberal feasting and left him enough to hire what George Hyde aptly terms a "small army of squawmen and mixed bloods" to lobby relatives and acquaintances. At Cheyenne River, for

---

[50] Little No Heart to My Great Father, 11 Dec. 1877, enclosed in SW to SI, 8 Jan. 1878, CRA, roll 130; Crook report, 169. Greene, "Sioux Land Commission," 48, notes the variety of Sioux opinion about Crook. I am grateful to Harvey Markowitz for discussing *skopa* with me.

example, Crook paid James Pearman (a squawman) and Joe Hodgkiss (a squawman or mixed blood) $20 each for four days' work "explaining Sioux act to the Indians." Old Clown and Brave Eagle received $30 each for fifteen days' "services as messengers."[51]

Even more important was the assistance of the reservation agents, whose services required not a dime. At Standing Rock, for example, Agent McLaughlin spent most of the evening of July 31, in the words of Crook's diary, "tuning up John Grass and others." McLaughlin later wrote of secret meetings with Grass, Gall, Mad Bear, and Big Head. If "the act was not concurred in," he told them, "a worse thing might happen: that legislation might be enacted which would open the reservation without requiring the consent of the Indians." McLaughlin followed this stick with a carrot. He promised that Crook would use his influence to secure an additional appropriation of $200,000 to compensate the Standing Rock and Cheyenne River Indians for ponies confiscated from them in 1876.[52]

In the end, Crook might have failed except for the simple fact that he offered more than Pratt. His bill contained better terms, although not by as much as the government claimed. More importantly, Crook made promises that went beyond the bill. The general told the Sioux that he would work for improving the annual issue of clothing, issuing beef on the hoof rather than the block, tolerating "social dances," funding on-reservation schools as an alternative to off-reservation education, constructing saw and grist mills, enforcing regulations against non-Indian grazing on reserves, increasing compensation for Indian police and judges, and providing additional cattle and agricultural assistance. As we saw in Chapter 3, when Crook used the idea of a northern agency to get Crazy Horse to surrender, making promises like these was part of Crook's standard method of operation.[53]

But beneath the velvet glove, there was always the iron fist. For many leaders, the risks of refusal became too high. As Gall told a newspaper reporter, "I have given my consent...after learning the Government could take our lands for nothing if it wanted to." There were other dangers. At Rosebud, High Hawk voiced widespread concerns that "those of us who refuse to sign this agreement will be disarmed and our rations taken from us." Even future generations might bear the consequences of opposing the government.

---

[51] Pratt report, 42; Kappler, ed., *Indian Affairs: Laws and Treaties*, 1:339; Hyde, *Sioux Chronicle*, 200; Charles McChesney to CIA, 26 Jan. 1891, OSI, file 3701–1891. Pearman was listed as a "white man" in Crook report, 290; I am unable to identify Hodgkiss.

[52] Crook diary, 31 July 1889 (1st qtn.); McLaughlin, *My Friend the Indian*, 283–85 (2d qtn., 285). Standing Rock was the last agency the commission visited; it had enough signatures to be close to its goal of three-fourths assent. Because of this, McLaughlin was under substantial pressure to deliver his agency. See Carole Barrett, "'March of Civilization': Standing Rock and the Sioux Act of 1889," in *Centennial West: Essays on the Northern Tier States*, ed. William L. Lang (Seattle, 1991), 88.

[53] Crook report, 25–31.

"[A]fter you are dead and gone, and somebody reads...the names of the people who signed this treaty," commissioner Foster ominously observed, "I think you will want your names to be read out."[54]

Hard-line opponents of the bill did all they could to prevent Crook from destroying their unity, sometimes resorting to intimidation and force. When Standing Bear signed the bill at Rosebud, "some of the Indians in the hall called out to kill him," while a "body of mounted soldiers" disrupted the commission's first meeting at Pine Ridge "to prevent any expression of opinion favoring acceptance." After several days of councils at Cheyenne River, Chasing Crow and a few others finally came forward to sign. When they did "two Indians in war paint and clubs jumped inside to club the men." At Standing Rock, members of Sitting Bull's Silent Eaters society, one of the last remaining war societies, tried to "stampede the Indians to prevent them from signing." Police lieutenant Henry Bullhead rushed a detachment of his men to the front and beat the Silent Eaters back.[55]

Government officials condemned these coercive tactics as revealing the tyranny of chiefly authority. By their way of thinking, the vast majority of Sioux men wanted to sign the bill, but a handful of reactionary chiefs stood in their way.[56] Although this interpretation helped officials feel better about what they were doing (most Sioux, they could later claim, agreed with them), it exaggerated the power of chiefs and seriously understated the depth of Sioux opposition. It also failed to acknowledge the forces at work on the other side. Even apart from the commissioners' threats and the larger context of economic dependency was the refusal to let Indians return to their homes. This *alone* undermined any pretense of free choice. Hyde hits the nail on the head: "all the 'no' men were to be kept right there until a sufficient number of them became 'yes' men and the land agreement was declared approved." Furthermore, Indians who signed the bill also used force to get others to join them. At Cheyenne River, police lieutenant Cook complained that some Indians were "trying to cow" those who didn't want to sign the bill. Florentine Digmann, a Jesuit at Rosebud, offered a specific example when he wrote that Yellow Hawk confided to him that Big Turkey "pushed me in to touch the pen." Ever since then, however, Yellow Hawk's heart had been "beating very hard" and he now regretted having "sold our land."[57]

---

54 *New York Times*, 7 Aug. 1889, p. 1 (1st qtn.); Crook report, 60, 67 (other qtns.). Hyde, *Sioux Chronicle*, 200, suggests that the decisive factor in Crook's success was his capacity (unlike Pratt's) to summon "regiment on regiment of cavalry." To the extent that Crook could call for troops, however, so could Pratt. In any case, neither of the commissions relied much on the threat of troops.

55 Crook report, 52, 18, 175, 213. See also Standing Bear, *My People the Sioux*, 214; *New York Times*, 17 June 1889, p. 1; Crook diary, 18 July 1889; McLaughlin, *My Friend*, 287.

56 See Crook report, 16.

57 Hyde, *Sioux Chronicle*, 210; Crook report, 179; Florentine Digmann, "History of the St. Francis Mission, 1886–1922," unpublished manuscript, n.d., series 7, box 14, folder 7,

Like Yellow Hawk, Sioux people who initially opposed the bill but eventually signed found themselves in a painful predicament. Consider the situation of John Grass. During the 1888 negotiations with Pratt, Grass had been brilliant. He had effectively countered the commissioners on their own terrain, authoritatively citing provisions of previous treaties and exposing flaws in the commissioners' arguments. Along with other leaders, he kept the Standing Rock Sioux united and sent Pratt packing. A year later, however, when Crook and McLaughlin twisted his arm into signing, Grass's position was extremely awkward. Knowing that he would face substantial criticism, Grass blamed the Sioux at other agencies who had already signed. Had they kept their pledge to refuse the bill, Grass would have said no. But now he had to sign. Otherwise, the Standing Rock Indians would be "at the mercy of those who are living at the other agencies."[58]

A minority refused to yield despite everything the government could do. At Pine Ridge there was an especially powerful trio of holdouts: Red Cloud, Little Wound, and Young Man Afraid of His Horses. When the Crook commissioners visited Pine Ridge in June, they were able only to secure the signatures of a simple majority of the adult men. Technically, the bill might not need a three-fourths majority at all of the agencies so long as it gained three-fourths overall. To remove all doubt, however, government officials tried several plans to win over the Pine Ridge opposition.[59]

One move involved William J. Pollock, who in 1878 had assisted with the Oglalas' move to Pine Ridge and four years later, as an Indian Office inspector, had written a report critical of McGillycuddy. With the commission's approval, Pollock came to Pine Ridge in mid-July. But after offering $200 each to the three holdouts to provide feasts for their bands, all he received in return was "a first class scolding from Little Wound."[60]

Agent Gallagher then tried his hand. Around August 6, Gallagher gave Little Wound a pass to Shoshone Agency for the purpose of "get[ting] him away" so Gallagher could "work on his people." When this produced nothing, Gallagher "read the riot act" to Red Cloud, but he remained "determined

---

p. 17, Holy Rosary Mission Records, Marquette University Special Collections, Milwaukee. This manuscript gives the name as "Yelling Hawk," but this must be either a mistake in the transcription or in Digmann's original diary, which, despite the valuable help of Mark Theil, I have been unable to locate. "Yelling Hawk," an improbable Lakota name, does not appear on the list of Rosebud signers (Crook report, 242–64), while Yellow Hawk signed as #364 (p. 248).

58 Crook report, 209.
59 William Warner to SI, 29 June 1889, OSI, file 3846–1889.
60 Charles Foster et al. to SI, 8 July 1889, OSI, file 132–1890; William Warner to SI, 3 July 1889, OSI, file 136–1890; Postmaster General to SI, 12 July 1889, OSI, file 4061–1889; William J. Pollock to SI, 31 July 1889, OSI, file 138–1890; Maj. Gen. George Crook to Charles Foster, 27 Aug. 1889, Crook Correspondence; H. D. Gallagher to Charles Foster, 24 July 1889, PR-KC, box 54 (qtn.). For Pollock's earlier activities at Pine Ridge, see Chapters 5 and 9.

to persevere." In late September, Gallagher made one last try. Realizing that Red Cloud's wife, Pretty Owl, was opposed to the bill and thinking that "her influence was holding him back," Gallagher asked William J. Godfrey, who for years had written letters for Red Cloud, and Jesuit missionary John Jutz to "drop in" on the Red Cloud family "as if by accident for the purpose of making a surprise effort to gain the old man over." Unable to persuade Red Cloud (or Pretty Owl), Godfrey left in anger. Never again, he told Red Cloud, would he write a letter for him. When Godfrey died two weeks later, Red Cloud "felt triumphant." By mid-October Gallagher concluded that it would be "useless" to do more.[61]

The Crook Commission left behind a people deeply divided. These divisions were all the more bitter precisely because the Sioux had worked so hard to forge a united front and came so close to sustaining it in the face of relentless pressure. As the Crook Commission left Standing Rock, one newspaper reporter asked Sitting Bull what the opening of the reservation would mean to the Indians. "Don't talk to me about Indians," the chief shot back, "there are no Indians left except those in my band." Faced with similar accusations at Pine Ridge, signers like American Horse lashed out against those who defined being an Indian as "to live in idleness and you feed me." American Horse did not accuse nonsigners of not being Indians. But his insistence that "I am an Indian as well as you" revealed his defensiveness in the face of widespread recriminations and allegations of betrayal.[62]

Government actions after Crook's departure only made things worse. The Crook Commission had repeatedly assured the Sioux that signing would not jeopardize their rations. Yet in late June – weeks before the commissioners departed – the Indian Office informed the Pine Ridge and Rosebud agents of a 20 to 25 percent reduction in their beef ration for the coming year.[63] U.S. officials kept this knowledge from the Pine Ridge and Rosebud Sioux; they probably did not learn about the cuts until fall.[64] When they found out, they were furious. Nonsigners accused signers of being "fools and dupes." Signers felt the commission had betrayed them; as Bishop William Hare observed,

[61] H. D. Gallagher to Charles Foster, 20 Aug., 3, 19 Oct. 1889, PR-KC, box 54.
[62] *New York Times*, 7 Aug. 1889, p. 1; Crook report, 113.
[63] The beef ration at Pine Ridge was reduced from 5 million pounds in fiscal year 1888–1889 to 4 million pounds in fiscal year 1889–1890. The cut at Rosebud was from 8.1 to 6 million pounds; at Cheyenne River it was from 2.1 million to 2 million pounds; the Standing Rock beef ration remained the same (4 million pounds). This information is in letters from the Acting CIA to the four relevant agencies, 31 July 1888, 24 June 1889, Record Group 75, Office of the Indian Affairs, Correspondence, Finance Division, vols. 139, 145, National Archives and Records Administration, Washington, D.C. On the Crook commissioners' assurances regarding rations, see Crook report, 23.
[64] The request for reversal of the beef reduction at Rosebud in J. George Wright to CIA, 19 Sept. 1889, RA-KC, book 16, implies that the Rosebud Indians weren't yet aware of the situation.

the Sioux thought that "the promises made by the Commissioners were, to all intents and purposes, part and parcel of the agreement."[65]

In an effort to defuse a growing crisis, Secretary of the Interior John Noble invited a delegation from the four western agencies as well as Crow Creek and Lower Brulé to meet with him and the Crook commissioners in December. Speaking for the Pine Ridge delegation on December 18, American Horse began politely enough. "My friends," he said, "I am very glad to meet you all." But with these niceties out of the way, Crook's major supporter at Pine Ridge turned to a topic that was "like cutting our heads off." American Horse observed that the commissioners had promised "that the beef... would not be touched," but "when we signed the treaty you struck us in the face... in taking the beef away from us."[66] Although government officials made vague promises to reverse the ration cuts and fulfill Crook's other promises, Congress failed to act. On February 10, 1890, President Benjamin Harrison declared the Sioux reservation open to settlement. As the months went by and the government continued to do nothing, nonsigners were more certain than ever that the signers had been fooled.[67]

The events of late 1889 and early 1890 provoked a crisis for the western Sioux. Against enormous pressures, the Sioux had managed to create a unified opposition against land cession, only to see this shattered. The government's reduction of rations and its failure to deliver additional promises not only discredited the signers on the land issue, it exposed serious problems with the strategy of selective cooperation that many leaders had been

---

[65] *ARCIA*, 1890, 49 (1st qtn.); W. H. Hare to William Welsh, 19 Jan. 1890, Indian Rights Association Papers, roll 5 (2d qtn.).

[66] Crook report, 221–22. Many historians have argued that Crook acted in good faith in assuring the Sioux that their rations would not be cut. See Robert M. Utley, *The Last Days of the Sioux Nation* (New Haven, 1963), 55; Hyde, *Sioux Chronicle*, 231; Greene, "Sioux Land Commission," 65; Robert W. Larson, *Red Cloud: Warrior-Statesman of the Lakota Sioux* (Norman, 1997), 261. It is true that Congress, not Crook, was to blame for the cuts in the annual Sioux appropriation that necessitated rations cuts. However, Congress cut the appropriation for Sioux subsistence (from $1 million to $900,000) in early March, months before Crook's commission began work. There is no direct evidence that Crook knew of this, although it is difficult to imagine that such an important fact escaped his notice. Furthermore, although the commission had already left Pine Ridge and Rosebud by the time the Indian Office informed the agents of the ration cuts at those two agencies, the commission probably learned of them while visiting Cheyenne River and Standing Rock. The commissioners' assurances at Cheyenne River and Standing Rock that rations would not be cut could be defended on the grounds that they applied only to Indians at *those* agencies, but at best this allows Crook to escape on a technicality.

[67] In opening the reserve, Harrison urged Congress to pass additional legislation to comply with the Crook Commission's recommendations. The Senate approved a bill for this purpose but it was gutted in the House. *Congressional Record*, 51st Cong., 1st sess., 1889–90, 21, pt. 2:1187; *Sioux Indians in Dakota*, 51st Cong., 1st sess., 1889–90, H. Rept. 2616, serial 2814; *ARCIA*, 1891, 134.

pursuing. Accommodationists had hoped that it might be possible to create a workable set of economic and political relationships with the government under the reservation system. By the end of the decade, however, the United States had not only launched a sustained assault on religious and cultural traditions, it had now taken almost half of the Sioux' remaining land as well. Farming was failing, as a drought settled on the Plains in the last years of the decade. The winter of 1889–1890 was especially hard. There was not enough to eat, and diseases like influenza and whooping cough claimed many lives.[68] Although many Sioux remained oriented to practical survival and working for gradual melioration, others were open to more radical possibilities. They were particularly interested when they learned of a new movement, the Ghost Dance, that promised the transformation of a world that had grown old and impossible to bear.

[68] Documentation for drought in summer 1889 and disease in winter 1889–1890 can be found in *ARCIA*, 1890, 37, 39, 44, 48, 57–58.

PART 3

ANTICOLONIALISM AND THE STATE

"When the Earth Shakes Do Not Be Afraid"

The Ghost Dance as an Anticolonial Movement

In late 1888 and early 1889 the Plains Sioux began to hear rumors of an Indian prophet with unusually strong spiritual powers. He lived someplace to the West, in or beyond *He Ska* (the White Mountains, known to Americans as the Rockies). News of this prophet came from several sources. William Selwyn, a Yankton Sioux who had been educated in the East and was postmaster at Pine Ridge, later stated that Utes, Shoshones, Crows, and Arapahoes who visited the agency in late 1888 brought word of a "New Messiah." Lakotas who traveled to the Wind River, Uintah, and other agencies the next summer undoubtedly heard more. Another source of information was letters. According to Selwyn, Oglalas at Pine Ridge frequently asked him to read correspondence they received from agencies throughout the West; some of these included reports of the prophet and his teachings.[1] Sometime in fall 1889, a council of Pine Ridge leaders appointed a delegation to journey west to learn more. Delegates were also chosen at Rosebud and Cheyenne River.[2]

---

[1] William T. Selwyn to Col. E. W. Foster, 25 Nov. 1890, SC 188, roll 1. For groups traveling between Pine Ridge and the Uintah and Wind River agencies, see H. D. Gallagher to U.S. Ind. Agent, Shoshone Agency, 3 July 1889, PR-KC, box 54; H. D. Gallagher to U.S. Ind. Agent, c. 3 July 1889, PR-KC, box 54.

[2] The sources for this delegation give different lists of names and dates. Selwyn to Foster, 25 Nov. 1890, states that the delegation departed in the fall and included Good Thunder, Short Bull, Kicking Bear, Yellow Breast, Broken Arm, Flat Iron, and two unnamed others. Another account by Short Bull, in "Wanagi Wacipi," *LT&T*, 277, states that a delegation left Pine Ridge in June 1889 and consisted of him, Kicking Bear, Brave Wolf, Thunder Horse, Turn Over Back, Scare Them, and Gray Horse. Another account by Short Bull, "As Narrated by Short Bull," Buffalo Bill Memorial Museum, Golden, Colo., evidently written sometime in the 1890s when Short Bull was employed by "Buffalo Bill" Cody, states that the delegation left in fall 1889 and included him, Kicking Bear, Twist Back (the same as Turn Over Back?), Scatter, He Dog, Flat Iron, Yellow Knife, Brave Bear, Yellow Breast, and Broken Arm (p. 2). To add to the confusion, Robert M. Utley, *The Last Days of the Sioux Nation* (New Haven, 1963), 61, uses the names in Selwyn's account for the fall 1889 delegation but adds Cloud Horse and Yellow Knife, who are mentioned in George Sword, "The Story of the Ghost Dance," *The*

The prophet they sought was a Northern Paiute (Numu) named Wovoka (Cutter or Wood Cutter), also known as Jack Wilson after the name of a local rancher who frequently employed him. Wovoka, shown in Illustration 9, was born sometime in the late 1850s or early 1860s, probably near the Walker River in the Mason Valley of Nevada. His father, Tavivo, was likely a follower of Wodziwob. In the late 1860s Wodziwob began holding dances and foretelling of the imminent return of the dead and the restoration of game and fish. Influenced by Wodziwob's teachings, Wovoka began to demonstrate spiritual powers. He introduced dancing and developed a set of teachings around 1886 or 1887.[3] On January 1, 1889, at the time of a solar eclipse, Wovoka "fell asleep" and "was taken up to the other world." In the words of ethnologist James Mooney, who interviewed him in January 1892, Wovoka

saw God, with all the people who had died long ago engaged in their oldtime sports and occupations, all happy and forever young. It was a pleasant land and full of game. After showing him all, God told him he must go back and tell his people they must be good and love one another, have no quarreling, and live in peace with the whites; that they must work, and not lie or steal; that they must put away all the old practices that savored of war; that if they faithfully obeyed his instructions they would at last be reunited with their friends in this other world, where there would be no more death or sickness or old age. He was then given the dance which he was commanded to bring back to his people. By performing this dance at intervals, for five consecutive days each time, they would secure this happiness to themselves and hasten the event.[4]

Much of our knowledge of Wovoka comes from Mooney, whose classic work *The Ghost-Dance Religion and the Sioux Outbreak of 1890*, published in 1896, has been by far the most influential study of the Ghost Dance. In many respects, Mooney offered a courageous interpretation of Wovoka and the movement he inspired. Against the dominant view at the time that the Ghost

Folk-Lorist 1 (July 1892): 28–29 (also in James Mooney, *The Ghost-Dance Religion and the Sioux Outbreak of 1890*, Fourteenth Annual Report of the Bureau of Ethnology, 1892–93, pt. 2 [Washington, D.C., 1896], 797–98), evidently without realizing that Sword reported these names from a second delegation in 1890. Utley also adds the names of Cloud Horse, Kicks Back (the same as Twist Back/Turn Over Back?), and Mash-the-Kettle (probably the same as Breaks-the-Pot-on-Him, mentioned in Luther Standing Bear, *My People the Sioux*, ed. E. A. Brininstool [1928; Lincoln, 1975], 218). Although it is impossible to resolve the discrepancies about the names in these accounts, the preponderance of evidence suggests that the first delegation did not leave until fall 1889, despite the June date in the *LT&T* account.

[3] For biographical information on Wovoka, see Michael Hittman, *Wovoka and the Ghost Dance*, expanded edition, ed. Don Lynch (Lincoln, 1997), 27–62; L. G. Moses, "'The Father Tells Me So!': Wovoka: The Ghost Dance Prophet," *American Indian Quarterly* 9 (Summer 1985): 336–38; Paul Bailey, *Wovoka: The Indian Messiah* (Los Angeles, 1957); Grace Dangberg, "Wovoka," *Nevada Historical Society Quarterly* 11 (Summer 1968): 5–53.

[4] Mooney, *Ghost-Dance Religion*, 771–72.

ILLUSTRATION 9. Wovoka (seated) with an unidentified man. National Anthropological Archives, 01659 A.

Dance was nothing more than the delusion of superstitious savages, Mooney treated it as the manifestation of the common human desire for a redeemer, which had found expression in the world's great religions, placing Wovoka on a par with Gautama, Mohammed, and Jesus.[5] To create a favorable impression of Wovoka for a skeptical American public, Mooney, following Wovoka's own lead, emphasized the peacefulness of Wovoka's teachings. In summarizing his January 1892 interview with Wovoka, Mooney reported that Wovoka "earnestly repudiated any idea of hostility toward the whites, asserting that his religion was one of universal peace."[6] Wovoka's insistence on the pacific character of his teaching was certainly understandable. Only a little more than a year had passed since the army had gunned down hundreds of his followers at Wounded Knee.[7]

Despite Mooney's overall emphasis on the peacefulness of Wovoka's teachings, he was aware that Wovoka had prophesied an apocalyptic event that would destroy European Americans or remove them from Indian lands. This is clear from Mooney's discussion of a document he described as "the genuine official statement of the Ghost-dance doctrine,"[8] which he obtained from members of a Cheyenne-Arapahoe delegation to Wovoka. According to their report, Wovoka said:

> When you get home you must make a dance to continue five days. Dance four successive nights, and the last night keep up the dance until the morning of the fifth day, when all must bathe in the river and then disperse to their homes. You must all do in the same way.
>
> I, Jack Wilson, love you all, and my heart is full of gladness for the gifts you have brought me. When you get home I shall give you a good cloud which will make you

---

[5] L. G. Moses, *The Indian Man: A Biography of James Mooney* (Urbana, 1984), 233; and Curtis M. Hinsley Jr., *Savages and Scientists: The Smithsonian Institution and the Development of American Anthropology, 1846–1910* (Washington, D.C., 1981), 207, suggest that Mooney's Irish background gave him empathy with oppressed peoples. Mooney's work can be faulted for its paternalism, but his emphasis on the similiarites within humanity marked a sharp contrast to that of John Wesley Powell, the director of the Bureau of American Ethnology, which consistently stressed the distance separating savagery and civilization. On this point, see Hinsley, *Savages and Scientists*, 213. Michael A. Elliott, "Ethnography, Reform, and the Problem of the Real: James Mooney's *Ghost-Dance Religion*," *American Quarterly* 50 (June 1998): 201–33, also comments on the advantages gained by Mooney's departure from Powell's and Lewis Henry Morgan's evolutionary schemes but suggests that the work's "circular emplotment" and "tragic realism" (p. 214) function to diminish agency and distance the reader from Lakota suffering by making it seem inevitable.

[6] Mooney, *Ghost-Dance Religion*, 772.

[7] The remark by Thomas W. Overholt, "The Ghost Dance of 1890 and the Nature of the Prophetic Process," *Ethnohistory* 21 (Winter 1974): 41, that Wounded Knee "would have been [a] strong motivator toward a doctrinal shift" acutely identifies the issue, although the notion of a "doctrinal shift," may misleadingly imply that Wovoka completely repudiated an earlier "doctrine" rather than that his comments to Mooney indicated a more subtle shift of emphasis.

[8] Mooney, *Ghost-Dance Religion*, 780.

feel good. I give you a good spirit and give you all good paint. I want you to come again in three months, some from each tribe there.

There will be a good deal of snow this year and some rain. In the fall there will be such a rain as I have never given you before.

Grandfather says, when your friends die you must not cry. You must not hurt anybody or do harm to anyone. You must not fight. Do right always. It will give you satisfaction in life. This young man has a good father and mother.

Do not tell the white people about this. Jesus is now upon the earth. He appears like a cloud. The dead are all alive again. I do not know when they will be here; maybe this fall or in the spring. When the time comes there will be no more sickness and everyone will be young again.

Do not refuse to work for the whites and do not make any trouble with them until you leave them. When the earth shakes do not be afraid. It will not hurt you.

I want you to dance every six weeks. Make a feast at the dance and have food that everybody may eat. Then bathe in the water. That is all. You will receive good words again from me some time. Do not tell lies.[9]

In commenting on this text, Mooney stressed its injunctions to peace. To underscore this theme, he selected pacific phrases from the text – "You must not fight. Do no harm to anyone. Do right always" – for the epigraph for his main chapter on Wovoka's teachings, titled "The Doctrine of the Ghost Dance." Nonetheless, Mooney did acknowledge the document's clear references to an apocalypse ("[w]hen the earth shakes do not be afraid"; "do not make any trouble with [the whites] until you leave them"), if only euphemistically, by observing that "[t]he great change will be ushered in by a trembling of the earth."[10]

Some scholars have gone beyond Mooney to reject altogether the idea that Wovoka prophesied the destruction or removal of European Americans.[11] Yet a substantial body of evidence shows that he did in fact forecast such an apocalyptic event. In late 1890, with the Ghost Dance threatening to unsettle government authority on reservations throughout the West,

---

[9] Ibid., 781 (bracketed comments omitted).

[10] Ibid., 777, 782.

[11] For statements of this view by its leading proponent, see Michael Hittman, "The 1890 Ghost Dance in Nevada," *American Indian Culture and Research Journal* 16, no. 4 (1992): 123–66; Hittman, *Wovoka and the Ghost Dance*. Hittman considers Wovoka as the leader of a "redemptive" movement for individual moral reformation rather than a "transformative" movement seeking a fundamental reversal of the world's order, categories that rely on David F. Aberle, *The Peyote Religion among the Navaho*, 2d ed. (Chicago, 1982), 316–17. Other interpretations of a nontransformative Wovoka include Joseph G. Jorgensen, "Religious Solutions and Native American Struggles: Ghost Dance, Sun Dance and Beyond," in *Religion, Rebellion, Revolution: An Interdisciplinary and Cross-Cultural Collections of Essays*, ed. Bruce Lincoln (London, 1985), 108; Åke Hultkrantz, "Ghost Dance," in *The Encyclopedia of Religion*, ed. Mircea Eliade (New York, 1987), 545. Omer C. Stewart, "The Ghost Dance," in *Anthropology on the Great Plains*, ed. W. Raymond Wood and Margot Liberty (Lincoln, 1980), 180, writes euphemistically of a "world renewal" during which "whites would be quietly removed."

and with newspapers offering conflicting and sometimes sensationalist reports of the movement, U.S. officials sought reliable intelligence. One man who offered information was John Mayhugh. He had lived near the Paiutes for thirty years and had recently conducted a special census of Nevada Indians. On November 24, 1890, Mayhugh reported that "Captain Jack Wilson known... by the Indian names of We-vo-kai and Co-we-jo" had told his followers not to "disturb the White Folks saying that the blanket – or Rabbit skin that was put over the moon by the Indians long ago will soon fall off and then the moon which is now on fire will destroy the whites."[12]

An army investigation into the possible closure of Fort Bidwell (in far northwestern California) provided additional evidence. On or shortly after November 22, the post's commander, Lieutenant Nathaniel P. Phister, interviewed a Paiute known as Indian George who stated that "Kvit-tsow... says that all the dead Indians and all the buffalo and other game will come back, and all the white people will die or be removed." Although Indian George had not heard anything about how this would happen, other Indians later told Phister that "[t]he Great Spirit will then send a mighty flood of mud and water to drown all the white people, and to utterly obliterate from the country all traces of their works and occupancy."[13]

The head of the Fort Bidwell investigation, Captain Jesse M. Lee, gained additional evidence in early December. Although Indian George had been

---

[12] John S. Mayhugh to CIA, 24 Nov. 1890, SC 188, roll 1. For Mayhugh's credentials, see John S. Mayhugh to President Benjamin Harrison, 9 Jan. 1891, SC 188, roll 1.

[13] Lieut. Nat P. Phister to Capt. J. M. Lee, 7 Dec. 1890, enclosed in Capt. J. M. Lee to AG, 10 Dec. 1890, RG 94, Records of the Adjutant General's Office, Records of Divisions, Military Reservation Division, early 1800s–1916, Reservation File, Ft. Bidwell, Calif., box 12, National Archives and Records Administration, Washington, D.C.; Nat. P. Phister, "The Indian Messiah," *American Anthropologist*, old ser., 4 (April 1891): 106. Hittman, "1890 Ghost Dance in Nevada," 151, quotes Phister, "Indian Messiah," 107, that "[t]he doctrine as preached by Kvit-tsów [Wovoka] is not at all in the nature of a crusade against the white people" to support his position that Wovoka did not prophesy the cataclysmic destruction or removal of European Americans, yet Phister was simply pointing out that Wovoka did not advocate armed resistance to achieve the removal of non-Indians.

A crucial part of Hittman's argument for a pacific Wovoka is that by the 1880s Paiutes no longer suffered from deprivation. Having become wage workers, "Numus [Northern Paiutes] received more food, clothing, and material than ever before seen and possibly even dreamed." Hittman, *Wovoka and the Ghost Dance*, 101; for a similar argument, see also Brad Logan, "The Ghost Dance among the Paiute: An Ethnohistorical View of the Documentary Evidence, 1889–1893," *Ethnohistory* 27 (Summer 1980): 267–88. Yet even if Paiutes were materially better off, it is doubtful that they were reconciled to the loss of their earlier ways of life and their new, subordinate position. As John Walton, *Western Times and Water Wars: State, Culture, and Rebellion in California* (Berkeley, 1992), 36–37, 105–11, makes clear, many Paiutes experienced wage labor as a sign of a broader loss of political and economic autonomy. Focusing on the Paiutes of California's Owens Valley, Walton documents several cases in which they burned the haystacks, ranch buildings, and mining equipment of current or former employers. These acts of "indigenous Luddism" protested the recent dispossession of Paiutes' land and resources and their status as wage workers.

unable to tell Phister the details of the cataclysm, he informed Lee that the "whites will be all snowed under." Indian George's new knowledge may have come from another Paiute, Jo Evans, who told Lee that one year before he had personally heard the "medicine man" known as "Kvist-tsów" and "Wo-po-kah-ti" say that "he destroy all the soldiers" and "will destroy all the white people. Destroy them with big snow or something like that." Another Paiute, Captain Dick, offered a different version of the apocalypse. Two years earlier, Captain Dick went to see "Indian Sam, a head man," who told him that he had just returned from hearing the "Indian medicine man." According to Indian Sam, Wovoka said that when "Old Man comes this way, then all the Indians go to mountains, high up away from whites. Whites can't hurt Indians then. Then while Indians way up high, big flood comes like water – and all white people die – get drowned. After that water go away and then nobody but Indians everywhere and game all kinds thick."[14]

Another pre–Wounded Knee report, one from army scout Arthur Chapman, at first glance appears to support the thesis of an entirely pacific Wovoka. Ordered to investigate "the supposed Messiah," Chapman interviewed Wovoka on December 1, 1890. Wovoka told Chapman that "God" had instructed him "that he must tell the Indians that they must work all the time and not lie down in idleness; that they must not fight the white people or one another; that we were all brothers and must remain in peace." Yet Chapman also reported that Wovoka told him that "God" had given him "the power to destroy this world and all the people in it and to have it made over again; and the people who have been good heretofore were to be made over again and all remain young." Although Wovoka did not directly name the people who would be destroyed, it is clear that it would be those who were not "good" (i.e., most, if not all, European Americans as well as non-believing Indians). In speaking to an army scout in early December 1890, Wovoka's description of the apocalypse was understandably oblique, but it is evident that he was thinking in these terms.[15]

It is clear, then, that although Wovoka counseled his followers not to take up arms against European Americans, he hoped to remove their presence and looked to a cataclysmic event to accomplish this. Wovoka taught peace, not because he sought permanent harmony between Indians and non-Indians but because he recognized the futility of armed resistance to U.S. power and feared that assertions of militancy would provoke a brutal crackdown. It was as though two forms of power were contending for supremacy. The spiritual powers that had once given Indian people freedom and abundance might ultimately prevail. But Indians must avoid the temptation of turning to non-Indian forms of power to bring about the new world. Indeed, until

---

[14] "Synopsis of Statements of Indians at Fort Bidwell, Cal.," enclosed in Lee to AG, 10 Dec. 1890 (Indian Dick statement also in Mooney, *Ghost-Dance Religion*, 784).
[15] A. I. Chapman to Gen. John Gibbon, 6 Dec. 1890, in *ARSW*, 1891, 191–94 (qtns., 193).

the new world arrived, it would be dangerous to antagonize the powers that lay behind European American domination.

Rather than seeing Wovoka as another Gautama or Jesus, at least as Mooney understood these figures, he might be better placed in the company of a group that Michael Adas calls "prophets of rebellion." By this term, Adas refers to leaders of several movements in the nineteenth and early twentieth century ranging from the Pai Mairire movement in New Zealand in the 1860s to the Maji Maji Rebellion in Tanzania in 1905–1906. Adas categorizes these movements as "prophet-inspired rebellions among non-Western peoples against European-dominated colonial regimes." Although some prophets of rebellion advocated armed resistance, others, like Wovoka, looked to spiritual power to overthrow colonial rule.[16]

Wovoka was hardly the first North American prophet of rebellion. American Indian prophets like the Delaware Neolin in the 1760s, the Shawnee Tenskwatawa (the Prophet) and his brother Tecumseh in the first years of the 1800s, the Wanapam Smohalla in the 1860s, and Wovoka's immediate predecessor, Wodziwob, in the 1870s criticized the new world that European Americans had imposed on Indian people and hoped for its overthrow. These prophets and the movements they inspired differed in significant ways, holding a variety of perspectives on issues ranging from moral reformation to the utility of western weapons. A common theme in all of them, however, was the use of spiritual power to achieve the destruction or removal of European Americans. It should not diminish Wovoka's stature, then, to place him in this tradition.[17]

[16] Michael Adas, *Prophets of Rebellion: Millenarian Protest Movements against the European Colonial Order* (1979; Cambridge, 1987), xix (italics omitted). Other works that relate the Ghost Dance to similar movements throughout the world include Vittorio Lanternari, *The Religions of the Oppressed: A Study of Modern Messianic Cults*, trans. Lisa Sergio (New York, 1963); Bryan R. Wilson, *Magic and the Millennium: A Sociological Study of Religious Movements of Protest among Tribal and Third-World Peoples* (New York, 1973); John S. Galbraith, "Appeals to the Supernatural: African and New Zealand Comparisons with the Ghost Dance," *Pacific Historical Review* 51 (May 1982): 115–33; Dominic J. Capeci Jr. and Jack C. Knight, "Reactions to Colonialism: The North American Ghost Dance and East African Maji-Maji Rebellions," *Historian* 52 (August 1990): 584–601; James O. Gump, "A Spirit of Resistance: Sioux, Xhosa, and Maori Responses to Western Dominance, 1840–1920," *Pacific Historical Review* 66 (February 1997): 21–52.

[17] The literature covering these leaders and the movements they were associated with is too extensive to cite in full, but see Alfred A. Cave, "The Delaware Prophet Neolin: A Reappraisal," *Ethnohistory* 46 (Spring 1999): 265–90; Gregory Evans Dowd, *A Spirited Resistance: The North American Indian Struggle for Unity, 1745–1815* (Baltimore, 1992); Joel Martin, *Sacred Revolt: The Muskogees' Struggle for a New World* (Boston, 1991); R. David Edmunds, *The Shawnee Prophet* (Lincoln, 1983); John Sugden, *Tecumseh: A Life* (New York, 1998); Robert H. Ruby and John A. Brown, *Dreamer-Prophets of the Columbia Plateau: Smohalla and Skolaskin* (Norman, 1989); Christopher L. Miller, *Prophetic Worlds: Indians and Whites on the Columbia Plateau* (New Brunswick, 1985); Gregory E. Smoak, *Ghost Dances and*

Lakotas first encountered Wovoka in late 1889. According to an account by Short Bull in 1915, transcribed in Lakota, the Sioux delegation that was appointed in fall 1889 traveled first to the Wind River Agency in Wyoming, then to *Wabanake Tipi* (the home of the Bannocks; i.e., Ft. Hall, Idaho). There they stayed a few days and participated in a *wakan wacipi* (sacred or powerful dance), which the Bannocks had earlier learned from Wovoka.[18] The delegates joined in the dance, painting themselves with vermillion and then standing in a circle, with men and women mixed together. After a while, some of the dancers became frenzied and fell down unconscious. Upon awakening, they related the visions they had seen. The next day, the delegates traveled to *Mastincala Ha Sina In Tipi* (the home of the Wearers of Rabbit Blankets; the Paiutes). After resting a few days, a Paiute led them up a high mountain, where they met Wovoka.[19]

Short Bull (see Illustration 10) described Wovoka as a powerful being (*wasicun*),[20] who spoke in unexpectedly beautiful Lakota. He further remarked that a Cheyenne and a Shoshone who were part of the group heard

Identity: American Indian Ethnicity, Race, and Prophetic Religion in the Nineteenth Century (Berkeley, forthcoming). There is little direct evidence of Wodziwob's teachings about the demise of non-Indians, though in a survey of the 1870 Ghost Dance among several tribes, Cora Du Bois, *The 1870 Ghost Dance*, University of California Anthropological Records, vol. 3, no. 1 (Berkeley, 1939), 130, points out that there was a general belief that "whites were to be exterminated at the time of the advent and there was no need to hasten matters by armed efforts."

[18] *LT&T*, 277–78. Based on the evidence in note 2, I am inclined to think the June date in this account is erroneous. Hittman, *Wovoka and the Ghost Dance*, 63, notes that the Paiutes referred to the dance as "dance in a circle." Judith Vander, *Shoshone Ghost Dance Religion: Poetry Songs and Great Basin Context* (Urbana, 1997), 17, points out that the Shoshone term for the "Ghost Dance," *Naraya*, referred to the "particular shuffling step" of the dance. According to Mooney, *Ghost-Dance Religion*, 791, only among the Sioux, Arapahoe, and some other "prairie tribes" was the dance called "ghost" or "spirit."

[19] *LT&T*, 278–80. Evidently following Eugene Buechel, comp., *A Dictionary – Oie Wowapi Wan of Teton Sioux*, ed. Paul Manhart (Pine Ridge, S.Dak., 1983), 333; Paul I. Manhart, trans., *Lakota Tales and Texts*, 2 vols. (Chamberlain, S.Dak., 1998), 2:476, 511, identifies *Mastincala Ha Sina In kin* as the Crees and therefore Wovoka as a Cree. Obviously, however, the text refers to Paiutes, not Crees. I have been unable to verify that the Sioux called Paiutes by this name, but the Cheyenne name for the Paiutes was "rabbit blanket people." See James Mooney, *The Cheyenne Indians*, Memoirs of the American Anthropological Association, vol. 1 (Lancaster, Pa., 1905–1907), 424. I am indebted to Father Manhart for providing me with an advance copy of his translation, which aided me in correcting errors and resolving ambiguities in my own.

[20] *LT&T*, 280. The context here seems to rule out a translation of *wasicun* as "white man." Rather, the meaning is "any person or thing that is *wakan*." See Buechel, comp., *Dictionary*, 551; and the discussion in Bruce M. White, "Encounters with Spirits: Ojibwa and Dakota Theories about the French and Their Merchandise," *Ethnohistory* 41 (Summer 1994): 384–85. Confirming this translation is the fact that another account of Short Bull's experience in Natalie Curtis, ed., *The Indians' Book* (New York, 1907), 45, uses the term *spirit-man* in a similar context.

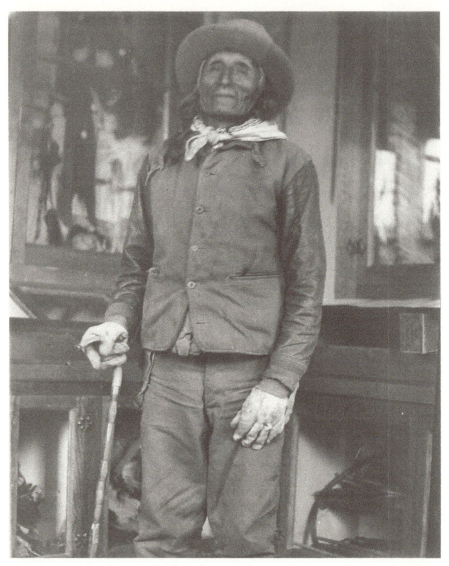

ILLUSTRATION 10. Short Bull. This photograph was taken several years after Short Bull's involvement in the Ghost Dance. Buechel Memorial Museum, St. Francis, S.Dak.

this being speak their own languages.[21] Short Bull related that the *wasicun* promised the Indians that in the future they would be reunited with their relatives who had died long ago. After instructing them not to kill one another, to love one another, and to have pity on each other, he then showed them a

[21] *LT&T*, 280–81, 283. The text at p. 280 is confusing, because there is either a missing or extra quotation mark. In my reading, the quotation mark before "*Iwatohanl*" (l. 77) is an

vision of their relatives living in a "smoky camp" (*osotaya wicoti*), a sign of the good life in earlier times. After this vision, Short Bull and his companions descended the mountain. They stayed with the Paiutes a few days before returning to Pine Ridge by way of Ft. Hall.[22] According to another account, this one a translation of a Lakota text written by George Sword, the "Son of God" showed Lakotas "a land created across the ocean on which all the nations of Indians were coming home." Later, "the Messiah" told them that if they grew weary on their return home, they could call on him for help. When they did, they awoke the next morning "at a great distance from where we stopped."[23]

The use of the English terms *Son of God* and *Messiah* in Sword's account, as in many others, conveys the impression that Lakotas understood Wovoka to be the biblical Christ. Here especially, however, it is important to be attentive to the meanings of Lakota words. Sword's account consistently uses the term *Wakan Tanka Cinca*, which the translator sometimes rendered as Son of God and other times as Messiah. Besides *wasicun*, Short Bull's account uses two names for Wovoka: *Wakan Tanka Cinca* and *ate* (father), a standard term of respect.[24] *Wakan Tanka* can be translated as God, hence Son of God for *Wakan Tanka Cinca*.

As discussed in Chapter 1, neither God nor the commonly used Great Spirit are very good translations for *Wakan Tanka*. Great Mystery is better, though the important point is that *Wakan Tanka* is not a person; instead the term refers to the collective spiritual powers of the universe, which can be manifested in myriad ways. For Short Bull to encounter the Son of *Wakan Tanka*, then, was something far different from a European American Christian's encounter with the Second Person of a triune God. Instead, Short Bull had experienced a specific manifestation of *Wakan Tanka* (i.e., of the sacred, mysterious, spiritual powers of the universe).[25] There was nothing particularly unprecedented about this.

---

error and the words following should be attributed to *Mastincala Ha Sina In kin* (Wovoka). Rather than translating *yusinyaye* (l. 79) as "afraid" (compare Manhart, trans., *Lakota Tales and Texts*, 2:, 477, 512), a better translation is "to hear, unexpectedly, something beautiful" (Buechel, comp., *Dictionary*, 653).

[22] *LT&T*, 281–84 (qtn., 282).

[23] Mooney, *Ghost-Dance Religion*, 797. According to Mooney, this account was originally written in Lakota by George Sword and was translated by an unnamed Indian for Emma S. Sickels. The translation can also be found in George Sword, "The Story of the Ghost Dance," *The Folk-Lorist* 1 (July 1892): 28–31; L. W. Colby, "Wanagi Olowan Kin," *Proceedings and Collections of the Nebraska State Historical Society* 1 (January 1895): 137–40. The Lakota version is George Sword, "Wanagi Wacipi Toranpi Owicakiyakapi Kin Lee," manuscript 936, Smithsonian Institution, National Anthropological Archives, Washington, D.C. Sword was not a participant in the Ghost Dance; his account was presumably based on knowledge he gathered from others.

[24] "Wanagi Wacipi Toranpi Owicakiyakapi Kin Lee"; *LT&T*, 283, 285.

[25] Black Elk used another term, *Wanikiye*, to refer to "the Messiah." See Raymond J. DeMallie, ed., *The Sixth Grandfather: Black Elk's Teachings Given to John G. Neihardt* (Lincoln, 1984), 266. This term, literally, "one who makes live," was the one that missionaries, seeking

Although Lakotas understood Wovoka in their own distinctively non-Christian context, they did attribute to him defining features of Christianity's Messiah. Good Thunder told Elaine Goodale that when he saw "the Christ," he "saw the prints of the nails on his hands and feet." Kicking Bear also reportedly observed that the "Son of the Great Spirit showed them the wounds in his hands and feet where he had been crucified by the whites when he came first upon this earth."[26] Short Bull did not explicitly mention scars, but he reported that the father said, "Look upon me, sons, long ago the white men killed me."[27]

It is possible that Lakotas' expectations of Wovoka were so strong that they attributed to him things he did not actually say or do. Perhaps, as Wovoka insisted to Mooney in early 1892, he never claimed to be "Christ, the Son of God" but was a "prophet who has received a divine revelation."[28] Yet the idea that Wovoka claimed to be the man whom the whites had killed was held not just by the Plains Sioux but by his followers from other tribes.[29] Given the universality of this view, it is certainly possible that in 1892 Wovoka understated his earlier claims. If so, Wounded Knee gave him ample reason to do so. To protect himself and his people, Wovoka undoubtedly wanted to distance himself from aspects of his teachings that Americans found objectionable.[30]

---

analogues in Sioux culture, used for "Savior." See also David Humphreys Miller, *Ghost Dance* (1959; Lincoln, 1985), 34.

[26] Kay Graber, ed., *Sister to the Sioux: The Memoirs of Elaine Goodale Eastman, 1885–91* (Lincoln, 1978), 143; "The 'Indian Messiah' doctrine," undated statement, MP, roll 20. An embellished account of this statement, along with the information that its source was One Bull, is in James McLaughlin, *My Friend the Indian* (1910; Lincoln, 1989), 185–89. Other Lakota accounts that report Wovoka's body bore the evidence of crucifixion are Selwyn to Foster, 25 Nov. 1890; Sword, "Story of the Ghost Dance," 29.

[27] "*Wanmayanka po, cinksi, miye kayes wasicun kin ehanni maktepelo.*" *LT&T*, 281.

[28] Mooney, *Ghost-Dance Religion*, 773. Moses, "'The Father Tells Me So,'" 340–41, relying mainly on Mayhugh to CIA, 24 Nov. 1890, makes a good case that Wovoka claimed only to be a prophet of God and not His Son.

[29] See the accounts of Porcupine (Northern Cheyenne) in Brig. Gen. Thomas H. Ruger to AG, 25 June 1890, SC 188, roll 1 (also in Mooney, *Ghost-Dance Religion*, 793–96); and Sitting Bull (Arapahoe) in George B. Grinnell, "Account of the Northern Cheyennes Concerning the Messiah Superstition," *Journal of American Folk-Lore* 4 (January–March 1891): 64. As additional evidence of the universality of this view of Wovoka, it is noteworthy that when Apiatan (Kiowa) encountered Wovoka in late 1890 or early 1891 he fully expected him to bear the marks of crucifixion (and his faith reportedly shattered when he learned he did not). See Mooney, *Ghost-Dance Religion*, 913; H. L. Scott, "Essay for the Fort Sill Lyceum, March 1892: Subject: The 'Messiah Dance' in the Indian Territory," Hugh L. Scott Papers, box 75, Library of Congress, Washington, D.C.

[30] Edward A. Dyer, a non-Indian who knew Wovoka well and helped persuade him to talk to Mooney, observed that Wovoka was "more than a little apprehensive" after learning of Wounded Knee and removed his camp to an isolated area. See E. A. Dyer Sr., "Wizardry," unpublished manuscript, p. 14, Nevada Historical Society, Reno (also in Hittmann, *Wovoka and the Ghost Dance*, 247–55 [qtn., 253]).

Whether Wovoka identified himself with the Christian Messiah, he and his followers were clearly influenced to some extent by Christianity.[31] It would be a mistake, however, to conclude that concepts like the renewal of the world or the need for moral reformation depended on Christianity[32]; these ideas were available through indigenous traditions that predated Europeans. Nor does it seem accurate to see Wovoka's teachings as an instance of syncretism. Talk of a messiah and the renewal of the world did not so much add something from Christianity to create a new blend as it used Christianity's central story to reject the entire world of which Christianity was a part. Indians could not overturn the world that westerners had imposed on them by ignoring their religion altogether. Somehow they had to take account of the religion of the people who had come to dominate them.

Rather than ignoring Christianity, ghost dancers contended with it in order to turn its powers to their advantage. The story of the messiah afforded Indians an effective opening to exploit one of Christian civilization's central contradictions. For if whites were the bearers of a superior way of life, how could they have rejected and killed God's Son? By pointing out that Europeans had killed the Messiah and then having him claim Indians as his chosen people, Wovoka and his followers hoped to reverse the flow of power. The moral powers of the universe would no longer support the strong. They would take pity on those who suffered. As Good Thunder said, when the Messiah "appeared to the white people, [they] scorned him and finally killed him. Now he came to red men only. He said their crying sounded loud in his ears. They were dying of starvation and disease."[33]

The Lakota delegates who visited Wovoka recognized that he held out the possibility of ending the European American presence through a cataclysmic event that would either destroy or remove non-Indians and usher in a new world in which game would be restored and deceased ancestors returned to life. Lakotas offered varying details about exactly how the apocalypse would occur. Some, like Kicking Bear, said that because the earth "was getting old,"

---

[31] Moses, "'The Father Tells Me So,'" 337, points out that Wovoka was aware of Christianity from his time living with David Wilson, a devout Presbyterian. Mooney, *Ghost Dance-Religion*, 763, suggests that Wovoka was influenced by Shakers, a view rebutted in Hittman, *Wovoka and the Ghost Dance*, 79–80. Bailey, *Wovoka*, 121–22; Lawrence G. Coates, "The Mormons and the Ghost Dance," *Dialogue: A Journal of Mormon Thought* 18 (Winter 1985): 110; Gregory E. Smoak, "The Mormons and the Ghost Dance of 1890," *South Dakota History* 16 (Fall 1986): 293–94; Smoak, *Ghost Dances and Identity*; Garold D. Barney, *Mormons, Indians and the Ghost Dance Religion of 1890* (Lanham, Md., 1986), 155, argue for or suggest Mormon influence.

[32] Utley, *Last Days*, 70; William K. Powers, *Oglala Religion* (Lincoln, 1975), 202.

[33] Graber, ed., *Sister to the Sioux*, 143. Short Bull recalled that Wovoka spoke similar words: "*lehanl mis mayuonihanpelo tka ikceye wicasa kin iyotikyeyakiyapi heon oicimani kin le cic'upi ca heon nitakuyepi tona t'api kin hena om tokata wanyecilakpi kte.*" ([N]ow they [the whites] honor me, but because you common people are suffering, I will give you a journey in which you will see many of your relatives who have died.) *LT&T*, 281.

the Messiah would "rebuild" it by sending a "wave" of "new soil" that would "cover over the Earth under which all the whites would be crushed." Others, like Kuwapi (They Chased After Him), explained that the "father is going to cause a big cyclone or whirlwind, by which he will have all the white people to perish." Years later, Short Bull recalled that Wovoka taught that the present world would be "consumed in flame." Rather than revealing competing doctrines, these accounts more likely indicate that the ghost dancers had a provisional sense of the cataclysm's details. The world might end through fire, but others ways would equally suffice.[34]

The Lakota delegates to Wovoka returned home in late 1889. After discussing Wovoka's teachings with others at the Pine Ridge, Rosebud, and probably Cheyenne River reservations, another delegation went to see the prophet early the next year. In the spring, when this group returned, they began to organize dances.[35]

Wanagi Wacipi ("Ghost" or "Spirit" Dances)[36] could be held during the day or night. They could include as many as four hundred dancers and a thousand or more observers. Participants prepared themselves to dance by fasting or eating only certain foods, purifying themselves in sweat lodges, painting themselves, and tying eagle feathers in their hair. A trader observed that the dancers formed a line and the leader "standing facing them, made a prayer and waved over their heads the 'ghost stick,' a staff of about 6 feet long, trimmed with red cloth and feathers of the same color." The leader then faced the sun and made a prayer, while a woman standing near a tree at the center held a pipe toward the sun. The dancers, men and women together, formed a circle around a center tree. At another dance, a Pine Ridge day school teacher observed that the center tree was "covered with strips of cloth of various colors, eagle feathers, stuffed birds, claws, and horns – all offerings to the Great Spirit."[37]

---

34 Kicking Bear, quoted in "'Indian Messiah' doctrine"; Kuwapi quoted in William T. Selwyn to Col. E. W. Foster, 22 Nov. 1890, SC 188, roll 1 (also in Mooney, *Ghost-Dance Religion*, 799); Short Bull quoted in Curtis, ed., *Indian's Book*, 46–47. Others sources that describe a belief in a new earth covering the old include Sword, "Story of the Ghost Dance," 29; Charles A. Eastman (Ohiyesa), *From the Deep Woods to Civilization: Chapters in the Autobiography of an Indian* (1916; Lincoln, 1977), 83; Standing Bear, *My People the Sioux*, 218; Mary C. Collins, "Sitting Bull and the Indian Messiah," *The Word Carrier* 19 (November 1890): 2 (also in Louis P. Olson, "Mary Clementine Collins: Dacotah Missionary," *North Dakota History* 19 [January 1952]: 75).
35 DeMallie, ed., *Sixth Grandfather*, 256–58.
36 The dances were also referred to by the generic *"wacipi wakan"* ("sacred" or "powerful" dance). See *LT&T*, 289.
37 Mooney, *Ghost-Dance Religion*, 915 (1st qtn.); ARCIA, 1891, 530 (2d qtn.), with the day school teacher identified as Mrs. Z. A. Parker in Mooney, *Ghost-Dance Religion*, 916; Collins, "Sitting Bull and the Indian Messiah," 2; Sword, "Story of the Ghost Dance," 31. An account of a dance by Henry Young Skunk in *LT&T*, 289, notes that dancers were

Once the participants were in a circle, all faced to the west, "the country of the messiah," and sang an opening song. As with many Lakota songs, the words to this one were simple yet highly evocative.

Ate heye eyayo	The father says so!
Ate heye eyayo	The father says so!
Ate heye lo	The father says so
Ate heye lo	The father says so
Nitunkansila wanyegalake kta eyayayo	Your grandfather you shall see!
Nitunkansila wanyegalake kta eyayayo	Your grandfather you shall see!
Ate heye lo	The father says so
Ate heye lo	The father says so
Nitakuye wanyegalake kta eyayo	Your relatives you shall see!
Nitakuye wanyegalake kta eyayo	Your relatives you shall see!
Ate heye lo	The father says so
Ate heye lo	The father says so[38]

After this, the dancers clasped each others' hands, closed their eyes, and began to move around the center, all the while singing songs inspired by the promise of a new world. One song envisioned a reunion with a lost child ("It is my own child"); another spoke of a brother "always crying," saying "Mother, come home; mother, come home." Many songs imagined the return of the buffalo. One saw "a buffalo bull walking," while another remembered the hunt: "Now they are about to chase the buffalo/Grandmother, give me back my bow." Several songs spoke of eating *wasna* (pemmican) and one recalled traditional female tasks of setting up a tipi, driving in its pegs, and commencing to cook. Many songs recalled "the father's" promises: "You shall grow to be a nation/Says the father"; "The buffalo are coming, the buffalo are coming.../The father says so, The father says so."[39]

---

instructed not to eat meat of any kind, but to eat only chokecherries ("*taku talo ke eyas yatapi kte sni yelo, na canpa esa luhapi he ci heca ee yatapi skelo*"). In describing the Ghost Dance I have tried to identify typical patterns while recognizing that there was considerable variation.

[38] Mooney, *Ghost-Dance Religion*, 1061, identifies this as "the opening song." William K. Powers, *Voices from the Spirit World: Lakota Ghost Dance Songs* (Kendall Park, N.J., 1990), 28, treats it as no different from other songs. I have slightly modified their translations.

[39] Quotations in this paragraph are from the songs in Mooney, *Ghost-Dance Religion*, 1061–75, in sequence by number, 11, 15, 4, 16, 6, 19. References to pemmican are found in songs numbered 7, 13, 24; the song about female domesticity is number 23. Although Mooney does not state how he obtained these Ghost Dance songs, the most likely source is George Sword, who provided most of the songs published in Colby, "Wanagi Olowan Kin."

After a while – an hour or two, sometimes less – some of the dancers "became affected" (*ececa*) and "fainted" or "died" (*t'a*).[40] While unconscious, they saw visions, and upon awakening, they related what they had seen. Many told of having seen relatives who had died. For example, when Henry Young Skunk fell unconscious at a dance on White Clay Creek, the first thing he saw was someone going on a road. As he followed up a hill, this person told Young Skunk to continue on. He went up another hill, where he saw another person, this one on horseback, coming toward him. The rider stopped but Young Skunk couldn't tell who it was because there was smoke all around. As the person approached, however, he could see it was a woman. As she came nearer, he recognized that it was his older sister, who had died long ago. Addressing him by the kinship term *misun* (younger brother), she said, "you came and so, in reply, I must come," and she embraced him (*poski mayuza*, literally, "took hold of me by the neck"). Then she cried, and he too wept.[41]

Those who "went to the land of the spirits" (*wanagiyata ipi*)[42] related that the people there were living well in a good land. In his second vision, Young Skunk traveled to "a country with many green leaves, a country that was green all over."[43] His sister came again and took him to a camp with a very spacious center filled with many people and then to a large tipi where there were several women. They sat Young Skunk in the "place of honor" (*catku*) and gave him some *wakapapi* (another word for pemmican). The contrast to the present world was all the more apparent when Young Skunk regained consciousness and saw that he was no longer in "a good country" (*makoce wan waste*), but in one "*sanyela*" (literally, grayish, i.e., bleak) where everything was "miserable" (*oiyokisica*) and all the people "smelled badly" (*sicamnapi*) and were "very dirty" (*lila sapsapapi*). Another dancer

---

[40] "*Na hihanna el ake wauncipi. Yunkan ake emaceca. Na wancak mat'a na ake paha wan el iyawahan.*" "And the next morning again we danced. Therefore, again, I was affected. And at once I fainted and again I went up a hill and stood." *LT&T*, 285.

[41] Ibid., 292. Young Skunk's account (ibid., 299) notes that many of the dancers "saw well their immediate relatives and told about it well" ("*titakuyepi kin tanyan wanwicaglakapi na tanyan woglakapi*"). Sword, "Story of the Ghost Dance," 30, reports that Good Thunder saw a son "who died in war long ago." Goodale in Graber, ed., *Sister to the Sioux*, 149, observed that upon regaining consciousness, an old woman stated that she had "'seen those dear ones we lost long ago.'" Little Wound, quoted in "Ghost-Dances in the West," *The Illustrated American* 5 (17 January 1891): 330, saw "the playmates of my childhood." This was one of a series of articles published in *The Illustrated American*, written by Warren K. Moorehead, which formed the basis for Warren K. Moorehead, "The Indian Messiah and the Ghost Dance," *The American Antiquarian and Oriental Journal* 13 (May 1891): 161–67; Warren K. Moorehead, "The Sioux Messiah," *The Archaeologist* 2 (May, June 1894): 146–49, 168–70. James P. Boyd, *Recent Indians Wars* (Philadelphia, 1891), drew heavily on Moorehead's initial articles.

[42] *LT&T*, 277.

[43] "*makoce wan lila canwape to na makoce kin toyela yunka*" (ibid., 293).

saw the people in the other world "living in a most beautiful country covered with buffalo!" Here, though, "everything looks hateful to me – how can I bear it!"[44]

Dancers brought back specific instructions from *Wakan Tanka Cinca* and others in the spirit world. At a dance at Pine Ridge, *Wakan Tanka Cinca* told Short Bull that he had "not reported well my words" and instructed him to tell the people to paint themselves properly and not to forget his teachings.[45] Henry Young Skunk received instructions from his sister. During his first vision, she told him that he could not visit the large camp, the one he later reached in his second vision, because he "smelled very badly" (*lila nisicamna*). She then told him that when he returned home, he should stop using metal of any kind.[46] Injunctions against metal, an especially obvious symbol of European American material culture, were common. Dancers also instructed one another to shun non-native clothing and foods. As Elaine Goodale pointed out, however, "[w]hile there was a noticeable trend in this direction, it was impossible to conform strictly. Knives, kettles, cotton cloth, blankets, and flour . . . had long since become indispensable."[47]

Visionaries also returned from the spirit world with gifts. In his third vision Young Skunk went to a tipi and saw a grandmother and five young women. Addressing him by the kinship term *takoja* (grandson), the grandmother told Young Skunk, "I will give you something to put on the faces of your people who want to see their relatives. Command them to put this on before they dance." After feeding him some *wasna*, she gave him some vermillion (*wase*). When Young Skunk regained consciousness, he held the vermillion in his hand. After telling what he had seen, he painted twelve dancers and when the dance resumed, "all were affected and lost consciousness for a long time and saw well their relatives."[48]

Ordinary people who joined the Ghost Dance surely knew about and accepted the idea that European Americans would be removed or destroyed, but the dance acknowledged this mostly by negation, as in the rejection of western material culture. Ghost dancers did not necessarily dwell on the

[44] Ibid., 293–95; Graber, ed., *Sister to the Sioux*, 149. Little Wound saw the people "riding the finest horses I ever saw, dressed in superb and most brilliant garments, and seeming very happy." Upon his return, the "Great Spirit" told him that "the earth was now *bad* and *worn out*." "Ghost-Dances in the West," 330.

[45] "*mioie k'on hena tanyan olakapi sni.*" *LT&T*, 286.

[46] "*maza wanjini ikoyakic'iye sni ye*," literally, "do not fasten yourself to any metal." Ibid., 292.

[47] Sword, "Story of the Ghost Dance," 31; Graber, ed., *Sister to the Sioux*, 149 (qtn.).

[48] "*Takoja, taku wan cic'u kte tka he tona titakuye wanglakapi cinpi kin hena itoksan wicayecic'un kte ca tonhal wacipi ca ecela itokam lena ate enanala wicaku ye, na hecon wicasi ye . . . owasin ececapi na lila tehanhan t'api na titakuyepi kin tanyan wanwicaglakapi.*" *LT&T*, 299. Sword, "Story of the Ghost Dance," 31, notes that many dancers brought back pieces of meat. See also Selwyn to Foster, 22 Nov. 1890.

actual process by which European Americans would disappear. What made the dance so immediately compelling was the visionary experience itself and the promises it carried. As dancers prepared themselves by praying in the sweat lodge and putting on paint, the present world began to seem remote. As they danced singing, it receded further, and in visionary experience vanished altogether.

Beginning with James Mooney, who contended that the Sioux gave Wovoka's teachings a "hostile meaning," a long line of scholars who have written on the Ghost Dance have argued that the Sioux ghost dancers fundamentally altered Wovoka's original teachings. The thesis of Sioux heterodoxy continues to have wide currency, appearing in works on Lakota history, Native American history, as well as military and policy history. Even a work on the Boxer Rebellion in China, which compares the Boxers to the ghost dancers, repeats this thesis.[49]

There is little question that Wovoka's followers modified his teachings. People from many tribes saw and heard Wovoka; naturally, they interpreted his instructions in different ways. When his followers returned to their own

---

[49] Mooney, *Ghost-Dance Religion*, 787. Mooney later abandoned this thesis; see James Mooney, "The Indian Ghost Dance," *Collections of the Nebraska State Historical Society* 16 (1911): 168–82. The authoritative modern study, Utley, *Last Days*, 87, argues that the Sioux "perverted Wovoka's doctrine into a militant crusade against the white man." Although Robert M. Utley, *The Lance and the Shield: The Life and Times of Sitting Bull* (New York, 1993), does not recapitulate the argument for Sioux heterodoxy, he nonetheless echoes his earlier interpretation in stating that "[a]t Cheyenne River, Rosebud, and Pine Ridge, the dances assumed an increasingly militant and alarming aspect" (p. 287). For other statements of Sioux heterodoxy, see Ralph K. Andrist, *The Long Death: The Last Days of the Plains Indian* (New York, 1964), 338–52; Miller, *Ghost Dance*, 45–57; Weston La Barre, *The Ghost Dance: Origins of Religion* (New York, 1972), 230; Rex Alan Smith, *Moon of Popping Trees* (1975; Lincoln, 1981), 74–75; Moses, *Indian Man*, 53; Francis Paul Prucha, *The Great Father: The United States Government and the American Indians*, 2 vols. (Lincoln, 1984), 2:727; Russell Thornton, *We Shall Live Again: The 1870 and 1890 Ghost Dance Movements as Demographic Revitalization* (Cambridge, 1986), 58; Joseph W. Esherick, *The Origins of the Boxer Uprising* (Berkeley, 1987), 317; Hultkrantz, "Ghost Dance," 545; Stephen Cornell, *The Return of the Native: American Indian Political Resurgence* (New York, 1988), 62; Alice Beck Kehoe, *The Ghost Dance: Ethnohistory and Revitalization* (New York, 1989), 13; Edward Lazarus, *Black Hills/White Justice: The Sioux Nation Versus the United States, 1775 to the Present* (New York, 1991), 114, 464; Michael F. Steltenkamp, *Black Elk: Holy Man of the Oglala* (Norman, 1993), 72; Robert Wooster, *Nelson A. Miles and the Twilight of the Frontier Army* (Lincoln, 1993), 176–78; Hittman, *Wovoka and the Ghost Dance*, 96; Larson, *Red Cloud*, 272; Vander, *Shoshone Ghost Dance*, 10, 55; John William Sayer, *Ghost Dancing the Law: The Wounded Knee Trials* (Cambridge, Mass., 1997), 20–21; Roger L. Nichols, *Indians in the United States and Canada: A Comparative History* (Lincoln, 1998), 241; Robert V. Hine and John Mack Faragher, *The American West: A New Interpretive History* (New Haven, 2000), 380; Guy Gibbon, *The Sioux: The Dakota and Lakota Nations* (Malden, Mass., 2003), 135.

communities and began to put the dance into practice, they and their own new followers experienced further revelations through visionary experiences. These additional forms of knowledge were interpreted and put into practice through complex social processes that varied from tribe to tribe. The Ghost Dance, in other words, was never static. It had no equivalent of the Apostle's Creed, no written catechism to memorize. It is therefore misleading to try to pin down a Ghost Dance "doctrine." Nonetheless, leaders of the Ghost Dance, Lakotas included, did their best to adhere to Wovoka's teachings.

As we will see in Chapter 13, the thesis that the Sioux transformed a peaceful teaching into a militant one originated in the army's attempts to justify its campaign to suppress the Sioux Ghost Dance. There is no evidence that leaders of the Lakota Ghost Dance departed from Wovoka's teachings in any fundamental way. Their predictions of a cataclysmic event that would destroy or remove European Americans were entirely consistent with the Paiute prophet's as well as those of ghost dancers among other tribes.[50] Lakota Ghost Dance leaders looked only to nonwestern sources of spiritual power to overthrow European American domination. Lakota ghost dancers were willing to defend themselves if necessary, and, as we will see in the next chapter, they devised means to make themselves invulnerable to western weapons once the threat of military action escalated. But Lakota ghost dancers never contemplated using arms to bring about the new world. In this sense, the Lakota ghost dancers were just as "pacific" as Wovoka.

To characterize a movement that defied the government's ban on the practice of Indian religion and called upon the spiritual powers of the universe to overthrow European American power as essentially peaceful, however, obscures a crucial element.[51] For entirely understandable reasons James

---

[50] Utley, *Last Days*, 73, contrasts the Northern Cheyenne Porcupine's account of Wovoka in Ruger to AG, 25 June 1890, with the summary of the Sioux version in Sword, "Story of the Ghost Dance," 29, and argues that Porcupine's account "displays no particular hostility toward the white man," while the "Sioux version of the same story took on decidedly militant overtones." It is true that in this particular account Porcupine said nothing about the coming apocalypse, but this may have been because he was being interviewed by military officials. In any case, according to Grinnell, "Account of the Northern Cheyennes," 65, Porcupine stated that Wovoka "told the people... that they should again have their own country, and that the world should be turned upside down and all the whites spilled out."

[51] To counter the thesis that the Lakota ghost dancers distorted an originally peaceful teaching into one of hostility, some writers have argued that the Lakota Ghost Dance was also peaceful. Dee Brown, *Bury My Heart at Wounded Knee: An Indian History of the American West* (New York, 1971), 409, describes the Ghost Dance among all tribes, the Lakotas included, as "entirely Christian" and emphasizes the Lakota ghost dancers' commitment to "nonviolence and brotherly love." Raymond J. DeMallie, "The Lakota Ghost Dance: An Ethnohistorical Account," *Pacific Historical Review* 51 (November 1982): 385–405, contests the view that the Lakotas altered Wovoka's original teachings and, like Brown, characterizes the Lakota Ghost Dance as pacific, though he does so by placing the Ghost Dance in the context of

Mooney downplayed Wovoka's apocalypticism, realizing that this was the only way to make Wovoka acceptable to the American public in the 1890s. But the categories Mooney created, (legitimate) pacifism and (illegitimate) militancy, are clearly inadequate to account for a movement that constituted an ideological, and in many ways a direct, challenge to U.S. authority. The ghost dancers engaged in illegal activities (dancing itself, withdrawing children from school, neglecting crops), realizing that these actions risked reprisals from government officials. Their project of cultural revival resisted government policies of assimilation and imagined nothing less than the end of colonial relations. Like many similar movements throughout the world, then, the Ghost Dance is best understood as an anticolonial movement.[52]

The Ghost Dance has often been seen as an example of a "revitalization movement." But, this category, too, fails to account for the movement's oppositional character. The ghost dancers' goal was not to find individual or group redemption in the existing world or to "construct a more satisfying culture" through reformulating a cultural "mazeway," to use Anthony F. C. Wallace's terms, although this may have been an unintended consequence over time.[53] Instead, they hoped to see the present world destroyed and a new one come into being. Nor was the Ghost Dance simply a new religion. It was certainly religious in the sense that it relied on spiritual power to achieve revolutionary purposes, but its ultimate purpose was not moral and social redemption in this world, but the destruction of that world and its replacement.

In instructing Indians to dance but to avoid hostilities that might provoke non-Indians to use the power of western weapons, Wovoka looked to a different kind of power. He focused on a spiritual power that recognized

---

Lakota religion. For DeMallie, cultural relativism, not Brown's universalism, allows the Lakota Ghost Dance to be understood as pacific. Other writers who have characterized the Lakota Ghost Dance as essentially peaceful include Stewart, "The Ghost Dance," 179–87; Trudy Thomas, "Crisis and Creativity: The Ghost Dance Art Style," in Alvin M. Josephy Jr., Trudy Thomas, and Jeanne Eder, *Wounded Knee: Lest We Forget*, with an introductory essay by George P. Horse Capture (Cody, Wyo., 1990), 37.

[52] For treatments of North American prophetic movements as anticolonial movements, see especially Dowd, *Spirited Resistance*; Martin, *Sacred Revolt*; Joel W. Martin, "Before and Beyond the Sioux Ghost Dance: Native American Prophetic Movements and the Study of Religion," *Journal of the Academy of Religion* 59 (Winter 1991): 677–701. For similar movements outside North America, see the works cited in this chapter, note 16.

[53] Anthony F. C. Wallace, "Revitalization Movements," *American Anthropologist* 58 (April 1956): 264–81 (qtns., 265–66); see also Richard White, *The Middle Ground: Indians, Empires, and Republics in the Great Lakes Region, 1650–1815* (Cambridge, 1991), 285. An exception, however, was the movement led by the Seneca prophet Handsome Lake in the first years of the nineteenth century. Handsome Lake did not imagine the removal of the descendants of European immigrants, but instead drew upon both Christian and "traditional" Seneca elements to revive Seneca ways of life. See Anthony F. C. Wallace, *The Death and Rebirth of the Seneca* (New York, 1969), 239–302. The Handsome Lake case formed the basis for Wallace's general theory of revitalization movements.

the sufferings of oppressed people and had the capacity to destroy and renew. It was this vision of transformation that drew representatives of tribes throughout the western United States – Lakotas included – to seek Wovoka in 1889 and 1890. It was this vision that Lakotas who journeyed to Nevada brought back with them and tried to put into practice in the months before Wounded Knee.

12

"To Bring My People Back into the Hoop"

The Development of the Lakota Ghost Dance

When the Lakota delegates to Wovoka returned with news of his teachings, it was unclear how Plains Sioux communities would respond to the new dance. The idea of sending delegates had been broadly sanctioned by tribal leaders, but this did not mean that the Ghost Dance would receive widespread support. Evaluating the new movement involved several considerations. Were the Ghost Dance's claims consistent with Lakota cosmology? What were the practical consequences of holding these dances? Would the government act to suppress the dance, and if so, would the powers of *Wakan Tanka Cinca* protect the dancers? Would the dance unify a badly divided people, or would it only aggravate these divisions? Although we lack evidence of the discussions that must have taken place within western Sioux communities about these and similar questions, we can consider some of the issues these questions would have raised.

When they first heard about the Ghost Dance, Plains Sioux people undoubtedly responded in different ways. One consideration surely would have been the extent to which the new dance was consistent with Lakota cultural and religious practices. Scholars have reached different conclusions on this question. Raymond J. DeMallie emphasizes the Ghost Dance's continuity with Lakota culture by explaining how the ghost dancers' expectation of the return of the bison was consistent with Lakota cosmology. On the other hand, William K. Powers stresses that the Ghost Dance was "foreign" by arguing that ideas of a cataclysm and of a return of deceased human and animal spirits was inconsistent with "sacred persons' knowledge of how the universe functions."[1] There are problems with both these positions. Too much emphasis on continuity understates the epistemological distance

---

[1] Raymond J. DeMallie, "The Lakota Ghost Dance: An Ethnohistorical Account," *Pacific Historical Review* 51 (November 1982): 385–406; William K. Powers, *Oglala Religion* (Lincoln, 1975), 202.

between historical Lakota practices and the new movement. An argument for radical disjuncture fails to account for connections between the Ghost Dance and past Lakota practices as well as Lakota culture's capacity for innovation.

Some elements of the Ghost Dance departed significantly from Plains Sioux traditions. One innovation was the form of the dance. Drawing on Great Basin practices, Wovoka instructed his followers to perform a round dance in which dancers held hands in a circle. This style of dance was new to the Sioux. In the Sioux Sun Dance, for example, dancers stood facing the center and then moved together around the center, stopping at each of the four directions, and they also danced toward and away from the center tree. They did not form a circle together or hold hands.[2] Lakota ghost dancers took great care that the circle not be broken. Leaders instructed the dancers to rub their hands with dust or sand and to interlock their fingers with the other dancers to prevent slippage. Although dancing with hands held in a circle was an innovation, it resonated with one of the basic motifs in western Sioux culture. Mary Crow Dog, who married into a family with oral histories of the Ghost Dance, explains that the sacred hoop was more than just a visual symbol. It was something experienced through one's own body and the bodies of others: "dancing in a circle holding hands was bringing back the sacred hoop – to feel, holding on to the hand of your brother and sister, the rebirth of Indian unity, feel it with your flesh, through your skin." After so many years of demoralization and factional fighting, it was now possible to experience the nation becoming strong again.[3]

The content and social context of the visionary experiences was also new. In the past, visions had given individuals particular powers that were vital to performing specific tasks. Whether visions came through a formal vision quest or occurred spontaneously, male visionaries obtained powers that were useful in warfare, hunting, or healing. Women did not usually seek visions; visions generally came to them unbidden. In either case, female visionaries also received powers that assisted them in particular tasks of healing and craftwork.[4]

[2] Of the many sources for the Sun Dance, Joseph Epes Brown, ed., *The Sacred Pipe: Black Elk's Account of the Seven Rites of the Oglala Sioux* (Norman, 1953), 67–100, pays more attention to describing the dancing itself than most others. The Omaha Dance complex and social dances are described in Ben Black Bear Sr. and R. D. Theisz, *Songs and Dances of the Lakota* (Rosebud, S.Dak., 1976).

[3] "Ghost-Dances in the West," *The Illustrated American* 5 (17 January, 1891): 329; ARCIA, 1891, 530; Kay Graber, ed., *Sister to the Sioux: The Memoirs of Elaine Goodale Eastman, 1885–91* (Lincoln, 1978), 148; Mary Crow Dog and Richard Erdoes, *Lakota Woman* (New York, 1990), 153 (qtn.).

[4] Marla N. Powers, *Oglala Women: Myth, Ritual, and Reality* (Chicago, 1986), 96, 194; Lee Irwin, *The Dream Seekers: Native American Visionary Traditions of the Great Plains* (Norman, 1994), 80–81, 215.

The Ghost Dance differed from prior visionary experiences in two ways. First, several individuals, male and female, had visions at the same time and immediately described them to the community. This practice contrasted with the past, when mostly men experienced visions in relative isolation and made their experiences known afterward. Earlier practices had allowed for the gradual accumulation and modification of spiritual knowledge; with the Ghost Dance, these processes accelerated significantly. This was one of the many sources of the Ghost Dance's dynamism.

The fact that women had equal public access to visions may also have involved a modest shift in gender relations. Previously, visionary powers had corresponded to gender roles that may have been "equal" in the sense of being complementary but belonged to distinctly separate spheres of activity. In the Ghost Dance, however, both men and women had similar visions for similar purposes. Other elements of the dance – its integrated form (men and women holding hands in the same circle) and the wearing of feathers by both sexes – also indicated this shift.[5] On the other hand, it would be a mistake to suggest a fundamental reorientation of gender roles, given that the movement's general emphasis on returning to past ways of life tended to reaffirm a "traditional" division of labor.

The other innovation in the visionary experience was that ghost dancers did not contact spiritual beings that conveyed powers to help living people. Rather, they saw people who had left this world and were living well in the world to come. For many participants, actually to see deceased loved ones must have been the dance's most compelling aspect. Even in "normal" times, the possibility of seeing departed friends and relatives would have been powerful. All the more so in a time of severe cultural loss and death. Virtually all Lakotas had mourned losses from war or disease. As we have seen, serious outbreaks of measles, whooping cough, and influenza occurred in the late 1880s.[6]

The best account we have of a religious leader's encounter with the Lakota Ghost Dance, Black Elk's, is particularly useful for thinking about the relationship between the new movement and existing cultural categories. In 1873, at the age of nine, Black Elk experienced an unusually powerful vision in which he was taken to the grandfathers of the six directions (west, north, east, south, above, and below). During his vision Black Elk received various powers. From the Thunder Beings (*Wakinyan*), Black Elk received a bow and

---

[5] For further discussion on gender and the Ghost Dance, see Judith Vander, *Shoshone Ghost Dance Religion: Poetry Songs and Great Basin Context* (Urbana, 1997), 270–72; Reginald Laubin and Gladys Laubin, *Indian Dances of North America: Their Importance to Indian Life* (Norman, 1977), 60.

[6] For these epidemics, see Chapter 7. Russell Thornton, *We Shall Live Again: The 1870 and 1890 Ghost Dance Movements as Demographic Revitalization* (Cambridge, 1986), correlates tribes' participation in the Ghost Dance to population losses.

arrow, symbolic of lightning's power to "destroy any enemies." Black Elk also received a sacred herb, a sacred wind, a sacred pipe, a flowering stick, and a sacred hoop to help his people walk the "red road" and prosper.[7]

For many years Black Elk kept his vision to himself, but as time went on, he grew increasingly "afraid of the spirits." During summer 1880, Black Elk felt uneasy every time a cloud appeared in the sky for fear that the Thunder Beings were coming to call him. In the fall the Thunder Beings went away, but that winter he was troubled by a voice saying, "[y]our grandfather told you to do these things. It is time for you to do them." Finally, Black Elk's father asked a holy man named Black Road to find out what might be wrong with his son. When Black Road inquired, the young man related what he had seen seven years before. Black Road told him that he must perform portions of his vision for the people.[8]

Over the next few years, Black Elk, with the assistance of Black Road and other holy men, chose particular parts of his vision and publicly enacted them. As he did, he became more capable of using the powers of his vision to help his people, especially by healing the sick.[9] One of Black Elk's performances, the buffalo ceremony, was designed to show his people how his powers could be used to help them walk the good red road. Black Elk staged this ceremony at Pine Ridge around 1884. To prepare for this ceremony, Black Elk asked Red Dog, an elderly holy man, for assistance, telling him "about the good road from the south to the north on which they [the people] were to walk."[10] Black Elk also explained that in the performance he was to resemble a buffalo. He would wear horns with an herb on one of the horns. On the left side of the buffalo would be a feather, representing the people who would feed on the buffalo. Red Dog responded to Black Elk's request:

Boy, you had a great vision, and I know that it is your place to see that the people might walk the good red road in a manner satisfactory to all its powers. It is the duty for you to see that the people will lead and walk the right road, because if it is not done, in the future our relatives-like [the animals] will disappear.[11]

Inside a tipi, Red Dog prepared for the ceremony by making a buffalo wallow on the east side of a circle and then a road – the red road – running from north to south across the circle. He also made buffalo tracks along the red road, leading to the north, where he placed a cup of water from Black Elk's vision. As Black Elk commented, this meant "that people would walk buffalo-like and as a result would be tough."[12] Red Dog then sang a buffalo song:

---

[7] Raymond J. DeMallie, ed., *The Sixth Grandfather: Black Elk's Teachings Given to John G. Neihardt* (Lincoln, 1984), 116–35 (qtn., 118).

[8] Ibid., 213–14.

[9] Ibid., 215–39.

[10] Ibid., 240.

[11] Ibid.

[12] Ibid.

> Revealing this they walk
> A sacred herb, revealing it, they walk.
> Revealing this they walk,
> The sacred life of the buffalo,
>   revealing it they walk. (four times)
> Revealing a sacred eagle father. Revealing it they walk.
> The eagle and buffalo, relative-like they walk.

Red Dog then "made a snorting sound of a buffalo" and from his breath came "visible red flames." After this, Black Elk, painted red and wearing horns, went outside the tipi:

The people were all eager to see me. In this act I represented the relationship between the people and the buffalo. From the buffalo, people had reared their children up. I went around acting like [a] buffalo and behind me followed One Side [a helper], representing [the] people. Everyone saw that my power was great.

Black Elk then returned to the tipi and people brought their children to be cured.[13]

To understand the meanings Lakota people would have found in Black Elk's ceremony, it is helpful to turn to insights offered by recent theorists of ritual. Such theorists have rejected an earlier notion of rituals as conservative mechanisms for social reproduction and resolving social and cultural contradictions and have instead seen them as a "site and a means of experimental practice, of subversive poetics, of creative tension and transformative action."[14] This approach not only underscores the obviously improvised character of Black Elk's buffalo ceremony, it also prompts us to search his story for meanings it may have carried at the time. In telling this story to John Neihardt fifty years later, Black Elk indicated that the ceremony's efficacy was manifested through an increase in his powers of healing. The account itself, however, contains hints that in 1884 Black Elk and other participants understood the ritual to have the potential to reverse the decline of the buffalo. The ceremony's imagery – the feather showing the people's dependence on the buffalo – suggests this possibility. A stronger indication is the comment Red Dog made to Black Elk (quoted earlier): if Black Elk did not do his duty to help the people walk the good road, "in the future our relatives-like will disappear."

Theorists of ritual offer another useful insight for thinking about Black Elk's buffalo ceremony by pointing out that ritual's meanings are created

---

[13] Ibid., 241 (brackets except after "One Side" in the original).

[14] Jean Comaroff and John Comaroff, "Introduction," in *Modernity and Its Malcontents: Ritual and Power in Postcolonial Africa*, ed. Jean Comaroff and John Comaroff (Chicago, 1993), xxix. For an excellent introduction to ritual theory, see Catherine Bell, *Ritual Theory, Ritual Practice* (New York, 1992).

through the physical actions of participants.[15] Black Elk did not simply describe his vision in words. To realize the vision's powers, it was necessary that he actually perform it. In some basic sense, Black Elk had to *become* a buffalo. His body moved like a buffalo; he snorted and stamped his feet. The audience could see and hear his strength. They could sense the bison's power – the animal's energy and capacities – in their own bodies. Realizing that One Side, Black Elk's helper, represented their community, they were reminded of their historic need for the buffalo, not only for food, but also as a source of life. Seeing One Side following Black Elk, they felt the necessity and the capability to imitate the buffalo, to become "tough" (*suta*).[16] This might simply mean that the people would need to endure and hope to find the red road under the new reservation conditions. But it was also possible that if the people became buffalo-like once again, the animals might return in their former abundance. The Plains Sioux could walk the red road in the old way.

How could becoming like the buffalo affect animal populations? As we saw in Chapter 1, the Plains Sioux' relationship to the buffalo was grounded in the White Buffalo Calf Woman's instructions about Sioux duties and responsibilities and her gift of the pipe. Proper moral behavior and ritual performance had allowed the Plains Sioux to become a Buffalo Nation. In recent years, though, their connection to the buffalo had been lost. As Raymond DeMallie explains, Lakotas believed that the "buffalo had originated within the earth before they emerged on the surface." During times of scarcity, Lakotas understood that the buffalo "went back inside the earth because they had been offended, either by Indians or whites."[17] By this logic, the severe decline in bison populations that Black Elk and his people had so painfully experienced could be reversed through proper ritual performance and moral reformation.

Although Lakota culture offered the possibility that the buffalo could return, it did not guarantee this would happen. Indeed, for several decades Plains Sioux people had offered various, sometimes conflicting opinions about the causes of game shortages and the likelihood that decline could be reversed.[18] In the early 1880s, faced with the unprecedented crisis of the bison's near extinction and the imposition of reservation life, the Sioux were uncertain how to find the red road. Many would have expressed strong doubts that the buffalo could return, at least any time in the near

[15] Bell, *Ritual Theory, Ritual Practice*, 94–117; Pierre Bourdieu, *Outline of a Theory of Practice*, trans. Richard Nice (Cambridge, 1977), 87–95, 114–24.

[16] *Suta*, the likely word Black Elk used, can be translated as "tough," but also as "hardy," "capable of endurance," and "strong."

[17] DeMallie, "Lakota Ghost Dance," 391.

[18] Jeffrey Ostler, "'They Regard Their Passing as *Wakan*': Interpreting Western Sioux Explanations for the Bison's Decline," *Western Historical Quarterly* 30 (Winter 1999): 475–97.

future, and placed their hopes in living well under new conditions.[19] Others, however, were willing, in Marshall Sahlins's terms, to "submit [their] cultural categories to empirical risks" in the hope that the spiritual powers of the universe might restore the world as it had been a generation or two before.[20]

Black Elk's account of his buffalo ceremony reveals, then, that Lakota culture was capable of generating at least some of the epistemological premises of the Ghost Dance. However, even for someone like Black Elk, who was unusually attuned to the creative possibilities of spiritual experimentation, accepting the Ghost Dance was not an obvious proposition. When word of the Ghost Dance first reached Pine Ridge, Black Elk was traveling in Europe with Cody's Wild West Show.[21] Shortly after his return, he learned of the delegation to Wovoka and heard reports of the dance they had begun. Black Elk could not help but recall his vision. It seemed "as though my vision were really coming true and that if I helped, probably with my power that I had I could make the tree bloom and that I would get my people back into that sacred hoop again where they would prosper." Though deeply interested, Black Elk was also reluctant to get involved. Finally, though, he "could no longer resist" and attended a dance near Manderson.[22]

When Black Elk arrived at the dance grounds, he was struck by the congruence between his vision and the scene before him. Employing what might be called a kind of mystical empiricism, Black Elk observed that the "sacred pole" in the center was "an exact duplicate of my tree that never blooms." In addition, the dancers' red-painted faces, the pipe, and the eagle feathers were "all from my vision." These elements recalled common themes in Lakota ceremonies and visionary experiences. They reveal how Sioux Ghost Dance leaders incorporated Wovoka's teachings into a familiar cultural context. As he watched the dance, Black Elk felt sad at first, but then "happiness overcame me all at once" as he realized that "I was to be intercessor for my people and yet I was not doing my duty. Perhaps it was this Messiah that had pointed me out and he might have se[n]t this to remind me to get to work again to bring my people back into the hoop and the old religion."[23]

---

[19] Documentary evidence such as the following statement by Pumpkin Seed before the Crook Commission offers some support for this observation: "If I wanted to talk about what is in the past, I would talk about the buffalo, when we had buffalo years back. But now I look out for my children to the future to come." See *Report and Proceedings of the Sioux Commission*, 51st Cong., 1st sess., 1889–90, S. Ex. Doc. 51, serial 2682, 112. The strongest evidence, however, is simply the fact that most Lakotas did not take up the Ghost Dance. Although there were many reasons for nonparticipation, a lack of confidence in its efficacy was undoubtedly a factor.

[20] Marshall Sahlins, *Islands of History* (Chicago, 1985), ix.

[21] DeMallie, ed., *Sixth Grandfather*, 245–55.

[22] Ibid., 257–58.

[23] Ibid., 258.

Black Elk then decided to participate in the Ghost Dance and over the next weeks had several powerful visions.

The account Black Elk gave John Neihardt in 1931 suggests that he had some doubts about the Ghost Dance all along. When firing broke out at Wounded Knee, Black Elk was at Pine Ridge and heard it. For someone who had become deeply involved in ghost dancing, Black Elk was surprisingly indecisive. He started for Wounded Knee, but on the way had second thoughts. He "doubted about this Messiah business and therefore it seemed that I should not fight for it." Although Black Elk continued toward Wounded Knee, he rode with uncertainty. Decades later, Black Elk continued to agonize over his involvement in the Ghost Dance. Instead of depending on his "Messiah vision," he told Neihardt, he should have relied on his "first great vision which had more power." This "might have been where I made my great mistake."[24]

For Black Elk, then, the Ghost Dance's validity was not immediately obvious and required testing. This process did not involve an abstract evaluation of Ghost Dance beliefs against tenets of Lakota cosmology. Some spiritual leaders may have taken such an approach, but Black Elk characteristically sought to work out the implications of his vision in existing historical circumstances. In doing so, Black Elk was acting on the assumption that Lakota culture permitted new ways to gain spiritual assistance to solve problems, especially in a moment of crisis. In the past, *Wakan Tanka* had given the Sioux new instructions and methods for accessing power. Accordingly, Black Elk first looked for empirical congruity between his vision and the practice of the Ghost Dance. Once the dance passed that test, he poured all his energies into the new movement, but his participation ultimately remained provisional.

Although Black Elk's experience was not necessarily typical of all ghost dancers, it suggests a complicated and dynamic relationship between a new set of practices and beliefs, themselves subject to alteration (the Ghost Dance), and a never-static multivalent set of prior practices and beliefs (Lakota culture). Some Ghost Dance leaders, especially those who had seen *Wakan Tanka Cinca*, might have been more certain of the dance than Black Elk. Yet because the dance's efficacy was contingent on proper moral behavior and ritual performance, ghost dancing was inherently uncertain.

For all that Black Elk's experiences reveal about how existing cultural categories could comprehend the Ghost Dance, the fact remains that the majority of Plains Sioux people never became committed ghost dancers. If, as I have suggested, the Ghost Dance was subject to being tested, it stands to reason that some experimenters reached negative conclusions. An account

---

[24] Ibid., 272, 266. It is possible that Black Elk was more uncertain about the Ghost Dance in 1931 than he was at the time, but the fact that he linked his uncertainty to specific recollections like the ride to Wounded Knee suggests that it was present at the time.

by school teacher Mrs. Z. A. Parker, although obviously biased, confirms that some doubters existed. After observing a dance at White Clay Creek in which one hundred lost consciousness, Parker talked with several of the dancers. One man said he saw an eagle flying around and around. As it drew near, he reached out to take it, but then it was gone. Parker asked the man "what he thought of it." His reply: "Big lie." Parker claimed that this man was typical and asserted that "not one in twenty believed in it."[25] Although Parker's conclusion that 95 percent of ghost dancers were nonbelievers is so absurd as to call into question her reliability, it would be a mistake to dismiss her account altogether. Parker wished to make it seem that the Indians she had been guiding toward the supposed rationalities of Christian civilization had progressed beyond what she regarded as the superstitions of the Ghost Dance. This led her to exaggerate the extent of Sioux skepticism. But her distortions should not prevent us from recognizing the kernel of truth in her description.

Most Plains Sioux never even saw a Ghost Dance, let alone danced in one. In some communities, as Powers suggests, spiritual leaders may well have rejected Wovoka's ideas of a cataclysm and the return of the dead as incompatible with Sioux cosmology. Yet although we lack direct evidence of how Sioux communities evaluated the Ghost Dance, it makes sense to think that it was not solely a matter of judging its relationship to religious and philosophical knowledge. It was in part a political decision. One reason this conclusion seems warranted is that the initial decision to send a delegation to visit Wovoka in fall 1889 was approved by a council of political leaders (see Chapter 11). The pattern of division about the Ghost Dance among Plains Sioux communities also suggests the importance of politics.

Bands with a history of strategic cooperation with U.S. officials generally rejected the Ghost Dance. Many leaders of these bands – American Horse and Young Man Afraid of His Horses at Pine Ridge, Hollow Horn Bear at Rosebud, White Swan and Charger at Cheyenne River, and John Grass and Gall at Standing Rock – worried about the Ghost Dance from the outset, fearing that it would only provoke government repression. The only bands seriously to consider the Ghost Dance were those with a history of direct resistance to the reservation system. Even among these bands, however, leaders appeared unsure how to respond to the new movement. Red Cloud, for example, had a long record of opposing government policies and could have been expected to join the Ghost Dance with great enthusiasm. Although some members of his band became ghost dancers, including his son Jack, Red Cloud himself did not.

A partial glimpse of Red Cloud's views can be found in the record of a conversation he had with General Nelson A. Miles in late October 1890. At

---

[25] *ARCIA,* 1891, 531. Parker is identified as the author of this account in Mooney, *Ghost-Dance Religion,* 916.

this time, the army was investigating the Sioux Ghost Dance, but had not yet decided to act against it.[26] Red Cloud told Miles that although he was "too old to dance," he had seen the Ghost Dance and recognized that "what they are doing is the teaching of the [Catholic] Church." Their "doctrines and belief and practice is what is taught by the scriptures." If this sounded like an endorsement of the dance, however, Red Cloud qualified this impression by saying: "If it is true they will go on with their dance, and it will go all over the world before it stops; on the other hand, if it is false, and there is nothing in it, it will go away like the snow under the hot sun."[27]

Clearly, Red Cloud's remarks were strategic. In equating the Ghost Dance and Christianity, he hoped Miles would conclude that the Ghost Dance was benign. And, in suggesting that the Ghost Dance might be "false" (Red Cloud surely knew this was Miles's opinion), Red Cloud hoped that Miles would leave it alone so that it could "melt." It is possible that Red Cloud's apparent admission that the Ghost Dance might be false was only strategic, but his conditional reasoning probably revealed something of his own views. Perhaps the Ghost Dance would work (or at least have a positive effect by promoting tribal sovereignty), but it might as easily provoke catastrophic repression. For someone in Red Cloud's position, it may have seemed best simply to watch. He could protect a space for resistance but take care that the dance not go too far.

In early 1890, when Lakotas began organizing ghost dances, they must have anticipated that the government would move against them. The crackdown on the Sun Dance, especially, had demonstrated U.S. officials' unwillingness to tolerate large public ceremonies. Surely, too, the ghost dancers would have realized that officials would disapprove of having children attend dances instead of school. Indeed, as soon as government agents became aware of ghost dancing, they moved to suppress it. In March, when Rosebud Agent J. George Wright learned that Short Bull was talking about his recent visit to "the Messiah," he summoned him, and, in Wright's words, "called [him] to account." In his recollections, Short Bull explained exactly what this meant: "The Agent...told me if I would tell this story to the Indians I would be a dead man."[28] The next month Pine Ridge Agent Hugh Gallagher, learning

---

[26] Miles had come to Pine Ridge as the chair of the Northern Cheyenne Commission to investigate the possibility of having the approximately four hundred northern Cheyennes at Pine Ridge join their relatives at Tongue River. See Orlan J. Svingen, *The Northern Cheyenne Indian Reservation, 1877–1900* (Niwot, Colo., 1993), 87.

[27] "Conversation between General Miles and Sioux Indian Chiefs 'Red Cloud' and 'Little Wound' at Pine Ridge Agency, S.D., October 27th, 1890, Regarding 'Ghost Dance,'" Nelson A. Miles Papers, box 4, folder D, U.S. Army Military History Institute, Carlisle Barracks, Pa.

[28] *ARCIA*, 1891, 411; Short Bull, "As Narrated by Short Bull," p. 8, Buffalo Bill Memorial Museum, Golden, Colo.

of plans to "organize the new religion," confined Good Thunder and two other emissaries in the guardhouse for a few days.[29]

Although some ghost dances were held at Rosebud and possibly elsewhere after the spring arrests, many potential dancers were evidently reluctant to proceed with the dance.[30] Some Ghost Dance leaders apparently decided to consult with other tribes. According to George Sword, Kicking Bear went to Wyoming to visit the Arapahoes shortly after the arrests. The fact that Kicking Bear was a key figure in the dance's late-summer revival suggests that he returned with a strong argument for continuing the dances even in the face of government opposition.[31] In any case, by late summer Lakota ghost dancers had apparently resolved whatever doubts they had. Ghost dancing resumed in earnest at Pine Ridge in August. Large ghost dances were held in September at Rosebud and Cheyenne River, and in early October Kicking Bear initiated dances at Standing Rock. By this time, the height of the Ghost Dance, between one-fourth and one-third of the Sioux at the four reservations were involved.[32]

As they revived the Ghost Dance in the summer and fall, participants were resolved to defy government interference with their activities. On August 22 Pine Ridge Agent Gallagher sent the Indian police to stop a dance at White Clay Creek. This dance was a much larger one than those performed in April. Including spectators, around two thousand people attended. When the police ordered "the gathering to disperse," the dancers simply ignored them. Unauthorized to use force and not wanting to provoke bloodshed anyway, the police had little choice but to return to the agency. Two days later, Gallagher went to White Clay Creek along with twenty policemen and Philip Wells, an agency interpreter. On the way, Wells observed that "the women and children were at the houses but no men were in sight." Because

[29] William T. Selwyn to Col. E. W. Foster, 25 Nov. 1890, SC 188, roll 1 (qtn.); George Sword, "The Story of the Ghost Dance," *The Folk-Lorist* 1 (July 1892): 30; Elaine Goodale Eastman, "The Ghost Dance War and Wounded Knee Massacre of 1890–91," *Nebraska History* 26 (January–March 1945): 31.

[30] *ARCIA*, 1891, 411, implies that there was no ghost dancing at Rosebud between April and September, but Short Bull, "As Narrated by Short Bull," 8–9, indicates that ghost dancing at Rosebud continued, although Short Bull himself did not participate.

[31] Sword, "Story of the Ghost Dance," 30; *ARCIA*, 1890, 49; James McLaughlin to CIA, 17 Oct. 1890, MP, roll 21.

[32] William J. Cleveland stated that the rate of participation in the Ghost Dance was 10 percent at Standing Rock, 15 percent at Cheyenne River, 30 percent at Rosebud, and 40 percent at Pine Ridge. See *Ninth Annual Report of the Executive Committee of the Indian Rights Association*, 1891 (Philadelphia, 1892), 29. My reading of the primary sources suggests that these estimates are close to the mark, although they may understate the percentages at Standing Rock and Cheyenne River. Based on population figures in *ARCIA*, 1890, I estimate that between four and five thousand Sioux (almost all from Lakota bands) were involved in the Ghost Dance.

women and children participated in the dance, it dawned on Wells that this "was a sign of some extreme resolution on the part of the warriors."

Once Gallagher's party reached the dance ground, they saw no one until a man ran out of a nearby house with his gun drawn. Another man, also armed, emerged from a thicket of brush, followed by eight or ten others. Gallagher approached the first man and (through Wells) asked, "What do you mean when I come as your agent to talk to you and you draw guns on me?" Seeking to defuse the situation, Wells, who knew the man and was a friend of his son, addressed him by the kinship term, *ate* (father), and asked him to put down the gun and come forward. The man responded, "Yes, my son, I will obey you." The man then asked Gallagher why, if he only wanted to talk, he had brought so many guns with him. The agent replied that it was the duty of the police to carry their weapons and that he shouldn't take offense. Suddenly, though, another man jumped out from behind a bank and threatened to shoot a policemen he held a grudge against. At this point, Young Man Afraid of His Horses, who was not a ghost dancer but lived nearby, arrived on the scene. Characteristically, in Wells's words, Young Man Afraid "set about to restore an amicable understanding and prevent bloodshed." Although Gallagher ordered the dancing stopped, he did not arrest anyone. The dances continued.[33]

From the perspective of the ghost dancers, Gallagher's lack of action surely validated their decision to resume the dances. Given their understanding of the dance's potential capacities (nothing less than the remaking of the entire world), they likely interpreted Gallagher's weakness as a sign of the powers of the dance. The ghost dancers' next encounter with government officials would have reinforced this impression. On September 20 Indian Office Special Agent E. B. Reynolds and some agency employees visited another Pine Ridge Ghost Dance. When they arrived, Reynolds instructed his interpreter to inform the dance leaders that "we came not to interfere with their exercises but simply to see for ourselves" and to ask them to announce that

---

[33] *ARCIA*, 1890, 49; Philip Wells interview, 1906, RT, tablet 5, roll 2 (qtns.). See also P. F. Wells to James McLaughlin, 19 Oct. 1890, in Stanley Vestal, ed., *New Sources of Indian History, 1850–1891* (Norman, 1934), 5–6. E. B. Reynolds to CIA, 25 Sept. 1890, SC 188, roll 1, gives a slightly different version of this event based on secondhand information. It is unclear why Gallagher allowed the dances to continue. Perhaps he thought arrests would only encourage further defiance and hoped the dance would die out in the months to come. Gallagher's status as a lame duck might also have played a role. As Philip S. Hall, *To Have This Land: The Nature of Indian/White Relations in South Dakota, 1888–1891* (Vermillion, S.Dak., 1991), 16, relates, in late 1889, when South Dakota was admitted as a state, the legislature chose Republican Richard F. Pettigrew as the state's leading senator, and the following March Pettigrew endorsed Daniel F. Royer, one of his political supporters, to replace Gallagher at Pine Ridge. Royer's appointment had not gone through, but Gallagher likely realized that it was just a matter of time before the Ghost Dance would be someone else's problem.

there would be a council at the agency in a few days. Torn Belly, the dance's "proclaimer" (probably *eyapaha*), said that because it was Sunday and they were in the middle of "their religious exercise," he was reluctant to make an announcement about the council, but he would consult with the leaders. After doing so, Torn Belly returned, shook hands with Reynolds, and said that the leaders "were glad to see us as we would learn there was no harm in their dance and the announcement was made." Reynolds and his party watched for a while, heard the dancers relate their visions, joined them when they broke for lunch, and then watched again before returning to the agency.[34]

It is clear from Reynolds's account that the ghost dancers hoped that familiarity with the new dance would promote tolerance. For the same reason, the Sioux had earlier accepted the presence of American visitors at the Sun Dance (see Chapter 8). Torn Belly's appeal to the Christian Sabbath afforded a particularly effective way to make an argument for cultural pluralism. Over the years, missionaries had told the Sioux that Sunday was a "holy day" and gave Sunday precisely that name (*Anpetu Wakan*). But if Sunday was a "holy" day, surely Indians had the right to do *wakan* things (pray, dance, and have visions) on this of all days.[35] When Torn Belly informed Reynolds it was Sunday, Reynolds was apparently caught off guard. He described himself as "dazed" by Torn Belly's words and evidently could not think of a reply.[36] This underscores the power in the Ghost Dance's tactic of taking ideas that Americans had imposed on Indians and turning them around. After returning to the agency, however, Reynolds reported that the dance was "exceedingly prejudicial to [the dancers'] physical welfare" and had the unfortunate effect of "binding them to the customs of their ancestors." He advised that "steps should be taken to stop it" and concluded that "[t]his can only be done by the military unless the cold weather accomplishes this end."[37] From the Pine Ridge ghost dancers' perspective, however, the evidence suggested that the government might leave the dancers alone.

At Rosebud, Agent Wright took a stronger stance; in mid-September he ordered the dances to cease. They were "interferring with schools, and causing a total neglect of stock and all belongings." Shortly after this order, while the Indians were at the agency drawing rations, a rumor began that troops were on the reservation. Ghost dancers immediately left the agency. Interestingly, they did not seek to avoid the soldiers. Rather, Wright found the

---

[34] Reynolds to CIA, 25 Sept. 1890.

[35] Using the same logic, ghost dancers frequently told agents and missionaries, "You have your churches, why can we not have ours." Graber, ed., *Sister to the Sioux*, 148.

[36] Reynolds to CIA, 25 Sept. 1890.

[37] Ibid.

dancers at the location where the troops were reported to be "clothed only in paint and ammunition, on horses, armed with rifles and waiting for developments." Wright persuaded them that the rumors were baseless and the gathering dispersed.[38]

Any thought that the absence of troops signaled a policy of toleration disappeared the next day when Wright ordered rations withheld until the dancing stopped. According to Wright's report, written months later, this approach worked until late October when he was suspended for allegedly pocketing money earmarked for rations. The Indians took advantage of the "change in authority" and started dancing with "renewed vigor." Possibly ghost dancing at Rosebud did subside in the weeks before Wright's suspension, but the agent's account of the reasons was self-serving. Although Wright was eventually exonerated and reinstated in December, he was nonetheless eager to avoid responsibility for the Ghost Dance and probably overstated his success in suppressing it.[39] If dancing did decline in October, it was because of the dancers' own timetable rather than the withdrawal of rations. Shortly after Wright's suspension, his temporary replacement, Special Agent Reynolds, reported that the ghost dancers had for some time been killing government-issue cattle intended as breeding stock, indicating that the dancers were undeterred by the loss of rations.[40]

Reynolds's report offered further evidence that the Rosebud dancers were fully resolved to keep dancing in the weeks before he assumed charge. Immediately after relieving Wright, Reynolds sent ten police to arrest two Sioux who had killed their cows for a ghost dance feast at Red Leaf's camp. When they arrived, seventy-five well-armed ghost dancers surrounded them. The police "unanimously agreed that an attempt to arrest the offenders would have resulted in death to the entire posse." A few days later (October 31), Reynolds sent the chief of police to try to talk the leaders into surrendering the two men. This effort also failed.[41]

At Cheyenne River the ghost dancers were similarly undeterred. On October 11, Agent Perain Palmer wrote that his police had been unable to stop ghost dances at Big Foot's camp. According to Palmer, the police were afraid to challenge the dancers, because the dancers had Winchester rifles while the police had only revolvers. Some policemen, in fact, resigned from the force. With his police unwilling to act, Palmer decided to try to convince key leaders

---

[38] *ARCIA*, 1891, 411. Luther Standing Bear, *My People the Sioux*, ed. E. A. Brininstool (1928; Lincoln, 1975), 221–22, offers a version of what appears to be the same event.

[39] *ARCIA*, 1891, 411. On Wright's suspension and reinstatement, see Robert M. Utley, *The Last Days of the Sioux Nation* (New Haven, 1963), 95, 133.

[40] E. B. Reynolds to CIA, 2 Nov. 1890, SC 188, roll 1.

[41] Ibid. See also Capt. C. A. Earnest to AAG DP, 19 Nov. 1890, enclosed in Brig. Gen. John R. Brooke to AAG DM, 2 Mar. 1891, RCWK, roll 2.

like Big Foot and Hump to give up the dance. When he told them that the "[Interior] Department is displeased with their actions," they retorted that they were "displeased with the Department and <u>will dance</u>."[42]

Ghost dancers also defied the authorities at Standing Rock. On October 9, when Kicking Bear arrived at Sitting Bull's camp to hold a ghost dance, agent James McLaughlin immediately sent thirteen police, including Captain Crazy Walking and Second Lieutenant David Chatka, to arrest Kicking Bear and escort him off the reservation. The police returned on the thirteenth without having done a thing, except to learn that Kicking Bear was planning to leave the following day. McLaughlin reported that Crazy Walking and Chatka returned "in a 'dazed' condition and fearing the powers of Kicking Bear's medicine." The next day, McLaughlin sent Chatka and another policeman back "to notify Sitting Bull that his insolence and bad behavior would not be tolerated [any] longer and that the 'Ghost Dance' must not be continued." When Chatka returned, he reported that he had ordered Kicking Bear to leave and the Ghost Dance to stop. Kicking Bear replied that he planned to return to Cheyenne River anyway. Sitting Bull was "determined to continue the 'Ghost Dance' as the Great Spirit had sent a direct message by Kicking Bear that to live they must do so" but promised nonetheless to stop the dances until he had a chance to come to the agency and talk with the agent. Despite this promise, however, dancing was again underway at Sitting Bull's camp on the sixteenth.[43]

By mid-October, Lakota ghost dancers had some reason to think that they could continue dancing without facing a serious government crackdown. Nonetheless, they could hardly be certain of this. Ghost dancers knew well that U.S. officials thus far had used only the least violent of their weapons of repression. Agents had tried verbal persuasion, issued orders, sent the police, and cut off rations. But they had not yet instructed the police to use force. Nor had they called on the army.

Even this level of repression exceeded the response of agents at most other reservations throughout the West. Near Wovoka's home, Nevada newspapers broadcast alarming and distorted accounts of the Ghost Dance, but U.S. officials countered these inflammatory reports. Agents on Nevada reservations generally let the Ghost Dance run its course. When pressured by Washington officials, they tried to convince Paiutes to give up the dance, but their tactics were relatively light-handed.[44] The response of officials in Oklahoma

---

[42] Perain Palmer to CIA, 11, 25, 29 Oct., 4, 6, 10 Nov. 1890, SC 188, roll 1 (qtns., 10 Nov., underlining in original).

[43] McLaughlin to CIA, 17 Oct. 1890. See also the account in James McLaughlin, *My Friend the Indian* (1910; Lincoln, 1989), 191.

[44] Sally S. Zanjani, "The Indian Massacre That Never Happened," *Nevada Historical Quarterly* 31 (Summer 1988): 119–29; William I. Plumb to CIA, 8 Nov., 6 Dec. 1890, 10 Jan. 1891, SC 188, roll 1; S. S. Sears to CIA, 17 Nov. 1890, SC 188, roll 1; John S. Mayhugh to CIA,

was similar. A typical reaction was the Anadarko agent's. He forbade the dance and "depriv[ed] the dancers of privileges whenever possible," but he "made no effort to use force in any way that would bring on a crisis."[45] Military officers in Oklahoma encouraged these policies. Ordered to investigate ghost dancing among the Kiowas, Arapahoes, and Caddoes, Lieutenant Hugh L. Scott concluded that the dances should be allowed to continue, because "this religious excitement can be utilized for the great benefit of the Indian." Through the Ghost Dance, Scott argued, Indians "have already received some of the essential elements of the [C]hristian religion." The dance, in fact, was "intended as worship of the white man's God." Should the dances be forcibly stopped, it would seem to the Indians "a violation of those rights common to every human being, viz: – the right to the pursuit of happiness, to personal liberty under the law and the right of each person without contravening the law to worship God according to the dictates of his own conscience." Scott's pluralism had limits; he was willing (at least publicly) to extend religious freedom only to Native spiritual practices that seemed to advance Christianity. Nonetheless, Scott's call for toleration departed sharply from the views of officials in the Dakotas and encouraged a far less repressive response in Oklahoma.[46]

In the north, however, the Lakota ghost dancers had reason to fear a possible escalation of repression. Consequently, they turned to the spiritual powers in the dance to seek protection from possible violence. As we have seen, the Ghost Dance was capable of providing new knowledge and practices. Visionaries could receive instructions and gifts from *Wakan Tanka Cinca*, other spiritual beings, and relatives living in the other world. Sometime in

24 Nov. 1890, SC 188, roll 1; C. C. Warner to CIA, 28 Nov. 1890, 6 Feb. 1891, SC 188, roll 1.

[45] Charles E. Adams to CIA, 4 Feb. 1891, SC 188, roll 2. See also Charles E. Adams to CIA, 5 Nov. 1890, 14 Jan. 1891, SC 188, roll 1; D. J. M. Wood to CIA, 21 Jan. 1891, SC 188, roll 1; Charles F. Ashley to CIA, 25 Nov. 1890, SC 188, roll 1; Anja Schaefers, "The Arapaho Ghost Dance: Religious Continuity and Change," M.A. thesis, University of Oklahoma, 1994, 54–61.

[46] Lieut. H. L. Scott to Post Adjt., Ft. Sill, 16 Dec. 1890, SC 188, roll 1. See also Maj. Wirt Davis to AAG DM, 23 Dec. 1890, SC 188, roll 1; Col. J. F. Wade to AAG DM, 26 Dec. 1890, enclosed in Brig. Gen. W. Merritt to AG, 21 Jan. 1891, SC 188, roll 2; Lieut. Col. C. H. Carlton to AAG DM, 11 Jan. 1891, enclosed in Meritt to AG, 21 Jan. 1891; Lieut. H. L. Scott to Post Adjt., Ft. Sill, 30 Jan. 1891, SC 188, roll 2; H. L. Scott, "Essay for the Fort Sill Lyceum, March 1892: Subject: The 'Messiah Dance' in the Indian Territory," Hugh L. Scott Papers, box 75, Library of Congress, Washington, D.C. Moderate policies were adopted at other agencies. For the Shoshone Agency (Wyoming), see E. R. Kellogg to AAG DP, 27 Oct. 1890, SC 188, roll 1; John Fisher to CIA, 3 Dec. 1890, SC 188, roll 1. For Fort Hall (Idaho), see S. G. Fisher to CIA, 26 Nov., 18, 23 Dec. 1890, SC 188, roll 1. For Fort Belknap (Montana), see A. O. Simons, 29 Nov. 1890, SC 188. For Uintah (Utah), see Robert Waugh to CIA, 2 Dec. 1890, SC 188, roll 1.

October (probably early in the month), some ghost dancers began to receive visions of dresses and shirts to be worn in the dance.[47] Lakotas initially referred to these articles of clothing as *cuwignaka wakan* (holy or powerful dresses) and *ogle wakan* (holy or powerful shirts). Soon, they came to be known as "ghost dresses" and "ghost shirts" (see Illustration 11).[48]

Ghost dresses and shirts had multiple purposes. One ghost dancer, Pretty Eagle, recalled a vision in which a person showed him a shirt with an eagle, stars, and a moon and instructed him to make two shirts and two dresses with these symbols. Upon regaining consciousness, Pretty Eagle related what he had seen and asked that two young men and two young women wear the new clothing. That evening Pretty Eagle painted two shirts and two dresses, just as he had seen. The following day the four dancers put on the clothing, lost consciousness, and had visions. Although Pretty Eagle did not explicitly state that the apparel's purpose was to facilitate visionary experiences, his narrative makes it clear that they "worked" in precisely that way. Black Elk's account confirms this logic. After participating in a few dances, Black Elk had a vision in which he was dressed in a ghost shirt. He then saw two men dressed the same way. They came and said to him, "It is not yet time to see your Father, but we shall present to you something [i.e., the shirts] that you will carry home to your people and with this they shall come forth to see their loved ones."[49]

Another purpose of the dresses and shirts – their most well-known property – was to make wearers invulnerable to weapons.[50] Protective clothing

---

[47] It is doubtful that ghost shirts were used prior to early October. Accounts of confrontations with ghost dancers in late August and mid-September dances indicate that men were painted but not wearing shirts. See Reynolds to CIA, 25 Sept. 1890; *ARCIA*, 1891, 411. Mrs. Z. A. Parker's account of a dance held sometime in October states that "they wore the ghost shirts or ghost dress for the first time that day." In this instance, instructions for making the dresses and shirts had come through a vision to a woman, whom Parker identifies as the wife of Return from Scout. See *ARCIA*, 1891, 530. At another dance center, ghost shirts were apparently introduced in a vision to Black Elk. See DeMallie, ed., *Sixth Grandfather*, 262.

[48] George Sword, "Wanagi Wacipi Toranpi Owicakiyakapi Kin Lee," manuscript 936, Smithsonian Institution, National Anthropological Archives, Washington, D.C., uses the term *cuwignaka wakan* for the dresses and *ogle wakan* and *ongloge wakan* for the shirts. This text also refers to *honska* (leggings) *wakan*; this disappeared in the translation in Sword, "Story of the Ghost Dance," 30.

[49] *LT&T*, 309–310; DeMallie, ed., *Sixth Grandfather*, 261.

[50] It is unclear when Lakota ghost dancers began to attribute invulnerability to the shirts and dresses. Elaine Goodale, an especially careful observer, states that "[a]fter troops had come it was asserted that the 'sacred shirts' were bullet-proof." See Graber, ed., *Sister to the Sioux*, 150. Nonetheless, Goodale wrote this account several years after the events, and was not in a position to know the day-to-day development of Ghost Dance practices. Black Elk did not mention invulnerability in relating his initial vision of the shirts, although he clearly understood his shirt to be "bullet-proof" by the time of Wounded Knee. See DeMallie, ed., *Sixth Grandfather*, 272. This suggests that some time elapsed before the dresses and shirts acquired invulnerability, although it is impossible to know for sure.

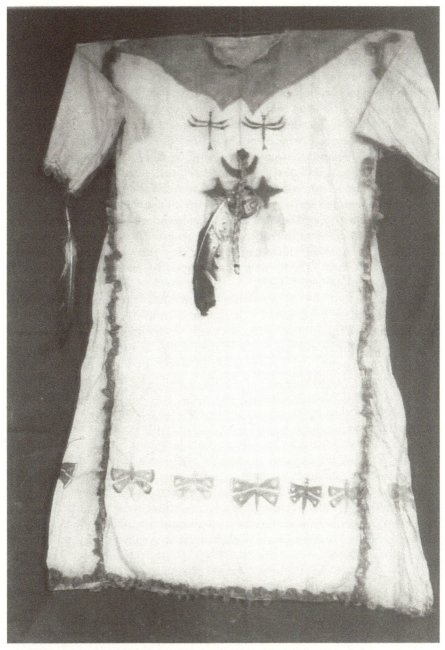

ILLUSTRATION 11. Ghost dress. Buechel Memorial Museum, St. Francis, S.Dak.

was another example of how the Lakota Ghost Dance, in response to particular historical conditions, developed practices that were innovative yet
resonated with past ways of doing things. For decades, if not centuries, the
Sioux had used a variety of techniques to obtain protection during warfare. To some extent, these methods depended upon the creation of devices
(shields) with physical properties that would prevent projectiles (arrows and
even bullets) from hitting the body. In the early 1830s, George Catlin witnessed a procedure he called "smoking the shield." A warrior applied coats
of glue to a piece of rawhide as it was heated. As the rawhide shrunk, it
absorbed the glue and eventually became thick and hard enough to make it
"arrow, and almost ball proof." In this case, the shield's efficacy depended
in part on material qualities (thickness/hardness). Importantly, though, the
shield also contained spiritual power. As the shield was being made, Catlin
explained, the warrior's "best friends . . . dance and sing around it, and solicit
the Great Spirit to instil into it the power to protect him harmless against
his enemies." Once the shield had cooled, the warrior painted it with his
"medicine or totem." Catlin mentioned eagles, owls, buffaloes, and other
animals as common emblems.[51]

Because rawhide shields, no matter how skillfully prepared, could not always repel bullets, some Sioux experimented with making metal shields.[52]
But most Indians continued to make shields from hides, as the effectiveness
of shields ultimately did not reside in their material characteristics. Shields
contained many spiritual powers, each of which operated in a somewhat
different way. High Bald Eagle, for example, painted a hawk in the center of
his shield so that when he charged an enemy he would (hawklike) not turn
away. On the other hand, one of the designs on Sitting Bull's shield was a
particular bird known for its ability to "dart rapidly up and down, here and
there, and [is] very hard to hit." Some shields contained lightning, an indication of the owner's capacity for sudden and overwhelming destruction.[53]
Over time, many Plains Sioux fighters stopped using shields at all and relied
on *wotawe* (charms or war medicines) they received directly through visions,
or from holy men and women. When Crazy Horse went to battle, he wore
an eagle-bone whistle, a feather in his hair, and a round stone held under
his left arm by a leather thong. Others gained invulnerability by rubbing

[51] George Catlin, *Letters and Notes on the Manners, Customs, and Condition of the North
American Indians*, 2 vols. (London, 1841), 1:241. See also accounts of making shields in
Royal B. Hassrick, *The Sioux: Life and Customs of a Warrior Society* (Norman, 1964),
231–33; Vestal, ed., *New Sources*, 152–56.

[52] There is a metal shield in the collections of the Buechel Memorial Lakota Museum, St.
Francis, S.Dak.

[53] John C. Ewers, *Plains Indian History and Culture: Essays on Continuity and Change* (Nor-
man, 1997), 52; Hassrick, *The Sioux*, 232; Vestal, ed., *New Sources*, 154 (qtn.); Clark
Wissler, *Some Protective Designs of the Dakota*, Anthropological Papers of the American
Museum of Natural History, vol. 1, pt. 2 (New York, 1907), 24.

the pulverized roots of certain plants over their bodies or wearing a sash of antelope hoofs across the chest.[54]

New methods for invulnerability were constantly being devised and tested. In the early 1870s a man named Long Holy announced that in a vision he had received power to make men bulletproof. Four young men volunteered to receive the power; Long Holy performed his vision for them. He dressed with a buffalo horn attached to each ear and painted his face with symbols from his vision, a moon on his forehead and a star at the bridge of his nose. He then performed his vision by stamping and making sounds "in imitation of the buffalo bull and the eagle." Long Holy showed the four young men how to paint themselves, told them to observe certain "taboos," and gave them a root to chew and rub on their bodies "to make them bullet-proof." Long Holy then tested the medicine by firing "point-blank" at one of the four young men, White Bull. The bullet almost knocked White Bull over, "but ricocheted off his bare body 'as if had hit a rock.'"[55] Although war medicines sometimes stopped bullets from entering the body, in other instances, they allowed someone whose body had been punctured to expel a projectile by coughing or retching, thus healing the wound.[56] War medicines could also prevent warriors from being hit at all. For example, a Cheyenne named Whirlwind wore a large war bonnet with a hawk. The feathers were shot off, but the hawk was not hit. "[B]alls went to the right and left, above and below me.... It was the Great Spirit and the hawk which protected me." High Dog, a Lakota, recalled that when warriors went to war they painted their horses and blew medicine on them: "Thus, bullets or arrows would perhaps not come near them."[57]

Lakota ghost dresses and shirts drew on these practices. Like shields and war charms in an earlier time, ghost dresses and shirts were containers (or

---

[54] Eleanor H. Hinman, ed., "Oglala Sources on the Life of Crazy Horse," *Nebraska History* 57 (Spring 1976): 13; Edward S. Curtis, *The North American Indian*, vol. 3 (Cambridge, Mass., 1908), 185; James R. Walker, *Lakota Belief and Ritual*, ed. Raymond J. DeMallie and Elaine A. Jahner (Lincoln, 1980), 274; High Dog, "Wotawe Koyakapi Na Tokel Econpi Kin He [Putting On War Charms and How They Work], *LT&T*, 173. Some "war medicine" carried "offensive" powers. See, for an example, Clark Wissler, *Societies and Ceremonial Associations in the Oglala Division of the Teton-Dakota*, Anthropological Papers of the American Museum of Natural History, vol. 11, pt. 1 (New York, 1912), 43.

[55] Stanley Vestal, *Warpath: The True Story of the Fighting Sioux Told in a Biography of Chief White Bull* (1934; Lincoln, 1984), 132–36. For a similar test, see Frances Densmore, *Teton Sioux Music and Culture* (1918; Lincoln, 1992), 175.

[56] Wilson D. Wallis, *The Canadian Dakota*, Anthropological Papers of the American Museum of Natural History, vol. 41, pt. 1 (New York, 1947), 83; Helen H. Blish, *A Pictographic History of the Oglala Sioux* (Lincoln, 1967), 39. See also Richard Lone Wolf, "Tatanka Kagapi Kin [Making Buffalo Medicine]," *LT&T*, 242–45, which describes an incident in which a man testing buffalo medicine was shot at and wounded and then expelled two bullets.

[57] W. P. Clark, *The Indian Sign Language* (1885; Lincoln, 1982), 248 (1st qtn.); "*Na hecel mazsu nains wahinkpe esa ikiyela hiyupi kte sni, heon econpi,*" *LT&T*, 173 (2d qtn.).

emblems) of power that could operate in various ways. At times, the apparel could function as a shield with both physical and spiritual properties that would stop projectiles. When Black Elk, who was living close enough to Wounded Knee to hear shots when they broke out, put on his ghost shirt and rode toward the massacre site, he quickly encountered firing. He felt the bullets hitting him with such force he almost fell off his horse, but because he was "bullet proof," he was uninjured.[58]

Sioux ghost dancers explained the workings of the ghost shirts in various ways. In an early reference to ghost dancers' claims of invulnerability in government sources, Agent McLaughlin reported that the dancers said that "the white man will be unable to make gunpowder in [the] future and all attempts at such will be a failure and that the gun powder now on hand will be useless as against Indians, as it will not throw a bullet with sufficient force to pass through the skin of an Indian."[59] With this statement in mind, there is more than one way to interpret a statement attributed to Little Wound that the "medicine-shirts" would cause "the bullets of any whites that desired to stop the Messiah Dance [to] fall to the ground without doing any one harm." Perhaps the dresses and shirts would stop bullets fired at normal speed. Or, following the logic in McLaughlin's report, the power within the shirts might counter the power behind the bullets, rendering the projectiles harmless. Certainly, for Little Wound, the spiritual power of the shirts operated beyond the physical boundaries of the garments themselves, for, as he went to say, "the person firing such shots would drop dead."[60]

Holy shirts and dresses also allowed potential targets to avoid being hit by bullets altogether. One common design on the clothing was a creature or series of creatures (dragonflies, butterflies, or small birds like swallows) painted on a background of small dots representing hail or bullets (*mazasu*, the word for bullets, means metal hail). Empirical observation indicated that hailstorms did not injure these insects and birds, evidently because hail did not strike them. The power specific to these creatures, then, would protect the wearers of ghost dresses and shirts. Another motif, the spider's web, suggests an additional logic. It was common knowledge among the Sioux that bullets and arrows did not destroy a spider's web but instead passed through it leaving only a hole. By this reasoning, bullets might pass through the dresses and shirts but not hit the wearer at all. Other animals represented on the dresses and shirts like turtles and lizards were powerful not so much

---

[58] DeMallie, ed., *Sixth Grandfather*, 273–74. Black Elk's account suggests that his ghost shirt protected him in other ways. Not long after being directly hit, he felt bullets passing through the ghost shirt, but this time, they grazed his body rather than actually hitting it. At the same time, Black Elk also depended on an element from his original vision, the "sacred bow," which made it so soldiers who were trying to run from him could not run fast as well as preventing bullets from hitting him.

[59] McLaughlin to CIA, 17 Oct. 1890.

[60] "Ghost-Dances in the West," 330–31.

because they could evade projectiles but simply because the Sioux observed that it was difficult to kill them.[61]

The dresses and shirts, then, could work in many ways, but their efficacy was not guaranteed under all circumstances. For a warrior's *wotawe* to be effective, it was necessary for him to observe certain taboos and, once in battle, to keep his mind focused on his power.[62] In the same way, the efficacy of the ghost dancers' apparel was contingent. Late in the fighting at Wounded Knee, Black Elk became afraid and doubted his power and a bullet pierced him near the belt. "My doubt and my fear killed my power and during that moment I was shot," he recalled.[63] Ghost shirts needed to be tested, as in Illustration 12, showing a ghost dancer riding through a "hail of bullets."

Many writers have seen the Lakotas' adoption of protective clothing as a sign of their distortion of Wovoka's pacific teachings, in the words of one, "into a militant crusade against the white man."[64] It is true that Wovoka did not make ghost shirts or instruct Indians to do so. He did, however, claim powers of invulnerability. Prior to Wounded Knee, Wovoka foresaw the possibility that the U.S. army might attack him. By one account, Wovoka said

---

[61] Wissler, *Protective Designs*, 31–40, 48–52. The importance of small birds' powers of evasion can also be seen in Densmore, *Teton Sioux Music*, 112–14, who reported that at Standing Rock sun dances, before the cutting of the sacred tree, the "intercessor" would speak of the attributes of the kingbeard, eagle, yellowhammer, and spider in war. The yellowhammer could not "overcome its enemies in open fight, but is expert in dodging them, darting from one side of the tree-trunk to another" (p. 113). Illustrations of ghost shirts, dresses, and other items from several tribes can be found in Harold Peterson, ed., *I Wear the Morning Star: An Exhibition of American Indian Ghost Dance Objects* (Minneapolis, 1976).

[62] See, for example, White Bull's account of a warrior who was shot through the neck "because he was wearing red aginst [*sic*] the orders of the med. man and the red was the string on his powder horn." Walter S. Campbell Collection, box 105, notebook 22, p. 87, Western History Collections, University of Oklahoma Library, Norman.

[63] DeMallie, ed., *Sixth Grandfather*, 277–78 (qtn., 278).

[64] Utley, *Last Days* 87 (qtn.). See also Mooney, *Ghost-Dance Religion*, 772, 789–91; George E. Hyde, *A Sioux Chronicle* (Norman, 1956), 258; Rex Alan Smith, *Moon of Popping Trees* (1975; Lincoln, 1981), 80–81; Powers, *Oglala Religion*, 121; Alice Beck Kehoe, *The Ghost Dance Religion: Ethnohistory and Revitalization* (New York, 1989), 13; Edward Lazarus, *Black Hills/White Justice: The Sioux Nation Versus the United States, 1775 to the Present* (New York, 1991), 114; Michael F. Steltenkamp, *Black Elk: Holy Man of the Oglala* (Norman, 1993), 72; Vander, *Shoshone Ghost Dance Religion*, 55; Robert W. Larson, *Red Cloud: Warrior-Statesman of the Lakota Sioux* (Norman, 1997), 266. For a treatment of the ghost shirts as defensive, see Richard E. Jensen, "Another Look at Wounded Knee," in *Eyewitness at Wounded Knee*, ed. Richard E. Jensen, R. Eli Paul, and John E. Carter (Lincoln, 1991), 7–10.

Mooney, *Ghost-Dance Religion*, 790, speculated that the source of Sioux ghost shirts was the "endowment robes" worn by Mormons in their temple ceremonies. Garold D. Barney, *Mormons, Indians and the Ghost Dance Religion of 1890* (Lanham, Md., 1986), 219, gives some credence to this theory; Lawrence G. Coates, "The Mormons and the Ghost Dance," *Dialogue: A Journal of Mormon Thought* 18 (Winter 1985): 98–103, 110, offers persuasive reasons to reject it.

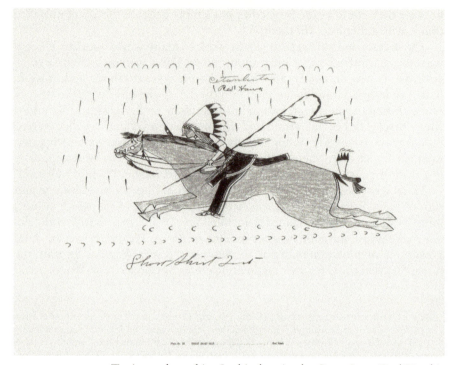

ILLUSTRATION 12. Testing a ghost shirt. In this drawing by Cetan Luta (Red Hawk), a ghost dancer tests a ghost shirt by riding through a hail of bullets. Milwaukee Public Museum.

that if soldiers "cut him all to pieces he would still live, and the soldiers would be killed."[65] Other evidence indicates that Wovoka demonstrated powers of invulnerability by having a relative shoot him with a gun at close range. The bullet fell harmlessly to the ground.[66] The idea of defensive invulnerability,

[65] Lieut. Nat. P. Phister to Capt. J. M. Lee, 7 Dec. 1890, enclosed in Capt. J. M. Lee to AG, 10 Dec. 1890, RG 94, Records of the Adjutant General's Office, Records of Divisions, Military Reservation Division, Early 1800s-1916, Reservation File, Ft. Bidwell, Calif., box 12, National Archives and Records Administration, Washington, D.C. Phister also reported that Wovoka could make his followers return to life if they were killed by soldiers, a point that he omitted in N. P. Phister, "The Indian Messiah," *American Anthropologist*, old ser., 4 (April 1891): 107.

[66] E. A. Dyer Sr., "Wizardry," unpublished manuscript, pp. 8–9, Nevada Historical Society, Reno (also in Michael Hittman, *Wovoka and the Ghost Dance*, expanded edition, ed. Don Lynch [Lincoln, 1997], 250–51). In December 1890, when army investigator Arthur Chapman asked Wovoka about this or a similar demonstration, Wovoka said "that was a joke." See A. I. Chapman to Brig. Gen. John Gibbon, 6 Dec. 1890, in *ARSW*, 1891, 193. Still, Wovoka was in the uncomfortable situation of being interrogated, and his claims to invulnerability were serious. As Willard Z. Park, "Paviotso Shamanism," *American Anthropologist*, new ser., 36 (January–March 1934): 109, notes, among Northern Paiutes invulnerability was often used as a demonstration of the strength of a shaman. Hittman, *Wovoka and the Ghost*

then, was not foreign to Wovoka's ways of thinking. Because, as I argued in the previous chapter, Wovoka knew that his prophesies of a cataclysmic event that would destroy or remove Americans threatened U.S. authority, he clearly anticipated the possibility of repression. As it turned out, the United States did not seriously threaten to use force against Wovoka (or, for that matter, against any tribe that adopted the Ghost Dance except the Lakota Sioux). Because of this, Wovoka never needed to decide if (and how) to implement his powers of invulnerability. We do not know what he would have done had the government used force against him, but it is certainly possible that he would have relied on spiritual power to protect himself and his followers.

Lakota ghost dancers took seriously Wovoka's injunctions to maintain peace in preapocalyptic time. Like ghost dancers everywhere, they would have preferred that the government leave them alone, thus allowing them to follow Wovoka's exhortations without having to think about defending themselves. As they faced an increasingly hostile environment, however, they faced difficult questions that did not have obvious answers. Should they abandon the dance altogether? If they continued, would it be permissible to use weapons to defend themselves if the Indian police or soldiers threatened to fire on them? Was it consistent with Wovoka's teachings to wear invulnerable clothing? As Lakota ghost dancers recalled what *Wakan Tanka Cinca* had told them in Nevada and in subsequent visions, and as they sought continued guidance from *Wakan Tanka*, they reached different conclusions about how to apply general principles to specific situations. Some ghost dancers may have rejected invulnerability as a departure from Wovoka's teachings. Descendants of Crow Dog maintain that he counseled his people that the "Paiute did not teach us this thing. These shirts cannot stop bullets no matter what is painted on them."[67] On the other hand, the dresses and shirts had been received in visionary experiences that occurred during dances that had so obviously manifested strong spiritual power. Most Lakota dancers concluded that the new clothing would allow them to continue dancing under conditions of escalating repression.

The Lakotas' decision to adopt invulnerable ghost dresses and shirts was, like most decisions, subject to debate, but it did not mark a radical departure from Wovoka's teachings. It did not signify a new level of hostility toward

Dance, 98, argues that Wovoka's claims to invulnerability indicate that he had no reason to modify his teachings after Wounded Knee. If he could make soldiers die, why would he fear them? It is conceivable that Wovoka managed an unwavering certainty that his powers of invulnerability would be effective under all foreseeable circumstances, but it is more likely that he understood the efficacy of spiritual power to have an element of contingency. Willard Z. Park, *Shamanism in Western North America: A Study in Cultural Relationships* (Evanston, Ill., 1938), 32, notes that a shaman "is never secure at any time in the possession of his power."

[67] Leonard Crow Dog and Richard Erdoes, *Crow Dog: Four Generations of Sioux Medicine Men* (New York, 1995), 45.

European Americans beyond what was already present in Wovoka's original prophesies of their cataclysmic removal or destruction. Nor did it indicate a plan to use violence or go to war. In fact, the situation was exactly the opposite of what has often been claimed. It was not the Lakota ghost dancers who were becoming hostile or threatening to use force; it was the United States.

In October, when the ghost dancers received invulnerable dresses and shirts, they accurately foresaw the possibility that the United States would send soldiers to stop them from dancing. But they probably did not anticipate that the army's invasion of Sioux country would be so massive.[68] When the government authorized troops in mid-November, army officials did not merely send a few detachments from local posts. Instead, they summoned troops from Kansas, Montana, Wyoming, Texas, and as far away as New Mexico and California. It was the single largest military operation since the Civil War.[69] Why did the government decide to use troops to suppress the Lakota Ghost Dance, and why was the operation so massive? To understand Wounded Knee, it is essential to have good answers to these questions.

[68] After Wounded Knee, Buffalo Bill Cody, who had taken some of the Ghost Dance leaders on his show, wrote to Nelson Miles that "[t]he hostiles say...they looked for only a few soldiers at a time, and they would ship them by detail, but you brought more than they ever seen before, and it frightened them." W. F. Cody to Nelson A. Miles, 4 May 1891, Nelson A. Miles Family Papers, box 1, Library of Congress, Washington, D.C.

[69] Jerry Green, ed., *After Wounded Knee: Correspondence of Major and Surgeon John Vance Lauderdale while Serving with the Army Occupying the Pine Ridge Indian Reservation, 1890–1891* (East Lansing, 1996), 26, points out that the 1890 mobilization was the "largest consolidated force of the U.S. Army since the Civil War."

13

"The Most Serious Indian War of Our History"

The Army's Invasion

The man who would direct the army's campaign to suppress the Lakota Ghost Dance, General Nelson A. Miles, first heard of the Ghost Dance in September 1890, a few months after his promotion to major general. When we last encountered Miles, he was trying to win the credit for ending the "Great Sioux War" (Chapter 3). Since then, his ambition had not flagged. Throughout the 1880s, Miles waged war against rival officers, criticizing them in private and planting stories against them in the press. At the same time, he curried favor with potential allies and demanded their support. Miles tirelessly promoted himself and his accomplishments, especially his role in securing the highly publicized surrenders of Chief Joseph and Geronimo. Although some generals and politicians were put off by Miles's unseemly tactics, his sheer relentlessness ultimately prevailed. An important obstacle between Miles and his second star was removed when one of the army's major generals conveniently vacated his position. Fittingly, it was Miles's archrival, General George Crook, who died of a heart attack on March 21, 1890.[1]

As soon as Miles was promoted, he began lobbying for bigger and better things. Currently in charge of the Division of the Pacific, Miles desired to command the more prestigious Division of the Missouri. He secured this post on September 1.[2] On his way to his new headquarters in Chicago, Miles stopped at Fort Keogh, Montana, near the Tongue River Agency, home of the Northern Cheyennes. It was during this visit that he first heard of the Ghost Dance.

Under the leadership of Porcupine, ghost dancing had begun at Tongue River in early 1890 at a time when ration shortages had caused widespread

---

[1] For Miles's career in these years, see Peter R. DeMontravel, *A Hero to His Fighting Men: Nelson A. Miles, 1839–1925* (Kent, Ohio, 1998), 137–95; Robert Wooster, *Nelson A. Miles and the Twilight of the Frontier Army* (Lincoln, 1993), 96–174.

[2] DeMontravel, *Hero to His Fighting Men*, 196–98; Wooster, *Miles*, 174–75.

hunger. Some Cheyenne leaders at Tongue River knew Miles well. Many of them, including White Bull and Two Moons, had surrendered to Miles in 1877 and had enlisted as scouts. When the Cheyennes learned that Miles was coming to Fort Keogh, they went to tell him of their "distressed condition" and "suffering for want of food." If they did not inform Miles about the Ghost Dance, the post's officers surely did.[3]

Miles's first impression of the Ghost Dance was shaped by his reading of the situation at Tongue River. He saw the conditions that had given rise to the Ghost Dance there as a particularly glaring example of the general failures of a system of civilian management. Like many western army officers, Miles was an inveterate critic of the Indian Office. Even the best civilian agents, Miles believed, lacked real knowledge of Indians. Most were incompetent and many were corrupt. In the late 1870s Miles had led the chorus of army officers who advocated transferring responsibility for Indian affairs from the Interior Department to the War Department. In an essay written for the *North American Review* in 1879, Miles argued that the army was far better equipped to manage Indians, especially the "wild and nomadic tribes," than civilian officials. Under the War Department, Indians would be managed by "officials having a knowledge of the Indian country and the Indian character." The army was also in a better position to avoid corruption and provide supplies and annuities in an efficient and timely manner.[4] For Miles, then, it was no wonder that Tongue River had serious problems. Nor was it surprising that in their desperation the Cheyennes had embraced the promises of "the Messiah delusion."[5] Miles did not approve of the Ghost Dance, but a paternalistic attitude toward "his" Cheyennes led him to adopt a sympathetic perspective.

Miles gained further knowledge of the Ghost Dance when he visited Pine Ridge on October 27. On this occasion, as we saw in the previous chapter, Red Cloud argued that the Ghost Dance was consistent with Christianity and appealed to Miles to let the ghost dancers alone. Miles responded favorably to this plea for religious toleration. "I have no objection to the dancing,"

---

[3] *ARSW*, 1891, 132 (qtn.); Orlan J. Svingen, *The Northern Cheyenne Indian Reservation, 1877–1900* (Niwot, Colo., 1993), 78–86.

[4] Nelson A. Miles, "The Indian Problem," *North American Review* 128 (March 1879): 304–14 (qtns., 311, 310); see also N. A. Miles, "Our Indian Question," *Journal of the Military Service Institution of the United States* 2, no. 7 (1881): 278–92. Indian affairs were under the War Department until 1849 when they were transferred to the newly created Interior Department. After the Civil War, the War Department tried several times to regain control. For discussions of the transfer issue, see Loring Benson Priest, *Uncle Sam's Stepchildren: The Reformation of United States Indian Policy, 1865–1887* (New Brunswick, 1942), 15–27; Donald J. D'Elia, "The Argument over Civilian or Military Control, 1865–1880," *Historian* 24 (February 1962): 207–25; Francis Paul Prucha, *The Great Father: The United States Government and the American Indians*, 2 vols. (Lincoln, 1984), 1:549–60.

[5] I infer Miles's attitudes from his later analysis of the reasons behind "Indian disaffection" in *ARSW*, 1891, 133–41 (qtn., 140).

Miles said. "I know there is nothing in it, and as Red Cloud said, it will in time disappear as the snow before the heat of the sun." If, however, the dancers' "frenzy and fanaticism" went too far, Miles warned, there might be "trouble." Miles exhorted Red Cloud and Little Wound to "control your people, and restrain them from any acts of violence."[6]

While at Pine Ridge, Miles consulted with the new agent, Daniel F. Royer, who had assumed charge a few weeks before. It is doubtful that Miles found Royer particularly impressive. A small-town businessman and some-time physician, Royer owed his appointment solely to his ability "to control votes in a county convention." As Valentine McGillycuddy self-servingly but not unjustly remarked, no one with any sense would appoint Royer to "superintend six men building a wood shed let alone handling six thousand Indians."[7] For Miles, Royer would have been a perfect example of all that was wrong with a civilian system.

Since taking over, Royer had been unable to stop ghost dancing. For months, as we saw in the previous chapter, the dancers had defied the authority of his predecessor, Hugh Gallagher. At first, as Royer reported on October 12, he resolved to "act very cautiously" and tried to "bring every influence to bear upon the chiefs to get them to pull out of [the Ghost Dance]." Already, however, he was contemplating asking for troops. "[I]f persuasive measures fail," he wrote, it would be necessary to "force them to obey by using the military." By late October, Royer believed the dance was "growing steadily each day and at this time over half or nearly two thirds of the Indians on this reserve are strong supporters of it." This overestimate revealed Royer's characteristic tendency to overreact.[8]

In reporting on his conversation with Miles, Royer noted that "the General is of the opinion that it [the Ghost Dance] will in the course of time die-out." Reading between the lines, it is easy to imagine Miles trying to calm the rattled new agent. Most likely, he pointed out that that even if the ghost dancers seemed out of control, winter was just around the corner. If Royer kept his head, the dances would soon stop. But Royer spurned Miles's voice of experience, insisting that "the only remedy for this matter is the use of [the] military."[9]

[6] "Conversation between General Miles and Sioux Indian Chiefs 'Red Cloud' and 'Little Wound' at Pine Ridge Agency, S.D., October 27th, 1890, Regarding 'Ghost Dance,'" in Nelson A. Miles Papers, box 4, folder D, U.S. Army Military History Institute, Carlisle Barracks, Pa.

[7] Valentine McGillycuddy to Herbert Welsh, 4 Dec. 1890, Indian Rights Association Papers, Historical Society of Pennsylvania, Philadelphia, microfilm (hereafter, IRA Papers), roll 6.

[8] D. F. Royer to CIA, 12 Oct. 1890, in *Letter from the Secretary of the Interior, Transmitting ... a Communication from the Commissioner of Indian Affairs ...*, 51st Cong., 2d sess., 1890–91, S. Ex. Doc. 9, serial 2818, 5 (1st qtn.); Acting CIA to SI, 24 Oct. 1890, OSI, file 16910–1890; D. F. Royer to Acting CIA, 30 Oct. 1890, SC 188, roll 1 (2d qtn.).

[9] Royer to Acting CIA, 30 Oct. 1890.

By this time, officials in Washington were concerned about what they described as "the unsettled condition of the Sioux."[10] Not only was Royer
calling for troops, Rosebud's temporary agent E. B. Reynolds had earlier
suggested that it would take either "the military" or "cold weather" to stop
the dancing. The Indian Office was receiving disturbing reports from other
agencies. On October 17 Standing Rock Agent James McLaughlin penned a
lengthy diatribe against Sitting Bull, the "high priest and leading apostle of
this latest Indian absurdity," excoriating him as "devoid of a single manly
principle," a "coward," a "polygamist," a "libertine," a "habitual liar," an
"active obstructionist," and the "most vain, pompous, and untruthful Indian
that I ever knew." Despite McLaughlin's near-pathological rage, however, he
did not "apprehend any immediate uprising or serious outcome" from the
Ghost Dance, nor did he call for troops. Instead, he recommended having
Sitting Bull and other recalcitrant leaders arrested sometime before spring.[11]
Cheyenne River Agent Perain Palmer favored a similar course of action, calling on October 29 for the arrest or removal of Hump and other Ghost Dance
leaders.[12]

By late October, then, Washington officials had received several conflicting assessments and recommendations. On October 30 Interior Secretary
John Noble forwarded the agents' reports to President Benjamin Harrison.
The next day, Harrison instructed Secretary of War Redfield Proctor to order
an investigation into "[t]his delusion as to the coming of an Indian Messiah
and the return of the dead Indian warriors for a crusade upon the whites."[13]
Whether Harrison himself wrote this description of the Ghost Dance or it
was drafted for him by someone else, it offers a revealing window on Washington officials' assumptions about Indians. These officials, it appears, were

[10] This phrase was used in AAG to AG, and AAG to Commanding Gen. DM, both dated 31
Oct. 1890, RCWK, roll 1.

[11] E. B. Reynolds to CIA, 25 Sept. 1890, SC 188, roll 1; James McLaughlin to CIA, 17 Oct.
1890, MP, roll 21. McLaughlin attributed Sitting Bull's "worsening" state to the presence
of Catherine Weldon, a member of the National Indian Defence Association. Weldon had
come to Standing Rock in June 1889 to help the Sioux defeat the Crook Commission and
returned again in spring 1890. Since then, McLaughlin wrote, Sitting Bull "has been a frequent visitor to her house and has grown more insolent and worthless with every visit he
has made there." Weldon's relationship with Sitting Bull became the subject of much gos-
sip among non-Indians. Newspapers, predictably, dubbed her "Sitting Bull's White Squaw."
Since then, historians have been unable to refrain from indulging in speculations of a "criminal" connection between the two. See Stanley Vestal, *Sitting Bull: Champion of the Sioux*
(1932; Norman, 1957), 264–68; Robert M. Utley, *The Lance and the Shield: The Life and
Times of Sitting Bull* (New York, 1993), 282–83. For an extended treatment of Weldon,
see Eileen Pollack, *Woman Walking Ahead: In Search of Catherine Weldon and Sitting Bull*
(Albuquerque, 2002).

[12] Perain P. Palmer to CIA, 29 Oct. 1890, SC 188, roll 1.

[13] Benjamin Harrison to SW, 31 Oct. 1890, Benjamin Harrison Papers, Library of Congress,
Washington, D.C., microfilm, roll 29.

dimly aware of the Ghost Dance's prophesies of the return to life of dead ancestors and the destruction of non-Indians. In describing dead warriors returning to fight a war against the whites, however, the author of this document seriously distorted the teachings of the Ghost Dance. Had U.S. officials taken this image more seriously, they might have concluded that the Ghost Dance posed little threat, because the dancers would not embark on their "crusade" until the "dead Indian warriors" returned. But this distortion did not emerge from a dispassionate attempt to evaluate the Ghost Dance. Instead, it revealed a deeply ingrained way of responding to Native American resistance. A movement like the Ghost Dance was not simply a challenge to U.S. authority; it was a potential threat to American lives.

The War Department assigned the task of investigating the Sioux Ghost Dance to Brigadier General Thomas H. Ruger, commander of the Department of Dakota. Ruger did not file his first report until November 13, a full two weeks after the investigation was ordered. At that time, Ruger had visited only one agency, Standing Rock, where he offered the bland observation that "the messiah craze affects families embracing some two hundred males, chiefly Sitting Bull's followers." Ruger also gave an assessment of the overall situation in the Dakotas. Consistent with the views Miles had earlier expressed at Pine Ridge, Ruger did not "think there is any probability of an outbreak at present, nor during the winter.... [T]he craze may subside before spring."[14]

Ruger's report suggested that the best course of action would be to let the Ghost Dance run its course. However, on the same day Ruger filed his report, but before it reached Washington, President Harrison ordered the War Department to dispatch a "body of troops sufficiently large to be impressive" to the western Sioux agencies. Troops were necessary for two reasons. First, at three of the agencies – Pine Ridge, Rosebud, and Cheyenne River – the "authority and power of the Agents and of the Indian police have been violently defied and set at nought." Second, "adequate and early steps [must be] taken to prevent any outbreak that may put in peril the lives and homes of the settlers in the adjacent states."[15]

It was true that the ghost dancers had defied the agents' authority, especially at Pine Ridge where Agent Royer continued to demand that the cavalry ride to the rescue. In his most recent report, dated November 13, Royer had related that a day or two before he had ordered the agency police to arrest a man named Little for "killing cattle promiscuously." The "offender drew a butcher knife on the police and in less than two minutes he was reinforced by two hundred ghost dancers all armed and ready to fight." By this time,

[14] Ruger's November 13 report was summarized in Maj. Gen. Nelson A. Miles to Maj. Gen. John M. Schofield, 14 Nov. 1890, RCWK, roll 1. Ruger made similar observations, reported in AAG to Maj. Gen. Nelson A. Miles, 16 Nov. 1890, RCWK, roll 1.

[15] Benjamin Harrison to SW, 13 Nov. 1890, RCWK, roll 1.

Royer was close to panicking and requested permission to travel to Washington to explain the situation and try to persuade the government to send troops. (A trip back East would also put some distance between himself and butcher knives.)[16]

Was there any evidence, however, to support the second rationale for military action, that an "outbreak" was likely? Interestingly, Royer, the most insistent voice for military intervention, did not advance the theory that the ghost dancers were a threat beyond Pine Ridge. Even in his hysterical and oft-quoted telegram of November 15 – "Indians are dancing in the snow & are wild & crazy" – Royer never expressed concerns about the lives of settlers.[17] On the other hand, Agent Reynolds at Rosebud contended that there were two "unmistakable indications" of an "imminent outbreak." First, Reynolds claimed that the ghost dancers had advanced the date of the "coming of the millenium [sic]" to December 11. Even if true, however, this proved nothing. In fact, officials could have regarded this new date as a fortuitous development that argued against military action. When the target date passed and nothing happened, they could have reasoned, the ghost dancers would lose faith. Reynolds's second "unmistakable sign" was that the ghost dancers were trading "horses and everything else" for arms and ammunition.[18] Yet these actions were not preparations for an "outbreak." The ghost dancers needed arms and ammunition to defend themselves in the event the United States used force against them and, because the Indian Office had cut off their rations, to kill game and cattle. Nor was there evidence that an outbreak might originate from Cheyenne River or Standing Rock. Since his anti–Sitting Bull tirade of October 17, McLaughlin had said nothing about the Ghost Dance. Perain Palmer, the Cheyenne River agent, suggested on November 6 that "it might be advisable to have a small detachment of

---

[16] D. F. Royer to CIA, 11 (1st qtn.), 13 (2d qtn.) Nov. 1890, SC 188, roll 1. D. F. Royer to CIA, 2 Dec. 1890, SC 188, roll 1, identifies the arrested man as Little. Charles A. Eastman (Ohiyesa), *From the Deep Woods to Civilization: Chapters in the Autobiography of an Indian* (1916; Lincoln, 1977), 92–96; Kay Graber, ed., *Sister to the Sioux: The Memoirs of Elaine Goodale Eastman, 1885–91* (Lincoln, 1978), 146–47, give accounts of this incident and credit American Horse with defusing the conflict. James Mooney, *The Ghost-Dance Religion and the Sioux Outbreak of 1890*, Fourteenth Annual Report of the Bureau of Ethnology, 1892–93, pt. 2 (Washington, D.C., 1896), 848, reports that Lakotas called Royer "Lakota Kokipa-Koshkala, 'Young-man-afraid-of-Indians.'"

[17] D. F. Royer to CIA, 15 Nov. 1890, SC 188, roll 1.

[18] E. B. Reynolds to CIA, 2 Nov. 1890, SC 188, roll 1. Reynolds did not give any source for his information about the December 11 date. Two detailed reports of the Rosebud Ghost Dance by Captain C. A. Earnest failed to mention anything about a new date. See Capt. C. A. Earnest to Bvt. Lieut. Col. M. V. Sheridan, 12 Nov. 1890, enclosed in Brig. Gen. John R. Brooke to AAG DM, 15 Nov. 1890, RCWK, roll 1; Capt. C. A. Earnest to AAG DP, 19 Nov. 1890, enclosed in Brig. Gen. John R. Brooke to AAG DM, 2 Mar. 1891, RCWK, roll 2.

troops sent here," but Palmer's goal was to restore order, not to prevent an outbreak.[19]

In fact, the agents' reports contained little evidence that the ghost dancers were planning an outbreak, thus suggesting that the decision to send troops involved something other than an objective response to external facts. Indeed, it is revealing of the weakness of the government's initial case to note that official justifications of military action in the weeks and months to come relied less on the agents' reports than on evidence that surfaced *after* the decision to send troops had been made.

One piece of evidence that became especially crucial, eventually assuming the status of a smoking gun, was a speech that Short Bull reportedly gave at Red Leaf's camp on October 31. According to the *Chicago Tribune*, which published this "sermon" on November 22, it was contained in a telegram dated three days earlier to General Miles from an unnamed officer at the Rosebud Agency. As reported in the *Tribune*, Short Bull told the ghost dancers, "I will soon start the thing in running order. I have told you that this [the new world] would come to pass in two seasons, but since the whites are interfering so much, I will advance the time from what my Father above told me. The time will be shorter." Should the soldiers surround his followers, Short Bull instructed:

three of you, upon whom I have put holy shirts will sing a song which I have taught you, and some of them will drop dead; then the rest will start to run, but their horses will sink into the earth . . . and you can do what you desire with them. Now, you must know this, kill all the soldiers, and that race will be dead; there will be only 5,000 of them left living on the earth.

Commenting on this speech in the *Tribune*, Miles observed that "[i]t will require the utmost care and prudence to prevent an outbreak, and then we may not succeed." Several months later, when Miles wrote his summary report of the campaign, he turned to this "public harangue" as the key piece of evidence in support of his argument for the necessity of military action. He called particular attention to Short Bull's announcement that "he would shorten the time for a general uprising."[20]

Relying on Miles, James Mooney's *The Ghost-Dance Religion* uses Short Bull's "sermon" to support his view, discussed in Chapter 11, that the Sioux ghost dancers gave Wovoka's pacific teachings a "hostile meaning." Later

[19] James McLaughlin, *My Friend the Indian* (1910; Lincoln, 1989), 201, states that during this time, "I was convinced that a military demonstration would precipitate a collision and bloodshed." For reports from Cheyenne River, see Perain Palmer to CIA, 4, 6 (qtn.), 10 Nov. 1890, SC 188, roll 1.

[20] *Chicago Tribune*, 22 Nov. 1890, p. 2. Similar versions also appeared in the *Chadron Democrat*, 27 Nov. 1890; "The Red Christ," *The Illustrated American* 5 (13 December 1890): 12–13. For Miles's report, see *ARSW*, 1891, 142–43 (qtn., 142).

in his study, as Mooney narrates the events leading up to the government's decision to send troops against the Sioux, he returns to Short Bull's decision to "advance the time for the great change and make it nearer," treating it as a genuinely alarming development implicitly requiring military action. Following Miles and Mooney, Robert Utley prominently features Short Bull's speech to support his conclusion that troops were necessary.[21]

There are good reasons to suspect that "Short Bull's sermon" was a fabrication. Although many scholars have cited this speech, none of them have provided a reference to the original telegram or to another extant source. This raises doubts that such a document ever existed. The archival record of original reports from officials in the field during these months is remarkably complete. Because correspondence was routinely copied and forwarded to multiple parties within the Interior and War departments, it is highly doubtful that no copy would have survived, even if the original had been lost.[22] Moreover, this account has Short Bull saying things that fly in the face of everything we know about the Ghost Dance. Most remarkable is Short Bull's instruction that men and women "take off all their clothing" as "[n]o one shall be ashamed of exposing their persons." Besides the fact that there is no corroboration in the sources for Lakota ghost dancers dancing without clothing, such a thing would have been so culturally foreign to Lakotas as to have been next to impossible even under the most liberal reading of the

---

[21] Mooney, *Ghost-Dance Religion*, 787–89, 849–50 (qtns., 787, 849); Robert M. Utley, *The Last Days of the Sioux Nation* (New Haven, 1963), 105–06. Although Utley describes Short Bull's speech as "militant" but only "defensive," he argues that "the distinction between offense and defense was fine" and that many of Short Bull's followers increasingly "talked of a holy war against the white man" (p. 106). To support this point, Utley refers to army reports, which he fails to identify, that "emissaries from Sitting Bull had urged tribes as far north as Canada to unite in the spring at Bear Butte...to drive the whites from the country" (pp. 106–07). The only source for this information, however, appears to be Miles's unsubstantiated assertions in Maj. Gen. Nelson A. Miles to AG, 28 Nov. 1890, RCWK, roll 1; *ARSW*, 1891, 143. Utley also cites the report of an incident, noted later, in which ghost dancers supposedly told a rancher named "Scotty" Philip that they were planning horrific acts of violence. Yet this incident occurred a few days after the government decided to send troops. Mostly likely, it was a product of the wild rumors that were sweeping the region at that time.

Not all writers who take a position in favor of Sioux heterodoxy (see Chapter 11, note 49) endorse the need for military action, but the two positions are linked in much of the literature.

[22] Mooney was apparently unaware that the first accounts of the speech attributed it to a November 19, 1890 telegram; in *Ghost-Dance Religion*, 1109, he states that he obtained it from George Bartlett, who, at the time, was a deputy U.S. marshall for the Pine Ridge reservation (see *Black Hills Weekly Times*, 15 Nov. 1890). Utley, *Last Days*, 106, n. 31, attributes the speech to Capt. C. A. Earnest, but without giving a source. Earnest was at Rosebud and one of his reports was dated November 19 (see Earnest to AAG DP, 19 Nov. 1890), but neither this nor an earlier report (Earnest to Sheridan, 12 Nov. 1890) said anything about a speech along these lines.

Ghost Dance's capacity for innovation. But even if Short Bull's sermon is authentic, all it shows is a change in the timing of the cataclysm. It provides no support for the idea that the ghost dancers were planning any action themselves.[23]

If officials had no real evidence of an outbreak when they ordered military action, another possible reason for their decision to send troops would be that they were under pressure from settlers living near the western Sioux reservations. Indeed, several historians have argued that settlers were deeply alarmed by the Sioux Ghost Dance and demanded military protection.[24] The evidence to support this theory is extremely thin. On November 6 Cheyenne River Agent Palmer wrote that "the settlers are somewhat alarmed at the action of the Indians," but his proof was hardly compelling. It consisted of a petition, dated September 26, signed by ten men, that did not even mention the Ghost Dance. Instead, the petitioners requested "military protection

[23] Scholars' uncritical use of Short Bull's speech is one example of a tendency to accept without question evidence the army offered to justify military action. Another is a report by William T. Selwyn to Col. E. W. Foster, 25 Nov. 1890, SC 188, roll 1, discussed in Mooney, *Ghost-Dance Religion*, 799–801; Utley, *Last Days*, 73–74. Selwyn, a mixed-blood Sioux, predicted a "general Indian war" on the basis that the ghost dancers had told him the previous spring, when he was postmaster at Pine Ridge, that "the father" had given them orders to "cause trouble on the whites" but they were to be "kept secret." It is odd, however, that Selwyn would have waited until after the military had intervened to provide this information and that the conspirators would have so easily revealed their plans to him. According to Selwyn, one of the conspirators was Red Cloud, yet we know from Miles's October conversation with Red Cloud that Red Cloud was not a firm adherent of the Ghost Dance (see Chapter 12). Red Cloud might have concealed his true position from Miles, but if so, that simply underscores the unlikelihood that he would have confided in Selwyn. In another report, in which Selwyn interviewed Kuwapi (They Chased After Him), a ghost dancer from Rosebud, he was clearly fishing for evidence of an "outbreak" and asked Kuwapi a series of leading questions. See William T. Selwyn to Col. E. W. Foster, 22 Nov. 1890, SC 188, roll 1.

[24] Utley, *Last Days*, 110, for example, writes that by late October "cries of anguish rang in the White House and had to be heeded." See also George E. Hyde, *A Sioux Chronicle* (Norman, 1956), 259; James C. Olson, *Red Cloud and the Sioux Problem* (Lincoln, 1965), 326; Rex Alan Smith, *Moon of Popping Trees* (1975; Lincoln, 1981), 94–96, 110–13; Edward Lazarus, *Black Hills/White Justice: The Sioux Nation Versus the United States, 1775 to the Present* (New York, 1991), 114; Utley, *Lance and the Shield*, 287; Wooster, *Miles*, 178; Robert W. Larson, *Red Cloud: Warrior-Statesman of the Lakota Sioux* (Norman, 1997), 266–67. Some historians have emphasized that the press stirred up rumors of an uprising and that these, independent of settlers' actual fears, played an important role in the government's decision to send troops. See Elmo Scott Watson, "The Last Indian War, 1890–91 – A Study of Newspaper Jingoism," *Journalism Quarterly* 20 (September 1943): 205–19; Christina Klein, "'Everything of Interest in the Late Pine Ridge War Are Held by Us for Sale': Popular Culture and Wounded Knee," *Western Historical Quarterly* 25 (Spring 1994): 51. Criticisms of the press are valid after the decision to send troops, but before that time, the press was fairly restrained and had little effect on officials' decisions. For a defense of the press after military intervention, see George A. Kolbenschlag, *A Whirlwind Passes: News Correspondents and the Sioux Indian Disturbances of 1890–1891* (Vermillion, S.Dak., 1990).

during the trouble on the opening [of the] Reservation."²⁵ Other than that, there is no mention in any government correspondence that settlers were worried. If they were, an army officer at one of the region's posts or one of the civilian agents would certainly have commented on it.

An examination of local newspapers shows no evidence of settler alarm. For example, the *Democrat*, a paper published in Chadron, Nebraska, under fifty miles from Pine Ridge Agency, was in an excellent position to detect settlers' perspectives. Before November 15, when the public became aware that the government was sending troops, the only item in the *Democrat* suggesting any fear of an Indian uprising was in its September 18 issue under the headline "An Indian Outbreak." This story's dateline was Boise City, Idaho, and it contained rumors about Nez Percé "warriors in war paint." A week later, under the headline "Pine Ridge Agency," the *Democrat* reported routine events at the agency (photographers from Rushville, Nebraska, had arrived) and added that "[t]he new dance among the Indians is said to be worth going many miles to see." This was probably a reference to the Ghost Dance, but it hardly indicates concern. Nor did newspapers in Rapid City, Deadwood, or Bismarck reveal the slightest fear of the Ghost Dance.²⁶

Correspondence received by two governors, John M. Thayer of Nebraska and Arthur C. Mellette of South Dakota, confirms that settlers were not worried about the Ghost Dance before the decision to send troops became public knowledge. In September, October, and early November, at a time when these officials were supposedly being inundated with demands for protection from "hostile Indians," they received not a single documented request. Settlers' overriding concerns, as expressed in their letters, were hot winds, the lack of rain, and withering crops.²⁷ As we will see, settlers did become alarmed about the Ghost Dance, but only *after* they learned that the government was sending the army to protect them.

In the absence of clear evidence of an impending outbreak and without a public demand for action, why did officials in Washington decide on a military solution? Unfortunately, we do not have sources that would enable a

²⁵ Palmer to CIA, 6 Nov. 1890 (petition enclosed). Philip Wells, an interpreter at the time, later stated that during summer 1890 settlers near Pine Ridge were "seized with alarm" several times and that he and Agent Gallagher had gone out to reassure them, but there is no corroboration of this in Gallagher's correspondence. See Philip Wells interview, 1906, RT, tablet 5, roll 2.

²⁶ *Chadron Democrat*, 18, 25 Sept., 1890; Jeffrey Ostler, "Conquest and the State: Why the United States Employed Massive Military Force to Suppress the Lakota Ghost Dance," *Pacific Historical Review* 65 (May 1996): 220–23.

²⁷ The earliest letters documenting settlers' fears in these papers are George H. Bowring to Gov. John M. Thayer, 20 Nov. 1890, box 6, Governor John M. Thayer Papers, Nebraska State Historical Society, Lincoln; A. H. Burns to Gov. A. C. Mellette, 22 Nov. 1890, box 8, Arthur C. Mellette Papers, South Dakota State Historical Society, Pierre.

full reconstruction of decision makers' thinking, but one plausible answer is that their primary concern was the ghost dancers' defiance of the agents' authority. They felt troops were necessary to restore order and cited threats to settlers to gain public support. On the other hand, America's leaders had always been prone to exaggerate threats from Indians. Harrison's description of the Ghost Dance as involving the return of "dead Indian warriors for a crusade upon the whites" (see earlier) reveals this tendency, as does a biography of Harrison written for his 1888 presidential campaign. To establish Harrison's credentials, this biography reminded Americans of his family's tradition of political leadership, most notably, his grandfather, William Henry Harrison, the ninth president of the United States. In the early 1800s, while governor of Indiana Territory, the elder Harrison had faced the movement led by Tenskwatawa and Tecumseh (see Chapter 11). The younger Harrison's campaign biography sought to convert his grandfather's victory over Tecumseh into political capital:

In 1806 these children of the forest dreamed of a universal confederation for all the tribes for the redemption of the Western world from the usurpations of the pale-faces, and to that end set a great conspiracy on foot. They had promises of support from the Father beyond the Great Lake. Eventually Tecumseh challenged the young governor at Vincennes to the conflict. There were at the time scalps of white women and children flying on a string at his wigwam door. The defiance was accepted. Harrison took the field in person. On the morning of November 7, 1811, he fought and won the Battle of Tippecanoe.[28]

Benjamin Harrison did not record his thoughts about the Ghost Dance, and it is unclear that he did anything more in the matter than routinely endorse decisions made by other officials. However, he might well have recalled stories of white scalps hanging from Tecumseh's door and concluded that just as Tecumseh threatened settlers' lives, so did the Sioux ghost dancers. In any case, a written and oral historiography of previous Indian treachery circulated widely in American culture and probably had some influence on him and other decision makers.[29]

Highly charged images of the Sioux in particular might also have affected Washington officials. In 1890 most Americans instantly associated the Sioux

---

[28] Lew Wallace, *Life of Gen. Ben Harrison* (Philadelphia, 1888), 28. Reginald Horsman, *Expansion and American Indian Policy, 1783–1812* (East Lansing, 1967), 169; John Sugden, *Tecumseh: A Life* (New York, 1998), 260, note that William Henry Harrison inflated the significance of the Battle of Tippecanoe and that his prediction that it would end Indian militancy was far off the mark.

[29] Unfortunately, Benjamin Harrison's biographers have said little about their subject's views about Indians in general let alone the Sioux, the Ghost Dance, or his role in these events. See Harry J. Sievers, *Benjamin Harrison: Hoosier President: The White House and after* (Indianapolis, 1968); Homer E. Socolofsky and Allan B. Spetter, *The Presidency of Benjamin Harrison* (Lawrence, 1987).

with Custer, dead for fourteen years. By this time, "Custer's Last Stand," a myth that began the day America tried to absorb the unfathomable news of the Seventh Cavalry's demise, had sunk deep roots in the national imagination. At the center of the Last Stand's iconography were images of demonic, frenzied savages surrounding and killing the heroic general and then ripping out his heart.[30] To some extent, these images existed safely in the past, to be experienced as entertainment through spectacles like Buffalo Bill Cody's Wild West Show. Yet faced with reports of Sioux ghost dancers defying the agents, decision makers may have recalled that many of Custer's killers remained alive and able to commit unspeakable crimes.

Whatever the reasons behind the November 13 decision to authorize military action, it is safe to say that officials acted rashly in choosing the course they did. Military operations are risky and costly, and alternatives are almost always available. Instead of sanctioning an open-ended military operation, officials could have ordered troops already in the region to back up agents as they arrested a few key leaders. Another approach would have been to send a small number of troops to Pine Ridge but not the other agencies. (Acting Commissioner of Indian Affairs R. V. Belt recommended this course on November 13.) Alternatively, officials might have replaced the obviously incompetent Royer.[31] Because there was no real evidence that the ghost dancers threatened settlers' lives, the decision to send troops arguably violated Article 1 of the 1868 Treaty, which states that the "Government of the United States desires peace, and its honor is hereby pledged to keep it."[32]

The decision to send troops to suppress the Lakota ghost dancers was an important one, as it set in motion the chain of events that led to Wounded Knee. When President Harrison learned of the massacre, he expressed

---

[30] For the creation of the Last Stand myth, see Robert M. Utley, *Custer and the Great Controversy: The Origin and Development of a Legend* (Los Angeles, 1962); Brian W. Dippie, *Custer's Last Stand: The Anatomy of an American Myth* (Missoula, 1976); Richard Slotkin, *The Fatal Environment: The Myth of the Frontier in the Age of Industrialization, 1800–1890* (Middletown, Conn., 1985), 502–11; Paul Andrew Hutton, "From Little Bighorn to Little Big Man: The Changing Image of a Western Hero in Popular Culture," in *The Custer Reader*, ed. Paul Andrew Hutton (Lincoln, 1992), 395–423; Shirley A. Leckie, *Elizabeth Bacon Custer and the Making of a Myth* (Norman, 1993).

[31] Acting CIA to SI, 13 Nov. 1890, RCWK, roll 1. Acting SI to President Benjamin Harrison, 13 Nov. 1890 (two letters), RCWK, roll 1, also focused solely on the situation at Pine Ridge. In pointing out these alternatives, my intention is not to endorse their legitimacy, only to note that even from a colonial perspective, there were other possibilities.

[32] Charles J. Kappler, ed., *Indian Affairs: Laws and Treaties*, 5 vols. (Washington, D.C., 1904–1941), 2:998. I am grateful to Steve Newcomb for alerting me to the argument that the army's invasion violated the treaty. One could argue that the ghost dancers violated Article 1's corresponding clause that "[t]he Indians desire peace, and they now pledge their honor to maintain it," but to do so would require adopting a position that the Sioux had no right to protest oppressive reservation conditions, a position that would imply that U.S. domination over the Sioux was legitimate.

disappointment to Miles for his "failure...to secure the settlement of the Sioux difficulties without bloodshed."[33] There is no reason to doubt Harrison's preference for a bloodless campaign. In ordering the military to subdue the ghost dancers, he and other officials hoped the threat of violence would be sufficient. Nonetheless, if officials truly believed their own statements that the Sioux were about to go to war, they must have realized that sending troops would be likely to provoke a clash. Even if talk of an outbreak was simply an expedient to build popular support, officials still had reason to anticipate that the threat of force might easily result in violence.

Within days after Washington ordered military action, army units from throughout the western United States began to converge on Sioux country. The first soldiers came from nearby posts. Troops from Fort Robinson, Nebraska, and Fort Omaha, Nebraska, arrived at Pine Ridge on November 20. On the same day, troops from Fort Niobrara, Nebraska, completed their march to Rosebud. Over the next few weeks, cavalry and infantry from places like Fort Riley and Fort Leavenworth (Kansas), Fort Logan (Colorado), Fort Wingate (New Mexico), and several posts in California took up positions on or near the Pine Ridge, Rosebud, Cheyenne River, and Standing Rock reservations. By the end of the first week of December, the U.S. Army had marshaled between six and seven thousand soldiers, about one-third of its total fighting strength, to subdue between four and five thousand ghost dancers, the majority of whom were women and children. The army's strategy was to use this huge display of force to intimidate the ghost dancers into surrendering.[34]

This approach was not the only possible one for the military. Instead of surrounding the western Sioux reservations with massive force, the army could have deployed a much smaller concentration of troops at two or three of the agencies.[35] This might not have avoided a massacre, but the army's decision to take the approach that it did shaped the course of events in crucial ways and contributed to the environment in which Wounded Knee took

[33] Harrison's words were conveyed in Maj. Gen. J. M. Schofield to Maj. Gen. Nelson A. Miles, 2 Jan. 1891, RCWK, roll 1.

[34] To follow troops movements and estimate numbers, I have used information in *ARSW*, 1890, 69–83; *ARSW*, 1891, 177–88. My estimates of troop numbers are corroborated in the *Chicago Tribune*, 8 Dec. 1890, p. 5, which reported between eight and nine thousand soldiers in the field, a figure that, unlike mine, included a little more than two thousand Indian scouts. A good overview of troop mobilization is R. Eli Paul, "'Your Country is Surrounded,'" in *Eyewitness at Wounded Knee*, ed. Richard E. Jensen, R. Eli Paul, and John E. Carter (Lincoln, 1991), 25–31. For the number of ghost dancers, see Chapter 12, note 32.

[35] In response to a revolt led by Sword Bearer, a disaffected young Crow, in 1887, which the government exaggerated as a "general outbreak" involving tribes in eastern Montana and western Dakota, the size of the military force was significantly smaller than that used against the Sioux three years later. See Frederick E. Hoxie, *Parading through History: The Making of the Crow Nation in America, 1805–1935* (Cambridge, 1995), 154–61 (qtn., 158).

place. Therefore, it is critical to understand why the government pursued the strategy it did to suppress the Lakota Ghost Dance.

The person most responsible for this decision was General Miles. Miles did not act alone. He had the support of higher army officers, the War Department, and the president. As commander of the Division of the Missouri, however, Miles formulated, implemented, and justified the army's strategy.[36] In late October, as we have seen, Miles had not been terribly concerned about the Ghost Dance. On November 14, when he received orders to deploy troops, Miles remained unalarmed. Miles responded to these orders by relaying to higher officials Ruger's conclusion that there was little possibility of an "outbreak" and promising to report his "own observations and recommendations" within the week. Miles did not say what he would advise, but the tone of his remarks suggests that he was not yet envisioning the enormous troop mobilization that would soon take place.[37]

Within the next few days, however, Miles's statements about the Ghost Dance began to undergo a dramatic shift. This first sign of this change appeared in a report of November 17 in which Miles contended that his forces were woefully outnumbered. The Division of the Missouri (encompassing Minnesota, the Dakotas, Montana, Wyoming, Nebraska, Kansas, and Utah), Miles wrote, contained a mere 1,400 cavalry troops. By contrast, there were "thirty thousand disaffected Indians, numbering six thousand warriors" in the same region. Accordingly, Miles requested higher officials to authorize troops outside his division "to prevent if possible another Indian war."[38]

After this request was granted, Miles wrote a lengthy report, dated November 28, that elaborated his sketchy reference to an "Indian war." This carefully crafted document began with a strong indictment of civilian management of western Indian tribes. After being "subjugated at different times by the U.S. Army," these tribes had been "turned over to the charge of civil agents, who are frequently changed, and often inexperienced." Under these conditions, western tribes remained capable of going to war against the United States. Although Indians had been "forced to adopt the ways of the whites," they still longed for the "pleasures, romance and freedom of their former Indian life." Knowing that they are a "doomed race," they "recount their woes and misfortunes, and their hatred of the white race becomes intensified." They pray that "their God may send them some super-natural power to destroy their enemies." Following this reference to the Ghost Dance, Miles

---

[36] For the discretion given Miles see, for example, SW to Maj. Gen. Nelson A. Miles, 1 Dec. 1890, RCWK, roll 1.

[37] Orders issued by Maj. Gen. J. M. Schofield, 14 Nov. 1890, RCWK, roll 1; Maj. Gen. Nelson A. Miles to Maj. Gen. J. M. Schofield, 14 Nov. 1890, RCWK, roll 1.

[38] Maj. Gen. Nelson A. Miles to AAG, 17 Nov. 1890, RCWK, roll 1. Miles later observed that "we have plenty of infantry," but "you cannot catch mounted Indians with white foot soldiers." *Chicago Tribune*, 3 Dec. 1890, p. 2.

observed that the original teaching of the movement had been "one of peace," but "false prophets" had convinced their followers that "<u>deeds</u> were necessary to show their faith, please the Messiah and hasten his coming." One of the "principal incendiaries" was Sitting Bull. He had sent emissaries to many tribes, "advising them to obtain arms and ammunition and be prepared to meet the warriors near the Black Hills in the spring." Western Indians were well-armed and had access to ample material resources. The common theory that the "construction of the railways, disappearance of the buffalo, and the scattered settlements over the western country has terminated Indian wars," Miles argued, was a "dangerous delusion." Indians "can now live better upon domestic stock than they could formerly upon the buffalo, and the many horse ranchers scattered over the great western country would furnish them re-mounts in almost every valley." In short, Miles concluded, "<u>There never has been a time when the Indians were as well armed and equipped for war as the present.</u>"[39]

Miles quickly made these arguments public. In a widely publicized newspaper interview of December 2, he contended that "[t]he seriousness of the situation...has not been exaggerated. The disaffection is more widespread than it has been at any time for years. The conspiracy...is a more comprehensive plot than anything ever inspired by the prophet Tecumseh, or even Pontiac."[40] As before, Miles blamed the Indian Office: "The Indian agents have persistently cheated the Indians out of their just dues – have robbed them of their rations until, in sheer desperation and goaded on by starvation, they have taken their present stand."[41] Miles had always linked the Ghost Dance to Indian Office mismanagement. What was new was his assessment of the Ghost Dance's potential for danger. Instead of a movement that would fade away like the melting snow, he now claimed that it portended a pantribal uprising of unprecedented proportions.

Why did Miles change his mind? One possible answer is that new evidence, reliable or otherwise, came to light. If so, however, Miles did not use it to offer any proof of a "comprehensive plot." Nor, months later, when Miles again asserted in his final report that "the most serious Indian war of our history was imminent" and that "[t]he states of Nebraska, the two Dakotas, Montana, Wyoming, Colorado, Idaho, and Nevada, and the Territory of Utah, were liable to be overrun by a hungry, wild, mad horde of savages," could he muster anything more than Short Bull's sermon, discussed earlier.[42] A much better answer results from thinking through the opportunities

---

[39] Miles to AG, 28 Nov. 1890 (underlining in original).

[40] *Chicago Tribune*, 3 Dec. 1890, p. 2. This interview originally appeared in the *Washington Evening Star*, 2 Dec. 1890. See also *New York Times*, 3 Dec. 1890, p. 2.

[41] *Chicago Tribune*, 6 Dec. 1890, p. 4.

[42] ARSW, 1891, 142–44 (qtn. 144). Historians have often reproduced Agent Royer's ravings, especially the highly quotable, "Indians are dancing in the snow & are wild & crazy" (see

Miles saw in the rapidly changing situation of mid-November. From this perspective, we can see the calculations behind his apparent hysteria.

The army was not simply a machine that responded to Washington's orders as to the touch of a switch. Both the army as an institution and the individuals within it had interests of their own. Bureaucracies have institutional imperatives, however internally incoherent and contested they may be. Members of bureaucracies desire to promote specific agendas and their own careers. Miles's most recent biographer concludes that "[a]mbition and the pursuit of power came to dominate his life."[43] It should not be surprising to learn that such a man saw the government's authorization of military action as an opportunity to advance his interests and those of the army as he understood them.

What, then, did Miles hope to gain through orchestrating a military campaign aimed at destroying what he defined as a serious uprising of several tribes throughout an extensive region? At the most obvious level, Miles's assertions of grave danger magnified the importance of his mission. Far better to prevent the most serious Indian uprising in the nation's history than subdue a handful of ghost dancers wielding butcher knifes against a terrified ex-physician turned Indian agent. Beyond this, Miles had a more specific goal in mind. He intended to use the Ghost Dance to demonstrate the continued importance of a strong military presence in the western United States.

After the end of the "Indian wars" the western army faced a difficult situation. In the 1880s military theorists began to argue that the army needed to make the transition from a western, Indian-fighting army to a more modern force. Proponents of a new, more professional army sought expanded opportunities in areas like preparation for foreign war and building seacoast fortifications.[44] Western army officers responded to these changes by arguing

note 16, this chapter), but they have given little attention to Miles's alarmist statements. Miles's 1891 report (p. 141) is also noteworthy for its veiled suggestion that the Mormons were behind the Ghost Dance. "[D]riven to desperation," Miles wrote, Indians

> were willing to entertain the pretensions or superstitions of deluded, fanatical people living on the western slope of the Rocky Mountains, whose emissaries first secretly appeared among the Indians prior to 1889.... They first aroused the curiosity of the Indians by some secret method scarcely realized by the savages themselves and persuaded delegations from the different tribes of Indians to leave their reservations in November, 1889.

43 Wooster, *Miles*, 269.

44 August V. Kautz, "Our National Military System," *Century* 36 (October 1888): 935; Stephen E. Ambrose, *Upton and the Army* (Baton Rouge, 1964), 106–07; Russell Weigley, *Towards an American Army: Military Thought from Washington to Marshall* (New York, 1962), 140–41; Stephen Skowronek, *Building a New American State: The Expansion of National Administrative Capacities, 1877–1920* (Cambridge, 1982), 111; Jerry M. Cooper, "The Army's Search for a Mission, 1865–1890," in *Against All Enemies: Interpretations of American Military History from Colonial Times to the Present*, ed. Kenneth J. Hagan and William R. Roberts (Westport, Conn., 1986), 182–83.

for the continued necessity of a military presence in the West. In 1887, for example, General Ruger warned of the inadvisability of reducing the number of western troops, since the threat of Indian hostility would remain for years. Furthermore, because more settlers were living near reservations than ever before, any outbreak would be far bloodier. Similarly, General Miles observed in 1889 that Indians would "have to be under military surveillance" for a long time to come. To meet this need, he urged that the western army be updated. In contrast to the traditional western army, in which troops were stationed at numerous small outposts, troops would be concentrated in larger, more comfortable garrisons. Should trouble break out on an Indian reservation, commanders could rapidly dispatch troops along the nation's new railway system and extinguish the flames of unrest before they spread. In this way, an updated western army would continue to have a vital role in the country's future.[45]

Given these views, it is easy to understand why Miles saw the government's authorization of military action as an excellent opportunity to demonstrate the capacity of a modernizing western army to respond to Indian unrest. The nation would be amazed at the speed and efficiency with which troops from several states could respond to the threat of a vast conspiracy and crush it before it had a chance to mature. A successful campaign would prove the western army's continued relevance and give it a strong claim to national resources in the future.

In late November 1890 Miles began to float the idea that the army be given permanent control over Indian affairs.[46] At first he suggested that the military assume "absolute general control" over only two reservations – Pine Ridge and Rosebud. Quickly, though, he expanded his recommendation to include the four western Sioux and Northern Cheyenne reservations.[47] Miles went even further in an article he drafted in early December for the *North American Review*. In this essay, Miles repeated his previous warnings about the most "serious and general uprising" in the "whole history of Indian warfare." To this he added lurid fantasies of Indians "prompted by some wild, savage religious frenzy" who might easily "ravage a country and brain the innocent prattling babe with fiendish delight."[48] Miles also elaborated

---

[45] *ARSW*, 1887, 137–38; *ARSW*, 1889, 172. For an overview of military operations on or near western Indian reservations in the 1880s, see Henry George Waltmann, "The Interior Department, War Department, and Indian Policy, 1865–1887," Ph.D. diss., University of Nebraska, 1962, 336–60.

[46] Although most army officials dropped the transfer issue after 1879, there were occasional calls for transfer in the 1880s. See, e.g., George B. McClellan, "The Militia and the Army," *Harper's New Monthly Magazine* 72 (January 1886): 294–303. On the transfer issue generally, see note 4, this chapter.

[47] SI to SW, 25 Nov. 1890, RCWK, roll 1 (qtn.); Miles to AG, 28 Nov. 1890.

[48] Nelson A. Miles, "The Future of the Indian Question," *North American Review* 152 (January 1891): 1–10 (qtns., 2, 10). Miles drafted this article in early December, as he referred to it

on his theories about the Indian Office's responsibility for the current unrest. Between 1877 and 1881, when the Sioux were under military control, they made progress. Since then, however, their condition had deteriorated. The Indian Office had failed to provide the Sioux with sufficient food, while at the same time allowing them to acquire arms and assume a "threatening attitude." For these reasons, Miles concluded, Indians who are "still a terror to the peace and good order of certain States and territories should be placed under some government just and strong enough to control them."[49]

Many military and civilian observers were critical of Miles's campaign against the ghost dancers. Some suggested that the general, infected by the "Presidential bee," was exaggerating the threat of an Indian war so that he could campaign for the White House as a war hero in 1892.[50] Miles undoubtedly contemplated the prospect of a Pennsylvania Avenue address. Yet, saving the nation from the largest Indian uprising in its history could have other salutary consequences. If it catapulted him to the presidency, so much the better, but Major General of the Army would also be a worthwhile reward.

The army's mobilization against the Sioux ghost dancers had several repercussions. One was that it caused settlers throughout the region to panic. For months, ranchers and farmers had paid little more than passing attention to the Ghost Dance, but like a sudden blizzard, dark rumors descended upon the northern Plains. Near Mandan, North Dakota, settlers reported that Indians "draw mysterious circles around their heads, indicating that there will be scalping done." From northern Nebraska came the news that "Indians are on the war path and pursuing their usual burning and slaughtering tactics."[51] James "Scotty" Philip, a rancher on the Bad River, claimed that twelve ghost dancers had recently accosted him. They were "surly and defiant in manner." One of them recalled the days "when he used to beat out the brains of children and drink women[']s blood" and said that "the time was coming when they will do it again."[52] In this climate, imaginations

in a letter to Herbert Welsh, 10 Dec. 1890, IRA Papers, roll 6. At the latest, this article appeared in print in early January as the *Chicago Tribune*, 3 Jan. 1891, p. 4, commented on it.

[49] Miles, "Future of the Indian Question," 5, 10.

[50] *New York Times*, 6 Dec. 1890, p. 1; C. C. Painter to Herbert Welsh, 28 Nov. 1890, IRA Papers, roll 6; "General Merritt's Opinion," *Army and Navy Journal* 28 (20 December 1890): 279 (qtn.). For a discussion of these charges, see Wooster, *Miles*, 181–82; Peter R. DeMontravel, "General Nelson A. Miles and the Wounded Knee Controversy," *Arizona and the West* 28 (Spring 1986): 25–26.

[51] R. M. Tuttle to Benjamin Harrison, 18 Nov. 1890, SC 188, roll 1 (1st qtn.); *Rapid City Journal*, 20 Nov. 1890 (2d qtn.).

[52] This incident supposedly occurred on November 18. A. C. Mellette to Maj. Gen. Nelson A. Miles, 26 Nov. 1890, enclosed in Maj. Gen. Nelson A. Miles to AG, 26 Nov. 1890, RCWK, roll 1.

ran wild. A young boy near Hot Springs, South Dakota, was certain he saw a war bonnet peeking above a ridge near his family's homestead and rode to town to summon the Hot Springs Home Guard to the rescue. When the guard arrived, they discovered the war bonnet to be a yucca plant.[53]

Frightened settlers fled to the relative safety of nearby towns, where they sought comfort in numbers and the hope of securing weapons. On November 19 the *Bismarck Daily Tribune* reported that in nearby Mandan "[p]eople who never before carried firearms are going around loaded down – veritable traveling batteries." Many settlers demanded that the government provide arms. The cashier of a bank in Stuart, Nebraska, well over one hundred miles from the nearest ghost dancer, wrote Governor Thayer: "We have no means of protecting ourselves and our farmers cannot stand the expense of buying arms. We therefore respectfully ask that you send us one hundred good rifles and one hundred rounds of ammunition to each rifle."[54]

Even towns did not seem safe. On November 18 rumors broke out at Mandan "that 200 Indians in war paint, well armed and mounted, were charging down upon the ill-fated little city." As it turned out, however, the greatest danger to Mandan's citizens was from among their own number. Prior to a mass meeting held to organize a defense of the city, a "thoroughly alarmed" man named Wilcox purchased a "huge revolver and put it in his pocket." As he squeezed his way into the crowd, Wilcox's "revolver fell to the floor and exploded, the ball taking effect in the body of Fred Clark." Clark was paralyzed from the waist down and observers feared his injury would prove fatal.[55]

Not all settlers lost their heads. In Rapid City a "Citizen's meeting" was called for November 23, but only thirty people turned up. According to the *Daily Journal*, the meeting failed because those with "experience in such affairs" opposed it. Among them was the city's mayor who thought that "calling for arms or organization of a company . . . would simply cause a panic and do no good." For its own part, the *Journal*, like many other newspapers in the region, sought at times to minimize the danger. Already, years of drought and declining prices for corn and wheat had driven many farmers from the northern Plains. Many editors feared that wild talk of an Indian uprising would further damage the region's fragile economy. Yet cold economic calculation could easily give way to the racist hysteria that gripped settlers and generals alike. For weeks the *Rapid City Daily Journal* cautioned readers against sensationalist accounts, but on December 20 the paper suddenly erupted with the prediction that "an uprising of the whole Indian race in the United States" was imminent. The

[53] Philip S. Hall, *To Have This Land: The Nature of Indian/White Relations, South Dakota, 1888–1891* (Vermillion, S.Dak., 1991), 63.
[54] *Bismarck Daily Tribune*, 19 Nov. 1890; Bowring to Thayer, 20 Nov. 1890.
[55] *Bismarck Daily Tribune*, 19 Nov. 1890.

evidence: "The Indians themselves say this is going to be the last great fight in history."[56]

Some newspapers openly encouraged genocide. On November 27, for example, the *Black Hills Daily Times* approvingly summarized a resolution passed by the newly formed Deadwood Rifle Club:

[T]he Indians must be killed as fast as they made an appearance and before they could do any damage. It was better to kill an innocent Indian occasionally than to take chances on his goodness, and to exterminate them it was necessary to employ first class killers, regardless of expense.[57]

Settlers did not launch a campaign of extermination, but their demands for action increased pressure on the army to take decisive action. If the lives of thousands (or, tens of thousands) were at risk, it was imperative for the army to subdue the "hostiles" without delay. Settlers would not sleep again until the last band of ghost dancers had been exterminated, taken away in chains, or at least disarmed. Contrary to what many historians have written, it was at this point – *after* military intervention – that settlers had some impact on the course of events.

The coming of troops also heightened the anxieties of missionaries and government employees living at the western Sioux agencies. Prior to mid-November the main concern of these "advance agents of civilization" was the Ghost Dance's threat to the progress of their work. On October 19, for example, Father Emil Perrig, a missionary at Holy Rosary Mission, noted in his diary: "Not one Indian attended Mass. They are dancing again." A month later, when the soldiers arrived at Pine Ridge, Perrig wrote that the "Day Schools on the reservation are closed and the teachers have been called to the Agency together with all other whitemen in the Government[']s employ. At the Agency everybody is said to get his weapons in order for defence." Over the next few days, non-Indians at Pine Ridge were buffeted by rumors of ghost dancers on the path to war. When these rumors failed to materialize, however, most concluded that the ghost dancers posed no direct threat to the agency. On November 23 Perrig observed that the "Indian troubles have been fearfully exaggerated" and asked, "Who is responsible for this costly and unwarranted scare?"[58]

Although most non-Indians at Pine Ridge and the other agencies quickly abandoned the kind of fantasies that would continue to torment settlers for weeks to come, they remained nervous about other, more realistic scenarios.

---

[56] *Rapid City Daily Journal*, 25 Nov., 20 Dec. 1890. For examples of press attempts to counter alarming rumors, see *Chadron Democrat*, 20, 27 Nov. 1890.

[57] *Black Hills Daily Times*, 27 Nov. 1890.

[58] Emil Perrig diary, 19 Oct., 20, 23 Nov. 1890, St. Francis Mission Records, series 7, box 5, Marquette University Special Collections, Milwaukee.

On November 20 William Keith, a day school teacher at Pine Ridge, wrote to a local newspaper that he was "much surprised" to see the troops arriving. Only a few nights before he had seen the Indians dancing "and they didn't seem to be excited or act any different from their usual manner." Now, though, the coming of the soldiers might "get them excited" and "precipitate a conflict." Louisa Riggs, a Congregationalist missionary at Oahe (Cheyenne River), voiced similar concerns. She assured her mother that she did "not anticipate any trouble here," but, "if measures are taken to stop the dancing by force, it may cause trouble. Left to itself the craze will probably dance itself out."[59]

Other experienced observers, like former Pine Ridge Agent Valentine McGillycuddy, also feared the consequences of military intervention. After his ouster in 1886, McGillycuddy had moved to Rapid City where he devoted his undiminished energies to various business enterprises. He became president of the Lakota Banking and Investment Company and vice president of the Black Hills National Bank. Banking alone "did not satisfy him," however, so he founded a "hydroelectric and power company." Besides meeting his need for "outdoor life," working with electricity allowed him to experience new forms of resistance. In handling the dynamos, his wife later wrote, McGillycuddy frequently "encountered an unexpected short circuit which sent him flying against the wall in an unconscious heap."[60]

McGillycuddy regarded military intervention as a serious mistake. In late November, when the ex-agent arrived at his former agency bearing the title of Assistant Adjutant General for the State of South Dakota, he promptly told Brigadier General John R. Brooke, commander of the Department of the Platte:

Were I still agent here ... I should let the dance continue. The coming of the troops has frightened the Indians. Winter is here – a time when they do not go on the warpath if it is possible to avoid it. If the Seventh-Day Adventists prepare their ascension robes for the second coming of the Saviour, the United States Army is not put in motion to prevent them. Why should not the Indians have the same privilege? If the troops remain, trouble is sure to come.[61]

[59] *Black Hills Daily Times*, 22 Nov. 1890; Louisa L. Riggs to Margaret Irvine, 28 Nov. 1890, South Dakota Conference United Church of Christ Archives, Oahe Mission Collection, box 12, Center for Western Studies, Augustana College, Sioux Falls, S.Dak. (underlining in original). For similar assessments, see Elaine Goodale to CIA, 18 Dec. 1890, SC 188, roll 1; Thomas L. Riggs to Alfred Riggs, 13 Dec. 1890, Oahe Mission Collection, box 4; America Evans Collins to an unnamed daughter, 9 Dec. 1890, in Ethel C. Jacobsen, "Life in an Indian Village," *North Dakota History* 26 (Spring 1959): 60; Thomas Stewart to Herbert Welsh, 25 Nov. 1890, IRA Papers, roll 6.

[60] Julia B. McGillycuddy, *Blood on the Moon: Valentine McGillycuddy and the Sioux* (1941; Lincoln, 1990), 255–56.

[61] Ibid., 261–62.

If McGillycuddy was afraid for the Sioux, however, he had the luxury of being on the safe side of the guns. Sioux people, whether ghost dancers or not, experienced the army's invasion of their country from a much different position. They feared for their own lives, the lives of their relatives, and the future of their communities.

Even before the soldiers arrived, nonghost dancers were worried about the potentially catastrophic impact of a military operation. On November 11, the day Little drew a knife on the Pine Ridge Indian police and armed ghost dancers backed him up (see earlier), American Horse appealed to the ghost dancers to think of the consequences of killing Indian policemen. "Your country is surrounded with a network of railroads; thousands of white soldiers will be here within three days," he warned.[62] Nine days later, when Oglalas saw clouds of dust in the distance and realized it was the cavalry, nonghost dancers fled to the agency. As Charles Eastman, a Santee Sioux who was agency physician, later explained, they feared that the "dreaded soldiers might attack their villages by mistake." Eastman assured them that "the troops were here only to preserve order, but their suspicions were not easily allayed."[63]

There were other disturbing possibilities. Only fourteen years earlier, troops had confiscated weapons and ponies from noncombatants at Cheyenne River and Red Cloud agencies. This could easily happen again. One Oglala, Turning Hawk, later testified that many Lakotas at Pine Ridge and Rosebud were convinced that "the soldiers had come there to disarm the Indians entirely and to take away all their horses." Indeed, once Pine Ridge Agent Royer got the troops he had been so loudly demanding, he began instructing higher officials how to use them. He wanted them to disarm all the Oglalas, ghost dancers and nonghost dancers alike.[64] Unlike Royer, General Brooke proceeded on the assumption that it would be easiest to subdue the ghost dancers by exploiting divisions between them and the nonghost dancers. Therefore, he did not antagonize nonghost dancers by taking their guns and horses. Instead, Brooke listened to nonghost dancers' grievances about rations and assured them that he "came as a friend, not as an enemy." Many Lakota leaders reciprocated these sentiments. On December 10 Red Cloud wrote that "I am the constant friend of the whites.... [T]he soldiers are here and treat us all very well; we have no fault to find with them." This,

---

[62] Eastman, *From the Deep Woods*, 94. Although Royer to CIA, 30 Oct. 1890, reported that American Horse, Sword, and Young Man Afraid of His Horses supported military intervention, with the possible exception of Sword, it is hard to believe that any support these leaders voiced for a military operation was not highly qualified.

[63] Eastman, *From the Deep Woods*, 101. See also J. George Wright to CIA, 5 Dec. 1890, SC 188, roll 1, who reported that Brulés were "asking for my assistance to protect them from the troops."

[64] *ARCIA*, 1891, 179 (qtn.); D. F. Royer to CIA, 27, 28 Nov. 1890, SC 188, roll 1. See also C. S. Cook to Herbert Welsh, 11 Dec. 1890, IRA Papers, roll 6.

however, did not reveal a great love for the men in blue, nor approval of their presence. Red Cloud's expression of friendship was a means of self-defense in a tense and volatile situation.[65]

The ghost dancers had the most to fear. Two Strike later related that when a "white man employed at a trader's store" brought news that "soldiers were coming to stop the dance," it "scared us." The men in Two Strike's band "put our women and children into wagons and got on our ponies and left our homes." Around the same time, rumors reached Short Bull that soldiers "were coming to arrest me and if I was not given up they would fire on us all."[66] Many ghost dancers were angry about military intervention. Little Wound confronted a day school teacher and "indignantly demanded of him why soldiers were coming." Torn Belly protested that "he did not know what the troops were on the reservation for." "We don't want to fight," he explained, "but this is our church. It's just the same as the white man's church except that we don't pass around the hat."[67]

Some ghost dancers immediately sought refuge at the agencies.[68] Others stayed away from the agencies and prepared to defend themselves should the troops attack. At Short Bull's camp, an old man "rode around our circle and stopped in the middle saying to us, 'My boys, save your Powder, Guns, Bows Arrows and Ammunition for the Agency is full of Soldiers.'" This man, like many ghost dancers, was angry at Lakotas who were not on his side. "[O]ur own people have caused the soldiers to come here by telling lies," he said, and named American Horse, Charging Thunder, Fast Thunder, Spotted Horse, and Good Back. The coming of the troops, then, aggravated tensions between ghost dancers and nonghost dancers and created new tensions as ghost dance communities divided. As Elaine Goodale recalled, "[m]any families were broken up, and feeling was intense."[69]

Some ghost dancers raided the possessions nonghost dancers left behind when they went to the agencies. They confiscated and destroyed household and farm items, appropriated horses and cattle, and may have burned a few houses. To some extent, these acts expressed bitterness that had been building for years under the reservation system. Like Luddites of another time, ghost dancers who destroyed hay rakes or mowing machines vented their rage at

[65] Brooke to AAG DM, 2 Mar. 1891 (1st qtn.); T. A. Bland, ed., *A Brief History of the Late Military Invasion of the Home of the Sioux* (Washington, D.C., 1891), 20 (2d qtn.).

[66] Bland, ed., *Brief History*, 8 (1st qtn.); Short Bull, "As Narrated by Short Bull," p. 11, Buffalo Bill Memorial Museum, Golden, Colo. (2d qtn.). See also John M. Carignan to James McLaughlin, 27 Nov. 1890, in Stanley Vestal, ed., *New Sources of Indian History, 1850–1891* (Norman, 1934), 9–10; statement by Dewey Beard, 12 Mar. 1917, in Wounded Knee 1890 Collection, folder 6, SC 11, Oglala Lakota College Archives, Kyle, S.Dak.

[67] Graber, ed., *Sister to the Sioux*, 150 (1st qtn.); *Chicago Tribune*, 22 Nov. 1890, p. 1 (2d qtn.)

[68] Short Bull, "As Narrated by Short Bull," 10, states that as soon as troops arrived "many of my people were moving toward Pine Ridge Agency."

[69] Ibid., 11–12; Graber, ed., *Sister to the Sioux*, 151.

a new order that was crushing an older way of life. Practical considerations also encouraged these raids. Ghost dancers could make use of clothing, blankets, rope, and saddles, not to mention flour, potatoes, coffee, wheat, and dried corn. By far the most important thing they obtained was cattle, not only from the abandoned homes of nonghost dancers but also from agency herds. Ghost dancers butchered some cattle on the spot but kept most of the animals alive for the days to come.[70] By causing nonghost dancers to seek refuge at the agencies, military intervention had the unintended consequence of redistributing resources to the ghost dancers. The transfer of cattle was especially important, because it increased the ghost dancers' capacity to hold out and may have prolonged the army's campaign.

In deploying such a large number of troops, the army intended to terrorize the ghost dancers into quickly surrendering. Some ghost dancers did come into the agencies right away. In the next chapter we see that others followed in late November and December. But many ghost dancers remained defiant. Some held out in remote villages, where it was difficult for troops to approach without being detected. Other ghost dancers sought refuge in the inaccessible terrain of the Badlands near Pine Ridge. Although the army was successful in creating widespread fear, this did not accomplish its desired result.

As the days and weeks wore on, army commanders found themselves in a difficult situation. Having promised the nation a lightning strike campaign, they were under mounting pressure to bring an expensive operation to a close. In mid-December it looked as though the remaining ghost dancers were about to surrender, but after an attempt to arrest Sitting Bull went awry, it suddenly seemed to the army that it was losing control. As officers grew frustrated at their inability to dictate the course of events, they became increasingly angry at the still-defiant dancers. By late December General Miles and his subordinates were more ready than ever to punish resistance.

---

[70] D. F. Royer and James A. Cooper to CIA, 30 Nov. 1890, SC 188, roll 1; D. F. Royer to CIA, 1, 4, 5 Dec. 1890, SC 188, roll 1; J. George Wright to CIA, 5 Dec. 1890, SC 188, roll 1; Herbert Welsh, "The Meaning of the Dakota Outbreak," *Scribner's Magazine* 9 (April 1891): 450–51; C. S. Cook to Herbert Welsh, 2 Dec. 1890, IRA Papers, roll 6; claims enclosed in report of James A. Cooper, 25 Feb. 1892, OIA, file 7805–1892. My analysis of the claims in Cooper's report indicates that most instances of burning houses or schools occurred after Wounded Knee.

14

"If He Fights, Destroy Him"
The Road to Wounded Knee

Army officers in charge of the campaign to subdue the Sioux ghost dancers would have been gratified if the initial mobilization of troops had caused all the ghost dancers immediately to surrender. As we saw in the previous chapter, however, by late November many ghost dancers had decided to remain in their villages or to seek refuge in remote areas. At this point, there were significant constraints on the army's capacity to use force. General Miles and his field commanders realized that troop movements against ghost dancers might easily provoke them to take flight. If the army did succeed in engaging the dancers the result might be very bloody. Officials in Washington had made clear their preference for a bloodless campaign, not only to avoid U.S. casualties but also to preserve the "humanitarian" image of U.S. Indian policy. Thus, the army was forced to rely, at least for a time, on diplomacy.

The army's earliest diplomatic initiative began around November 20, 1890, when General Miles learned that Buffalo Bill Cody had just returned from a European tour. Miles promptly summoned Cody to Chicago to ask him if he would pay a visit to Sitting Bull. As Cody later wrote, Miles "knew that I was an old friend of the chief, and he believed that if any one could induce the old fox to abandon his plans for a general war I could."[1] It is hard to believe that Cody swallowed Miles's theory that Sitting Bull was at the center of the largest Indian uprising in American history. But Cody was never overly troubled by facts. Although Cody was more than two hundred miles from the Little Bighorn on June 25, 1876, in his Wild West show's "Custer's Last Charge," he placed himself at mythic ground zero, arriving moments after the martyr's expiration. How could a showman like Cody turn down a chance to make history yet again?[2]

---

[1] W. F. Cody, *An Autobiography of Buffalo Bill* (New York, 1923), 305.

[2] Brian W. Dippie, *Custer's Last Stand: The Anatomy of an American Myth* (Missoula, 1976), 90–91; Don Russell, *The Lives and Legends of Buffalo Bill* (Norman, 1960), 214–35.

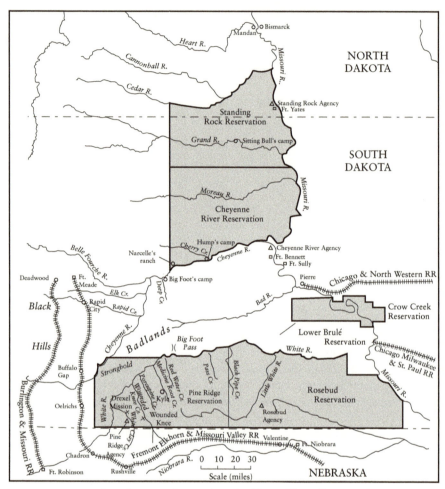

MAP 5. Army's campaign against the Sioux Ghost Dance, 1890.

On November 28 Buffalo Bill arrived at Standing Rock Agency (see Map 5) with two companions, Frank "White Beaver" Powell and Robert "Pony Bob" Haslan, and presented Miles's orders to "secure the person of Sitting Bull [and] deliver him to the nearest com'g officer of U.S. troops." Standing Rock Agent James McLaughlin was not happy to see Buffalo Bill. After shaking hands with the famous showman, McLaughlin hurried back to his office and wrote an urgent telegram to the Indian Office. Cody's mission, McLaughlin warned, was "unnecessary and unwise as it will precipitate a fight." "I have matters well in hand," he assured his superiors. When the "proper time arrives," he would be able to "arrest Sitting Bull by Indian police without bloodshed." McLaughlin requested that Cody's orders be rescinded.[3]

Some historians, taking McLaughlin's words at face value, have concluded that the agent truly feared that Cody "would get himself killed and start a full-fledged war." In all probability, however, McLaughlin was more concerned that Cody's mission would succeed. Unlike McLaughlin, whose relationship with Sitting Bull had soured, Cody had a reasonable chance of persuading Sitting Bull to turn himself over to U.S. authorities. What really irked McLaughlin was the thought of letting General Miles, through Cody, interfere with the management of "his" agency.[4]

After wiring the Indian Office, McLaughlin's next task was to prevent Cody from reaching Sitting Bull's village before the orders could be reversed. To achieve this, he enlisted the help of army officers at nearby Fort Yates. To detain Cody, they "entertained" him at the officers' club well into the night. Much to everyone's surprise, however, the next morning found Buffalo Bill "smiling and happy" and ready to carry out his mission. McLaughlin then devised another scheme. He sent Louis Primeau, an agency interpreter, ahead of Cody. Twenty-five miles from the agency, Primeau intercepted Cody and gave him the (false) news that Sitting Bull was traveling to the agency on another road. By the time Cody returned to the agency, his orders had been suspended. Buffalo Bill returned to Chicago, his arrest of Sitting Bull never to assume a place in the lore of the Wild West.[5]

Historians have usually treated the Cody incident as an inconsequential moment of comic relief. Yet Cody's visit resulted in something more than empty whiskey bottles. Prior to Cody's arrival at Standing Rock, McLaughlin had not intended to arrest Sitting Bull anytime soon. Instead, he planned to try to persuade Sitting Bull to give up the Ghost Dance. If he failed,

---

[3] Russell, *Lives and Legends*, 359 (1st qtn.); W. F. Cody to Nelson A. Miles, 3 Dec. 1890, Nelson A. Miles Papers, box 4, folder D, U.S. Army Military History Institute, Carlisle Barracks, Pa.; *Chicago Tribune*, 28 Nov. 1890, p. 2; James McLaughlin to CIA, 28 Nov. 1890, SC 188, roll 1 (2d qtn.).

[4] Robert Wooster, *Nelson A. Miles and the Twilight of the Frontier Army* (Lincoln, 1993), 181 (qtn.). Russell, *Lives and Legends*, 359–60; Robert M. Utley, *The Last Days of the Sioux Nation* (New Haven, 1963), 124; Robert M. Utley, *The Lance and the Shield: The Life and Times of Sitting Bull* (New York, 1993), 294, offer similar interpretations to Wooster's. For views more consistent with my own, see Stanley Vestal, *Sitting Bull: Champion of the Sioux: A Biography* (1932; Norman, 1957), 281; Bobby Bridger, *Buffalo Bill and Sitting Bull: Inventing the Wild West* (Austin, 2002), 379.

[5] M. F. Steel, "Buffalo Bill's Bluff," *South Dakota Historical Collections* 9 (1918): 478 (1st qtn.); Peter E. Traub, "The First Act of the Last Sioux Campaign," *Journal of the United States Cavalry Association* 15 (April 1905): 874–75 (2d qtn., 874); Lieut. Col. W. F. Drum to AAG DD, 30 Nov. 1890, MP, roll 31; James McLaughlin to CIA, 1 Dec. 1890, SC 188, roll 1; Cody to Miles, 3 Dec. 1890; *Chicago Tribune*, 2 Dec. 1890, p. 1; SW to Maj. Gen. Nelson A. Miles, 28 Nov., 1 Dec. 1890, RCWK, roll 1.

McLaughlin would withhold rations from any Sioux who refused to camp at the agency, thus isolating Sitting Bull and forcing him to come in to the agency. To get Cody's orders rescinded, however, McLaughlin had to agree to arrest Sitting Bull at the earliest possible moment.[6]

Civilian and military officials cooperated better at the Cheyenne River Agency. In late November, at the confluence of Cherry Creek and the Cheyenne River, sixty miles west of the agency, Minneconjous of Big Foot's and Hump's bands were holding large Ghost Dances. To weaken the ghost dancers, Palmer turned to interpreter and agency farmer Narcisse Narcelle, who lived near Cherry Creek. Day after day, Narcelle tried to convince the dancers to stop dancing and to travel to the agency and turn in their weapons. Palmer also sent Christian Indians to Hump's and Big Foot's villages. At the same time, Miles made an overture to Hump. Several years before, at the end of the Great Sioux War, Hump had surrendered to Miles and had enlisted as a scout. To try to persuade Hump to do the same thing again, Miles summoned Captain Ezra P. Ewers, who had spent several years at Fort Bennett, the military post near the Cheyenne River Agency, from his current post in Texas. Around December 5 Ewers rode to Hump's camp with an offer to enlist Hump and others of his band as scouts. They would be allowed to keep their weapons and their people would be fed. On December 9 Hump and most of his band decided to go in to the agency, though a few joined Big Foot.[7]

During this time, the army was also beginning negotiations with the Pine Ridge and Rosebud ghost dancers. By late November ghost dancers from Rosebud under Two Strike, Crow Dog, Short Bull, and Kicking Bear had joined the dancers from Pine Ridge, who were camped on the White River. On November 27 Big Road and Little Wound decided to surrender at Pine Ridge. Shortly after, the remaining ghost dancers (1,500 people including 500 to 600 men of fighting age) decided to move deep into the Badlands. By December 1 they occupied a place called *Onajince Kin*, the Stronghold.[8]

---

[6] James McLaughlin to CIA, 19 Nov. 1890, MP, roll 21. Though there is no record of a compromise along the lines I'm suggesting, I infer that there was one from the fact that by December 12 McLaughlin was under orders to arrest Sitting Bull as soon as possible. See Lieut. Col. W. F. Drum to AAG DD, 27 Feb. 1891, in *ARSW*, 1891, 194–97.

[7] Perain P. Palmer to CIA, 28 Nov., 1, 9 Dec. 1890, SC 188, roll 1; Maj. Gen. Nelson A. Miles to AG, 10 Dec. 1890, RCWK, roll 1; *ARSW*, 1891, 147; Wooster, *Miles*, 181.

[8] T. A. Bland, ed., *A Brief History of the Late Military Invasion of the Home of the Sioux* (Washington, D.C., 1891), 8; A. T. Lea to James A. Cooper, 22 Nov. 1890, SC 188, roll 1; E. B. Reynolds to CIA, 26 Nov. 1890, SC 188, roll 1; D. F. Royer and James A. Cooper to CIA, 30 Nov. 1890, SC 188, roll 1; Maj. Gen. Nelson A. Miles to AG, 27 Nov. 1890, RCWK, roll 1; Raymond J. DeMallie, ed., *The Sixth Grandfather: Black Elk's Teachings Given to John G. Neihardt* (Lincoln, 1984), 269. According to "Sioux on the War-Path," *The Illustrated American* 5 (10 January 1891): 268, Louis Shangrau counted 262 lodges at the Stronghold on December 10 and reported that 145 of these went to Pine Ridge a few days later; Brig. Gen. John R. Brooke to AAG DM, 2 Mar. 1891, RCWK, roll 2, reported that the 145 lodges

The Stronghold was a small piece of tableland, half a square mile, that was connected to the much larger Cuny Table by a narrow neck of land about thirty feet wide. Otherwise, the Stronghold was surrounded by cliffs too steep for soldiers to ascend without serious difficulty. After they arrived in the Stronghold, the ghost dancers erected breastworks at the point where the Stronghold joined Cuny Table, thus making themselves secure against an attack from any direction.[9]

Rather than assaulting the Stronghold, the officer in charge at Pine Ridge, General John R. Brooke, hoped to persuade the ghost dancers there to surrender. To do this, he needed emissaries. Brooke was aware of Young Man Afraid of His Horses's reputation as a skilled peacemaker, but unfortunately Young Man Afraid was on his way to visit the Crows.[10] Another possibility presented itself on December 2 when Father John Jutz of the Holy Rosary Mission told Brooke that Red Cloud was willing to accompany him to the Ghost Dance camp. Brooke quickly approved the plan, although Red Cloud decided to send his son Jack rather than go himself.[11]

When Jutz reached the Stronghold on the fourth, he told the ghost dancers that he had come "only in their own interest" and invited them to state their grievances. According to Jutz, they responded by saying that their rations were inadequate and that many of them who lived on Pass Creek were angry that the Indian Office wanted to relocate them several miles to the east. They also feared that the government would punish them for damaging property and killing cattle. After promising to support them on these issues, Jutz convinced the dancers to send a delegation to the agency to meet with Brooke. The sources emphasize Jutz's role, but Jack Red Cloud was probably influential in the negotiations. The next day, Two Strike, Big Turkey, Turning Bear, Short Bull, Bull Dog, High Pipe, and twenty-eight others left the Stronghold. After spending a night at the Holy Rosary Mission, they went to Brooke's headquarters. Throughout their journey, the delegates feared they

---

consisted of 850 people. Thus, assuming a constant ratio, there would have been 1,535 in the 262 lodges. Shangrau reported 250 men of fighting age in the remaining 117 lodges, suggesting a figure of 550 in the 262 lodges.

9 Jerry Green, ed., *After Wounded Knee: Correspondence of Major and Surgeon John Vance Lauderdale while Serving with the Army Occupying the Pine Ridge Reservation, 1890–1891* (East Lansing, 1996), 27; Virginia I. Kain Lautenschlager, *A History of Cuny Table, 1890–1983* (Rapid City, S.Dak., 1983), 1–2; William Denver McGaa interview, 1906, RT, tablet 7, roll 2.

10 Brig. Gen. John R. Brooke to Francis Warren, 21 Nov. 1890, RCWK, roll 1.

11 Emil Perrig diary, 2, 3 Dec. 1890, St. Francis Mission Records, series 7, box 5, Marquette University Special Collections, Milwaukee; John Jutz, "Historic Data on the Causes of the Dissatisfaction among the Sioux Indians in 1890," *Woodstock Letters* 47 (1918): 319. Other unsuccessful diplomatic efforts are noted in "Sioux on the War-Path," 266; Man Above interview, 1906, RT, tablet 12, roll 3; Julia B. McGillycuddy, *Blood on the Moon: Valentine McGillycuddy and the Sioux* (1941; Lincoln, 1990), 263.

would be arrested or killed, but Father Jutz offered them reassurances to the contrary.[12]

Hoping to win the trust of the delegates, Brooke told them that the soldiers had not come to "fight" but to "keep peace." Should they surrender, he would "give them plenty to eat and would employ many of their young men as scouts." As for their grievances, these could easily be settled "after they had shown a disposition to come in." The delegates' spokesman, Turning Bear, pointed out that it would be impossible for the ghost dancers to camp at Pine Ridge, because there was not enough grass or water for additional horses. Turning Bear also wondered why Brooke wanted to employ scouts if "there was no enemy to be watched." The delegates agreed to return to the Stronghold and discuss matters with the others, but nothing more.[13]

To follow up on these talks, Brooke requested interpreters Louis Shangrau and Baptiste "Little Bat" Garnier to take a detachment of Indian scouts and follow the delegation back to their camp. On December 10 the Shangrau party, probably a day behind the delegates, approached the Stronghold. When twenty ghost dancers intercepted them, Shangrau said that they "had come on a mission of peace" and the dancers allowed them to proceed.[14] Once in the Stronghold Shangrau and No Neck, the scouts' spokesman, tried to convince the ghost dancers that they would not be harmed if they came into the agency. Short Bull was skeptical. "We have been lied to so many times that we will not believe any words that your agent sends to us," Shangrau quoted him as saying. "If we return he will take away our guns and ponies, put some of us in jail for stealing cattle and plundering houses." On December 13, after several councils, Shangrau finally convinced Two Strike and Crow Dog to return to the agency. At this point, according to Shangrau, Short Bull told Two Strike and Crow Dog: "These men from the agency are not telling us the truth; they will conduct you back to the agency and they will place you in jail there. Louis [Shangrau] is at the bottom of this affair. *I know he is a traitor; kill him, kill him!*" Then, Short Bull grabbed his gun and threatened to kill Shangrau, No Neck, Two Strike, and Crow

[12] Perrig diary, 5 (qtn.), 6 Dec. 1890; Jutz, "Historic Data," 320–21; William Fitch Kelley, *Pine Ridge 1890: An Eye Witness Account of the Events Surrounding the Fighting at Wounded Knee*, edited and compiled by Alexander Kelley and Pierre Bovis (San Francisco, 1971), 93–94; Ross Alexander Enochs, *The Jesuit Mission to the Lakota Sioux: Pastoral Theology and Ministry, 1886–1945* (Kansas City, 1996), 57–58. The Indian Office wanted to relocate the Pass Creek people so that they would continue to draw rations at Rosebud even though a boundary change had recently placed them under Pine Ridge. See J. George Wright to CIA, 5 Dec. 1890, SC 188, roll 1.
[13] *Chicago Tribune*, 7 Dec. 1890, p. 3 (qtns.); Perrig diary, 6 Dec. 1890; Jutz, "Historic Data," 321–22; Brooke to AAG DM, 2 Mar. 1891. According to Maj. Gen. Nelson A. Miles to AG, 7 Dec. 1890, RCWK, roll 1, Brooke reported that the delegates had agreed to come in, but my reading of the sources indicates that they agreed only to consider it.
[14] Brooke to AAG DM, 2 Mar. 1891; "Sioux on the War-Path," 266–68 (qtn., 268).

Dog. Crow Dog sat on the ground and pulled his blanket over his head, not wishing to know who "should commit the dastardly act – murdering a brother Dakota." Fortunately, "wiser heads prevailed" and conflict was avoided. Whether this was an accurate account of events, it is clear that tensions among the ghost dancers were high.[15]

Like the militants during the winter of 1876–1877 (Chapter 3), the ghost dancers faced painful choices in early December 1890. As always, a major consideration was food. Although the ghost dancers had live cattle and meat from their earlier raids, grass was scarce in the Stronghold and their supplies were dwindling. A woman from Rosebud later reported being in a "starving condition, having no coffee, sugar, flour or vegetables of any description."[16] As time went on, many ghost dancers grew tired of being on the run. The prospect of going to the agency seemed increasingly appealing, especially if they found reasonable treatment. Other ghost dancers, however, doubted that the same people who had stolen the Black Hills and broken countless promises could be trusted to provide adequate food and refrain from arresting (or killing) Ghost Dance leaders and their followers. If the people continued to dance, as they were during Shangrau's visit,[17] *Wakan Tanka Cinca* would provide for their needs.

As Crow Dog and Two Strike led about 850 people out of the Stronghold toward Pine Ridge on December 13,[18] the army's campaign was nearly a month old. Military officials could point to some success. The first appearance of the troops had driven many ghost dancers into the agencies. Since then, diplomacy had led Hump's band and the majority of the Stronghold ghost dancers to give up the dance. Before the military campaign began, between 4,000 and 5,000 Lakotas were living in Ghost Dance camps. A month later there were no more than 1,300 people at the three remaining Ghost Dance sites (Sitting Bull's and Big Foot's camps and the Stronghold).[19] But diplomacy was a slow process. When the army mobilized troops against the ghost dancers, the implicit idea was that the campaign would be brief.

---

[15] "Sioux on the War-Path," 269 (italics in original). Leonard Crow Dog and Richard Erdoes, *Crow Dog: Four Generations of Sioux Medicine Men* (New York, 1995), 45–46, offers a similar version of this story; Short Bull, "As Narrated by Short Bull," p. 13, Buffalo Bill Museum, Golden, Colo., relates a similar incident, though with Short Bull covering his head with a blanket to avoid seeing who would kill him.

[16] Shangrau ("Sioux on the War-Path," 268) observed that the dancers had "tons of jerked beef" and access to two good springs; Green, ed., *After Wounded Knee*, 26–27, suggests that their resources were more limited. The testimony of the woman from Rosebud was reported in the *Omaha World Herald*, 17 Dec. 1890, p. 2.

[17] "Sioux on the War-Path," 268.

[18] Ibid., 269; Brooke to AAG DM, 2 Mar. 1891; *Chicago Tribune*, 17 Dec. 1890, p. 1.

[19] For participation in the Ghost Dance at its height, see Chapter 12, note 32. I estimate that on December 15 there were 300 people in Sitting Bull's camp, 330 in Big Foot's, and 650 in the Stronghold.

By mid-December army officers were under pressure to bring the campaign to a close. Their patience was wearing thin.

By December 14 Miles and Brooke were ready to use force against the remaining ghost dancers in the Stronghold.[20] Their plan was to send the Seventh Cavalry, Custer's old regiment, from Pine Ridge into the Badlands. Cavalry and infantry units at Fort Meade, Rapid City, Buffalo Gap, and Oelrichs would join the South Dakota state militia and move upon the Stronghold from the north and west. Troops were scheduled to leave Pine Ridge on the morning of the sixteenth. The day before, however, shocking news reached Pine Ridge. The Standing Rock Indian police had killed Sitting Bull and members of his band. Lakotas at Pine Ridge feared that this news meant the army was about to arrest or kill them. Fearing that troop movements might cause Lakotas to flee the agency, Miles and Brooke canceled the operation.[21]

The death – some would say murder – of yet another of the Lakotas' preeminent leaders deserves careful analysis. Not only was it an important event in itself, but it had a crucial impact on subsequent developments, as it triggered a series of events that contributed to the massacre at Wounded Knee. Understanding why Sitting Bull was killed involves more than a simple determination of what happened when the Indian police arrived in Sitting Bull's camp early on the morning of December 15. We also need to understand why U.S. officials ordered the Indian police to arrest Sitting Bull in the first place.

We began to answer that question when we observed that, during the Cody affair, the Indian Office had agreed to have Sitting Bull arrested as soon as possible. McLaughlin initially decided to delay carrying out the arrest until December 20 when most of Sitting Bull's people would be at the agency to receive rations and his village would be virtually deserted.[22] This tactic might have minimized the chances of violence, but using the Indian police to arrest Sitting Bull was inherently a risky proposition. The risk was especially high because of deep animosities between the police and Sitting Bull's people. Though McLaughlin failed to acknowledge the existence of these animosities in his reports or autobiography, he was well aware of them. Hatred was especially strong between Lieutenant Henry Bullhead, the highest ranking officer on the police force, and Sitting Bull and his old friend Catch the Bear.[23]

---

[20] Reports that ghost dancers had raided a ranch on French Creek, not far from the Stronghold, on December 12 may have encouraged Brooke to use force, yet this event did not determine his decision. For this raid, see Philip S. Hall, *To Have This Land: The Nature of Indian/White Relations, South Dakota, 1888–1891* (Vermillion, S.Dak., 1991), 90–94.

[21] *Chicago Tribune*, 15 Dec. 1890, p. 1, 17 Dec. 1890, p. 1; Brooke to AAG DM, 2 Mar. 1891.

[22] ARCIA, 1891, 334.

[23] A better translation for Catch the Bear's name (Mato Wawoyuspa) would be Bear that Catches or Bear that Seizes.

Stories about this feud stress its personal dimensions. By one account, Bullhead was "jealous" of Catch the Bear and Sitting Bull and ridiculed them for being "women." Another has Sitting Bull calling Bullhead an "old woman."[24] Like so many instances of factionalism, this one, too, was inextricably bound up with colonialism. Though Bullhead and Sitting Bull had once fought side by side against the U.S. cavalry, on the reservation they found themselves on opposite sides of divisive issues. In July 1889 Bullhead and his men stopped Sitting Bull and his Silent Eaters from blocking the signing of the Crook land reduction (see Chapter 10). More recently, Bullhead had prevented Catch the Bear from buying empty flour sacks, because he suspected they would be used to make ghost shirts.[25]

On December 14 McLaughlin decided to abandon his plan of waiting until the twentieth. Instead, he ordered the reservation police to arrest Sitting Bull the next morning. McLaughlin later argued that this change was necessary because he discovered that Sitting Bull was about to leave Standing Rock and join Short Bull and Kicking Bear in the Stronghold. "I knew that Sitting Bull contemplated putting himself at the head of the fugitives," he wrote in his autobiography. "[H]e had sure news from Pine Ridge that he, only, was needed to lead the hostiles there in a war of extermination against the white settlers."[26]

The proposition that Sitting Bull intended to lead the ghost dancers in a "war of extermination" was sheer propaganda. On the other hand, McLaughlin did have some possible proof that Sitting Bull was planning to leave Standing Rock, perhaps for Pine Ridge. One piece of evidence was a letter from Sitting Bull that Bull Ghost, a Ghost Dance leader, brought to the agent on the evening of December 12. Sitting Bull, unable to write in English, had dictated this letter to his son-in-law, Andrew Fox, who translated it. Because Fox's written English was not very good, however, the letter was, as McLaughlin later described it, "so incoherent as to be difficult to understand." Despite this, McLaughlin focused on one passage in the letter, which read, "I got to go to Pine Ridge agency, and to know this pray." Most historians have interpreted the phrase "to know this pray" as meaning that Sitting Bull's reason for going to Pine Ridge was to learn more about the Ghost Dance.[27]

---

[24] Frank B. Zahn to W. S. Campbell, 3 Nov. 1929, Walter S. Campbell Collection, box 107, folder 5, Western History Collections, University of Oklahoma Library, Norman; Frank B. Fiske, *Life and Death of Sitting Bull* (Fort Yates, N.Dak., 1933), 50.

[25] Utley, *Lance and the Shield*, 69; Zahn to Campbell, 3 Nov. 1929. Gary Clayton Anderson, *Sitting Bull and the Paradox of Lakota Nationhood* (New York, 1996), 149, adds that Bullhead frequently "taunted" Sitting Bull when he came in for rations.

[26] James McLaughlin, *My Friend the Indian* (1910; Lincoln, 1989), 214, 220.

[27] Ibid., 215–16; Louis L. Pfaller, *James McLaughlin: The Man with an Indian Heart* (New York, 1978), 149; Vestal, *Sitting Bull*, 282–83; Anderson, *Sitting Bull*, 164; Utley, *Lance and the Shield*, 296–97. Utley, *Lance and the Shield*, 296, further argues that McLaughlin

The closest we can come to the original of this letter is a transcription in Walter Campbell's biography of Sitting Bull. On the key line about Sitting Bull's intentions – "I got to go to Pine Ridge agency, and to know this pray" – the words "Pine Ridge" appear in brackets, indicating a third party's (probably Campbell's) interpolation. It appears, then, that the letter actually read: "I got to go to agency, and to know this pray."[28] With this in mind, it becomes possible that Sitting Bull was referring not to Pine Ridge but to his own (Standing Rock) agency.

Such an interpretation is consistent with what we know of ongoing discussions between McLaughlin and Sitting Bull in the weeks before. On November 19 McLaughlin reported on a recent conversation he had with Sitting Bull during a visit to Grand River. During this conversation, Sitting Bull proposed that McLaughlin accompany him on a journey to the Ghost Dance's place of origin. If they could not find "the new Messiah," Sitting Bull would conclude that the Indians had "been too credulous." On the other hand, if they found the Messiah, the Indians should be "permitted to continue their medicine practices." McLaughlin countered with practical objections (to do this would be "to catch up the wind that blew last year") and proposed instead that Sitting Bull visit him at the agency so that McLaughlin could convince him "of the absurdity of this foolish craze." Sitting Bull said he would consider coming to the agency but made no promises.[29]

It is clear, then, that McLaughlin and Sitting Bull had talked about the possibility of Sitting Bull coming to the agency to discuss religion (including, but not limited to the Ghost Dance). It is reasonable to think that Sitting Bull's December 12 letter referred to this earlier conversation. If so, the letter also explains why Sitting Bull had not yet come to Standing Rock. Directly after the phrase, "I got to go to agency, and to know this pray," Sitting Bull wrote, "So I let you know that & the Police man. told me you going to take all our Poneys, gun[s], too; so I want you let me know that. I want answer back soo[n]."[30] Although some historians have interpreted this passage to mean that Sitting Bull was asking for a pass to go to Pine Ridge,[31] an equally plausible reading is that he was telling the agent that he would come to the Standing Rock Agency to follow up on their earlier discussions, but only if McLaughlin would promise not to confiscate his people's ponies and guns. Given the garbled quality of Fox's translation, however, it is impossible to understand Sitting Bull's intentions from this letter.

obtained clarification of Sitting Bull's intentions from Bull Ghost when he brought the letter, but neither of the sources he cites (McLaughlin, *My Friend*, 215; James McLaughlin to Mary Collins, 26 Dec. 1890, Mary Collins Family Papers, box 1, folder 15, South Dakota Historical Society, Pierre) states this.

[28] Vestal, *Sitting Bull*, 285. Vestal was Campbell's pseudonym.
[29] McLaughlin to CIA, 19 Nov. 1890.
[30] Vestal, *Sitting Bull*, 285.
[31] Ibid., 283; Anderson, *Sitting Bull*, 164.

McLaughlin had another piece of evidence that Sitting Bull intended to leave Standing Rock. This was a report from John Carignan, a day school teacher at Grand River, which arrived in McLaughlin's hands at 4:00 P.M. on December 14. According to Carignan, Lieutenant Bullhead had recently learned (from spies) that Sitting Bull had received a message "from the Pine Ridge outfit, asking him to come over there as God was to appear to them." No matter how McLaughlin responded to Sitting Bull's earlier request for permission to leave the agency, Carignan reported, "he is going to go anyway; he has been fitting up his horses to stand a long ride and will go on horseback in case he is pursued." Bullhead wanted permission to arrest Sitting Bull "before he has the chance of giving them the slip, as he thinks that if he gets the start, it will be impossible to catch him." Thirty minutes after reading this report, McLaughlin ordered Bullhead to arrest the chief.[32]

As McLaughlin himself later noted, for several weeks Bullhead and other policemen had been urging the agent to arrest Sitting Bull.[33] Given Bullhead's animosity toward Sitting Bull, it would hardly be surprising if he misread the situation or simply invented evidence of the chief's imminent departure.[34] Sitting Bull's relatives later claimed that he never intended to leave the agency. In the early 1930s One Bull, Sitting Bull's nephew and son by adoption, contended that Sitting Bull's enemies "kept lying and informing about [Sitting Bull]'s intention to go to Red Cloud [and] other false reports to McLaughlyn [sic] and helped to cause his death."[35]

Defenders of McLaughlin have argued that even if Sitting Bull was not planning to leave Standing Rock, the agent cannot be faulted for believing Bullhead.[36] Yet, McLaughlin knew enough about Bullhead's hatred of Sitting Bull to have questioned the accuracy of his information. McLaughlin also realized (or should have) that having Bullhead and his men arrest Sitting Bull might easily result in a bloody confrontation. A better defense of McLaughlin would be that he had no choice but to act on Bullhead's information. Having assumed responsibility for arresting Sitting Bull after the

---

[32] John M. Carignan to James McLaughlin, 14 Dec. 1890, in Stanley Vestal, ed., *New Sources of Indian History, 1850–1891* (Norman, 1934), 13–14. For the timing of the receipt of the letter, see *ARCIA*, 1891, 335; for the timing of the orders, see James McLaughlin to J. M. Carignan, 14 Dec. 1890, in Vestal, ed., *New Sources*, 14–15; for the orders, see James McLaughlin to Afraid of Bear [Bullhead] and Shave Head, 14 Dec. 1890, in Vestal, ed., *New Sources*, 15–16.

[33] *ARCIA*, 1891, 334.

[34] Vestal, *Sitting Bull*, 288, suggests this possibility.

[35] Henry Oscar One Bull, "Regarding Sitting Bull's Life from the Custer Fight until His Surrender," Campbell Collection, box 104, folder 11. One Bull singled out Gray Eagle, who was the brother of Sitting Bull's first two wives, Four Robes and Seen by the Nation. Gray Eagle and Sitting Bull had once been close, but during the 1880s Gray Eagle increasingly sided with McLaughlin and advocated Sitting Bull's arrest. Utley, *Lance and the Shield*, 100–01, 271.

[36] Utley, *Lance and the Shield*, 297.

Cody episode, McLaughlin could ill afford to risk having him escape. On the other hand, McLaughlin's eagerness to arrest Sitting Bull cannot be understood without taking into account his long-standing hostility toward his adversary. As we know, McLaughlin was a strong proponent of assimilation. Like many "friends of the Indian," however, he was quick to turn against Indians who refused his friendship on the terms he offered it. Having tried and failed to gain Sitting Bull's friendship, McLaughlin had come to hate him with a consuming passion.

What happened at 5:50 A.M.[37] on December 15 when Lieutenant Bullhead and forty-two Indian police burst into Sitting Bull's camp was entirely predictable. Within the hour, Sitting Bull, seven of his people, and six policemen were dead or mortally wounded.

Most of the eyewitness accounts of the events are those of the *Ceska Maza* (Metal Breasts), as the police were known at Standing Rock. The police later told how they entered Sitting Bull's cabin, found him in bed, helped him dress (or, in some versions, watched him dress himself), and then escorted him toward the door. By this time, many of Sitting Bull's allies had gathered outside. According to John Loneman, one of the police, Sitting Bull's fourteen-year-old son Crow Foot said to his father, "You always called yourself a brave chief. Now you are allowing yourself to be taken by the Ceska maza." Up to this point, Sitting Bull had shown no signs of resistance, but now he changed his mind. "Then I will not go," he said. After this, according to Loneman, three policemen took hold of Sitting Bull and pulled him outside, where the "whole camp was in commotion." The police "tried to keep order," Loneman related, but "it was like trying to extinguish a treacherous prairie fire." In the "heat of the excitement," Catch the Bear pulled his gun and fired at Bullhead. Although wounded, Bullhead was able to aim his gun and hit Sitting Bull. The details in other police accounts varied. Shoots Walking, for example, omitted the Crow Foot story and instead stated that Sitting Bull had simply urged his friends to attack. But the police were unanimous that Catch the Bear fired first and hit Bullhead, who, in turn, shot Sitting Bull.[38]

---

[37] *ARSW*, 1891, 198.

[38] John Loneman, "The Arrest and Killing of Sitting Bull," in Vestal, ed., *New Sources*, 45–55 (qtns., 51–52). The Loneman account is also in John M. Carroll, ed., *The Arrest and Killing of Sitting Bull: A Documentary* (Glendale, Calif., 1986), 77–85, which also contains accounts by Shoots Walking, Black Hills, and Little Soldier. These accounts, based on interviews by Walter Camp in the early 1910s and Walter Campbell in the late 1920s and early 1930s, are consistent with contemporary government reports. See James McLaughlin to CIA, 16 Dec. 1890, SC 188, roll 1; *ARCIA*, 1891, 335–38; *ARSW*, 1891, 194–99. The police version is also supported in E. G. Fechet, "The True Story of the Death of Sitting Bull," *Proceedings and Collections of the Nebraska State Historical Society*, 2d ser., 2 (1898): 179–90; McLaughlin, *My Friend*, 218–21. The Crow Foot story also appears in the Higheagle Manuscript, Campbell Collection, box 104, folder 22, p. 53. One Bull, who was not in Sitting Bull's camp at the time but had many relatives there, disputed the Crow Foot story and stated that one of Sitting Bull's wives sang a "brave heart song" that encouraged

An account by Four Robes, one of Sitting Bull's two wives, provides a much different perspective on the events. When the police burst into the cabin, Four Robes related, they "smelled of whiskey" and used insulting language. Seeing Crow Foot hiding in the bedding, they shot him and then, also in "cold blood," shot Little Assiniboine, a captive whom Sitting Bull had adopted as a brother years before. Then, the police rushed Sitting Bull "out of the house naked," where they and their comrades "closed in around Sitting Bull and fired into and killed each other." Four Robes concluded that the "friends of Sitting Bull had no chance to help him, and could not have done so even if they had been well armed." Another witness, Scarlet Whirlwind, married to One Bull and living in another cabin, told a similar story. When she "heard the trouble" she ran outside and "saw Sitting Bull brought out naked." Sitting Bull called out to have his horse saddled and offered no resistance. "At that time," Scarlet Whirlwind continued, "I saw a flash of a gun from behind and he was shot." Evidently aware of the police claim that Catch the Bear fired first, she noted that Catch the Bear was present and was "very angry" but insisted that "[t]he shot that hit Sitting Bull was the first one fired."[39]

Historians have generally based their narratives on the police version of events.[40] How can we be sure, however, that the police were not lying? The statements of Four Robes and Scarlet Whirlwind may just as easily be nearest the truth. Lieutenant Colonel William F. Drum later argued that "[i]f it had been the intention of the police to assassinate Sitting Bull, they could easily have done so before his friends arrived."[41] True, the police could have burst into Sitting Bull's cabin, killed him, and quickly rode away before the others were aroused. To support their claim that they had tried to arrest Sitting Bull, however, they needed to secure his body, and this required time.

In the end, it is impossible to prove or disprove either of the conflicting sets of accounts. Whatever transpired, however, it is fair to say that U.S. officials – McLaughlin as well as others – bear the primary responsibility for Sitting Bull's death. There is no doubt that officials genuinely regarded Sitting Bull as an obstacle to "civilization." Some may have truly believed that he threatened white lives. Yet to defend their actions on the grounds that they were sincere seems inadequate.[42] This rationale can be used to justify virtually any historical act, no matter how reprehensible. Sitting Bull posed a threat to no one. Although officials claimed he did, they possessed no clear

Sitting Bull to resist. See "Information in Sioux and English with Regard to Sitting Bull," Campbell Collection, box 104, folder 11.

[39] Carroll, ed., *Arrest and Killing*, 69, 72, 77. Four Robes is identified in this source as Four Blanket Woman, an alternative translation of Tashina Topawin.

[40] Vestal, *Sitting Bull*, 293–300; Pfaller, *James McLaughlin*, 155, 158–59; Utley, *Lance and the Shield*, 299–302; Anderson, *Sitting Bull*, 165–67.

[41] Drum to AAG DD, 27 Feb. 1891, in *ARSW*, 1891, 195.

[42] Utley, *Lance and the Shield*, 311.

evidence of this. The main reason the government regarded Sitting Bull as a criminal was because of his opposition to its policy of assimilation.

After Sitting Bull's death, some members of his band fought with the police in a brief, but intense, close-quarter fight, while most of the three hundred people in the village sought cover in a nearby grove of trees. At 7:30 A.M. a detachment of troops arrived and firing continued sporadically for a few more hours. Later that day, all but about thirty of Sitting Bull's band decided to leave their homes on the Grand River. With little food or spare clothing, terrified that the army would pursue them, they headed south to seek refuge with Big Foot's and Hump's people on the Cheyenne River.[43]

The killing of Sitting Bull marked an important turning point in the army's campaign. It triggered the flight of his band and thus substantially increased the volatility of the situation. Up until this moment, the army's strategy of using diplomacy to induce the ghost dancers to surrender had been effective. Now, however, the commanding officers lost control of events. Over the next two weeks, while they struggled to regain control, the commanders grew more frustrated and prone to demonize uncooperative Lakotas. They labeled Indians who refused to behave as they wished "defiant and hostile."[44]

As Sitting Bull's people moved south, the army's immediate fear was that they would set off a chain reaction that would wind up strengthening the ghost dancers in the Stronghold. One possibility was that Two Strike and Crow Dog, having just reached Pine Ridge Agency, might lead their people back to the Badlands. (As it turned out, they remained camped at the agency.) Another possibility was that Sitting Bull's people would encourage ghost dancers in Big Foot's and Hump's camps to accompany them to the Stronghold. To prevent this from happening, on December 18 General Ruger ordered Colonel Henry C. Merriam to lead troops from forts Bennett and Sully on the Missouri up the Cheyenne River. Ruger also ordered troops under Lieutenant Colonel Edwin V. Sumner to move from the mouth of the Belle Fourche down the Cheyenne. Merriam and Sumner would converge on Big Foot's camp and cut off possible escape routes. Ruger did not order Sumner to arrest Big Foot but told him this would be "desirable."[45] With Sitting Bull dead, army officers now identified Big Foot as the major malefactor outside the Stronghold.

[43] *ARSW*, 1891, 197–198. According to this source, about thirty of Sitting Bull's people went into the Standing Rock Agency.

[44] Capt. M. P. Maus to Col. E. V. Sumner, 23 Dec. 1890, in *ARSW*, 1891, 231. See also Maj. Gen. Nelson A. Miles to AG, 22 Dec. 1890, RCWK, roll 1, which characterized Big Foot as "one of the most defiant and threatening."

[45] Brig. Gen. Thomas Ruger to Col. H. C. Merriam, 18 Dec. 1890, in *ARSW*, 1891, 204; Acting AAG DD to Col. E. V. Sumner, 16 Dec. 1890, in *ARSW*, 1891, 229 (qtn.).

Big Foot, also known as Spotted Elk, was the son of the Minneconjou chief Lone Horn, a brilliant diplomat who had brokered peace agreements between the Minneconjous and the Cheyennes and Crows in the 1840s and 1850s. Though willing to fight to protect his people's interests, Lone Horn was a voice for moderation when conflicts erupted with the United States. Big Foot inherited his father's style. He was with the militants in the winter of 1876–1877 but was among the first to surrender. Once on the reservation, Big Foot consistently opposed accommodation. He refused to sign the Crook agreement and defended the rights of his band to hold Ghost Dances. Unlike many other leaders, however, his resistance was tempered by an effort to avoid antagonizing U.S. officials. Among the western Sioux, Big Foot was seen as a diplomat, someone who could find common ground between contending parties.[46]

Big Foot learned of the killing of Sitting Bull on December 19, as he was leading a portion of his band down the Cheyenne River to the agency. Their plan was to draw rations and annuities and return to their village. After that, they were considering going to Pine Ridge Agency. Some days before, Big Foot had received a letter from Red Cloud, No Water, and Big Road. One member of Big Foot's band, Dewey Beard (also known as Iron Hail), recalled that these chiefs invited Big Foot to come to Pine Ridge to "help us to put it [a fire] out and make a peace."[47]

Just west of Hump's village at Cherry Creek, Big Foot's party came upon two men from Sitting Bull's band. After they told their story, Big Foot sent ten of his men, including Dewey Beard, to locate the rest of refugees and tell them "he would feed and clothe them." A little farther down the Cheyenne River, these ten men found two groups of Sitting Bull's people. One, mostly women and children, "were keeping themselves warm by the fires" and "mourning... Sitting Bull and the others killed." The other group, mostly men, were at Hump's village just across the Cheyenne River. Beard and his companions went to the council and told the men that Big Foot was willing to help them. Two weeks earlier, Big Foot and Hump might have cooperated, but Hump was now a government scout. He offered Sitting Bull's people a much different choice: He would take them to the Cheyenne River Agency

---

[46] Kingsley M. Bray, "Lone Horn's Peace: A New View of Sioux-Crow Relations, 1851–1858," *Nebraska History* 66 (Spring 1985): 28–47; Utley, *Lance and the Shield*, 126; James H. McGregor, *The Wounded Knee Massacre from the Viewpoint of the Sioux* (1940; Rapid City, S.Dak., 1993), 14–19; Frank C. Armstrong to SI, 25 Mar. 1890, OIA, file 9858–1890; Perain P. Palmer to CIA, 29 Oct. 1890, SC 188, roll 1.

[47] ARSW, 1891, 224; Dewey Beard interview, 1907, RT, tablet 30, roll 5. In a separate interview, Beard's younger brother, Joseph Horn Cloud, stated that Big Foot had been receiving overtures from Red Cloud, No Water, Big Road, and also Calico and Young Man Afraid of His Horses. See Joseph Horn Cloud interview, 1906, RT, tablet 12, roll 3. The Beard, Horn Cloud, and other useful interviews can also be found in Donald F. Danker, ed., "The Wounded Knee Interviews of Eli S. Ricker," *Nebraska History* 62 (Summer 1981): 151–243.

and see that they were fed and clothed. According to Beard, Hump backed this promise with a threat. "You people want to fight," he told Big Foot's emissaries, "and I will bring some infantry to help you."[48] Besides serving as a warning to Big Foot, Hump's message offered a powerful inducement for Sitting Bull's people to accept his invitation. Otherwise, they too would face the infantry. Two days later, Captain Joseph H. Hurst, an emissary from Colonel Merriam, amplified the alternatives. If they surrendered, Hurst told Sitting Bull's people, he would spare their lives, but "if they chose to join Big Foot...the result would be the certain destruction of themselves and probably their families." Faced with the threat of annihilation, 175 turned over the few weapons they had and followed Hurst to an uncertain future. A few days later 50 more followed, and the remaining 38 joined Big Foot's band.[49]

When the ten Minneconjou messengers returned to their camp and reported that "Hump was talking about war," Big Foot decided that it was too risky to continue to the agency. It would be better, he thought, to return to his permanent village at the mouth of Deep Creek. As Big Foot and his party moved back up the river, they encountered the rest of his band. A day or two before, they had learned that Sumner's troops were coming from the west and had fled from their village. Realizing he was pinned down, Big Foot sent word to Sumner on December 20 that he was his "friend and wished to talk." The next day Big Foot found Sumner four miles east of Narcisse Narcelle's ranch.[50]

Like any army officer, Sumner was expected to be tough with Indian leaders who were not under government control and so scolded Big Foot for helping Sitting Bull's people. Big Foot replied by pointing to two men from Sitting Bull's camp who were with him. These men, he told Sumner, were "brothers and relations; that they had come to him and his people almost naked, were hungry, footsore, and weary; that he had taken them in, had fed them, and no one with any heart could do any less." Sumner had to agree that the two Indians were a "pitiable sight," so much so that he "dropped all thought of their being hostile or even worthy of capture."[51]

Sumner probably considered arresting Big Foot at this point, but an arrest risked provoking conflict with others in Big Foot's band. It might easily cause many of his band to flee, possibly to the Stronghold. The best course of action was to keep Big Foot under close watch until he could convince him

[48] *ARSW*, 1891, 224; Beard interview (qtns.).

[49] Capt. J. H. Hurst to AAG DD, 9 Jan. 1891, in *ARSW*, 1891, 202. For the numbers, I am relying on dispatches in *ARSW*, 1891, 202, 207, 209, 212, 224. Those who surrendered were held at Fort Sully until May 1891 when they returned to Standing Rock. See James McLaughlin to CIA, 9 June 1891, MP, roll 34.

[50] Beard interview (1st qtn.); *ARSW*, 1891, 224 (2d qtn.).

[51] *ARSW*, 1891, 224.

to surrender voluntarily. This reasoning likely explains why Sumner asked Big Foot to follow him to his camp at the mouth of the Belle Fourche. From there, Sumner evidently hoped, he could convince Big Foot to agree to take his people to one of the nearby forts. Although Big Foot agreed with this plan, he had cause to fear the worst. Later that day, after Sumner issued some cattle, mixed-blood interpreter Felix Benoit advised Big Foot not to have his people kill the cattle and offered to shoot them himself. The reason, Benoit explained, was that Sumner's men planned to watch Big Foot's people kill the cattle to see who had guns and how many there were. Armed with this intelligence, the soldiers would confiscate their guns that evening.[52]

On the morning of the twenty-second, when Big Foot's people began moving up the Cheyenne, some of their wagons became locked together while passing through a gate. As soldiers shouted orders for the Indians to hurry up, terrified children began to cry. A man named Black Coyote, angry at the soldiers for "treating the Indians as though they were mere animals," took his gun from his wagon. He and several young men on horses rode past the jammed wagons, overtaking the soldiers at the head of the column. When the troops drove them back, many of the women "got into a panic from fright, supposing they were going to be killed." Although things calmed down, and Big Foot's people proceeded, when came to their village at Deep Creek later in the day, they refused to take another step. Sumner wanted Big Foot to keep his people moving, but the chief replied that "there will be trouble in trying to force these women and children, cold and hungry as they are, away from their homes."[53]

Sumner was reluctant to force the issue. He later wrote that he was unable to justify "making an attack on peaceable, quiet Indians on their reservation and at their homes, killing perhaps many of them." At the same time, however, unless he was willing to jeopardize his career, Sumner could not take these humane observations to their logical conclusion and simply leave Big Foot's people alone. Instead, he demanded that Big Foot visit him the next day. At that time, Sumner decided, he would pressure Big Foot into taking his people to Fort Bennett.[54]

The next day, when Big Foot failed to appear at his camp, Sumner issued an ultimatum. He asked John Dunn, a long-time local rancher, to inform Big Foot that Sumner was ordering him to take his people to Fort Bennett. If they refused to go, Sumner would use force. According to Dunn's testimony a month later, Big Foot explained that he had been unable to meet his appointment with Sumner because he was sick (this was true – Big Foot was developing a serious case of pneumonia) and that he would comply with Sumner's orders: "When I left Big Foot," Dunn swore, "I had not the

[52] Ibid., 224–25; Beard interview.
[53] Horn Cloud interview (1st qtn.); Beard interview (2d qtn.); *ARSW*, 1891, 225 (3d qtn.).
[54] *ARSW*, 1891, 225.

least doubt that he would go to Fort Bennett." Dewey Beard and his brother Joseph Horn Cloud (also known as White Lance) told a different story. They recalled that Dunn (Red Beard) advised the leaders of Big Foot's band to go to Pine Ridge, since "there were more Indians there." If they stayed where they were, Dunn said, they would all be killed.[55]

Despite this discrepancy in the sources, it is clear that Big Foot and others of his band were fearful of Sumner and unsure what to do. After Dunn left, the leaders met to discuss their options. Some advocated going to Pine Ridge, while others said they should remain where they were. As a compromise, the leaders decided to have their people retreat into the cedars of nearby canyons and watch. If the soldiers came, they would leave; if they did not, the people would return to their village. Big Foot's people moved into the hills south of their village around sunset. A few hours later, when scouts reported the approach of troops, Big Foot's people left for Pine Ridge.[56]

Keeping an anxious eye to the rear, Big Foot's band of four hundred traveled quickly. By daylight, they reached a fork of the Bad River, twenty miles south of their village. As the sun traced a tight arc low across the sky before them, they raced across the prairie, driving wagons and cattle, helping along the weak, old, and sick. Near dark they arrived at the northern wall of the Badlands. In under twenty-four hours they had covered fifty miles, an astonishing distance. Before them, steep cliffs dropped two hundred feet toward a valley below. As it was growing dark, they somehow managed to lower their wagons down the cliffs and then travel the few remaining miles to the White River. There they stopped, exhausted, but for the moment safe.[57]

By this time, Big Foot's pneumonia was getting worse. Because of this, band leaders decided to move the next morning (the twenty-fifth) to a spring on Red Water Creek and rest for two or three days. They also sent three messengers to Pine Ridge, in Dewey Beard's words, "to give notice that Big Foot was on his way to the Agency, and was very sick" and that he was coming in "openly and peaceably." Two of these messengers, Bear Comes and Lies and Shaggy Feather, reached Pine Ridge on the twenty-sixth and conveyed Big Foot's plans to Oglala leaders. In turn, the Oglalas related that Short Bull was moving toward the agency and would arrive within two days. They hoped Big Foot would come and help "make peace," but they warned that the "cavalry was out at Wounded Knee and for him [Big Foot]

---

[55] Ibid., 236–37 (1st qtn., 237); Horn Cloud interview (2d qtn.); Beard interview.

[56] Horn Cloud and Beard interviews. Sumner reached Big Foot's village about 7:00 P.M. but decided to spend the night there and pursue in the morning. See Col. E. V. Sumner to Col. E. A. Carr, 23 Dec. 1890, in *ARSW*, 1891, 234.

[57] Beard and Horn Cloud interviews. For the number in Big Foot's band, which includes the thirty-eight Hunkpapa refugees, I am relying on Richard E. Jensen, "Big Foot's Followers at Wounded Knee," *Nebraska History* 71 (Fall 1990): 198.

to go around these and avoid them."[58] As these discussions revealed, Lakota leaders were working desperately to avoid bloodshed. Had the army allowed Big Foot to come into the agency without interference, they probably would have succeeded.

The effort of Oglala leaders to gain Big Foot's help was only one of many diplomatic initiatives they pursued. On December 16 when the news of Sitting Bull's death led Brooke and Miles to call off the attack on the Stronghold, Oglala and Brulé leaders at Pine Ridge had immediately renewed negotiations with Short Bull and Kicking Bear. At first, they sent a delegation of 40 to the Stronghold. When these delegates returned without success, the leaders decided to call all the Lakotas at Pine Ridge into council. In an extraordinary meeting, attended by close to 7,000 people, the Indians decided to send a large delegation to the Stronghold. Around December 22, 140 men, led by Little Wound, Fast Thunder, and Big Road, departed Pine Ridge.[59]

The ensuing negotiations were undoubtedly more complex than the available sources reveal. Little Wound, Fast Thunder, and Big Road must have offered the ghost dancers assurances that Brooke would not punish them and that the United States would address their grievances. Not surprisingly, the sources reveal serious tensions between the delegates and the ghost dancers. Short Bull recalled that Fast Thunder pointed to him and accused him of "trying to have your people fight" and then challenged him to "do something wonderful that this Messiah told you to do." Short Bull responded to this challenge by putting on his ghost shirt and telling Fast Thunder to shoot at him, but Jack Red Cloud intervened.[60]

For many in the Stronghold, especially those who continued to hope that the Ghost Dance's possibilities might soon be realized, it must have been difficult to stop dancing and go in to the agency. An account by Henry Young Skunk offers some insight into how it was possible to disengage. According to Young Skunk, Kicking Bear related a vision in which "father" told him that the "Lakotas killed Sitting Bull because of the dance" and that "the white men have surrounded you in this place, and you are badly penned up in a small place." Soon after, with an awareness of the ghost dancers' predicament, Young Skunk had a vision in which he received from his older sister a "root that was little and very yellow and good smelling." Upon regaining consciousness and returning to the present world ("a very bad place"), Young Skunk burned this root and his sister appeared, laughing, outside his lodge. She gave him some pemmican and then said she was returning home. As she departed, Young Skunk kept his eyes on her until she was no longer

[58] Beard (qtns.) and Horn Cloud interviews. The third messenger, Big Voice Thunder, returned to Big Foot's camp to report on the presence of troops at Wounded Knee.

[59] Brooke to AAG DM, 2 Mar. 1891; *Chicago Tribune*, 23 Dec. 1890, p. 1.

[60] Short Bull, "As Narrated by Short Bull," 15–16 (qtns., 15).

visible.[61] Soon after, Young Skunk left the Stronghold, carrying with him the memory of his sister and the possibility that he might see her again. By December 27 the last of the ghost dancers were on their way to Pine Ridge.[62] They had decided to quit dancing for now, but the hope of the dance would remain.

At this point, two days before Wounded Knee, the army was in an excellent position to ends its campaign without violence. The Stronghold was now empty, and the only other ghost dancers, Big Foot's people, were on their way to Pine Ridge. Had Miles and Brooke allowed Big Foot's people to travel to the agency without interference, almost certainly the massacre would not have happened. With terrible consequences, however, they insisted on intercepting Big Foot's people and disarming them. To understand the reasons for their decision, it is necessary to examine their attitude toward Big Foot in the week before the massacre.

On the morning of December 24, when General Miles learned that Big Foot had escaped Sumner, he was at his temporary headquarters in Rapid City. It was not the news the general had been hoping to hear the day before Christmas. Only two days earlier, a jubilant Miles had informed Washington that "the followers of Sitting Bull have been captured, and Colonel Sumner reports the capture of Big Foot's band of Sioux." This was an especially positive development, he instructed a newspaper reporter, because it prevented the ghost dancers on the Cheyenne River from joining those in the Stronghold. Had "the conjunction been effected," Miles gravely observed, "these Indians...could have massacred as many settlers as the Sioux did in the Minnesota troubles of 1862." But Miles was a little too eager to proclaim victory. Sumner's dispatches had indicated that he was *close* to securing Big Foot's surrender but nothing more. Now, Miles was forced to retract his earlier report and notify his superiors that Big Foot had "deceived [Sumner] and eluded his command."[63]

After contacting Washington Miles erupted at Sumner for "miss[ing] your opportunity" and instructed him to find "Big Foot and his immediate followers" and have them "arrested, disarmed, and held until further orders." Miles further reminded Sumner that the Minneconjou chief "has been defiant both to the troops and to the authorities, and is now harboring outlaws

---

[61] *LT&T*, 300–304. *"Tatanka Iyotake Lakota ktepi keyelo wowaci kin le on....Iho wanna le oyanke etanhan wasicun aogluteniyanpi tka cik'ayela sicaya yelo"* (p. 300); *"pejuta ca cik'ala na lila zi na wastemna na omnapi iyowicakipi"* (p. 303); *"makoce wan lila sicaya"* (p. 303).

[62] *Chicago Tribune*, 28 Dec. 1890, p. 4; *Omaha World-Herald*, 28 Dec. 1890, p. 2.

[63] Col. E. V. Sumner to Maj. Gen. Nelson A. Miles, 23 Dec. 1890, in *ARSW*, 1891, 234; Maj. Gen. Nelson A. Miles to AG, 22 Dec. 1890, RCWK, roll 1 (1st qtn.); *Chicago Tribune*, 23 Dec. 1890, p. 1 (2d qtn.); *ARSW*, 1891, 232–33; Maj. Gen. Nelson A. Miles to AG, 24 Dec. 1890, RCWK, roll 1 (3d qtn.).

and renegades from other bands."[64] Thinking that Big Foot's people were on their way to the Stronghold, Miles hoped that Sumner, Merriam, or Colonel Eugene Carr's Sixth Cavalry, positioned at the mouth of Rapid Creek, would quickly intercept them and bring the situation back under control. Operating on the same theory, Brooke ordered Major Guy V. Henry's Ninth Cavalry to march toward the Badlands.[65]

The language in Miles's dispatches reveals a strong disposition to treat Big Foot as a dangerous criminal and to assume the worst about his motives and intentions. Not only was Big Foot "deceitful" and "harboring outlaws and renegades," he intended to join the other ghost dancers with the likely result an assault on innocent settlers. Only two months before, Miles had been trying to calm down Royer at Pine Ridge, but now he was ignoring his own advice. Why did Miles insist that Big Foot was dangerous? One possible answer is that, since he was now in charge of a military campaign, Miles had no choice but to anticipate the worst from Big Foot and the other ghost dancers; to do otherwise would be to risk the lives of his troops and those of settlers. Yet Miles's response to Big Foot exceeded the requirements of military prudence. From Miles's perspective, it was possible that Big Foot intended to go the Stronghold, but he had no intelligence indicating this, and alternatives were possible. Even if Big Foot intended to go to the Stronghold, there was a remote possibility that his people and other ghost dancers would do some damage at nearby ranches, perhaps even killing a few settlers, but this was a far cry from the dangers Miles was predicting and was likely to happen only if troop movements provoked the ghost dancers to panic. It is impossible to know whether Miles convinced himself that Big Foot was as dangerous as he said he was, or whether he consciously created a false sense of crisis. It is easy to see, however, that Miles's attitude toward Big Foot was a logical consequence of the alarmism and demonization of the ghost dancers that he had promoted from the beginning of the campaign. Miles's growing obsession with Big Foot was a measure of his frustration at losing control of the situation.

On the morning of the twenty-sixth the army finally received news of Big Foot's location. As General Brooke later wrote, he was "south of White River and moving towards the Agency."[66] The army now had reliable information that Big Foot was not going to the Stronghold. This might have caused Miles to reevaluate his assessment of Big Foot, but he continued to regard Big Foot's

---

[64] Maj. Gen. Nelson A. Miles to Col. E. V. Sumner, 24 Dec. 1890 (two telegrams), in *ARSW*, 1891, 234–35.

[65] Maj. Gen. Nelson A. Miles to Commanding Officer, Ft. Bennett, 24 Dec. 1890, in *ARSW*, 1891, 209–10; Miles to Sumner, 24 Dec. 1890; Sumner to Carr, 23 Dec. 1890; Brooke to AAG DM, 2 Mar. 1891. Miles established another line of defense when Brooke ordered Major Guy V. Henry to take a position east of the Stronghold. See Brooke to AAG DM, 2 Mar. 1891.

[66] Brooke to AAG DM, 2 Mar. 1891.

people as dangerous criminals who must be disarmed. Later that day, Miles fired off three telegrams to Brooke. At 4:00 P.M.: "Big Foot is cunning and his Indians are very bad.... I hope you will round up the whole body of them, <u>disarm and keep them all under close guard</u>." At 5:50: "It is very important to secure the men with Big Foot with as little delay as possible." At 6:48: "I shall be exceedingly anxious till I know [the orders] are executed." The next day Miles reiterated his orders to disarm Big Foot's people and added: "If he fights, destroy him."[67]

Military historians have taken these orders for granted, failing to ask if they were warranted.[68] This question is crucial, because the decision to disarm Big Foot's people created the immediate circumstances in which Wounded Knee took place. A week after the massacre Brooke testified that it was necessary to disarm them; otherwise "the presence at Pine Ridge Agency of Big Foot and his people would complicate matters then in progress of settlement, and possibly defeat them."[69] This, however, seems an ex post facto justification for a decision that had no tactical imperative at the time. For several weeks, ghost dancers had been coming into Pine Ridge without being forced to give up their weapons in advance, and there were no orders to disarm the last dancers coming in under Short Bull and Kicking Bear.[70] Rather than explaining Miles's orders to disarm Big Foot's people in tactical terms, it makes more sense to see these orders as the result of his earlier classification of them as criminals.

At one level, Miles's decision to disarm Big Foot's band was his own, as were his efforts to manufacture a theory of conspiracy to foment a massive uprising and his obvious frustration at having lost control of the situation in late December. Another commander charged with subduing the Lakota Ghost Dance might have made different choices. Nonetheless, Miles's actions were consistent with general patterns we have seen in this book. From the time Lewis and Clark informed Sioux people that the "Great Father" would destroy them if they refused to comply with Lewis and Clark's demands, U.S. officials had consistently regarded Indians who resisted their will as "hostile" and threatened to use force against them.

---

[67] Testimony of Brig. Gen. John R. Brooke, 17 Jan. 1891, RCWK, roll 1 (underlining in original); Lieut. Fayette W. Roe to Maj. S. M. Whitside, 27 Dec. 1890, RCWK, roll 1.

[68] Utley, *Last Days*, 193, 197; Wooster, *Miles*, 185. Peter R. DeMontravel, *A Hero to His Fighting Men: Nelson A. Miles, 1839–1925* (Kent, Ohio, 1998), 204, attributes the orders to General Brooke.

[69] Testimony of Brooke.

[70] I can find no record of orders to disarm any of the ghost dancers coming in from the Stronghold, nor were such orders reported in the press. Two articles by Susette La Flesche, an Omaha Indian, in the *Omaha World Herald*, 27 Dec. 1890, p. 5, 28 Dec. 1890, p. 2, objecting to disarming the Indians at Pine Ridge once the last ghost dancers arrived, confirm that the army had allowed the ghost dancers who had earlier surrendered to retain their arms and that there were no plans to disarm the last dancers until after they reached Pine Ridge.

On the afternoon of December 27 Big Foot and his people left the camp at Red Water Creek, where they had been since the twenty-fifth. Although band leaders realized they would probably encounter soldiers, Big Foot's worsening illness forced them to take the most direct route to the agency. At midnight they stopped a few miles from Kyle, and the next morning took the main road to Pine Ridge. In the early afternoon, as Big Foot's people crossed the ridge between Medicine Root and Porcupine creeks, they could see government scouts and, farther on, close to 240 soldiers just east of Porcupine Butte.[71] To signal their intentions, they raised a white flag above Big Foot's wagon, and the men in the band, in Dewey Beard's words, went "right up to the soldiers calmly and confidently showing no fear." This was a difficult thing to do, especially when the soldiers seemed to be loading their weapons and appeared to be taking aim at them.[72] Beard thought he was going to die but rode forward anyway. Dismounting near one of the two Hotchkiss guns (small cannons; see Illustration 13), he shoved his hand down the barrel. In a long tradition of Sioux warriors, Beard had made himself courageous by confronting his fear head on.[73]

Soon after, Big Foot's wagon arrived, and Major Samuel M. Whitside, commander of the first squadron of the Seventh Cavalry, looked inside and saw blood from Big Foot's nose pooling on the wagon floor. Whitside then opened Big Foot's blanket to see his face. When Big Foot extended his hand, Whitside asked his destination. Big Foot replied that he was going into the agency and did not intend to fight. Whitside asked him to give up twenty-five guns as proof. According to Beard, Big Foot said, "[I]f I give you the 25 guns I am afraid you are going to do harm to my people in such country. I am willing to give you the 25 guns; but wait till we get to the Agency, and I will give you whatever you ask." One of Whitside's scouts, John Shangrau (Louis's brother), later recalled that he advised Whitside not to force the issue, as there was "liable to be a fight." Beard remembered Whitside telling Big Foot, "I had heard that you were hostile; but they had lied about you." Whitside shook hands with Big Foot and offered to transfer him to a much more comfortable army ambulance.[74] Although Beard's account suggests that Whitside had some compassion for Big Foot and quickly concluded he was not dangerous, he remained subject to Miles's orders. Whitside decided to escort Big Foot's

[71] Beard and Horn Cloud interviews. The soldiers were the first squadron of the Seventh Cavalry and a detachment of the Second Artillery. For troop strength, see Utley, *Last Days*, 201.

[72] Beard interview. John Shangrau, a scout with Whitside, recalled that when the troops saw Big Foot's band, they assumed battle formation. See John Shangrau interview, 1906, RT, tablet 27, roll 5.

[73] Beard interview; Royal B. Hassrick, *The Sioux: Life and Customs of a Warrior Society* (Norman, 1964), 32–34.

[74] Testimony of Maj. S. M. Whitside, 7 Jan. 1891, RCWK, roll 1; Maj. S. M. Whitside to Regimental Adjt., 7th Cavalry, 1 Jan. 1891, in *Army and Navy Journal* 28 (24 January 1891): 366; Beard interview (1st and 3d qtns.); Shangrau interview (2d qtn.).

ILLUSTRATION 13. Hotchkiss gun. Library of Congress Prints and Photographs Division, LC-USZ62–11970.

people to his camp five miles away on Wounded Knee Creek and call for reinforcements. "The object I had in view," he later testified, was that a large force would "overawe the Indians, and so they would submit quietly to be disarmed."[75]

After transferring Big Foot to the ambulance, Whitside's troops conducted Big Foot's people to Wounded Knee, arriving in the late afternoon. Some soldiers issued the Lakotas rations and set up a tent for Big Foot, while others took the two Hotchkiss guns to the top of a nearby hill and pointed them toward the Lakota camp. In the meantime, Brooke had responded to Whitside's request for additional force. At 4:40 P.M. Colonel James W. Forsyth left Pine Ridge with the remaining troops of the Seventh, a troop of Oglala scouts, and two more Hotchkiss guns, arriving four hours later. Once Forsyth was settled, the officers of the Seventh Cavalry tapped into a barrel of whiskey a trader had brought from the agency. For some time thereafter, the officers passed from tent to tent drinking congratulatory toasts.[76]

---

[75] Testimony of Whitside.

[76] Whitside to Regimental Adjt., 1 Jan. 1891; Col. James W. Forsyth to Acting AAG DP, 31 Dec. 1890, RCWK, roll 1; Richard C. Stirk interview, 1906, RT, tablet 8, roll 2; Charles W. Allen interview, 1907, RT, tablet 11, roll 2.

Most of Big Foot's people spent a restless, fearful night. Peter Stand recalled that some women went out to get water and returned with word that "the infantry and the cavalry had surrounded us." Dewey Beard, "impressed with fear and foreboding," did not sleep at all, nor could he eat. "There was great uneasiness among the Indians all night," Beard explained. "[T]hey were up most of the night – were fearful that they were to be killed." Before it grew light, Beard's father, Horned Cloud, told his seven sons that there was sure to be a fight. "Try to die in the front of your relations, the old folks, and the little ones," he said. "I will be satisfied if you die trying to help them." Soon after, reveille sounded in the soldiers' camp.[77]

[77] McGregor, *Wounded Knee Massacre*, 116 (1st qtn.); Beard interview (2d qtn.).

15

"A Valley of Death"

Wounded Knee

To carry out his orders to disarm Big Foot's band, Colonel Forsyth first positioned his troops. As shown in Map 6, he placed troops in three lines to the west, south, and east of an open space between the Indian and cavalry camps. Farther to the south, across a dry ravine, he positioned three additional lines, one consisting of the Indian scouts. To the northwest, two detachments assumed positions near the Hotchkiss guns. Once his forces were in place, Forsyth ordered the Lakota "warriors" to assemble in council in the open space. As most of the approximately 120 Lakota men and older boys gathered, they were surrounded by nearly 500 soldiers. The four Hotchkiss guns, each capable of firing exploding cartridges weighing two and a half pounds with a range of over two miles, were trained on them and their camp.[1]

According to Major Whitside's testimony before an army court of inquiry a week later, once the men had gathered, Forsyth instructed twenty of the "bucks" to return to their camp and bring back their weapons. When these men produced only "two broken carbines, and stated that that was all they had," Forsyth then ordered Big Foot to "demand of his band their arms." Big Foot replied that "they had no arms, that they, the arms, had all been destroyed on the Cheyenne." At this point, mixed-blood interpreter Philip Wells testified, Forsyth accused Big Foot of "lying to me in return for all

---

[1] Robert M. Utley, *Last Days of the Sioux Nation* (New Haven, 1963), 200–05, provides a good overview of the troop disposition and strength. For troop strength, see also Jerry Green, "The Medals of Wounded Knee," *Nebraska History* 75 (Summer 1994): 201. Col. James W. Forsyth to Acting AAG DP, 31 Dec. 1890, RCWK, roll 1, reported that 106 Lakota men assembled at 7:30 A.M. There were probably 10 or 20 men and older boys remaining in the Indian camp, as the total number of adult men was between 120 and 125. See Brig. Gen. John R. Brooke to Maj. Gen. Nelson A. Miles, 28 Dec. 1890, in testimony of Brig. Gen. John R. Brooke, 17 Jan. 1891, RCWK, roll 1; Joseph Horn Cloud interview, 1906, RT, tablet 12, roll 3. The Hotchkiss Breach-Loading Mountain Rifle is described in Edward S. Farrow, *Farrow's Military Encyclopedia: A Dictionary of Military Knowledge* (New York, 1905), 57.

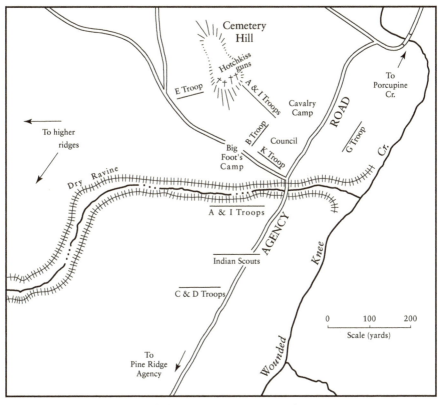

MAP 6. Wounded Knee Massacre, December 29, 1890.

my kindness to you." Forsyth and Whitside then ordered a search of the camp.[2]

Lakotas later told a different story. Big Foot's brother, Frog, informed the court of inquiry that "[a]n officer told us he wanted our guns, and as soon as we gave them up he would give us provisions, and we could go on our way. We, the older men, consented willingly, and began giving them up." In his 1906 account Joseph Horn Cloud stated that at the beginning of the council an officer told Big Foot, "I want 25 guns. Yesterday everybody had a gun. I want 25 of them." With blood still flowing from his nose, Big Foot asked

---

[2] Testimony of Maj. S. M. Whitside, 7 Jan. 1891, RCWK, roll 1; testimony of P. F. Wells, 11 Jan. 1891, RCWK, roll 1 (see also Philip F. Wells, "Ninety-Six Years among the Indians of the Northwest," *North Dakota History* 15 [October 1948]: 285). Similar accounts can be found in Forsyth to Acting AAG DP, 31 Dec. 1890; testimony of Francis M. J. Craft, 11 (?) Jan. 1891, RCWK, roll 1; testimony of Lieut. L. S. McCormick, 10 Jan. 1891, RCWK, roll 1; Major L. S. McCormick, "Wounded Knee and Drexel Mission Fights," unpublished manuscript, 1904, p. 11, Newberry Library, Chicago.

his people to comply with this demand. The "young men" went to the camp and returned with twenty-five guns. The officer then asked for five more, the young men again complied, and the officer then asked for the rest. The men "answered back to Big Foot, 'There are no more guns.'" Then came the order to search the camp.[3]

Whitside's claim that the Sioux yielded only two carbines (and those "broken") is almost certainly inaccurate. Even Forsyth said they produced a "few," and Wells, whose general perspective was consistent with the officers', saw "about a dozen old rifles."[4] Given the fact that most of the men in Big Foot's band probably owned guns, Horn Cloud's statement that the Lakotas surrendered thirty weapons is certainly plausible. Whatever the precise number, however, the evidence indicates that the Lakotas did not fully comply with Forsyth's orders. Horn Cloud noted that when firing broke out, "a few of the warriors ... still had guns." Dewey Beard's account offers a specific example of concealment. When Forsyth called the men to the council, Beard stayed in his lodge until he heard soldiers were searching the camp. At that point, he "dug a little hole and laid my gun in and covered some dirt over it." After hiding cartridges beneath some manure, Beard finally joined the other men. Indeed, it is quite possible that Big Foot advised his men, as interpreter John Shangrau recalled, to "give them some of the bad guns, but keep the good ones."[5] In the days and years after the massacre, survivors probably felt the need to construct a narrative of compliance rather than defiance. On the morning of December 29, however, outnumbered by a ratio of more than four to one, it would have been entirely reasonable for Big Foot's people to try to keep as many of their weapons as possible. Still, though, at the end of the first phase of the disarming, they had even fewer weapons than before.

The next phase of the disarming began when Forsyth ordered Captain Charles A. Varnum and Captain George D. Wallace to send two details

---

[3] Statement of Frog, 7 Jan. 1891, RCWK, roll 1; Horn Cloud interview. For other statements of the Indians' initial willingness to give up their weapons, see James H. McGregor, *The Wounded Knee Massacre from the Viewpoint of the Sioux* (1940; Rapid City, S.Dak., 1993), 109, 121, 125, 127; "Statement of Hehakawanyakape [Elk that Looks]," Wounded Knee 1890 Collection, folder 1, box 1, Oglala Lakota College Archives, Kyle, S.Dak. (also in Wells, "Ninety-Six Years," 292–93).

[4] Forsyth to Acting AAG DP, 31 Dec. 1890; testimony of Wells. Other witnesses later gave higher numbers, too. John Shangrau gave a figure of seven or eight (John Shangrau interview, 1906, RT, tablet 27, roll 5); Sergeant Ragnar Ling-Vannerus gave a figure of eight in an account written in 1894. See Christer Lindberg, ed., "Foreigners in Action at Wounded Knee," *Nebraska History* 71 (Fall 1990): 175.

[5] Horn Cloud interview; Dewey Beard interview, 1907, RT, tablet 30, roll 5; Shangrau interview. Interestingly, in the 1930s, when Dewey Beard made a statement as part of the survivors' efforts to gain compensation, he did not mention having a gun. See McGregor, *Wounded Knee Massacre*, 96.

to the Indian camp in search of hidden weapons. The Lakota men were told to remain in the council area.[6]

The soldiers looked everywhere. According to Dog Chief, they "would go right into the tents and come out with bundles and tear them open." Joseph Black Hair stated that they "unpacked the packs of the women and looked for weapons," while Charlie Blue Arm saw them "hunting the bed rolls and blankets." The cavalrymen also searched the wagons, as Bertha Kills Close to Lodge recalled, "throwing down our dishes" as they did. Although Joseph Horn Cloud mentioned that the soldiers found "some old shot guns," most of the survivors' testimony says very little about guns and instead emphasizes that they confiscated everything with a sharp edge or point: knives, axes, awls, crowbars, tomahawks, arrows, even tent stakes.[7]

Army officers' accounts noted that the two details confiscated domestic tools but gave greater emphasis to guns. Some gave particular attention to finding weapons beneath the bodies of Lakota women. Whitside testified that "the squaws [made] every effort to conceal [weapons], by hiding and sitting on them and in various other ways, evi[n]cing a most sullen mien." Captain Varnum offered strikingly specific details: "the first rifle I found was under a squaw who was moaning and was so indisposed to the search that I had her displaced, and under her was a beautiful Winchester rifle." He found another gun "under the skirts of a squaw, and we had to throw her on her back to get it."[8] Although another officer involved in the search, Lieutenant James D. Mann, claimed that when the soldiers found "squaws" concealing weapons, they "lifted them as tenderly and treated them as nicely as possible," Varnum's testimony undoubtedly comes closer to the truth and reveals a hostility toward the women that he and other officers continued to feel when they testified a week later. This hostility is evident in their use of the word *squaw*, a term that invoked the racist stereotype of Indian women as ugly and degraded (an image that Varnum accentuated by reserving the description "beautiful" for the rifle). It also appears in Varnum's highly sexualized language (the first woman "moaning" atop a rifle, the second being thrown on her back), suggestive of a rape fantasy.[9] In the days after the

---

[6] Testimony of Whitside; Forsyth to Acting AAG DP, 31 Dec. 1890.

[7] McGregor, *Wounded Knee Massacre*, 101–30 (qtns., 125, 124, 128, 107); Horn Cloud interview. These accounts are confirmed in testimony of Capt. Charles A. Varnum, 7 Jan. 1891, RCWK, roll 1; Shangrau interview; Charles W. Allen, *From Fort Laramie to Wounded Knee: In the West That Was*, edited and with an introduction by Richard E. Jensen (Lincoln, 1997), 195.

[8] Testimony of Whitside; testimony of Varnum. With a couple of exceptions (see McGregor, *Wounded Knee Massacre*, 105, 110), the survivors' testimony says little about the mistreatment of women during the search, perhaps because they did not want to talk about female relatives in this way.

[9] Mann was wounded in the Drexel Mission fight on December 30 and dictated this account to his brother shortly before dying a month later. See Frazer Arnold, "Ghost Dance and Wounded

massacre, the Seventh Cavalry was under intense pressure to explain the high number of casualties among women and children. The officers claimed that they tried to avoid shooting women, but that because the women were mixed up with the men, it was impossible to tell them apart.[10] By indicting the women for concealing weapons, they further blurred the distinction between men and women, at the same time making the women complicit in the events that led to their deaths.

Although the Lakota men were fifty yards or more from the camp as it was being searched, they could see some of what was happening. Their anxiety and anger must have increased as they were forced to wait. At the same time, according to Horn Cloud, an officer informed the Lakota men that he wanted some of them to stand in a line. He told them that a soldier would then stand in front of each of them and "take their cartridges out of their guns and cock them and aim at their [the Indians'] foreheads and pull the triggers." The officer apparently did not actually carry out this threat, but "[s]ome of the Indians were getting wild at such talk," and protested "[w]e are not children to be talked to like this." Although most other accounts do not mention this incident, Horn Cloud's recollection accurately captures the Lakotas' humiliation at being disarmed, as well as their fear that they were about to be killed.[11]

As the camp was being searched, a medicine man began walking around the outside of the council circle.[12] According to Wells, who was interpreting for Forsyth at the time, the medicine man was "throwing up his hands and

---

Knee," *Cavalry Journal* 43 (May–June 1934): 19–29 (qtn., 20). For a discussion of the image of the "squaw" in American culture, see Rayna Green, "The Pocahontas Perplex: The Image of Indian Women in American Culture," *Massachusetts Review* 16 (Autumn 1975): 698–714; for images of Indian women among western army officers, see Sherry L. Smith, *The View From Officers' Row: Army Perceptions of Western Indians* (Tucson, 1990), 55–91.

[10] For this testimony, see note 20, this chapter.

[11] Horn Cloud interview. The only other source that mentions this incident is the Beard interview, but the other survivors' accounts are much briefer and undoubtedly omitted many things they could have recalled.

[12] Although most scholars have followed James Mooney, *The Ghost-Dance Religion and the Sioux Outbreak of 1890*, Fourteenth Annual Report of the Bureau of Ethnology, 1892–93, pt. 2 (Washington, D.C., 1896), 868, in identifying this medicine man as Yellow Bird, only two of the sources give this name and both of these likely depend on other sources for this detail. See Lindberg, ed., "Foreigners in Action," 176; Alice Ghost Horse, "A True Story of What Happened at Wounded Knee (in South Dakota) in December 1890," in U.S. Senate Select Committee on Indian Affairs, *Proposed Wounded Knee Park and Memorial: Hearing before the Select Committee on Indian Affairs, United States Senate*, 102d Cong., 1st sess., 30 April 1991, 64. Most sources give no name at all, while the Horn Cloud interview identifies him as Shakes Bird and "Statement of Hehakawanyakape" gives the name as Stose Yanka (the "St" in this handwritten document misleadingly looks like an "H"). Richard E. Jensen, "Another Look at Wounded Knee," in *Eyewitness at Wounded Knee*, ed. Richard E. Jensen, R. Eli Paul, and John E. Carter (Lincoln, 1991), 21, plausibly argues that Stose Yanke (Sits Up Straight) was a nickname for Good Thunder and that he was the medicine man.

occasionally picking up dust and throwing it towards the soldiers." After a while, he addressed the men, saying, "We are well aware that there are lots of soldiers about us and they have lots of bullets, but I have received assurance that their bullets cannot penetrate us; the prairie is large and the bullets will not go towards you; they will not penetrate you." These words, consistent with the Ghost Dance's ideas about defensive invulnerability, were likely intended to calm the agitated men. Father Francis Craft, a missionary at Pine Ridge, testified that the medicine man's words "indicat[ed] that the Indians were afraid of what might happen to them when their guns would be taken." Forsyth, however, stated that the medicine man had at first told "the Indians to be quiet and submit," but then changed his message and began "talking of wiping out the whites." Wells's testimony says that he told Forsyth that the medicine man was "making mischief" and "inciting trouble," not exactly the same as "talking of wiping out the whites."[13]

Eventually, the medicine man stopped speaking, or was ordered to stop. Soon after, the soldiers completed their search of the Indian camp. At this point, Forsyth ordered Wallace and Varnum to come to the council circle and search the men.[14] While the men were being searched a shot was fired. An instant later, the Seventh Cavalry began firing on the Indians in the council area.

When the firing began, those in the Indian camp, mostly women and children, ran as fast as they could. A few on the east side of the camp went around the council circle toward the north. Joined by some of the men who had been in the council, they faced heavy fire from the cavalry and Hotchkiss guns. Many were cut down but some made it to Wounded Knee Creek and hid beneath the banks. Others in the camp fled on a road to the northwest, where they also came under fire from the Hotchkiss guns. A few of Big Foot's people tried to get beyond the nearby ridges, but most sought shelter in the ravine that ran to the west and south of the camp.[15]

---

[13] Testimony of Wells; testimony of Craft; Forsyth to Acting AAG DP, 31 Dec. 1890. In 1990 Mario Gonzalez, attorney for the Cheyenne River and Pine Ridge Wounded Knee Survivors associations, and Renée Sansom Flood, writing in behalf of these associations, offered persuasive evidence indicting Wells's abilities as an interpreter. See U.S. Senate Select Committee on Indian Affairs, *Wounded Knee Memorial and Historic Site, Little Big Horn National Monument Battlefield: Hearing before the Select Committee on Indian Affairs, United States Senate*, 101st Cong., 2d sess., 25 September 1990, 35, 123; Renée Sansom Flood, *Lost Bird of Wounded Knee: Spirit of the Lakota* (New York, 1995), 28. Despite doubts about Wells's abilities as an interpreter, however, my reading of the evidence indicates that the reason army officers misread the situation was not because of Wells but because of their own predispositions.

[14] Testimony of Wells; testimony of Whitside; Forsyth to Acting AAG DP, 31 Dec. 1890.

[15] Testimony of Whitside; testimony of Craft; testimony of Lieut. W. J. Nicholson, 7 Jan. 1891, RCWK, roll 1; testimony of Lieutenant Charles W. Taylor, 8 Jan. 1891, RCWK, roll 1; testimony of Lieut. W. W. Robinson Jr., 9 Jan. 1891, RCWK, roll 1; McCormick, "Wounded

The few Lakota men who still had guns or knives returned fire or attacked soldiers in hand-to-hand combat. Some men grabbed weapons from the pile of those earlier confiscated. A few Lakotas wrested guns and knives from soldiers, while others took weapons and ammunition from the bodies of soldiers who were dead or dying. Still, only a minority of Lakota men were armed. Some men escaped through the lines and ran into the nearby ravines. A few hid behind hay bales or wagons or in the tipis. The Hotchkiss guns rained shells on them, shredding the canvas tipis and silencing resistance. Within ten minutes of the first shot, the army had killed or seriously wounded the majority of the men in Big Foot's band. Forsyth later reported that eighty-three of the men in Big Foot's band were found dead "in and near the camp." No more than forty escaped to the ravines and open country beyond.[16]

For the next several hours, the Seventh Cavalry hunted the remaining people of Big Foot's band. With most of the men already killed, the large majority were women and children. Rough Feather's wife recalled that she ran to a "cut bank and lay down there. I saw some of the other Indians running up the coulee so I ran with them, but the soldiers kept shooting at us and the bullets flew all around us." Her father, mother, grandmother, and two brothers were killed, and her two-year-old son was shot in the mouth and later died. As people sought shelter in ravines and thickets of brush, artillery gunners pounded them with exploding shells.[17] As the Hotchkiss guns fired, Dewey Beard recalled, "there went up from these dying people a medley of death songs that would make the hardest heart weep." Some shells scored direct hits. According to Beard, one man "was penetrated in the pit of the stomach by a Hotchkiss shell which tore a hole through his body six inches in diameter." Shrapnel caused many wounds, some fatal. The Hotchkiss guns also broke down the protective banks of the ravines and flushed people from thickets, making them more vulnerable to cavalry fire.[18]

The carnage might have been even worse had not some of the surviving men fought back. Although many of the soldiers who were killed and wounded in the first few minutes were the victims of crossfire from their own ranks, others fell because of Lakota bullets and knives. Over the next several hours, Lakotas were able to kill or wound a few additional cavalrymen

Knee and Drexel Mission Fights," 14; Louis Mousseau interview, 1906, RT, tablet 26, roll 5; Ghost Horse, "True Story of What Happened at Wounded Knee," 65–66; McGregor, *Wounded Knee Massacre*, 107, 112, 122, 126; Utley, *Last Days*, 216.

[16] Testimony of Varnum; testimony of Taylor; testimony of Wells; testimony of Craft; Arnold, "Ghost Dance and Wounded Knee," 20; Lindberg, ed., "Foreigners in Action," 176; Beard interview; McGregor, *Wounded Knee Massacre*, 99–128; Forsyth to Acting AAG DP, 31 Dec. 1890; Utley, *Last Days*, 218–19.

[17] McGregor, *Wounded Knee Massacre*, 120.

[18] Beard interview. For a perspective from behind the Hotchkiss guns, see an account by Corporal Paul H. Weinert in W. F. Beyer and O. F. Keydel, eds., *Deeds of Valor from Records in the Archives of the United States Government*, 2 vols. (Detroit, 1906), 1:325–26.

and at times deter soldiers' pursuit. Sergeant Ragnar Ling-Vannerus recalled advancing up one ravine – a "valley of death" – when "all of a sudden a couple of shots cracked." Having already sustained more casualties than he "considered the whole of the Sioux nation to be worth," Ling-Vannerus ordered his unit to retreat. Big Foot's people also received assistance from Oglalas who rode from Pine Ridge and other nearby communities when they heard the firing. Upon reaching the scene of the slaughter, they began rescuing wounded people and shooting at the U.S. soldiers. These efforts undoubtedly saved lives.[19]

At the court of inquiry army officers contended that they took great pains to avoid killing women and children. Captain Henry J. Nowlan's testimony was typical: "It came under my personal observation during that day that it was the cry all over the field, both on the part of officers and enlisted men, not to kill women or children – 'Don't fire, let them go, they are squaws.'" With the entire Seventh Cavalry imploring each other to avoid killing women and children, why did they so abysmally fail? To explain this, officers turned to a time-honored argument, in the words of Captain Edward S. Godfrey: "we could not discern the distinction between bucks and squaws."[20]

An inability to distinguish women from men is a poor excuse for the killing fields of Wounded Knee. At times, especially in the first few minutes after the firing began, smoke and dust obscured soldiers' vision. Later, as the cavalry and artillery fired at Indians huddled in ravines or fleeing across the prairie, the sex of individuals would not have always been apparent. Nonetheless, the officers' defense collapses under the weight of horrific facts. By the late afternoon, when the firing finally subsided, between 270 and 300 of the 400 people in Big Foot's band were dead or mortally wounded. Of these, 170 to 200 were women and children, almost all of whom were slaughtered while fleeing or trying to hide.[21]

---

[19] Lindberg, ed., "Foreigners in Action," 177; McGregor, *Wounded Knee Massacre*, 126; Raymond J. DeMallie, ed., *The Sixth Grandfather: Black Elk's Teachings Given to John G. Neihardt* (Lincoln, 1984), 271–75. One of the main issues before the court of inquiry was whether or not Forsyth's deployment of troops resulted in them shooting each other. The evidence seems clear that some of the cavalrymen were killed by cross-fire, though how many remains unclear. For a discussion of this issue, see Green, "Medals of Wounded Knee," 201.

[20] Testimony of Capt. H. J. Nowlan, 10 Jan. 1891, RCWK, roll 1; testimony of Capt. Edward S. Godfrey, 8 Jan. 1891, RCWK, roll 1. These kinds of statements ran so consistently through officers' testimony that it is impossible to avoid the impression that they were rehearsed. On the general use of the inability to distinguish men from women to justify massacres, see Richard Slotkin, "Massacre," *Berkshire Review* 14 (1979): 122. Some officers also argued that the Indians' initial fire killed many of their own people (e.g., testimony of Nicholson), but even under the army's scenario of several Lakotas firing first, this would account for only a small percentage of the casualties to women and children.

[21] For a good discussion of the varying estimates of the numbers killed, see Richard E. Jensen, "Big Foot's Followers at Wounded Knee," *Nebraska History* 71 (Fall 1990): 194–212. It could be argued that because the soldiers were receiving fire from men in mixed groups, they

Lakota people today tell how in the days following Wounded Knee, Oglalas living nearby came across bodies several miles from the massacre's origin. Found in the fetal position with powder burns near fatal wounds, these bodies offer clear evidence of point-blank executions.[22] Contemporary sources confirm that such atrocities took place. Charles Eastman, who went to Wounded Knee three days after the slaughter, found the bodies of young girls who had "wrapped their heads with shawls and buried their faces with their hands." Eastman surmised that "they did that so that they would not see the soldiers come up to shoot them."[23] American Horse, having talked to many survivors after Wounded Knee, stated that "[l]ittle boys who were not wounded came out of their places of refuge, and as soon as they came in sight a number of soldiers surrounded them and butchered them there."[24]

Military sources provide additional evidence of atrocities. On January 21, 1891, Captain Frank D. Baldwin, a member of the court of inquiry, discovered the bodies of one adult woman, two girls (one seven years old, the other eight), and a ten-year-old boy. They were three miles from Wounded Knee and had been killed "on the day of the Wounded Knee fight." Baldwin concluded that each had been shot once "at so close a range that the person or clothing of each was powder-burned."[25]

---

had no choice but to fire back. But Lakota fire was sporadic and, where it occurred, obviously defensive. Instead of bombarding the ravines and pursuing Lakotas who were trying to flee, Colonel Forsyth could have ordered his men to cease firing and then proceeded to round up the terrified survivors. A few armed men might have escaped, but they would have posed little danger.

[22] I am grateful to Steve Emery for telling me about these stories.

[23] Charles A. Eastman to Mr. Wood, in *Boston Journal*, 8 Jan. 1891, Elmo Scott Watson Papers, box 6, Newberry Library, Chicago. See also Charles A. Eastman (Ohiyesa), *From the Deep Woods to Civilization: Chapters in the Autobiography of an Indian* (1916; Lincoln, 1977), 111.

[24] *ARCIA*, 1891, 181. John Little Finger recalled that from his hiding place in a ravine, he heard an Indian calling out that "the Indians were to come out of there because fighting is not to be continued." With gunshot wounds in the leg and foot, Little Finger could not stand up, but he watched as several others came out of the ravine and sat in a circle. Soldiers surrounded them "and they started to shoot them again and killing them." McGregor, *Wounded Knee Massacre*, 112. Another possible, but uncorroborated, atrocity was reported by Warren K. Moorehead, "The Indian Messiah and the Ghost Dance," *The American Antiquarian and Oriental Journal* 13 (May 1891): 166. Without naming his source, Moorehead stated that "[f]our babies were found on the battle-field with crushed skulls, showing that they had been struck on the head with either the butt of a musket or some heavy club."

[25] Capt. Frank D. Baldwin to AAG DM, 21 Jan. 1891, RCWK, roll 1. Baldwin stated that men under the command of Captain Edward S. Godfrey were responsible for these killings. Godfrey's version was that his men, fearing they were being drawn into a trap, opened fire on two women, two children, and a fourteen-year-old boy, but not at point-blank range. Upon reaching the bodies, one of Godfrey's men discovered that the boy wasn't dead and so shot him in the head out of "fright and the well-known sentiment in the Army at that time to take no chance with a Wounded Indian." See Brig. Gen. E. S. Godfrey to Chief of the Historical Section, Army War College, 29 May 1931, Godfrey Family Papers, box 14,

From the moment the firing subsided, there were disputes about what had happened and who was responsible. Over the decades, one of the most controversial questions about Wounded Knee has been who fired the first shot. Most army officers told a story of several Indians firing on a prearranged signal. Lieutenant W. J. Nicholson, for example, testified, "[t]he first thing I saw of a disturbance was in a buck who started up with a handful of dirt, which he threw in the air. I immediately heard a shot fired from the circle...and then immediately the whole lot of bucks rose, threw off their blankets, faced about and delivered a volley."[26] Embellished versions of the theory that the first shots were fired by fanatical ghost dancers, deluded by the belief that their ghost shirts would protect them, were widely circulated in the press. Within weeks of the massacre, for example, Lieutenant John C. Gresham wrote in *Harper's Weekly*:

[T]he search was hardly begun when the whole body of painted, bedizened fanatics sprang as one man, or rather as one demon, flung off their blankets, and with nothing but breech clouts and light ghost shirts to impede their marvellous agility, began emptying their magazine rifles into the ranks of the soldiers.... The medicine-man gave the signal by throwing in the air a handful of sand and blowing a whistle. Poor deluded savages! Nothing less could give efficient test of their talisman, the ghost shirt.[27]

Most Lakota sources state that the cavalry fired first. Big Foot's grandson, John Little Finger, recalled that he saw some of the soldiers loading their

---

U.S. Army Military History Institute, Carlisle Barracks, Pa.; compare "Statement of Captain E. S. Godfrey," enclosed in Maj. P. D. Vroom to AAG DM, 24 Mar. 1891, RCWK, roll 2.

[26] Testimony of Nicholson. Though not all army officers mentioned a signal from a medicine man, their accounts all support the view that the Lakotas fired first and often suggest a prearranged plan. The only real difference in the military sources is whether the soldiers returned fire immediately. Whitside testified that the Indians fired "at least 50 shots" before the troops returned fire, which not only enhanced his argument for the soldiers' restraint toward the Indians but also deflected criticism that some of the soldiers were killed by cross-fire. See testimony of Whitside. Some sources support Whitside on this point (see, e.g., testimony of Craft), but others indicate that the soldiers fired immediately. See testimony of Robinson; Arnold, "Ghost Dance and Wounded Knee," 20; McCormick, "Wounded Knee and Drexel Mission Fights," 13; Brig. Gen. Guy H. Preston to Historian of the Order of Indian Wars, 5 Apr. 1931, in John M. Carroll, ed., *The Unpublished Papers of the Order of Indian Wars*, book 7 (New Brunswick, 1977), 30; Lindberg, ed., "Foreigners in Action at Wounded Knee," 176.

[27] John C. Gresham, "The Story of Wounded Knee," *Harper's Weekly* 35 (7 February 1891): 107. See also Frederic Remington, "The Sioux Outbreak in South Dakota," *Harper's Weekly* 35 (24 January 1891): 57, 61; *Chadron Democrat*, 1 Jan. 1891, quoted in Allen, *From Fort Laramie to Wounded Knee*, 200–02; William Fitch Kelley, *Pine Ridge 1890: An Eye Witness Account of the Events Surrounding the Fighting at Wounded Knee*, edited and compiled by Alexander Kelley and Pierre Bovis (San Francisco, 1971), 187–88, 198; *Omaha Weekly Bee*, 31 Dec. 1890, p. 6. An instantly produced history, Henry Davenport Northrop, *Indians Horrors Or, Massacres by the Red Men* (Philadelphia, 1891), 539, argued that the Indians fired first "as though" on a "signal."

guns, so he tried to get away. Just then, though, he "heard a white man's voice...sound just like somebody calling like, 'hey.'" In the next instant, "the report of the guns came in one sound. The soldiers commenced to shoot at that moment." Afraid of the Enemy stated that an officer gave "some command and right after the command it sounded like a lightning crash." Most other survivors told similar stories of the soldiers firing on command. Many emphasized that "a white flag" or a "flag of truce" was flying at the time.[28]

The most detailed Lakota accounts of Wounded Knee, those by Dewey Beard and Joseph Horn Cloud, offer a somewhat different version of the first shot. Both Beard and Horn Cloud stated that when the soldiers searched the men in the council circle, they came to a deaf man, whom Beard identified as Black Coyote, and tried to take his gun from him. According to Horn Cloud, the man was holding his gun above his head, "telling the Indians that this was his own gun, that it had cost him a good deal of money." As two or three sergeants struggled with Black Coyote for his gun, Dewey Beard noticed that many of the Indians' faces "changed as if they were wild with fear." He turned and saw that "the guns of the soldiers were pointing at the Council." Suddenly, the deaf man's gun discharged, and "[i]n an instant a volley followed as one shot, and the people began falling." The only Lakota eyewitness to state that an Indian fired first was Help Them, an Oglala traveling with Big Foot's people. He testified: "I saw some of the Indians throw off their blankets, and raise their guns, one of the Indians fired a shot."[29]

Although it is impossible to know for certain who fired the first shot, some scenarios are more plausible than others.[30] The army's contention that

[28] McGregor, *Wounded Knee Massacre*, 111–12, 118 (see also pp. 97, 114, 116, 117, 122, 125, 128).

[29] Horn Cloud and Beard interviews; statement of Help Them, 7 Jan. 1891, RCWK, roll 1. In later testimony, reported in McGregor, *Wounded Knee Massacre*, 97, 109, Beard again focused on the struggle for a gun, while Horn Cloud (White Lance) instead emphasized an officer giving a command, followed by the firing. Other accounts that emphasize a struggle over a weapon include Richard C. Stirk interview, 1906, RT, tablet 8, roll 2; Mousseau interview.

[30] Until recently, the weight of scholarly authority supported the army's version of who fired the first shot. Mooney, *Ghost-Dance Religion*, 868–69, relates that a medicine man had been "urging...resistance, telling them...that the bullets would be unavailing against the sacred 'ghost shirts,'" This man "stooped down and threw a handful of dust into the air, when, as if this were a signal, a young Indian...drew a rifle from under his blanket and fired at the soldiers." Utley, *Last Days*, 212, incorporates Beard's and Horn Cloud's story of Black Coyote's struggle to keep his gun, but he gives priority to the army's perspective by relating that at the exact moment when Black Coyote's gun accidentally fired, the medicine man "gathered a handful of dirt and threw it into the air." Five or six young men then "threw aside their blankets, turned toward K troop, and leveled their rifles." Although some works challenged this perspective before the 1970s, it was not until that decade that scholarly opinion began to shift toward an interpretation more consistent with the Lakota testimony. The best known of these works is Dee Brown, *Bury My Heart at Wounded Knee:*

several Lakotas fired first on a prearranged signal is among the least likely, as it rests on a dubious interpretation of the ghost dancers' understanding of invulnerability. As we saw in Chapter 12, the ghost dancers began wearing protective clothing as a means of self-defense. As they were being disarmed at Wounded Knee, Big Foot's people surely hoped that their ghost shirts and dresses would protect them if the army started firing, but this attitude was far from believing that they could initiate an attack without suffering catastrophic consequences. It is highly doubtful that the medicine man incited the men to fire. As Wells explained in a later interview, his gesture of throwing dirt made visible a logic of invulnerability: Just as dust "floated away, so will the bullets float away harmlessly over the prairies."[31] In all likelihood, army officers, recalling that the medicine man threw dirt as he circled the council, inaccurately placed this gesture at the moment of the first shot. They may have done this consciously, or under pressure to justify their actions, they may have conflated two separate events. In any case, their story of Indians firing on signal enhanced their narrative of treachery.

A more plausible scenario is that under the chaotic and stressful conditions of being disarmed, a single Lakota, acting on his own, fired without premeditation. Charles Eastman, a mixed-blood physician at Pine Ridge who attended to the dying and wounded, wrote that the survivors he spoke with all said that the soldiers searched a "wretch of an Indian, who was known as good for nothing." This man "made the first shot and killed one of the soldiers."[32] Based on similar discussions with survivors, Oglala leaders who visited Washington in February 1891 also testified that the first shot was fired by a "crazy man, a young man of very bad influence, and, in fact, a nobody among that bunch of Indians." (One of their sources may have been Help Them, who, as noted earlier, testified that an Indian fired first.)[33] Another likely scenario, following Beard and Horn Cloud, is that the first shot was

An Indian History of the American West (New York, 1971), 416–17. Even so, several works published in the 1990s repeat the army's version of events. See Edward Lazarus, *Black Hills/ White Justice: The Sioux Nation Versus the United States, 1775 to the Present* (New York, 1991), 115; Robert Wooster, *Nelson A. Miles and the Twilight of the Frontier Army* (Lincoln, 1993), 185–86; Robert W. Larson, *Red Cloud: Warrior-Statesman of the Lakota Sioux* (Norman, 1997), 278. Recent works that argue that the army fired first include Richard E. Jensen, "Another Look at Wounded Knee," in Jensen, Paul, and Carter, eds., *Eyewitness at Wounded Knee*, 19; James O. Gump, *The Dust Rose Like Smoke: The Subjugation of the Zulu and the Sioux* (Lincoln, 1994), 114; Flood, *Lost Bird*, 40; James Wilson, *The Earth Shall Weep: A History of Native America* (New York, 1998), 285. Jerry Green, ed., *After Wounded Knee: Correspondence of Major and Surgeon John Vance Lauderdale while Serving with the Army Occupying the Pine Ridge Reservation, 1890–1891* (East Lansing, 1996), 32, offers the useful observation that the question of who fired first "may never be satisfactorily answered." For an approach that allows multiple sources to speak for themselves, see William S. E. Coleman, *Voices of Wounded Knee* (Lincoln, 2000), 295–301.

[31] Philip F. Wells interview, 1906, RT, tablet 4, roll 1.
[32] Eastman to Wood, 8 Jan. 1891. See also Eastman, *From the Deep Woods*, 112.
[33] *Washington Post*, 12 Feb. 1891, p. 5 (also in Mooney, *Ghost-Dance Religion*, 885).

fired during a struggle for a weapon. If so, Beard's and Horn Cloud's accounts do not necessarily contradict the testimony that Eastman and Oglala leaders summarized but can instead be read as a more detailed version of what they meant when they said an Indian fired first.

Another theory remains possible, but less likely: Army officers ordered their men to fire, either as part of a preconceived plan or as a result of their growing frustration with their perceived lack of success in disarming Big Foot's people. It is possible that survivors who stated in the weeks after the massacre that an Indian fired first did so from an understandable fear of suffering the adverse consequences of contradicting the army. Yet these pressures would not have shaped Beard's and Horn Cloud's testimony, which was given years later under noncoercive conditions.[34] To question the theory that the army simply opened fire does not mean rejecting the narratives of the survivors who heard what they thought was a command just before the shooting broke out. If the first shot was fired by a Lakota, an officer might easily have yelled either a command or some other exclamation just before the first shot. The survivors heard the firing break out, but few actually saw it happen.

Too much weight, however, has been placed on the first shot, as though this alone is the decisive factor in interpreting Wounded Knee. Regardless of who fired the first shot, the United States ultimately bears responsibility for the massacre. Even under the highly unlikely scenario of several Indians agreeing in advance to fire, the eruption of firing was a direct consequence of the army's decision to disarm Big Foot's band. As we have seen, army officers had sufficient information to realize that Big Foot's people were coming peacefully to Pine Ridge. They had no tactical reason to disarm them. Nor can the first shot be considered in isolation from the government's unwarranted decision to send troops in mid-November or, for that matter, the long history of conquest and colonialism that led Sioux people to turn to the Ghost Dance in the first place. Nor can it be considered apart from what happened after the firing began. Even if one or more Lakotas fired first, what followed was an unjustified massacre. From the instant firing began and for several hours thereafter, the Seventh Cavalry and its artillery attachments ruthlessly carried out higher officials' orders to destroy Big Foot's people should they fight.[35]

---

[34] Beard and Horn Cloud gave lengthy interviews in 1907 and 1906, respectively, to Eli S. Ricker, a retired judge and newspaper editor, who appears genuinely interested in understanding Sioux perspectives. On Ricker, see Donald F. Danker, ed., "The Wounded Knee Interviews of Eli S. Ricker," *Nebraska History* 62 (Summer 1981): 152–53.

[35] For these orders, see Chapter 14, note 67. On this point, the key studies disagree. Mooney, *Ghost-Dance Religion*, 869, writes that "the pursuit was simply a massacre." Utley, *Last Days*, 212–30, uses the term *battle* instead of *massacre* and takes pains to defend the army's conduct after the firing broke out.

Some members of the Seventh Cavalry gloried in the massacre as revenge for the Little Bighorn. Three weeks before Wounded Knee, William Kelley of the *Nebraska State Journal* reported that the Seventh Cavalry was "fairly itching" to pursue the "Indians who mercilessly shot down the gallant Custer and 300 men of the Seventh Cavalry on that memorable day of June 25, 1876." Should "an opportunity occur" for the Seventh to "wreak out vengeance for . . . the Little Big Horn," Kelley continued, "the Sioux will receive no quarter." No wonder, then, that with the slaughter underway, an unnamed lieutenant said to John Shangrau, "Scout, we've got our revenge now." To Shangrau's question, "What revenge?," the officer replied, "Why, don't you know, the Custer massacre?"[36] After Wounded Knee, stories circulated that the battlefield was filled with cries of "Remember Custer."[37]

To what extent can the massacre ultimately be explained as an act of vengeance for Custer?[38] One possible answer is that the generals in charge of the campaign conspired days in advance to give the Seventh the opportunity for revenge. Such an overarching theory, however, suffers from the problem that the generals could not have anticipated, let alone controlled, the events that led to the Seventh's interception of Big Foot's band. Had Miles and Brooke had their way, the *Eighth* Cavalry under Sumner would have contained Big Foot's band a week before Wounded Knee. Once Big Foot eluded Sumner, the generals placed their initial hopes in the Seventh Infantry, the Sixth Cavalry, and the Ninth Cavalry. That the Seventh Cavalry intercepted Big Foot was, to some extent, a historical accident. A more modest theory would be that once the Seventh Cavalry captured Big Foot's people, Miles and Brooke realized that circumstances, though unplanned, offered a fortuitous opportunity for revenge and gave Forsyth permission (tacit or

---

[36] Kelley, *Pine Ridge 1890*, 103; Shangrau interview. See also *Washington Post*, 12 Feb. 1891, p. 5; T. A. Bland, ed., *A Brief History of the Late Military Invasion of the Home of the Sioux* (New York, 1891), 17.

[37] Unidentified to O. R. Ainsworth, 1 Mar. 1891, "A Wounded Knee Letter, March 1891," accession H75.I57, box 3543A, South Dakota Historical Society, Pierre. See also Emily H. Lewis, *Wo'Wakita Reservation Recollections: A People's History of the Allen Issue Station District on the Pine Ridge Reservation of South Dakota* (Sioux Falls, S.Dak., 1980), 122; *Omaha World Herald*, 3 Jan. 1891, p. 4.

[38] For a discussion of some of the earlier literature on this question, see Merrill J. Mattes, "The Enigma of Wounded Knee," *Plains Anthropologist* 5 (May 1960): 9; Michael A. Sievers, "The Historiography of 'The Bloody Field . . . That Kept the Secret of the Everlasting Word': Wounded Knee," *South Dakota History* 6 (Winter 1975): 39–40. For recent Lakota statements that Wounded Knee was revenge for the Little Big Horn, see Senate Select Committee on Indian Affairs, *Wounded Knee Memorial*, 35; Mario Gonzalez and Elizabeth Cook-Lynn, *The Politics of Hallowed Ground: Wounded Knee and the Struggle for Indian Sovereignty* (Urbana, 1999), 254; Severt Young Bear and R. D. Theisz, *Standing in the Light: A Lakota Way of Seeing* (Lincoln, 1994), 140; Esther Black Elk DeSersa et al., *Black Elk Lives: Conversations with the Black Elk Family*, ed. Hilda Neihardt and Lori Utecht (Lincoln, 2000), 22.

otherwise) to open fire. Or, perhaps Forsyth, acting in concert with his own officers, decided in advance to open fire to avenge the Seventh's most famous martyr. It is impossible prove or disprove premeditation, but the more likely scenarios for the first shot discussed earlier argue against it.

In more subtle ways, however, memories of the Little Bighorn may have played a role by contributing to the decision to disarm Big Foot's people as well as the Seventh's conduct. Officers of another unit might have carried out orders to disarm in an equally authoritarian way, but those of the Seventh were especially sensitive to the fact that the Sioux had killed their unit's former commander. Eleven of the nineteen officers at Wounded Knee were at the Little Bighorn. Others who joined later quickly imbibed what was known as the "GarryOwen Esprit," after the regimental song. Soldiers of another unit might have slaughtered defenseless Indians for hours and urged their comrades to "Remember Custer," but the desire for revenge burned strongest in the ranks of Custer's own regiment.[39]

Some observers have suggested that alcohol played a decisive role. Although it is true that the officers were drinking whiskey the night before the massacre, it is doubtful that they were drunk the next morning, or that the aftereffects of alcohol influenced their actions. It is also unlikely that enlisted men had access to whiskey. An argument that the Seventh was inebriated offers a powerful way to contest racist stereotypes of drunken Indians, but the chilling fact is that the officers and their men were in their right minds on December 29.[40] Some writers have suggested that the inexperience of the

---

[39] My count of the officers is based on information in notebooks on the Seventh Cavalry at the U.S. Army Military History Institute, Carlisle Barracks, Pa.; William H. Powell, *List of Officers of the Army of the United States from 1779 to 1900* (New York, 1900); Utley, *Last Days*, 201. On the "GarryOwen Esprit" and the regimental song, see Melbourne C. Chandler, *Of Garry Owen in Glory: The History of the Seventh United States Cavalry Regiment* (Annandale, Va., 1960), 412–13, 446. W. P. Richardson, "Some Observations on the Sioux Campaign of 1890–91," *Journal of the Military Service Institution of the United States* 18 (1896): 526, suggests that the "sudden rage" of the soldiers was in part because the Seventh "still carried the memory of Custer and the Little Big Horn." This is rebutted in H. L. Hawthorne, "The Sioux Campaign of 1890–91," *Journal of the Military Service Institution of the United States* 19 (1896): 185, who states that there were only five officers and very few soldiers present at Wounded Knee who had been in the regiment in 1876. Besides understating the number of officers, Hawthorne's argument misses the larger point that to have memories of the Little Big Horn, one did not have to have been there. Joining the Seventh provided access to a powerful set of collectively held memories.

[40] Robert Gessner, *Massacre: A Survey of Today's American Indian* (New York, 1931), 415; Senate Select Committee on Indian Affairs, *Wounded Knee Memorial*, 35–36, 117–20; Flood, *Lost Bird*, 82. Richard Stirk, a trader who was at Wounded Knee, noted that among the officers "whiskey was very abundant the night before the battle" but he did not think the "soldiers had any" nor did he think the "officers were intoxicated next morning." Stirk was not an apologist for the Seventh – he believed that the unit had committed several "barbarities." See Stirk interview. One source that has been used to support the theory of intoxication is B. J. Peterson, *The Battle of Wounded Knee* (Gordon, Nebr., 1941), 26–27,

troops contributed to the duration and intensity of the slaughter. This may have been a factor, yet lack of restraint was pervasive among the enlisted men and received sanction from the officers in the field.[41]

Independent of the empirical issues, exclusive attention to factors like the troops' desire to avenge Custer or their drunkenness or inexperience can obscure the broader context in which Wounded Knee occurred. The actions of the Seventh Cavalry and its officers deserve condemnation, but higher officials who were in Rapid City or Washington when the massacre occurred also bear responsibility.

From the moment they received news of Wounded Knee, U.S. officials moved to deflect any blame that might fall on themselves. As we saw two chapters ago, President Benjamin Harrison assumed no responsibility for the killing and instead expressed disappointment with Miles for failing "to secure the settlement of the Sioux difficulties without bloodshed."[42] Miles in turn blamed his subordinates. Had the campaign ended without violence, Miles would have claimed credit for overseeing its minutest detail, but with blood on the ground, he was suddenly innocent of any connection to events in the field. The day after Wounded Knee he wrote his wife Mary: "Two nights ago I thought I had the whole difficulty in my hand, and without the loss of a single life. But all my efforts to prevent a war appear to have been destroyed by the action of Lt. Col. Sumner and Col. Forsyth."[43] On January 4 Miles relieved Forsyth of his command and ordered a court of inquiry. The two members of this court, Major J. Ford Kent and Captain Frank D. Baldwin, began hearing testimony on January 7 and issued their report six days later. Though Kent and Baldwin criticized Forsyth's disposition of troops, they rejected Miles's view that Forsyth was guilty of either "blind stupidity or criminal indifference." Miles ordered Kent and Baldwin to continue their inquiry. On the eighteenth Kent and Baldwin issued a new report. Though slightly more critical of Forsyth, once again they refused to issue the scathing indictment Miles had in mind. Forsyth was eventually exonerated.[44]

which relates that when the bodies of soldiers killed at Wounded Knee were exhumed for reburial at Fort Riley, Kansas, in 1905 they were not fully decomposed and attributes this to heavy alcohol use. However, alcohol oxidizes quickly and, if anything, would accelerate processes of decomposition.

[41] Mooney, *Ghost-Dance Religion*, 870; Sievers, "Historiography of 'The Bloody Field,'" 52–53; Green, ed., *After Wounded Knee*, 33. According to Hawthorne, "Sioux Campaign," 186, about one-fifth of the enlisted men were recent recruits; Utley, *Last Days*, 202, gives the same figure and points out that the majority had never been under fire.

[42] Chapter 13, note 33.

[43] Quoted in Virginia Weisel Johnson, *The Unregimented General: A Biography of Nelson A. Miles* (Boston, 1962), 288–89.

[44] Utley, *Last Days*, 245–49; Peter R. DeMontravel, "General Nelson A. Miles and the Wounded Knee Controversy," *Arizona and the West* 28 (Spring 1986): 34–38 (qtn., 35); Wooster, *Miles*, 188–91; statements of Maj. J. Ford Kent and Capt. Frank D. Baldwin, 13,

After Wounded Knee, Miles continued to advance in the army, eventually becoming commanding general (see Illustration 14). As the years went by, Miles continued to condemn Forsyth. In 1917 Miles characterized Wounded Knee as a "massacre" in which "not only the warriors but the sick Chief Big Foot, and a large number of women and children who tried to escape by running and scattering over the prairie were hunted down and killed." Forsyth's actions were "most reprehensible" and "the whole affair [w]as most unjustifiable and worthy of severest condemnation." The "least the government can do," Miles concluded, would be "to make a suitable recompense to the survivors."[45]

Miles's argument for compensation was (and remains) compelling. At the same time, it disguises his own culpability. There is plenty of blame to distribute for Wounded Knee, but of all those who shaped the events that led to the massacre, Miles had the largest hand. More than anyone else, it was Miles who demonized the Sioux ghost dancers and defined the terms of the army's campaign. He insisted that Big Foot's people be disarmed and gave Forsyth the orders – "if he fights, destroy him" – that sanctioned the slaughter. Twenty-seven years after Wounded Knee, Miles could shed a tear for "sick Chief Big Foot," but at the time he characterized the Minneconjou leader as a treacherous savage who had to be captured and punished.

One day after the massacre, the winter's first blizzard descended on the northern Plains. Temperatures, well above freezing on December 29, plunged to zero and below. On New Year's Day parties of Indian scouts, soldiers, and civilians went from Pine Ridge to Wounded Knee to bring in any wounded and bury the dead. The parties found several survivors, including a few infants whose mothers' dying bodies had provided enough warmth to keep them alive.[46] Most of these infants remained in Lakota families, but one, Zintkala Nuni (Lost Bird), was taken away. The commander of the Nebraska National Guard, Brigadier General Leonard W. Colby, purchased her from a trader, and he and his wife adopted her. Before returning to his home in Beatrice, Nebraska, General Colby showed his "most interesting Indian relic" to the men under his command.[47] Lost Bird was not the only

---

18 Jan. 1891, RCWK, roll 1; Maj. Gen. Nelson A. Miles to AG, 4 Feb. 1891, RCWK, roll 2; SW to Maj. Gen. John M. Schofield, 12 Feb. 1891, RCWK, roll 2.

[45] Lieut. Gen. Nelson A. Miles to CIA, 13 Mar. 1917, Wounded Knee Compensation Papers, South Dakota Historical Society, Pierre.

[46] Eastman to Wood, 8 Jan. 1891; Eastman, *From the Deep Woods*, 111–13; *New York Times*, 3 Jan. 1891, p. 5; L. W. Colby, "The Sioux Indian War of 1890–91," *Transactions and Reports of the Nebraska State Historical Society* 3 (1892): 159; Paddy Starr interview, 1907, RT, tablet 11, roll 2; Mooney, *Ghost-Dance Religion*, 876–77.

[47] Flood, *Lost Bird*, 56–61, 70–71, 86 (qtn., 71). See also Acting CIA to John R. Brennan, 7 Aug. 1901, copy in Pine Ridge Diary, John Brennan Papers, South Dakota Historical Society, Pierre.

83902

ILLUSTRATION 14. Nelson A. Miles. By the time of this 1895 portrait, Miles had become Commanding General of the U.S. Army. Arizona Historical Society, 1156.

"relic" of Wounded Knee. According to Captain F. A. Whitney, in charge of the burial party, "[t]he camp and bodies of the Indians had been more or less plundered before my command arrived here." Ghoulish collectors were especially interested in ghost shirts and dresses, and this exotic plunder eventually found its way into museums and private collections throughout the world. Only recently have a few of these items been returned to Lakota communities.[48]

The burial party was unable to complete its work on January 1 and so returned to Wounded Knee three days later. Most of the dead were heaped into wagons and dumped in a long trench atop the hill where the Hotchkiss guns had stood. This hill later became known as Cemetery Hill. During the burial, John Blunt Horn, a lay reader for the Episcopal Church, came from his nearby home to ring a bell for the dead so that their spirits would ascend to heaven. Blunt Horn knew many of the people in Big Foot's band; several had received Christian baptism.[49] A very different event was staged by commercial photographer George Trager, who asked the burial party to pose above their partially completed work. Trager's camera recorded a shockingly brutal image (see Illustration 15). Though some of the men in the burial party have shovels, most hold rifles. A soldier at the far right goes so far as to point his weapon toward the bodies on the lip of the grave, as though to assert once more the army's "victory" six days before. The bodies are treated, both by the burial party and the photographer, as an undifferentiated mass. They are nothing more than a pile of "dead Indians," undeserving of consideration as fully individual human beings.[50]

The military campaign did not end with the destruction of Big Foot's band. Indeed, Wounded Knee was a serious setback to the army's goal of gaining control over the ghost dancers. On the morning of December 29 the last remaining dancers under Short Bull and Kicking Bear had decided to surrender and were within a few miles of Pine Ridge Agency. Newspapers had already declared "the great Indian conspiracy" to be "crushed without bloodshed, and peace, quiet, and security restored" to the West.[51] When they heard

---

[48] Capt. F. A. Whitney to Acting AAG DP, 3 Jan. 1891, RCWK, roll 1; R. Eli Paul, "Wounded Knee and the 'Collector of Curios,'" *Nebraska History* 75 (Summer 1994): 209–15; "Sioux Seek Return of Sacred Shirt," *London Times*, 10 Apr. 1995, p. 3.

[49] *Washington Post*, 4 Jan. 1891, p. 1; *Inter Ocean* (Chicago), 7 Jan. 1891, p. 9; Capt. Frank D. Baldwin to AAG DM, 5 Feb. 1891, RCWK, roll 2. I am grateful to Mike Her Many Horses for the Blunt Horn story and permission to use it.

[50] Mooney, *Ghost-Dance Religion*, 878–79; John E. Carter, "Making Pictures for a News-Hungry Nation," in Jensen, Paul, and Carter, eds., *Eyewitness at Wounded Knee*, 49; Christina Klein, "'Everything of Interest in the Late Pine Ridge War Are Held by Us for Sale': Popular Culture and Wounded Knee," *Western Historical Quarterly* 25 (Spring 1994): 55–56.

[51] *Inter Ocean* (Chicago), 28 Dec. 1890, p. 1.

ILLUSTRATION 15. Mass burial at Wounded Knee. Nebraska State Historical Society, RG2845:13–12.

the guns of Wounded Knee, however, Short Bull's and Kicking Bear's people scattered. Many vowed to fight. Ghost dancers who had already come to the agency, Little Wound's and Big Road's people, fled Pine Ridge. Hundreds of Oglalas who had never participated in the Ghost Dance joined them. Some Lakotas took up positions in nearby hills and fired on the agency, wounding two soldiers.[52]

In their rage and with an eye toward needed supplies, some Indians raided the agency herd and the homes and stock herds of nonghost dancers. Far more plundering took place after Wounded Knee than before.[53] On the thirtieth a party of forty to fifty Oglalas and Brulés rode toward the Holy Rosary Mission (also known as Drexel Mission) and set fire to a nearby log cabin.

[52] Short Bull, "As Narrated by Short Bull," pp. 16–17, Buffalo Bill Memorial Museum, Golden, Colo.; *ARSW*, 1891, 150; Brig. Gen. John R. Brooke to AAG DM, 2 Mar. 1891, RCWK, roll 2; DeMallie, ed., *Sixth Grandfather*, 271–74; Thisba Hutson Morgan, "Reminiscences of My Days in the Land of the Ogallala Sioux," *South Dakota Historical Collections* 29 (1958): 54–56; Eastman, *From the Deep Woods*, 107–108; Kay Graber, ed., *Sister to the Sioux: The Memoirs of Elaine Goodale Eastman, 1885–91* (Lincoln, 1978), 160; Utley, *Last Days*, 231–34.

[53] This observation is based on my sampling of depredations claims enclosed in report of James A. Cooper, 25 Feb. 1892, OIA, file 7805–1892 (see Chapter 6, note 39).

Seeing the smoke, General Brooke dispatched Forsyth's Seventh once again. Finding no "hostiles" at the mission, Forsyth continued down White Clay Creek. As the valley narrowed beneath steep cliffs, Forsyth came under heavy fire from Sioux on nearby tablelands and sent a courier to Pine Ridge with an urgent plea for help. The nearest unit was the Ninth Cavalry, African Americans known as buffalo soldiers under the command of white officers. Though the Ninth's troopers had just completed a forty-mile overnight march from the Badlands to Pine Ridge, they rode down White Clay Creek and drove off the Indians. Forsyth's command suffered one killed and five wounded, one mortally.[54] If not for the "valiant Buffalo soldiers of the 9th," the Chicago *Inter Ocean* wrote, the "massacre of 1876 would have been repeated." Although this judgment was surely exaggerated, the Seventh did owe much to the Ninth. As the militants abandoned the fight, men from the two regiments "hugged one another on the field."[55] But although the Ninth had saved Forsyth from becoming a second Custer, army officials quickly relegated the buffalo soldiers to their former status, closer to the Sioux than their white comrades. When the campaign finally ended in late January, the army ordered the Seventh and other units to return to their posts, but the Ninth remained at Pine Ridge with only canvas tents to shelter them from the brutal winds.[56]

After the Drexel Mission fight, General Miles feared the Sioux were planning a full-blown assault on Pine Ridge. Miles moved his headquarters from Rapid City to Pine Ridge and began erecting defensive fortifications at the

---

[54] *ARSW*, 1891, 151; Brooke to AAG DM, 2 Mar. 1891; Col. E. M. Heyl to AAG DM, 28 Jan. 1891, RCWK, roll 2; Emil Perrig diary, 30, 31 Dec. 1890, St. Francis Mission Records, series 7, box 5, Marquette University Special Collections, Milwaukee; Wells interview; Alex W. Perry, "The Ninth United States Cavalry in the Sioux Campaign of 1890," *Journal of the United States Cavalry Association* 4 (1891): 39–40; William H. Leckie, *The Buffalo Soldiers: A Narrative of the Negro Cavalry in the West* (Norman, 1967), 256–58; Frank N. Schubert, *Black Valor: Buffalo Soldiers and the Medal of Honor, 1870–1898* (Wilmington, Del., 1997), 121–25; Charles L. Kenner, *Buffalo Soldiers and Officers of the Ninth Cavalry, 1867–1898: Black and White Together* (Norman, 1999), 127–28; Utley, *Last Days*, 236–41.

[55] *Inter Ocean* quoted in *Army and Navy Journal* 28 (17 January 1891): 355 (1st qtn.); Charles G. Seymour, "The Sioux Rebellion," *Harper's Weekly* 35 (7 February 1891): 106 (2d qtn.).

[56] A ballad by W. H. Prather, a private in the Ninth Cavalry, which generally celebrated the army's subjugation of the Sioux, concluded by protesting the unfair treatment of the Ninth:

> The rest have gone home; and to meet the blizzard's wintry blast
> The Ninth, the willing Ninth, is camped here till the last.
> We were the first to come; will be the last to leave;
> Why are we compelled to stay; why this reward receive?
> In warm barracks our recent comrades take their ease,
> While we, poor devils, and the Sioux are left to freeze.

Mooney, *Ghost-Dance Religion*, 883; *Army and Navy Journal* 28 (7 March 1891): 483 (qtn.); see also Quintard Taylor, *In Search of the Racial Frontier: African Americans in the American West, 1528–1990* (New York, 1998), 172.

agency on January 2.[57] These actions triggered a new round of wild rumors. Under headlines like "REDSKINS WANT BLOOD" and "PINE RIDGE IN DIRE PERIL," the *Chicago Tribune* reported that an "Indian army," four thousand strong, was planning a major attack.[58] The *Tribune* quoted no less an authority than Buffalo Bill Cody, now an officer in the Nebraska National Guard, that "a big battle is almost sure to occur within a few days in the immediate vicinity of Pine Ridge." Building on the emerging theory that fanatical ghost dancers in Big Foot's band had "committed suicide," Cody informed the *Tribune* that the Indians "have reached that stage of their madness in which they will court death." The "Messiah craze," Cody explained, "has made them fatalists to that degree that they firmly believe that if they go under in battle they will come to life again in the spring."[59]

Fear of an Indian attack spread far beyond Pine Ridge. In northern Nebraska settlers believed they were in "great peril." Women and children from Rushville, Chadron, and Haysprings took the train east to the security of Sioux City, Iowa, leaving the men to defend civilization's most vulnerable outposts. A dispatch from southern Idaho indicated that the town of Pocatello was "in a great state of excitement over the action of the Shoshone Indians," who the night before had "indulged in a war dance." Anywhere Indians danced, or were thought to dance, word spread that fanatical savages were preparing for war.[60] In the end, Indians spared both Pocatello and Pine Ridge. The far more likely possibility that a new incident would spark another outbreak of violence against the Sioux did not happen either. Conflict threatened to erupt when Plenty Horses, a Carlisle graduate, killed Lieutenant Edward Casey on January 7, and, in an unrelated incident four days later, when white settlers killed Few Tails, the leader of a small hunting party.[61] But the army's campaign against the Sioux ghost dancers came to a close without additional serious violence.

Many Americans wanted more Indians to die. One citizen wrote the Secretary of War to propose "establishing an electric plant at Pine Ridge and stretching a wire around the hostile camp. Then, turning on the current, the Indians are to be driven down to the wire, which is to be drawn closer and closer. Contact... would cause general death." Retired General William Tecumseh Sherman shared these genocidal impulses, though he was willing to rely on existing technology. Sherman wrote his niece, Miles's wife Mary,

[57] *ARSW,* 1891, 151; *Chicago Tribune,* 3 Jan. 1891, p. 1.
[58] *Chicago Tribune,* 5, 6 Jan. 1891, p. 1.
[59] For Cody's interview, see *Chicago Tribune,* 7 Jan. 1891, p. 1. The phrase "committed suicide" appeared in a dispatch from Pine Ridge in the *Inter Ocean* (Chicago), 5 Jan. 1891, p. 1.
[60] *Chicago Tribune,* 7 Jan. 1891, p. 1 (1st qtn.); *New York Herald,* 6 Jan. 1891, p. 3; *Rocky Mountain News* (Denver) quoted in *Chicago Tribune,* 9 Jan. 1891, p. 5 (2d qtn.).
[61] On these incidents, see Utley, *Last Days,* 257–58, 261–64; Robert M. Utley, "The Ordeal of Plenty Horses," *American Heritage* 26 (December 1974): 15–19, 82–86.

that the more Sioux her husband "kills now, the less he will have to do later."[62] But Miles rejected this approach and turned instead to diplomacy. By demonstrating the validity of the humanitarian criticism that the army was a machine for killing, Wounded Knee had seriously damaged Miles's goal of having the army assume control over western Indian reservations. Additional violence would further decrease the chances of realizing this objective.

Lakota leaders also wanted to avoid further bloodshed, though for very different reasons. In the first few days of January these leaders faced a chaotic and volatile situation. Their people were grieving, angry, and frightened. Many were in no mood for peace. When Miles sent scouts with a letter to the "hostile camp," fifteen miles from the agency on White Clay Creek, the Indians tore it "to fragments and threw them into the fire, saying, 'We want no treaty; we are here to fight.'"[63] Faced with this rebuff, Miles turned to Oglala leaders, among them Young Man Afraid of His Horses, who had recently returned from the Crow Agency. These intermediaries brokered an agreement between Miles and the militants that brought the campaign to a close. Although newspapers reported that Miles took a hard line, he offered significant concessions. One, clearly apparent in the historical record, was that the Oglalas could send a delegation to Washington to discuss their grievances. Another, evident through the unfolding of events, was that he would not disarm them.[64] Several Ghost Dance leaders agreed to be arrested, but their term of imprisonment was set at only six months. The last of the ghost dancers rode into Pine Ridge on January 15. Two weeks later, thirty prisoners left for Fort Sheridan, Illinois. As it turned out, the ghost dancers were out of prison by spring. Buffalo Bill took them on a European tour.[65]

---

[62] *Washington Post*, 10 Jan. 1891, p. 1 (1st qtn.); W. T. Sherman to Mary Miles, 7 Jan. 1891, Nelson A. Miles Family Papers, box 4, Library of Congress, Washington, D.C. (2d qtn.).

[63] Perrig diary, 4 Jan. 1891 (1st qtn.); *Inter Ocean* (Chicago), 5 Jan. 1891, p. 1 (2d qtn.).

[64] On the negotiations, see *Inter Ocean* (Chicago), 5 Jan. 1891, p. 1, 7 Jan. 1891, p. 1; Maj. Gen. Nelson A. Miles to AG, 5, 14 Jan. 1891, RCWK, roll 1; Maj. Gen. Nelson A. Miles to AG, 27 Jan. 1891, RCWK, roll 2; AAG to Maj. Gen. Nelson A. Miles, 15 Jan. 1891, RCWK, roll 1; Joseph Agonito, "Young Man Afraid of His Horses: The Reservation Years," *Nebraska History* 79 (Fall 1998): 126. In ARSW, 1891, 153, Miles reported that "between 600 and 700 guns" were surrendered. Newspaper accounts suggest that this was probably an inflated number, but even if accurate, it probably accounted for less than half the weapons. Newspaper reports offer varying figures for the number of arms, though, taken together, they make it clear that hundreds of weapons remained cached or hidden away. See *New York Times*, 16 Jan. 1891, p. 2, 17 Jan. 1891, p. 5, 19 Jan. 1891, p. 2; *Omaha World Herald*, 17 Jan. 1891, p. 1, 18 Jan. 1891, p. 2; *Chicago Tribune*, 26 Jan. 1891, p. 1.

[65] Maj. Gen. Nelson A. Miles to AG, 15 Jan. 1891, RCWK, roll 1; *New York Times*, 16 Jan. 1891, p. 2; *Chicago Tribune*, 28 Jan. 1891, p. 1; Short Bull, "As Narrated By Short Bull," 14; Utley, *Last Days*, 271–72.

Conclusion

After Wounded Knee

At the end of *Black Elk Speaks*, John G. Neihardt's famous interpretation of Black Elk's life, Black Elk recalls the terrible slaughter of Wounded Knee. "I can still see the butchered women and children lying heaped and scattered all along the crooked gulch," Black Elk says. "And I can see that something else died there in the bloody mud, and was buried in the blizzard. A people's dream died there." The dream was "beautiful," Black Elk continues, but now "the nation's hoop is broken and scattered. There is no center any longer, and the sacred tree is dead." These are sad and moving words, but as recent scholarship has shown, Black Elk never said them. In fact, according to the transcripts of Neihardt's interviews with Black Elk, he ended his story of Wounded Knee with the words: "Two years later I was married." Drawing on deeply ingrained images of American Indians as a vanishing race, Neihardt invented the imagery of the broken and scattered hoop to give his narrative the desired tragic ending.[1]

The massacre at Wounded Knee was certainly a traumatic event for the Plains Sioux. It was particularly devastating for the survivors (see Illustration 16) and their relatives and the Minneconjous, who lost close to twenty

---

[1] John G. Neihardt, *Black Elk Speaks: Being the Life Story of a Holy Man of the Ogalala Sioux* (1932; Lincoln, 1979), 270; Raymond J. DeMallie, ed., *The Sixth Grandfather: Black Elk's Teachings Given to John G. Neihardt* (Lincoln, 1984), 282. For a range of interpretations about the relationship between Black Elk and Neihardt's text and the life of Black Elk, see Sally McCluskey, "*Black Elk Speaks*: And So Does John Neihardt," *Western American Literature* 6 (Winter 1972): 231–42; Julian Rice, *Black Elk's Story: Distinguishing Its Lakota Purpose* (Albuquerque, 1991); Michael F. Steltenkamp, *Black Elk: Holy Man of the Oglala* (Norman, 1993); Clyde Holler, *Black Elk's Religion: The Sun Dance and Lakota Catholicism* (Syracuse, 1995); Clyde Holler, ed., *The Black Elk Reader* (Syracuse, 2000); Esther Black Elk DeSersa et al., *Black Elk Lives: Conversations with the Black Elk Family*, ed. Hilda Neihardt and Lori Utecht (Lincoln, 2000). For the idea of Indians as a "vanishing race," see Brian W. Dippie, *The Vanishing American: White Attitudes and U.S. Indian Policy* (Middletown, Conn., 1982).

ILLUSTRATION 16. Blue Whirlwind and children. Survivors of Wounded Knee. National Anthropological Archives, 3200A1.

percent of their people.[2] Nonetheless, hope did not die at Wounded Knee, nor did the massacre mark the end of the Sioux nation. Plains Sioux communities continued to struggle to survive and search for ways to return to the red road. As always, people chose different paths.

[2] Based on population figures in *ARCIA*, 1888, 25.

Some Lakotas continued to hold ghost dances. At first glance, this might seem surprising. Hadn't the slaughter at Wounded Knee discredited the Ghost Dance by disproving its claims about the invulnerability of ghost dresses and shirts?[3] Not necessarily. Lakotas had always understood invulnerablity as contingent on human action. Thus, rather than indicting the Ghost Dance itself, the "failure" of the ghost dresses and shirts could be attributed to improper preparation of the garments or inadequacies in wearers' mental/spiritual condition, as when Black Elk became afraid and doubted his power (see Chapter 12). Or, the "failure" of invulnerability might only mean that protective clothing had been a mistaken departure from Wovoka's original teachings.[4] For many who had experienced visions of the new world to come and had seen deceased relatives, the powers of the Ghost Dance remained strong.

Richmond Clow has pointed out that Indians at Pine Ridge and Rosebud continued to hold ghost dances after Wounded Knee. In early 1892 the Pine Ridge agent reported that "a considerable number of the Indians are still clinging to their old belief of the Messiah and general change of things when he comes." Reports of ghost dancing and praying to "Jack Wilson, Indian Messiah" persisted into the early twentieth century. As time went on, ghost dancers continued to recall their experiences. This very recounting kept alive the movement's possibilities, although themes of transformation became less pronounced.[5] The Ghost Dance persisted among other tribes into the twentieth century, often interacting with other spiritual practices and undergoing significant modification.[6]

---

[3] For affirmative answers to this question, see James Mooney, *The Ghost-Dance Religion and the Sioux Outbreak of 1890*, Fourteenth Annual Report of the Bureau of Ethnology, 1892–93, pt. 2 (Washington, D.C., 1896), 927; Robert M. Utley, *The Last Days of the Sioux Nation* (New Haven, 1963), 284.

[4] The statement in Leonard Crow Dog and Richard Erdoes, *Crow Dog: Four Generations of Sioux Medicine Men* (New York, 1995), 45, that Crow Dog repudiated invulnerable clothing as foreign to Wovoka's teachings may reflect the emergence of this kind of interpretation. For a useful analysis of Indians' assessment of the "failure" of spiritual power in a similar situation, see Gregory Evans Dowd, *A Spirited Resistance: The North American Indian Struggle for Unity, 1745–1815* (Baltimore, 1992).

[5] Richmond L. Clow, "The Lakota Ghost Dance after 1890," *South Dakota History* 20 (Winter 1990): 323–33 (1st qtn., 331); William Iron Crow et al. to H. M. Tidwell, 12 Dec. 1917, in folder labeled "Wounded Knee," Record Group 75, National Archives and Records Administration, Kansas City (2d qtn.). Although a Ghost Dance was held during the American Indian Movement's occupation of Wounded Knee in 1973 (see Crow Dog and Erdoes, *Crow Dog*, 126–31), it does not form part of the contemporary religious life of the Plains Sioux. See Stephen E. Feraca, *Wakinyan: Lakota Religion in the Twentieth Century* (Lincoln, 1998).

[6] Alexander Lesser, *The Pawnee Ghost Dance Hand Game: Ghost Dance Revival and Ethnic Identity* (1933; Lincoln, 1996); James H. Howard, *The Canadian Sioux* (Lincoln, 1984), 173–79; Judith Vander, *Shoshone Ghost Dance Religion: Poetry Songs and Great Basin Context* (Urbana, 1997); Benjamin R. Kracht, "Kiowa Religion in Historical Perspective," in *Native American Spirituality: A Critical Reader*, ed. Lee Irwin (Lincoln, 2000), 246–48. Based on

In recent years, Indians have seen the increase in bison populations and the revival of traditional cultural and religious practices as at least partial fulfillment of the Ghost Dance's potential. At the same time, Native American novelists and poets have used the Ghost Dance as a metaphor to express the ongoing possibilities of liberation. To many Native people, it is abundantly clear that western civilization will inevitably collapse under the weight of its technological madness and moral bankruptcy. Whether in ten, one hundred, or five hundred years, Wovoka's prophesy will eventually be fulfilled.[7]

Although some Lakotas continued pursuing the Ghost Dance after Wounded Knee, most turned to different methods in their effort to walk the red road. As we saw at the end of the last chapter, in early January 1891 nonghost dance leaders successfully negotiated the right to send a delegation to Washington. Oglala delegates left Pine Ridge for Washington on January 26 and were joined by representatives from Rosebud, Cheyenne River, Standing Rock, and Lower Brulé.[8] On February 8 the delegates presented their grievances to Commissioner of Indian Affairs Thomas Jefferson Morgan. Morgan was unable to make concrete promises, but he expressed the hope that Congress would respond. A month later, Congress appropriated sufficient funds to restore rations to their pre-1890 level for the coming fiscal year and to fund a commission to adjust the Pine Ridge–Rosebud boundary.[9]

---

an analysis of the persistence of the Ghost Dance among Shoshones and Bannocks of Fort Hall, Idaho, Gregory E. Smoak, *Ghost Dances and Identity: American Indian Ethnicity, Race, and Prophetic Religion in the Nineteenth Century* (Berkeley, forthcoming), shows how ghost dancing encouraged processes of ethnic and racial identity formation.

[7] On the return of the buffalo, see Ernest Callenbach, *Bring Back the Buffalo!: A Sustainable Future for America's Great Plains* (Washington, D.C., 1996); David Cournoyer, "Return of the Buffalo: The Efforts to Restore Bison to Native Americans," *Tribal College: Journal of American Higher Education* 7 (Spring 1996): 14–18. For examples of the Ghost Dance in literature, see Leslie Marmon Silko, *Almanac of the Dead* (New York, 1991), 721–25; Sara Little-Crow Russell, "Ghost Dance," quoted in Winona LaDuke, *All Our Relations: Native Struggles for Land and Life* (Cambridge, Mass., 1999), 69–70. On the future realization of Wovoka's prophesies, see Mike Davis, *Dead Cities and Other Tales* (New York, 2002), 30.

[8] From newspaper accounts, I have compiled the following, incomplete list of names: George Sword, Young Man Afraid of His Horses, American Horse, Big Road, Spotted Elk, Hump, Two Strike, High Pipe, High Hawk, Little Wound, Spotted Horse, Fire Lightning, Fast Thunder, He Dog, John Grass, Hollow Horn Bear, High Horse, Medicine Bull, White Ghost, Little No Heart, Mad Bear, Big Mane, Turning Hawk, White Bird. See *Chicago Tribune*, 28 Jan. 1891, p. 1; *Washington Post*, 8 Feb. 1891, p. 2, 9 Feb. 1891, p. 5, 10 Feb. 1891, p. 6, 12 Feb. 1891, p. 5.

[9] *Washington Post*, 8 Feb. 1891, p. 2; *ARCIA*, 1891, 137, 139–40. Another issue was whether the delegates wanted army officers as agents. Higher authorities, including the army brass, had already rebuffed Miles's efforts to have the War Department reassume responsibility for western Indian reservations. Miles had been able to appoint an army officer at Pine Ridge, however, and it remained possible that this and the other western Sioux agencies would remain under military control. The delegates repudiated this idea. Maj. Gen. J. M. Schofield to Maj. Gen. Nelson A. Miles, 7 Jan. 1891, RCWK, roll 1; *Washington Post*, 10 Feb. 1891, p. 6.

These concessions were painfully inadequate, but the Sioux had little choice but to take what they could and work from there.

In 1892, 792 Sioux signed a petition demanding compensation for the United States' theft of the Black Hills.[10] The Sioux continued to fight for compensation throughout most of the twentieth century. In 1979 the Indian Claims Commission ruled in their favor, and the U.S. Supreme Court affirmed this decision in 1980. By this time, however, most Lakotas had become committed to the actual return of the Black Hills and rejected monetary compensation. In 1877 Americans thought they had permanently acquired the Black Hills from a people whose fate was extinction, but the future has always been less predictable and more open than nineteenth-century Americans imagined. The Plains Sioux may yet regain the Black Hills.[11]

While in Washington in February 1891, the delegates also wanted to talk about Wounded Knee. Most of them had been critical of the dancers for risking a military crackdown. After the massacre, however, they did not lash out against the ghost dancers but instead vigorously contested the army's story that the ghost dancers were to blame. American Horse, for example, observed:

Yes, sir; they were fired right down, and there was a woman with her infant in her arms, who was killed as she almost reached the flag of truce. . . . The women as they were fleeing with their babes on their backs were killed together, shot right through and the women who were very heavy with child were also killed.

American Horse informed Morgan that he had been "very loyal to the Government," but now he came "with a very great blame against the Government on my heart." Had only men been killed, "we would feel almost greatful [*sic*] for it," but the killing of women and children, "the future strength of the Indian people," made him feel "very sorely."[12]

A portion of the American public was receptive to Lakotas' criticisms of army conduct at Wounded Knee, but the majority was not. The delegates did not convince army officers to change their story, but they may have

---

[10] Joseph Agonito, "Young Man Afraid of His Horses: The Reservation Years," *Nebraska History* 79 (Fall 1998): 129.

[11] Edward Lazarus, *Black Hills/White Justice: The Sioux Nation Versus the United States, 1775 to the Present* (New York, 1991); Mario Gonzalez and Elizabeth Cook-Lynn, *The Politics of Hallowed Ground: Wounded Knee and the Struggle for Indian Sovereignty* (Urbana, 1999); Alexandra New Holy, "The Heart of Everything That Is: Paha Sapa, Treaties, and Lakota Identity," *Oklahoma City University Law Review* 23 (Spring/Summer 1998): 317–52; Jill E. Martin, "Returning the Black Hills," *Journal of the West* 39 (Summer 2000): 31–37; Dennis M. Christafferson, "Sioux, 1930–2000," in *Plains*, ed., Raymond J. DeMallie, vol. 13, pt. 2, *Handbook of North American Indians*, ed. William C. Sturtevant (Washington, D.C., 2001), 836–38.

[12] *Washington Post*, 12 Feb. 1891, p. 5. Much of this testimony appeared in *ARCIA*, 1891, 179–81. See also T. A. Bland, ed., *A Brief History of the Late Military Invasion of the Home of the Sioux* (Washington, D.C., 1891), 15–16.

ILLUSTRATION 17. Oscar Howe, *Wounded Knee Massacre*. Painted in 1960. Dwight D. Eisenhower Library and Museum, Abilene, Kans. Copyright, Adelheid Howe, 1983.

increased the army's defensiveness. If so, this may partly explain why army officials recommended in late 1891 that twenty-five men receive the Medal of Honor for supposed deeds of valor at Wounded Knee. That twenty of these recommendations were approved, a suspiciously high number given the circumstances, suggests that military officials felt the need to bolster a flimsy narrative of courage under fire.[13]

During the twentieth century Sioux people continued to contest the United States' official version of Wounded Knee. One way of doing this was through visual representation. Dakota artist Oscar Howe's 1960 painting, *Wounded Knee Massacre* (Illustration 17), recalled George Trager's by then well-known photograph of the mass grave (see Chapter 15, Illustration 15), while dissenting from its colonial vantage point.

To distill the essence of the massacre, Howe conflated several elements and made them synchronous. In the background to the left, a Hotchkiss gun fires, while to the right, a soldier takes point-blank aim at a woman pleading for

[13] Jerry Green, "The Medals of Wounded Knee," *Nebraska History* 75 (Summer 1994): 200–08.

her life beneath the American flag. The painting's massive foreground brings these emblematic details into a deeply disturbing coherence. There, soldiers stand shoulder to shoulder as their commander lifts his eyes to the heavens, beseeching, or perhaps thanking, a demonic god. Though one soldier, to the far left, looks questioningly at his commander, the others, in orchestrated unison, fire into the space below them. This space suggests both "the pit," the ravine to the west of Big Foot's camp where the army's firing was fiercest, and the mass grave atop Cemetery Hill. Some of Big Foot's people have already died, but most writhe in the agony of the living resisting their slaughter. In its treatment of Big Foot's people as individuals, Howe's painting contests the perspective in Trager's photograph. At the same time, the reference to the mass grave shows that Wounded Knee was not made up of a series of discrete, unconnected events. Instead, from the disarming to the burial of the dead, it consisted of a series of acts held together by an underlying logic of racist domination.[14]

Although Howe's painting served the general purpose of interrogating American society's assumptions about Wounded Knee and its violent propensities, survivors of the massacre and their descendants have had a more specific goal in mind. They have contested the army's version of Wounded Knee in order to secure compensation. In 1938 members of the Wounded Knee Survivors' Association, led by James Pipe on Head, testified in support of a congressional bill to provide $1,000 to each survivor or heirs. The War Department responded that the January 1891 army investigation had "completely vindicated" the Seventh Cavalry. Therefore, there was "no reason why the surviving Sioux Indians or their next of kin should be reimbursed by the United States Government for the result of an action, for which, insofar as the records of the Department show, they were responsible." Renewed agitation in the 1970s resulted in consideration of a new bill to provide $3,000 to descendants of the survivors. Once again, the army opposed compensation, citing the absence of "credible evidence . . . of a premeditated intention on the part of the troops to injure the innocent."[15]

One hundred years after the massacre, descendants of survivors once again came before Congress, this time to seek a formal apology as well as monetary compensation. Congress passed a resolution expressing "its deep regret

[14] Howe himself described the painting as "giv[ing] the impression of an open grave with a structure-like tombstone of soldiers." See *The Bulletin* (Institute of American Indian Studies, University of South Dakota), no. 124 (Winter 1990): 3. Elsewhere, he described this impression as "unintentional." See Elaine Mitchell, "Oscar Howe, Sioux Artist: A Biographical, Cultural, and Stylistic Analysis," M.A. thesis, University of New Mexico, 1996, 106.

[15] U.S. House Subcommittee on Indian Affairs, *Sioux Indians: Wounded Knee Massacre: Hearings before the Committee on Indian Affairs, House of Representatives*, 75th Cong., 3d sess., 7 March, 12 May 1938, 7; U.S. Senate Committee on the Judiciary, *Wounded Knee Massacre: Hearings before the Committee on the Judicary, United States Senate*, 94th Cong., 2d sess., 5, 6 February 1976, 214.

to the Sioux people and in particular to the descendants of the victims and survivors for this terrible tragedy" and commended South Dakota's proclamation of 1990 as a "Year of Reconciliation."[16] But it rejected compensation. "If reparations were to be paid in this instance," South Dakota Senator Larry Pressler argued, "what of the descendants of the appalling massacre of Indians at Sand Creek or the children of white settlers killed in other incidents?" To further the goal of reconciliation, Pressler advised Indians to "look to the future," not to the past. History is full of "[t]errible tragedies," Pressler admonished, but "we cannot and should not attempt to change history with a checkbook." For Lakotas, however, history is not a series of equally weighted "tragedies" that cancel each other out and can then be forgotten. Reconciliation requires non-Indians to acknowledge a long and ongoing history of injustice. From this perspective, Mario Gonzalez, attorney for the Wounded Knee survivors' associations, argued that compensation was necessary to make an apology for Wounded Knee "meaningful and substantive." Otherwise, it would be "insincere and hollow."[17]

Although most Sioux people would have welcomed compensation and were disappointed by its rejection, they realized that overcoming the painful legacy of Wounded Knee could not ultimately depend on the goodwill of U.S. politicians. For this reason, they undertook initiatives of their own. One of these began in late December 1986 when nineteen Lakotas retraced the journey of Big Foot and his people from their camp on the Cheyenne River to Wounded Knee, thus inaugurating the *Si Tanka Wokiksuye* (Big Foot Memorial Ride). Each December thereafter the Big Foot Riders repeated this journey until 1990, the centennial of the massacre, when 350 people participated. That year, on December 29, the riders joined other Lakotas at the mass grave site and performed a ceremony in which they released the spirits of those who had died at Wounded Knee and wiped away their own tears. As Arvol Looking Horse, the keeper of the Sacred Calf Pipe, explained, the Wiping of Tears Ceremony signified "the rebirth of our nation after 100 years of mourning." Alex White Plume, one of the organizers of the Big Foot Memorial Ride, spoke of the event as the "mending of the hoop."[18]

---

[16] S. Con. Res. 153, 101st Cong., 2d sess., *Congressional Record*, 136, no. 148, pt. 2, daily ed. (25 October 1990): H13640.

[17] U.S. Senate Select Committee on Indian Affairs, *Wounded Knee Memorial and Historical Site, Little Big Horn National Monument Battlefield: Hearing before the Select Committee on Indian Affairs, United States Senate*, 101st Cong., 2d sess., 25 September 1990, 82–83 (1st qtn.), 8 (2d qtn.). A bill drafted by an Oglala organization, the Wounded Knee Centennial Commission, sought an appropriation of $100 million, with 60 percent devoted to education, 30 percent for a memorial, and 10 percent to the descendants. See "Sixth Working Draft of an Act to Compensate the Descendants of the 1890 Wounded Knee Massacre and for Other Purposes," SC 12, box 1, folder 4, Oglala Lakota College Archives, Kyle, S.Dak.

[18] Robert Allen Warrior, "Dances with Ghosts: Pain and Suffering on the Big Foot Trail," *Village Voice*, 15 Jan. 1991, pp. 33–36; *Indian Country Today*, Jan. 11–18, 1999, p. A1;

The Wiping of Tears Ceremony did not mean that Plains Sioux communities would suddenly escape high levels of poverty and unemployment, poor housing and health, domestic violence, and alcoholism. Yet, it was one sign among many that Lakotas and other western Sioux people remained determined to improve the conditions of their lives and the possibilities for future generations. In many ways – fighting for the return of their land, promoting the recovery of bison populations, preserving their language, reviving religious ceremonies and cultural activities, developing new methods to heal collective and individual trauma, and establishing programs to improve economic and social conditions – the Plains Sioux continue to try to live well as a distinctive people in their own land.[19]

At one time, European Americans saw this goal as incompatible with their own ideas of progress and declared that the Sioux, like other tribes, would eventually cease to exist. If the end of the twentieth century found the Plains Sioux surviving and the nation's hoop being mended, the beginning of the twenty-first holds the possibility of an end to economic and political colonialism and the reemergence of fully sovereign Indian communities in Sioux country and throughout North America. The realization of this possibility will certainly depend on the agency of Native people and communities. It will also require non-Indians to recognize the legitimacy of Native aspirations and to alter powerful structures that continue to constrain their realization.

Charmaine White Face Wisecarver, "Wounded Knee: Mending the Sacred Hoop," *Native Peoples* 3 (Spring 1990): 8–16; *Rapid City Journal*, 29 Dec. 1990, pp. A1-A2 (1st qtn., A2); *St. Paul Pioneer Press*, 30 Dec. 1990, p. 3G (2d qtn.); *New York Times*, 30 Dec. 1990, p. A1. The 1990 ceremony was based on the Spirit Keeping Ceremony discussed in Chapters 7 and 8.

[19] Ian Frazier, *On the Rez* (New York, 2000), provides a one-sided portrait of Pine Ridge; for criticisms, see "Reviews of Ian Frazier's *On the Rez*," *American Indian Quarterly* 24 (Spring 2000): 279–305. For an approach to healing historical trauma, see Maria Yellow Horse Brave Heart-Jordan, "The Return to the Sacred Path: Healing from Historical Trauma and Historical Unresolved Grief among the Lakota," Ph.D. diss., Smith College, 1995. For overviews of reservation conditions in recent decades, see Christafferson, "Sioux, 1930–2000," 824–36; Guy Gibbon, *The Sioux: The Dakota and Lakota Nations* (Malden, Mass., 2003), 190–201.

Index